COMPLETE GUIDE TO

CREDIT AND COLLECTION LAW

SECOND EDITION

ARTHUR WINSTON

JAY WINSTON

PRENTICE HALL

To Audrey
and
Elizabeth

Library of Congress Cataloging-in-Publication Data

Winston, Arthur,
  Complete guide to credit and collection law / Arthur Winston, Jay Winston.—2nd ed.
    p. cm.
  ISBN 0-13-084752-6 (cloth)
    1. Debtor and creditor—United States.   2. Executions (Law)—United States.   3.
  Bankruptcy—United States.   4. Credit—Law and legislation—United States.   5. Collection
  laws—United States.   I. Winston, Jay.   II. Title.
  KF1501 .W56 2000
  346.7307′7—dc21

                                                                    99-089707

Printed in the United States of America.

10 9 8 7 6 5 4 3 2 1

This publication is designed to provide accurate and authoritative information in regard
to the subject matter covered. It is sold with the understanding that the publisher is not
engaged in rendering legal, accounting, or other professional service. If legal advice or
other expert assistance is required, the services of a competent professional person should
be sought.

  . . From the Declaration of Principles jointly adopted by a Committee of the American Bar
Association and a Committee of Publishers and Associations.

ISBN 0-13-084752-6

ATTENTION: CORPORATIONS AND SCHOOLS
Prentice Hall books are available at quantity discounts with bulk purchase for
educational, business, or sales promotional use. For information, please write to:
Prentice Hall Special Sales, 240 Frisch Court, Paramus, NJ 07652. Please supply:
title of book, ISBN number, quantity, how the book will be used, date needed.

PRENTICE HALL
www.phdirect.com

ABOUT THE AUTHORS

ARTHUR WINSTON is the founding partner of Winston & Winston, P.C., New York, New York. The firm consists of a staff of over 100 and is engaged primarily in the collection of delinquent accounts, commercial litigation, and defending collection agencies and law firms for violations of the FDCPA, FCRA, TIL, ECOA and other consumer protection legislation. Arthur Winston has over 30 years of experience in commercial practice and commercial litigation. The firm represents a large core of clients in the collection area, ranging from the major money center banks, financial institutions, credit card companies, credit unions, large wholesalers, and manufacturers to some of the major direct marketing firms, hotels, and hospitals in the country. Winston & Winston, P.C. also represents distributors, franchisees, and a large variety of other businesses.

Arthur Winston was one of the founding members of the National Association of Retail Collection Attorneys, and served on the Board of Directors and was Chairman of the Education Committee for a period of three years. In the 1990s, he conducted a seminar for the Direct Marketing Association entitled "Credit and Collection Law" for several years and also conducted day seminars on the subject of credit and collection before both national and regional trade associations. He is the author of the *Complete Guide to Telephone Collection Techniques*, published by Prentice Hall. He attended New York University and received a degree in law from New York University Law School.

JAY WINSTON is a partner of Winston & Winston, P.C. and is admitted to practice law in the states of New York, New Jersey, and Connecticut. Together with Arthur Winston, he writes a column for the "Credit and Collection Manager's Newsletter," one of the oldest credit and collection newsletters. He has a strong programming background by virtue of studying electrical engineering at Cornell University. He has conducted day seminars on the subject of credit and collection and privacy before several regional trade associations. Jay Winston graduated from Cornell University and received a degree in law from New England School of Law.

ACKNOWLEDGMENTS

I would like to specifically thank the following persons and organizations for some of the appendix material appearing in the book:

The National Association of Credit Management (NACM) for Summary of State Laws Governing Claims Against Estates.

The American College of Mortgage Attorneys for allowing us to use the Foreclosure Fact Sheet which was contained in their National Mortgage Law Summary.

Steven O. Weise of the firm Heller, Ehrman, White & McAuliff, Los Angeles, CA for the comparison under the current Article 9 and the Draft New Article 9, including a table showing the distinctions between the old and new sections.

The American Lawyers Quarterly for the table on Statute of Limitations, Collection Agency Bonding and Licensing and Garnishment Exemptions state by state.

PREFACE

The purpose of this book is to identify and explain the key laws that affect credit and collection. Most credit and collection managers are well informed as to what procedures to use in the extension of credit and the practices used to collect both consumer and business debts. The major question that concerns them is summarized in one short sentence: "Can I do it legally?" This book is a comprehensive effort to answer that question.

Because credit and collection managers want to read the actual law as much as someone else's explanation and opinion of what the law means, I have attempted to include in the appendices the actual federal law and the commentaries to the federal law (which are explanations of the federal law) as well as examples of the various state laws in the more populated states.

My primary goal is to present to the credit and collection manager a broad overview of the laws that affect the credit and collection effort, with more emphasis on the collection effort. Most of the federal laws deal with consumer debtors and these are covered extensively. Several chapters are exclusively devoted to the collection of debts from businesses, including chapters dealing with primary concepts of the corporate and business relationship. Furthermore, Section 2 (Sales) and Section 9 (Security Interests) of the Uniform Commercial Code are included in the appendices.

The first chapter provides the credit and collection manager with an insight into the operation of the office of a collection attorney. Legal terminology is defined so that the manager understands what the attorney is talking about. An explanation of the progress of the suit and the alternative options open to the client are presented. With the knowledge of the laws affecting credit and collection that the rest of the book provides, credit and collection managers will be able to more effectively communicate with their collection agencies and attorneys to effectively collect the accounts and at the same time meticulously and carefully comply with the laws.

While Chapter 2 covers the concepts of business, including the corporation, partnership, and limited liability company, Chapter 3 covers some of the avenues open to a creditor to collect debts from a business, and the various types of liens that may be created from the business transaction. A special section is devoted to Personal Liability for Corporate Debts.

The legal issues of consumers are treated in Chapter 4 and a comprehensive analysis is made of the responsibility of family members for the debts of other family members. The recent ability to garnish members of the military service together with the enforcement of gambling debts are also covered. Divorces, deceased parties, jointly held property, relationships of husbands, wives and children, social security, and welfare recipients are all discussed in the chapter.

Chapter 5 covers the basic ingredients of the bankruptcy code and the appendices contain the actual law that deals with automatic stays and preferences. The question of reaffirmation of debts has been before the media recently and receives significant attention. We explore the ability of the creditor to attend the first meeting of creditors and the options open to the creditor when he receives a bankruptcy notice.

Selecting, working with, and monitoring outside attorneys or collection agencies are covered in Chapter 6.

The legal consequences of checks, notes, and guarantees are specifically discussed including certified checks, stale checks, unsigned checks, postdated checks, stop payments on checks, and bad check charges. The distinction between negotiable instruments and checks is carefully explained and the obligations of the guarantor from the simple guarantee to the three-page small print guarantee offered by a financial institution is examined. Section 3-311 covering paid-in-full checks is explored.

The repossession of property including whether it be an automobile or real estate is the principal topic of Chapter 8. With regard to the automobile, the issue of a commercially reasonable sale and peaceful repossession is considered in depth. The Ship Mortgage Act is contained in the appendices.

Chapter 9, dealing with harassment, intimidation, malicious prosecution, and the invasion of privacy, clearly spells out the dangers to the creditor of being exposed to this type of liability.

Chapter 10 undertakes to explain the new UCC 9 and sets forth some of the major changes in the new UCC 9 from the old UCC 9. The significant changes in preparing and filing a financing statement are set forth and the chapter covers the preparation and drafting of security agreements as well as covering some of the problems and dangers in foreclosing on a real estate mortgage.

The Fair Debt Collection Practices Act has received a great deal of publicity by virtue of the cottage industry of consumer attorneys who continually seek to sue for technical violations. In Chapter 11, we have made an effort to present some of the most recent court decisions. One of the major effects of the litigation is that more consumer attorneys are suing the creditor jointly with the debt collector.

Chapter 12, 13 and 15 deal respectively with the Truth and Lending Act, the Equal Credit Opportunity Act, and the Fair Credit Billing Act. Copies of the Acts are in the appendices.

Chapter 14 covers the new Fair Credit Reporting Act and in the appendix a copy of the new Act appears. A summary of the distinctions between the new Act and the old Act is presented.

Locating a debtor who has disappeared in covered in Chapter 16, on Skiptracing.

An effort is being made to present the book as a one-stop guide to the various laws affecting credit and collection that you will refer to again and again in addressing your legal questions.

NOTE

No attempt has been made here to review, include, or comment upon all the relevant laws and statutes. The major federal laws mentioned in the text or set forth in the Appendices must be considered in light of the laws passed by each of the fifty states. Some states have passed separate laws which directly subject creditors to regulations. Other states have passed more oppressive or burdensome mirror images of the federal law.

Most of the general statements presented are representative of the laws in the majority of states, but some states have passed laws that modify or change the legal consequences of the general statement. Exceptions exist to every general statement. Therefore, a general statement should not be used to fit a particular set of circumstances until after a thorough examination of the facts and laws plus a review of the decisions of the court of the appropriate state.

Laws and statutes are continually amended, revised, and repealed and court decisions may be reversed or rendered obsolete by more recent decisions or decisions of higher courts. The limited material presented here reflects what generally existed at the time this book was written. By the time this second edition reaches the reader, the reader must be aware that there may have been changes in the statutes and that more recent cases may have affected the contents. The author recommends that a review of all the state laws and federal laws as well as the court decisions of the federal courts and the state courts should be done before any decision is made with regard to any legal problem involved with the credit or collection effort and consultation with an attorney is always recommended before proceeding.

While we attempt to cover all the major amendments as well as the major decisions that affect the industry, we know that it is impossible to be comprehensive and complete. There are certainly many changes in the laws of the various states as well as decisions that we have not addressed, either because we are not aware of them or because of the limited space available.

The tables offered were probably prepared months or much longer prior to publication, and thus the information should be verified.

We welcome any reader to bring to our attention any state law or court decision which significantly affects the credit and collection industry. Please forward any material to: Winston and Winston p.C., 18 East 41st Street, New York, New York 10017, Attn: Arthur Winston.

This book is not intended to be a substitute for consultation with an attorney. Consultation is not only recommended, but encouraged. We hope that this volume provides you with additional compliance guidance in your credit and collection efforts.

CONTENTS

Chapter 6   LAW FIRMS AND COLLECTION AGENCIES **253**

Chapter 7   CHECKS, NOTES AND GUARANTEES **289**

Chapter 8   REPOSSESSION OF PROPERTY 327

Chapter 9   HARASSMENT, INTIMIDATION AND INVASION OF PRIVACY 355

CHAPTER 1

An Explanation of Legal Terminology in a Collection Case

The credit and collection manager will frequently have direct dealings with the in-house attorney or the outside attorney. A strong working knowledge of legal terminology is critical during the course of these conversations. This chapter will present an explanation of legal terminology as it affects a civil collection case against a business or a consumer.

Our firm conducts collection efforts throughout the country, but we practice primarily in the New York courts and therefore are exposed to the terminology commonly used in the New York court system. While the legal terms may vary from state to state, the institution of a lawsuit, the entry of a judgment, and the procedures to collect a judgment are similar in almost all of the states (with the exception of Louisiana, which still operates in some ways under the Napoleonic code).

The listings and explanations set forth here are for the purpose of furnishing general information and are not intended to be specific definitions of particular terms or a particular set of circumstances. The definitions or explanations should not be relied on as comprehensive and accurate in view of the limited space available in a book of this size. They are provided as a general overview with the understanding that each statement may have exceptions, may not be complete, and may have limitations or restrictions. For a full interpretation of any term, we recommend consulting with counsel.

1

JURISDICTION OF THE COURT

The "jurisdiction" of a court means the conditions and terms which must be satisfied to enable a party to commence suit or a proceeding in that particular court. Certain courts of the state, usually the lower courts, are considered "original" jurisdiction, which means that an individual or business may commence a proceeding initially in that court. Other courts are deemed to be courts of appellate jurisdiction in that the only way a proceeding can be brought into that court is to appeal a decision from a lower court. The highest courts in most states are considered appellate courts whose only function is to review appeals from the lower courts.

The courts of original jurisdiction set forth the requirements to be met before a suit is commenced. The courts are often divided into criminal courts, family courts, landlord-tenant courts, small claims courts, or civil courts. In most instances, credit and collection matters are instituted in civil courts or small claims courts. The major requirement to commence a suit is that the dollar amount of the claim is less than the ceiling set by the court or greater than the floor set by a second level of courts. For example, in New York City, the small claims court will only hear cases involving damages of twenty-five hundred dollars or less; the Civil Court in the City of New York will hear cases involving damages up to twenty-five thousand dollars; the Supreme Court of the state will hear all cases involving damages in excess of twenty-five thousand dollars. Jurisdiction varies from state to state, from county to county as well as from city to city. Consultation with your counsel is recommended.

The Justice or Magistrate Courts are courts of original jurisdiction, and usually prohibit suits in excess of a certain amount, generally between $1,000 and $10,000. The opportunity for discovery is limited, and after the defendant interposes an answer, the court sets a date for trial. Sometimes the judge will hold a preliminary conference to settle the case. In many jurisdictions a corporation must be represented by an attorney. Adjournments of the trial are not readily granted. The costs to commence suit are significantly less than city, town, county or state courts. Justice and Magistrate Courts usually handle consumer disputes and problems. This is not an advantageous forum for collection cases since the plaintiff must appear in court by a witness, and, in some cases, by an attorney. These appearances are expensive if the debtor defaults, and exceed the savings in court costs. In metropolitan areas, the equivalent court is usually denoted as the "small claims court," and often holds court in the evening hours.

SELECTION OF JURISDICTION

There are various rules which determine the court used by a plaintiff in suing a defendant. If a business or individual is suing a consumer, the Fair Debt

Collection Practices Act requires the suit against the consumer to be instituted in the county in which the consumer resides or where the transaction occurred regardless of where the business is located. One business suing another business constitutes a commercial transaction, which may be brought either where the defendant corporation is located or in the county in which the transaction took place. Where the business defendant is located outside of the state, the plaintiff may commence a suit within the state if the transaction took place within the plaintiff's state, and jurisdiction is obtained under a "Long Arm" statute which allows service on the defendant in another state. Sometimes the business agreement will identify what court should be used and what state law will govern. In some instances, the federal court may be utilized.

LONG ARM JURISDICTION

Most states have what is known as the "Long Arm Statute" which enables a plaintiff to institute suit in the state where the plaintiff resides and to serve the defendant in a distant state. The Long Arm Statute varies from state to state but, in general, provides that if the transaction took place in the state where the plaintiff resides, the plaintiff may serve the defendant in a distant state and the defendant will have to appear in the state in which the plaintiff is located. Thus, if the defendant has a plant in Texas, but signed a contract while in New York, the state court of New York has jurisdiction and the summons and complaint may be served in Texas.

Service on the defendant is usually accomplished by forwarding the summons to a sheriff (or other authorized process server) in the county where the defendant resides; the sheriff will serve the defendant in that county. The defendant then must decide whether to defend the case or permit the case to proceed to a default judgment. In most instances where a state will give full faith and credit to a default judgment (as opposed to a judgment obtained after contested litigation) obtained in another state, the plaintiff certainly has a distinct advantage in instituting suit in the state in which the creditor is located. Before any creditor embarks upon this course, the creditor should examine the laws of the state in which the judgment is to be enforced to be certain that the state will docket the judgment and enable the creditor to enforce the judgment without the institution of a new suit in a distant state. For example, New York will not docket a default judgment obtained in another state. A new suit would have to be started. If the defendant appeared in the action and a judgment was ultimately entered, all states give full faith and credit to the judgment.

Long Arm jurisdiction may not be available to use against a consumer in a suit when the obligation is to pay money arising out of a transaction in which the money, property, insurance or services are primarily for personal, family or household purposes. The Fair Debt Collection Practices Act requires that such a suit be brought in the judicial district in which the consumer signed the contract or where such consumer resides at the commencement of the action.[1]

ATTACHMENT

Attachment is a proceeding that enables a creditor to seize assets of the debtor simultaneously with the institution of the suit by service of a summons and complaint. This powerful remedy assures a creditor that the judgment will be paid from the assets attached. The court is allowing the creditor to secure the claim even though the debtor may have valid defenses and may be successful in dismissing the creditor's claim. During the attachment the debtor is unable to use or sell the assets attached, i.e., the bank account, the real estate. If the debtor is later successful in dismissing the complaint, the creditor may be severely penalized since the debtor has been deprived of the use of assets and will undoubtedly sue the creditor for damages. For example, if the debtor is about to buy a house, and the funds for the closing are in a bank account which has been attached, the debtor cannot perform, loses the house, and forfeits the deposit. It follows that the requirements for a creditor to obtain an attachment are burdensome (see Chapter 3).

PROPER NAME OF DEFENDANT

Suits must be instituted against the proper party whether a business or individual. If you institute suit and use the incorrect name of the individual, the judgment will be filed against the incorrect name of the individual and you will be unable to execute on the judgment against the assets of the debtor.

In many instances the debtor provides a social security number along with the proper name. All credit applications should contain provisions instructing the debtor to print his name on the appropriate line, instead of having the creditor to ask verbally for the name and then writing it on the application. If a mistake is made in the spelling of the first or last name, a suit instituted against this incorrect name may be attacked. Credit applications should be reviewed carefully to be certain that the debtors name is accurate.

Suits are instituted against individuals by using the first and the last name of the party and if a middle initial is provided, we include the middle initial to differentiate that person from other people with the same first and last name. Additional information to identify an individual is the address of the party, the social security number and the date of birth.

A post office box address is not considered adequate because a party cannot be served at a post office box. An individual must be served at their residential address or place of business.

Sometimes individuals operate under alias names or maiden names and if the alias is known, it should be provided to the attorney to enable the process

---

[1]Fair Debt Collection Practices Act, 15 USC, 1692 I(2).

server to serve the summons and complaint on the correct person. If the defendant is operating under an alias and the process server is not aware of the alias, service of the summons of complaint may not be made.

Businesses operate as sole proprietorships, partnerships or corporations. When instituting suit against a business, we must determine whether the debtor falls within one of these three categories. Many of the states have separate requirements for institution of suits against unions, trade associations, charitable associations and other types of entities which do not fall within the criteria of the three types of business operations.

A sole proprietorship occurs when an individual is doing business under a trade name or its own individual name. The proper party to sue is John Jones individually and d/b/a Jones Advertising (d/b/a means "doing business as"). If we sue him individually, we would be able to reach the assets of the business of Jones Advertising since he is personally operating under the name of Jones Advertising plus his own personal assets. If we just sue the business, Jones Advertising Company, this would be useless since Jones Advertising Company does not exist except as a trade name.

A partnership is similar to a sole proprietorship except instead of one person operating under a trade name, two or more people operate under a trade name (John Jones and Mary Jones d/b/a Jones Advertising). In both sole proprietorships and partnerships, the business may end in "co." or "company." A corporation can operate under a trade name such as "Jones Corp." d/b/a as "Jones Advertising."

Corporations must be sued under their proper corporate name. In most states corporations are identified by the words and letters which are at the end of the name such as "Corp", "Corporation", "Inc.", "Co. Inc.", "Incorporation", "Ltd". Separate identifications are designated for professional corporations such as attorneys or accountants (in New York designated as "P.C."). With the new limited liability companies, we have a new designation ie: "LLC".

The key to meeting these problems is a proper credit application. A designation should appear on the credit application as to whether the business defendant is an individual partnership, sole proprietorship or corporation. We also recommend that a copy of the first check received from the customer be photocopied since the proper business name is on the check.

For partnerships and individual d/b/a under a trade name, the assets of the individual and partners may be reached.

COMMENCING A SUIT

SUMMONS. In a civil action, the summons is the instrument initially served upon the defendant to commence the suit. The summons identifies the court in which the action is being brought and the address of the court. The summons sets forth the time period within which the defendant must answer or the date and time that the defendant must appear in court. The summons also may contain other local rules, such as indicating a particular room where the defendant must appear.

COMPLAINT. The complaint is a recitation of what the party commencing the suit (the plaintiff) is claiming from the defendant. The complaint states a claim for monies loaned to the defendant and not paid, or a claim for merchandise sold to the defendant which remains unpaid. The complaint may contain several claims, i.e., "causes of action" or "counts." The complaint is attached to the summons or incorporated into the summons depending upon the rules of the local court, and is usually served on the defendant along with the summons. Sometimes a summons is served, and a complaint is served after the defendant appears. The defendant appears by serving a paper (Notice of Appearance) stating that the defendant appears.

SERVICE OF PAPERS. In most jurisdictions, the plaintiff must file the summons and complaint with the court *before service* of the summons and complaint with a fee ranging as high as $150 to $300. (The purpose of this filing fee is to raise funds for the court.) Most statutes provide that the summons and complaint must be served within a period of time after the filing, i.e., 90 to 120 days. If service is not effected, a new fee must be paid. In some jurisdictions service may be first made and then the fee paid. If service is not made, no fee is paid. Upon payment of the fee, the court will issue an index number (or case number of docket number) to identify and create a file for the case, similar to a file number system used in most businesses. The same problems occur in court as in any business. Papers are misfiled and files are lost. Even when counsel can replace lost papers, valuable time is lost and sometimes proceedings must be repeated and started over.

Summons and complaints are usually served by the Sheriff of the County. A flat fee is paid plus an additional fee based on the mileage. In the Justice, Magistrate and small claims court, state law allows the summons and complaint to be served by certified mail. Many states permit the use of process servers.

SERVICE OF SUMMONS AND COMPLAINT. Although the law varies from state to state, three methods are generally available to serve a summons and complaint:

a. Personal Service: The individual is personally served by placing the paper in the hands of the debtor or at the feet of the debtor.

b. Substituted Service: This is done in several ways: by serving on a suitable person at the business or in the household; by serving a neighbor plus mailing the papers to the debtor; serving a doorman or nailing the papers to the door of the last known residence of the debtor (Nail and Mail). State laws allow one or more combinations of these procedures, and usually provide strict details as well as conditions when this type of service may be used.

c. Service by Publication: This type of service is used when the defendant cannot be found, but assets of the defendant (such as real estate) are located in the jurisdiction. Publication of the summons in newspapers for several weeks several times a week is generally required. Application to court to use this method is necessary. Each state has its own procedures, conditions and time frames but due diligence must be exercised in attempting to locate the party before publication is available. This method of service is expensive, because of the application to court and the cost of publishing notices in the newspaper.

SERVICE ON A CORPORATION. A corporation is usually served by personal service on an officer or managing agent of the corporation who apparently is the party in charge of the office where the corporation is located. In addition, every state has a requirement that a corporation, when filing a certificate of incorporation, designate the Secretary of State as authorized to accept service of papers for the corporation. Thus, a creditor can serve the Secretary of State's office (or the proper office designated by the state) and service would be effective. The Secretary of State mails the summons to the address designated on the certificate of incorporation; any corporation moving to a new address should so notify the Secretary of State of the new address.

SERVICE ON A PARTNERSHIP. Normally, the only effective way to serve a partnership is to serve one of the partners in the same way an individual is served.

DEFECTIVE SERVICE. Sometimes the debtor will claim improper service. The process server may have served the wrong person by personal service; the summons may have been mailed to the wrong address; the debtor may have been staying at a hotel when service is alleged to have been made; or the corporation may allege that the managing agent served was not a managing agent and was not authorized to accept service. The procedure is for the defendant to assert defective service in the answer, and thereafter an application to court is made by either party for a hearing to be held to determine if service was proper. If the hearing officer determines proper service was made, the application will be denied and the case will proceed. If service is held to be defective, the case will be dismissed and the creditor will be forced to start all over again (assuming the Statute of Limitations has not expired).

Accordingly, if the transaction is covered by the Fair Debt Collection Practices Act, the creditor is required to institute suit where the consumer resides or where the transactions occurred.

ANSWERS OR DEMURRERS

An answer or demurrer is the response to the complaint and states how the defendant disputes the claim set forth in the complaint. The normal answer may contain denials of each claim made in the complaint taking the form of "deny each and every allegation of paragraph 4 of the complaint." Affirmative defenses may also be set forth, including:

1. Statute of Limitations—The law recognizes that a claim against another party should be resolved within a reasonable time. Accordingly, the statute provides that a suit must be started within a certain prescribed time or else the claim is deemed abandoned. The time limits vary from state to state. One state may provide a statute of limitations of four years for goods sold and delivered while another state may provide only three years. The time limit usually starts from the time the transaction took place; so that if the merchandise was shipped in April of 1988, and the Statute of Limitations was four years, a suit would have to be started by April of 1992. A key issue is choice of law if the 2 states have different time periods.

2. Payment—Usually payment must be alleged as an affirmative defense.

3. Fraud—Inducing the defendant to enter into the agreement by fraud usually is an affirmative defense.

4. Lack of proper service or jurisdiction—For example, an attack on the personal jurisdiction of the Court over the defendant or defective service of the summons.

5. Failure to state a claim upon which relief can be granted.

6. Latches—an unreasonable delay in prosecuting.

7. Estoppel—where an act of plaintiff prevents or prohibits plaintiff from instituting suit.

COUNTERCLAIM

Whenever a suit is started against a defendant, the defendant may assert defenses to the suit; in addition, the defendant may plead a complaint against the plaintiff on a totally separate claim that may or may not have a connection with the claim of the plaintiff. This is described as a *counterclaim*. If an attorney or doctor sues for services rendered, for instance, the defendant may counterclaim for damages due to a typewriter owned by the doctor negligently falling on the defendant's foot.

RESPONSE OR REPLY TO COUNTERCLAIM

In the event the defendant asserts a counterclaim, the plaintiff has an opportunity to respond or reply to the counterclaim. This is the equivalent of an answer by the defendant to the complaint, except the plaintiff is answering the defendant's counterclaim. In some courts if you do not file a reply or answer to the counterclaim, the defendant can obtain a default against the plaintiff on the counterclaim. In other courts, the counterclaim is assumed to be denied.

CROSS CLAIM

When the defendant has a claim against a third party arising out of the transaction, the defendant may cross claim against the third party defendant or co-defendant in the same suit (a cross claim against an insurance company for indemnification for example). The cross claim is then served on the third party together with the complaint and answer.

COMPULSORY ARBITRATION

In many of the metropolitan courts the judges use a system of compulsory arbitration. Discovery is usually not allowed and both parties must submit the dispute to an arbitrator or panel of arbitrators, somewhat similar to private arbitration (see Arbitration). The difference from private arbitration is that the loser still receives the option to seek a trial in the court system, for the loser has not waived the right to trial by a judge or jury. Sometimes the loser must pay minor additional costs or expenses to exercise this right.

DISCOVERY PROCEEDINGS

Discovery proceedings occur after an answer has been interposed by a defendant denying the allegations in the complaint. The purpose of discovery proceedings is to enable either party to a lawsuit to obtain the details of the claim or defense of the other party. By determining these details, the parties can narrow the issues and prevent surprise at the trial. Often the information obtained or furnished leads the parties to dispose of the case prior to trial.

There are five major devices used to obtain information about the other party's claim: demand for a bill of particulars, interrogatories, depositions of parties and witnesses, production of documents, and notices to admit. These pleadings can be served by either party since the defendant requests information concerning the plaintiff's claim and the plaintiff seeks information as to the defenses asserted by the defendant.

Demand for a Bill of Particulars—This device is not available in all states, but where available, a set of questions is submitted to the plaintiff to explain the details of the complaint. An example might be a request to set forth how plaintiff arrives at $100,000 damages for a breach of contract. A bill of particulars is similar to interrogatories, but confined to questions about the complaint and not as broad. Many attorneys prefer interrogatories, and include any question about the complaint in the interrogatories. If the questions are improper or the answers inadequate, the defendant may apply to court for relief.

Interrogatories—Interrogatories are a set of written questions submitted to the other party who is required to answer. Sometimes the questions are inappropriate, or not applicable to the claim or defense, or are too broad and too general. In this instance the party to whom the questions are addressed may apply to the court to limit or omit the particular questions. On the other hand, the responses to questions may be inadequate or omitted and the party seeking the answers may make an application to court to compel the party to answer the questions adequately.

Depositions of Parties and Witnesses—The defendant may seek to examine the plaintiff under oath as to the claim in the complaint, and plaintiff may examine the defendant as to the defenses in the answer. During this deposition any question may be asked that is permitted to be asked at a trial of this matter and thus a broad interrogation may take place. The proceeding is commenced by serving a notice of an "examination before trial" (or deposition) which sets forth the day, time and place of the examination which can take place either at an attorney's office or at the courthouse. The notice will also describe what documents, books or records must be produced. The opposing party will appear and a court stenographer will be present to record the questions and answers. Examinations before trial are frequently adjourned, often for 30 day periods. Thus either side may delay the prosecution of the case by seeking several adjournments for a variety of reasons, i.e., attorney is engaged at a trial, party is sick, etc. If the opposing party is uncooperative, sometimes an application to court is necessary to compel the party to appear. Either party has a right to examine witnesses. The most common reason to examine your own witness is if the witness is located at a distant place or will be unable to travel to the location of the court where the trial is taking place.

Production of Documents—Either party may require production of documents in the other party's possession which are connected with or relevant to the claim or defense. The party served with this "notice to produce" must produce the documents if they are available. If the party does not produce the documents, the other party may make an application to court to compel compliance. On the other hand, if the document request is unreasonable or has no connection with the claim or defense, the party served may then make application to court to "quash" (cancel) the notice to produce. If the documents are unavailable or lost, the party does not have to produce them. However, a miraculous discovery on the eve of trial will be treated skeptically by the court.

Notice to Admit—A notice to admit is designed to save time at the trial by having the parties agree prior to the trial on certain facts or the validity of certain documents. Certain facts will be set forth for the opposing party to admit. An example would be if monies were loaned, the plaintiff asks the defendant to admit the execution of the promissory note (a copy of which is attached to the notice to admit). If the defendant executed the note, the defendant would not respond. A non-response is an admission and the note then may be offered as evidence at the trial. On the other hand, if the party denies the execution of the note, the note must be identified by a knowledgeable witness at the trial. If proving the note is expensive because money is paid to bring witnesses to attend the trial and the note is admitted as evidence, the cost and expense of offering proof at the trial is borne by the party who refused to admit the execution of the note.

ADJOURNMENTS

In depositions, interrogatories, production of documents, bills of particulars and notices to admit, the parties to whom the papers are addressed frequently request additional time to respond. These adjournments are generously allowed; for if an attorney refuses to grant the adjournment, the other party will normally apply to court and the judge will grant a reasonable adjournment. Furthermore, if plaintiff's attorney refuses a reasonable adjournment, the defendant's attorney may later refuse a reasonable adjournment to plaintiff's attorney. Nevertheless, after one or two adjournments are granted, with each one being for less time, an attorney will allow an adversary one last adjournment providing the adversary agrees not to ask for any more. Although discovery proceedings require an extensive amount of time in complicated actions because of frequent adjournments, discovery is crucial to the success or failure of a case.

MOTIONS AND APPLICATIONS

A motion or an application is a request to the judge or court to order or prohibit a particular action of the plaintiff or the defendant. Motions and applications serve many purposes.

a. A motion to dismiss the complaint based on the fact that even if everything is true in the complaint, it does not form the basis upon which relief can be granted.

b. A motion to allow the filing of a paper notwithstanding the fact that the paper was filed late. The party making the application will usually provide a reasonable excuse.

c.   A motion by an attorney to be relieved from representing a party because the attorney feels that the relationship between the parties has deteriorated, that further representation would not be in the best interest of the client, or for the simple reason that the attorney has not been paid.

d.   A motion to compel the party to answer the questions specified in the interrogatories or a motion to compel the party to appear on a given date at a given place to submit to an examination before trial.

In any motion or application to the court, the party seeking the relief must notify the other party so that the opposing party may also either consent to the relief that is being sought by defaulting (failing to appear at the designated date) or oppose the relief by submitting affidavits and documents. The court will review the application and the affidavits in support of the motion by the moving party and the affidavit submitted in opposition by the other party. The court may require the parties to appear in court in "contested" motions (where the party opposes the motion) and argue orally before the court. The party making the application must provide the opposing party usually with at least ten to fourteen days notice before the date set in court to hear the motion. The date that is set is usually referred to as the "return date." As in discovery proceedings, the party seeking the relief may grant several adjournments to the other party before all affidavits and documents are submitted to the court so that the judge may decide the motion.

Order to Show Cause—Under certain circumstances, the party cannot wait for relief for the ten to fourteen days. In that case, an "order to show cause" is used. This enables the party seeking the relief to set the return date (the day on which both parties must appear in court) within twenty-four to seventy-two hours rather than to wait seven to fourteen days. The party seeking the short return date applies to the judge *prior to giving notice to the defendant* so that the judge will review the emergency situation and approve a short two or three day period for the "return date." The judge must sign "the order to show cause," before it is served on the other side, usually by personal service.

Summary Judgment—A summary judgment is a motion (an application to court) supported by affidavits to court stating that either the plaintiff or the defendant is entitled to win the case as a matter of law *without a trial* based on the documentary evidence (such as a note or lease), testimony at a deposition, or other evidence. One party states that sufficient documentary evidence is before the court to warrant a decision in favor of that party. An application to court for a summary judgment will save time and the expense of a trial. A summary judgment may be made either before, during, or after discovery proceedings, and will suspend the discovery proceedings pending a decision. Sometimes the discovery proceedings provide evidence and testimony to support a motion for summary judgment, and in that event the motion is made after discovery. A presentation to the court of the testimony, the answers to the interrogatories, and documentary evidence may be sufficient for the court to render a decision without a formal trial. If the facts are disputed, the court usually denies the motion for summary judgment on the grounds that a factual dispute must be resolved by a trial.

Order—After each application (motion) is made to court, a judge renders a decision on whether the motion is denied or granted. This decision is contained in an "order" signed by the judge and is usually sent to each attorney. The winning side must serve a copy on the other side, and file an affidavit in court that service was made. This process is a "notice of entry" of the order. In federal courts the judge mails the decision to both parties. This procedure ensures that the losing side receives a copy of the order and causes the appeal time period to begin.

STIPULATIONS

A stipulation is an agreement entered into between the plaintiff and the defendant. A stipulation extending the time to answer is an agreement between the attorney for the plaintiff and the attorney for the defendant that the time within which the defendant must serve an answer has been extended to a certain date. A stipulation extending the time to respond to a set of interrogatories or adjourn an examination of a party is a similar document.

A stipulation can be entered to discontinue an action commenced by the plaintiff against the defendant. An action may be discontinued "on the merits," which means that an action cannot be commenced in a new suit based on the same facts. On the other hand, an action discontinued "without prejudice" means that the action can be commenced in a new suit based upon the same set of facts. An action is discontinued "without prejudice" due to jurisdictional failure, the wrong court, wrong name, wrong summons, wrong address of the court, or reasons other than "on the merits" of the case.

CONFERENCE

Prior to a trial most state courts, federal courts and other active courts of original jurisdiction schedule a preliminary conference. The judge, or the judge's clerk, will convene both attorneys in a room to discuss whether the case can be settled, and the judge will often counsel both parties as to the best way to settle so the court's time is not wasted. Either side always has the option to refuse to settle, and exercise the right to a trial.

SETTLEMENT NEGOTIATIONS

Many books have been written about negotiating a deal and the same number of books can be written about negotiating a settlement of a debt. The key ingredients in negotiating any type of indebtedness are the same key ingredients that are self-evident in negotiating any type of a deal. Preparation, a consideration of all the facts and circumstances, and plain old-fashioned common sense are the basics.

Clients should recognize the fact that their attorneys have much more experience in negotiating a settlement, but unfortunately many clients refuse to accept this self-evident fact and persist in controlling the negotiation themselves, ignoring or disregarding the advice of their attorney. The argument most often offered is that the attorney is acting in his self-interest when negotiating a settlement. If the attorney's recommended offer is not accepted, the case will ultimately be tried and the attorney will be generating fees for himself. On the other side of the coin, if the attorney is handling the matter on a contingency basis, the client usually argues that the attorney is recommending a settlement for the purpose of earning the contingency fee and that much more would be collected if a suit were started.

If the client seriously believes that the attorney is only interested in generating fees and that any negotiation that the attorney embarks on will be designed for this purpose, the client should immediately discharge the attorney and find another attorney to negotiate in the best interest of the client. I assure you that there are many attorneys out there who successfully retain their clients by negotiating in the best interest of the client.

The important thing to remember is that the attorney is negotiating these types of situations on a day-to-day basis. Every negotiation of a settlement must be considered upon the facts and circumstances then and there prevailing, but there are certain recommendations that can be made that apply to every negotiation of a settlement of a debt.

A. The classic rule that must never be violated is not to "bid against yourself." For example, if you are requesting the full amount, the response should be negative to an inquiry such as "well, give me the best figure you will take" before the debtor has made any offer. The response should be that "we do not bid against ourselves." If the debtor feels that a settlement is in order, let him make a reasonable offer and then consider the grounds upon which the debtor is making the reduced offer.

B. Probably the most basic reason that the debtor may offer for seeking an adjustment in price or a payout plan is the fact that the debtor has financial problems. Again, this is a circumstance that the creditor must consider in any negotiation. The problem is that many creditors do not seek sufficient financial information from the debtor to make a valued judgment. If it is a corporate debt, the ability to obtain financial information is only limited by time and effort. Most creditor's attorneys have financial forms to be completed by the debtor's business or request financial statements from the debtor. If the debtor claims he cannot furnish statements prepared by an accountant, the creditor should obtain the financial statements under a representation by the individual principal that the statements are true and accurate. Then he can state that he relied on these financial statements to enter into the final settlement agreement with the debtor.

C. Many creditors take the position that they want the full amount and allow little room for their attorney to make a settlement. If any leeway is allowed, it is to permit a 20% to 30% discount from the face amount. Some creditors will *establish this as a policy.* In the banking and credit card areas, this will happen frequently. Nevertheless, this reasoning is flawed because every debt must be reviewed on a case-by-case basis. The financial problems of the debtor are extremely important in settling any debt. It is far better to retain a small cash payment than be faced with a bankruptcy petition where there will probably be no payment or a small payment of less than 10%.

D. Another factor which must be considered when demanding the full amount is that the attorney for the debtor may make the following recommendation to the debtor as follows:

> "The creditor wants the full amount or else he is going to sue. We can drag this case through the courts for at least a year and maybe longer. The very worst that can happen is that if we lose the case, we will pay the full amount plus interest of a few hundred dollars. In addition, we may win because the creditor is located across the country and may not send a witness."

E. Dealing with a debtor asserting financial difficulties, the reasonable assumption that a creditor should make is that the debtor is not paying several other creditors as well. The number is not important. There may be only five pieces of pie to feed 10 or 15 hungry creditors. Most creditors who address the problem with information, investigation, and common sense will walk away with their hunger at least partially satisfied. The remaining creditors may go hungry for a long time and ultimately may starve.

F. The most advantageous time to commence negotiation is when the matter reaches the attorney's office. At this point, the debtor is faced with the inevitable conclusion that the debt has been referred to an attorney and that a suit is imminent. If a settlement cannot be negotiated at this point, the next best time to open negotiation is immediately after a summons and complaint is served upon the debtor and, hopefully, before an attorney is retained by the debtor.

G. While the creditor must have absolute control over the settlement negotiations, the effort must be joint and both parties must recognize the function of the other party to achieve a fair and reasonable settlement. Remember that settlements make both parties *partially unhappy.* A settlement that makes one party totally happy and the other party totally unhappy will probably never be consummated.

H. The client usually does not wish to accept the uncertainties of litigation. The attorney, on the other hand, is well aware that even with a "rock solid" case, a case may be lost in litigation for any number of reasons including, but not limited to, witnesses inadvertently offering the wrong answers, documents being lost or unavailable, witnesses leaving for parts unknown or passing away, judges rendering decisions subjectively rather than objectively, cases being reversed on appeal for technical errors during the trial, and, of course, the fact that mistakes in strategy may be made by both the client and the attorney. How many times over the past 30 years have I seen cases that I expected to lose turn out to be winners and some cases I thought to be sure winners turn out to be losers? There is no such thing as a "rock solid" case. Rock solid cases are won at summary judgments, not at trial. For this reason, most attorneys are more attuned to the settlement process than clients.

STIPULATION OF SETTLEMENT

If a collection matter is settled, most attorneys have prepared a standard stipulation of settlement. The stipulation usually provides that the defendant has appeared in the action and waives any defenses to the jurisdiction of the court. The reason for this waiver is so that the defendant cannot claim improper service of the summons and complaint or that the court has no jurisdiction over the defendant. The amount of the settlement and the terms of the settlement are included. The stipulation provides for interest, since the creditor is extending credit to the defendant over a longer period of time. If the original agreement provides for attorney's fees, this can be added to the settlement.

Provisions are usually made that in the event of default, the creditor can enter judgment for the full amount. Any payments made will be credited to the amount of the judgment. A provision for attorney's fees may be made in the event of a default even if not in the original agreement.

The defendant should state that he or she is not subject to military service because this is necessary to enter judgment. (Under the new law that amended the Soldiers and Sailors Civil Relief Act, judgments can be obtained against members of the military under certain circumstances and by complying with certain procedures).

If the defendant has interposed an answer and counterclaim to the complaint, the stipulation usually provides that the defendant will withdraw the answer and counterclaim, if any. If the defendant withdraws the answer and not the counterclaim, the counterclaim may still be asserted by the defendant. The attorney shall have the right to enter the judgment based on the affidavit of the attorney that the defendant has failed to make payments as provided for in the stipulation.

COURT PROCEDURES

The court systems in each state have their own different procedures with regard to the conduct of litigation. Most courts require attorneys to attend a conference for purposes of settlement before the trial. At these conferences, the judges will exert a significant amount of pressure on the attorneys to settle the case. Other judges will treat these conferences perfunctorily by asking the attorneys whether they have attempted to settle the case and, upon receiving a negative response, will set a date for trial. In the Federal Court, the judges will set a schedule for discovery, i.e., set the dates within which time interrogatories must be served and answered and depositions must be taken. Some state courts utilize the same procedures that are used in the Federal Court.

In some state courts, the judges require their consent for adjournments in the scheduling process, whereas in most of the lower courts, adjournments can be obtained with the consent of both attorneys. Each system tends to set its own rules with regard to the procedure for the case.

On the other hand, the federal bankruptcy court has totally different procedures with regard to the examination of the bankrupt and the devices available to the creditors to obtain information concerning the bankrupt.

TRIAL PREPARATION

Cases are not won at trial, but at the office. Trial preparation is the key ingredient to a successful outcome. If a case is going to trial, the client should devote the necessary time to prepare. The attorney will review the witnesses' testimony as well as the documentary evidence. It is essential to provide your attorney with the original file at least 1-3 weeks prior to trial. Evidence that appears useless to the client may be gold to the attorney. To go to trial without seeing the original file is setting the attorney up for failure. Time and privacy are necessary. Meeting at the courthouse early in the morning to prepare a case for trial that afternoon is a certain ticket to losing.

TRIAL

If the parties cannot settle the case, the case will proceed to trial. Either party may serve the other party and file a *notice of trial,* which is a request to the clerk to issue a trial calendar number. This notice identifies the parties, the type of case and other information to enable the clerk to classify when the case will be tried and, in larger jurisdictions, what courtroom in the courthouse. In smaller jurisdictions, the clerk will notify the parties when the trial will take place. Some courts require affidavits stating that all discovery proceedings have been completed.

In the metropolitan areas, the clerk issues a trial number in consecutive order, and both parties wait for the court to reach the number. A special room is designated where the clerk calls the numbers each day, each week, or each month. Both parties appear and indicate they are ready for trial. The clerk assigns a judge for the case. The attorneys then appear before the assigned judge. Both parties and the judge agree when the trial will begin. Since the judge, attorneys, and clients are often not ready on the day when the case is called, adjournments occur frequently. But the attorneys must be in court for the calendar calls, the requests for adjournments, and the decision of the judge to adjourn. Many times the judge requires both sides to be ready on a given day with the expectation that the current case before the judge will be completed; when it is not, the client's case is adjourned to another day. For this reason actual trials are expensive due to the waiting time in court. The adjournment time and waiting time for a trial are probably the best reasons to settle a case.

JUDGMENT

A judgment is the final effect of a decision on a motion addressed to the merits of a case such as a summary judgment or a verdict after a trial. A contested judgment is when the defendant appeared and answered the complaint. A default judgment is where the defendant has not appeared or answered the complaint.

Vacating a Default Judgment—Sometimes the creditor will enter a default judgment, and the creditor will then attach assets of the debtor, either a bank account, inventory, or even real estate. The debtor will claim that service was never made, and the default resulted only because the debtor never knew a suit was started. The procedure is a motion to vacate the judgment for improper service. A hearing is held. If the creditor cannot prove proper service, the judgment is vacated and the creditor must begin again. If the creditor proves proper service, the proceeding by the creditor continues with regard to the assets.

The debtor may also vacate a judgment on the grounds that the court has no jurisdiction over the debtor. For example, the amount claimed exceeds the amount permitted by the court, or the corporation is located in another state and service has not been properly made. Many other reasons may be offered; and while some are valid and result in dismissal, many are frivolous and interposed by debtors merely to delay and stall the proceedings.

CONFESSION OF JUDGMENT

A *confession of judgment* allows a judgment to be entered in favor of a creditor automatically when the debtor breaches the terms of the confession of judgment. The debtor normally will confess the judgment, i.e., admit liability for the debt, either before or after suit is instituted. The debtor is basically waiving any right to assert any defenses to a suit to recover the debt.

A confession of judgment sometimes appears in commercial leases or loan documents. Under the Credit Practices Act, consumer credit contracts that include the use of confession of judgment involving individuals or consumers are unenforceable; some states had already prohibited them even before enactment of the Act. On the other hand, the use of confessions of judgment under business transactions, leases of real estate or property, or in lending situations with financial institutions are quite common though varied, across the fifty states. The laws in a particular state should be examined carefully.

Any confession of judgment obtained under duress will be set aside and rendered unenforceable. To be valid, a confession of judgment must contain several important terms, including a confession as to the fact that the plaintiff's claim is valid and that the debtor consents to the entry of the judgment (filing the judgment with the clerk of the court). Naturally, the amount of the judgment and the terms of any payout plan must also be set forth. In most instances, the debtor authorizes entering the judgment (filing in court) once the attorney for the creditor files an affidavit with the court stating that the debtor breached the terms of the confession of judgment. Most states permit a confession of judgment prior to the maturity of the obligation; on the other hand, a few prohibit judgments confessed prior to maturity or before commencement of suit. In the minority states, a confession of judgment is not enforceable unless executed by the debtor after an action is instituted on the matter. In many states, once a confession of judgment is entered, to preserve the due process rights of the debtor, certain notice provisions must be complied with to enable the debtor to have an opportunity to vacate the judgment for the reasons set forth in the statute.

CREDIT AND COLLECTION TIP: *Most states provide that confessions of judgment must be entered within a specified time from the date of the signing of the judgment, i.e., one to three years from date of signing. Thus, confessions are not used where payouts or performance extend beyond the time limitations. Failure to enter (file the judgment with the clerk) within the prescribed time will render it void and useless.*

DAMAGES

The general standard for most damages is compensatory damages. The courts recognize damages which may fairly and reasonably be considered as arising naturally from a breach of contract and any damages that may reasonably be supposed to have been in the contemplation of both parties as the probable result of a breach of contract. Reasonable, foreseeable, and consequential damages usually must be those type of damages that both parties would be able to foresee in the event the contract was breached. Some courts have placed strict interpretations on consequential damages which are permitted to be recovered in special circumstances only if sufficiently impressed upon the breaching party.

Punitive damages are usually not awarded in a breach of contract case. Nevertheless, if the breach of contract is also a tort, the court may still award punitive damages. Examples of tort claims are fraud, a willful misrepresentation to induce entering a contract, or a conversion of funds. Most punitive damage awards are in tort litigation involving accidents, an intentional infliction of bodily harm, or other types of injuries suffered by a large number of consumers with the purpose being to deter the wrongdoer from similar conduct in the future and to deter others from engaging in such type of conduct. The courts normally do not award damages for mental distress or emotional upset in a breach of contract suit because the damages are too vague and uncertain to be considered as foreseeable by the parties to the contract.

The insured party's obligation to mitigate damages is always present, but the courts only require that the party mitigating the damages use a reasonable effort. The injured party need not act if the cost of avoidance is an unreasonable expense and he need not commit a wrong by breaching other contracts to mitigate damages.

ENFORCEMENT AND COLLECTION OF A JUDGMENT

Transcript of Judgment—A judgment is recognized in the county where it is obtained. If suit was started in the Supreme Court of Clark County, the judgment would be recognized in Clark County and would enable the sheriff to levy on the real or personal property of the defendant located in Clark County. This would apply whether the judgment was a contested judgment or a default judgment where the defendant did not appear. A transcript of judgment is a document issued under the signature of the county clerk, in the county where the judgment is entered, listing the plaintiff, the defendant, the amount of the judgment, the date it was obtained, the county in which it was obtained, and the index number issued. If the defendant owns property in another county, a transcript of judgment must be filed in the other county to conduct enforcement proceedings in that county. Thus, if the debtor had property in Cook County and judgment was entered in Clark County, a transcript of the judgment from Clark County must be filed in Cook County to proceed against property in Cook County.

Garnishment of Wages—After a judgment has been obtained, the creditor has a right to garnishee the salary of the debtor. To garnishee a salary means to issue a document (execution) reciting the details of the judgment to a sheriff or marshal who notifies the employer of the debtor to deduct a percentage of the wages of the debtor and send this amount to the sheriff, who deducts fees and sends the balance to the creditor. The amount permitted to be deducted from the salary is between 10% and 25% and varies from state to state.

The salaries of federal employees and the military are now subject to garnishment, effective in 1994. The garnishment process for federal employees is simple and similar to state garnishment proceedings. As for members of the military, the Department of Defense issued rules which are available from the Department of Defense, Finance and Accounting Service, Code L., P.O. Box 998002, Cleveland, Ohio 44119, telephone number 216-522-5301. In most states, employees of the state or city government are subject to garnishment.

In some states, the sheriff must first notify the debtor of the fact that a garnishment will be served on the employer and allow the debtor to make voluntary payments equivalent to what would be deducted from the salary and avoid the notification to the employer. Failing this the debtor knows the employer will be notified.

Garnishment of Property—Once a judgment is obtained, the creditor is entitled to garnish or attach assets (such as wages) of the debtor in the hands of third parties. (To garnish, attach, or restrain assets requires the third party to transfer the monies or properties of the debtor to the creditor.) The method used is to serve the third party with a garnishment (execution) that lists the amount of the judgment, date of entry, name of court, plaintiff and defendant, and the balance due. A prime example of third parties holding assets of the debtor is a bank account where the bank is holding money of the debtor. The garnishment is served on the bank, and monies on deposit are paid to the creditor up to the amount of the judgment. Another example would be third parties who owe money to the debtor such as a tenant owing money to the landlord (debtor) or a mortgagor owing money to the mortgagee (debtor). In each instance a restraining notice (garnishment) served upon the tenant or the mortgagor would require payment of the monies directly to the creditor (rent due landlord, mortgage payment due mortgagee).

This powerful tool should be used where the creditor knows that monies belonging to the debtor are resting in the hands of third parties who owe money to the debtor. The procedure is simple and usually only requires service of a notice upon the third party. In some jurisdictions notice must be also sent to the debtor.

Executions—Wage executions and property executions are directions to a marshal or sheriff to take possession of assets of the debtor. Wage executions are more properly called "garnishees," as described previously. A property execution is an instrument delivered to the sheriff reciting the amount of the judgment, date of entry, court, plaintiff and defendant, and the location of the assets to be levied upon. In property executions the sheriff levies and executes on the assets of the debtor, sells the assets at public sale by auction, collects the proceeds from the sale, and remits the proceeds to the creditor, less any fees or expenses incurred in the process of the sale by the sheriff or the marshal.

After a judgment has been obtained by a creditor, the creditor's attorney may issue an execution to the sheriff or marshal of the county in which the debtor resides if the debtor is operating a business or has other types of assets. Real estate is heavily regulated and controlled by statute and specific requirements must be met before a judgment creditor can sell real property to satisfy a debt. The execution or garnishment is a document which directs the sheriff to collect the judgment by selling any property that the debtor may have for cash and then remitting the cash to the creditor. The sheriff usually performs this function for a fee of about 5% plus his expenses.

The execution contains the date of judgment was entered, the court, the index number, the amount of the judgment, the amount of interest, the location of the debtor, and, in most instances, the location of the property which the sheriff is to sell. When the sheriff receives the document, he will mail or deliver personally the same type of information to the debtor and allow the debtor a certain time period within which to voluntarily pay the judgment or arrange for an installment plan. In the event the judgment is not paid voluntarily by a specified time or arrangements are not made, the sheriff proceeds to levy on the assets (visiting the premises and identifying the assets).

The sheriff then publishes a notice of sale in the newspaper in the same geographic area as the debtor and publishes the date of sale, description of property to be sold, and other information. The judgment creditor pays in advance the fees to hold a sale, which include the cost of tagging the property, advertising in the newspaper, and conducting the auction of the property. The cost may approach several hundred dollars or substantially more, depending upon the amount of the property and whether it is real estate. On the date set for sale an auction is conducted on all the property or specific parts of the property. If a bid of all the property is greater than the bid for the specific property, the property is sold to the party who bid for all of the property. If the bid for the specific property is greater than the bids for all of the property, the sheriff will sell the parts rather than the whole. A down payment of around 10% is required and the balance is due when the property is removed by the purchaser from the premises. The proceeds first are used to pay off a specific judgment and the remainder of the proceeds, if any, may be used to pay other creditors in a surplus money proceeding which is regulated by specific state laws.

Prior to the auction the sheriff visits the debtor's place of business to conduct an inventory of any assets. The debtor may oppose this levy on the grounds that the property had been mortgaged to a bank or another secured creditor. Under these circumstances, the levy by the sheriff will be subject to the prior lien and the sheriff will have to announce at the public sale that the purchaser is buying the assets subject to the prior lien. This happens frequently with regard to automobiles or boats, which are usually subject to prior liens to a bank or a financial institution.

Information Subpoenas—In most states, after a judgment has been obtained, the creditor can serve an information subpoena upon any third party who may have information concerning the debtor or who owes the debtor any money. Landlords, telephone companies, accountants, utility companies, banks, prior owners of residences, past and present employers are all types of third parties upon whom information subpoenas may be served. In some jurisdictions, witness information subpoenas may be served upon relatives and friends of the debtor. The information subpoena lists questions asking the third party where the debtor is residing, the name and address of the debtor's employer, and similar questions helpful to the creditor in locating assets of the debtor. With certain third parties, such as banks and telephone companies, questions are used to determine if the bank has monies on deposit or whether the debtor has a telephone deposit with the telephone company. Sometimes landlords have security deposits and are able to furnish information as to the whereabouts of the debtor, or where the debtor works. (In some states, landlord's security deposits may be exempt.)

Subpoenas—Subpoenas are documents served upon the debtor or witnesses requiring an appearance at a given time and place to be examined under oath. After a judgment is obtained, a creditor is entitled to examine the debtor under oath as to the whereabouts of any assets that the debtor may own or information where the debtor is employed. The subpoena also may be served upon a witness who may have information concerning the debtor. Such witnesses may be the debtor's spouse, relatives, or former employers. With regard to judgments against businesses, the subpoena is available to be served upon its officers, directors or employees who have information concerning its assets.

Contempt Orders—If a subpoena is served upon the debtor or a witness who does not appear, the creditor may make an application to court to punish the debtor for contempt of court. In New York this is called an "order to show cause to punish the debtor for contempt of court," or just a contempt order. The creditor alleges that the debtor was served and that the debtor failed to appear. The judge will issue an order requiring the debtor to appear on a specified day at the courthouse to cure said default. The difficulty with contempt orders is that usually they must be served personally upon the debtor and if the debtor is evading service, the likelihood of success is slim. Failure to serve within the specified time requires preparing a new contempt order. If the debtor is served and does not appear, in most jurisdictions the creditor may apply to court for a warrant to arrest the debtor. This order is issued to the sheriff who arrests and produces the debtor in court to be examined under oath. After the debtor is examined, the judge usually releases the debtor.

The judges rarely incarcerate a debtor for failure to appear pursuant to a subpoena. Many sophisticated debtors will respond only to a contempt order; and some will wait for notice of an arrest order (the sheriff notifies the debtor before executing the arrest order) before submitting to an examination.

Freedom of Information—Under the terms of the Freedom of Information Act, information can be obtained from federal and state governmental agencies about the debtor. For example, if the debtor is using a post office box number, a service of the proper papers upon the U.S. Postal Service will require it to furnish you with the street address of the owner of the post office box. In a new policy change this device is only available to attorneys, process servers, and plaintiffs appearing in person (see Chapter 16).

Skip Tracing—This is a term used to locate either the residence, the place of employment, or the bank account of the debtor. Businesses in every state provide this type of service (see Chapter 16).

Order To Compel Payment—Sometimes a creditor obtains a judgment against a debtor who has no visible assets or stream of income. Nevertheless, the debtor appears to be living in an expensive accommodation and apparently enjoying expensive means of transportation, travel, food and other luxuries.

Most states have statutes which allow the creditor to request the court to compel the debtor to make monthly payments because the debtor is spending money which should be paid to the creditor. For example, one particular debtor was sending three children to private prep school, was renting a Cadillac, and paying several thousand dollars each month for an apartment in New York. In addition, he took a yearly vacation for two weeks to the Caribbean and maintained a membership in a country club. His source of income could not possibly cover all of these expenses. When he was examined, he testified to an income barely enough to cover the obvious living expenses. After the obvious expenses were deducted from his stream of income, the debtor had barely enough to cover food, clothing and medical expenses for maybe a few days out of each month. After a hearing on an application to court to compel the debtor to make payments, the court directed the debtor to make a substantial payment each month.

In the event the debtor defaults on a payment plan, the creditor has the right to ask the court to punish the debtor for contempt of court. The application to court to punish for contempt is a function of the judge's discretion. Some judges fashion severe punishments, but most judges will just allow the debtor more time to make the payments or may even reduce the payments. Consultation with counsel is recommended.

ARBITRATION

Arbitration is the method by which a plaintiff and a defendant avoid the use of the court system and agree between themselves, usually in writing, to submit their disputes to binding arbitration. In most instances, they will seek an arbitration board in the state in which they are located or will use the American Arbitration Association, which will present a selection of some twenty to twenty-five arbitrators. The plaintiff and the defendant will each select one to three arbitrators; the association will then choose from this selection either one arbitrator who is acceptable to both parties or a panel of three arbitrators acceptable to both parties. The parties then will offer their evidence before the arbitrators who will render a decision. The main distinction in resolving a dispute by arbitration as distinguished from a lawsuit is as follows:

a.   In an arbitration, little discovery is available in the way of examinations of witnesses before trial, interrogatories, or production of documents. Because discovery prior to the arbitration is severely limited, the savings in legal fees are substantial.

b. The rules of evidence are not as closely followed during an arbitration hearing and the arbitrator will normally listen to everything offered.

c. No appeal on the merits of the case is allowed from a decision by the arbitrator. The arbitrator's decision is final unless a conflict of interest exists or one of the arbitrators acted improperly due to personal reasons. If an unfavorable decision is rendered, the losing party must live with that decision. In the court system, if a bad decision is rendered by a judge, the option to appeal to the appellate court is available.

d. Arbitrations usually are arranged more quickly than are trials in the present court system.

Many written commercial agreements, purchase orders, lease agreements, and other types of complicated written contracts contain "boiler plate" terminology providing for arbitration. Attorneys often are opposed to arbitration, because of the lack of any opportunity to appeal a bad decision. On the other hand, some businessmen find arbitration exceptionally advantageous because of the speed of resolution of the dispute and the savings in legal fees. In most arbitration proceedings, both parties share the fees.

SATISFACTION OF JUDGMENT

When a judgment is paid, the debtor is entitled to have the judgment marked *"paid"* at the clerk's office where the judgment was recorded (docketed or entered). The attorney for the plaintiff prepares a *satisfaction of judgment,* an instrument which identifies the judgment by name of plaintiff and defendant, index number, court, recites that the judgment is paid, and is filed with the clerk of the court where the judgment is recorded.

GENERAL RELEASE

The general release is a statement by the creditor that releases the debtor from any and all claims the creditor may have against the debtor. A general release is normally requested after the payment of a claim. Instead of using a general release, a creditor in a large firm should use a limited general release restricted only to the debt that was paid rather than releasing all debts when a debtor may have two or three debts to the same creditor. The general release form, available at stationery stores, should contain an additional statement that the release is limited to the particular debt which the debtor is paying.

SUBORDINATION AGREEMENT

Often a lender wishes to extend credit to a borrower who already has a lien or a mortgage on the property which the borrower wishes to offer as collateral to the creditor. The borrower enters an agreement with the existing mortgagee so that the mortgagee will become subordinate to the new mortgage being placed on the property by the bank. For example, real estate worth $200,000 carries a $10,000 mortgage. The owner seeks a loan of $100,000. The existing mortgagee agrees to subordinate the $10,000 mortgage to the $100,000 mortgage which is being placed on the premises by the bank. Some form of consideration may be paid to the existing mortgagee, such as a prepayment or an increase in interest. As a result, the $100,000 is the first mortgage and $10,000 is the second mortgage. The agreement between the borrower and the existing mortgagee is the subordination agreement.

GUIDELINES FOR TESTIMONY AT DEPOSITION

This material is taken from a memorandum our office uses for the purpose of preparing a person for a deposition.

Either party is entitled to examine the witness before the trial to attempt to obtain information, to narrow the client's testimony, and cause the client to commit to as many positions as possible. The general purpose is to prevent surprise at the trial, and reduce the number of issues.

Some comments as to conduct at a deposition follow:

1. The client should volunteer no information, should answer only the questions asked as briefly as possible and should be thoroughly prepared.

2. The reporter serves to record the testimony and at the end certifies that it is a true record of what took place at the examination before trial.

3. The testimony may be used at the trial. The procedure is for the opposing attorney to read the reporter's record of the testimony into the record at the trial.

4. If an answer to a question at the examination before trial is different from an answer to the same question at the trial, the credibility of the witness is severely impaired. The client should provide a truthful answer at the examination and the same answer at the trial.

5. The attorneys may agree prior to the examination before trial that all objections, except as to the form of the questions, are reserved for the trial. The purpose of this stipulation is to permit the examination to go forward but to enable the other side to object to the question and answer at the trial.

6. During the examination the attorney may not wish the client to respond to the question. When the attorney interrupts the question-and-answer proce-

dure, the client should stop talking immediately and permit the attorney to speak.

7. The client should create a small pause before each answer to enable the attorney to object to that specific question. Once the question is answered by the client, it cannot be erased from the transcript.

8. An examination before trial is usually conducted in a friendly atmosphere between the attorneys. Do not be misled by this friendly atmosphere into volunteering any information or discussing with the attorney for the opposing side or the adversary any details of the case.

9. It is permissible to ask the attorney to repeat the question and to ask the court reporter to read the question back when you state that you did not understand it. This procedure should be utilized whenever appropriate.

10. If you are testifying and you have kept some notes to refresh your recollection at the examination, do not refer to those notes in the presence of the opposing attorney. The attorney for the other side is then entitled to examine all of those notes, including the notes you did not use. Furthermore, the notes can be used at the trial to cross-examine. The best course is to review these notes prior to the examination and out of the sight of the opposing attorney.

GUIDELINES FOR TESTIMONY AT TRIAL

1. The oath warrants repeating "to tell the truth, the whole truth, and nothing but the truth." Accordingly, the truth should be stated at all times. The truth always hangs together.

2. Do not try to evaluate whether your answer is hurting your side or helping the other side. Answer the question to the best of your recollection.

3. Do not try to color or exaggerate your answer, nor use intonations of indignation or sincerity, to help or hurt your side. Give your answer truthfully and in a level and sincere tone of voice.

4. Listen carefully to the questions. Remember that the other attorney is attempting to help his or her client. Failure to understand the question may produce an answer which is harmful to your side, especially since everyone else in the Courtroom will have heard the question correctly. If necessary, ask that the question be repeated.

5. Do not respond quickly to a question, nor should you respond slowly to a question. The reason you do not respond quickly is to afford your attorney an opportunity to lodge an objection. If your attorney does so, do not answer the question until the Court directs you. If you answer the question slowly and spend too much time deliberating, the impression may be that you are framing or fabricating an answer.

6. The most important thing to remember when answering a question is that the answer should respond only to the question. Do not furnish information that is not sought. Furnishing additional information creates more material about which the opposing attorney will ask questions.

7. Where possible, an answer of "yes" or "no" is preferred. Nevertheless, if the answer needs an explanation, furnish the explanation.

8. If during your testimony you remember that a prior question was answered improperly, stop, state that you would like to change an answer to a prior question, and change the answer.

9. Do not memorize any answers prior to the trial. Answer the questions truthfully and to the best of your recollection.

10. If you finish an answer and the other attorney remains silent, do not continue to speak. The attorney is hoping you will offer more information.

DEMEANOR

1. Maintain a serious attitude. Don't laugh or talk loud in the hallways, restrooms, or anywhere in the Courthouse.

2. Do not try to approach or talk to any members of the jury if you should meet them in the hall or in the Courtroom.

3. While testifying, direct your answers directly at the attorney or the jury. Look at them most of the time and speak to them openly and frankly as you would to any friend or neighbor. Do not cover your mouth with your hand. Do not look down at the floor. Do not gaze up at the ceiling. Do not try to look up at the judge and answer the question to the judge. The answer should be responsive to the attorney, or preferably to the jury if one is present.

4. Be polite to the attorney and to the judge. Do not be argumentative. Do not be curt or brief.

5. Do not be a conceited or a wise-guy type of witness.

6. Do not act nervous. Avoid mannerisms which will make the jury think you are scared or not telling the truth.

7. Sit upright and do not slump in the chair.

8. As a general rule, the male's attire should be a suit and tie. Women should wear a dress or suit. Conservative colors are advisable. Neatness counts in your overall appearance.

SUGGESTIONS AS TO TESTIMONY

1. The Court and the jury want the facts. They do not want conclusions, opinions, or what you heard other people say. Testifying as to conclusions, opinions, or what other people say normally produce objections by the other attorney.

2. Do not say "that's all that was said," "nothing else was said," or "nothing else happened." Use the words "that's all I recall," "that's all I remember," or "that's all I recollect." You may use "to the best of my recollection," or "at this time all I remember." This leaves an opening in case your recollection is refreshed in the future and you wish to add facts or certain statements.

3. Give firm answers whenever possible. If you do remember something, do not say "I think," "I believe," or "in my opinion." If you do not know something, answer "I do not know" or "I do not remember." If the other attorney is seeking minor and small details, it is best to say that you do not remember them. Of course, you should remember major points.

CONDUCT

1. Do not ask the judge for advice or ask the judge to help you.

2. If you feel that the question is improper or you feel you should not be answering, wait for your attorney to object. If your attorney does not object, you must answer the question.

3. Do not argue with the other attorney or be flippant. It is best to respond with no side remarks, no comments, no groans, or any other physical move which would offend the attorney, the judge, or the jury.

4. Do not use your head for "yes" or "no" answers. Speak out.

FATIGUE

Fatigue always enters into cross examination of a witness. After being on the witness stand for an hour, or being examined before trial for an hour, it is easy to become fatigued, short-tempered, and anxious for the next question to be the last. Do not lose your temper. When you become tired, and you feel you are nervous or angry or careless, be aware of these symptoms and attempt to control the fatigue. Other symptoms are crossness, nervousness, a willingness to answer any questions, a desire to stand up out of your seat and walk around, a slight headache or an impatience in waiting for the next question. Remember that many attorneys on cross examinations attempt to induce this fatigue and cause you to lose your temper to provoke you into careless answers. Do not let this happen. Request a recess when fatigue is present.

DOWN THE GARDEN PATH

Some attorneys lead you down the garden path with trick questions that have been used many times before.

1. *Have you talked to anyone about the case?* If you say no, the jury knows lawyers always talk to their witnesses before a trial.

2. *Has your attorney told you what to say at this trial?* This is the same type of question. The answer is that the case was discussed with you and you were told to tell the truth.

3. *Are you getting paid to testify in this case?* If you are being paid, your answer should be that you are paid to compensate for your time off from work and the expenses to appear at the trial or whatever the arrangement is.

4. Often an attorney will try to narrow down "time," "days," "hours," and "approximate values":

Q. When was the last time you saw the car before it struck your car?

A. I don't know.

Q. Well, was it a minute, ten seconds, five seconds, two seconds?

A. I don't know; perhaps two seconds.

Q. Well, you must realize that a car can travel somewhere around 60 to 80 feet in two seconds. If you saw a car 60 to 80 feet away from you, you could have certainly done something to avoid the collision.

The same principle applies when you are recollecting a conversation that took place several years ago and the attorney asks you when the conversation took place. For example:

Q. Was it in January, February, the first week in January, the first week in February?

If you do not remember the exact time, and only remember that it happened during the first half of the year, the testimony is:

A. It happened during the first half of the year. I don't remember exactly when during that period of time.

The same line of questioning may apply when you are asked:

Q. How many boxes did you see? Did you see ten, twenty, fifty, a hundred boxes?

If you don't remember how many you saw, and all you remember is that you saw a lot of boxes, the answer should be:

A. I saw a lot of boxes. I don't remember how many there were.

5. The client should not adopt the attorney's friendly questions as the testimony or adopt a summary of the situation furnished by the attorney where it appears to be substantially correct, although not exactly correct. In short, the client should testify as to exactly what happened and not adopt any summary provided by the attorney requesting a "yes" or "no" answer, as follows:

Q. The borrower was at your desk and signed the note.
A. Yes.

The attorney for the other side failed to mention that one of the defenses is that the defendant was not wearing glasses and could not read the note. The witness, on the other hand, failed to tell the defendant that the borrower spent about two minutes reading the note carefully (without glasses).

SPECIAL TESTIMONY

1. As a general rule, you may testify as to what you saw, heard, felt, touched or smelled.
2. You are not permitted to testify as to opinion, conclusions, what someone said about something happening, what you believe to have happened, what you hope to happen, etc.

TELEPHONE CONVERSATIONS

There are special foundations which must be laid in order to permit a telephone conversation or a letter to be admitted as evidence.

The key to a telephone conversation is the recognition of a voice. An essential part to this is that you spoke to the party either before the telephone conversation took place, or after the telephone conversation took place, and you can state that you recognize the voice on the telephone. A series of questions might be as follows:

Q. Did you speak to John Smith before July 4th?
A. Yes.

Q. On July 4th, did you or did you not telephone him?

A. I telephoned him on July 4th.

Q. Did you dial his number?

A. Yes.

Q. Did you recognize the voice on the telephone as the voice of John Smith?

A. Yes.

Q. What did he say and what did you say?

A. He said …

MAILING A LETTER

A similar problem may arise with regard to offering a copy of a letter as evidence.

The key to this line of questioning is that you compared the original to the copy, and that the envelope was mailed in a depository of the United States, i.e., a mailbox. A line of questioning might be as follows:

Q. Did you write (dictate) the letter dated July 4, 1976?

A. Yes.

Q. Did you see the original letter before it was mailed?

A. Yes.

Q. Did you compare the original with the copy?

A. Yes.

Q. Then what did you do with the letter?

A. I sealed it in an envelop, affixed postage to it and mailed it in a mailbox at Fifth Avenue and 42nd Street.

CONCLUSION

When you leave the witness stand, try to have a confident expression and not a downcast one. It is best not to discuss the case, and if you have been excused, you should leave the Courtroom and the Courthouse.

CHAPTER 2

Legal Concepts
of Business

To properly extend credit to and collect money from a debtor, you must understand the structure of the debtor's business as well as the basic ingredients of a contract. Each type of business creates different exposures to liability. This chapter will describe the various types of business organizations and the liabilities of the organization and its principals. Also, the basic contract will be reviewed, to determine if a contract actually existed.

AN INDIVIDUAL IN BUSINESS

The simplest form of doing business is an individual conducting a business under his or her own name or a trade name. An example of a trade name would be "Joe's Shoe Repair Shop." This designation could indicate either an individual or a partnership, but not a corporation. Corporations must be designated as "Corporation," "Corp.," "Inc," "Co. Inc.," "Ltd." (Some state laws may vary these designations.) To determine whether the business is an individual or a partnership, a search of the filing records in the county where the business is located should be performed by your attorney. A limited liability company requires the designation of "Limited Liability Company" or abbreviations "L.L.C." or "LLC."

> **CREDIT AND COLLECTION TIP:** *You can include a designation on your credit application as follows:*
> ___ *Individual* ___ *Partnership* ___ *Corporation* ___ *Limited Liability*

The credit application should provide space for listing all the partners and all the stockholders and directors of corporations. In lieu of the stockholders and directors, you might provide for the "principals" of the corporation.

PARTNERSHIP

A partnership is a group of two or more persons who contribute capital and engage in a business enterprise. Most states have laws regulating the creation of partnerships and the liabilities of partners. The individuals are liable in the same manner as they would be if they were operating the business as a single individual. Some states require a creditor to first proceed against the assets of the partnership before proceeding against the individual partners. Partners are only taxed once.

A special type of partnership is a *limited partnership*. General partners operate the partnership, and limited partners invest money. The liability of limited partners extends only to the amount of capital contributed to the partnership, whereas general partners are liable for all of the debts of the partnership. If limited partners act as a general partner or are perceived by the creditor as a general partner, the limited partner may be liable as a general partner.

Before the states enacted statutes setting forth the exact liability of partners, the common law rule was that partners must be sued in the names of all the partners and that a suit against a partnership must name all of the partners. The state laws changed this by enacting various statutes which are now known as "common name" or "joint debtor" statutes.

A partner is always considered the agent of the partnership. Even if all the partners are not served, a judgment creditor can still proceed against the partnership assets under a common name statute (California). The judgment creditor is limited to the assets of the individual partner who is served and may not proceed against the assets of any partner who is not served.

On the other hand we have what is known as "joint debtor" statutes (New York) which are not the same but have the same affect. Usually they apply only to contract claims and not to tort liabilities (accidents). In "joint debtor" statutes a plaintiff may name all of the partners but only serve some of them. With regard to the partners that have been served, no problem exists. The end result is the same because the judgment remains against the property of all the partners (partnership) and against the separate property of the defendants actually served.

The Uniform Partnership Act has been adopted in almost every state but with changes which produce either joint debtor statutes or common name statutes. Nevertheless, the Act adopted in New Jersey provides for joint and several liability for the contract obligations of the partnership but joint liability for other debts and obligations of the partnership that were not created by means of a contract. The New Jersey Act seems to place partners in a position more vulnerable than stockholders but less vulnerable than guarantors of payment. Partners were held liable for partnership contract debts, but their assets were not at risk until it was shown that the partnership could not discharge the debt. Therefore, the court held that partners are more like guarantors of collection as distinguished from guarantors of payment.

> CREDIT AND COLLECTION TIP: *Most states have adopted the common name statutes so suits against partners and partnerships may proceed simultaneously. Again, the particular partnership law of the particular state must be reviewed before proceeding.*

CORPORATION

A corporation is created solely by law and therefore only has the powers and the rights that the law provides. One basic right is perpetuity—the corporation can operate forever. Thus, groups of people, endlessly replacing each other, may devote themselves to a particular purpose to achieve a particular goal, as if one person had lived forever. Double taxation occurs in corporations since the corporation is taxed on income and the shareholder is taxed when a dividend is declared.

A corporation is created in three tiers. The first tier is the stockholders who contribute the money and capital by purchasing the shares of stock. This ownership share is represented by stock certificates. If it is a public corporation that has complied with the registration statutes of the state and the Securities and Exchange Commission, the stock certificates can be traded publicly either through the National Association of Security Dealers (NASDAQ) or through one of the exchanges, such as the New York Stock Exchange. The shareholder is not personally liable for corporate debts except to the extent of the money used to purchase stock in the corporation. The only money the shareholder can lose is the money invested.

The second tier of the corporation consists of the Board of Directors, which is elected by the stockholders at an annual meeting. The Board of Directors then elects the officers of the corporation at the first meeting of the directors. Directors have a fiduciary duty to the stockholders—and, to some degree, to the creditors—to conduct the affairs of the corporation in a proper manner. Directors are not personally liable to creditors of a corporation except in unusual circumstances.

The third tier of the corporation is the officers who operate the corporation on a day-to-day basis. The officers of the corporation include the President, Vice Presidents, Secretaries, Controllers, Treasurers, etc., who have the authority to sign checks and to execute contracts and purchase orders. Officers are not personally liable for corporate debts except in unusual circumstances.

LIABILITIES OF STOCKHOLDERS, DIRECTORS AND OFFICERS. For a corporate debt to be valid, an officer or an authorized person (see "Apparent Authority") of the corporation must execute the instrument binding the corporation. The officers, directors and stockholders are generally not personally liable for the debt, with certain exceptions.

The officer of the corporation who signs or supervises the issuing of payroll checks may be personally liable to the Internal Revenue Service for withholding taxes if they have not been set aside and paid to the government at the same time the salary was paid to the employees. Liability for failure to collect and remit sales taxes also may apply to officers pursuant to state law. Sometimes individual business debtors rely on this liability to the IRS to support their inability to continue to pay their business debt. You should verify before accepting this excuse. While the circumstances may exist, the IRS will normally allow long periods (running into years) to discharge this liability, and a thorough investigation may reveal substantial monies or income available to pay business debts.

Stockholders usually do not have any liability for debts, but the directors of the corporation would probably be liable to the creditors for the declaration of an improper or illegal dividend.

In some instances the principals of the corporation do not operate it either as a business or a corporation. Corporate books are not kept, corporate bank accounts are used for personal debts, and the individuals commingle their personal affairs under the "corporate veil." Under these circumstances, the courts have recognized a theory of law entitled "piercing the corporate veil" wherein a creditor can sue the individuals as well as the corporation and hold the individuals liable for a corporate debt because the individuals were not operating the corporation as a corporation solely for corporate purposes.

> **CREDIT AND COLLECTION TIP:** *If an officer or agent of a corporation commits an act of fraud to obtain property or services from you, consult with counsel to evaluate the circumstances. If fraud, collusion or conspiracy are involved in the transaction, you may be able to look to the individual officer or the agent for payment. A fraudulent application, forgery or misrepresentations as to solvency may be sufficient grounds.*

LIMITED LIABILITY COMPANY

The limited liability company (LLC) is a new concept in forming a business entity, somewhere between a corporation and a partnership. With an LLC, individual partners have all the tax advantages of a partnership to avoid double taxation plus the limited liability of the partners similar to the stockholders in a corporation. The partners are only liable for the partnership debts up to the amount of the investment in the LLC. The limited liability company may or may not have the characteristic of continuity of existence, even perpetuity, depending upon the state's statute. The LLC may resemble the corporate characteristic of free transferability of the interest of a partner in a manner similar to the transfer of a stock certificate.

The four characteristics that the IRS considers in taxing an LLC are:

1. the continuity of life.
2. whether the central management is an individual or a board.
3. the ability of the partners to limit their liability to the investment.
4. the extent of the transferability of the interest of the limited liability partner.

The general theory is that if the new organization lacks two of these four corporate ingredients, the IRS will tax the limited liability company as a partnership and not as a corporation.

The major question surrounding Limited Liability Companies is whether the courts will "pierce the veil" of the LLC on the grounds that the LLC has not complied with the statute's requirements; and thus the partners are personally liable.

Each state's statute is somewhat different and there are many specific requirements with which the LLC must comply before the LLC attains the status of a properly organized Limited Liability Company. The LLC must operate carefully within the parameters of the partnership agreement and in compliance with the requirements of the laws of the state in which it is located. The creditor should examine the books of the LLC, the filings, as well as the day-to-day operations of the company to determine if it has complied not only with its partnership agreement, but also with the requirements set forth in the state law.

Failure to comply may expose the partners to personal liability for the debts of the partnership. Where the debt is substantial, it may be worthwhile to spend the money to search the records of the state with regard to the filings of the Limited Liability Company and the operation of the Limited Liability Company. Certainly, if the partners are individuals of substance and the debt is substantial, these activities may be warranted.

Almost all the states have passed laws to authorize the use of a limited liability company. The appropriate laws should be reviewed with counsel.

BUSINESS TRUST

In several states, a *business trust* may be created to operate a business for the benefit of investors. Property is transferred to a trustee under a specified agreement which sets forth the purpose and the powers of the trustee and how the trustee is to pay the benefits. Certificates are issued to the beneficiaries according to their investment and these parties are entitled to receive any income or dividend from the trust. Although some state statutes attempt to regulate trusts, a trust is primarily regulated by the agreement that created the trust. Whereas the trust may be considered a partnership, at the same time the certificate holders (similar to shareholders of a corporation) may be relieved from any liability and only the trustee is liable for the obligations and the business dealings of the trust.

A careful examination of the trust agreement and the state law is necessary before extending credit.

PRINCIPAL-AGENT RELATIONSHIP

A recent case involving the rental of mailing lists analyzed in depth the relationship between a principal, the agent (broker) and a third party who is dealing with the agent. In that case, a list owner engaged a firm, known as a list broker, to rent mailing lists to a mailer. The agreement stated as follows:

> "Greenfield Direct Response, Inc. acts only as agent to the list owner and does not guarantee payment under this order. Upon receipt of payment from the mailer who was solely responsible for payment of this order, Greenfield Direct Response, Inc. will remit to the list owner, less the standard 20% commission."

The case arose because the list broker was in bankruptcy and a bank had issued a letter of credit secured by accounts receivable. The bank believed that all this money that the list broker was collecting from mailers belonged to the list broker. The list owners contended that the list broker was merely an agent, and that all the monies (less commissions) belong to the list owners for the rental of their lists.

The list owners took the position that the wording in the contract delineated that the broker acted only as agent for the list owner. The bank contended that the funds belonged to the broker and that the broker was not an agent because the broker was not subject to the control of the list owner, that the funds were commingled with those of other list owners and no agency relationship existed because there was no such understanding between the parties. In addition, the contractual writing was merely "boilerplate."

The usual test of what creates an agency is whether the principal has authority to control the method or manner of accomplishing a task by the agent and whether the agent has authority to subject the principal to liability. Existence of an agency relationship is a question of fact. However, where an agency's authority has been conferred in writing and there is no dispute concerning the parties' relationship, the question becomes one of law.

The word "agent" is broader than the word "broker" and more comprehensive in its legal scope. Though every broker is in a sense an agent, every agent is not a broker. Attorneys, brokers, auctioneers and similar persons are employed for a single transaction of agency, although as to their physical activities, they are independent contractors.

The court seemed to conclude that the broker could have been a limited agent for both the mailer and the list owner as to different tasks and responsibilities. The broker contended that it was really retained by the mailer to search for a customer list owned by a list owner which would meet the criteria of the mailer. The court emphasized the fact that if the broker held itself out to be a broker, it represented itself as an agent to someone and in the "collection" paragraph of the agreement, the broker stated that the broker was an "agent for the list owner." Thus, the broker was an agent of the list owner for purposes of collection and prompt remittance, notwithstanding whether it might have been an agent for the mailer in searching out the proper list for the mailer to use.

Extrinsic evidence to alter the terms of the contract was disallowed even though it was a "boilerplate" contract. Whether or not it was a boilerplate contract, it was a contract. The court dismissed the lack of control by the principal since there was no control that the principal had to exercise to be certain that the broker remitted collections for the rental of the lists. Accordingly, an agent who collects money on behalf of the principal does not become the owner of such money, and the court decided that the money belongs to the list owners and not to the creditor of the list broker (less commissions due the list broker).

One of the interesting aspects of this case was the distinction the court drew with another case where the party held the funds for sixty (60) days by agreement and the monies actually became the property of the party holding the money because he was entitled to ownership for a period of 60 days. However, in the mailing list broker case, the broker had to remit the monies (less commission) immediately upon receipt.

The fact that brokers or agents sometimes act for one party for a certain part of the transaction and for the other party for a different part of the transaction will lead to different results depending upon which transaction is involved in a dispute. The method to solve this type of situation is to be certain that the contract is clear as to the responsibility of the broker or agent.[1]

RELYING ON APPARENT AUTHORITY

An agent is a party who represents a principal, and binds the principal. Businesses utilize agents for a wide variety of purposes: an officer of a corporation is the agent for the corporation; a partner is the agent for the partnership; a salesman is the agent for sales of merchandise. Individuals or businesses may also act as agents of other businesses. An attorney, accountant, stockbroker, real estate broker, or food broker, all are agents of the business.

Doing business with an agent is the same as doing business with the principal. Sometimes agents are appointed for all business transactions and other times for limited or specific transactions. When dealing with an agent, the best protection is to obtain the written authority of the agent to act on behalf of the principal, but if a written agreement cannot be obtained, you may rely on the "apparent authority" of the agent to act for the business.

---

[1]Greenfield Direct Response, Inc. v. Adco List Management, 171 B.R. 848 (Bankr. N.D. Ill. 1994).

The question of a valid agency will turn on this "apparent authority," and "apparent authority" comes in many different forms. The decision to start suit may depend upon whether an agency relationship has been established, or, more to the point, whether the "apparent authority" of the party is sufficient to create an agency. Some examples follow:

(1) The scope of the employee's duties may entitle a businessperson to rely on the "apparent authority" of the agent, such as dealing with the sales manager. Even if the sales manager is not an officer of the corporation or a partner, the title of sales manager is adequate "apparent authority" to bind the business to a sale of merchandise.

(2) Prior dealings where past orders were accepted and delivered will support the "apparent authority." For example, the owner of a business alleges that the party who ordered the merchandise did not have the authority to order and did not bind the business to a contract. The owner states that the individual is no longer employed or was employed in such a position that the creditor had no right to rely on the employee's authority to order. The fact the party is no longer employed is not relevant. The only question is whether "apparent authority" was present, and whether prior activities enabled a reasonable businessman to rely on the representations of the employee. If the employee ordered in the past and the bills were paid, the employee has "apparent authority" to bind the business.

(3) Accepting the benefits of the transaction will also support "apparent authority." For example, a bookkeeper orders merchandise. The seller (creditor) ships the merchandise directly to the customer (the employer of the bookkeeper). The customer retains the merchandise and the benefits of the transaction, but refuses to pay on the grounds the bookkeeper had no authority to order merchandise. The seller may recover for "unjust enrichment" in addition to breach of contract. If the bookkeeper had no authority, the breach of contract claim may fail, but the seller would recover for "unjust enrichment" since the buyer cannot retain the goods and not pay for them. At the same time, an argument may be offered that a bookkeeper in a small business may have "apparent authority" to order at least office supplies.

(4) Officers of corporations and partners of partnerships have the authority to bind the corporation and partnership. Whether other employees or staff can do so depends upon "apparent authority."

CREDIT AND COLLECTION TIP: *When dealing with professional agents, such as real estate brokers, attorneys, accountants, or stockbrokers, reliance on a written agreement is recommended.*

CONTRACTS

To understand whether a debtor is legally liable on a debt requires the creditor to understand whether or not a contract was actually formed and thus would be enforceable. Whether a contract is enforceable has continually confronted the courts and the legislators. Contract law covers hundreds of pages of the Uniform Commercial Code. In each state, hundreds of cases each year interpret the terms and conditions of a contract between two parties. Nevertheless, certain ingredients are essential to the formation of a contract. With that in mind, we will review some basic contract law.

AN OFFER AND ACCEPTANCE. Until the two parties agree on the terms of the contract, no contract exists. For there to be a contract, an offer has to be made by the creditor and the debtor has to accept. If the debtor counteroffers with new terms, the debtor is making a new offer awaiting the acceptance by the creditor of the new terms. After agreement on the terms, a contract is formed.

A contract does not have to be in writing (for exceptions see *Statute of Frauds*), but reducing an agreement to writing is the most desirable form of a contract because the uncertainty of the memory of either party is removed.

An offer is open for acceptance for a reasonable time or at least until it is revoked. If an offer is open for a specific time period, the offer automatically terminates at the end of that period.

Another way that a contract can be formed, despite the fact that the parties did not agree on all the terms, is by performance. If the creditor and the debtor agreed on most, but not all, the terms of the contract, and thereafter the creditor performed the contract by shipping the goods, and the debtor accepted the goods, the parties have entered a contract by virtue of performance.

AGREEING ON MATERIAL TERMS. Every contract contains material terms and minor terms. Material terms consist of identifying the subject of the contract (building, merchandise, service, commodity), price, delivery terms, and the important ingredients necessary to complete the transaction. If the material terms of a contract are acceptable to both parties, a contract will be formed even if certain minor or trivial terms are not mentioned or agreed upon. Minor or trivial terms may be the place of signing, method of delivery, etc. Nevertheless, the courts lean to the concept that where a written agreement is contemplated, no contract has been entered into until the written agreement has been executed.

If partial performance by either party is added, the court is more likely to enforce the contract to the extent performed. A breach of a material term of a contract may enable the other party to refuse to perform. A breach of a minor term may not release the other party from performance, although a claim for damages may be made. Each contract is different, and what is a "material" term is a question of fact to be decided by a judge or jury.

IS THE PARTY COMPETENT TO MAKE THE OFFER? The party making the offer must be competent to make the offer. An individual who is conducting a business is empowered to bind the business. If an offer is being made by a partnership, a contract with one of the partners, or an authorized agent, will bind the partnership. In dealing with a corporation, a contract with an officer of the corporation or authorized party is necessary to bind the corporation. A salesman should be able to bind a business to a sales contract since the salesman has "apparent authority" to purchase goods, but only officers as a rule have the "apparent authority" to borrow money.

CONSIDERATION AND PAYMENT. Some form of consideration is generally necessary to support a contract. The most common example of consideration is the payment of money. Nevertheless, other forms of considerations which do not involve payment of money may be sufficient to form a binding contract. Agreeing to do something or to perform an act in return for the promise of another is consideration. The surrender of a legal right or the forbearance of a right to act, such as a right to sue, is sufficient to constitute consideration. An example is when one party agrees not to sue if the other party enters a payment arrangement or agrees to perform an act.

On the other hand, if no consideration is received, the agreement may be unforceable. For example:

A. "Joe, you've known me for 40 years. I need about $10,000 to clear up my debts. So, instead of giving $10,000 to United Way, give me $10,000."

J. "Allen, you have been a good friend for many years and I am going to give you the $10,000 you need."

Allen cannot enforce this promise for there is no "consideration" for the promise. Allen has not done anything or performed any act or service in return for the promise to give him $10,000.

The interpretation of consideration by the courts creates many exceptions to this rule. The courts enforce contracts even though no apparent consideration is present, either because the contract falls into an exception, or the circumstances of the contract present what appears to be consideration. In certain states and in certain circumstances, consideration is not necessary if the contract is entered into in writing, or if there has been partial or full performance of the contract. In the example above, if the promise to give Allen $10,000 was in writing, in certain circumstances and in some states, the contract may be binding.

MISTAKES IN CONTRACT

Where both parties entered into a contract and made a mistake concerning one of the material ingredients of the contract, no offer and acceptance of the terms and conditions exists since the parties mutually misunderstood an essential element, and no "meeting of the minds" took place. An example is where the seller offers to sell a pentium computer but only has a pentium II in inventory, which the seller believes is a pentium computer and the buyer wants to purchase a pentium computer. The buyer accepts the pentium II believing it to be a pentium. This is considered a mutual mistake of fact, and the contract for the pentium II computer could not be enforced.

On the other hand, if a mistake was made by one of the parties, that party cannot evade liability by alleging a mistake was made. A loan is made and the documents recite the interest rate as the prime rate. The borrower thought the prime rate was 6% when in fact it was 7%. This is a mistake by one party.

Nevertheless, where consumers are involved, the courts seem to produce different results. A classic example is where the store owner mistakenly advertises a ridiculously low price for a product, such as thirty dollars ($30.00) for a camcorder on sale when three hundred dollars ($300) was meant. The store owner argues that the consumer knew that the advertised price was a mistake and refuses to sell at that price. Some courts treat such an advertisement as an offer to negotiate, and not an offer to contract. The cases go both ways with the majority probably requiring the store owner to honor the advertised offer.

STATUTE OF FRAUDS

Almost all states have a Statute of Frauds which requires certain types of contracts to be in writing. A review of each state law is necessary since the laws differ from state to state. The following types of contracts usually must be in writing:

A. Contracts for sale or lease of real estate.
B. Agreements that cannot be fully performed within a period of one year from the date of the agreement.
C. A guarantee of the debt of another party.
D. Contracts for the sale of goods (not services) in excess of $500.

Section 2-201 of the Uniform Commercial Code recites certain exceptions. A contract where the goods are specifically manufactured for the buyer and are not suitable for sale to others is one exception, as well as if the goods have been received and accepted. In these instances, a failure to have a written contract cannot be asserted under the Statute of Frauds (only to the extent the contract is completed).

An important ingredient of UCC 2-201 is subdivision 2 which provides a ten-day period between merchants to object to any of the terms and conditions set forth in a written confirmation which arrives after an oral contract. An oral agreement is entered into over the telephone and then one of the parties confirms this oral agreement by writing to the other party setting forth what they believe are the terms of the agreement. Under the UCC the receiving party has a ten-day period to object to any of these terms and conditions set forth in the written confirmation. If no objection is made within that ten-day period, the written confirmation becomes the written contract between the parties.

If the written confirmation does not specifically agree with what the party understood over the telephone, that party has an obligation to object in writing within ten days and his failure to object may result in a written agreement to which he did not agree.

If the agreement cannot be completed by its own terms within one year, UCC 2-201 provides that you must have a written agreement. If the terms of performance are possible within one year, however unlikely or improbable that performance may be, the agreement or promise is usually not within the statute of frauds and a written agreement is not needed. Contracts that are of an indefinite time period are usually not within this provision of the statute.

Another provision of the Statute of Frauds states that a contract must be executed by the party to be charged. Some courts add additional criteria such as identifying both contracting parties, setting forth the subject matter of the contract and the essential terms of the contract and requiring consideration to be described. The courts are still uncertain as to exactly what the criteria should be and the decisions seem to vary from state to state and from court to court even within the same state.

One case analyzed the question of an alleged contract bearing no signature of the party against whom they are trying to enforce the contract. The court relied on the commentary to the U.C.C., which acknowledges that a complete signature is not necessary. It may be printed, stamped, or written and may be by initials or even by a thumb print. It may be on a part of the document and in appropriate cases may be found in a bill head or a letterhead.[2] The court must use common sense and commercial experience in passing upon these matters. If we translate, it means that the courts must look at these situations on a case-by-case basis. Actually, the courts sometimes utilize any symbol executed or adopted by a party with the present intention to authenticate a writing. An examination of other cases will reveal the creation of other criteria to create a signature.

If the specific agreement is listed in the Statute of Frauds of the particular state, the contract is unenforceable in the courts of that state unless it is in writing. Exceptions and defenses to the Statute of Frauds vary from state to state, but they usually include the following:

1. Part performance—a contract is not in writing, but one party has partially performed the contract with knowledge of the other party.
2. Equitable estoppel—where one party's conduct leads the other party to reasonably rely on the activity or representation of the first party and their positions is changed to their detriment.

A printer enters an agreement with a customer and sends the customer a contract. The customer calls on the telephone and pressures the printer (because

---

[2]*Owen v. Kroger Co.*, 936 F. Supp. 579 (S.D. Ind. 1996).

of prior business dealings) to run the job even though the contract was not received by the customer. The printer runs the job, and on the same day, the customer calls for a progress report. After half the job is run, the customer cancels and refuses to pay since no contract was signed. Elements of both part performance and equitable estoppel would support a suit in this instance.

TERMS OF CONTRACT OFFERS

There is significant litigation over UCC Section 2-207, which states as follows:

(1) A definite and seasonable expression of acceptance or a written confirmation which is sent within a reasonable time operates as an acceptance even though it states terms additional to, or different from those offered or agreed upon, unless acceptance is expressly made conditional on assent to the additional or different terms.

(2) The additional terms are to be construed as proposals for additions to the contract. Between merchants such terms become a part of the contract unless

(a) the offer expressly limits acceptance to the terms of the offer

(b) they materially alter it

(c) notification of objection to them has already been given or is given within a reasonable time after notice of them is received.

(3) Conduct by both parties which recognizes the existence of a contract is sufficient to establish a contract for sale, although the writings of the parties do not otherwise establish a contract. In such case the terms of the particular contract consists of those terms on which the writings of the parties agreed, together with any supplementary terms incorporated under any other provision of this act.

The wording of UCC Section 2-207 is confusing and at best promotes a considerable amount of litigation in the courts. Subdivision 1 states in essence that the accepting party can accept the terms of a contract and still add additional or different terms unless the acceptance is made conditional by the accepting party, so that the offering party must assent to the additional or different terms. On the other hand, subdivision 2 states that the additional terms are to be construed as proposals only for additions to the contract.

The problem arises that between merchants such terms become a part of the contract unless the conditions of a, b and c are met, because the code uses the word "additions" and does not refer to different terms. Therefore, it seems that if you disagree and your terms are different from the terms submitted by the other party over the same subject matter, the different terms will cancel themselves out.[3]

---

[3]*Northrop Corp. v. Litronic Indus.*, 29 f.3d 1173 (7th Cir. 1994).

From a practical point of view, the important thing to remember in negotiating contracts is that if you offer different or additional terms and it is your intent to make the consummation of the contract conditional upon these material different or additional terms, it should be spelled out in clear and unequivocal language that you will not enter the contract unless the party agrees to these material different or additional terms. Unless the language is vividly clear as to what your intentions are with regard to these different and additional terms, in the event a dispute should arise later, the end result will be litigation and a further opportunity for some court to interpret Section 2-207.

The majority view of most courts is that different terms cancel themselves out. The definition of different terms is those terms which both parties have considered. Additional terms are terms upon which only one party has made a proposal and the other party has not responded. Whether additional terms or different terms are one and the same is a question upon which the courts certainly disagree. In any event, the last sentence of UCC 2-207 subdivision 1 is most important: "unless acceptance is expressly made conditional on assent to the additional or different terms." It is recommended to utilize this phraseology in any proposal of additional or different terms.

GOOD FAITH CONTRACT

In most state laws, there are provisions stating that unconscionable contracts are not enforced and somewhere in case lore, the courts have adopted a policy that every party to a contract must act in good faith. The definition of an unconscionable contract and what is and is not good faith or fair dealing are usually subjective questions which may vary significantly from court to court. While the definitions of the two terms are somewhat similar, the application of the terms to a set of circumstances will differ from judge to judge depending upon the subjective point of view of each particular judge. In a recent case in New Jersey, the court attempted to attack the question of whether the party acted in good faith:

> "The obligation to perform in good faith exists in every contract including those contracts that contain express and unambiguous provisions permitting either party to terminate the contract without cause."

The court relied on a Fourth Circuit case which evaluated the covenant of good faith and fair dealing and cited the following:

> "What is wrong with Colgate's conduct in this case is not its failure to communicate a decision to terminate…, but its cessation of performance. Clearly, it had an obligation of good faith performance up until its right of termination was actually effec-

tive. The contract expressly obliged it to use its best efforts in the promotion of Banbeanos. Instead of doing that, it simply ceased performance..., quite simply, it broke its contract when it terminated its performance, which was United Roasters' contractual due."

The court then cited another case:

"While the contractual relation of manufacturer and exclusive territorial distributor continued between the parties, an obligation of reciprocal good faith dealing persisted between them."

The court adopted a proposition that a party to a contract may breach the implied covenant of good faith and fair dealing in performing its obligations even when it exercises an express and unconditional right to terminate.

The fact that a party has not violated one single express term of a contract does not mean that the party cannot violate the implied covenant of good faith and fair dealing. The duty to act in good faith is independent of the express terms of a given contract.

In this particular case, the defendant knew that the plaintiff depended upon the income from its contract and yet the defendant continually breached the contract by refusing the required amount of merchandise. The defendant also knew that the plaintiff was borrowing money to enable them to continue the contract. Evidence of bad faith abounded in this case.

The problem left unanswered is what degree of bad faith is necessary. Probably there is no answer to that question since a defendant either acts in bad faith or does not act in bad faith and the demarcation point is the subjective view of the trier of the fact who is a human being and has made a determination of what is and what is not good faith.[4]

USURY

Usury is charging a rate of interest in excess of the legal rate provided by the statute in the state where the law is to be enforced. Aside from certain usury laws contained in federal laws, most states have usury laws which affect the extension of credit or the lending of money. A contract may be declared unenforceable in the event it is usurious.

Contracting for an interest rate in excess of the legal rate would constitute usury. Although banks and credit card companies charge in excess of that rate

---

[4]*Sons of Thunder, Inc. v. Borden Inc.,* 148 N.J. 396, 690 A.2d 575 (N.J. Sup. Ct. 1997).

allowed by the state, federal law permits these rates for consumer credit transactions. In some states charging a corporation an interest rate in excess of fifteen percent constitutes usury. The legal rate of interest to charge a corporation or a consumer varies from state to state. Notwithstanding the variations, the state laws also provide a wide range of exceptions to the legal rate of interest that may be charged a consumer or a corporation. Review the state laws for these exceptions.

If there is a violation of the usury law of a particular state, the consequences vary from state to state and may include any of the following:

A. Sometimes the creditor may lose only the amount of the interest that exceeds the legal rate of interest, and in other instances the creditor may lose the entire amount of interest.

B. Some state laws expressly provide that the creditor has no right to enforce the debt.

C. In some states, charging usurious interest may be punishable as a crime.

Penalties for a late payment are usually treated as interest and included as interest for purposes of the usury law.

EXCULPATORY CLAUSE

An exculpatory clause enables a party to a contract to escape liability for a particular act. A typical clause used is the "Act of God" phrase where one party seeks absolution from responsibility for failure to deliver merchandise on time due to an "Act of God," such as a flood, a fire, an act of war, or some other natural phenomenon.

Although such clauses are usually upheld by the courts, an exculpatory clause which permits one party to escape liability for performing an activity under the contract in a negligent way presents different problems. An example would be a printer who states that the printing firm shall not be liable for any damages due to printing errors. Courts frown on exculpatory clauses unless the words specify the exact activity that is being pardoned, such as "negligence." For instance, if the terms and conditions on the order form eliminate liability for printing errors due to "negligence," the printer has a better chance of relying on that clause in a court of law. If the clause is not specific or the word "negligence" is totally omitted, the courts usually will not enforce this type of clause, even between merchants. Where a consumer is the aggrieved party, the courts are more inclined not to enforce any type of exculpatory clause even when "negligence" is used and the specificity of the activity is present.

LIQUIDATED DAMAGE CLAUSE

A liquidated damage clause is an example of the exculpatory clause. The purpose of the liquidated damage clause is not to remove liability, but to limit the liability of one of the contracting parties. For example, a liquidated damage clause may be used in the printing contract instead of or in addition to the exculpatory clause. With regard to printing errors, the clause may provide that "the printer will only be liable to the extent of reprinting the job and will not be liable for any damages resulting from the distribution of the printed material."

The courts will usually not enforce a liquidated damage clause if the damages are reasonably ascertainable and can be determined with a degree of effort. Furthermore, the amount of liquidated damages must bear a reasonable relationship to the actual amount of damages sustained. The courts normally will frown on liquidated damage clauses unless they are fair and equitable to both parties and are not excessive as to amount to a penalty which will not be allowed.

> CREDIT AND COLLECTION TIP: *Exculpatory clauses and liquidated damage clauses do not have to be accepted when they are contained in printed order forms or printed contracts. Printed contracts can be changed. If the clause is unreasonable, consultation with counsel is advised and the clause should be modified.*

BAILMENTS

A "bailment" is created when one party (bailor) delivers property to another party (bailee) for a specific purpose and the agreement between the parties is that the property will be returned after the purpose is accomplished. Bailments are encountered by consumers almost every day. The shoes are delivered to the shoemaker, the dress to the cleaners, and the automobile to the mechanic. But bailments are also created in a wide number of business situations. An example would be an original document delivered for the purpose of printing several hundred copies and thereafter returned to the owner. Other examples of a bailment are delivering computer discs to a computer service bureau for the purpose of adding to a data base; the delivery of property to a trucker for the purpose of transport; the delivery of securities to a transfer agent for the purpose of transferring the stock certificates to a new ownership; or delivering printed brochures and envelopes to a fulfillment house for the purpose of affixing labels, folding, inserting and mailing the envelopes.

The basic intent of the parties is that the property is to be delivered for a specific reason and thereafter the property is to be returned to the owner or, as in the case of the envelopes, sent to the potential customers of the owner. If the recipient of the goods (bailee) is entitled to return to the party who delivers the goods anything other than the property itself, such as cash, then the transaction does not create a bailment, but may create a sale. In certain circumstances where a bailment is created, the party who receives the merchandise is entitled to a lien on the property to the extent of the services that were rendered by the party. (See chapter on Legal Remedies.)

Under a bailment, the bailee (the party receiving the goods for a specific purpose) has the exclusive right to possession during the bailment as long as the bailee is performing in accordance with the bailment agreement. Thus, the bailee may recover any property taken by any third party, including the bailor (if the property was taken before the end of the bailment). The bailee cannot use the property other than to perform the specific purpose.

A gratuitous bailee, such as a neighbor who collects your mail when you are away, receives no compensation. Gratuitous bailees are usually liable only for gross negligence. In normal bailments for compensation, the bailee is liable for ordinary negligence.

Special statutes control common carriers such as trucks and trains, and other statutes regulate innkeepers, such as hotels.

CONSIGNMENT

Where merchandise is delivered to a merchant by the owner and the agreement is that the merchant will sell the merchandise, but the title of the merchandise shall remain with the owner, the arrangement is known as a consignment. The merchant has no obligation to pay for the merchandise until sold. If the merchandise is never sold, it will be returned to the owner. If the merchant sells the merchandise, the proceeds from the sale should technically be segregated and remitted to the owner, less the commission that the merchant has earned by selling the merchandise. If the agreement between the parties is that the merchant has an obligation to pay for the merchandise, the arrangement is not a consignment, but a sale. The key ingredient of a consignment is that no obligation exists on the part of the merchant to pay.

Sometimes determining whether the actual transaction constituted a consignment or a sale is difficult. Whether the owner had the right to determine the price of the merchandise, the right to set the periods of time within which the merchant had the right to sell the merchandise, or the right to terminate the transaction at any time and require the return of the merchandise to the owner are factors which indicate that the transaction was fundamentally a consignment. The ability to set the price and demand a return are elements of a consignment as opposed to a sale.

Even with a reservation of title to the owner, an obligation on the part of the merchant to pay for the merchandise would be an indication that the contract was a sale and not a consignment. The courts will look to all the ingredients which lead to the contract and will consider the substance of the transaction as opposed to what label is affixed.

ESTABLISHING A POWER OF ATTORNEY

Often an individual is unable to be present at the time that it is necessary to enter into a contract or execute documents necessary to consummate a business transaction. In these circumstances the party executes a power of attorney in favor of another party. The power of attorney clearly authorizes the other party to perform certain acts for the authorizing party. The power of attorney must clearly authorize what must be done and the language must be clear and specific.

A power of attorney normally authorizes the agent to perform all necessary acts in connection with a particular purpose, such as executing a contract between two parties, operating a business, or receiving or transporting goods or merchandise. A general power of attorney will authorize the agent to act for the principal generally. Before accepting the agent's authority, be certain that the party executing the power of attorney is alive at the time the transaction takes place, for a power of attorney is automatically terminated upon the death of the principal.

GENERAL INTANGIBLES

The average businessman does not encounter the term "general intangibles" often, but general intangibles often are encountered without recognizing that the item is a general intangible.

An "account" is generally defined as any right to payment for goods sold or leased or for services rendered which is not evidenced by an instrument, whether or not it has been earned by performance. An account cannot be a general intangible. "General intangibles," on the other hand, means any personal property including "things in actions" other than goods, accounts, chattel paper, instruments and money (UCC Section 9-106). "Things in action" is a personal right to demand money or property by an action. For example, the term includes a wide variety of contracts, and promises which confer on one party a right to recover a chattel or sum of money from another party. An interest in a pension or profit-sharing plan or a payment due to a beneficiary under an insurance policy are examples. In some special cases, a right to receive money not yet earned by performance creates not an account, but more likely a general intangible: it is the right to payment of money that is *not* "for goods sold or leased or for services rendered." An example of this is a right to receive a refund of a purchase price paid by reason of a retroactive volume discount or a right to receive payment under a license of a copyright where in both instances there are no services rendered and no goods sold.

Goods defined as property which is moveable at the time the security agreement attaches is not a general intangible. Such things as rights to thoughts, ideas, and concepts protected by patent law and copyright are widely accepted as not constituting goods and therefore are not accounts. Goodwill and literary rights are also examples of general intangibles. Assignment of the proceeds of a personal injury action is also considered a general intangible.

The Uniform Commercial Code specifically allows a security agreement on a general intangible. Some types of general intangibles are not subject to being covered by a security agreement and a financing statement. These items are sometimes called "choses in action" such as stock certificates, treasury notes, promissory notes, bonds. To allow these types of documents to be subject to a security interest would defeat the purpose of the negotiability of such types of documents. If these documents could be subject to a lien such as a security interest and a financing statement, it would place a difficult burden on each party who purchased the stock or treasury note to investigate to see whether a perfected lien has been filed. Such a requirement would disrupt the relative ease by which such interests are transferred in the marketplace.

THE UNIFORM COMMERCIAL CODE

The Uniform Commercial Code has been adopted in similar form in all 50 of the United States. The purpose of the code was to establish in all the states the same laws which apply to negotiable paper, credit transactions, and bank and commercial businesses so that businesses can deal with their counterparts in other states based on a fairly uniform code throughout the country. Nevertheless, the code as adopted in each state is somewhat distinct from that adopted in every other state, since the legislatures of each state at the time of adoption made changes and modifications. For that reason, it is necessary to review the code with respect to the state's law that affects a particular transaction.

The code runs hundreds of pages; text books analyzing the code run thousands of pages; literally hundreds of cases are decided each year interpreting the code. So covering each section of the code in this particular book would be nearly impossible. However, the following list of sections of the Uniform Commercial Code will give you a general awareness of the topics the code covers:

1. General Provisions
2. Sales
   a. Leases (adopted by most states)
3. Commercial paper
4. Bank deposits and collection
   a. Funds transfer
5. Documentary letters of credit
6. Bulk transfers
7. Warehouse receipt, bills of lading and other documents of title
8. Investment securities
9. Secured transactions (recently revised)
10. Effective date and transition provision

CHAPTER 2
APPENDIX I

EXCERPTS FROM ILLINOIS LAW
STATUTE OF FRAUDS

80/1 WRITING-NECESSITY-SIGNATURE

1. No action shall be brought, whereby to charge any executor or administrator upon any special promise to answer any debt or damages out of his own estate, or whereby to charge the defendant upon any special promise to answer for the debt, default or miscarriage of another person, or to charge any person upon any agreement that is not to be performed within the space of one year from the making thereof, unless the promise or agreement upon which such action shall be brought, or some memorandum or note thereof, shall be in writing, and signed by the party to be charged therewith, or some other person, thereunto by him lawfully authorized.

80/2 LAND-WRITING-SIGNATURE-EXCEPTIONS

2. No action shall be brought to charge any person upon any contract for the sale of lands, tenements or hereditaments or any interest in or concerning them, for a longer term than one year, unless such contract or some memorandum or note thereof shall be in writing, and signed by the party to be charged therewith, or some other person thereunto by him lawfully authorized in writing, signed by such party. This section shall not apply to sales for the enforcement of a judgment for the payment of money or sales by any officer or person pursuant to a judgment or order of any court in this State.

80/3 CONSIDERATION-PROOF

3. The consideration of any such promise or agreement need not be set forth or expressed in the writing, but may be proved or disproved by parol or other legal evidence.

80/8 BONA FIDE SALES

8. This act shall not extend to any estate or interest in any lands, goods or chattels, or any rents, common or profit, out of the same, which shall be upon good consideration, and bona fide lawfully conveyed or assured to any person, bodies politic or corporate.

CHAPTER 3

Legal Remedies for Business Creditors

While compliance by the creditor with the state and federal laws is essential to enable the creditor to take advantage of the law, sometimes the debtor uses the law to avoid payment of the debt or fails to comply. The creditor should be alert to any suspicions that the debtor has not complied with the law, is evading the intent and purpose of the law or is even engaging in actions to defraud the creditor. This chapter discusses some of the more common remedies available to business creditors and some of the alternatives offered to business debtors. Consultation with counsel is recommended.

ASSIGNMENT FOR THE BENEFIT OF CREDITORS

An "assignment for the benefit of creditors" may be considered an alternative to bankruptcy. The debtor (assignor) transfers the property, assets, and receivables of the business to a person, usually an attorney (assignee, trustee), in trust to convert the property into cash and distribute the proceeds to the creditors of the debtor. Any surplus is returned to the debtor. Almost all states, excepting Connecticut, Maine, Maryland, Illinois, Nebraska, Nevada, Oregon, and Wyoming, have provisions providing for an assignment for the benefit of creditors.

Usually, the debtor executes a written "assignment for the benefit of creditors" in favor of a trustee. This assignment transfers to the assignee (trustee) all the assets of the business. The consent of the creditor is not required although notice to the creditors is required under the laws of most states. The assignee's duties are to distribute the assets in accordance with the provisions of the state law. The priorities of general creditors and secured creditors are specifically set forth. The duties and powers of the assignee (to sell, to settle disputes, to sue and to liquidate the business) are set forth in the instrument of assignment or in the provisions of the state law.

After the assignee mails a notice to the creditors, a proof of claim must be filed by a creditor with the assignee within a specific time.

The assignee sells all the property, as well as any real estate, receivables, intangibles (trademark) and other assets, at the best possible price, and converts the property into cash. The assignee is authorized to pay the expenses of the sale and is entitled to retain counsel and other professionals necessary to effectuate the sale. After all the assets are sold and converted to cash, the assignee distributes the proceeds, less fees, to the creditors. Compensation of the assignee is fixed by the statute. In many states, the fee is usually five percent of the total value of the assets after conversion to cash.

Only the debtor may voluntarily file an assignment for the benefit of creditors. The creditor *may favor use* of this remedy because it is quick and relatively cheap compared with a bankruptcy, but unlike a bankruptcy, a creditor cannot make a debtor use this device. Also, the sale of assets should provide the maximum amount for creditors. On the other hand, the process in most states does not allow creditors to examine the debtor under oath, and there is little supervision by the judicial system. Thus, the remedy becomes attractive to the unscrupulous debtor who sells the assets to a friend for pennies, and then sets up a new business around the corner.

But the power lies with creditors to file an involuntary petition in bankruptcy if they suspect fraud, improper transfers or self-dealing by the debtor, notwithstanding that the debtor has filed an assignment for the benefit of creditors. An involuntary petition in bankruptcy filed by the creditors terminates the assignment for the benefit of creditors. Therefore, if preferential payments or transfers of property to family members or other creditors for little value are suspected, a creditor should consider an involuntary petition in bankruptcy.

A distinction exists between a "common law" assignment for the benefit of creditors and a statutory assignment under the respective state law. "Common Law" assignments are rarely used in today's environment primarily because the consent of all the creditors is required. A common law assignment usually operates under the court decisions rendered in the particular state.

Assignments in the various states range from simple types of assignments to extremely comprehensive and complex types. The statutory law as well as the case law requires that an assignment include all of the debtor's property and must be for the benefit of all the creditors. Within 20 days after the assignment, the debtor must file a copy of the schedules and if he does not file a copy of his schedules, the assignee must file schedules. The assignee's duties in many respects are similar to those of a trustee in bankruptcy. In New York, the creditors are entitled to receive ten-days notice of a proposed sale of property, payment of dividends, and other proceedings under the assignment. The courts provide a wide brush to supervise the entire proceeding and creditors may seek relief in the court in the event these proceedings do not proceed in accordance with the requirements of the statute. New York provides only for voluntary assignments at the initiation of the debtors. Most states do not provide for procedures to set aside preferential or fraudulent transfers.

The question of a discharge in an assignment proceeding has been treated by the Supreme Court, which has held that a discharge of a debt is a unique feature of bankruptcy legislation which cannot be superseded by the states. Those creditors who have actually consented to an assignment have effectively granted the debtor a discharge. In that respect, the Supreme Court has upheld the assignment statute by virtue of the fact that the consenting creditors are effectively releasing the debtor from any claims. Of course, creditors who do not consent do not discharge the debtor from the claim.

The extent of court supervision over state assignments is limited and the procedures before the court are often before different judges regarding the same assignment. The major reason that the debtors do not use state assignment is because of the inability to obtain a complete and valid discharge. This is an important consideration for an individual who is conducting a business although it is not particularly important with respect to a corporate debtor. Individuals rarely file assignments.

A debtor using an assignment proceeding who owns property in two states is faced with separate problems. Local creditors of the other state may assert a claim superior to that of the assignee. A transfer of a debtor's property is usually determined by the law of the state that has the most significant relationship and that would usually be the state where the debtor is domiciled or incorporated.

The major advantage of an assignment is that it is cheaper to conduct than a bankruptcy proceeding. On the other hand, creditors have a better chance of realizing a distribution in bankruptcy.

If you receive a notice of an assignment for the benefit of creditors, you should do the following:

1. Obtain the basic information from the court in which the proceeding has been started: the date of the filing, the index number, the list of creditors, the value of the property transferred, the name and address of the assignee, and the name and address of the attorney for the assignee, as well as the name and address of the attorney for the debtor.

2. If the creditor is a secured creditor (the debtor executes a security agreement in favor of the creditor covering specific property such as machinery, equipment, automobiles, trucks—see Chapter 10, Secured Lending), determine the location of the property and consult with your counsel.

3. Obtain a proof of claim from your counsel and file it with the assignee. The proof of claim should be filed by certified mail to obtain a receipt, or enclose a post card for the assignee to return.

In the event the creditor does not feel that the assignment is filed in good faith, three options are available.

1. Contact the other creditors to determine whether they share the same feeling, and if so, consider whether to file an involuntary petition of bankruptcy against the debtor. An involuntary petition will provide a wide latitude for the creditors to examine the debtor and to determine what has happened to the assets and why the debtor is presently insolvent. These activities should be conducted through an attorney.

2. Obtain information from the assignee, or the attorney for the assignee, as to the financial condition of the debtor and such other information as is necessary to determine whether to accept the assignment or file an involuntary petition. These activities also should be conducted through an attorney.

3. File a proof of claim. The form for filing a proof of claim is usually provided by the assignee or can be obtained from a stationery store. It requires a listing of the debt similar to the bankruptcy proof of claim except the form is less complicated.

ATTACHMENT

"Attachment" is a proceeding where the property, whether it be real estate, bank accounts, automobiles or boats etc. of the debtor, is segregated by a court order so that the debtor is unable to transfer said property until such time as the suit is finally decided, and the property is held as security to pay any judgment rendered against the debtor.

General Attachment Statutes—In some New England states, such as Connecticut and New Hampshire, general attachment is available. The creditor prepares "a writ of attachment," listing the debtor's real property or bank accounts, and serves it on those parties in whose name the property is registered. A copy is filed with the appropriate court officer to prohibit the transfer of any real property. The only option for the debtor is to obtain a bond to release the attachment. The bond stands as security for any judgment. Thus, any judgment later obtained in these states after a writ is filed is satisfied immediately, providing enough property is attached to cover the amount of the judgment. The attaching party is usually not required to file a bond.

Obviously, in those states where attachment is available, this proceeding is a substantial remedy which should be used where the creditor can identify real estate owned by the defendant. If bank accounts can be identified and a likelihood exists that a substantial amount is on deposit (not exempt), or if a defendant owns a boat or automobile with substantial equity, the remedy is ideal for the creditor to attach these assets.

Because of due process concerns and the hardship that might be inflicted upon the debtor, most states have abolished this ideal scenario for the plaintiff.

Limited Attachment Statutes—In the great majority of the states the power to attach is limited by requiring the creditor to post a bond (usually in an amount double the value of the property attached) and by providing several restrictions before an attachment is effective. Most states allow attachment only under the following circumstances:

1. The debtor is not a resident of a state but has property within the state.
2. The debtor is a resident of the state, but has left the state and is secreting property within the state, and the creditor has identified that secreted property.
3. The debtor has left or is leaving the state and is about to remove, conceal, or dispose of property for the sole purpose of defrauding creditors.

In some states, if the claim against the debtor is based on fraud, an attachment may be available.

The creditor must post a bond equal to twice the amount of the claim to protect the debtor if the creditor should not be successful. The debtor may file a counter bond to release the attachment.

In the New England states, the writ of attachment is prepared by the attorney and filed with the court, and the legal charges are usually minimal. The attachment in most other states requires the preparation of an extensive set of papers to warrant the attachment. In marginal cases, the attorney may not be assured of success and often the court will deny the remedy unless the party petitioning the court has clearly met the criteria for obtaining the attachment. The creditor must allege a fact situation reflecting one of the reasons mentioned above and an allegation that the creditor is likely to succeed in obtaining a judgment against the debtor.

Rarely does a defendant leave personal property in that state; real estate is usually transferred before the debtor leaves. To prove that the debtor is about to leave the state or has left the state while concealing property in the state is a difficult task. For these reasons, the remedy is seldom used except in the New England states.

CREDIT AND COLLECTION TIP: *The creditor should be certain of success before attachment is used in a law suit. If the debtor is successful, the creditor may be liable for substantial damages, which is the reason for a bond.*

BULK SALES

Most states have statutes compelling a debtor who wishes to sell all or most of its goods, wares, merchandise, and fixtures for an amount less than its liabilities to comply with the procedures set forth in the "bulk sales" law. The merchant must notify creditors of an intention to consummate said sale and afford the creditors an opportunity to object to the sale if fraud is detected. The Uniform Commercial Code adopted by most states controls the terms and conditions under which a merchant must effectuate a bulk sale. Assignments for the benefit of creditors, transfers and settlements of liens or other security interests and sales by executors, administrators, receivers or trustees in bankruptcy are exempt.

The procedure used in a bulk sale is for the purchaser to require the seller (debtor) of the business to furnish a list of all the creditors. The purchaser then notifies the creditors of the date of the intended sale and whether the proceeds will be sufficient to pay all the creditors of the seller. Creditors have a limited time to act, only ten days in some states. The list of creditors must be available for inspection by all the creditors.

A common situation for a bulk sale arises where a debtor has borrowed money from a bank, has collaterized (mortgaged) the loan with an assignment of all inventory and accounts receivable, and has executed a security agreement (mortgage) on all of its equipment. The debtor becomes insolvent and at this stage obtains a purchaser for inventory, receivables and equipment. The device used by the debtor is a bulk sale. A bulk sale is set up and a statement is made that the creditors will not be paid from the proceeds of the sale, because the inventory, accounts receivable and equipment are mortgaged to the bank. Since the bank has a prior lien, the bank will be paid first. Usually the sale of the inventory and accounts receivable rarely produces enough money to pay the bank, and *thus creditors of the seller never receive payment.*

What motivates the debtor to sell the inventory, receivables and equipment when he or she will not receive any of the proceeds of said sale? The probable answer is that the principal owner of the debtor personally guaranteed the corporate debt to the bank. The proceeds of the sale of all the assets are paid to the bank, reducing the balance due to the bank, and reducing the personal obligation of the principal owner to the bank. In this type of situation the creditor has few options. If the sale is made to a purchaser at arms length and a valid obligation exists with the bank, the resulting transaction leaves no assets to pay creditors.

An alternative scenario of a bulk sale is where the notice of bulk sale states that some payments will be made to the creditors. In this situation, the key factors are who the purchaser is and whether the sale of the assets is an arms-length transaction with the purchaser paying full value for the assets. If the purchaser is a new corporation organized by the principal owner of the selling corporation, sufficient reasons exist to make a full investigation as to whether the price paid is fair and reasonable. A valid obligation may exist to the bank, but the assets of the business may be substantially greater than the bank loan. Thus, with the inventory, receivables and equipment valued in excess of the bank loan, the corporation does have a net worth and monies should be available to pay the creditors. The creditors should be certain that the sale of these assets is made for a fair price to an "arms-length" purchaser (a purchaser not connected or affiliated in any way to the seller).

Sometimes a creditor learns about a bulk sale weeks or months after it has taken place, because notice has not been received. The failure to notify the creditor may have been intentional or accidental. The seller at the time of the sale may have deliberately omitted the creditor's name from the list of creditors since the debtor suspected that this creditor might have been more aggressive in efforts to investigate and review the bulk sale. On the other hand, the purchaser may have accidentally forgotten to include the name of this creditor for any number of reasons, including the fact that the purchaser was careless. The remedy available to the creditor at this stage is to move to set aside the transfer with respect to this particular debt. The procedure available to the creditor varies from state to state, and a careful reading of the statute is necessary.

Only persons with claims at the time of the bulk sale or transfer are creditors within the framework of the bulk sales law. Persons who extend credit or whose claims come into existence after the sale or transfer are not covered. Liquidated claims at the time of sale or transfer are entitled to the law's protection even though the claim or loan may not be due. In one case, a claim for future rent was beyond the scope of the bulk transfer act. Having a claim that is contingent but becomes certain upon the happening of a subsequent event or circumstance does not fall within the protection of the act.

The Uniform Commercial Code does include disputed claims, but the claim must meet the other criteria of being a liquidated claim at the time of the bulk sale.[1]

SALE OF DEBTOR'S ASSETS

After a judgment has been obtained by a creditor, the creditor may issue an execution to the sheriff of the county in which the debtor resides. The creditor is notifying the sheriff in writing of the judgment and directing the sheriff to collect the judgment by selling the property of the debtor for cash. After deducting appropriate fees (about 5% of the amount collected), the sheriff will remit the balance to the creditor to satisfy the judgment.

The execution contains the date the judgment was entered, the court, the docket number, the amount of the judgment, the amount of interest, the location of the debtor and, in some instances, the location of the property which the sheriff is to sell. The sheriff will mail or deliver personally the same type of information to the debtor and may allow the debtor a certain period of time within which to voluntarily pay the judgment. In the event the judgment is not paid voluntarily by the specified time, the sheriff will proceed to levy on the debtor's assets (visiting the premises of the debtor and identifying the assets).

The sheriff will then publish a notice of the sale in a newspaper in the same geographic area as the debtor, and publish the date of the sale, description of

---

[1]*Schlussel v. Emmanuel Roth Co.*, 270 N.J. Super. 628, 637 A.2d 944 (N.J. Super. Ct. App. Div. 1994).

property to be sold, and other pertinent information. The judgment creditor pays in advance the fees to hold a sale, which include the costs of tagging all the property, advertising in the newspaper, and auctioning the property. The cost may approach hundreds of dollars or more for personal property, and substantially more for real estate.

On the date set for the sale, the sheriff conducts an auction of all the property or specific parts of the property. If the bid for all the property is greater than the bid for the specific machinery or the specific inventory, the property will be sold to the party who bid for all of the property. Usually a down payment of 10% is required at the auction and the balance is due when the property is removed by the purchaser. The proceeds will then be used to pay off the specific judgment and the remainder of the proceeds will be paid to other judgment creditors. If a balance remains, the amount will be paid to the debtor.

Prior to the auction, the sheriff will visit the debtor at the place of business to determine the presence of any assets. On arrival the sheriff will make a levy. A levy is the tagging and identifying all the equipment and inventory at the place of business. However, the debtor may oppose this levy on the grounds that the property has been mortgaged to a bank or another secured creditor. Under these circumstances, the levy will be subject to the prior lien and the sheriff would have to announce at the public sale that the purchaser would be buying the particular merchandise or equipment subject to the prior lien. This means that the purchaser would have to pay off the lien before full and unencumbered title to the property could be acquired. This happens often in the situation where the sheriff levies and executes on an automobile or a boat which is subject to a prior lien to a bank.

After a levy is made, the debtor often voluntarily tries to make arrangements with the sheriff to pay off the lien. The sheriff will communicate this offer to the attorney who, in turn, will communicate the offer to the creditor. The creditor should recognize that where a payout plan is offered, and the payments are sent directly to the attorney or the creditor, the sheriff still must be paid a fee (of approximately five percent of the amount collected).

In the event the debtor has insufficient money to pay the judgment or to enter a payout plan over a period of time, the debtor will probably walk away and allow the sheriff to proceed with the sale. The levy may be withdrawn or continued.

Occasionally, an unscrupulous debtor arranges to have a friendly creditor sue him or her for an amount greater than is owed to the friendly creditor. The friendly creditor then obtains a judgment, engages a sheriff to execute, and arranges a sale under the judgment. The friendly creditor's judgment is larger than the amount of the assets of the debtor, and the friendly creditor is the purchaser of all the assets at the sheriff's sale. The assets then are sold by the friendly creditor to a new corporation organized by the debtor. In effect, the friendly creditor is the conduit to help the debtor start a new business using the assets of the old business.

When this type of situation develops, consult with an attorney because it is obvious that this "friendly" sale was held to defraud the creditors. The attorney may recommend a bankruptcy or a suit against the individual based upon fraud, conspiracy, or other grounds.

SALE OF ASSETS BY LENDER

Often a small business, such as a restaurant, a retail store, or a service business, will need financing and will mortgage all of its assets to a bank, a financial institution, or the seller of merchandise (such as the kitchen equipment for a restaurant). For example, the owner of a restaurant purchases kitchen equipment by paying $10,000 down and the balance over three years in equal monthly payments. A trucker sells his two old trucks and uses the proceeds as a down payment on two new trucks, and agrees to pay the balance of this purchase price over four years in equal monthly payments. The owner of the restaurant and the trucker execute security agreements (mortgages) on the kitchen equipment and the trucks.

Unfortunately, the food preparation is poor in the restaurant, and the number of customers declines. The trucking business almost stops since the trucker's major client terminates all shipments because of a strike. Both enterprises fail to make the required payments and decide to abandon their businesses. They surrender the collateral to the sellers who extended them credit.

The seller/lenders take possession of the equipment and the trucks and publish a notice of sale at auction in a newspaper. A sale is held at the premises of the debtors. The sale may be attended by dealers in kitchen equipment or truck brokers, and these parties may bid at the sale. In most instances, the sellers/lenders themselves will bid up to the amount of their indebtedness, and will acquire title to the vehicles or the kitchen equipment.

One day the vendor who sells paper products to the restaurant telephones the restaurant and the number has been disconnected. A visit to the premises reveals that the restaurant is closed, and the landlord has put a "For Rent" sign in the window. Little can be done if it is a proper lien. While this may be a worst-case scenario where the debtor owes a substantial sum of money for paper products, almost every vendor has faced this set of circumstances at one time or another. If you haven't, consider yourself lucky.

When the debtor surrenders the collateral (kitchen equipment or trucks), the debtor has effectively gone out of business. The lender usually must comply with state laws that require the lender to sell the collateral in a "commercially reasonable manner." Some states still allow a private sale, but most require a public sale which is advertised in a recognized newspaper. The definition of "commercially reasonable manner" is the subject of many court decisions, but in general the state laws encourage a public sale at auction after notice to the debtor and other secondary lienors on the property. The laws that permit a private sale should be reviewed carefully to be certain the lender complied. Consult with counsel to investigate whether there are suspicious circumstances that may include fraud, or transfers to the owner prior to the sale.

NEW OWNER

A creditor may contact a debtor. The conversation develops as follows:

Cr: Is Charlie there?

N.O: Charlie's no longer here. We bought the business from Charlie.

Cr: When did this happen? I spoke to Charlie two weeks ago.

N.O.: We purchased the business as of last Monday. Charlie has left for Florida.

Cr: What about my debt for a thousand dollars for paper bags that I sold to Charlie?

N.O.: We are not liable for Charlie's debt.

Cr: What do you mean you're not liable for Charlie's debt? You have the business. You have the same phone number.

N.O.: We purchased only the video tapes in the store. This is a new corporation which was formed by me. We are not liable for the debts of Charlie's corporation.

Cr: But you have the same phone number and you are at the same place and using the same name.

N.O.: We entered a new lease with the landlord and took Charlie's phone number and trade name.

In this instance the buyer formed a new corporation to purchase only the inventory, the video tapes. In the contract of sale executed with Charlie's former corporation, the telephone number and the trade name also were purchased.

The purchaser rarely buys the stock of the prior corporation, but instead purchases the assets and organizes a new corporation, since the new owner does not want to be liable for the debts of the old corporation. If the purchaser acquires the stock of the prior corporation, the prior corporation continues to exist and the purchaser is liable for the debt (and no new corporation is created).

Extensive questioning as to the transfer is recommended or have your attorney contact the attorney for the purchaser.

Cr: I don't understand. Was Charlie in financial trouble?

N.O.: I really don't know.

Cr: Did you purchase these video tapes at a sheriff's sale?

N.O.: No, there was no sheriff's sale, there was no judgment. I entered into a purchase and sale contract with Charlie when I purchased the video tapes.

Cr: How much did you pay for these video tapes?

N.O.: I paid $23,000.

Cr: What happened to the $23,000?

N.O.: I really don't know what happened to the $23,000.

Cr: Was this a bulk sale? Did you send out a notice to the creditors? Did you get a list of the creditors from Charlie?

N.O.: No, it was not a bulk sale. I have no list of creditors from Charlie and I had no interest in whether Charlie had any creditors or not. I issued a check to him for $23,000.

Cr: But this is all his assets.

N.O.: I never made any inquiry as to whether it was all his assets or not. I merely issued a check for $23,000 to Charlie and Charlie turned over the entire stock of video tapes to my corporation.

Cr: What's the name of your corporation?

N.O.: My corporation's name is the XYZ corporation.

Cr: How did you get a lease at Charlie's store? Did Charlie transfer the lease to you?

N.O.: No, he did not transfer the lease to me. Charlie's lease expired about a month ago. He hadn't paid any rent and the landlord was about to evict him. I approached the landlord and entered into a new lease with the landlord. I am now occupying the premises under the lease.

Cr: Why are you using Charlie's name and phone number?

N.O.: I'm using Charlie's name because it was known in the neighborhood. Part of that $23,000 was for Charlie's name and some also was for the telephone number, because people would call up to see whether we had a particular movie and I thought it would be best to keep the same phone number.

Cr: So all you did was enter into a new contract with Charlie for the name, the phone number, and all the video tapes.

N.O.: That's right.

Cr: Did you know that these were the only assets Charlie had?

N.O.: I told you once and I'll tell you a second time that I made no inquiry to see whether this was all the assets or wasn't all the assets. And I think I've answered enough questions up to now.

Cr: Could you please give me the name of your attorney.

N.O.: My attorney's name is John Eagle at 25 Main Street, Centerville, New Jersey. His telephone number is 201-555-1234.

Cr: Do you know the name of Charlie's attorney?

N.O.: I think the attorney's name is Sparrow and Hawk at 15 Spring Street, Centerville, New Jersey.

Cr: Do you know the telephone number?

N.O.: No, I don't know the telephone number, but I suppose the number is in the book.

Cr: Do you know where Charlie is conducting business now?

N.O.: I don't have the foggiest idea.

Cr: Thank you very much.

> **CREDIT AND COLLECTION TIP:** *If assets are purchased, the next question is the disposition of the money paid for the assets. Was the money used to pay off certain creditors and not others? Were there any liens on Charlie's property? Was the money used to pay only those debts which were personally guaranteed? Was the money used to form a new corporation for the principal owner or for other personal uses such as travel, boats, entertainment, etc.? Did Charlie violate the bulk sales law? The money should be used to pay the creditors. Consultation with counsel is advised.*

RECEIVERSHIP

In some instances the debtor is depleting the assets of a business either by neglecting them or by willfully selling the assets piece by piece for less than fair market value. In most states where the creditor obtains a judgment, and in some states (Mass.) before suit, the creditor may make an application to court to appoint a receiver of the assets. A receivership also may be requested where the debtor owns real estate, permits the real estate to fall into disrepair, collects the rents, but fails to use the rents to maintain the property. In these instances, the mortgagee will make an application to court to appoint a receiver, but the remedy is also available to a creditor who improved the property by performing construction work, or by furnishing other equipment or services. A receiver who is appointed by the court takes possession of the real estate, collects the rents, uses the rents to maintain the property, and uses the surplus monies to pay off the creditors.

Some states allow a receiver to be appointed during a foreclosure proceeding. The application is simple, and if unopposed, usually granted quickly. The mortgagee uses the income generated by tenants to maintain the property and to pay off debt. A review of the state law is necessary. In some states receivership is your best remedy because the state law does not provide for a sheriff's sale of the debtor's property.

DISCOVERY OF INSOLVENCY

If a creditor discovers that the debtor is insolvent, or the debtor reveals an inability to meet his or her debts, the creditor may cancel an order by the debtor providing the merchandise is in possession of the creditor. If the merchandise is in transit, the creditor may cancel, providing the debtor has not taken possession of the property. If the merchandise has already been delivered to the debtor, consult with counsel as to section UCC 2.702 to see if it may be utilized. (See Appendix UCC Sec. 2.)

MECHANICS LIEN

A *mechanics lien* is an additional right available to those vendors who perform work and labor or furnish materials to repair and improve real property. Each state has passed specific laws which enable this class of vendors to file a lien on the property.

The lien form generally sets forth the value of the work, labor and materials furnished, when the work was done, the location of the property, and a description of work. The filing of the lien creates the effect of a mortgage on the property at the time of the filing of the lien. The mechanics lien is subject to those liens and mortgages which were filed prior to the date of the lien, and is ahead and prior to those liens or mortgages filed after the date the lien was filed. The lienor (electrician, plumber, carpenter) usually has a period of approximately three or four months after the time the work is completed to file the lien, and sometimes up to seven or eight months. (This time period may vary from state to state depending upon the type of property affected and other circumstances.)

The debtor may make an application to court to remove the lien or the debtor may wait until the lienor commences a foreclosure suit under the lien. Since a mechanics lien normally expires after a certain period of time and requires renewal by the lienor, the debtor may permit the mechanics lien to expire with the hope that the lienor will not renew the lien.

A further device available to the debtor is to bond the lien. The debtor arranges with the insurance company to obtain a bond at least in the amount of the lien (in some states a greater amount is required). Upon receipt of said bond, counsel will make an appropriate application to court to have the lien removed and will utilize the bond to secure the lienor who filed the lien. A bond is usually used when the owner of the property is preparing to sell the property or the property is already under a contract of sale. In this instance, the lienor files the mechanics lien to exert pressure on the owner of the property to pay the bill at the closing or else the purchaser will deduct the amount of the lien from the purchase price. For this reason, the use of the bond is uniquely designed to prevent an unscrupulous lienor from interfering with the prospective sale of real estate in the event the owner disputes the amount due under the lien.

The mechanics lien is a powerful tool protecting the construction firm that repairs or improves real estate. If the bill is not paid promptly, the recourse of the creditor is to file a lien with the county clerk in the county in which the property is located. This remedy was created by the state, and therefore each state has its own requirements and procedures with regard to filing and foreclosing a lien, and providing notice and information. A review of each state law is essential.

MECHANICS LIEN—HAZARDOUS WASTE REMOVAL

Black's Law Dictionary defines the phrase "improvement of property" as meaning a valuable addition made to real property (usually real estate) for an amelioration of its condition, amounting to more than mere repairs or replacement, costing labor or capital and intended to enhance its value, beauty or utility, or to adapt it for a new or further purpose.[2]

In most states' statutes, mechanics liens are allowed to be filed where there has been an "improvement of real property." Nevertheless, there are variations from state to state dealing with this particular verbiage and a review of the state law is absolutely necessary before filing a mechanics lien.

A particular statute was carefully analyzed in a Kansas case albeit the decision left some questions. The statute read as follows:

> Any person furnishing labor, equipment, material, or supplies used or consumed for the improvement of real property, under a contract with the owner or with the trustee, agent or spouse of the owner, should have a lien upon the property for the labor, equipment, material or supplies furnished and for the cost of transporting same.

In the removal of hazardous waste material, the court reasoned that no construction was ever commenced and there were no visible or physical manifestations of the contractor's work on the property. The court acknowledged that there is no necessity for a visible effect on the real property for the activity to be lienable, as long as the services did enhance the value of the land. The equipment, material, or supplies must be used or consumed for the improvement of the property. The court zeroed in on the fact that material purchased must actually be added to the land and that no lien could be created for material purchased for a building on the land, unless in fact it is added to the building and becomes a part of the realty. For a mechanics lien to attach, such items must be used and consumed for the improvement of the realty.

After a thorough analysis, the court set down several observations concerning the definition of "improvement of real property":

---

[2]*Black's Law Dictionary*, 757 (6th ed. 1990).

1. What is or is not an improvement of real property must be based upon the circumstances of each case;

2. Improvement of the property does not require the actual construction of a physical improvement;

3. The improvement of the property need not necessarily be visible, although in most instances it is;

4. The improvement of the real property must enhance the value of the real property, although it need not enhance the selling value of the property;

5. For labor, equipment, material or supplies to be lienable items, they must be used or consumed and thus become part of the real property;

6. The nature of the activity performed is not necessarily a determining factor of whether there is an improvement of real property within the meaning of the statute; rather, the purpose of the activity is more directly concerned in the determination of whether there is an improvement of property which is thus lienable; and

7. The furnishing of labor, equipment, material or supplies used or consumed for the improvement of real property may become lienable if it is established as part of an overall plan to enhance the value of the property, its beauty or utility, or to adapt it for a new or further purpose, or if the furnishing of labor, equipment, materials or supplies is a necessary feature of plaintiff's construction of a physical improvement to the real property.

Needless to say, the court decided that removal of a hazardous waste product did not qualify under this seven-pronged test and that the contractor did not have a right to file a mechanics lien.[3]

This court emphasized the necessity to increase value. The analysis seems sound, but other courts might favor the contractor and measure the labor and material. In addition, environmental cleanup is desirable, and penalizing a contractor may not be in the best interest of the community.

> **CREDIT AND COLLECTION TIP:** *After the lien is filed, the creditor also has the option to commence a suit against the debtor for the debtor's failure to pay for services or materials, or foreclose against the property by reason of the mechanics lien.*

GARAGE LIEN

In many states the law allows a garageman to assert a lien on an automobile, boat or similar vehicle for repairs completed. This lien, in some states, may cover storage charges for the vehicles. The garageman may exercise the lien by selling the

---

[3]*Haz-Mat Response, Inc. v. Certified Waste Services Limited,* 259 Kan. 166, 910 P.2d 839 (Kan. 1996).

vehicle to satisfy the bill for repairs and storage, but must notify the owner of the vehicle of the proposed sale. The garageman's lien is also a creation of the state and its procedures and requirements are specific to each state.

In New York, the garage keeper's superior lien is a specific one, attaching only to the motor vehicle that was subject to the unpaid charges. The garage owner must establish:

1) a bailment of the motor vehicle (delivered for repairs, and to be returned);
2) that it has performed garage services or stored the vehicle with the vehicle owner's consent;
3) that there was an agreed price, or if no agreement as to price has been reached, the charges are reasonable for the services supplied;
4) that the garage is a duly registered motor vehicle repair shop, as required under state law.

Normally, the garageman must notify the owner of the vehicle by mailing a copy of the lien under the specific terms of the statute. Upon receipt of the lien, the debtor has a right to contest the lien providing appropriate action is taken within a fixed period of time. If the debtor does not contest the lienor's storage charges, the garageman (without making application to the court in some states) may then sell the vehicle to satisfy the bill for repairs and storage.

In situations where the vehicle or the boat is secured by either a mortgage or a lease, the rights of the garageman as opposed to the rights of the secured party come into conflict and a careful reading of the state statute is necessary. In some states the owner of the vehicle must consent to the repairs or storage. If the vehicle is leased, consent of the owner/lessor (financial institution) is required. On the other hand, if the vehicle is mortgaged, the owner of the vehicle would be the debtor who has the power to consent to the repairs and storage.

The garage lien, like the mechanics lien, is a creation of statute and a careful reading of the statute must be made to determine the rights of the garageman. Some states do not allow the garageman to assert a lien for storage.

The lien is a powerful weapon. In most states, the vehicle may be sold to satisfy the charges. The paperwork is minimal for the garageman. On the other hand, for the owner of the vehicle (which may be the leasing company) to stop the sale, an attorney will have to be retained and an application to court is required. If a credit grantor is faced with such a situation, consultation with counsel is recommended not only to analyze the statute, but also to review the case law of the particular state as to its application to the garageman's lien.[4]

---

[4]*National Union Fire Insurance Co. of Pitt. v. Eland Motor Car Co., Inc.*, 87 N.Y.2d 1002, 665 N.E.2d 656 N.Y.S.2d 855 (N.Y. 1996).

WAREHOUSE LIEN

We have included in Appendix II a portion of Article 7 of the Uniform Commercial Code entitled "Warehouse Receipts, Bills of Lading and other Documents of Title." The use of warehouses and warehouses receipts is quite common. Each state has passed a slightly different version of Article 7 and a careful review of the state law applicable to the warehouse transaction must be reviewed before any steps are taken.

A recent case came before the bankruptcy court in North Carolina involving a situation where Airway entered into an agreement with Aerospace to move certain personal property consisting of aircraft parts, furniture and tools and equipment stored in a building in Wilmington, North Carolina. Airway proceeded to pack the property in containers which were brought to the premises by Frederickson, an interstate motor carrier. Frederickson took two trailers full of property with them from the location to a terminal operated by Frederickson. Other equipment were placed on flatbed trailers. At that point, Airway made demand upon Aerospace for payment and Aerospace did not pay the amount demanded. Airway drove the remaining property still located at the original location to their warehouse in Wilmington and the two flatbeds were also transferred to the warehouse of Airway. Airway also communicated with the interstate carrier and advised them not to deliver the two trailers in their possession without getting paid.

A special North Carolina statute states that any person who tows, alters, repairs, stores or services property has a lien on said property. Nevertheless another statute in North Carolina says a warehouseman has a lien against the bailor of the goods covered by a warehouse receipt. Airway was in the moving and storage business and that business also included storage for hire. Unfortunately, the court relied on Section 7-209 which states "a warehouseman has a lien against the bailor of the goods covered by the warehouse receipt" and stated that in the absence of a warehouse receipt being issued for the goods, even where the warehouseman has possession, no lien is acquired.

Under Section 7-202 a warehouse receipt does not have to be in any particular form, but there are certain terms which must be included for a document to constitute a warehouse receipt. Included among these terms are the location of the warehouse, where the goods are stored, the date of issue of the receipt, the consecutive number of the receipt, a statement whether the goods received will be delivered to the bearer or to specified person, the rate of storage and handling charges, a description of the goods or the package containing the goods, the signature of the warehouseman, and other information contained in Section 7-202 of the Uniform Commercial Code. An invoice or bill from the warehouseman which simply itemizes the charges of the warehouseman and states the total amount due does not qualify as a warehouse receipt. Aside from the receipt, other problems were present.

The problem here was that the arrangement between Airway and Aerospace did not call for Airway to store the property at its premises. Airway was hired primarily to move the property. The reason the property was removed from the location was not to carry out the terms of the agreement or any consensual arrangement between Airway or Aerospace for storage. Airway was acting unilaterally and without the consent of Aerospace in removing the property and taking it to their warehouse.

Merely packing and loading a truck does not mean "repairing, servicing, treating or improving personal property" within the meaning of the specific North Carolina statute.

The lesson to be learned is that whereas the state may have adopted the Uniform Commercial Code, the state may have also passed specific laws dealing with warehouse receipts. Whereas the state laws may conform closely to the Uniform Commercial Code, variations may affect the situation.[5]

When a firm is dealing with a warehouse situation, they should be familiar with the laws of that particular state. Needless to say, the warehouseman is familiar with the law and accordingly it is only fair that the person who deals with the warehouseman should also be familiar with the law.

PIERCING THE CORPORATE VEIL

Sometimes under unique circumstances, creditors may proceed on corporate obligations personally against the principals of a privately held corporation if the principals are not operating the corporation either as a business or as a corporation. They may be utilizing the corporation to pay their personal debts and the debts of their spouses, thereby commingling their personal affairs with their corporate affairs and not distinguishing one from the other. Usually when the corporation is paying personal debts along with corporate debts, corporate books are not kept and corporate bank accounts are used for personal debt. Under these circumstances, the courts have recognized the theory of law entitled "piercing the corporate veil" wherein a creditor can sue individuals as well as the corporation and hold them liable for corporate debt.

Corporations must be operated under the laws in the state in which they are incorporated. The corporation should deposit all checks and income in the corporate bank account and the only checks issued from the bank account should be for corporate purposes. The board of directors, which may consist only of a husband and wife, should meet periodically and the minutes of the meeting should be recorded. The stock of the corporation may be held by only one person, but that doesn't eliminate the need to have a meeting of stockholders at least once a year, to ratify the acts of the officers and to record the fact that a board of directors has been elected and is properly operating.

A close examination of the law in the respective states should be made with regard to liquidation of corporations who leave outstanding debts that were

---

[5]*In re Aerospace Technologies, Inc.*, 199 B.R. 331 (Bankr. M.D.N.C. 1996).

incurred prior to the time of the dissolution. Sometimes, the creditors may bring actions against the officers, directors, or even the individual stockholders of the defunct corporations on the grounds that the corporation did not properly liquidate or did not file the necessary papers for liquidation in compliance with the particular statute of the state. Other times the question of fraud or misrepresentations in self dealing are involved and sometimes the assets have been diverted from the corporation into the individual hands of the directors, officers, or stockholders. In some cases, the property of the corporation may be in the hands of a third party. Consultation with experienced counsel is recommended.[6]

UNIFORM FRAUDULENT TRANSFER ACT

The Uniform Fraudulent Transfer Act is the successor act to the Uniform Fraudulent Conveyance Act. (See Appendix II.) The act that is set forth in the appendix was adopted at the National Conference of Commissioners on Uniform State Laws. Nevertheless, when the act was adopted by the various states, changes and modifications in the act may have been made, and a careful review of the law in the particular state must be made.

The key section of the Uniform Fraudulent Transfer Act states that a transfer made by a debtor is fraudulent as to a creditor if the debtor made the transfer or incurred a new obligation with actual intent to hinder, delay, or defraud any creditor of the debtor, or in the alternative, without receiving a reasonably equivalent value in exchange for the transfer. A transfer is also fraudulent if the debtor intended to incur, or believed or reasonably should have believed debts would be incurred, beyond the ability to pay for the debts as they became due. The statute provides eleven suggestions for determining the actual intent:

1. The transfer to an insider.
2. The debtor retains possession or control of the property.
3. The transfer obligation was disclosed or concealed.
4. Before the transfer was made or the obligation was incurred, the debtor had been sued or threatened with a suit.
5. The transfer was substantially of all the debtor's assets.
6. The debtor absconded.
7. The debtor removed or concealed assets.
8. The value of the consideration received by the debtor was reasonably equivalent to the value of the assets transferred or the amount of the obligation incurred.

[6]*Brunson Bonding and Insurance Agency v. Elm,* 540 So. 2d 530 (La. App 1st Cir. 1989); *Kyle v. Stewart,* 360 F. 2d 753 (5th Cir. 1996); *Exxon Corp. v. Fisher,* 817 F. 2d 1429 (9th Cir. 1987); *Travelers Insurance Company v. Jacob C. Mol Inc,* 898 F. Supp. 528 (W.D. Mich. 1995); *James Rodney Moore, Sr. V. Principal Credit Corp.,* 1998 WL 378387 (N.D. Miss. 1998).

9. The debtor was insolvent or became insolvent shortly after the transfer was made or the obligation was incurred.

10. The transfer occurred shortly before or shortly after a substantial debt was incurred.

11. The debtor transferred the essential assets of the business to a lienor who transferred the assets to an insider of the debtor.

Some of the remedies available include setting aside the transfer to satisfy the creditor's claim or an attachment using the applicable principles of equity. The court may prohibit further disposition of the property or perhaps appoint a receiver to take charge of the assets transferred.

One of the key problems faced in utilizing the remedies available under the Uniform Fraudulent Transfer Act is the question of the Statute of Limitations and the definition of a creditor.

A key feature of the Uniform Fraudulent Transfer Act is that a creditor is permitted, but not required, to maintain an action to annul a fraudulent conveyance before the debt has matured. It is no longer necessary that a creditor reduce its claim to judgment before seeking the benefit of the Uniform Fraudulent Transfer Act. The law actually gives the creditor an option. The creditor may establish its debt, whether matured or unmatured, and challenge the conveyance in a single suit or may pursue the unmatured claim to judgment, and follow it by a suit to set aside the fraudulent transfer.

The next question is the effect of the Statute of Limitations on this new option. One court opined that the date of the underlying judgment, combined with the creditor's knowledge of the transfer, were the key factors in determining when the Statute of Limitations begins to run. If the debtor chooses the old procedure, and sues upon its debt to judgment in ordinary fashion, the time for a later suit to set aside a fraudulent conveyance runs from the date of judgment. If the creditor exercises the other option and initially commences its suit to set aside the transfer, then the limitation period runs from the time when the transfer was made or the obligation was incurred, or at least from the time the transfer or obligation was or could reasonably have been discovered by the creditor.[7] (See Section 9 of the Uniform Fraudulent Transfer Act, Appendix II.)

LIQUOR LICENSES

The question of whether a liquor license is subject to execution by a creditor after obtaining a judgment is treated with various approaches by the states. In a recent case in Maryland, the Court of Appeals reviewed the situation and came to the conclusion that a creditor may execute on a liquor license absent a statutory prohibition.[8]

---

[7]*Cortez v. Vogt*, 52 Cal. App. 4th 917, 60 Cal. Rptr. 2d. 841 (Cal. App. Div. 1, 4th Dist. 1997).

[8]*Dodds vs. Shamer*, 339 Md. 540, 663 A.2d 1318 (1995).

The question being faced by the court was whether a liquor license is property which may be executed upon or whether it is merely an intangible license by the state to conduct a business under certain restrictions.

The court opined that a liquor license is property if it exhibits the attributes of property. One of the attributes of property is that the liquor license was transferable, salable or assignable by the holder or the holder's receiver or trustee (at least in Maryland). Whereas the discussion centered upon the fact that a liquor license may not be property between the licensing authority and the holder and possesses no constitutionally protective property rights that restrain the state's authorized licensing authority from exercising its power over the licensee, the particular case at hand was a situation between two private individuals and did not concern the licensing authority of the state.

Property is a term that has a broad and comprehensive significance and embraces everything which has exchangeable value or is used to make up a person's wealth. Property may reasonably be construed to include obligations, rights and other intangibles, as well as physical things.

The question of whether licenses are subject to execution is checkered and the states are divided on this subject. In the case above, the court acknowledged that there were five counties in Maryland that expressly prohibited execution on a liquor license. Several states, including Alaska, Illinois, Kansas, Nebraska, New Jersey, Oklahoma, Oregon, Texas, and Wyoming expressly have stated that liquor licenses are not subject to a right of execution. Even in those states where no statutory prohibition exists, the execution on a liquor license has been prohibited on the grounds that the liquor license is transferable only with the express permission of the state (Ohio and Pennsylvania). The position of the Attorney General of New York is that a liquor license is not subject to execution since the license is not transferable or assignable.

Other jurisdictions have found that liquor licenses are subject to execution (Florida, Massachusetts, Montana, the District of Columbia, and California), and now add Maryland (at least in some of the counties) to this list.

CREDIT AND COLLECTION TIP: *When considering whether to execute against other types of licenses such as for taxi cabs, beauty salons, plumbers, electricians, etc., a review of the state law and consultation with counsel are recommended.*

CORPORATE SIGNATURE

A new amendment to revised Article 3 & 4 of the Uniform Commercial Code provides that a representative will not be liable if the capacity of the person (representative) signing is ambiguous, and the name of the principal is not disclosed and the representative proves by oral evidence that the parties to the agreement did not intend to make the representative personally liable. This codifies the rule using oral evidence to resolve a situation where ambiguity exists as to whether the representative has or has not signed in a representative capacity. It is best to remove ambiguity by setting forth the corporate name and the title of the officer on all instruments signed, including checks and notes.

Another danger that appears is a situation where an officer enters into an oral agreement with another party and only refers to the business under a name which does not indicate that the business is a corporation, such as referring to "ABC Restaurant" instead of "ABC Restaurant Corporation." Several courts have held that the other party was led to believe that the business was an individual or a partnership because the officer did not mention that it was a corporation or mention the full corporate name. Under those circumstances officers may expose themselves to personal liability.

CONTACTING DEBTOR AT HOME

A recent case held that collection telephone calls to a business debtor at his home may transfer the business debt into a consumer debt under the Fair Debt Collection Practices Act. In the instance case, the debtor owned a grocery store and the collection agency called the owner at home at night. The reasoning of the court was that once the agency called the debtor at home, it suggested to the debtor that he may be personally liable on the debt and, as such, the Fair Debt Collection Practices Act would cover him because of his personal liability. The court seemed to be stretching, since the FDCPA covers only personal, family, or household goods. Nevertheless, it seems the phone calls were flagrant and the court subjectively decided that it is unfair to the particular consumer to receive these phone calls and not have a remedy.[9]

---

[9]*James Rodney Moore, Sr. V. Principal Credit Corporation* 4:96 C.V. 338-S-B (N.D. Miss. 3/30/98).

CHAPTER 3
APPENDIX I

UNIFORM COMMERCIAL CODE: SECTION 2
UNIFORM COMMERCIAL CODE
TWELFTH EDITION
THE AMERICAN LAW INSTITUTE AND THE
NATIONAL CONFERENCE OF COMMISSIONERS ON UNIFORM
STATE LAWS
OFFICIAL TEXT-1990

PART 1
SHORT TITLE, GENERAL CONSTRUCTION AND SUBJECT MATTER

2-101. SHORT TITLE.

This Article shall be known and may be cited as Uniform Commercial Code—Sales.

2-102. SCOPE; CERTAIN SECURITY AND OTHER TRANSACTIONS EXCLUDED FROM THIS ARTICLE.

Unless the context otherwise requires, this Article applies to transactions in goods; it does not apply to any transaction which although in the form of an unconditional contract to sell or present sale is intended to operate only as a security transaction nor does this Article impair or repeal any statute regulating sales to consumers, farmers or other specified classes of buyers.

2-103. DEFINITIONS AND INDEX OF DEFINITIONS.

(1) In this Article unless the context otherwise requires

    (a) Buyer" means a person who buys or contracts to buy goods.

    (b) "Good faith" in the case of a merchant means honesty in fact and the observance of reasonable commercial standards of fair dealing in the trade.

    (c) "Receipt" of goods means taking physical possession of them.

    (d) "Seller" means a person who sells or contracts to sell goods.

(2) Other definitions applying to this Article or to specified Parts thereof, and the section in which they appear are:

"Acceptance".	Section 2-606.
"Banker's credit".	Section 2-325.
"Between merchants".	Section 2-104.
"Cancellation".	Section 2-106(4).
"Commercial unit".	Section 2-105.
"Confirmed credit".	Section 2-325.
"Conforming to contract".	Section 2-106.
"Contract for sale".	Section 2-106.
"Cover".	Section 2-712.
"Entrusting".	Section 2-403.
"Financing agency".	Section 2-104.
"Future goods".	Section 2-105.
"Goods".	Section 2-105.
"Identification".	Section 2-501.
"Installment contract".	Section 2-612.
"Letter of Credit".	Section 2-325.
"Lot".	Section 2-105.
"Merchant".	Section 2-104.
"Overseas".	Section 2-323.
"Person in position of seller".	Section 2-707.
"Present sale".	Section 2-106.
"Sale".	Section 2-106.
"Sale on approval".	Section 2-326.
"Sale or return".	Section 2-326.
"Termination".	Section 2-106.

(3) The following definitions in other Articles apply to this Article:

"Check".	Section 3-104.
"Consignee".	Section 7-102.
"Consignor".	Section 7-102.
"Consumer goods".	Section 9-109.
"Dishonor".	Section 3-507.
"Draft".	Section 3-104.

(4) In addition Article 1 contains general definitions and principles of construction and interpretation applicable throughout this Article.

2-104. Definitions: "Merchant"; "Between Merchants"; "Financing Agency".

(1) "Merchant" means a person who deals in goods of the kind or otherwise by his occupation holds himself out as having knowledge or skill peculiar to the practices or goods involved in the transaction or to whom such knowledge or skill may be attributed by his employment of an agent or broker or other intermediary who by his occupation holds himself out as having such knowledge or skill.

(2) "Financing agency" means a bank, finance company or other person who in the ordinary course of business makes advances against goods or documents of title or who by arrangement with either the seller or the buyer intervenes in ordinary course to make or collect payment due or claimed under the contract for sale, as by purchasing or paying the seller's draft or making advances against it or by merely taking it

for collection whether or not documents of title accompany the draft. "Financing agency" includes also a bank or other person who similarly intervenes between persons who are in the position of seller and buyer in respect to the goods (Section 2-707).

(3) "Between merchants" means in any transaction with respect to which both parties are chargeable with the knowledge or skill of merchants.

2-105. DEFINITIONS: TRANSFERABILITY; "GOODS"; "FUTURE" GOODS; "LOT"; "COMMERCIAL UNIT".

(1) "Goods" means all things (including specially manufactured goods) which are movable at the time of identification to the contract for sale other than the money in which the price is to be paid, investment securities (Article 8) and things in action. "Goods" also includes the unborn young of animals and growing crops and other identified things attached to realty as described in the section on goods to be severed from realty (Section 2-107).

(2) Goods must be both existing and identified before any interest in them can pass. Goods which are not both existing and identified are "future" goods. A purported present sale of future goods or of any interest therein operates as a contract to sell.

(3) There may be a sale of a part interest in existing identified goods.

(4) An undivided share in an identified bulk of fungible goods is sufficiently identified to be sold although the quantity of the bulk is not determined. Any agreed proportion of such a bulk or any quantity thereof agreed upon by number, weight or other measure may to the extent of the seller's interest in the bulk be sold to the buyer who then becomes an owner in common.

(5) "Lot" means a parcel or a single article which is the subject matter of a separate sale or delivery, whether or not it is sufficient to perform the contract.

(6) "Commercial unit" means such a unit of goods as by commercial usage is a single whole for purposes of sale and division of which materially impairs its character or value on the market or in use. A commercial unit may be a single article (as a machine) or a set of articles (as a suite of furniture or an assortment of sizes) or a quantity (as a bale, gross, or carload) or any other unit treated in use or in the relevant market as a single whole.

2-106. DEFINITIONS: "CONTRACT"; "AGREEMENT"; "CONTRACT FOR SALE"; "SALE"; "PRESENT SALE"; "CONFORMING" TO CONTRACT; "TERMINATION"; "CANCELLATION".

(1) In this Article unless the context otherwise requires "contract" and "agreement" are limited to those relating to the present or future sale of goods. "Contract for sale" includes both a present sale of goods and a contract to sell goods at a future time. A "sale" consists in the passing of title from the seller to the buyer for a price (Section 2-401). A "present sale" means a sale which is accomplished by the making of the contract.

(2) Goods or conduct including any part of a performance are "conforming" or conform to the contract when they are in accordance with the obligations under the contract.

(3) "Termination" occurs when either party pursuant to a power created by agreement or law puts an end to the contract otherwise than for its breach. On "termination" all obligations which are still executory on both sides are discharged but any right based on prior breach or performance survives.

(4) "Cancellation" occurs when either party puts an end to the contract for breach by the other and its effect is the same as that of "termination" except that the canceling party also retains any remedy for breach of the whole contract or any unperformed balance.

2-107. GOODS TO BE SEVERED FROM REALITY: RECORDING.

(1) A contract for the sale of minerals or the like (including oil and gas) or a structure or its materials to be removed from realty is a contract for the sale of goods within this Article if they are to be severed by the seller but until severance a purported present sale thereof which is not effective as a transfer of an interest in land is effective only as a contract to sell.

(2) A contract for the sale apart from the land of growing crops or other things attached to realty and capable of severance without material harm thereto but not described in subsection (1) or of timber to be cut is a contract for the sale of goods within this Article whether the subject matter is to be severed by the buyer or by the seller even though it forms part of the realty at the time of contracting, and the parties can by identification effect a present sale before severance.

(3) The provisions of this section are subject to any third party rights provided by the law relating to realty records, and the contract for sale may be executed and recorded as a document transferring an interest in land and shall then constitute notice to third parties of the buyer's rights under the contract for sale.

PART 2
FORM, FORMATION AND READJUSTMENT OF CONTRACT

2-201. FORMAL REQUIREMENTS; STATUTE OF FRAUDS.

(1) Except as otherwise provided in this section a contract for the sale of goods for the price of $500 or more is not enforceable by way of action or defense unless there is some writing sufficient to indicate that a contract for sale has been made between the parties and signed by the party against whom enforcement is sought or by his authorized agent or broker. A writing is not insufficient because it omits or incorrectly states a term agreed upon but the contract is not enforceable under this paragraph beyond the quantity of goods shown in such writing.

(2) Between merchants if within a reasonable time a writing in confirmation of the contract and sufficient against the sender is received and the party receiving it has reason to know its contents, it satisfies the requirements of subsection (1) against such party unless written notice of objection to its contents is given within 10 days after it is received.

(3) A contract which does not satisfy the requirements of subsection (1) but which is valid in other respects is enforceable

(a) if the goods are to be specially manufactured for the buyer and are not suitable for sale to others in the ordinary course of the seller's business and the seller, before notice of repudiation is received and under circumstances which reasonably indicate that the goods are for the buyer, has made either a substantial beginning of their manufacture or commitments for their procurement; or

(b) if the party against whom enforcement is sought admits in his pleading, testimony or otherwise in court that a contract for sale was made, but the contract is not enforceable under this provision beyond the quantity of goods admitted; or

(c) with respect to goods for which payment has been made and accepted or which have been received and accepted (Sec. 2-606).

2-202. FINAL WRITTEN EXPRESSION: PAROL OR EXTRINSIC EVIDENCE.

Terms with respect to which the confirmatory memoranda of the parties agree or which are otherwise set forth in a writing intended by the parties as a final expression of their agreement with respect to such terms as are included therein may not be contradicted by evidence of any prior agreement or of a contemporaneous oral agreement but may be explained or supplemented

(a) by course of dealing or usage of trade (Section 1-205) or by course of performance (Section 2-208); and

(b) by evidence of consistent additional terms unless the court finds the writing to have been intended also as a complete and exclusive statement of the terms of the agreement.

2-203. SEALS INOPERATIVE.

The affixing of a seal to a writing evidencing a contract for sale or an offer to buy or sell goods does not constitute the writing of a sealed instrument and the law with respect to sealed instruments does not apply to such a contract or offer.

2-204. FORMATION IN GENERAL.

(1) A contract for sale of goods may be made in any manner sufficient to show agreement, including conduct by both parties which recognizes the existence of such a contract.

(2) An agreement sufficient to constitute a contract for sale may be found even though the moment of its making is undetermined.

(3) Even though one or more terms are left open a contract for sale does not fail for indefiniteness if the parties have intended to make a contract and there is a reasonably certain basis for giving an appropriate remedy.

2-205. FIRM OFFERS.

An offer by a merchant to buy or sell goods in a signed writing which by its terms gives assurance that it will be held open is not revocable, for lack of consideration, during the time stated or if no time is stated for a reasonable time, but in no event may such period of irrevocability exceed three months; but any such term of assurance on a form supplied by the offeree must be separately signed by the offeror.

2-206. OFFER AND ACCEPTANCE IN FORMATION OF CONTRACT.

(1) Unless otherwise unambiguously indicated by the language or circumstances

   (a) an offer to make a contract shall be construed as inviting acceptance in any manner and by any medium reasonable in the circumstances;

   (b) an order or other offer to buy goods for prompt or current shipment shall be construed as inviting acceptance either by a prompt promise to ship or by the prompt or current shipment of conforming or nonconforming goods, but such a shipment of nonconforming goods does not constitute an acceptance if the seller seasonably notifies the buyer that the shipment is offered only as an accommodation to the buyer.

(2) Where the beginning of a requested performance is a reasonable mode of acceptance an offeror who is not notified of acceptance within a reasonable time may treat the offer as having lapsed before acceptance.

2-207. ADDITIONAL TERMS IN ACCEPTANCE OR CONFIRMATION.

(1) A definite and seasonable expression of acceptance or a written confirmation which is sent within a reasonable time operates as an acceptance even though it states terms additional to or different from those offered or agreed upon, unless acceptance is expressly made conditional on assent to the additional or different terms.

(2) The additional terms are to be construed as proposals for addition to the contract. Between merchants such terms become part of the contract unless:

   (a) the offer expressly limits acceptance to the terms of the offer;

   (b) they materially alter it; or

   (c) notification of objection to them has already been given or is given within a reasonable time after notice of them is received.

(3) Conduct by both parties which recognizes the existence of a contract is sufficient to establish a contract for sale although the writings of the parties do not otherwise establish a contract. In such case the terms of the particular contract consist of those terms on which the writings of the parties agree, together with any supplementary terms incorporated under any other provisions of this Act.

2-208. COURSE OF PERFORMANCE OR PRACTICAL CONSTRUCTION.

(1) Where the contract for sale involves repeated occasions for performance by either party with knowledge of the nature of the performance and opportunity for objection to it by the other, any course of performance accepted or acquiesced in without objection shall be relevant to determine the meaning of the agreement.

(2) The express terms of the agreement and any such course of performance, as well as any course of dealing and usage of trade, shall be construed whenever reasonable as consistent with each other; but when such construction is unreasonable, express terms shall control course of performance and course of performance shall control both course of dealing and usage of trade (Section 1-205).

(3) Subject to the provisions of the next section on modification and waiver, such course of performance shall be relevant to show a waiver or modification of any term inconsistent with such course of performance.

2-209. MODIFICATION, RESCISSION AND WAIVER.

(1) An agreement modifying a contract within this Article needs no consideration to be binding.

(2) A signed agreement which excludes modification or rescission except by a signed writing cannot be otherwise modified or rescinded, but except as between merchants such a requirement on a form supplied by the merchant must be separately signed by the other party.

(3) The requirements of the statute of frauds section of this Article (Section 2-201) must be satisfied if the contract as modified is within its provisions.

(4) Although an attempt at modification or rescission does not satisfy the requirements of subsection (2) or (3) it can operate as a waiver.

(5) A party who has made a waiver affecting an executory portion of the contract may retract the waiver by reasonable notification received by the other party that strict performance will be required of any term waived, unless the retraction would be unjust in view of a material change of position in reliance on the waiver.

2-210. DELEGATION OF PERFORMANCE; ASSIGNMENT OF RIGHTS.

(1) A party may perform his duty through a delegate unless otherwise agreed or unless the other party has a substantial interest in having his original promisor perform or control the acts required by the contract. No delegation of performance relieves the party delegating of any duty to perform any liability for breach.

(2) Unless otherwise agreed all rights of either seller or buyer can be assigned except where the assignment would materially change the duty of the other party, or increase materially the burden or risk imposed on him by his contract, or impair materially his chance of obtaining return performance. A right to damages for breach of the whole contract or a right arising out of the assignor's due performance of his entire obligation can be assigned despite agreement otherwise.

(3) Unless the circumstances indicate the contrary a prohibition of assignment of "the contract" is to be construed as barring only the delegation to the assignee of the assignor's performance.

(4) An assignment of "the contract" or of "all my rights under the contract" or an assignment in similar general terms is an assignment of rights and unless the language or the circumstances (as in an assignment for security) indicate the contrary, it is a delegation of performance of the duties of the assignor and its acceptance by the assignee constitutes a promise by him to perform those duties. This promise is enforceable by either the assignor or the other party to the original contract.

(5) The other party may treat any assignment which delegates performance as creating reasonable grounds for insecurity and may without prejudice to his rights against the assignor demand assurances from the assignee (Section 2-609).

PART 3
GENERAL OBLIGATION AND CONSTRUCTION OF CONTRACT

2-301. GENERAL OBLIGATIONS OF PARTIES.

The obligation of the seller is to transfer and deliver and that of the buyer is to accept and pay in accordance with the contract.

2-302. Unconscionable Contract or Clause.

(1) If the court as a matter of law finds the contract or any clause of the contract to have been unconscionable at the time it was made the court may refuse to enforce the contract, or it may enforce the remainder of the contract without the unconscionable clause, or it may so limit the application of any unconscionable clause as to avoid any unconscionable result.

(2) When it is claimed or appears to the court that the contract or any clause thereof may be unconscionable the parties shall be afforded a reasonable opportunity to present evidence as to its commercial setting, purpose and effect to aid the court in making the determination.

2-303. Allocation or Division of Risks.

Where this Article allocates a risk or a burden as between the parties "unless otherwise agreed", the agreement may not only shift the allocation but may also divide the risk or burden.

2-304. Price Payable in Money, Goods, Realty, or Otherwise.

(1) The price can be made payable in money or otherwise. If it is payable in whole or in part in goods each party is a seller of the goods which he is to transfer.

(2) Even though all or part of the price is payable in an interest in realty the transfer of the goods and the seller's obligations with reference to them are subject to this Article, but not the transfer of the interest in realty or the transferor's obligations in connection therewith.

2-305. Open Price Term.

(1) The parties if they so intend can conclude a contract for sale even though the price is not settled. In such a case the price is a reasonable price at the time for delivery if

    (a) nothing is said as to price; or

    (b) the price is left to be agreed by the parties and they fail to agree; or

    (c) the price is to be fixed in terms of some agreed market or other standard as set or recorded by a third person or agency and it is not so set or recorded.

(2) A price to be fixed by the seller or by the buyer means a price for him to fix in good faith.

(3) When a price left to be fixed otherwise than by agreement of the parties fails to be fixed through fault of one party the other may at his option treat the contract as canceled or himself fix a reasonable price.

(4) Where, however, the parties intend not to be bound unless the price be fixed or agreed and it is not fixed or agreed there is no contract. In such a case the buyer must return any goods already received or if unable so to do must pay their reasonable value at the time of delivery and the seller must return any portion of the price paid on account.

2-306. Output, Requirements and Exclusive Dealings.

(1) A term which measures the quantity by the output of the seller or the requirements of the buyer means such actual output or requirements as may occur in good faith, except that no quantity unreasonably disproportionate to any stated estimate or in the absence of a stated estimate to any normal or otherwise comparable prior output or requirements may be tendered or demanded.

(2) A lawful agreement by either the seller or the buyer for exclusive dealing in the kind of goods concerned imposes unless otherwise agreed an obligation by the seller to use best efforts to supply the goods and by the buyer to use best efforts to promote their sale.

2-307. Delivery in Single Lot or Several Lots.

Unless otherwise agreed all goods called for by a contract for sale must be tendered in a single delivery and payment is due only on such tender but where the circumstances give either party the right to make or demand delivery in lots the price if it can be apportioned may be demanded for each lot.

2-308. Absence of Specified Place for Delivery.

Unless otherwise agreed

(a) the place for delivery of goods is the seller's place of business or if he has none his residence; but

(b) in a contract for sale of identified goods which to the knowledge of the parties at the time of contracting are in some other place, that place is the place for their delivery; and

(c) documents of title may be delivered through customary banking channels.

2-309. Absence of Specific Time Provisions; Notice of Termination.

(1) The time for shipment or delivery or any other action under a contract if not provided in this Article or agreed upon shall be a reasonable time.

(2) Where the contract provides for successive performances but is indefinite in duration it is valid for a reasonable time but unless otherwise agreed may be terminated at any time by either party.

(3) Termination of a contract by one party except on the happening of an agreed event requires that reasonable notification be received by the other party and an agreement dispensing with notification is invalid if its operation would be unconscionable.

2-310. Open Time for Payment or Running of Credit; Authority to Ship Under Reservation.

Unless otherwise agreed

(a) payment is due at the time and place at which the buyer is to receive the goods even though the place of shipment is the place of delivery; and

(b) if the seller is authorized to send the goods he may ship them under reservation, and may tender the documents of title, but the buyer may inspect the goods after their arrival before payment is due unless such inspection is inconsistent with the terms of the contract (Section 2-513); and

(c) if delivery is authorized and made by way of documents of title otherwise than by subsection (b) then payment is due at the time and place at which the buyer is to receive the documents regardless of where the goods are to be received; and

(d) where the seller is required or authorized to ship the goods on credit the credit period runs from the time of shipment but post-dating the invoice or delaying its dispatch will correspondingly delay the starting of the credit period.

2-311. OPTIONS AND COOPERATION RESPECTING PERFORMANCE.

(1) An agreement for sale which is otherwise sufficiently definite (subsection (3) of Section 2-204) to be a contract is not made invalid by the fact that it leaves particulars of performance to be specified by one of the parties. Any such specification must be made in good faith and within limits set by commercial reasonableness.

(2) Unless otherwise agreed specifications relating to assortment of the goods are at the buyer's option and except as otherwise provided in subsection (1) (c) and (3) of Section 2-319 specifications or arrangements relating to shipment are at the seller's option.

(3) Where such specification would materially affect the other party's performance but is not seasonably made or where one party's cooperation is necessary to the agreed performance of the other but is not seasonably forthcoming, the other party in addition to all other remedies

(a) is excused for any resulting delay in his own performance; and

(b) may also either proceed to perform in any reasonable manner or after the time for a material part of his own performance treat the failure to specify or to cooperate as a breach by failure to deliver or accept the goods.

2-312. WARRANTY OF TITLE AND AGAINST INFRINGEMENT; BUYER'S OBLIGATION AGAINST INFRINGEMENT.

(1) Subject to subsection (2) there is in a contract for sale a warranty by the seller that

(a) the title conveyed shall be good, and its transfer rightful; and

(b) the goods shall be delivered free from any security interest or other lien or encumbrance of which the buyer at the time of contracting has no knowledge.

(2) A warranty under subsection (1) will be excluded or modified only by specific language or by circumstances which give the buyer reason to know that the person selling does not claim title in himself or that he is purporting to sell only such right or title as he or a third person may have.

(3) Unless otherwise agreed a seller who is a merchant regularly dealing in goods of the kind warrants that the goods shall be delivered free of the rightful claim of any third person by way of infringement or the like but a buyer who furnishes specifications to the seller must hold the seller harmless against any such claim which arises out of compliance with the specifications.

2-313. Express Warranties by Affirmation, Promise, Description, Sample.

(1) Express warranties by the seller are created as follows:

   (a) Any affirmation of fact or promise made by the seller to the buyer which relates to the goods and becomes part of the basis of the bargains creates an express warranty that the goods shall conform to the affirmation or promise.

   (b) Any description of the goods which is made part of the basis of the bargain creates an express warranty that the goods shall conform to the description.

   (c) Any sample or model which is made part of the basis of the bargain creates an express warranty that the whole of the goods shall conform to the sample or model.

(2) It is not necessary to the creation of an express warranty that the seller use formal words such as "warrant" or "guarantee" or that he have a specific intention to make a warranty, but an affirmation merely of the value of the goods or a statement purporting to be merely the seller's opinion or commendation of the goods does not create a warranty.

2-314. Implied Warranty: Merchantability; Usage of Trade.

(1) Unless excluded or modified (Section 2-316), a warranty that the goods shall be merchantable is implied in a contract for their sale if the seller is a merchant with respect to goods of that kind. Under this section the serving for value of food or drink to be consumed either on the premises or elsewhere is a sale.

(2) Goods to be merchantable must be at least such as

   (a) pass without objection in the trade under the contract description; and

   (b) in the case of fungible goods, are of fair average quality within the description; and

   (c) are fit for the ordinary purposes for which such goods are used; and

   (d) run, within the variations permitted by the agreement, of even kind, quality and quantity within each unit and among all units involved; and

   (e) are adequately contained, packaged, and labeled as the agreement may require; and

   (f) conform to the promise or affirmations of fact made on the container or label if any.

(3) Unless excluded or modified (Section 2-316) other implied warranties may arise from course of dealing or usage of trade.

2-315. Implied Warranty: Fitness for Particular Purpose.

Where the seller at the time of contracting has reason to know any particular purpose for which the goods are required and that the buyer is relying on the seller's skill or judgment to select or furnish suitable goods, there is unless excluded or modified under the next section an implied warranty that the goods shall be fit for such purpose.

2-316. EXCLUSION OR MODIFICATION OF WARRANTIES.

(1) Words or conduct relevant to the creation of an express warranty and words or conduct tending to negate or limit warranty shall be construed wherever reasonable as consistent with each other; but subject to the provisions of this Article on parol or extrinsic evidence (Section 2-202) negation or limitation is inoperative to the extent that such construction is unreasonable.

(2) Subject to subsection (3), to exclude or modify the implied warranty of merchantability or any part of it the language must mention merchantability and in case of a writing must be conspicuous, and to exclude or modify any implied warranty of fitness the exclusion must be by a writing and conspicuous. Language to exclude all implied warranties of fitness is sufficient if it states, for example, that "There are no warranties which extend beyond the description on the face hereof."

(3)   Notwithstanding subsection (2)

    (a)   unless the circumstances indicate otherwise, all implied warranties are excluded by expressions like "as is", "with all faults" or other language which in common understanding calls the buyer's attention to the exclusion of warranties and makes plain that there is no implied warranty; and

    (b)   when the buyer before entering into the contract has examined the goods or the sample or model as fully as he desired or has refused to examine the goods there is no implied warranty with regard to defects which an examination ought in the circumstances to have revealed to him; and

    (c)   an implied warranty can also be excluded or modified by course of dealing or course of performance or usage of trade.

(4) Remedies for breach of warranty can be limited in accordance with the provisions of this Article on liquidation or limitation of damages and on contractual modification of remedy (Sections 2-718 and 2-719).

2-317. CUMULATION AND CONFLICT OF WARRANTIES EXPRESS OR IMPLIED.

Warranties whether express or implied shall be construed as consistent with each other and as cumulative, but if such construction is unreasonable the intention of the parties shall determine which warranty is dominant. In ascertaining that intention the following rules apply:

    (a)   Exact or technical specifications displace an inconsistent sample or model or general language of description.

    (b)   A sample from an existing bulk displaces inconsistent general language of description.

    (c)   Express warranties displace inconsistent implied warranties other than an implied warranty of fitness for a particular purpose.

2-318. THIRD PARTY BENEFICIARIES OF WARRANTIES EXPRESS OR IMPLIED.

Note: If this Act is introduced in the Congress of the United States this Section should be omitted. (States to select one alternative.)

ALTERNATIVE **A**

A seller's warranty whether express or implied extends to any natural person who is in the family or household of his buyer or who is a guest in his home if it is reasonable to expect that such person may use, consume or be affected by the goods and who is injured in person by breach of the warranty. A seller may not exclude or limit the operation of this section.

ALTERNATIVE **B**

A seller's warranty whether express or implied extends to any natural person who may reasonably be expected to use, consume or be affected by the goods and who is injured in person by breach of the warranty. A seller may not exclude or limit the operation of this section.

ALTERNATIVE **C**

A seller's warranty whether express or implied extends to any person who may reasonably be expected to use, consume or be affected by the goods and who is injured by breach of the warranty. A seller may not exclude or limit the operation of this section with respect to injury to the person of an individual to whom the warranty extends. As amended in 1966.

2-319. F.O.B. AND F.A.S. TERMS.

(1) Unless otherwise agreed the term F.O.B. (which means "free on board") at a named place, even though used only in connection with the stated price, is a delivery term under which

   (a) when the term is F.O.B. the place of shipment, the seller must at that place ship the goods in the manner provided in this Article (Section 2-504) and bear the expense and risk of putting them into the possession of the carrier; or

   (b) when the term is F.O.B. the place of destination, the seller must at his own expense and risk transport the goods to that place and there tender delivery of them in the manner provided in this Article (Section 2-503);

   (c) when under either (a) or (b) the term is also F.O.B. vessel, car or other vehicle, the seller must in addition at his own expense and risk load the goods on board. If the term is F.O.B. vessel the buyer must name the vessel and in an appropriate case the seller must comply with the provisions of this Article on the form of bill of lading (Section 2-323).

(2) Unless otherwise agreed the terms F.A.S. vessel (which means "free alongside") at a named port, even though used only in connection with the stated price, is a delivery term under which the seller must

   (a) at his own expense and risk deliver the goods alongside the vessel in the manner usual in that port or on a dock designated and provided by the buyer; and

   (b) obtain and tender a receipt for the goods in exchange for which the carrier is under a duty to issue a bill of lading.

(3) Unless otherwise agreed in any case falling within subsection (1) (a) or (c) or subsection (2) the buyer must seasonably give any needed instructions for making delivery, including when the term is F.A.S. or F.O.B. the loading berth of the vessel and in an appropriate case its name and sailing date. The seller may treat the failure of needed instructions as a failure of cooperation under this Article (Section 2-311). He

may also at his option move the goods in any reasonable manner preparatory to delivery or shipment.

(4) Under the term F.O.B. vessel or F.A.S. unless otherwise agreed the buyer must make payment against tender of the required documents and the seller may not tender nor the buyer demand delivery of the goods in substitution for the documents.

2-320. C.I.F. AND C. & F. TERMS.

(1) The term C.I.F. means that the price includes in a lump sum the cost of the goods and the insurance and freight to the named destination. The term C. & F. or C.F. means that the price so includes cost and freight to the named destination.

(2) Unless otherwise agreed and even though used only in connection with the stated price and destination, the term C.I.F. destination or its equivalent requires the seller at his own expense and risk to

(a) put the goods into the possession of a carrier at the port for shipment and obtain a negotiable bill or bills of lading covering the entire transportation to the named destination; and

(b) load the goods and obtain a receipt from the carrier (which may be contained in the bill of lading) showing that the freight has been paid or provided for; and

(c) obtain a policy or certificate of insurance, including any war risk insurance, of a kind and on terms then current at the port of shipment in the usual amount, in the currency of the contract, shown to cover the same goods covered by the bill of lading and providing for payment of loss to the order of the buyer or for the account of whom it may concern; but the seller may add to the price the amount of the premium for any such war risk insurance; and

(d) prepare an invoice of the goods and procure any other documents required to effect shipment or to comply with the contract; and

(e) forward and tender with commercial promptness all the documents in due form and with any endorsement necessary to perfect the buyer's rights.

(3) Unless otherwise agreed the term C. & F. or its equivalent has the same effect and imposes upon the seller the same obligations and risks as a C.I.F. term except the obligation as to insurance.

(4) Under the term C.I.F. or C. & F. unless otherwise agreed the buyer must make payment against tender of the required documents and the seller may not tender nor the buyer demand delivery of the goods in substitution for the documents.

2-321. C.I.F. OR C. & F.: "NET LANDED WEIGHTS"; "PAYMENT ON ARRIVAL"; WARRANTY OF CONDITION ON ARRIVAL.

Under a contract containing a term C.I.F. or C. & F.

(1) Where the price is based on or is to be adjusted according to "net landed weights", "delivered weights", "out turn" quantity or quality or the like, unless otherwise agreed the seller must reasonably estimate the price. The payment due on tender of the documents called for by the contract is the amount so estimated, but after final adjustment of the price a settlement must be made with commercial promptness.

(2) An agreement described in subsection (1) or any warranty of quality or condition of the goods on arrival places upon the seller the risk of ordinary deterioration, shrink-

age and the like in transportation but has no effect on the place or time of identification to the contract for sale or delivery or on the passing of the risk of loss.

(3) Unless otherwise agreed where the contract provides for payment on or after arrival of the goods the seller must before payment allow such preliminary inspection as is feasible; but if the goods are lost delivery of the documents and payment are due when the goods should have arrived.

2-322. DELIVERY "EX-SHIP".

(1) Unless otherwise agreed a term for delivery of goods "ex-ship" (which means from the carrying vessel) or in equivalent language is not restricted to a particular ship and requires delivery from a ship which has reached a place at the named port of destination where goods of the kind are usually discharged.

(2) Under such a term unless otherwise agreed

   (a) the seller must discharge all liens arising out of the carriage and furnish the buyer with a direction which puts the carrier under a duty to deliver the goods; and

   (b) the risk of loss does not pass to the buyer until the goods leave the ship's tackle or are otherwise properly unloaded.

2-323. FORM OF BILL OF LADING REQUIRED IN OVERSEAS SHIPMENT; "OVERSEAS".

(1) Where the contract contemplates overseas shipment and contains a term C.I.F. or C. & F. or F.O.B. vessel, the seller unless otherwise agreed must obtain a negotiable bill of lading stating that the goods have been loaded in board or, in the case of a term C.I.F. or C. & F., received for shipment.

(2) Where in a case within subsection (1) a bill of lading has been issued in a set of parts, unless otherwise agreed if the documents are not to be sent from abroad the buyer may demand tender of the full set; otherwise only one part of the bill of lading need be tendered. Even if the agreement expressly requires a full set

   (a) due tender of a single part is acceptable within the provisions of this Article on cure of improper delivery (subsection (1) of Section 2-508); and

   (b) even though the full set is demanded, if the documents are sent from abroad the person tendering an incomplete set may nevertheless require payment upon furnishing an indemnity which the buyer in good faith deems adequate.

(3) A shipment by water or by air or a contract contemplating such shipment is "overseas" insofar as by usage of trade or agreement it is subject to the commercial, financing or shipping practices characteristic of international deep water commerce.

2-324. "NO ARRIVAL, NO SALE" TERM.

Under a term "no arrival, no sale" or terms of like meaning, unless otherwise agreed,

   (a) the seller must properly ship conforming goods and if they arrive by any means he must tender them on arrival but he assumes no obligation that the goods will arrive unless he has caused the non-arrival; and

(b) where without fault of the seller the goods are in part lost or have so deteriorated as no longer to conform to the contract or arrive after the contract time, the buyer may proceed as if there had been casualty to identified goods (Section 2-613).

2-325. "Letter of Credit" Term; "Confirmed Credit".

(1) Failure of the buyer seasonably to furnish an agreed letter of credit is a breach of the contract for sale.

(2) The delivery to seller of a proper letter of credit suspends the buyer's obligation to pay. If the letter of credit is dishonored, the seller may on seasonable notification to the buyer require payment directly from him.

(3) Unless otherwise agreed the term "letter of credit" or "banker's credit" in a contract for sale means an irrevocable credit issued by a financing agency of good repute and, where the shipment is overseas, of good international repute. The term "confirmed credit" means that the credit must also carry the direct obligation of such an agency which does business in the seller's financial market.

2-326. Sale on Approval and Sale or Return; Consignment Sales and Rights of Creditors.

(1) Unless otherwise agreed, if delivered goods may be returned by the buyer even though they conform to the contract, the transaction is

(a) a "sale on approval" if the goods are delivered primarily for use, and

(b) a "sale or return" if the goods are delivered primarily for resale.

(2) Except as provided in subsection (3), goods held on approval are not subject to the claims of the buyer's creditors until acceptance; goods held on sale or return are subject to such claims while in the buyer's possession.

(3) Where goods are delivered to a person for sale and such person maintains a place of business at which he deals in goods of the kind involved, under a name other than the name of the person making delivery, then with respect to claims of creditors of the person conducting the business the goods are deemed to be on sale or return. The provisions of this subsection are applicable even though an agreement purports to reserve title to the person making delivery until payment or resale or uses such words as "on consignment" or "on memorandum". However, this subsection is not applicable if the person making delivery

(a) complies with an applicable law providing for a consignor's interest or the like to be evidenced by a sign, or

(b) establishes that the person conducting the business is generally known by his creditors to be substantially engaged in selling the goods of others, or

(c) complies with the filing provisions of the Article on Secured Transactions (Article 9).

(4) Any "or return" term of a contract for sale is to be treated as a separate contract for sale within the statute of frauds section of this Article (Section 2-201) and as contradicting the sale aspect of the contract within the provisions of this Article on parol or extrinsic evidence (Section 2-202).

2-327. SPECIAL INCIDENTS OF SALE ON APPROVAL AND SALE OR RETURN.

(1) Under a sale on approval unless otherwise agreed

    (a) although the goods are identified to the contract the risk of loss and the title do not pass to the buyer until acceptance; and

    (b) use of the goods consistent with the purpose of trial is not acceptance but failure seasonally to notify the seller of election to return the goods is acceptance, and if the goods conform to the contract acceptance of any part is acceptance of the whole; and

    (c) after due notification of election to return, the return is at the seller's risk and expense but a merchant buyer must follow any reasonable instructions.

(2) Under a sale or return unless otherwise agreed

    (a) the option to return extends to the whole or any commercial unit of the goods while in substantially their original condition, but must be exercised seasonably; and

    (b) the return is at the buyer's risk and expense.

2-328. SALE BY AUCTION.

(1) In a sale by auction if goods are put up in lots each lot is the subject of a separate sale.

(2) A sale by auction is complete when the auctioneer so announces by the fall of the hammer or in other customary manner. Where a bid is made while the hammer is falling in acceptance of a prior bid the auctioneer may in his discretion reopen the bidding or declare the goods sold under the bid on which the hammer was falling.

(3) Such a sale is with reserve unless the goods are in explicit terms put up without reserve. In an auction with reserve the auctioneer may withdraw the goods at any time until he announces completion of the sale. In an auction without reserve, after the auctioneer calls for bids on an article or lot, that article or lot cannot be withdrawn unless no bid is made within a reasonable time. In either case a bidder may retract his bid until the auctioneer's announcement of completion of the sale, but a bidder's retraction does not revive any previous bid.

(4) If the auctioneer knowingly receives a bid on the seller's behalf or the seller makes or procures such a bid, and notice has not been given that liberty for such bidding is reserved, the buyer may at his option avoid the sale or take the goods at the price of the last good faith bid prior to the completion of the sale. This subsection shall not apply to any bid at a forced sale.

PART 4
TITLE, CREDITORS AND GOOD FAITH PURCHASERS

2-401. PASSING OF TITLE; RESERVATION FOR SECURITY; LIMITED APPLICATION OF THIS SECTION.

Each provision of this Article with regard to the rights, obligations and remedies of the seller, the buyer, purchasers or other third parties applies irrespective of title to the goods except where the provision refers to such title. Insofar as situations are not covered by the other provisions of this Article and matters concerning title become material the following rules apply:

(1) Title of goods cannot pass under a contract for sale prior to their identification to the contract (Section 2-501), and unless otherwise explicitly agreed the buyer acquires by their identification a special property as limited by this Act. Any retention or reservation by the seller of the title (property) in goods shipped or delivered to the buyer is limited in effect to a reservation of a security interest. Subject to these provisions and to the provisions of the Article on Secured Transactions (Article 9), title to goods passes from the seller to the buyer in any manner and on any conditions explicitly agreed on by the parties.

(2) Unless otherwise explicitly agreed title passes to the buyer at the time and place at which the seller completes his performance with reference to the physical delivery of the goods, despite any reservation of a security interest and even though a document of title is to be delivered at a different time or place; and in particular and despite any reservation of a security interest by the bill of lading

   (a) if the contract requires or authorizes the seller to send the goods to the buyer but does not require him to deliver them at destination, title passes to the buyer at the time and place of shipment; but

   (b) if the contract requires delivery at destination, title passes on tender there.

(3) Unless otherwise explicitly agreed where delivery is to be made without moving the goods,

   (a) if the seller is to deliver a document of title, title passes at the time and the place where he delivers such documents; or

   (b) if the goods are at the time of contracting already identified and no documents are to be delivered, title passes at the time and place of contracting.

(4) A rejection or other refusal by the buyer to receive or retain the goods, whether or not justified, or a justified revocation of acceptance revests title to the goods in the seller. Such revesting occurs by operation of law and is not a "sale".

2-402. RIGHTS OF SELLER'S CREDITORS AGAINST SOLD GOODS.

(1) Except as provided in subsections (2) and (3), rights of unsecured creditors of the seller with respect to goods which have been identified to a contract for sale are subject to the buyer's rights to recover the goods under this Article (Sections 2-502 and 2-716).

(2) A creditor of the seller may treat a sale or an identification of goods to a contract for sale as void if as against him a retention of possession by the seller is fraudulent under any rule of law of the state where the goods are situated, except that retention of possession in good faith and current course of trade by a merchant-seller for a commercially reasonable time after a sale or identification is not fraudulent.

(3) Nothing in this Article shall be deemed to impair the rights of creditors of the seller

   (a) under the provisions of the Article on Secured Transactions (Article 9); or

   (b) where identification to the contract or delivery is made not in current course of trade but in satisfaction of or as security for a pre-existing claim for money, security or the like and is made under circumstances which under any rule of law of the state where the goods are situated would apart from this Article constitute the transaction of a fraudulent transfer or voidable preference.

2-403. Power to Transfer; Good Faith Purchase of Goods; "Entrusting".

(1) A purchaser of goods acquires all title which his transferor had or had power to transfer except that a purchaser of a limited interest acquires rights only to the extent of the interest purchased. A person with voidable title has power to transfer a good title to a good faith purchaser for value. When goods have been delivered under a transaction of purchase the purchaser has such power even though

   (a) the transferor was deceived as to the identity of the purchaser, or

   (b) the delivery was in exchange for a check which is later dishonored, or

   (c) it was agreed that the transaction was to be a "cash sale", or

   (d) the delivery was procured through fraud punishable as larcenous under the criminal law.

(2) Any entrusting of possession of goods to a merchant who deals in goods of that kind gives him power to transfer all rights of the entruster to a buyer in ordinary course of business.

(3) "Entrusting" includes any delivery and any acquiescence in retention of possession regardless of any condition expressed between the parties to the delivery or acquiescence and regardless of whether the procurement of the entrusting or the possessor's disposition of the goods have been such as to be larcenous under the criminal law.

   [**Publisher's Editorial Note:** If a state adopts the repealer of Article 6—Bulk Transfers (Alternative A), subsec. (4) should read as follows:]

(4) The rights of other purchasers of goods and of lien creditors are governed by the Articles on Secured Transactions (Article 9) and Documents of Title (Article 7).

   [**Publisher's Editorial Note:** If a state adopts Revised Article 6—Bulk Sales (Alternative B), subsec. (4) should read as follows:]

(5) The rights of other purchasers of goods and of lien creditors are governed by the Articles on Secured Transaction (Article 9), Bulk Sales (Article 6) and Documents of Title (Article 7).

As amended in 1988.

For material relating to the changes made in text in 1988, see section 3 of Alternative A (Repealer of Article 6—Bulk Transfers) and Conforming Amendment to Section 2-403 following end of Alternative B (Revised Article 6—Bulk Sales).

Part 5
Performance

2-501. Insurable Interest In Goods; Manner of Identification of Goods.

(1) The buyer obtains a special property and an insurable interest in goods by identification of existing goods as goods to which the contract refers even though the goods

so identified are non-conforming and he has an option to return or reject them. Such identification can be made at any time and in any manner explicitly agreed to by the parties. In the absence of explicit agreement identification occurs

(a) when the contract is made if it is for the sale of goods already existing and identified;

(b) if the contract is for the sale of future goods other than those described in paragraph (c), when goods are shipped, marked or otherwise designated by the seller as goods to which the contract refers;

(c) when the crops are planted or otherwise become growing crops or the young are conceived if the contract is for the sale of unborn young to be born within twelve months after contracting or for the sale of crops to be harvested within twelve months or the next normal harvest season after contracting whichever is longer.

(2) The seller retains an insurable interest in goods so long as title to or any security interest in the goods remains in him and where the identification is by the seller alone he may until default or insolvency or notification to the buyer that the identification is final substitute other goods for those identified.

(3) Nothing in this section impairs any insurable interest recognized under any other statute or rule of law.

2-502. BUYER'S RIGHT TO GOODS ON SELLER'S INSOLVENCY.

(1) Subject to subsection (2) and even though the goods have not been shipped a buyer who has paid a part or all of the price of goods in which he has a special property under the provisions of the immediately preceding section may on making and keeping good a tender of any unpaid portion of their price recover them from the seller if the seller becomes insolvent within ten days after receipt of the first installment on their price.

(2) If the identification creating his special property has been made by the buyer he acquires the right to recover the goods only if they conform to the contract for sale.

2-503. MANNER OF SELLER'S TENDER OF DELIVERY.

(1) Tender of delivery requires that the seller put and hold conforming goods at the buyer's disposition and give the buyer any notification reasonably necessary to enable him to take delivery. The manner, time and place for tender are determined by the agreement and this Article, and in particular

(a) tender must be at a reasonable hour, and if it is of goods they must be kept available for the period reasonably necessary to enable the buyer to take possession; but

(b) unless otherwise agreed the buyer must furnish facilities reasonably suited to the receipt of the goods.

(2) Where the case is within the next section respecting shipment tender requires that the seller comply with its provisions.

(3) Where the seller is required to deliver at a particular destination tender requires that he comply with subsection (1) and also in any appropriate case tender documents as described in subsections (4) and (5) of this section.

(4) Where goods are in the possession of a bailee and are to be delivered without being moved

   (a) tender requires that the seller either tender a negotiable document of title covering such goods or procure acknowledgment by the bailee of the buyer's right to possession of the goods; but

   (b) tender to the buyer of a non-negotiable document of title or of a written direction to the bailee to deliver is sufficient tender unless the buyer seasonably objects, and receipt by the bailee of notification of the buyer's rights fixes those rights as against the bailee and all third persons; but risk of loss of the goods and of any failure by the bailee to honor the non-negotiable document of title or to obey the direction remains on the seller until the buyer has had a reasonable time to present the document or direction, and a refusal by the bailee to honor the document or to obey the direction defeats the tender.

(5) Where the contract requires the seller to deliver documents

   (a) he must tender all such documents in correct form, except as provided in this Article with respect to bills of lading in a set (subsection (2) of Section 2-323); and

   (b) tender through customary banking channels is sufficient and dishonor of a draft accompanying the documents constitutes non-acceptance or rejection.

2-504. SHIPMENT BY SELLER.

Where the seller is required or authorized to send the goods to the buyer and the contract does not require him to deliver them at a particular destination, then unless otherwise agreed he must

(a) put the goods in the possession of such a carrier and make such a contract for their transportation as may be reasonable having regard to the nature of the goods and other circumstances of the case; and

(b) obtain and promptly deliver or tender in due form any document necessary to enable the buyer to obtain possession of the goods or otherwise required by the agreement or by usage of trade; and

(c) promptly notify the buyer of the shipment.

Failure to notify the buyer under paragraph (c) or to make a proper contract under paragraph (a) is a ground for rejection only if material delay or loss ensues.

2-505. SELLER'S SHIPMENT UNDER RESERVATION.

(1) Where the seller has identified goods to the contract by or before shipment:

   (a) his procurement of a negotiable bill of lading to his own order or otherwise reserves in him a security interest in the goods. His procurement of the bill to the order of a financing agency or of the buyer indicates in addition only the seller's expectation of transferring that interest to the person named.

   (b) a non-negotiable bill of lading to himself or his nominee reserves possession of the goods as security but except in a case of conditional delivery (subsection (2) of Section 2-507) a non-negotiable bill of lading naming the buyer as consignee reserves no security interest even though the seller retains possession of the bill of lading.

(2) When shipment by the seller with reservation of a security interest is in violation of the contract for sale it constitutes an improper contract for transportation within the preceding section but impairs neither the rights given to the buyer by shipment and identification of the goods to the contract nor the seller's powers as a holder of a negotiable document.

2-506. RIGHTS OF FINANCING AGENCY.

(1) A financing agency by paying or purchasing for value a draft which relates to a shipment of goods acquires to the extent of the payment or purchase and in addition to its own rights under the draft and any document of title securing it any rights of the shipper in the goods including the right to stop delivery and the shipper's right to have the draft honored by the buyer.

(2) The right to reimbursement of a financing agency which has in good faith honored or purchased the draft under commitment to or authority from the buyer is not impaired by subsequent discovery of defects with reference to any relevant document which was apparently regular on its face.

2-507. EFFECT OF SELLER'S TENDER; DELIVERY ON CONDITION.

(1) Tender of delivery is a condition to the buyer's duty to accept the goods and, unless otherwise agreed, to his duty to pay for them. Tender entitles the seller to acceptance of the goods and to payment according to the contract.

(2) Where payment is due and demanded on the delivery to the buyer of goods or documents of title, his right as against the seller to retain or dispose of them is unconditional upon his making the payment due.

2-508. CURE BY SELLER OF IMPROPER TENDER OR DELIVERY; REPLACEMENT.

(1) Where any tender or delivery by the seller is rejected because non-conforming and the time for performance has not yet expired, the seller may seasonably notify the buyer of his intention to cure and may then within the contract time make a conforming delivery.

(2) Where the buyer rejects a non-conforming tender which the seller had reasonable grounds to believe would be acceptable with or without money allowance the seller may if he seasonably notifies the buyer have a further reasonable time to substitute a conforming tender.

2-509. RISK OF LOSS IN THE ABSENCE OF BREACH.

(1) Where the contract requires or authorizes the seller to ship the goods by carrier

(a) if it does not require him to deliver them at a particular destination, the risk of loss passes to the buyer when the goods are duly delivered to the carrier even though the shipment is under reservation (Section 2-505); but

(b) if it does require him to deliver them at a particular destination and the goods are there duly tendered while in the possession of the carrier, the risk of loss passes to the buyer when the goods are there duly so tendered as to enable the buyer to take delivery.

(2) Where the goods are held by a bailee to be delivered without being moved, the risk of loss passes to the buyer

(a) on his receipt of a negotiable document of title covering the goods; or

(b) on acknowledgment by the bailee of the buyer's right to possession of the goods; or

(c) after his receipt of a non-negotiable document of title or other written direction to deliver, as provided in subsection (4) (b) of Section 2-503.

(3) In any case not within subsection (1) or (2), the risk of loss passes to the buyer on his receipt of the goods if the seller is a merchant; otherwise the risk passes to the buyer on tender of delivery.

(4) The provisions of this section are subject to contrary agreement of the parties and to the provisions of this Article on sale on approval (Section 2-327) and on effect of breach on risk of loss (Section 2-510).

2-510. Effect of Breach on Risk of Loss.

(1) Where a tender or delivery of goods so fails to conform to the contract as to give a right of rejection the risk of their loss remains on the seller until cure or acceptance.

(2) Where the buyer rightfully revokes acceptance he may to the extent of any deficiency in his effective insurance coverage treat the risk of loss as having rested on the seller from the beginning.

(3) Where the buyer as to conforming goods already identified to the contract for sale repudiates or is otherwise in breach before risk of their loss has passed to him, the seller may to the extent of any deficiency in his effective insurance coverage treat the risk of loss as resting on the buyer for a commercially reasonable time.

2-511. Tender of Payment by Buyer; Payment by Check.

(1) Unless otherwise agreed tender of payment is a condition to the seller's duty to tender and complete any delivery.

(2) Tender of payment is sufficient when made by any means or in any manner current in the ordinary course of business unless the seller demands payment in legal tender and gives any extension of time reasonably necessary to procure it.

(3) Subject to the provisions of this Act on the effect of an instrument on an obligation (Section 3-802), payment by check is conditional and is defeated as between the parties by dishonor of the check on due presentment.

2-512. Payment by Buyer Before Inspection.

(1) Where the contract requires payment before inspection non-conformity of the goods does not excuse the buyer from so making payment unless

(a) the non-conformity appears without inspection; or

(b) despite tender of the required documents the circumstances would justify injunction against honor under the provisions of this Act (Section 5-114).

(2) Payment pursuant to subsection (1) does not constitute an acceptance of goods or impair the buyer's right to inspect or any of his remedies.

2-513. BUYER'S RIGHT TO INSPECTION OF GOODS.

(1) Unless otherwise agreed and subject to subsection (3), where goods are tendered or delivered or identified to the contract for sale, the buyer has a right before payment or acceptance to inspect them at any reasonable place and time and in any reasonable manner. When the seller is required or authorized to send the goods to the buyer, the inspection may be after their arrival.

(2) Expenses of inspection must be borne by the buyer but may be recovered from the seller if the goods do not conform and are rejected.

(3) Unless otherwise agreed and subject to the provisions of this Article on C.I.F. contracts (subsection (3) of Section 2-321), the buyer is not entitled to inspect the goods before payment of the price when the contract provides

    (a) for delivery "C.O.D." or on other like terms; or

    (b) for payment against documents of title, except where such payment is due only after the goods are to become available for inspection.

(4) A place or method of inspection fixed by the parties is presumed to be exclusive but unless otherwise expressly agreed it does not postpone identification or shift the place for delivery or for passing the risk of loss. If compliance becomes impossible, inspection shall be as provided in this section unless the place or method fixed was clearly intended as an indispensable condition failure of which avoids the contract.

2-514. WHEN DOCUMENTS DELIVERABLE ON ACCEPTANCE; WHEN ON PAYMENT.

Unless otherwise agreed documents against which a draft is drawn are to be delivered to the drawee on acceptance of the draft if it is payable more than three days after presentment; otherwise, only on payment.

2-515. PRESERVING EVIDENCE OF GOODS IN DISPUTE.

In furtherance of the adjustment of any claim or dispute

    (a) either party on reasonable notification to the other and for the purpose of ascertaining the facts and preserving evidence has the right to inspect, test and sample the goods including such of them as may be in the possession or control of the other; and

    (b) the parties may agree to a third party inspection or survey to determine the conformity or condition of the goods and may agree that the findings shall be binding upon them in any subsequent litigation or adjustment.

PART 6
BREACH, REPUDIATION AND EXCUSE

2-601. BUYER'S RIGHTS ON IMPROPER DELIVERY.

Subject to the provisions of this Article on breach in installment contracts (Section 2-612) and unless otherwise agreed under the sections on contractual limitations of remedy

(Sections 2-718 and 2-719), if the goods or the tender of delivery fail in any respect to conform to the contract, the buyer may

(a) reject the whole; or

(b) accept the whole; or

(c) accept any commercial unit or units and reject the rest.

2-602. MANNER AND EFFECT OF RIGHTFUL REJECTION.

(1) Rejection of goods must be within a reasonable time after their delivery or tender. It is ineffective unless the buyer seasonably notifies the seller.

(2) Subject to the provisions of the two following sections on rejected goods (Section 2-603 and 2-604),

   (a) after rejection any exercise of ownership by the buyer with respect to any commercial unit is wrongful as against the seller; and

   (b) if the buyer has before rejection taken physical possession of goods in which he does not have a security interest under the provisions of this Article (subsection (3) of Section 2-711), he is under a duty after rejection to hold them with reasonable care at the seller's disposition for a time sufficient to permit the seller to remove them; but

   (c) the buyer has no further obligations with regard to goods rightfully rejected.

(3) The seller's rights with respect to goods wrongfully rejected are governed by the provisions of this Article on Seller's remedies in general (Section 2-703).

2-603. MERCHANT BUYER'S DUTIES AS TO RIGHTFULLY REJECTED GOODS.

(1) Subject to any security interest in the buyer (subsection (3) of Section 2-711), when the seller has no agent or place of business at the market of rejection a merchant buyer is under a duty after rejection of goods in his possession or control to follow any reasonable instructions received from the seller with respect to the goods and in the absence of such instructions to make reasonable efforts to sell them for the seller's account if they are perishable or threaten to decline in value speedily. Instructions are not reasonable if on demand indemnity for expenses is not forthcoming.

(2) When the buyer sells goods under subsection (1), he is entitled to reimbursement from the seller or out of the proceeds for reasonable expenses of caring for and selling them, and if the expenses include no selling commission then to such commission as is usual in the trade or if there is none to a reasonable sum not exceeding ten per cent of the gross proceeds.

(3) In complying with this section the buyer is held only to good faith and good faith conduct hereunder is neither acceptance nor conversion nor the basis of an action for damages.

2-604. BUYER'S OPTIONS AS TO SALVAGE OF RIGHTFULLY REJECTED GOODS.

Subject to the provisions of the immediately preceding section on perishables if the seller gives no instructions within a reasonable time after notification of rejection the buyer may store the rejected goods for the seller's account or reship them to him or resell them for the seller's account with reimbursement as provided in the preceding section. Such action is not acceptance or conversion.

2-605. WAIVER OF BUYER'S OBJECTIONS BY FAILURE TO PARTICULARIZE.

(1) The buyer's failure to state in connection with rejection a particular defect which is ascertainable by reasonable inspection precludes him from relying on the unstated defect to justify rejection or to establish breach

    (a) where the seller could have cured it if stated seasonally; or

    (b) between merchants when the seller has after rejection made a request in writing for a full and final written statement of all defects on which the buyer proposes to rely.

(2) Payment against documents made without reservation of rights precludes recovery of the payment for defects apparent on the face of the documents.

2-606. WHAT CONSTITUTES ACCEPTANCE OF GOODS.

(1) Acceptance of goods occurs when the buyer

    (a) after a reasonable opportunity to inspect the goods signifies to the seller that the goods are conforming or that he will take or retain them in spite of their non-conformity; or

    (b) fails to make an effective rejection (subsection (1) of Section 2-602), but such acceptance does not occur until the buyer has had a reasonable opportunity to inspect them; or

    (c) does any act inconsistent with the seller's ownership; but if such act is wrongful as against the seller it is an acceptance only if ratified by him.

(2) Acceptance of a part of any commercial unit is acceptance of that entire unit.

2-607. EFFECT OF ACCEPTANCE; NOTICE OF BREACH; BURDEN OF ESTABLISHING BREACH AFTER ACCEPTANCE; NOTICE OF CLAIM OR LITIGATION TO PERSON ANSWERABLE OVER.

(1) The buyer must pay at the contract rate for any goods accepted.

(2) Acceptance of goods by the buyer precludes rejection of the goods accepted and if made with knowledge of a non-conformity cannot be revoked because of it unless the acceptance was on the reasonable assumption that the non-conformity would be seasonably cured but acceptance does not of itself impair any other remedy provided by this Article for non-conformity.

(3) Where a tender has been accepted

    (a) the buyer must within a reasonable time after he discovers or should have discovered any breach notify the seller of breach or be barred from any remedy; and

    (b) if the claim is one for infringement or the like (subsection (3) of Section 2-312) and the buyer is sued as a result of such a breach he must so notify the seller within a reasonable time after he receives notice of the litigation or be barred from any remedy over for liability established by the litigation.

(4) The burden is on the buyer to establish any breach with respect to the goods accepted.

(5) Where the buyer is sued for breach of a warranty or other obligation for which his seller is answerable over

    (a) he may give his seller written notice of the litigation. If the notice states that the seller may come in and defend and that if the seller does not do so he will be bound in any action against him by his buyer by any determination of fact common to the two litigations, then unless the seller after seasonable receipt of the notice does come in and defend he is so bound.

    (b) if the claim is one for infringement or the like (subsection (3) of Section 2-312) the original seller may demand in writing that his buyer turn over to him control of the litigation including settlement or else be barred from any remedy over and if he also agrees to bear all expense and to satisfy any adverse judgment, then unless the buyer after seasonable receipt of the demand does turn over control the buyer is so barred.

(6) The provisions of subsections (3), (4) and (5) apply to any obligation of a buyer to hold the seller harmless against infringement or the like (subsection (3) of Section 2-312).

2-608. REVOCATION OF ACCEPTANCE IN WHOLE OR IN PART.

(1) The buyer may revoke his acceptance of a lot or commercial unit whose non-conformity substantially impairs its value to him if he has accepted it

    (a) on the reasonable assumption that its non-conformity would be cured and it has not been seasonably cured; or

    (b) without discovery of such non-conformity if his acceptance was reasonably induced either by the difficulty of discovery before acceptance or by the seller's assurances.

(2) Revocation of acceptance must occur within a reasonable time after the buyer discovers or should have discovered the ground for it and before any substantial change in condition of the goods which is not caused by their own defects. It is not effective until the buyer notifies the seller of it.

(3) A buyer who so revokes has the same rights and duties with regard to the goods involved as if he had rejected them.

2-609. RIGHT TO ADEQUATE ASSURANCE OF PERFORMANCE.

(1) A contract for sale imposes an obligation on each party that the other's expectation of receiving due performance will not be impaired.

When reasonable grounds for insecurity arise with respect to the performance of either party the other may in writing demand adequate assurance of due performance and until he receives such assurance may if commercially reasonable suspend any performance for which he has not already received the agreed return.

(2) Between merchants the reasonableness of grounds for insecurity and the adequacy of any assurance offered shall be determined according to commercial standards.

(3) Acceptance of any improper delivery or payment does not prejudice the aggrieved party's right to demand adequate assurance of future performance.

(4) After receipt of a justified demand failure to provide within a reasonable time not exceeding thirty days such assurance of due performance as is adequate under the circumstances of the particular case is a repudiation of the contract.

2-610. ANTICIPATORY REPUDIATION.

When either party repudiates the contract with respect to a performance not yet due the loss of which will substantially impair the value of the contract to the other, the aggrieved party may

(a) for a commercially reasonable time await performance by the repudiating party; or

(b) resort to any remedy for breach (Section 2-703 or Section 2-711), even though he has notified the repudiating party that he would await the latter's performance and has urged retraction; and

(c) in either case suspend his own performance or proceed in accordance with the provisions of this Article on the seller's right to identify goods to the contract notwithstanding breach or to salvage unfinished goods (Section 2-704).

2-611. RETRACTION OF ANTICIPATORY REPUDIATION.

(1) Until the repudiating party's next performance is due he can retract his repudiation unless the aggrieved party has since the repudiation canceled or materially changed his position or otherwise indicated that he considers the repudiation final.

(2) Retraction may be by any method which clearly indicates to the aggrieved party that the repudiating party intends to perform, but must include any assurance justifiably demanded under the provisions of this Article (Section 2-609).

(3) Retraction reinstates the repudiating party's rights under the contract with due excuse and allowance to the aggrieved party for any delay occasioned by the repudiation.

2-612. "INSTALLMENT CONTRACT"; BREACH.

(1) An "installment contract" is one which requires or authorizes the delivery of goods in separate lots to be separately accepted, even though the contract contains a clause "each delivery is a separate contract" or its equivalent.

(2) The buyer may reject any installment which is non-conforming if the non-conformity substantially impairs the value of that installment and cannot be cured or if the non-conformity is a defect in the required documents; but if the non-conformity does not fall within subsection (3) and the seller gives adequate assurance of its cure the buyer must accept that installment.

(3) Whenever non-conformity or default with respect to one or more installments substantially impairs the value of the whole contract there is a breach of the whole. But the aggrieved party reinstates the contract if he accepts a non-conforming installment without seasonably notifying of cancellation or if he brings an action with respect only to past installments or demands performance as to future installments.

2-613. Casualty to Identified Goods.

Where the contact requires for its performance goods identified when the contract is made, and the goods suffer casualty without fault of either party before the risk of loss passes to the buyer, or in a proper case under a "no arrival, no sale" term (Section 2-324) then

(a) if the loss is total the contract is avoided; and

(b) if the loss is partial or the goods have so deteriorated as no longer to conform to the contract the buyer may nevertheless demand inspection and at his option either treat the contract as avoided or accept the goods with due allowance from the contract price for the deterioration or the deficiency in quantity but without further right against the seller.

2-614. Substituted Performance.

(1) Where without fault of either party the agreed berthing, loading, or unloading facilities fail or an agreed type of carrier becomes unavailable or the agreed manner of delivery otherwise becomes commercially impracticable but a commercially reasonable substitute is available, such substitute performance must be tendered and accepted.

(2) If the agreed means or manner of payment fails because of domestic or foreign governmental regulation, the seller may withhold or stop delivery unless the buyer provides a means or manner of payment which is commercially a substantial equivalent. If delivery has already been taken, payment by the means or in the manner provided by the regulation discharges the buyer's obligation unless the regulation is discriminatory, oppressive or predatory.

2-615. Excuse by Failure of Presupposed Conditions.

Except so far as a seller may have assumed a greater obligation and subject to the preceding section on substituted performance:

(a) Delay in delivery or non-delivery in whole or in part by a seller who complies with paragraphs (b) and (c) is not a breach of his duty under a contract for sale if performance as agreed has been made impracticable by the occurrence of a contingency the non-occurrence of which was a basic assumption on which the contract was made or by compliance in good faith with any applicable foreign or domestic governmental regulation or order whether or not it later proves to be invalid.

(b) Where the causes mentioned in paragraph (a) affect only a part of the seller's capacity to perform, he must allocate production and deliveries among his customers but may at his option include regular customers not then under contract as well as his own requirements for further manufacture. He may so allocate in any manner which is fair and reasonable.

(c) The seller must notify the buyer seasonably that there will be delay or non-delivery and, when allocation is required under paragraph (b), of the estimated quota thus made available for the buyer.

2-616. PROCEDURE ON NOTICE CLAIMING EXCUSE.

(1) Where the buyer receives notification of a material or indefinite delay or an allocation justified under the preceding section he may by written notification to the seller as to any delivery concerned, and where the prospective deficiency substantially impairs the value of the whole contract under the provisions of this Article relating to breach of installment contracts (Section 2-612), then also as to the whole,

    (a) terminate and thereby discharge any unexecuted portion of the contract; or

    (b) modify the contract by agreeing to take his available quota in substitution.

(2) If after receipt of such notification from the seller the buyer fails so to modify the contract within a reasonable time not exceeding thirty days the contract lapses with respect to any deliveries affected.

(3) The provisions of this section may not be negated by agreement except in so far as the seller has assumed a greater obligation under the preceding section.

PART 7
REMEDIES

2-701. REMEDIES FOR BREACH OF COLLATERAL CONTRACTS NOT IMPAIRED.

Remedies for breach of any obligation or promise collateral or ancillary to a contract for sale are not impaired by the provisions of this Article.

2-702. SELLER'S REMEDIES ON DISCOVERY OF BUYER'S INSOLVENCY.

(1) Where the seller discovers the buyer to be insolvent he may refuse delivery except for cash including payment for all goods theretofore delivered under the contract, and stop delivery under this Article (Section 2-705).

(2) Where the seller discovers that the buyer has received goods on credit while insolvent he may reclaim the goods upon demand made within ten days after the receipt, but if misrepresentation of solvency has been made to the particular seller in writing within three months before delivery the ten day limitation does not apply. Except as provided in this subsection the seller may not base a right to reclaim goods on the buyer's fraudulent or innocent misrepresentation of solvency or of intent to pay.

(3) The seller's right to reclaim under subsection (2) is subject to the rights of a buyer in ordinary course or other good faith purchaser under this Article (Section 2-403). Successful reclamation of goods excludes all other remedies with respect to them. As amended in 1966.

2-703. SELLER'S REMEDIES IN GENERAL.

Where the buyer wrongfully rejects or revokes acceptance of goods or fails to make a payment due on or before delivery or repudiates with respect to a part or the whole, then with respect to any goods directly affected and, if the breach is of the whole contract (Section 2-612), then also with respect to the whole undelivered balance, the aggrieved seller may

    (a) withhold delivery of such goods;

(b) stop delivery by any bailee as hereafter provided (Section 2-705);

(c) proceed under the next section respecting goods still unidentified to the contract;

(d) resell and recover damages as hereafter provided (Section 2-706);

(e) recover damages for non-acceptance (Section 2-708) or in a proper case the price (Section 2-709);

(f) cancel.

2-704. SELLER'S RIGHT TO IDENTIFY GOODS TO THE CONTRACT NOTWITHSTANDING BREACH OR TO SALVAGE UNFINISHED GOODS.

(1) An aggrieved seller under the preceding section may

    (a) identify to the contract conforming goods not already identified if at the time he learned of the breach they are in his possession or control;

    (b) treat as the subject of resale goods which have demonstrably been intended for the particular contract even though those goods are unfinished.

(2) Where the goods are unfinished an aggrieved seller may in the exercise of reasonable commercial judgment for the purposes of avoiding loss and of effective realization either complete the manufacture and wholly identify the goods to the contract or cease manufacture and resell for scrap or salvage value or proceed in any other reasonable manner.

2-705. SELLER'S STOPPAGE OF DELIVERY IN TRANSIT OR OTHERWISE.

(1) The seller may stop delivery of goods in the possession of a carrier or other bailee when he discovers the buyer to be insolvent (Section 2-702) and may stop delivery of carload, truckload, planeload or larger shipments of express or freight when the buyer repudiates or fails to make a payment due before delivery or if for any other reason the seller has a right to withhold or reclaim the goods.

(2) As against such buyer the seller may stop delivery until

    (a) receipt of the goods by the buyer; or

    (b) acknowledgment to the buyer by any bailee of the goods except a carrier that the bailee holds the goods for the buyer; or

    (c) such acknowledgment to the buyer by a carrier by reshipment or as warehouseman; or

    (d) negotiation to the buyer of any negotiable document of title covering the goods.

(3) (a) To stop delivery the seller must so notify as to enable the bailee by reasonable diligence to prevent delivery of the goods.

    (b) After such notification the bailee must hold and deliver the goods according to the directions of the seller but the seller is liable to the bailee for any ensuing charges or damages.

    (c) If a negotiable document of title has been issued for goods the bailee is not obligated to obey a notification to stop until surrender of the document.

    (d) A carrier who has issued a non-negotiable bill of lading is not obliged to obey a notification to stop received from a person other than the consignor.

2-706. Seller's Resale Including Contract for Resale.

(1) Under the conditions stated in Section 2-703 on seller's remedies, the seller may resell the goods concerned or the undelivered balance thereof. Where the resale is made in good faith and in a commercially reasonable manner the seller may recover the difference between the resale price and the contract price together with any incidental damages allowed under the provisions of this Article (Section 2-710), but less expenses saved in consequence of the buyer's breach.

(2) Except as otherwise provided in subsection (3) or unless otherwise agreed resale may be at public or private sale including sale by way of one or more contracts to sell or of identification to an existing contract of the seller. Sale may be as a unit or in parcels and at any time and place and on any terms but every aspect of the sale including the method, manner, time, place and terms must be commercially reasonable. The resale must be reasonably identified as referring to the broken contract, but it is not necessary that the goods be in existence or that any or all of them have been identified to the contract before the breach.

(3) Where the resale is at private sale the seller must give the buyer reasonable notification of his intention to resell.

(4) Where the resale is at public sale

   (a) only identified goods can be sold except where there is a recognized market for a public sale of futures in goods of the kind; and

   (b) it must be made at a usual place or market for public sale if one is reasonably available and except in the case of goods which are perishable or threaten to decline in value speedily the seller must give the buyer reasonable notice of the time and place of the resale; and

   (c) if the goods are not to be within the view of those attending the sale the notification of sale must state the place where the goods are located and provide for their reasonable inspection by prospective bidders; and

   (d) the seller may buy.

(5) A purchaser who buys in good faith at a resale takes the goods free of any rights of the original buyer even though the seller fails to comply with one or more of the requirements of this section.

(6) The seller is not accountable to the buyer for any profit made on any resale. A person in the position of a seller (Section 2-707) or a buyer who has rightfully rejected or justifiably revoked acceptance must account for any excess over the amount of his security interest, as hereinafter defined (subsection (3) of Section 2-711).

2-707. "Person in the Position of a Seller".

(1) A "person in the position of a seller" includes as against a principal an agent who has paid or become responsible for the price of goods on behalf of his principal or anyone who otherwise holds a security interest or other right in goods similar to that of a seller.

(2) A person in the position of a seller may as provided in this Article withhold or stop delivery (Section 2-705) and resell (Section 2-706) and recover incidental damages (Section 2-710).

2-708. Seller's Damages for Non-Acceptance of Repudiation.

(1) Subject to subsection (2) and to the provisions of this Article with respect to proof of market price (Section 2-723), the measure of damages for non-acceptance or repudiation by the buyer is the difference between the market price at the time and place for tender and the unpaid contract price together with any incidental damages provided in this Article (Section 2-710), but less expenses saved in consequence of the buyer's breach.

(2) If the measure of damages provided in subsection (1) is inadequate to put the seller in as good a position as performance would have done then the measure of damages is the profit (including reasonable overhead) which the seller would have made from full performance by the buyer, together with any incidental damages provided in this Article (Section 2-710), due allowance for costs reasonably incurred and due credit for payments or proceeds of resale.

2-709. Action for the Price.

(1) When the buyer fails to pay the price as it becomes due the seller may recover, together with any incidental damages under the next section, the price

(a) of goods accepted or of conforming goods lost or damaged within a commercially reasonable time after risk of their loss has passed to the buyer; and

(b) of goods identified to the contract if the seller is unable after reasonable effort to resell them at a reasonable price or the circumstances reasonably indicate that such effort will be unavailing.

(2) Where the seller sues for the price he must hold for the buyer any goods which have been identified to the contract and are still in his control except that if resale becomes possible he may resell them at any time prior to the collection of the judgment. The net proceeds of any such resale must be credited to the buyer and payment of the judgment entitles him to any goods not resold.

(3) After the buyer has wrongfully rejected or revoked acceptance of the goods or has failed to make a payment due or has repudiated (Section 2-610), a seller who is held not entitled to the price under this section shall nevertheless be awarded damages for non-acceptance under the preceding section.

2-710. Seller's Incidental Damages.

Incidental damages to an aggrieved seller include any commercially reasonable charges, expenses or commissions incurred in stopping delivery, in the transportation, care and custody of goods after the buyer's breach, in connection with return or resale of the goods or otherwise resulting from the breach.

2-711. Buyer's Remedies in General; Buyer's Security Interest in Rejected Goods.

(1) Where the seller fails to make delivery or repudiates or the buyer rightfully rejects or justifiably revokes acceptance then with respect to any goods involved, and with respect to the whole if the breach goes to the whole contract (Section 2-612), the

buyer may cancel and whether or not he has done so may in addition to recovering so much of the price as has been paid

    (a) "cover" and have damages under the next section as to all the goods affected whether or not they have been identified to the contract; or

    (b) recover damages for non-delivery as provided in this Article (Section 2-713).

(2) Where the seller fails to deliver or repudiates the buyer may also

    (a) if the goods have been identified recover them as provided in this Article (Section 2-502); or

    (b) in a proper case obtain specific performance or replevy the goods as provided in this Article (Section 2-716).

(3) On rightful rejection or justifiable revocation of acceptance a buyer has a security interest in goods in his possession or control for any payment made on their price and any expenses reasonably incurred in their inspection, receipt, transportation, care and custody and may hold such goods and resell them in like manner as an aggrieved seller (Section 2-706).

2-712. "COVER"; BUYER'S PROCUREMENT OF SUBSTITUTE GOODS.

(1) After a breach within the preceding section the buyer may "cover" by making in good faith and without unreasonable delay any reasonable purchase of or contract to purchase goods in substitution for those due from the seller.

(2) The buyer may recover from the seller as damages the difference between the cost of cover and the contract price together with any incidental or consequential damages as hereinafter defined (Section 2-715), but less expenses saved in consequence of the seller's breach.

(3) Failure of the buyer to effect cover within this section does not bar him from any other remedy.

2-713. BUYER'S DAMAGES FOR NON-DELIVERY OR REPUDIATION.

(1) Subject to the provisions of this Article with respect to proof of market price (Section 2-723), the measure of damages for non-delivery or repudiation by the seller is the difference between the market price at the time when the buyer learned of the breach and the contract price together with any incidental and consequential damages provided in this Article (Section 2-715), but less expenses saved in consequence of the seller's breach.

(2) Market price is to be determined as of the place for tender or, in case of rejection after arrival or revocation of acceptance, as of the place of arrival.

2-714. BUYER'S DAMAGES FOR BREACH IN REGARD TO ACCEPTED GOODS.

(1) Where the buyer has accepted goods and given notification (subsection (3) of Section 2-607) he may recover as damages for any non-conformity of tender the loss resulting in the ordinary course of events from the seller's breach as determined in any manner which is reasonable.

(2) The measure of damages for breach of warranty is the difference at the time and place of acceptance between the value of the goods accepted and the value they

would have had if they had been as warranted, unless special circumstances show proximate damages of a different amount.

(3) In a proper case any incidental and consequential damages under the next section may also be recovered.

2-715. BUYER'S INCIDENTAL AND CONSEQUENTIAL DAMAGES.

(1) Incidental damages resulting from the seller's breach include expenses reasonably incurred in inspection, receipt, transportation and care and custody of goods rightfully rejected, any commercially reasonable charges, expenses or commissions in connection with effecting cover and any other reasonable expense incident to the delay or other breach.

(2) Consequential damages resulting from the seller's breach include

(a) any loss resulting from general or particular requirements and needs of which the seller at the time of contracting had reason to know and which could not reasonably be prevented by cover or otherwise; and

(b) injury to person or property proximately resulting from any breach of warranty.

2-716. BUYER'S RIGHT TO SPECIFIC PERFORMANCE OR REPLEVIN.

(1) Specific performance may be decreed where the goods are unique or in other proper circumstances.

(2) The decree for specific performance may include such terms and conditions as to payment of the price, damages, or other relief as the court may deem just.

(3) The buyer has the right of replevin for goods identified to the contract if after reasonable effort he is unable to effect cover for such goods or the circumstances reasonably indicate that such effort will be unavailing or if the goods have been shipped under reservation and satisfaction of the security interest in them has been made or tendered.

2-717. DEDUCTION OF DAMAGES FROM THE PRICE.

The buyer on notifying the seller of his intention to do so may deduct all or any part of the damages resulting from any breach of the contract from any part of the price still due under the same contract.

2-718. LIQUIDATION OR LIMITATION OF DAMAGES; DEPOSITS.

(1) Damages for breach by either party may be liquidated in the agreement but only at an amount which is reasonable in the light of the anticipated or actual harm caused by the breach, the difficulties of proof of loss, and the inconvenience or nonfeasibility of otherwise obtaining an adequate remedy. A term fixing unreasonably large liquidated damages is void as a penalty.

(2) Where the seller justifiably withholds delivery of goods because of the buyer's breach, the buyer is entitled to restitution of any amount by which the sum of his payments exceeds

(a) the amount to which the seller is entitled by virtue of terms liquidating the seller's damages in accordance with subsection (1), or

    (b)   in the absence of such terms, twenty per cent of the value of the total performance for which the buyer is obligated under the contract or $500, whichever is smaller.

(3) The buyer's right to restitution under subsection (2) is subject to offset to the extent that the seller establishes

    (a)   a right to recover damages under the provisions of this Article other than subsection (1), and

    (b)   the amount or value of any benefits received by the buyer directly or indirectly by reason of the contract.

(4) Where a seller has received payment in goods their reasonable value or the proceeds of their resale shall be treated as payments for the purposes of subsection (2); but if the seller has notice of the buyer's breach before reselling goods received in part performance, his resale is subject to the conditions laid down in this Article on resale by an aggrieved seller (Section 2-706).

2-719. CONTRACTUAL MODIFICATION OR LIMITATION OF REMEDY.

(1) Subject to the provisions of subsections (2) and (3) of this section and of the preceding section on liquidation and limitation of damages,

    (a)   the agreement may provide for remedies in addition to or in substitution for those provided in this Article and may limit or alter the measure of damages recoverable under this Article, as by limiting the buyer's remedies to return of the goods and repayment of the price or to repair and replacement of non-conforming goods or parts; and

    (b)   resort to a remedy as provided is optional unless the remedy is expressly agreed to be exclusive, in which case it is the sole remedy.

(2) Where circumstances cause an exclusive or limited remedy to fail of its essential purposes, remedy may be had as provided in this Act.

(3) Consequential damages may be limited or excluded unless the limitation or exclusion is unconscionable. Limitation of consequential damages for injury to the person in the case of consumer goods is prima facie unconscionable but limitation of damages where the loss is commercial is not.

2-720. EFFECT OF "CANCELLATION" OR "RESCISSION" ON CLAIMS FOR ANTECEDENT BREACH.

Unless the contrary intention clearly appears, expressions of "cancellation" or "rescission" of the contract or the like shall not be construed as a renunciation or discharge of any claim in damages for an antecedent breach.

2-721. REMEDIES FOR FRAUD.

Remedies for material misrepresentation or fraud include all remedies available under this Article for non-fraudulent breach. Neither rescission or a claim for rescission of the contract for sale nor rejection or return of the goods shall bar or be deemed inconsistent with a claim for damages or other remedy.

2-722. WHO CAN SUE THIRD PARTIES FOR INJURY TO GOODS.

Where a third party so deals with goods which have been identified to a contract for sale as to cause actionable injury to a party to that contract

(a) a right of action against the third party is in either party to the contract for sale who has title to or a security interest or a special property or an insurable interest in the goods; and if the goods have been destroyed or converted a right of action is also in the party who either bore the risk of loss under the contract for sale or has since the injury assumed that risk as against the other;

(b) if at the time of the injury the party plaintiff did not bear the risk of loss as against the other party to the contract for sale and there is no arrangement between them for disposition of the recovery, his suit or settlement is, subject to his own interest, as a fiduciary for the other party to the contract;

(c) either party may with the consent of the other sue for the benefit of whom it may concern.

2-723. PROOF OF MARKET PRICE: TIME AND PLACE.

(1) If an action based on anticipatory repudiation comes to trial before the time for performance with respect to some or all of the goods, any damages based on market price (Section 2-708 or Section 2-713) shall be determined according to the price of such goods prevailing at the time when the aggrieved party learned of the repudiation.

(2) If evidence of a price prevailing at the times or places described in this Article is not readily available the price prevailing within any reasonable time before or after the time described or at any other place which in commercial judgment or under usage of trade would serve as a reasonable substitute for the one described may be used, making any proper allowance for the cost of transporting the goods to or from such other place.

(3) Evidence of a relevant price prevailing at a time or place other than the one described in this Article offered by one party is not admissible unless and until he has given the other party such notice as the court finds sufficient to prevent unfair surprise.

2-724. ADMISSIBILITY OF MARKET QUOTATIONS.

Whenever the prevailing price or value of any goods regularly bought and sold in any established commodity market is in issue, reports in official publications or trade journals or in newspapers or periodicals of general circulation published as the reports of such market shall be admissible in evidence. The circumstances of the preparation of such a report may be shown to affect its weight but not its admissibility.

2-725. STATUTE OF LIMITATIONS IN CONTRACTS FOR SALE.

(1) An action for breach of any contract for sale must be commenced within four years after the cause of action has accrued. By the original agreement the parties may reduce the period of limitation to not less than one year but may not extend it.

(2) A cause of action accrues when the breach occurs, regardless of the aggrieved party's lack of knowledge of the breach. A breach of warranty occurs when tender of delivery is made, except that where a warranty explicitly extends to future performance of the goods and discovery of the breach must await the time of such performance the cause of action accrues when the breach is or should have been discovered.

(3) Where an action commenced within the time limited by subsection (1) is so terminated as to leave available a remedy by another action for the same breach such other action may be commenced after the expiration of the time limited and within six months after the termination of the first action unless the termination resulted from voluntary discontinuance or from dismissal for failure or neglect to prosecute.

(4) This section does not alter the law on tolling of the statute of limitations nor does it apply to causes of action which have accrued before this Act becomes effective.

CHAPTER 3
APPENDIX II

UNIFORM FRAUDULENT TRANSFER ACT

1. DEFINITIONS

As used in this Act:

(1) "Affiliate" means:

    (i) a person who directly or indirectly owns, controls, or holds with power to vote, 20 percent or more of the outstanding voting securities of the debtor, other than a person who holds the securities,

        (A) as a fiduciary or agent without sole discretionary power to vote the securities; or

        (B) solely to secure a debt, if the person has not exercised the power to vote;

    (ii) a corporation 20 percent or more of whose outstanding voting securities are directly or indirectly owned, controlled, or held with power to vote, by the debtor or a person who directly or indirectly owns, controls, or holds, with power to vote, 20 percent or more of the outstanding voting securities of the debtor, other than a person who holds the securities,

        (A) as a fiduciary or agent without sole power to vote the securities; or

        (B) solely to secure a debt, if the person has not in fact exercised the power to vote;

    (iii) a person whose business is operated by the debtor under a lease or other agreement, or a person substantially all of whose assets are controlled by the debtor; or

    (iv) a person who operates the debtor's business under a lease or other agreement or controls substantially all of the debtor's assets.

(2) "Asset" means property of a debtor, but the term does not include:

    (i) property to the extent it is encumbered by a valid lien;

    (ii) property to the extent it is generally exempt under non-bankruptcy law; or

    (iii) an interest in property held in tenancy by the entireties to the extent it is not subject to process by a creditor holding a claim against only one tenant.

(3) "Claim" means a right to payment, whether or not the right is reduced to judgment, liquidated, unliquidated, fixed, contingent, matured, unmatured, disputed, undisputed, legal, equitable, secured, or unsecured.

(4) "Creditor" means a person who has a claim.

(5) "Debt" means liability on a claim.

(6) "Debtor" means a person who is liable on a claim.

(7) "Insider" includes:

    (i) if the debtor is an individual,

        (A) a relative of the debtor or of a general partner of the debtor;

        (B) a partnership in which the debtor is a general partner;

        (C) a general partner in a partnership described in clause (B); or

        (D) a corporation of which the debtor is a director, officer, or person in control;

    (ii) if the debtor is a corporation,

        (A) a director of the debtor;

        (B) an officer of the debtor;

        (C) a person in control of the debtor;

        (D) a partnership in which the debtor is a general partner;

        (E) a general partner in a partnership described in clause (D); or

        (F) a relative of a general partner, director, officer, or person in control of the debtor;

    (iii) if the debtor is a partnership,

        (A) a general partner in the debtor,

        (B) a relative of a general partner in, a general partner of, or a person in control of the debtor;

        (C) another partnership in which the debtor is a general partner;

        (D) a general partner in a partnership described in clause (C), or

        (E) a person in control of the debtor;

    (iv) an affiliate, or an insider of an affiliate as if the affiliate were the debtor; and

    (v) a managing agent of the debtor.

(8) "Lien" means a charge against or an interest in property to secure payment of a debt or performance of an obligation, and includes a security interest created by agreement, a judicial lien obtained by legal or equitable process or proceedings, a common-law lien, or a statutory lien.

(9) "Person" means an individual, partnership, corporation, association, organization, government or governmental subdivision or agency, business trust, estate, trust, or any other legal or commercial entity.

(10) "Property" means anything that may be the subject of ownership.

(11) "Relative" means an individual related by consanguinity within the third degree as determined by the common law, a spouse, or an individual related to a spouse within the third degree as so determined, and includes an individual in an adoptive relationship within the third degree.

(12) "Transfer" means every mode, direct or indirect, absolute or conditional, voluntary or involuntary, of disposing of or parting with an asset or an interest in an asset, and includes payment of money, release, lease, and creation of a lien or other encumbrance.

(13) "Valid lien" means a lien that is effective against the holder of a judicial lien subsequently obtained by legal or equitable process or proceedings.

2. INSOLVENCY

(a) A debtor is insolvent if the sum of the debtor's debts is greater than all of the debtor's assets at a fair valuation.

(b) A debtor who is generally not paying his or her debts as they become due is presumed to be insolvent.

(c) A partnership is insolvent under subsection (a) if the sum of the partnership's debts is greater than the aggregate, at a fair valuation, of all of the partnership's assets and the sum of the excess of the value of each general partner's nonpartnership assets over the partner's nonpartnership debts.

(d) Assets under this section do not include property that has been transferred, concealed, or removed with intent to hinder, delay, or defraud creditors or that has been transferred in a manner making the transfer voidable under this Act.

(e) Debts under this section do not include an obligation to the extent it is secured by a valid lien on property of the debtor not included as an asset.

3. VALUE

(a) Value is given for a transfer or an obligation if, in exchange for the transfer or obligation, property is transferred or an antecedent debt is secured or satisfied, but value does not include an unperformed promise made otherwise than in the ordinary course of the promisor's business to furnish support to the debtor or another person.

(b) For the purposes of Sections 4(a)(2) and 5, a person gives a reasonably equivalent value if the person acquires an interest of the debtor in an asset pursuant to a regularly conducted, noncollusive foreclosure sale or execution of a power of sale for the acquisition or disposition of the interest of the debtor upon default under a mortgage, deed of trust, or security agreement.

(c) A transfer is made for present value if the exchange between the debtor and the transferee is intended by them to be contemporaneous and is in fact substantially contemporaneous.

4. TRANSFER FRAUDULENT AS TO PRESENT AND FUTURE CREDITORS

(a) A transfer made or obligation incurred by a debtor is fraudulent as to a creditor, whether the creditor's claim arose before or after the transfer was made or the obligation was incurred, if the debtor made the transfer or incurred the obligation:

(1) with actual intent to hinder, delay, or defraud any creditor of the debtor; or

(2) without receiving a reasonably equivalent value in exchange for the transfer or obligation, and the debtor:

- (i) was engaged or was about to engage in a business or a transaction for which the remaining assets of the debtor were unreasonably small in relation to the business or transaction; or

- (ii) intended to incur, or believed or reasonably should have believed that he or she would incur, debts beyond his or her ability to pay as they became due.

(b) In determining actual intent under subsection (a)(1), consideration may be given, among other factors, to whether:

(1) the transfer or obligation was to an insider;

(2) the debtor retained possession or control of the property transferred after the transfer;

(3) the transfer or obligation was disclosed or concealed;

(4) before the transfer was made or obligation was incurred, the debtor had been sued or threatened with suit;

(5) the transfer was of substantially all the debtor's assets;

(6) the debtor absconded;

(7) the debtor removed or concealed assets;

(8) the value of the consideration received by the debtor was reasonably equivalent to the value of the asset transferred or the amount of the obligation incurred;

(9) the debtor was insolvent or became insolvent shortly after the transfer was made or the obligation was incurred;

(10) the transfer occurred shortly before or shortly after a substantial debt was incurred; and

(11) the debtor transferred the essential assets of the business to a lienor who transferred the assets to an insider of the debtor.

5. TRANSFERS FRAUDULENT AS TO PRESENT CREDITORS

(a) A transfer made or obligation incurred by a debtor is fraudulent as to a creditor whose claim arose before the transfer was made or the obligation was incurred if the debtor made the transfer or incurred the obligation without receiving a reasonably equivalent value in exchange for the transfer or obligation and the debtor was insolvent at that time or the debtor became insolvent as a result of the transfer or obligation.

(b) A transfer made by a debtor is fraudulent as to a creditor whose claim arose before the transfer was made if the transfer was made to an insider for an antecedent debt, the debtor was insolvent at that time, and the insider had reasonable cause to believe that the debtor was insolvent.

6. WHEN TRANSFER IS MADE OR OBLIGATION IS INCURRED

For the purposes of this Act:

(1) a transfer is made:

- (i) with respect to an asset that is real property other than a fixture, but including the interest of a seller or purchaser under a contract for the sale of the asset, when the transfer is so far perfected that a good-faith purchaser of the asset from the debtor against whom applicable law permits the transfer to be perfected cannot acquire an interest in the asset that is superior to the interest of the transferee; and

    (ii) with respect to an asset that is not real property or that is a fixture, when the transfer is so far perfected that a creditor on a simple contract cannot acquire a judicial lien otherwise than under this Act that is superior to the interest of the transferee;

(2) if applicable law permits the transfer to be perfected as provided in paragraph (1) and the transfer is not so perfected before the commencement of an action for relief under this Act, the transfer is deemed made immediately before the commencement of the action;

(3) if applicable law does not permit the transfer to be perfected as provided in paragraph (1), the transfer is made when it becomes effective between the debtor and the transferee;

(4) a transfer is not made until the debtor has acquired rights in the asset transferred;

(5) an obligation is incurred:

    (i) if oral, when it becomes effective between the parties; or

    (ii) if evidenced by a writing, when the writing executed by the obligor is delivered to or for the benefit of the obligee.

7. REMEDIES OF CREDITORS

(a) In an action for relief against a transfer or obligation under this Act, a creditor, subject to the limitations in Section 8, may obtain:

(1) avoidance of the transfer or obligation to the extent necessary to satisfy the creditor's claim;

(2) an attachment or other provisional remedy against the asset transferred or other property of the transferee in accordance with the procedure prescribed by;

(3) subject to applicable principles of equity and in accordance with applicable rules of civil procedure,

    (i) an injunction against further disposition by the debtor or a transferee, or both, of the asset transferred or of other property;

    (ii) appointment of a receiver to take charge of the asset transferred or of other property of the transferee; or

    (iii) any other relief the circumstances may require.

(b) If a creditor has obtained a judgment on a claim against the debtor, the creditor, if the court so orders, may levy execution on the asset transferred or its proceeds.

8. DEFENSES, LIABILITY, AND PROTECTION OF TRANSFEREE

(a) A transfer or obligation is not voidable under Section 4(a)(1) against a person who took in good faith and for a reasonably equivalent value or against any subsequent transferee or obligee.

(b) Except as otherwise provided in this section, to the extent a transfer is voidable in an action by a creditor under Section 7(a)(1), the creditor may recover judgment for the value of the asset transferred, as adjusted under subsection (c), or the amount necessary to satisfy the creditor's claim, whichever is less. The judgment may be entered against:

   (1) the first transferee of the asset or the person for whose benefit the transfer was made; or

   (2) any subsequent transferee other than a good faith transferee who took for value or from any subsequent transferee.

(c) If the judgment under subsection (b) is based upon the value of the asset transferred, the judgment must be for an amount equal to the value of the asset at the time of the transfer, subject to adjustment as the equities may require.

(d) Notwithstanding voidability of a transfer or an obligation under this Act, a good-faith transferee or obligee is entitled, to the extent of the value given the debtor for the transfer or obligation, to

   (1) a lien on or a right to retain any interest in the asset transferred;

   (2) enforcement of any obligation incurred; or

   (3) a reduction in the amount of the liability on the judgment.

(e) A transfer is not voidable under Section 4(a)(2) or Section 5 if the transfer results from:

   (1) termination of a lease upon default by the debtor when the termination is pursuant to the lease and applicable law; or

   (2) enforcement of a security interest in compliance with Article 9 of the Uniform Commercial Code.

(f) A transfer is not voidable under Section 5(b):

   (1) to the extent the insider gave new value to or for the benefit of the debtor after the transfer was made unless the new value was secured by a valid lien;

   (2) if made in the ordinary course of business or financial affairs of the debtor and the insider; or

   (3) if made pursuant to a good-faith effort to rehabilitate the debtor and the transfer secured present value given for that purpose as well as an antecedent debt of the debtor.

9. EXTINGUISHMENT OF CLAIM FOR RELIEF—CAUSE OF ACTION

A claim for relief—cause of action with respect to a fraudulent transfer or obligation under this Act is extinguished unless action is brought:

(a) under Section 4(a)(1), within 4 years after the transfer was made or the obligation was incurred or, if later, within one year after the transfer or obligation was or could reasonably have been discovered by the claimant;

(b) under Section 4(a)(2) or 5(a), within 4 years after the transfer was made or the obligation was incurred; or

(c) under Section 5(b), within one year after the transfer was made or the obligation was incurred.

10. SUPPLEMENTARY PROVISIONS

Unless displaced by the provisions of this Act, the principles of law and equity, including the law merchant and the law relating to principal and agent, estoppel, laches, fraud, misrepresentation, duress, coercion, mistake, insolvency, or other validating or invalidating cause, supplement its provisions.

11. UNIFORMITY OF APPLICATION AND CONSTRUCTION

This Act shall be applied and construed to effectuate its general purpose to make uniform the law with respect to the subject of this Act among states enacting it.

12. SHORT TITLE

This Act may be cited as the Uniform Fraudulent Transfer Act.

13. REPEAL

The following acts and all other acts and parts of acts inconsistent herewith are hereby repealed:

CHAPTER 3
APPENDIX III

EXCERPTS FROM TENNESSEE CODE ANNOTATED TITLE 47 COMMERCIAL INSTRUMENTS AND TRANSACTIONS

CHAPTER 13 ASSIGNMENTS FOR BENEFIT OF CREDITORS

47-13-101 TRUSTEES OR ASSIGNEES FOR CREDITORS, ETC.—BOND—OATH.

Every trust or assignee to whom property exceeding the value of five hundred dollars ($500) is conveyed in trust for the benefit of creditors, sureties, or other persons, unless by them released, in writing, from the obligations hereinafter prescribed, before entering upon the discharge of such trustee's or assignee's duty, shall give bond, with two (2) or more good and sufficient sureties, or one (1) corporate surety, in an amount equal tot he value of the property mentioned in the deed or assignment, payable to the state of Tennessee, conditioned for the faithful performance of all the duties imposed upon the trustee or assignee by law and by the terms of the deed or assignment, and shall take and subscribe, before the person performing the duties of the county clerk of the county in which the trustee or assignee resides, an oath to the effect that the trustee or assignee will:

(1) Honestly and faithfully execute and perform all the duties imposed upon such trustee or assignee by law and by the deed or assignment;

(2) Cause to be made a full, true, and perfect inventory of the goods, chattels, lands, or other assets, all and singular, contained in the trust deed or assignment which have or may come into the trustee's or assignee's hands or into the hands of any other person for such trustee or assignee, and

(3) Return, or cause to be filed in the office of the person performing the duties of the county clerk, a full and true account of all the sales of the effects, and of all moneys received or securities taken.

47-13-102 FILING OF BOND AND OATH.

The bond and affidavit shall be filed and preserved by the person performing the duties of the county clerk in such person's office.

47-13-103 SETTLEMENT BY TRUSTEE OR ASSIGNEE.

Any trustee or assignee to whom property has been conveyed in trust for the benefit of creditors, under the provisions of this chapter, shall be required to make settlement with the person performing the duties of the county clerk of the county in which the deed or trustor assignment was made, as soon after qualification as the nature of the deed or assignment will admit, showing what funds the trustee or assignee has received, how the trustee or assignee has disposed of the trust property, what expenses the trustee or assignee has paid out, and what amount of the funds remain in the trustee's or assignee's hands for payment to beneficiaries under the deed or assignment.

47-13-104 FAILURE TO SETTLE—CITATION UPON APPLICATION OF INTEREST PARTY.

Should any such trustee or assignee fail or refuse to make settlement as required by the provisions of 47-13-103, the person performing the duties of the county clerk shall be required, upon application of anyone interested in the trust property, to issue a citation to such trustee or assignee, requiring the trustee or assignee to appear before the person performing the duties of the county clerk on a given day and make settlement as required by 47-13-103, a copy of which citation shall be served by the sheriff or any constable of the county at least five (5) days before the day appointed in the citation for such settlement or casting of account.

47-13-105 FAILURE TO SETTLE—CITATION WITHOUT APPLICATION.

The person performing the duties of the county clerk, after the expiration of two (2) years from the qualification of such trustee or assignee, shall have power, without application for anyone interested in the trust property, to compel such trustee or assignee to make settlement by citation, as prescribed in 47-13-104.

47-13-106 FAILURE TO SETTLE—PENALTY.

Any such trustee or assignee, who fails or refuses to settle, as above required, after such citation or notice, commits a Class A misdemeanor, and shall be liable to indictment or presentment in the same manner as administrators who fail or refuse to settle as required of them by law.

47-13-107 FAILURE TO SETTLE—REMOVAL OF TRUSTEE.

(a) In addition to the foregoing penalties for failure to settle, the court having the jurisdiction of the monthly county court has the power, and it is its duty, upon application, by petition, unless satisfactory reasons be shown why the same shall not be done, to revoke the appointment of such trustee and remove the trustee, and appoint another, who shall be subject to the provisions of 47-13-103–47-13-109.

47-13-108 APPLICABILITY OF 47-13-103–47-13-109

Nothing in 47-13-103–47-13-109 shall be construed to exempt trustees or assignees from qualifying, giving bond, and returning inventories, as prescribed by law, nor shall these sections be construed to make them applicable to deeds or mortgages given purely as security for money lent or advanced, but the sections apply only to conveyances made for the benefit of creditors.

47-13-109 FEES FOR SERVICES UNDER 47-13-103–47-13-108.

The person performing the duties of the county clerk, and the sheriff or constable, for the services performed by them under 47-13-103–47-13-108, shall be entitled to and be allowed the same fees as are allowed them by law for like services in other cases.

47-13-110 COMPENSATION OF TRUSTEES.

The court having the jurisdiction of the monthly county court, upon application, or the chancery court, if the trust is administered in the chancery court, may allow a trustee or assignee compensation exceeding the compensation of clerks and masters, if the character of the services rendered entitle the trustee or assignee to such compensation in the opinion of such court, but such compensation in no case shall exceed five percent (5%).

47-13-111 NONCOMPLIANCE BY TRUSTEES—APPOINTMENT OF RECEIVER.

If any trustee or assignee fails or refuses to comply with this chapter, the court having the jurisdiction of the monthly county court, upon application of any person interested, shall, in lieu of the delinquent, appoint a trustee or receiver who, upon executing the bond and taking the oath aforementioned, may execute the trust or assignment.

47-13-112 DEATH, RESIGNATION, OR REMOVAL OF TRUSTEE.

The chancery court or the court having the jurisdiction of the monthly county court is empowered, upon suggestion and proof of the death, resignation, or removal beyond the limits of this state, of any trustee named as such in any deed of trust conveying realty or personalty as security for the payment of debts or other obligations, to appoint and qualify a trustee in lieu of the trustee dead, resigned, or removed as aforementioned.

47-13-113 POWERS OF SUCCESSOR TRUSTEE.

Any trustee so appointed and qualified shall be vested with all the power and authority given in the deed of trust to the original trustee and be subject to all the conditions and limitations therein imposed upon the original trustee.

47-13-114 RELEASE OF SURETIES.

The sureties of a trustee or assignee for the benefit of creditors may be released in the manner prescribed in title 29, chapter 33.

47-13-115 GENERAL ASSIGNMENTS—PREFERENCE OF CREDITORS.

(a) Preference of creditors in general assignments of all a debtor's property for the benefit of creditors shall be illegal and voidable, and all general assignments shall operate for the benefit of all the debtor's creditors pro rata, whether all the creditors are named in the assignment or not.

(b) The insertion of a clause in the assignment giving a preference shall not render the assignment itself invalid, but the clause only shall be nugatory, and all the debtor's creditors shall share ratably in property assigned.

47-13-116 GENERAL ASSIGNMENTS—PRIOR CONVEYANCE FOR BENEFIT OF PARTICULAR CREDITOR.

Any mortgage, deed of trust, security interest under the Uniform Commercial Code, or any other conveyance of a portion of a debtor's property for the benefit of any particular creditor or creditors, made within three (3) months preceding a general assignment and in contemplation of making a general assignment, shall be void in the event a general assignment is made within three (3) months thereafter, and the property conveyed by such conveyance shall be shared ratably by all creditors just as that embraced in general assignments.

47-13-117 GENERAL ASSIGNMENTS—PRIOR JUDGMENT BY CONFESSION OR DEFAULT.

Any confession of judgment by a debtor, or permitting judgment to be taken by default, or by collusion, within three (3) months preceding a general assignment, and in contemplation of such assignment, shall be void, in the event a general assignment is made within three (3) months after the judgment.

47-13-118 GENERAL ASSIGNMENTS—INVENTORY—TRUSTEE'S RIGHTS TO PROPERTY.

The debtor making a general assignment shall annex thereto a full and complete inventory or schedule under oath of all the debtor's property or every description, and the trustee or assignee shall be entitled to any other property of the debtor not embraced in the assignment, and not exempt from execution, and also to property conveyed in violation of 47-13-116, and to the property or its proceeds assigned to satisfy judgments rendered in violation of 47-13-117.

47-13-119 MORTGAGES, DEEDS OF TRUST OR SECURITY AGREEMENTS.

The provisions of this chapter shall not prevent any person from making a mortgage, deed of trust, or security agreement under the Uniform Commercial Code to secure the payment for property bought or money lent, or for necessary advancements of supplies, stock, or farming implements to be made, to enable the owner of crops to make and save the same; provided, that the mortgage, deed of trust, or security agreement is executed at the time of buying the property, or borrowing the money, or making the contract for the advancements to be made, of the mortgage, deed of trust, or security agreement fixes the amount of advancement to be made under the contract.

47-13-120 TIME FOR PRESENTING CLAIMS—NOTICE.

(a) A trustee under a general assignment made for the benefit of creditors shall give notice for a reasonable time by advertisement for four (4) consecutive issues in the nearest newspaper to or within the county in which the trustee is qualified, and by posting at the courthouse door of the county, for all persons having claims secured by the assignment to present the claims to the trustee, taking the trustee's receipt therefor, on or before a day fixed in such notice, which day shall not be less than twelve (12) months after the day of notice.

(b) Any claims not presented to the trustee on or before the day so fixed, or before an appropriation of the trust funds, shall be forever barred, both in law and equity.

CHAPTER 3
APPENDIX IV

ARTICLE 7
WAREHOUSE RECEIPTS, BILLS OF LADING AND OTHER DOCUMENTS OF TITLE

PART 1
GENERAL

7-101. SHORT TITLE.

This Article shall be known and may be cited as Uniform Commercial-Documents of Title.

7-102. DEFINITIONS AND INDEX OF DEFINITIONS.

(1) In this Article, unless the context otherwise requires:

    (a) "Bailee" means the person who by a warehouse receipt, bill of lading or other document of title acknowledges possession of goods and contracts to deliver them.

    (b) "Consignee" means the person named in a bill to whom or to whose order the bill promises delivery.

    (c) "Consignor" means the person named in a bill as the person from whom the goods have been received for shipment.

    (d) "Delivery order" means a written order to deliver goods directed to a warehouseman, carrier or other person who in the ordinary course of business, issues warehouse receipts or bills of lading.

    (e) "Document" means document of title as defined in the general definitions in Article 1 (Section 1-201).

    (f) "Goods" means all things which are treated as movable for the purposes of a contract of storage or transportation.

    (g) "Issuer" means a bailee who issues a document except that in relation to an unaccepted delivery order it means the person who orders the possessor of goods to deliver. Issuer includes any person for whom an agent or employee purports to act in issuing a document if the agent or employee has real or apparent authority to issue documents, notwithstanding that the issuer received no goods or that the goods were misdescribed or that in any other respect the agent or employee violated his instructions.

    (h) "Warehouseman" is a person engaged in the business of storing goods for hire.

(2) Other definitions applying to this Article or to specified Parts thereof, and the sections in which they appear are:

"Duly negotiate". Section 7-501.

"Person entitled under the document". Section 7-403 (4) .

(3) Definitions in other Articles applying to this Article and the sections in which they appear are:

"Contract for Sale". Section 2-106.

"Overseas". Section 2-323.

"Receipt" of goods. Section 2-103.

(4) In addition, Article 1 contains general definitions and principles of construction and interpretation applicable throughout this Article.

7-103. RELATION OF ARTICLE TO TREATY, STATUTE, TARIFF, CLASSIFICATION OR REGULATION.

(1) To the extent that any treaty or statute of the United States, regulatory statute of this State or tariff, classification or regulation filed or issued pursuant to thereto is applicable, the provisions of this Article are subject thereto.

7-104. NEGOTIABLE AND NON-NEGOTIABLE WAREHOUSE RECEIPT, BILL OF LADING OR OTHER DOCUMENT OF TITLE.

(1) A warehouse receipt, bill of lading or other document of title is negotiable

   (a) if by its terms the goods are to be delivered to bearer or to the order of a named person; or

   (b) where recognized in overseas trade, if it runs to a named person or assigns.

(2) Any other document is non-negotiable. A bill of lading in which it is stated that the goods are consigned to a named person is not made negotiable by a provision that the goods are to be delivered only against a written order signed by the same or another named person.

7-105. CONSTRUCTION AGAINST NEGATIVE IMPLICATION.

The omission from either Part 2 or Part 3 of this Article of a provision corresponding to a provision made in the other Part does not imply that a corresponding rule of law is not applicable.

PART 2
WAREHOUSE RECEIPTS: SPECIAL PROVISIONS

7-201. WHO MAY ISSUE A WAREHOUSE RECEIPT: STORAGE UNDER GOVERNMENT BOND.

(1) A warehouse receipt may be issued by any warehouseman.

(2) Where goods including distilled spirits and agricultural commodities are stored under a statute requiring a bond against withdrawal, or a license for the issuance of

receipts in the nature of warehouse receipts, a receipt issued for the goods has like effect as a warehouse receipt even though issued by a person who is the owner of the goods and is not a warehouseman.

7-202. FORM OF WAREHOUSE RECEIPT: ESSENTIAL TERMS; OPTIONAL TERMS.

(1) A warehouse receipt need not be in any particular form.

(2) Unless a warehouse receipt embodies within its written or printed terms each of the following, the warehouseman is liable for damages caused by the omission to a person injured thereby:

    (a) the location of the warehouse where the goods are stored;

    (b) the date of issue of the receipt;

    (c) the consecutive number of the receipt;

    (d) a statement whether the goods received will be delivered to the bearer, to a specified person, or to a specified person or his order;

    (e) the rate of storage and handling charges, except that where the goods are stored under a field warehousing arrangement a statement of that fact is sufficient on a non-negotiable receipt;

    (f) a description of the goods or of the packages containing them;

    (g) the signature of the warehouseman, which may be made by his authorized agent;

    (h) if the receipt is issued for goods of which the warehouseman is owner, either solely or jointly or in common with others, the fact of such ownership; and

    (i) a statement of the amount of advances made and of liabilities incurred for which the warehouseman claims a lien or security interest (Section 7-209). If the precise amount of such advances made or of such liabilities incurred is, at the time of the issue of the receipt, unknown to the warehouseman or to his agent who issues it, a statement of the fact that advances have been made or liabilities incurred and the purpose thereof is sufficient.

(3) A warehouseman may insert in his receipt any other terms which are not contrary to the provisions of this Act and do not impair his obligation of delivery (Section 7-403) or his duty of care (Section 7-204). Any contrary provisions shall be ineffective.

7-203. LIABILITY FOR NON-RECEIPT OR MISDESCRIPTION.

A party to or purchaser for value in good faith of a document of title other than a bill of lading relying in either case upon the description therein of the goods may recover from the issuer damages caused by the non-receipt or misdescription of the goods, except to the extent that the document conspicuously indicates that the issuer does not know whether any part or all of the goods in fact were received or conform to the description, as where the description is in terms of marks or labels or kind, quantity or condition, or the receipt or description is qualified by "contents, condition and quality unknown," "said to contain" or the like, if such indication be true, or the party or purchaser otherwise has notice.

7-204. Duty of Care; Contractual Limitation of Warehouseman's Liability.

(1) A warehouseman is liable for damages for loss of or injury to the goods caused by his failure to exercise such care in regard to them as a reasonably careful man would exercise under like circumstances but unless otherwise agreed he is not liable for damages which could not have been avoided by the exercise of such care.

(2) Damages may be limited by a term in the warehouse receipt or storage agreement limiting the amount of liability in case of loss or damage, and setting forth a specific liability per article or item, or value per unit of weight, beyond which the warehouseman shall not be liable; provided, however, that such liability may on written request of the bailor at the time of signing such storage agreement or within a reasonable time after receipt of the warehouse receipt be increased on part or all of the goods thereunder, in which event increased rates may be charged based on such increased valuation, but that no such increase shall be permitted contrary to a lawful limitation of liability contained in the warehouseman's tariff, if any. No such limitation is effective with respect to the warehouseman's liability for conversion to his own use.

(3) Reasonable provisions as to the time and manner of presenting claims and instituting actions based on the bailment may be included in the warehouse receipt or tariff.

(4) This section does not impair or repeal....

Note: Insert in subsection (4) a reference to any statute which imposes a higher responsibility upon the warehouseman or invalidates contractual limitations which would be permissible under this Article.

7-205. Title Under Warehouse Receipt Defeated in Certain Cases.

A buyer in the ordinary course of business of fungible goods sold and delivered by a warehouseman who is also in the business of buying and selling such goods takes free of any claim under a warehouse receipt even though it has been duly negotiated.

7-206. Termination of Storage at Warehouseman's Option.

(1) A warehouseman may on notifying the person on whose account the goods are held and any other person known to claim an interest in the goods require payment of any charges and removal of the goods from the warehouse at the termination of the period of storage fixed by the document, or if no period is fixed, within a stated period not less than thirty days after the notification. If the goods are not removed before the date specified in the notification, the warehouseman may sell them in accordance with the provisions of the section on enforcement of a warehouseman's lien (Section 7-210).

(2) If a warehouseman in good faith believes that the goods are about to deteriorate or decline in value to less than the amount of his lien within the time prescribed in subsection (1) for notification, advertisement and sale, the warehouseman may specify in the notification any reasonable shorter time for removal of the goods and in case

the goods are not removed, may sell them at public sale held not less than one week after a single advertisement or posting.

(3) If as a result of a quality or condition of the goods of which the warehouseman had no notice at the time of deposit the goods are a hazard to other property or to the warehouse or to persons, the warehouseman may sell the goods at public or private sale without advertisement on reasonable notification to all persons known to claim an interest in the goods. If the warehouseman after a reasonable effort is unable to sell the goods he may dispose of them in any lawful manner and shall incur no liability by reason of such disposition.

(4) The warehouseman must deliver the goods to any person entitled to them under this Article upon due demand made at any time prior to sale or other disposition under this section.

(5) The warehouseman may satisfy his lien from the proceeds of any sale or disposition under this section but must hold the balance for delivery on the demand of any person to whom he would have been bound to deliver the goods.

7-207. Goods Must Be Kept Separate; Fungible Goods.

(1) Unless the warehouse receipt otherwise provides, a warehouseman must keep separate the goods covered by each receipt so as to permit at all times identification and delivery of those goods except that different lots of fungible goods may be commingled.

(2) Fungible goods so commingled are owned in common by the persons entitled thereto and the warehouseman is severally liable to each owner for that owner's share. Where because of overissue a mass of fungible goods is insufficient to meet all the receipts which the warehouseman has issued against it, the persons entitled include all holders to whom overissued receipts have been duly negotiated.

7-208. Altered Warehouse Receipts.

Where a blank in a negotiable warehouse receipt has been filled in without authority, a purchaser for value and without notice of the want of authority may treat the insertion as authorized. Any other unauthorized alteration leaves any receipt enforceable against the issuer according to its original tenor.

7-209. Lien of Warehouseman.

(1) A warehouseman has a lien against the bailor on the goods covered by a warehouse receipt or on the proceeds thereof in his possession for charges for storage or transportation (including demurrage and terminal charges), insurance, labor, or charges present or future in relation to the goods, and for expenses necessary for preservation of the goods or reasonably incurred in their sale pursuant to law. If the person on whose account the goods are held is liable for like charges or expenses in relation to other goods whenever deposited and it is stated in the receipt that a lien is claimed for charges and expenses in relation to other goods, the warehouseman also has a lien against him for such charges and expenses whether or not the other goods have been delivered by the warehouseman. But against a person to whom a negotiable

warehouse receipt is duly negotiated, a warehouseman's lien is limited to charges in an amount or at a rate specified on the receipt or if no charges are so specified then to a reasonable charge for storage of the goods covered by the receipt subsequent to the date of the receipt.

(2) The warehouseman may also reserve a security interest against the bailor for a maximum amount specified on the receipt for charges other than those specified in subsection (1), such as for money advanced and interest.

Such a security interest is governed by the Article on Secured Transactions (Article 9).

(3) (a) A warehouseman's lien for charges and expenses under subsection (1) or a security interest under subsection (2) is also effective against any person who so entrusted the bailor with possession of the goods that a pledge of them by him to a good faith purchaser for value would have been valid but is not effective against a person as to whom the document confers no right in the goods covered by it under Section 7-503.

(b) A warehouseman's lien on household goods for charges and expenses in relation to the goods under subsection (1) is also effective against all persons if the depositor was the legal possessor of the goods at the time of the deposit. "Household goods" means furniture, furnishings and personal effects used by the depositor in a dwelling.

(4) A warehouseman loses his lien on any goods which he voluntarily delivers or which he unjustifiably refuses to deliver.

7-210. ENFORCEMENT OF WAREHOUSEMAN'S LIEN.

(1) Except as provided in subsection (2), a warehouseman's lien may be enforced by public or private sale of the goods in block or in parcels, at any time or place and on any terms which are commercially reasonable, after notifying all persons known to claim an interest in the goods. Such notification must include a statement of the amount due, the nature of the proposed sale and the time and place of any public sale. The fact that a better price could have been obtained by a sale at a different time or in a different method from that selected by the warehouseman is not of itself sufficient to establish that the sale was not made in a commercially reasonable manner. If the warehouseman either sells the goods in the usual manner in any recognized market therefor, or if he sells at the price current in such market at the time of his sale, or if he has otherwise sold in conformity with commercially reasonable practices among dealers in the type of goods sold, he has sold in a commercially reasonable manner. A sale of more goods than apparently necessary to be offered to insure satisfaction of the obligation is not commercially reasonable except in cases covered by the preceding sentence.

(2) A warehouseman's lien on goods other than goods stored by a merchant in the course of his business may be enforced only as follows:

(a) All persons known to claim an interest in the goods must be notified.

(b) The notification must be delivered in person or sent by registered or certified letter to the last known address of any person to be notified.

(c) The notification must include an itemized statement of the claim, a description of the goods subject to the lien, a demand for payment within a specified time not less than ten days after receipt of the notification, and a conspicuous statement that unless the claim is paid within that time the goods will be advertised for sale and sold by auction at a specified time and place.

(d) The sale must conform to the terms of the notification.

(e) The sale must be held at the nearest suitable place to that where the goods are held or stored.

(f) After the expiration of the time given in the notification, an advertisement of the sale must be published once a week for two weeks consecutively in a newspaper of general circulation where the sale is to be held. The advertisement must include a description of the goods, the name of the person on whose account they are being held, and the time and place of the sale. The sale must take place at least fifteen days after the first publication. If there is no newspaper of general circulation where the sale is to be held, the advertisement must be posted at least ten days before the sale in not less than six conspicuous places in the neighborhood of the proposed sale.

(3) Before any sale pursuant to this section any person claiming a right in the goods may pay the amount necessary to satisfy the lien and the reasonable expenses incurred under this section. In that event the goods must not be sold, but must be retained by the warehouseman subject to the terms of the receipt and this Article.

(4) The warehouseman may buy at any public sale pursuant to this section.

(5) A purchaser in good faith of goods sold to enforce a warehouseman's lien takes the goods free of any rights of persons against whom the lien was valid, despite noncompliance by the warehouseman with the requirements of this section.

(6) The warehouseman may satisfy his lien from the proceeds of any sale pursuant to this section but must hold the balance, if any, for delivery on demand to any person to whom he would have been bound to deliver the goods.

(7) The rights provided by this section shall be in addition to all other rights allowed by law to a creditor against his debtor.

(8) Where a lien is on goods stored by a merchant in the course of his business the lien may be enforced in accordance with either subsection (1) or (2).

(9) The warehouseman is liable for damages caused by failure to comply with the requirements for sale under this section and in case of willful violation is liable for conversion.

CHAPTER 3
APPENDIX V

EXCERPTS FROM MASSACHUSETTS GENERAL LAWS

CHAPTER 255. MORTGAGES, CONDITIONAL SALES AND PLEDGES OF PERSONAL PROPERTY, AND LIENS THEREON OTHER LIENS

25. GARAGE KEEPERS; EFFECTS OF LIENS ON MOTOR VEHICLES OBTAINED BY FRAUD; ETC. LIEN FOR CHARGES REIMBURSED BY INSURANCE COMPANY

Persons maintaining public garages for the storage and care of motor vehicles brought to their premises or placed in their care by or with the consent of the owners thereof and persons engaged in performing work upon or in connection with the inspection, reconditioning and repairing of motor vehicles shall have a lien upon such motor vehicles for proper charges due them for the storage, work and care of the same.

If the owner of such motor vehicle obtains possession of the same by fraud, trick or by check, draft or order upon any depository or bank which is not honored, the lien on said motor vehicle shall not be deemed to have been discharted and the lien holder may thereafter continue to enforce said lien until the proper charges due him have been paid.

In any instance where a lien arises under this section for charges due that are to be paid or reimbursed by any insurance company licensed in the commonwealth, upon written notice by the holder of such lien to the insurance company, the check or draft issued by such insurance company for such charges shall name the holder of the lien, together with the holder of a security interest as defined by ARTICLE 9 of chapter one hundred and six, as a loss payee, unless otherwise provided by law. The holder of a security interest that does not have priority over the lien established under this section shall be required to endorse any check or draft issued for payment of such charges by such insurance company over to the holder of such lien, whether or not such lien has then been released by the holder; provided, however, that the holder of a security interest other than the lien provided by this section, may, within two business days of notice of a request to endorse any such check require the owner of the vehicle to make said vehicle available for inspection at a time and place convenient to the owner and lienholder, to reinspect the repaired vehicle, and, as a prerequisite for such endorsement, the holder of such security interest may require the holder of the lien established under this section to provide it with an itemized list of repairs and other services which it certifies, in writing, have been completed or provided, and a copy of any repair certification form required by law to be provided to the insurance company.

Nothing in this section shall affect or modify the provisions of any direct payment plans implemented by an insurer pursuant to section thirty-four O of chapter ninety.

39A. VEHICLES, SALE FOR STORAGE; PROCEDURE

Any motor vehicle removed from the scene of an accident and placed for storage in the care of a garage, which in this section also include a parking lot or other place for the storage of motor vehicles, by a member of the state police force, by a member of the metropolitan district police, by a member of the police force of any city or town or by any inspector, supervisor, investigator, examiner or instructor appointed by the registrar of motor vehicles under section twenty-nine of chapter ninety, shall be so stored at the prevailing rates. At the time such motor vehicles is so placed the officer or person placing it shall furnish the owner or operator of such garage the name and address of the registered owner of said motor vehicle; and if such information is not then available, said officer or person shall obtain such information and forthwith in writing the said owner or operator.

Upon receipt of such information the owner of the garage shall notify the registered owner of the motor vehicle by registered mail, return receipt requested, that such motor vehicle has been placed in his care as provided by this section, and shall inform him of the storage rates therefor, and shall inquire if he is to continue to hold the motor vehicle subject to such storage rates.

If the registered owner of the motor vehicle assents to the continued storage of such motor vehicle, the owner of the garage shall continue to hold said motor vehicle in storage and shall have a lien thereon, as provided in section twenty-five.

If the registered owner of the motor vehicle fails to answer said notice within twenty-one days after receipt thereof, the motor vehicle shall continue to be stored at the prevailing rates.

If, after the expiration of sixty days from the date when the vehicle was brought to the garage or placed in the care of the owner of said garage, the owner of the motor vehicle has not claimed said vehicle, the owner of the garage may give notice to the owner by registered mail at his last known place of abode stating the amount of the storage charges and informing him that if the vehicle is not claimed within twenty-one days the vehicle will be sold. If the owner does not claim the vehicle within said twenty-one days, the owner of the garage may sell said motor vehicle at public or private sale after publishing notice of such sale for three successive weeks in a newspaper published or having circulation in the city or town in which the property is located; provided that he shall notify the chief of police in the city or town in which the garage is located at least five days prior to such sale that the vehicle is to be sold. Upon such sale the owner of the garage may deduct therefrom his charges for storage and the costs of sending notices and of holding the sale, and shall furnish the registered owner of such motor vehicle a statement of the amount received at such sale, together with the amount of his charges and costs, and the balance, if any. If the owner of the garage knows the address of the registered owner of said motor vehicle he shall pay such balance to him; if not, he shall deposit the same with the clerk of the district court who shall give him a receipt therefor and deposit said balance in a savings bank in the name of the justice of the district court n trust for said owner of the motor vehicle.

CHAPTER 3
APPENDIX VI

EXCERPTS FROM NEW YORK LAW

ARTICLE 8—OTHER LIENS ON PERSONAL PROPERTY

180. ARTISANS' LIEN ON PERSONAL PROPERTY

A person who makes, alters, repairs or performs work or services of any nature and description upon, or in any way enhances the value of an article of personal property, at the request or with the consent of the owner, has a lien on such article, while lawfully in possession thereof, for his reasonable charges for the work done and materials furnished, and may retain possession thereof until such charges are paid.

184. LIEN ON BAILEE OF MOTOR VEHICLES, MOTOR BOATS OR AIRCRAFT

(1) A person keeping a garage, hangar or place for the storage, maintenance, keeping or repair of motor vehicles are defined by the vehicle and traffic law, or of motor boats as defined by article seven of the navigation law, or of aircraft as defined by article fourteen of the general business law, and who in connection therewith tows, stores, maintains, keeps or repairs any motor vehicle, motor boat, or aircraft or furnishes gasoline or other supplies therefor at the request or with the consent of the owner or, subject to the provisions of subdivision two of this section, tows and stores any motor vehicle at the request of a law enforcement officer authorized to remove such motor vehicle whether or not such motor vehicle, motor boat or aircraft is subject to a security interest, has a lien upon such motor vehicle, motor boat or aircraft for the sum due for such towing, storing, maintaining, keeping or repairing of such motor vehicle, motor boat or aircraft or for furnishing gasoline or other supplies therefor and may detain such motor vehicle, motor boat or aircraft at any time it may be lawfully in his possession until such sum is paid, except that if the lienor, subsequent to thirty days from the accrual of such line, allows the motor vehicle, motor boat or aircraft out of his actual possession the lien provided for in this section shall thereupon become void as against all security interests, whether or not perfected, in such motor vehicles, motor boat or aircraft and executed prior to the accrual of such lien, notwithstanding possession of such motor vehicle, motor boat or aircraft is thereafter acquired by such lienor.

However, if the bailee of a motor vehicle, motor boat or aircraft has furnished a written estimate of the cost of towing, storage, maintenance, repair or any other service

136

on such motor vehicle, motor boat or aircraft, any lien sought by such bailee for such service may not be in an amount in excess of the written estimate.

(2) A person who tows and stores a motor vehicle at the request of a law enforcement officer authorized to remove such motor vehicle shall be entitled to a lien for the reasonable costs of such towing and storage, provided that such person, within five working days from the initial towing, mails to the owner of said motor vehicle a notice by certified mail return requested that contains the name of the person who towed and is storing said motor vehicle, the amount that is being claimed for such towing and storage, and the address and times at which said motor vehicle may be recovered. Such notice shall further state that the person mailing said notice claims a lien on said motor vehicle and that said motor vehicle shall be released to the owner thereof or his or her lawfully designated representative upon full payment of all charges accrued to the date that said motor vehicle is released. A person who mails the foregoing notice within said five day period shall be entitled to a lien for storage from and after the date of initial towing, but a person who fails to mail such notice within said five day period shall only be entitled to a lien for storage from and after the date that the notice was mailed. A failure to mail such notice in a timely fashion shall not affect a lien for towing.

(3) The provisions of this section shall not apply to a person who tows and stores a motor vehicle at the request of a law enforcement officer where such request is made pursuant to the provisions of a local law or ordinance regulating the towing and safekeeping of stolen or abandoned vehicles within such locality and which requires such motor vehicle to be turned over to the locality after a specified period of time.

(4) The lien provided shall not inure to the benefit of any person required to be registered as a motor vehicle repair shop pursuant to article twelve-A of the vehicle and traffic law who is not so registered.

APPENDIX VII

EXCERPTS FROM BULK SALES CALIFORNIA DIVISION 6—BULK SALES

SECTION 6101. SHORT TITLE

SECTION 6102. DEFINITIONS AND INDEX OF DEFINITIONS

SECTION 6103. BULK SALES GOVERNED BY THIS DIVISION; EXCEPTIONS

(a) Except as otherwise provided in subdivision (c), this division applies to a bulk sale if both of the following are satisfied:

    (1) The seller's principal business is the sale of inventory from stock, including those who manufacture what they sell, or that of a restaurant owner.

    (2) On the date of the bulk-sale agreement the seller is located in this state or, if the seller is located in a jurisdiction that is not a part of the United States, the seller's major executive office in the United States is in this state.

(b) A seller is deemed to be located at its place of business. If a seller has more than one place of business, the seller is deemed located at its chief executive office.

(c) This division does not apply to any of the following:

    (1) A transfer made to secure payment or performance of an obligation.

    (2) A transfer of collateral to a secured party pursuant to Section 9503.

    (3) A sale of collateral pursuant to Section 9504.

    (4) Retention of collateral pursuant to Section 9505.

    (5) A sale of an asset encumbered by a security interest or lien if (i) all the proceeds of the sale are applied in partial or total satisfaction of the debt secured by the security interest or lien or (ii) the security interest or lien is enforceable against the asset after it has been sold to the buyer and the net contract price is zero.

    (6) A general assignment for the benefit of creditors or to a subsequent transfer by the assignee.

    (7) A sale by an executor, administrator, receiver, trustee in bankruptcy, debtor in possession, or any public officer under judicial process.

    (8) A sale made in the course of judicial or administrative proceedings for the dissolution or reorganization of an organization.

    (9) A sale to a buyer whose principal place of business is in the United States and who satisfies each of the following:

        (i) Not earlier than 21 days before the date of the bulk sale, (A) obtains from the seller a verified and dated list of claimants of whom the seller has notice three days before the seller sends or delivers the list to the buyer or (B) conducts a reasonable injury to discover the claimants.

(ii) Assumes in full the debts owed to claimants of whom the buyer has knowledge on the date the buyer receives the list of claimants from the seller or on the date the buyer completes the reasonable inquiry, as the case may be.

(iii) Is not insolvent after the assumption.

(iv) Records and publishes notice of the assumption not later than 30 days after the date of the bulk sale in the manner provided in Section 6105.

(10) A sale to a buyer whose principal place of business is in the United States and who satisfies each of the following:

(i) Assumes in full the debts that were incurred in the seller's business before the date of the bulk sale.

(ii) Is not insolvent after the assumption.

(iii) Records and publishes notice of the assumption not later than 30 days after the date of the bulk sale in the manner provided by Section 6105.

(11) A sale to a new organization that is organized to take over and continue the business of the seller and that has its principal place of business in the United States if each of the following conditions are satisfied:

(i) The buyer assumes in full the debts that were incurred in the seller's business before the date of the bulk sale.

(ii) The seller receives nothing from the sale except an interest in the new organization that is subordinate to the claims against the organization arising from the assumption.

(iii) The buyer records and publishes notice of the assumption not later than 30 days after the date of the bulk sale in the manner provided in Section 6105.

(12) A sale of assets having either of the following:

(i) A value, net of liens and security interests, of less than ten thousand dollars ($10,000). If a debt is secured by assets and other property of the seller, the net value of the assets is determined by subtracting from their value an amount equal to the product of the debt multiplied by a fraction, the numerator of which is the value of the assets on the date of the bulk sale and the denominator of which is the value of all property securing the debt on the date of the bulk sale.

(ii) A value of more than five million dollars ($5,000,000) on the date of the bulk-sale agreement.

(13) A sale required by, and made pursuant to, statute.

(14) A transfer of personal property, if the personal property is leased back to the transferor immediately following the transfer and either there has been compliance with subdivision (h) of Section 3440.1 of the Civil Code or the transfer is exempt under subdivision (k) of Section 3440.1 of the Civil Code.

(15) A transfer which is subject to and complies with Article 5 (commencing with Section 24070) of Chapter 6 of Division 9 of the Business and Professions Code, if the transferee records and publishes notice of the transfer at least 12 business days before the transfer is to be consummated in the manner provided in Section 6105 and the notice contains the information set forth in paragraphs (1) to (4) inclusive, of subdivision (a) of Section 6105.

(16) A transfer of goods in a warehouse where a warehouse receipt has been issued therefore by a warehouseman (Section 7102) and a copy of the receipt is kept at

the principal place of business of the warehouseman and at the warehouse in which the goods are stored.

(d) The notice under subparagraph (iv) of paragraph (9) of subdivision (c) shall state each of the following:

    (1) That a sale that may constitute a bulk sale has been or will be made.

    (2) The date or prospective date of the bulk sale.

    (3) The individual, partnership, or corporate names and the addresses of the seller and buyer.

    (4) The address to which inquiries about the sale may be made, if different from the seller's address.

    (5) That the buyer has assumed or will assume in full the debts owed to claimants of whom the buyer has knowledge on the date the buyer receives the list of claimants from the seller or completes a reasonable inquiry to discover the claimants.

(e) The notice under subparagraph (iii) of paragraph (10) of subdivision (c) and subparagraph (11) of subdivision (c) shall state each of the following:

    (1) That a sale that may constitute a bulk sale has been or will be made.

    (2) The date or prospective date of the bulk sale.

    (3) The individual, partnership, or corporate names and the addresses of the seller and buyer.

    (4) The address to which inquiries about the sale may be made, if different from the seller's address.

    (5) That the buyer has assumed or will assume the debts that were incurred in the seller's business before the date of the bulk sale.

(f) For purposes of paragraph (12) of subdivision (c), the value of assets is presumed to be equal to the price the buyer agrees to pay for the assets. However, in a sale by auction or a sale conducted by a liquidator on the seller's behalf, the value of assets is presumed to be the amount the auctioneer or liquidator reasonably estimates the assets will bring at auction or upon liquidation.

SECTION 6104. BUYERS' SELLER'S LIST; NOTICE; COMPLIANCE WITH SECTION 6106.2

In a bulk sale as defined in subparagraph (ii) of paragraph (3) of subdivision (a) of Section 6102 the buyer shall do each of the following:

(a) Obtain from the seller a list of all business names and addresses used by the seller within three years before the date the list is sent or delivered to the buyer.

(b) Give notice of the bulk sale in accordance with Section 6105.

(c) Comply with section 6106.2 if the bulk sale is within the scope of that section.

SECTION 6105. NOTICE; REQUIREMENTS FOR COMPLIANCE

In order to comply with subdivision (b) of Section 6104 each of the following shall be satisfied:

(a) The notice shall comply with each of the following:

    (1) State that a bulk sale is about to be made.

    (2) State the name and business address of the seller together with any other business name and address listed by the seller (subdivision (a) of Section 6104) and the name and business address of the buyer.

(3) State the location and general description of the assets.

(4) State the place and the anticipated date of the bulk sale.

(5) State whether or not the bulk sale is subject to Section 6106.2 and, if so subject, the matters required by subdivision (f) of Section 6106.2

(b) At least 12 business days before the date of the bulk sale, the notice shall be:

(1) Recorded in the office of the county recorder in the county or counties in this state in which the tangible assets are located and, if different, in the county in which the seller is located (paragraph (2) of subdivision (a) of Section 6103).

(2) Published at least once in a newspaper of general circulation published in the judicial district in this state in which the tangible assets are located and in the judicial district, if different, in which the seller is located and (paragraph (2) of subdivision (a) of section 6103), if in either case there is one, and if there is none, then in a newspaper of general circulation in the county in which the judicial district is located.

(3) Delivered or sent by registered or certified mail to the county tax collector in the county or counties in the state in which the tangible assets are located. *If delivered during the period from March 1 to the last Friday in May, inclusive, the notice shall be accompanied by a completed business property statement with respect to property involved in the bulk sale pursuant to Section 441 of the Revenue and Taxation Code.*

If the tangible assets are located in more than one judicial district in this state, the publication required in paragraph (2) shall be in a newspaper of general circulation published in the judicial district in this state in which a greater portion of the tangible assets are located, on the date the notice is published, than in any other judicial district in this state and, if different, in the judicial district in which the seller is located (paragraph (2) of subdivision (a) of Section 6103). As used in this subdivision, "business day" means any day other than a Saturday, Sunday or day observed as a holiday by the state government.

SECTION 6106.2 PAYMENT OF CONSIDERATION TO SATISFY CLAIMS OF SELLER'S CREDITOR'S DISPUTED CLAIMS; ATTACHMENT, INTERPLEADER; NOTICE; SECURITY INTEREST

SECTION 6106.4 ESCROW; FILING CLAIMS; DISTRIBUTION; NOTICE

SECTION 6107. LIABILITY FOR NONCOMPLIANCE

(a) Except as provided in subdivision (c), and subject to the limitation in subdivision (d), a buyer who fails to comply with the requirements of Section 6104 with respect to a claimant is liable to the claimant for damages in the amount of the claim, reduced by any amount that the claimant would not have realized if the buyer had complied.

(b) In an action under subdivision (a), the claimant has the burden of establishing the validity and amount of the claim, and the buyer has the burden of establishing the amount that the claimant would not have realized if the buyer had complied.

(c) A buyer who made a good faith and commercially reasonable effort to comply with the requirements of Section 6104 or to exclude the sale from the application of this division under subdivision (c) of Section 6103 is not liable to creditors for failure to comply with the requirements of Section 6104. The buyer has the burden of establishing the good faith and commercial reasonableness of the effort.

(d) In a single bulk sale the cumulative liability of the buyer for failure to comply with the requirements of Section 6104 may not exceed an amount equal to any of the following:

(1) If the assets consist only of inventory and equipment, twice the net contract price, less the amount of any part of the net contract price paid to or applied for the benefit of the seller or a creditor except to the extent that the payment or application is applied to a debt which is secured by the assets and which has been taken into consideration in determining the net contract price.

(2) If the assets include property other than inventory and equipment, twice the net value of the inventory and equipment less the amount of the portion of any part of the net contract price paid to or applied for the benefit of the seller or a creditor which is allocable to the inventory and equipment except to the extent that the payment or application is applied to a debt which is secured by the assets and which has been taken into consideration in determining the net contract price.

(e) For the purpose of paragraph (2) of subdivision (d), the "net value" of an asset is the value of the asset less each of the following:

(1) The amount of any proceeds of the sale of an asset, to the extent the proceeds are applied in partial or total satisfaction of a debt secured by the asset.

(2) The amount of any debt to the extent it is secured by a security interest or lien that is enforceable against the asset before and after it has been sold to a buyer. If a debt is secured by an asset and other property of the seller, the amount of the debt secured by a security interest or lien that is enforceable against the asset is determined by multiplying the debt by a fraction, the numerator of which is the value of all property securing the debt on the date of the bulk sale. The portion of a part of the net contract price paid to or applied for the benefit of the seller or a creditor that is "allocable to the inventory and equipment" is the portion that bears the same ratio to that part of the net contract price as the net value of the inventory and equipment bears to the net value of all the assets.

(f) A payment made by the buyer to a person to whom the buyer is, or believes it is, liable under subdivision (a) reduces pro tanto the buyer's cumulative liability under subdivision (d).

(g) No action may be brought under subdivision (a) by or on behalf of a claimant whose claim is unliquidated or contingent.

(h) A buyer's failure to comply with the requirements of Section 6104 does not do any of the following:

(1) Impair the buyer's rights in or title to the assets.

(2) Render the sale ineffective, void, or voidable.

(3) Entitle a creditor to more than a single satisfaction of its claim.

(4) Create liability other than as provided in this division.

(i) Payment of the buyer's liability under subdivision (a) discharges pro tanto the seller's debt to the creditor.

(j) Unless otherwise agreed, a buyer has an immediate right of reimbursement from the seller for any amount paid to a creditor in partial or total satisfaction of the buyer's liability under subdivision (a).

SECTION 6108. AUCTION SALES. . .

SECTION 6110. LIMITATION OF ACTIONS. . .

SECTION 6111. APPLICATION OF DIVISION. . .

CHAPTER 3
Appendix VIII

Excerpts From Texas Law

Mechanics Lien

53.021. Persons Entitled to Lien

(a) A person has a lien if:

    (1) the person labors, specially fabricates material, or furnishes labor or materials for construction or repair in this state of:

        (A) a house, building, or improvement;

        (B) a levee or embankment to be erected for the reclamation of overflow land along a river or creek; or

        (C) a railroad; and

    (2) the person labors, specially fabricates the material, or furnishes the

53.022. Property to Which Lien Extends

(a) The lien extends to the house, building, fixtures, or improvements, the land reclaimed from overflow, or the railroad and all of its properties, and to each lot of land necessarily connected or reclaimed.

(b) The lien does not extend to abutting sidewalks, streets, and utilities that are public property.

(c) A lien against land in a city, town, or village extends to each lot on which the housed building, or improvement is situated or on which the labor was performed.

(d) A lien against land not in a city, town, or village extends to not more than 50 acres on which the house, building, or improvement is situated or on which the labor was performed.

53.023. Payment Secured by Lien

The lien secures payment for:

    (1) the labor done or material furnished for the construction or repair;

    (2) the specially fabricated material, even if the material has not be delivered or incorporated into the construction or repair, less its fair salvage value; or

(3) the preparation of a plan or plat by an architect, engineer, or surveyor in accordance with Section 53.021(c).

53.024. LIMITATION ON SUBCONTRACTOR'S LIEN

The amount of a lien claimed by a subcontractor may not exceed:

(1) an amount equal to the proportion of the total subcontract price that the sum of the labor performed, materials furnished, materials specially fabricated, reasonable overhead costs incurred, and proportionate profit margin bears to the total subcontract price; minus

(2) the sum of previous payments received by the claimant on the subcontract.

53.052. FILING OF AFFIDAVIT

(a) Except as provided by Subsection (b), the person claiming the lien must file an affidavit with the county clerk of the county in which the property is located or into which the railroad extends not later than the 15th day of the fourth calendar month after the day on which the indebtedness accrues.

(b) A person claiming a lien arising from a residential construction project must file an affidavit with the county clerk of the county in which the property is located not later than the 15th day of the third calendar month after the day on which the indebtedness accrues.

(c) The county clerk shall record the affidavit in records kept for that purpose and shall index and cross-index the affidavit in the names of the claimant, the original contractor, and the owner. Failure of the county clerk to properly record or index a filed affidavit does not invalidate the lien.

53.054. CONTENTS OF AFFIDAVIT

(a) The affidavit must be signed by the person claiming the lien or by another person on the claimant's behalf and must contain substantially:

(1) a sworn statement of the amount of the claim;

(2) the name and last known address of the owner or reputed owner;

(3) a general statement of the kind of work done and materials furnished by the claimant and, for a claimant other than an original contractor, a statement of each month in which the work was done and materials furnished for which payment is requested.

(4) the name and last known address of the person by whom the claimant was employed or to whom the claimant furnished the materials or labor;

(5) the name and last known address of the original contractor;

(6) a description, legally sufficient for identification, of the property sought to be charged with the lien;

(7) the claimant's name, mailing address, and, if different, physical address; and

(8) for a claimant other than an original contractor, a statement identifying the date each notice of the claim was sent to the owner and the method by which the notice was sent.

(b) The claimant may attach to the affidavit a copy of any applicable written agreement or contract and a copy of each notice sent to the owner.

(c) The affidavit is not required to set forth individual items of work done or material furnished or specially fabricated. The affidavit may use any abbreviations or symbols customary in the trade.

53.055. NOTICE OF FILED AFFIDAVIT

(a) A person who files an affidavit must send a copy of the affidavit by registered or certified mail to the owner or reputed owner at the owner's last known business or residence address not later than one business day after the date the affidavit is filed with the county clerk.

(b) If the person is not an original contractor, the person must also send a copy of the affidavit to the original contractor at the original contractor's last known business or residence address within the same period.

CHAPTER 3
APPENDIX IX

SELLER'S REMEDIES—NEW YORK

UCC 2702—SELLER'S REMEDIES ON DISCOVERY OF BUYER'S INSOLVENCY

(1) Where the seller discovers the buyer to be insolvent he may refuse delivery except for cash including payment for all goods theretofore delivered under the contract, and stop delivery under this division (Section 2705).

(2) Where the seller discovers that the buyer has received goods on credit while insolvent he may reclaim the goods upon demand made within 10 days after the receipt, but if misrepresentation of solvency has been made to the particular seller in writing within three months before delivery the 10-day limitation does not apply. Except as provided in this subdivision the seller may not base a right to reclaim goods on the buyer's fraudulent or innocent misrepresentation of solvency or of intent to pay.

(3) The seller's right to reclaim under subdivision (2) is subject o the rights of a buyer in ordinary course or other good faith purchaser under the division (Section 2403). Successful reclamation of goods excludes all other remedies with respect to them (Stats. 1963, c. 819, 2702).

CHAPTER 4

Legal Issues of Consumers

The cliché phrase that used to permeate our society was "buyer beware." But during the 1970s the phrase gradually changed to "seller beware." At the same time, the federal and state governments enacted significant legislation designed to protect the consumer from abusive and coercive credit and collection practices (See Chapters 11, 12, 13, 14). In today's environment, the creditor must be careful to review these laws before proceeding with the collection effort. In this chapter, we will attempt to provide information concerning consumer exemptions and relationships between consumers which may affect the collection effort.

EXEMPTIONS

The federal government and the state authorities, always sympathetic to the impoverished citizen, have slowly and deliberately passed laws to protect the essential property of every citizen. An "exemption" means that this essential property may not be taken from the consumer before a law suit, during a lawsuit, or after a judgment has been obtained against the consumer.

The Fair Debt Collection Practices Act provides in Section 807, Subdivision 5, that:

> a debt collector may not use any false, deceptive or misleading representations or means in connection with the collection of any debt. Without limiting the general application of the foregoing, the following conduct is a violation of this debt ... the

threat to take any action that cannot legally be taken or that is not intended to be taken.

Thus the creditor may not take or threaten to take property that is "exempt." The particular assets may be cash, personal property, real estate, or a stream of income from a particular source such as wages, dividends, or interest income.

CREDIT AND COLLECTION TIP: *A frustrated telephone collector may easily violate this section of the act. Threats to take possession of jewelry, clothes, or farm animals are obvious violations. But a threat to attach alimony payments or social security, or suggesting to the consumer that the social security must be used to pay the debt also suffices as a violation.*

Household furniture is an example of "exempt" property. A prohibited telephone conversation would be as follows:

JUDGMENT CREDITOR:	Is Mrs. Smith there?
DEBTOR:	This is Mrs. Smith.
DEBT COLLECTOR:	This is the ABC Finance Company and I am calling about your loan. You haven't made any payments for the last three months. This is an attempt to collect a debt and any information obtained will be used for that purpose.
DEBTOR:	What are you talking about? I'm not behind three months; I'm only behind one month.
DEBT COLLECTOR:	Mrs. Smith, you are behind three months and it is going on four months. You were supposed to bring your loan up to date last time I spoke to you. You were three payments in arrears and you only made two payments at that time, so even then you were over a month behind and now in three days you are going to be three months behind.
DEBTOR:	I'm out of work right now and there is just nothing I can do to make payment. You will have to do whatever you want to do.
DEBT COLLECTOR:	Mrs. Smith, you wouldn't want us to come in there and take all your furniture and your bed and your chairs, would you? If you don't pay your bill, that's what will happen.

Since household furnishings are exempt, the debt collector has no right to threaten to remove them. If the property was not exempt, the debt collector would have to make a statement that suit would be started first. If the creditor is successful in obtaining a judgment and the property is not exempt, then the property could be sold. Therefore, the creditor should be careful to avoid any threats to seize any exempt assets, for such a threat may be a violation of the state laws which often apply to creditors. In addition, this threat is prohibited because it consists of a threat that must be fulfilled.

The federal law sets forth a list of exemptions and each of the fifty states has its own specified list. If the exemption in a particular state is broader or larger than the federal exemption, the consumer will be able to take advantage of the state exemption.

FEDERAL EXEMPTIONS: Under the federal law there are several exemptions which are well-known and recognized in the credit field.

1. When garnishing a salary, the federal law (as well as most state laws) allows the creditor to attach only a small percent of the salary of the individual. The amount depends upon the state.
2. Retirement income is exempt under the Employee Retirement Income Security Act (E.R.I.S.A.) 29 USC 1056 (D).
3. Veterans benefits are also exempt under 38 USC 30101 (A).
4. Social security payments are exempt under 42 USC 407 (A).
5. Civil Service Retirement Benefits are exempt under 5 UFSC 8346 (A).
6. Railroad Retirement Act annuities and pensions are exempt under 45 USC section 231 subdivision M (A).
7. Payments under the Longshoreman and Harbor Workers Compensation Act 33 USC 916 are exempt.

These exemptions are in addition to, and are to be distinguished from, the exemptions under the federal bankruptcy law, which are applicable only in a bankruptcy filing.

STATE EXEMPTIONS: Under the various state laws, a broad range of income and assets is exempt from execution. Examples of the types of exemptions are:

A. Alimony and support payments.
B. Appliances.
C. Cemetery plots.
D. Community property.
E. Homestead exemption. This is an exemption for the home occupied by the consumer. Each state protects the home of the resident in varying degrees, usually measured in dollars ranging from $5,000 to $10,000 in such states as New York or up to one million dollars in Florida. In a foreclosure or bank-

ruptcy, the amount set by the state is exempt, and may not be reached by the creditor conducting the sale. If real property (the principal residence) is sold at foreclosure and money is realized in excess of the amount of the mortgages, that money must be paid over to the owner of the property in an amount equal to the state or federal exemption.

F. Disability benefits.
G. Farm animals and feed.
H. Financial aid to students.
I. Household furnishings.
J. Insurance proceeds.
K. Jewelry.
L. Livestock.
M. Pension plan—in most states.
N. Personal effects—in most states a provision allows for an exemption for personal effects.
O. Public employee retirement benefits, vacation credits or other benefits.
P. Rental security deposits.
Q. Welfare benefits.
R. Unemployment benefits and contributions.
S. Wearing apparel.
T. Workman's compensation.
U. Wrongful death damages.

The list is far from inclusive, but the general area of exemptions is obvious. The lawmakers are primarily interested in protecting the debtor's household furniture and personal effects, and the stream of income from pension, retirement, and other payments which are necessary for the maintenance of the consumer.[1]

CREDIT AND COLLECTION TIP: *IRA and Keogh plans are not exempt under the federal law nor under many state laws where they can be attached, but this is changing in some states.*

The question of whether an exemption under the federal law will be recognized by the state has led to court decisions interpreting the preemption motivation of Congress. In some instances, the states have held that the federal exemp-

---

[1]California Exemptions Section Code of Civil Procedure Section 703.010 et seq.; Illinois Code of Civil Procedure Section 735 ILCS 5/12-1001 et seq; New York exemptions of certain insurance and annuity contracts Insurance Law Section 3212 New York C.P.L.R. section 5205 et seq.

tion does not pre-empt the laws of the state, whereas in most instances the federal law explicitly pre-empts the state law.[2]

Some of the district courts look upon the Fair Debt Collection Practices Act as a strict liability statute. Under these circumstances, debt collectors may be acting at their own peril in any effort to persuade debtors to utilize exempt income or exempt property.

A sample conversation might go as follows:

DEBT COLLECTOR: This mortgage is almost six month in arrears.

DEBTOR: I've been out of work for the last six months and I have been unable to make the payments. As a matter of fact, my wife and I had to go on welfare.

DEBT COLLECTOR: How much do you receive each month from welfare?

DEBTOR: We get food stamps and we receive $125 a week.

DEBT COLLECTOR: So, basically, you are getting $125 a week.

DEBTOR: Yeah, but I need the money for my wife and children and there's just no money to make the payments on this loan.

DEBT COLLECTOR: Maybe you can squeeze out a $25 payment to us once a month in order to keep this loan open, so I don't have to take any action under the judgment I have.

DEBTOR: You mean to tell me you can take my welfare benefits away?

DEBT COLLECTOR: I didn't say that exactly. I just want you to make a $25 payment.

DEBTOR: In the last letter you sent to me, you said you can levy on all my assets. Does that mean that the sheriff can take my welfare benefits to pay the debt?

DEBT COLLECTOR: I didn't say that exactly.

DEBTOR: You did say it in the letter. Isn't it a fact that you can't take my welfare benefits?

The use of a letter threatening a levy on the assets of a consumer may create an embarrassing situation. Sometimes collection letters are written with broad strokes and tend to include general terms referring to property and income. The letter must not mislead the consumer into believing that any exempt income or property can be subject to execution under the judgment. The question should not be evaded in the hope that the debtor might be persuaded to make a payment from the welfare income, as in the example above. A review of the collection letters should address those general and broad strokes.

---

[2]*Lanier Collection Agency & Service v. Mackey*, 2546 Ga. 499, 350 S.E. 2d 439 (Ga. 1986).

FLORIDA EXEMPTION

Some creditors are intimidated by the exemption laws in Florida, Texas and one or two other states. When a debtor moves to one of those states, the creditor may abandon an attempt to collect a debt and refuse to spend any money to collect the debt in the other state, because of the exemption laws.

In Florida, the exemption laws date back to 1868, when the state constitution was enacted and the homestead was originally restricted to the heads of household. Considerable litigation revolved around the question of whether or not a particular debtor qualified as head of the household. In 1985, the exemption was amended to apply to any person keeping a household of half an acre within a municipality or 160 acres outside of a municipality. Thus, any person who owns a home of any value on 160 acres of land outside of a municipality would be entitled to the exemption even if the home is valued at over a million dollars. If the husband and wife maintain separate residences, both parties may enjoy a homestead exemption under Florida law. Wages of a Florida resident are also exempt, as are bank accounts, but if both husband and wife work and live in the same household, the wages of only one spouse are exempt.

Florida has thus become a magnet for people seeking to avoid paying their debts, but sometimes they find that the homestead exemption is not available. The Florida courts insist that the party's legal residence be in Florida to take advantage of the exemption, and they require some form of corroboration of the intent of the party. Merely stating what your intent is without substantiation is not sufficient.

The Florida courts will consider where the party is employed, where he or she is registered to vote, the address on the driver's license and the address on the federal income tax return. People who visit Florida are not necessarily entitled to the benefits of the exemption. The debtor must intend to use Florida as a residence and must be present in Florida on a continuing basis. The fact that the debtor is present in the state for a period of time without any intention of remaining will usually be insufficient. The debtor must offer some evidence of the intention to reside in Florida, at least in the foreseeable future.[3]

The above analysis applies to a greater or lesser degree to the other states which are favorable to debtors, such as Texas, North Carolina, South Carolina, and Pennsylvania, in which creditors are prohibited from garnishing salaries of debtors.

If the amount is substantial, the creditor should not abandon pursuing a debtor in a "debtor's state," but should determine whether the debtor still maintains personal and business ties within the original state. If that is the fact, counsel may be able to pursue the debtor in both states.

---

[3]*Judd v. Schooley*, 158 So.2d 514 (Florida, 1963) (separate residence). *In re Cooke*, 412 So.2d 340 (Florida, 1982) (tourist or temporary residence not entitled to exemption). *Bloomfield v. City of St. Petersburg Beach*, 82 So.2d 364 (Florida, 1955) (intention).

CREDIT AND COLLECTION TIP: *In recent years, our experience has found that recording judgment liens from other states under full faith and credit is worthwhile, especially in Florida. With interest rates low, and parties refinancing, our firm has seen many loans paid so that the debtor could refinance the mortgage at a lower rate. It may be worthwhile to consider this procedure depending on the debtor's financial position.*

CREDIT PRACTICES ACT

The Credit Practices Act was enacted by the Federal Trade Commission to prohibit creditors from using certain contract provisions that the Commission found to be unfair to consumers. In addition, the new Act requires creditors to inform consumers who co-sign obligations about their liability if the borrower fails to pay the obligation. Finally, the rule sets certain restrictions on assessing late charges.

The Credit Practices Act prohibits creditors from including the following provisions in any consumer credit contract.

(A) CONFESSION OF JUDGMENT: Confessions of judgment, or "cognovit" notes, are agreements wherein the debtor is obligated to make payment. These notes authorize the creditor to appear in court and confess judgment on behalf of the debtor in the event the payment schedule is breached or the agreed payment is not made when due. A confession of judgment allows a judgment to be entered in favor of the creditor automatically when the debtor is in breach of the contract. "Automatically" means that the creditor does not usually have to appear in court, and in some states is allowed to submit an affidavit in lieu of that appearance. Based upon this affidavit by the attorney that the debtor has not made payments as agreed in the confession of judgment, the clerk of the court will enter the judgment without any further court proceedings (such as allowing the debtor to appear and contest the entry of judgment). The Credit Practices Act prohibits creditors from using a confession of judgment provision in a consumer credit contract. (This is still permitted in commercial transactions.)

(B) WAIVER OF EXEMPTION: Some consumer credit contracts previously contained a waiver of exemption provision which permitted creditors to seize specific property even if the property was exempt under state law. Such provisions are expressly prohibited.

(C) ASSIGNMENT OF WAGES: In some states, consumers were permitted to assign their wages, or a part of their wages, to creditors in the event of a default under an obligation, such as a loan or a purchase of goods on time. The problem with this device is that the debtor lost a portion of the salary without notice and without being able to assert any defense. Over the past 20 years, most states have prohibited this practice by passing specific laws. Under the new rule, such an assignment of wages is expressly prohibited. The only way a creditor can take a portion of a consumer's salary is to institute a suit, obtain a judgment and issue a garnishment to the sheriff.

(D) SECURITY AGREEMENT—HOUSEHOLD GOODS: The rule provides that a creditor is prohibited from obtaining a security agreement on household goods whether or not the household goods are exempt under state law. Certain personal property such as works of art, electronic entertainment equipment and other items acquired as antiques and jewelry (except wedding rings) as well as pianos, musical instruments, boats, snowmobiles, bicycles, cameras, and similar items may be offered to creditors as security under a security agreement to secure the loan.

(E) CO-SIGNER: The new rule requires a co-signer of a loan to be specifically informed of the potential liability before signing the obligation of the debt. A specific written statement must be included in the loan document in which the liability of the co-signer is specifically described. The law sets forth the wording of the document and informs the co-signer that the debt must be paid directly to the creditor if the borrower does not pay, and that the creditor may proceed against the co-signer without proceeding against the borrower. The co-signer must also be informed that if the debt should be in default, the default and loan will become a part of the credit record of the co-signer. The state may provide for a different notice, which must be included in addition to the notice under the Credit Practices Act. The law also requires that the notice be in the same language as the agreement to which it applies so that if the agreement is in Spanish, the notice must be in Spanish.

A co-signer is different from a co-buyer, co-borrower, or co-applicant, because a co-signer receives no tangible benefits from the agreement, but usually undertakes the liability as a favor to the principal debtor who would not otherwise qualify for credit. On the other hand, co-buyers, co-borrowers, or co-applicants do receive certain benefits. They are not considered co-signers under the rule and are not entitled to the required notice.

(F) LATE FEES: "Pyramiding of late charges" occurs when one payment is made after its due date and a late fee is assessed, but not paid promptly. All future payments are considered delinquent even though they are paid in full within the required time period. As a result, late fees are assessed on all future payments. This particular practice is now prohibited.

GARNISHMENT AND HOMESTEAD EXEMPTION

The Consumer Credit Protection Act limits the maximum amount that can be garnished to 30 times the minimum wage (currently $5.15). The great majority of states have an exemption of either 30 or 40 times the federal minimum wage, and most states also permit 75% of net weekly take-home pay as an exemption, whichever amount is greater. Florida, North Carolina, Pennsylvania, and Texas completely exempt the wages of the heads of household from any form of garnishment, although there are signs North Carolina and Pennsylvania legislatures are reviewing these exemptions. Some of the other states have fairly liberal exemption laws such as:

A. Connecticut–75% of the weekly wages

B. Missouri–90% for the head of a family

C. Illinois–85% of weekly disposable earnings or an amount by which such earnings exceed 40 times the minimum wage.

Some states allow only a minimum percentage of the salary to be garnished, such as 15% in Illinois, and only 10% in Missouri and New York.

Florida has a $500-a-week exemption for heads of household, but not for their spouses. Alaska has an exemption of 65 times the state minimum wage for heads of household. South Dakota has an exemption of 80% or 40 times the minimum wage plus $25 for each dependent. The garnishee in Wisconsin is also 80% exempt.

With regard to homestead exemptions for the household residence of the debtor and family, only Connecticut, Delaware, Maryland, New Jersey, Pennsylvania, and the District of Columbia do not provide for some sort of exemption. The most favorable state is Florida, which allows an exemption up to 160 acres and no minimum dollar amount. Accordingly, a debtor could purchase a residence for a million dollars and every dollar of it would be exempt. Massachusetts allows for $100,000 for a principal family residence, but the exemption is not available for debts arising after the purchase of the homestead nor for support payments for spouses or children. Arizona is also liberal in allowing $100,000 as an exemption on a personal residence. Many of the states make distinctions between heads of households as opposed to individuals and also do not exempt the personal residence where the debts involve child support or alimony.

Under the federal law, there are many exemptions which are well-known and recognized such as retirement income under the Employment Retirement Income Security Act, Veterans' Benefits, Social Security payments, Civil Service Retirement Benefits, Railroad Retirement Benefits and longshoremen and harbor workers' compensation.

CREDIT AND COLLECTION TIPS: *These exemptions are to be distinguished from exemptions under the Federal Bankruptcy Law which are only applicable in the event of a bankruptcy filing.*

DIRECT DEPOSIT AND GARNISHMENT

While some states prohibit wage garnishing, they do not prohibit execution on a debtor's bank account.

What happens when a debtor has a direct deposit account? This situation enables a creditor to obtain an entire paycheck or even two payments before the debtor can notify his employer. In some states, it's not considered wage garnishment and you can take all non-exempt monies in the account. In other states, the courts consider it a wage garnishment and the creditor is only entitled to a percentage of the wage check proportioned to the statutory scheme. (Failure to reduce the hold to that balance could constitute a violation of the exemption.)

WELFARE RECIPIENTS

Welfare income is exempt from attachment, and therefore cannot be attached even if the welfare check is deposited in a bank account. If the creditor attaches the bank account, the consumer may assert that the monies attached are the proceeds from a welfare check and, upon application, the court would order the creditor to release the account.

Nevertheless, welfare recipients can be sued for a just debt and a judgment can be obtained against them. A welfare recipient is still liable for the debt notwithstanding that he or she is receiving welfare payments. When the recipient returns to the work force, welfare payments cease and the wages can be garnished. If the debtor owns a car, a boat, or other assets from more prosperous times, they may be attached providing no exemption exists under federal or state law.

SOCIAL SECURITY

As with welfare, social security is also exempt under state law. Social security recipients are not prohibited from receiving a certain limited amount of income which can be from a job, from consulting or from doing part-time work as an independent contractor. While social security may be exempt from execution, the other stream of income or other assets acquired when the consumer worked may be subject to levy or execution, depending upon the nature of the income and assets. A telephone conversation with the debtor may proceed as follows:

CREDITOR: Your credit card account is past due almost five months and we must have some form of payment arrangement.

DEBTOR: I just retired and right now I'm on social security so you can do what you want.

CREDITOR: How much social security do you receive a month?

DEBTOR: My social security is about $1,500 a month.

CREDITOR: Do you earn or receive any other income outside of your social security?

DEBTOR: I told you I receive social security and what I do otherwise is none of your business.

CREDITOR: You didn't answer the question as to whether you receive any additional income. Do you hold a part-time job?

In the above instance, the debtor may be earning or receiving other income (such as holding a part-time job). Social security is intended to replace earnings lost because of the retirement of the wage earner. Any income received from savings, investments or insurance, which may be substantial, will not affect the monthly benefits. However, certain social security recipients work. The general rule is that if earnings are more than the annual exempt amount, the social security payment will be reduced one dollar for each two dollars of earnings above the annual exempt amount. (Once people reach the age of seventy the debtor may earn any amount and still collect social security.) Social security is an indication of age, but not necessarily ability to pay.

CREDIT AND COLLECTION TIP: *When the party acknowledges receiving social security, this should be the beginning, not the end, of the telephone conversation. The creditor should then inquire as to what the personal assets are and whether the debtor has any other income.*

RESPONSIBILITY OF PARENTS

The position of most states is that necessities for children are the responsibility of the parents. Unless the parents are divorced, separated or living apart, both parents are jointly liable for the debts of the children, and each parent is liable individually for the debts of the children.

CREDIT AND COLLECTION TIP: *Submit to the parent an agreement acknowledging liability. Several gray areas exist in which a product or service may or may not be a necessity.*

The parent who has custody of the child is normally liable for the necessities of that child which consist of food, lodging, medical, educational and clothing needs. Necessities do not include luxury items and probably not educational items purchased by the child which are partly educational and partly for amusement, such as video cassettes which are marginally educational.

Accordingly, clothing, shoes, medical supplies, doctor's bills, prescriptions, school supplies and similar items would fall under the classification of "necessities." On the other hand, bicycles, athletic equipment, records, CD tapes, audio tapes, toys, Nintendo and other items for entertainment or amusement would not.

A child may disaffirm a contract entered into while he or she was under the age of eighteen. Sometimes the merchandise is designed for children under the age of 18, and the order form bears only the child's signature. In these instances, the creditor cannot proceed against the child or parent, but may only request that the parents pay the debt. Any letters or communications must be addressed to the parents of the child and should clearly and conspicuously state that parents have no obligation to pay the child's debt. Most reputable law firms and collection agencies include this wording in their collection letters and in their telephone calls:

DEBT COLLECTOR: May I speak to the parents of Robert Arnold Smith?

MOTHER: Yes, this is his mother.

DEBT COLLECTOR: We sent Robert a set of video tapes on dinosaurs and reptiles, and we have not received payment for those tapes.

MOTHER: He did order them, but we didn't even know about him ordering them. He should know better than to order that kind of material.

DEBT COLLECTOR: He did receive the tapes and I assume that he used them.

MOTHER: He looked at them once and one of the tapes got broken. I don't even know where they are anymore. I don't think I have any obligation to pay for the tapes. You should not have accepted an order from a child.

DEBT COLLECTOR: But, the child did accept the tapes and he did use the tapes and therefore he is responsible to pay for the tapes.

MOTHER: I'm sorry. He may have used the tapes. I don't know whether he is responsible for payment. I don't even know if he understands at the age of twelve years old that he has to pay. If you speak to my husband, he'll tell you that none of the children knows the value of a dollar.

DEBT COLLECTOR: I don't know whether your son knows the value of a dollar, but the tapes were sent and the price was $49.95 and we must insist upon payment.

MOTHER: Well, you can insist upon payment, but I don't think that I have any obligation to pay for this debt.

The debt collector avoided communicating to the consumer that she actually had no obligation to pay the debt, but inferred that the child did. Both of these failures would probably constitute a violation of the Fair Debt Collection Practices Act. The debt collector has misrepresented to the debtor that both mother and child may be obligated for this debt. In fact, the child has an absolute right to disaffirm the contract and the parent is not responsible for the child's debt except to the extent of food, lodging, and necessities. A tape on the lifestyle of dinosaurs and reptiles does not fall under the heading of necessities, and whether it is educational may be debatable. On the other hand, if the parent made the purchase and signed the document or personally ordered the merchandise, then the parent would be liable. The problem arises only when the child makes the purchase.

HUSBANDS AND WIVES

Under common law, a married woman's legal identity merged with that of her husband, a condition known as coverture. The wife was unable to own any property, she could not enter into contracts, nor did anyone extend credit to her. A married woman was dependent upon her husband for maintenance and support and, as a result, he was under a duty to provide his wife with food, clothing, and shelter, as well as medical services. The doctrine of necessities mitigated the possible effects of coverture in the event the husband failed to fulfill his support obligation. Therefore, her husband was liable to any third party for any necessities that the third party creditor provided to the wife. Because the duty of this support was unique to the husband's obligation, and because coverture restricted the wife's access to the economic realm of credit, the doctrine normally did not impose a similar liability upon married women.

The wife's "necessities" are much broader and more general in scope than are those of a child. The wife's necessities certainly include food, clothing, lodging, and medical expenses and probably exclude education, entertainment, amusement, and athletics. If the husband makes the purchase for the wife, the husband is liable whether or not it is a necessity. On the other hand, if the wife makes the purchase, the husband is liable only for a necessity.

While the general law is that the husband is liable for the necessities of the wife, the law in the various states is a mixture and is changing on a day-to-day basis.

A recent case in Florida held that the husband was no longer liable for the wife's necessities. The court acknowledged the fact that the disability of coverture was basically abrogated and that the responsibilities between husband and wife in many instances are now reciprocal obligations.[4] The courts in other states have split on this question of necessities, which is treated differently both from a statutory viewpoint and as to the way the courts evaluate the obligation.[5]

---

[4]*Connor v. Southwest Florida Regional Medical Center, Inc.*, 668 So.2d 175 (Fla. 1995).

[5]Ibid.

The court pointed out that some states have abrogated the doctrine entirely, leaving to the legislature the final decision, such as in Alabama, Maryland and Virginia. Other states have extended the common law doctrine to apply reciprocally, so that the husband is liable for the wife's necessities and the wife is liable for the husband's necessities, such as in Indiana, Kansas, New Jersey, North Carolina, Rhode Island and South Carolina. Two states, Oklahoma and Kentucky, have codified the doctrine in its original common law form requiring the husband to be liable for the wife, but the wife is not liable for the husband. Minnesota recently altered the common law "doctrine of necessities" and limited the ability of creditors and collectors to hold a spouse liable for the debts of the other spouse. The law clearly states that the spouse is not liable to a creditor for any debts of the other spouse. If the spouses are living together, they are jointly and severely liable for necessary household articles and supplies furnished to and used by the family. Either spouse is allowed to close a credit card account for the other's unsecured consumer line of credit on which both spouses are liable if they give a written notice to the creditor. North Dakota imposes joint and several liability for debts incurred by either spouse for the necessities of food, clothing, fuel and shelter, but expressly excludes medical care. A review of the state law is essential before proceeding against either a husband or wife based on the theory of necessities; the law on this subject is changing radically state by state, year to year.

The wife may not be liable even if she executes an instrument as a guarantor or co-signer for the husband's obligations under circumstances when the bank is not relying on her financial condition to extend the credit to the husband (see Chapter on Equal Credit Opportunity). In eight states (Arizona, California, Idaho, Louisiana, Nevada, New Mexico, Texas, and Washington) which have community property laws, whatever is purchased after marriage belongs to both the husband and wife, and they both jointly and severally would be liable for the said purchases. A decision in 1998 held that a retail installment contract which contained an arbitration clause was enforceable even if only the husband signed it and the wife did not sign it.[6]

JOINTLY HELD PROPERTY

When a young couple purchases their first home, the title is normally transferred to both the husband and the wife. Usually the designation on the deed is "joint tenants with right of survivorship" or words of similar import. The legal effect of such a transfer of title to a husband and wife is that if one of the spouses dies, the surviving spouse acquires title to the property free and clear of any claims or judgments against the deceased spouse.

---

[6]*Nationwide of Bryan Inc. d/b/a Nationwide Housing Systems Inc. v. Daryll D. Dyer & Sherry Dyer*, 968 S.W. 2d 518 (S.W. App. 1998).

The net effect of joint ownership is that most creditors do not execute on a judgment against jointly owned property. In the event a creditor obtains a judgment against the husband, the recourse of the creditor is to sell the husband's interest at a sheriff's sale and use the proceeds to satisfy the judgment. The creditor—wearing a different robe—becomes a buyer at the sale, buys, and thus becomes the owner of the husband's interest. Whatever was paid at the sale is used to pay the judgment, similar to moving money from one pocket to the other pocket: the creditor bids $1,000 at the sale, the sheriff deducts the fees for the sale and remits $900 to the creditor to pay the judgment.

The creditor now is a joint owner with the wife. The creditor cannot evict either the husband or wife, but must wait to see which spouse survives. If the husband dies first, the creditor has no claim against the wife and the wife becomes the owner of the property free of any claims of the creditor. However, if the wife dies first, the creditor becomes the owner of the property.

The better course for the creditor is to have the judgment recorded as a lien against the real estate and hope that a time will come when the husband and wife will sell their home. The lien will remain on record from 10 to 20 years, depending upon state law. At the time of the sale, any purchaser of the property will require the husband and wife to discharge the debt, since the purchaser does not want to own the property with a lien in favor of a judgment creditor.

The first evidence of this occurrence is a telephone call from the judgment debtor who has not been heard from for several years. The judgment debtor will probably offer a settlement of substantially less than the face amount of the judgment. In most instances, when a judgment debtor makes a telephone call to the creditor after many years, the judgment debtor probably owns real estate and is attempting to sell the property, but the purchaser wants the debtor to discharge the judgment lien. In many instances, the judgment creditor may not have known that the debtor owned real estate, but the attorney took the precaution of filing the judgment as a lien against any property in the county where the judgment debtor resided.

The same rules apply to personal property owned jointly between a husband and wife, such as a joint checking account or joint ownership of a boat. In each of these instances, the disadvantaged judgment creditor must wait to determine who the survivor is.

Sometimes property is owned by a husband and wife as "tenants in common." Property may be held in this way by any two persons who do not have to be husband and wife. The distinction between "tenants in common" and "joint tenants with the right of survivorship" is that tenants in common own a separate undivided one-half of the property. The undivided one-half would be subject to execution by the creditor. The creditor who obtains a judgment may hold a sheriff's sale and cause the one-half interest in the property to be sold at public sale. In the event there is no purchaser at the sale, the judgment creditor could purchase the interest and thus become the one-half owner with the other tenant in common. The distinct advantage is that the creditor may then either seek to partition the property or apply to court for an order directing the entire property to be sold, and the creditor/owner would be entitled to one half of the sale price less expenses.

COMMUNITY PROPERTY

There are currently eight states which still enforce community property laws: Arizona, California, Idaho, Louisiana, Nevada, New Mexico, Texas, and Washington. The main reason for the law of community property is to allocate any property acquired after the marriage to each party on a fifty-fifty basis. The theory behind this is that marriage is similar to a partnership and that any property acquired after the marriage should be equally divided between the husband and wife. Thus, the heir of the husband and wife will receive the share that the husband and wife are entitled to from the property acquired after marriage.

If properties were acquired before the marriage, and were owned separately by the wife, the creditor may treat them as belonging to the wife and the said properties may be used as collateral for a loan without the other spouse's signature or consent. When the wife and husband conduct a business, in some states the income and profits from that business will belong to the individual who is conducting the business, whereas in other states it may become part of the community property.

The laws of the community property states are different in many respects with regard to creditors. For example, in some states community property may be subject to execution even if the debt was incurred solely by one spouse. In other states, the result is almost the opposite. In some states, the husband may incur the debt for the total community property and in other states only the husband and wife jointly may incur debt for the community property. In some states, clear distinctions are drawn if the indebtedness is secured by the residence. A careful review of the laws of the community property states must be made before extending credit or using collection efforts against the community property.

DIVORCES

Parties engaged in obtaining a divorce frequently stop paying their debts until the divorce proceedings is finalized either by written agreement or court order. If the only wage earner is the husband, the wife must look to him for payment of debts and the husband may deliberately withhold payment as a negotiating tool. Lawyers tend to thrive on these situations, and creditors are then faced with the unusual situation where money is available, but debts are not paid.

A hypothetical telephone conversation:

CREDITOR:	We have sent you several notices and we still have not received any payment.
DEBTOR:	I'm divorcing my husband and he is going to pay all my debts.
CREDITOR:	When will he start making the payments?
DEBTOR:	I don't know exactly when. My attorneys are fighting with his attorneys and we're still arguing over the house and the BMW and the dog and tickets to the U.S. Open, but I think we should have everything settled pretty quickly.
CREDITOR:	What do you mean pretty quickly?
DEBTOR:	I really don't know. Pretty quickly. As soon as it's settled, my husband said that he will continue to pay the balance on my credit card. If you want, I can give you my husband's name and the address at which he is now living, but it's a hotel and I think he will be checking out shortly.

The first important consideration is that the debt is based on the wife's credit card and therefore the wife is primarily liable. While the husband may also be liable, the wife is primarily liable for payment since she obligated herself to pay the debt and is over the age of eighteen years. The creditor's approach is that the wife is liable for the debt, and suit may be instituted against her. The creditor has no interest in the negotiations between the husband and the wife, and is not bound by them, even though circumstances exist under which the husband may be liable for payment of the debt by reason of a necessity furnished to the wife.

After the couple separates, the husband is usually not responsible for the debts incurred by the wife for luxury items and, in some instances under state laws, for necessities. A review of the state laws is absolutely necessary.

Sometimes a husband will publish advertisements to notify creditors not to extend further credit to his wife. In some states, such a notice can relieve the husband of future liability.

CREDIT AND COLLECTION TIP: *Divorce negotiations can drag on indefinitely and wives are often overly optimistic about the obligations to be undertaken by their husbands to pay off their debts. Where the wife is primarily or jointly liable, the creditor should rely on the wife's ability to repay the debt, and proceed quickly to obtain a judgment as other creditors are doing the same thing. A judgment creditor is in a better bargaining position since the debt cannot be disputed. Many joint debts are usually paid pursuant to the divorce agreement.*

DECEASED PERSONS

The first notification that the debtor has died usually happens during a collection telephone call to the debtor's number. The response is frequently that since the relative has passed away, the family does not want to be bothered by any collection calls. The fact that a party has died does not mean the debt is uncollectible, although there are some difficulties.

A major problem is property owned jointly between the husband and the wife. If a husband and a wife jointly own a private home, the property will pass to the surviving spouse automatically and the deceased party will have no further interest. A creditor cannot proceed against the house owned by the surviving spouse for any debt of the deceased spouse. The same rule applies to bank accounts which are held jointly between a husband and wife. Upon presentation of a death certificate to the bank, the money automatically is transferred into the surviving spouse's name and the creditor will be unable to attach or levy on the account.

Where the property is held in the individual name of the debtor (which is most cases), papers must be filed with the proper Surrogate Court (probate court) to commence a "probate" proceeding in order to distribute the property to beneficiaries. A "probate" is a proceeding where the administrator or executor of the estate collects all the assets of the deceased, pays all the debts, deducts the expenses of administration and distributes the balance to the beneficiaries under the will, or if there is no will, according to the state law. Creditors are allowed to assert in the probate proceedings their claims for any debts owed to the creditor by the deceased party. The normal method is to inquire whether a probate proceeding (estate) has been filed. The information needed is the name of the court in which the estate has been filed and the index number of the filing. The names and addresses of the executor or administrator of the estate and the attorney for the executor or administrator are helpful.

A typical conversation follows:

CREDITOR: May I please speak to Mrs. Smith?

DEBTOR: Mrs. Smith just passed away two days ago.

CREDITOR: To whom am I speaking?

DEBTOR: This is her daughter.

CREDITOR: I'm sorry to hear that. I will call in a few weeks.

DEBTOR: Thank you very much. Goodbye.

At this particular time it would be futile to try to determine whether the decedent has property and whether the beneficiaries are filing an estate. The procedures to probate a will (file an estate) are usually delayed for several weeks to months after the date of death. The follow-up conversation:

CREDITOR: This is Mr. Grant from the XYZ department store and I'm calling about the open charge account bill of Mrs. Ann Smith.

DEBTOR: Mrs. Smith died.

CREDITOR:	When did she die?
DEBTOR:	She died about two months ago.
CREDITOR:	Has someone retained an attorney to handle her affairs?
DEBTOR:	Yes, we've retained an attorney. What's this about?
CREDITOR:	This is about a debt owed to the XYZ department store. She had a charge account here and there's a balance of $550 still open. We'd like to know the name of the attorney handling the estate.
DEBTOR:	The attorney is John Mitchell at 14 Main Street, Centerville. Telephone number 555-1212.
CREDITOR:	Tell me, have probate papers been filed?
DEBTOR:	Yes, we did sign some papers to file them in court.
CREDITOR:	Could you tell me what court that is?
DEBTOR:	Probate court of the County of Centerville.
CREDITOR:	Do you know the index number?
DEBTOR:	No, the attorney would probably know that.
CREDITOR:	Who's the executor of the estate?
DEBTOR:	My sister and I.
CREDITOR:	What's your name and address?
DEBTOR:	I told you that my name is Frank Smith and my sister is Marilyn Smith. Speak to our attorney.
CREDITOR:	Thank you very much. I will get in touch with your attorney.

At this stage of the proceedings, obtain from the attorney the proper index number and name of the estate under which the papers have been filed so that a proof of claim can be filed. A proof of claim may be furnished by the attorney for the executor for the estate or may be obtained from a stationery store or from the court itself. Consult with counsel to file the proper papers.

If efforts to contact survivors prove futile, your attorney may search the record of the Surrogate Court where the debtor died to determine if the debtor has filed an estate.

Probate proceedings are only necessary where property is in the name of the deceased and must be transferred to a beneficiary. In many cases the assets of the deceased were transferred prior to death, and thus the deceased has no assets at the time of death. In other cases the only assets are jointly owned with a spouse or relative, such as the house or bank account, and in such case the property "automatically" is transferred to the survivor without a probate proceeding. If no probate proceeding is filed with the court, and the creditor suspects the debtor had assets at his death, consult with counsel for there are remedies available.

CREDIT CARDS

The increase in the use of phones to sell merchandise, now known as telemarketing, and the explosion of the direct marketing industry over the past ten years, have presented certain credit and collection problems that were once rare but are now quite common. In today's environment, a merchant frequently will take an order over the telephone for which a customer will use a credit card. In order to control fraud, certain procedures should be followed.

A. Always obtain:
1. the name and address of the purchaser.
2. the card number and the name of the credit card.
3. the expiration date of the credit card.
4. the name and address of the issuing bank.
5. the telephone number of the customer.
B. If an individual is ordering, obtain a home telephone number and, if necessary an office or work telephone number.
C. If a company is placing the order, obtain its telephone number and the home address of the individual placing the order.
D. Obtain the source code, if used. In direct marketing the source code is on the mailing label and identifies the specific mailing.
E. If the merchandise is unique to an advertisement over radio or TV, ask when the offer was made or when the TV advertisement was seen.

Where the purchaser is seeking credit, the creditor is entitled to ask any question that relates to the credit of the individual providing the creditor complies with the Equal Credit Opportunity Act and does not discriminate. Asking the home address of a business employee who is placing an order for merchandise over the telephone, where the individual is acting on behalf of the business, is a reasonable request before the creditor extends credit. The purpose of asking questions is to smoke out credit card fraud or a stolen credit card. The more questions asked, the more likely a stolen credit card or a credit card fraud will be identified. If the customer has problems in answering the questions or refuses to answer, the creditor may decide to withhold shipment. The above questions may be expanded depending upon how much time the merchant allocates to the credit checking process which is usually a function of the amount of the order.

The merchant could call the telephone number furnished to verify if the individual is there or whether the company is a viable business. Such a call may furnish more significant information than verifying a bank account or obtaining a credit report on a business.

An example of a telephone conversation:

CREDITOR:	Can I help you?
DEBTOR:	Yes, I would like to order some office equipment from your catalog. I need two boxes of fine point pens, and a box of computer paper, a magnifying glass, a ruler, and a box of tape.
CREDITOR:	Is this your first time ordering from our company?
DEBTOR:	Yes, it is.
CREDITOR:	How do you intend to pay for this?
DEBTOR:	A credit card.
CREDITOR:	Do you have a business corporate card by American Express or Diner's Club?
DEBTOR:	No, I'm using my boss' Visa Card.
CREDITOR:	What is your name?
DEBTOR:	My name is Mary Jones.
CREDITOR:	The items you wanted are two boxes of fine point pens, product number 5749, a magnifying glass, product number 9485, a ruler, product number 3968, a box of tape, product number 3958, and a box of computer paper, product number 3963.
DEBTOR:	Yes, those are the items and product numbers.
CREDITOR:	Do you wish to order anything else?
DEBTOR:	No, just those things.
CREDITOR:	What is the name and address of the company?
DEBTOR:	The Smith Plumbing Supply Company and the address is 420 Main Street, Centerville.
CREDITOR:	Do you want the merchandise shipped to that address?
DEBTOR:	Yes.
CREDITOR:	Is there any room number or floor number?
DEBTOR:	No.
CREDITOR:	What is your job there?
DEBTOR:	I am the bookkeeper.
CREDITOR:	What is the name of the principal owner?
DEBTOR:	Charlie Smith.
CREDITOR:	How long have you been working there?
DEBTOR:	Why is that any of your business?
CREDITOR:	You are placing an order for Mr. Smith and we would like to know how long you have been working there.
DEBTOR:	I've been working here about a year or so.
CREDITOR:	What is your home address?

DEBTOR: I don't have to give you my home address.

CREDITOR: You're placing an order and we would like to verify who you are and that you are the bookkeeper. We will call back at another time to verify this order. Do you have an objection to that?

DEBTOR: I don't have an objection to that. I gave the name and address of the firm. You haven't even asked for the credit card number.

CREDITOR: Yes, I do want Mr. Smith's credit card number.

DEBTOR: The card is a Visa Card. The number is 1111-3333-6666-1212.

CREDITOR: What is the expiration date?

DEBTOR: The date is December of 1996.

CREDITOR: Issuing bank?

DEBTOR: Citibank.

CREDITOR: Can you tell me how long Mr. Smith has been in business?

DEBTOR: About ten years or so.

CREDITOR: How many people does he employ?

DEBTOR: I guess about 5 or 6 people.

CREDITOR: I'm just trying to get information concerning your employer so that we can approve shipping the merchandise you are ordering.

DEBTOR: Do you need any more information?

CREDITOR: No, that will be good for now. Thank you.

The creditor probably was suspicious about the nature of the order for the business. Each item was very small and could be used by an individual at home as opposed to a business. Not one product ordered, such as one box of computer paper or one roll of tape, is indigenous to a business. Usually several rolls of tape are ordered. The bookkeeper's reluctance to answer the questions and her uncertainty about the size of the business also might lead the creditor to be suspicious. The next step would be for the creditor to make a call back to the debtor and attempt to contact Mr. Smith himself.

When a credit card is offered for payment of merchandise, the merchant should not accept the order simply based on the fact that the credit card company has advised the merchant that the card number represents a valid account and that the customer has not used up the credit line. The merchant has no assurance that the party placing the order is the same person who actually owns the credit card. The mere fact that the credit card company has approved the account only assures the merchant that a valid account is under that name and card number, but it does not assure that the party signing the credit card slip or furnishing a credit card number over the telephone is the person entitled to use the credit card.

MERCHANT AGREEMENT

A merchant enters into an agreement with its bank and not with Visa or Mastercard. Each bank prepares a separate agreement with any merchant who accepts its Visa and Mastercard and each agreement prepared by the bank is different from any other agreement. A standard agreement does not really exist, although Visa and Mastercard do require certain terms and conditions. The legal liabilities of the merchant and the cardholder are controlled by the written agreements and should be reviewed by an attorney prior to execution.[7] Remember that agreements are negotiable if the terms and conditions are not satisfactory to the merchant. Said terms and conditions may be compromised, modified and adjusted providing the bank wants the business of the merchant. If the bank is independent and not anxious for the business, the agreement will be presented as a "fait accompli" and the bank will accept no changes.

CHARGE BACKS

Charge backs occur when the customer claims that the merchandise was returned, was never delivered, or for some reason the customer refuses to accept the charge. Normally, the merchant will accept a reasonable amount of charge backs from customers without questioning their bank. Sometimes the merchant agreement states charge backs cannot be disputed if the customer ordered by phone or not on site and the merchant may have to absorb a substantial loss. Nevertheless, when the charge back is not warranted, the merchant is urged to persuade its bank to return the charge to the cardholder bank. Frequently, the merchant will ask its bank not to accept the charge back for 60 days to enable the merchant to collect and submit documentation to its bank. The bank sends this documentation to the cardholder's bank showing that the merchandise was delivered to the customer, that the customer signed for the merchandise, and that the customer retained the merchandise for a month or longer. Based on this set of circumstances or other convincing documentation, the cardholder's bank should charge the cardholder's account.

SOLDIERS AND SAILORS CIVIL RELIEF ACT

The Soldiers and Sailors Civil Relief Act expressly provides for a moratorium on all suits against members of the military service. The purpose of the Act is to allow persons in military service to appear in court and to properly defend a suit brought against them. If the debtor is reassigned by the Army or Navy to another post or

---

[7]*Franklin National Bank vs. Kass*, 19 Misc. 2d 280 (1959), *American Express Co. vs. Geller*, 343 NYS 2d 644 (1973).

overseas, the person in military service will not be able to defend a suit and the plaintiff will not be able to obtain a judgment because of his or her default.

But what about the professional soldier who remains in service for twenty or thirty years? The courts address this situation by stating that this law is designed to protect the serviceperson's right to appear in court and properly defend a lawsuit. If he or she is not at a disadvantage by reason of military service, the lawsuit may proceed. If the serviceperson is in the regular army and has been assigned to one post for a long time, the plaintiff may institute suit in the jurisdiction where the post is located, allege to the court that the party has been located at this post on an almost permanent basis for may years and will not suffer prejudice since relocation is unlikely. Thus, the serviceperson is able to appear and defend the action. If there is a failure to appear, the court may permit the creditor to enter a default judgment against the serviceperson. We recommend consulting with an attorney before a suit is abandoned against a member of the military service, especially in peace time when the military are assigned to a post for an extensive period of time. Furthermore, in 1994, garnishment of the wages of a member of the military service is available.

FEDERAL GARNISHMENT

Under the federal garnishment law, the wages of federal employees or members of the military may be garnished. A judgment must be obtained in the state and county in which the debtor works and service must be made on the payroll office in the location where the debtor works. If the debtor resides in one state and works in a second state, suit must first be instituted in the state in which the debtor resides. Notwithstanding the federal garnishment, Pennsylvania, Texas, Florida (head of household), South Carolina, North Carolina still prohibit garnishment.

With regard to suits against the military, the Soldiers and Sailors Civil Relief Act still provides for a moratorium on suits against personnel in the military. On the other hand, the Soldiers and Sailors Act has always allowed suits against career military personnel who maintain offices at one base for an extensive period of time so that they have sufficient time to defend themselves in any legal proceeding. With garnishment now available, suits against military personnel should be reviewed.

Another important part of the law is that federal garnishments are available for any judgments which have been entered in the past, prior to the enactment of the law. Therefore, if you do have old judgments against federal government employees, reactivate them and utilize this law.

The law permits the creditor to deduct up to 25% of the debtor's wages unless state law provides for a lesser amount, which is the case in many states. The creditor must only provide a copy of judgment, and the amount of interest set forth in the judgment can be collected. (In the initial rules, suit had to be instituted separately for the interest.) If the commander determines that the debtor's absence was due to exigencies of military duty, the rule provides a right of appeal.

A garnishment may be denied because of a prior garnishment which is using the maximum deductions. The state laws provide that the garnishments line up, and as soon as one is paid, the next in line begins to operate.

Forms can be obtained from the Defense Finance and Accounting Service and the request should be for the form "Involuntary Allotment Application, DD Form 2635." The branch of service and the social security number are required. The current duty station and address of the military member should be furnished. The garnishment is sent to:

Defense Finance and Accounting Service
Cleveland Center, Code L
P.O. Box 998002
Cleveland, Ohio 44199-8002

If the military member is attached to the Coast Guard, the garnishment should be sent to:

Coast Guard Pay and Personnel Center (LGL)
444 S.E. Quincy Street
Topeka, Kansas 66683-3591

RENT TO OWN TRANSACTIONS

Rent to own agreements are common among consumers who cannot afford to buy on credit. In most of these transactions, the customer pays in advance to rent the items, usually on a weekly or a monthly basis. At the end of each week or the end of each month, the customer renews the rental for a new period of time, and, of course, pays the rental fee in advance. Many states regulate this type of transaction.

The courts have not been sympathetic to the owners of the rent to own businesses. In several recent cases, they have decided there was noncompliance with the particular statute in the state, or the rent to own was a consumer-credit transaction which failed to comply with the states' laws. Rent to own businesses must be careful with their compliance if their intention is to repossess the equipment.

GAMBLING DEBTS

At one time the collection of a gambling debt presented severe problems in many of the states since the whole question of legalized gambling was confined to the state of Nevada. When New Jersey entered the arena, followed by American

Indian tribes across the country, the treatment of gambling debts radically changed.

Collecting gambling debts today is probably easier than it was in the past, but really not that much easier as many problems and pitfalls exist. The courts still seem to favor the consumer and seem to look for some reason to find a gambling debt unenforceable. Many states will look to the state in which the debt was incurred to see whether the debt was enforceable. Sometimes the creditor will sue in the state in which the debt was incurred and then attempt to sue on the judgment in another state on the theory that the other state will give full faith and credit to the judgment that was acquired in the state where the gambling debt was incurred, as most states do. In a few states (New York, for one) a new suit would have to be started on a default judgment and the court might review whether a gambling debt was enforceable in the state where the consumer resides.

Gambling debts have also presented problems in the bankruptcy courts when the consumer has used a credit card. The credit grantor has objected to the discharge of the credit card debt on the grounds that the consumer (gambler) used a credit card to gamble and did not intend to repay the debt. The courts seem to shrug off this argument by stating that the gambler always intends to pay back a debt because the gambler intends to win. In one case where the debtor used his credit card over a period of six months and did make some payments on the credit card, the court denied the credit grantor's claim that the debt should be non-dischargeable. Timing of the cash advances and the facts of each case are important to the Bankruptcy Judge. Only clear abuses should be pursued.

With regard to debts incurred on American Indian reservations, one must look to the Indian Gaming Regulatory Act.[8] The act requires a compact (agreement) between the reservation and the state which will determine the enforceability of gambling debts. Sometimes these agreements contain provisions about the extension of credit to persons who gamble. The question of whether an acceptance of a check from a resident of the hotel is "per se" an extension of credit for the purpose of gambling merely because the hotel has a casino is a question of fact to be decided by the court. In many of the agreements the casinos are not allowed to extend credit for the sole purpose of gambling.[9]

TOTTEN TRUST

A Totten Trust arises when an individual deposits money in a bank account in trust for a beneficiary with the intent that money will pass to the beneficiary upon the death of the individual. The Totten Trust is recognized in most states. It is a cardinal characteristic of a Totten (or tentative) trust that while it is effective as a testamentary device upon the death of a depositor, the subject property can be

---

[8]IGRA (Indian Gaming Regulatory Act) 25 U.S.C. 2701-21 (1988).

[9]In Re Anastas, 947 3d 1280 (9th Cir. 1996); *CBA Credit Services of N.D. v. Azar*, 551 N.W. 2d 787 (N.D. 1996).

withdrawn by the depositor and is within reach of creditors during the debtor's lifetime.[10]

A recent case dealt with the question of whether the Totten Trust property becomes part of the bankrupt estate. Section 541 of the Bankruptcy Code calls for inclusion in the bankruptcy estate of "all legal or equitable interest of the debtor in property as of the commencement of the case." Under this section, the court held that a Totten Trust poses no obstacle to the full inclusion of the bank account funds in a bankruptcy estate. Nevertheless, a review of state law may be necessary to determine whether other criteria or restrictions exist concerning Totten Trusts.

USE OF CREDIT CARD BY COLLECTION AGENCIES

Collection agencies and attorneys sometimes offer to the consumer the option to utilize payment by credit card. The credit card company wishes the option only to be afforded to those debtors who are current on their debts, for otherwise the credit card company is acquiring a delinquent debt. Once the account is referred to a collection agency or an attorney for collection, the debtor is now delinquent and the credit card company does not want to have a charge being made by a debtor who has already defaulted in the payment of his debt. As a result, collection agencies and attorneys cannot process credit card charges directly, and the only way collection agencies or attorneys can utilize the credit card option is either

1. Forward the credit card charge to their client and then the client processes it through their normal channels.
2. Process the credit card charge through a third party agency which processes credit charges for a fee.

The option most often used by attorneys or collection agencies that are offering this to the debtor is to forward the charge directly to the client and the client thereafter processes the charge. This type of procedure presents several problems:

1. The agency or the attorney may be violating the FDCPA which states that they cannot add any incidental charges unless those charges were created in the agreement creating the debt or permitted by law. The additional charge that the consumer will incur by using the credit card is not permitted by law and the additional charge has not been recited in the agreement creating the debt.
2. The merchant agreement between the creditor and the bank usually provides that the creditor will not process credit card charges for delinquent

---

[10]In re Totten, 179 N.Y. 112, 71 N.E. 748 (1904); *Seymour v. Seymour*, 85 So.2d 726 (Fla. 1956).

accounts. Although unlikely, it is possible that a breach of this contract might cause the bank to terminate the merchant agreement or possibly even have Visa and Mastercard terminate the merchant agreement.

For the above reasons, it is not recommended that collection agencies and attorneys use the credit card option after the account has become delinquent for consumer accounts.

WITNESS PROTECTION PROGRAM

The Federal Witness Protection Program is mentioned frequently on television police programs such as "Law & Order", "NYPD Blue", "Homicide: Life on the Street" and "The Practice". The program is designed to protect witnesses against bodily harm from organized crime (or even unorganized crime), so that the witness will not be injured and, furthermore, to set an example so that future witnesses may testify freely without risk of harm. Many of the people in the witness program have a record of prior violations of law.

It would seem that if such a person is indebted to a creditor, the debt is going to be extremely difficult to collect in view of the fact that the witness has assumed a totally different identity. Nevertheless, the US Code provides that the Attorney General shall make reasonable efforts to serve a copy of process (summons of complaint) upon any person in the program. After service, the Attorney General will notify the plaintiff whether the particular process has been served. If a judgment is entered against the debtor, the Attorney General will make reasonable efforts to find out whether the witness actually complied with the judgment and may take certain actions to persuade the person to comply with the judgment. Payment will usually be made through the Attorney General's office and not directly to the creditor.

If the witness refuses to pay, and has the ability to pay, the Attorney General may at that point, upon request, disclose the identity and location of the debtor to the creditor. Before this would be done, the Attorney General would have to consider the danger of physical harm to the particular individual and would probably do a balancing of the equity depending upon the ability of the witness to pay, the risk that the witness would entail if his identity was disclosed, and other factors.

The usual procedure is for the creditor to make a request to the Department of Justice to disclose the identity. If the above efforts fail completely, the opportunity is available to make an application to court if the Attorney General refuses to reveal the identity and location of the witness. The procedure is complex and the court must be provided with substantial persuasion to release the identity of a witness in the program. The nature of the proceeding is to appoint a guardian for the witness and thereafter the guardian effectively consummates the collection of the debt if the creditor should ultimately be successful.

CHAPTER 4
APPENDIX I

These summaries were prepared in 1996 and are provided for information and guidelines. Significant material changes may have been enacted since 1996.

SUMMARY OF STATE LAWS GOVERNING CLAIMS AGAINST ESTATES

ALABAMA

1. TIME FOR FILING.—Within six months after grant of letters of administration or letters testamentary are issued or within five months from first publication of notice to creditors of appointment or forever barred.
2. WHERE FILED.—Probate Court which issues letters of administration or letters testamentary.
3. MUST CLAIM BE SWORN TO?—Yes.
4. REMARKS.—If estate is insolvent, claim must be filed within six months after declaration of insolvency.

ALASKA

1. TIME FOR PRESENTMENT.—Within four months after date of the first publication of notice to creditors or within three years after decedent's death if notice to creditors has not been published. For claims against decedent's estate which arise at or after the death of the decedent, claims must be presented within four months after performance of contract by personal representative or four months after claim arises.
2. WHERE PRESENTED.—To representative or to clerk of court.
3. MUST CLAIM BE SWORN TO?—No.

ARIZONA

1. TIME FOR FILING.—Claims arising before death must be presented within four months from first publication. If claimant can show by affidavit he was not within the state and, therefore, had no notice, he may file at any time prior to entry of decree for distribution. If no notice was published, claims must be filed within three years of decedent's death. Claims arising at or after death must be presented within four months

Reprinted with the permission of The National Association of Credit Management.

176   *Chapter Four*

after performance by personal representative is due if based on a contract with him or four months after claim arises.

2. WHERE FILED.—Presented to representative for allowance or rejection. Upon rejection, suit must be commenced within 60 days of mailing of notice of disallowance.

3. MUST CLAIM BE SWORN TO?—No particular form of proof of claim is required.

ARKANSAS

1. TIME FOR FILING.—Within three months from the date of the first publication of the notice or forever barred. If no notice was published claims are barred at the end of five years of decedent's death. Claims for injury or death caused by negligence of decedent shall be filed within six months. If estate is under $1,000 notice may be posted in courthouse.

2. WHERE FILED.—Presented to representative or filed with the court.

3. MUST CLAIM BE SWORN TO?—Yes. Affidavit must state nature and amount of claim, that nothing has been paid, that there are no offsets, and that the sum demanded is justly due.

CALIFORNIA

1. TIME FOR FILING.—Within four months after letters are issued to a general personal representative or thirty days after date notice of administration is given to creditors provided such notice is timely. Court can extend time under special circumstances.

2. WHERE FILED.—With Clerk of the Court which issued letters. Copy must also be mailed to personal representative.

3. MUST CLAIM BE SWORN TO?—Yes, must be verified. Supported by affidavit showing that the amount is justly due, that no payments have been made which are not credited, and that there are no offsets.

4. REMARKS.—If claim is allowed it must be presented to the Judge of the Superior Court for his approval and thirty days thereafter must be filed with the Court. When claim is rejected by either the court or the representative, the holder must, under penalty of being barred, bring suit within three months if claim is then due, or within two months if claim is not due.

COLORADO

1. TIME FOR FILING.—Within four months after the date of the first publication of notice to creditors or such other time set forth in publication or within 60 days, if notice is mailed or delivered or within 1 year after decedent's death if notice has not be published. Claims arising at or after death must be presented within four months after performance by personal representative is due or four months after claim arises.

2. WHERE FILED.—With court where estate is being administered or with personal representative.

3. MUST CLAIM BE SWORN TO?—No particular form of proof of claim is required.

CONNECTICUT

1. TIME FOR FILING.—Stated in notice published by representative; usually not less than three months or more than 12 months from the time of granting of the order. In cases of insolvency of an estate, creditor has 150 days from date of determination of insolvency to present claim.

2. WHERE FILED.—Exhibited to representative, or if fiduciary resides outside the jurisdiction, claims may be filed with the judge of probate in the district where such estate is in settlement.

3. MUST CLAIM BE SWORN TO?—Yes, if required by representative or probate court. Must inform representative of the extent and character of the demand if required by the representative or probate court.

4. REMARKS.—Claim is barred if suit is not brought within 120 days after notice of disallowance.

DELAWARE

1. TIME FOR FILING.—Within eight months of decedent's death, whether or not notice was given. Claims arising at or after death must be presented within six months after claim arises or after performance by representative is due. Claims based on bond secured by mortgage must be presented within 8 months.

2. WHERE FILED.—With representative or with Register of Wills or presented by commencing a proceeding against personal representative in any court in which he is subject to its jurisdiction.

3. MUST CLAIM BE SWORN TO?—No; basis of claim must be indicated with name and address of claimant and amount claimed.

DISTRICT OF COLUMBIA

1. TIME FOR FILING.—Claims must be presented within six months after date of first publication of notice of appointment. Suit may be brought to recover amount due, even though no claim is filed, subject to general three-year statute of limitation, provided representative has not distributed estate.

2. WHERE FILED.—Presented to representative and entered upon claims docket of the Register of Wills or to Register with copy to representative.

3. MUST CLAIM BE SWORN TO?—Yes, with statement that the account as stated is true and just, that no part of the claim has been paid, and that all credits have been made.

FLORIDA

1. TIME FOR FILING.—Within three months from the first publication of notice to present claims or within 30 days after date of service of notice to creditor or within three years after the decedent's death, if notice of administration has not been published; otherwise barred.

2. WHERE FILED.—With the Clerk of Court who serves a copy to the representative.

3. MUST CLAIM BE SWORN TO?—Yes, must be verified.

4. REMARKS.—Objection to claims may be filed within four months from the first publication of notice to creditors. The court may extend the time for filing objections for good cause shown. If such objection is filed, the claimant has 30 days from such service within which to bring suit.

GEORGIA

1. TIME FOR FILING.—Within three months from publication of last notice. If filed thereafter, it loses right to equal participation with claims of equal dignity paid before the representative has notice of such unrepresented claims. Representative must give four weeks' notice to present claims.

2. WHERE FILED.—With representative.

3. MUST CLAIM BE SWORN TO?—Verification is not required, but is advisable.

4. REMARKS.—No suit to recover a debt may be commenced against representative until six months after his qualification.

HAWAII

1. TIME FOR FILING.—Claims are barred if not presented by creditors within four months after the first publication of notice by executor or administrator or within three years after the death of the decedent if no notice is published. Claims arising at or after death must be presented within four months after performance by representative, any other claims within four months after claim arises.

2. WHERE FILED.—With representative.

3. MUST CLAIM BE SWORN TO?—There is not statutory form of proof of claim. It is advisable that claims be itemized and an affidavit attached stating that the claim is due and unpaid and that there are no offsets or counterclaims thereto.

4. REMARKS.—Secured creditors may foreclose on security held without filing a claim.

IDAHO

1. TIME FOR FILING.—Within four months after the first publication of notice or within 60 days after mailing or delivery of the notice, whichever is later, if notice is published or mailed or forever barred. Where claimant had no notice by reason of being out of state, the court may permit presentation before decree of distribution is entered. Barred within 3 years after the decedent's death whether or not notice has been published.

2. WHERE FILED.—With representative.

3. MUST CLAIM BE SWORN TO?—No.

4. REMARKS.—If claim is rejected, suit must be brought within 60 days after date of rejection, if claim is due; if not due, then within two months after becoming due, otherwise claim is barred. Representative or court may order an extension of the period, but in no event shall the extension run beyond the applicable statute of limitations.

ILLINOIS

1. TIME FOR FILING.—All claims must be presented within six months from date of publication or within three months from date of mailing or delivery of notice of decedent's death or are barred as to property inventoried within such period.

2. WHERE FILED.—With Probate Court administering the estate or with representative.

3. MUST CLAIM BE SWORN TO?—Yes. When based on contract, an affidavit must accompany the claim and must state that claim is just, and unpaid, after allowing all credits, deductions, and setoffs.

4. REMARKS.—If an additional list of inventory is filed not covering previously inventoried property and clerk of court publishes notice of a new claim date, all claims not filed before such date are barred as to such additional property. All claims filed on or before such date share pro-rata in such additional property according to the classification of the claims.

INDIANA

1. TIME FOR FILING.—Claim should be filed within five months after first published notice to creditors or three months after the court has revoked probate of will if claimant was named as beneficiary in will, whichever is later or within one year after date of death.

2. WHERE FILED.—In office of clerk where estate proceedings are pending.

3. MUST CLAIM BE SWORN TO?—Affidavit must be attached to claim stating that it is justly due and wholly unpaid, after deducting all credits, setoffs, and deductions.

IOWA

1. TIME FOR FILING.—Within four months after the date of publication of notice to creditors, or forever barred.

2. WHERE FILED.—Filed with the Clerk of the District Court of county in which estate is being administered.

3. MUST CLAIM BE SWORN TO?—Yes. If founded on written instrument, it must be attached; if upon account, an itemized copy showing the balance should be attached.

KANSAS

1. TIME FOR FILING.—Within four months from the date of first published notice to creditors, or forever barred.

2. WHERE FILED.—With the Probate Court. If under $1500, may be allowed by representative without filing with court.

3. MUST CLAIM BE SWORN TO?—Yes, but if amount exceeds $200, then competent evidence must be produced before the Probate Court to establish claim.

KENTUCKY

1. TIME FOR FILING.—Within six months after appointment of personal representative. If no personal representative is appointed, then two years after decedent's death.

2.   WHERE FILED.—With representative or with clerk of court.

3.   MUST CLAIM BE SWORN TO?—Representative may pay claim without verification when he is satisfied the estate is solvent and that claim is just and owing. Otherwise, claim must be sworn to.

4.   REMARKS.—If debt is on a written contract, nothing further than affidavit of claimant required; if upon account, in addition to claimant's affidavit, that of a disinterested person is required.

LOUISIANA

1.   TIME FOR FILING.—No particular time specified. Representative must file an account every 12 months. Claims are passed upon and allowed at that time.

2.   WHERE FILED.—With representative.

3.   MUST CLAIM BE SWORN TO?—Yes.

MAINE

1.   TIME FOR FILING.—Within four months after the date of first publication of the notice, barred nine months after death of decedent. Claims arising at or after death must be presented within four months after the performance by representative is due, all other claims within four months after they arise.

2.   WHERE FILED.—With representative or clerk of the court.

3.   MUST CLAIM BE SWORN TO?—No.

MARYLAND

1.   TIME FOR FILING.—Within six months after publication of notice of appointment of representative and for all deaths after May 19, 1989, earlier of nine months after decedent's death or two months after personal representative gives required notice. Suit against the estate must be commended within six months after appointment unless decedent was covered by insurance, in which case the statute of limitations for the particular action governs. Six-month limitation period extended if first published.

2.   WHERE FILED.—With representative or Register of Wills with a copy sent to personal representative.

3.   MUST CLAIM BE SWORN TO?—Yes, verified statement is required.

MASSACHUSETTS

1.   TIME FOR FILING.—No time specified unless estate is insolvent, then within four months from the date of giving bond or the claim will be barred. For estates of decedents dying on or after January 1, 1990 action must be commenced or process served upon or accepted by representative or notice filed in registry of probate within one year of date of death. If representative, if after end of six month period after death, has no notice of demand sufficient to warrant his representing the estate as insol-

vent, he may pay debts of estate and is not personally liable for demands of creditors of which he had no notice.

2. WHERE FILED.—With representative.

3. MUST CLAIM BE SWORN TO?—No, but preferable practice.

MICHIGAN

1. TIME FOR FILING.—Hearing date is fixed by court after approval of bond of fiduciary, not more than four months nor less than two months from date of first publication of notice to file claims.

2. WHERE FILED.—With court, and copy must be served on fiduciary.

3. MUST CLAIM BE SWORN TO?—Yes. Claim must be in writing, under oath, and contain sufficient detail to inform fiduciary of nature and amount of same. Copy of any writing on which claim is based must be attached.

4. REMARKS.—Creditor may, within 18 months after last date to file claims and before estate is closed, file application to file claim and application shall be granted not more than one month thereafter, upon payment of costs. After the 18 months, the court may permit a claim to be filed for special cause.

MINNESOTA

1. TIME FOR FILING.—Within four months after the date of publication of the clerk of court's notice to creditors. If notice is not so published, within three years after the decedent's death.

2. WHERE FILED.—In the Probate Court or sent to the personal representative.

3. MUST CLAIM BE SWORN TO?—No, if sent to personal representative. If filed with court, see local court rules.

MISSISSIPPI

1. TIME FOR FILING.—Within 90 days from the first publication of notice to creditors. Otherwise barred.

2. WHERE FILED.—With Clerk of the Chancery Court.

3. MUST CLAIM BE SWORN TO?—Yes, must be duly verified.

4. REMARKS.—Before clerk will accept claims, affidavit of claim must be probated and registered. The affidavit of creditor must be attached to the written evidence of the indebtedness. Such affidavit must state that the claim is just, correct, and owing from the deceased, that it is not usurious, and that no part of it has been paid.

MISSOURI

1. TIME FOR FILING.—Within six months after first published notice of letters testamentary or of administration.

2. WHERE FILED.—Probate Court.

3. MUST CLAIM BE SWORN TO?—Yes.

4.   REMARKS.—Claim must be served on representative in writing stating the nature and amount of his claim with a copy of the written evidence of indebtedness.

MONTANA

1.   TIME FOR FILING.—Within one year from date of death if notice has not been published. Personal representative may give written notice to creditors to present claims within 4 months from date of publication or 30 days from date of mailing of notice. Claims that arise at or after death must be filed within four months after performance by representative is due if based on a contract with the representative, any other claim within four months after it arises.

2.   WHERE FILED.—With representative by mail, return receipt requested, or with the clerk of court.

3.   MUST CLAIM BE SWORN TO?—Yes, with statement that the amount is justly due, that no payments have been made thereon, and that there are not offsets. Basis of claim must be indicated.

NEBRASKA

1.   TIME FOR FILING.—The time for filing claims is two months. Claims that arise at or after death must be filed within four months after performance by representative is due if based on a contract with the representative, any other claim within four months after it arises.

2.   WHERE FILED.—Clerk of the Probate Court.

3.   MUST CLAIM BE SWORN TO?—Yes.

4.   REMARKS.—If claim is not presented within stipulated time, it shall be forever barred unless good cause is shown. If notice to claimant is not published, claim is barred within three years after decedent's death.

NEVADA

1.   TIME FOR FILING.—Within 90 days from date of first publication of notice to creditors or of mailing of notice to creditors for claims against the deceased, within 60 days for creditors of the estate.

2.   WHERE FILED.—Clerk of Court.

3.   MUST CLAIM BE SWORN TO?—Yes. If claim is for $250 or more, an affidavit must state that the amount is justly due (or date it will be due), that no payments have been made thereon which are not credited, and that there are no offsets to the same.

4.   REMARKS.—If claim is rejected, suit must be brought within 30 days from date of notice of rejection. Claim will not be barred if claimant can prove that he did not receive notice.

NEW HAMPSHIRE

1.   TIME FOR FILING.—Within six months from grant of letters. If estate is insolvent, no presentation is required and notice sent to representative by registered mail stating nature and amount of claim is sufficient.

2.   WHERE FILED.—Presented to representative.

3.   MUST CLAIM BE SWORN TO?—At discretion of representative.

NEW JERSEY

1.   TIME FOR FILING.—Within six months after entry of order of publication to creditors by the Superior Court or surrogate.

2.   WHERE FILED.—Presented to representative.

3.   MUST CLAIM BE SWORN TO?—Yes, with statement of amount and particulars of claim.

4.   REMARKS.—If claim is not presented in time, claimant may file before distribution of assets and the court may direct payment.

NEW MEXICO

1.   TIME FOR FILING.—Within two months of first publication of notice of appointment of executor or administrator or within three years of the decedent's death if notice to creditors has not been published. Claims arising at or after death based on a contract with personal representative must be presented within four months after performance by representative is due, any other claim within four months after it arises.

2.   WHERE FILED.—With district court or representative.

3.   MUST CLAIM BE SWORN TO?—No.

NEW YORK

1.   TIME FOR FILING.—Claims should be presented to fiduciary on or before date fixed in the notice to creditors or, if no notice is published, within seven months from the date of the issue of letters.

2.   WHERE FILED.—With the representative at the location stated in the notice.

3.   MUST CLAIM BE SWORN TO?—The fiduciary may require the claimant to present proof by affidavit with satisfactory vouchers and affidavit stating the claim is justly due, that no payments have been made thereon, and that there are no offsets against the same to the knowledge of the claimant.

4.   REMARKS.—If claim is rejected, creditor must commence suit against representative within 60 days after rejection; if claim is not then due, then sue within 60 days after claim becomes due or issue can be tried on a judicial accounting.

NORTH CAROLINA

1.   TIME FOR FILING.—Within time specified in general notice to creditors, but it must be at least six months from the day of first publication or posting of notice. Claims arising at or after death must be presented within six months after performance by representative is due if based on contract with him, all other claims within six months after claim arises. In certain cases, 90 days after delivery of notice from person representative if said period is later. Except certain claims covered by insurance.

2.   WHERE FILED.—Collector or Clerk of Superior Court.

3. MUST CLAIM BE SWORN TO?—Within discretion of representative or collector.

4. REMARKS.—Claim must contain name and address of claimant, amount claimed, and basis of the claim. Upon failure to file within six months, creditor may recover from the representative if he still has funds; if not, he may proceed against the heirs. To the extent that the decedent or the decedent's personal representative is protected by insurance coverage with respect to a claim, that claim is not automatically barred if not presented within six months.

NORTH DAKOTA

1. TIME FOR FILING.—Within three months after the date of the first publication of notice to creditors—provided that claims barred by a nonclaim statute in the state of the decedent's domicile are barred in this state. Within three years after decedent's death if no notice is published, claims at or after death based on contract with representative or collector must be presented within 4 months after which performance is due, all other claims within three months after they arise.

2. WHERE FILED.—Present to personal representative or file with clerk of court.

3. MUST CLAIM BE SWORN TO?—No, if filed with personal representative. If filed with clerk of court, consult local court rules.

OHIO

1. TIME FOR FILING.—Written one year after date of death, executor or administrator can shorten notice period by giving notice to creditor to file claim within 30 days. If claim is not filed within four months, claimant may petition for leave to file upon showing lack of notice or other good cause as set forth in statute. If not filed within six months, claim is forever barred.

2. WHERE FILED.—With representative.

3. MUST CLAIM BE SWORN TO?—If representative so requires, affidavit must state that such claim is justly due, that no payments have been made thereon, and that there are no offsets against the same.

OKLAHOMA

1. TIME FOR FILING.—Claims have to be presented by the presentment date stated in the notice to creditors. The presentment date shall be a date certain which is at least two months following the date said notice is filed. The first publication of said notice shall appear on or before the tenth day after the filing of said notice. The claim may be presented at any time before a final decree of distribution is entered. The claimant may prove by affidavit that he had no notice by reason of being out of state and that a copy of the notice was not mailed to such claimant.

2. WHERE FILED.—Presented at place specified in notice.

3. MUST CLAIM BE SWORN TO?—No form for proof of claim is prescribed by statute; but claimant must, if requested by executor or administrator, file with clerk affidavit in support of his claim.

OREGON

1. TIME FOR FILING.—Claims presented within four months after date of first publication of notice have priority. If notice is published, claims not presented before expiration of twelve months after date of first publication or before date personal representative files his final account, whichever occurs first, are barred from payment. If no notice is published to interested persons, claims are barred after three years after death if not statute-barred before.

2. WHERE FILED.—Presented to representative.

3. MUST CLAIM BE SWORN TO?—Yes, with necessary vouchers.

PENNSYLVANIA

1. TIME FOR FILING.—Within statute of limitations, which continues to run despite death of decedent. If statute would toll within one year after death, however, claim will not be barred until one year after death. Claims may be unenforceable against grantee of real property after one year.

2. WHERE FILED.—With representative.

3. MUST CLAIM BE SWORN TO?—It is not necessary that a claim be verified, but it must be presented and proved in Orphans' Court at audit of account, unless admitted by representative.

RHODE ISLAND

1. TIME FOR FILING.—Within six months from first publication of notice to creditors.

2. WHERE FILED.—In the office of the Probate Court together with affidavit that copy was delivered by hand or registered mail, return receipt requested, to executor or administrator or his attorney.

3. MUST CLAIM BE SWORN TO?—No form for proof of claim is prescribed by statute but claimant must, if requested by executor or administrator, file with clerk affidavit in support of his claim.

4. REMARKS.—For sufficient cause shown, the Probate Court may permit a claim to be filed after six months.

SOUTH CAROLINA

1. TIME FOR FILING.—Within eight months after first publication of notice, or claim will be barred. Within three years if no notice has been published. Claims arising at or after death: if claim is based on a contract with representative, within eight months after performance by representative is due, any other claim within eight months after it arises.

2. WHERE FILED.—With representative and Probate Clerk.

3. MUST CLAIM BE SWORN TO?—No.

SOUTH DAKOTA

1. TIME FOR FILING.—Within four months from time of first publication of notice or within 30 days after mailing of notice. In any event claims are barred if not filed within three years of date of death.

2. WHERE FILED.—Claims must be filed with clerk of court where proceedings are pending; a copy thereof must be mailed to the representative.

3. MUST CLAIM BE SWORN TO?—Yes.

4. REMARKS.—Suit on claim must be commenced no more than 30 days after personal representative has mailed notice of disallowance except for claims that are not due or are contingent, in which event extension may be obtained from court.

TENNESSEE

1. TIME FOR FILING.—Claims must be filed within six months after the first publication or posting. If creditor receives actual notice less than 60 days before expiration of the six month period or after expiration of the six month period, such creditor's claim is barred unless filed within 60 days from date of receipt of actual notice. In any event, claims are barred if not filed within 12 months of decedent's date of death.

2. WHERE FILED.—Triplicate copies of claim to be filed with clerk of court in which estate is being administered.

3. MUST CLAIM BE SWORN TO?—Claim must be verified by affidavit of creditor stating that the claim is a correct, just, and valid obligation of the estate and that no payment or security has been received except as indicated therein.

TEXAS

1. TIME FOR FILING.—Those exhibited within six months after the grant of letters are entitled to priority.

2. WHERE FILED.—Exhibited to the representative or Clerk of Court.

3. MUST CLAIM BE SWORN TO?—Yes.

UTAH

1. TIME FOR FILING.—Within three months after the first publication of notice to creditors, or forever barred. Within three years if no notice has been published. Claims arising at or after death must be presented within three months after performance by representative is due, if based on a contract with him all other claims within three months after they arise.

2. WHERE FILED.—Presented to representative or clerk of court.

3. MUST CLAIM BE SWORN TO?—No.

VERMONT

1. TIME FOR FILING.—Claims must be filed within four months of first publication of notice, if no notice is published, then within three years. Claims arising at or after death: four months.

2. WHERE FILED.—With representative and probate court.

3. MUST CLAIM BE SWORN TO?—No.

VIRGIN ISLANDS

1. TIME FOR FILING.—Within six months. Claims not presented within six months are not barred, but cannot be paid until properly presented claims are satisfied.

2. WHERE FILED.—With representative.

3. MUST CLAIM BE SWORN TO?—Yes.

VIRGINIA

1. TIME FOR FILING.—Within six months of qualification of representative.

2. WHERE FILED.—With personal representative or court-appointed Commissioner of Accounts.

3. MUST CLAIM BE SWORN TO?—No form prescribed but claim should be in writing.

WASHINGTON

1. TIME FOR FILING.—Within four months after the first publication of notice to creditors or date of filing copy of notice or within 30 days after giving actual notice to creditor, whichever is later. Claims against a casualty insurer of decedent can be made within 18 months.

2. WHERE FILED.—Presented to representative who must indorse on claim his allowance or rejection. Claim is then filed with court.

3. MUST CLAIM BE SWORN TO?—Claims need not be supported by an affidavit. The statement should include that the claim is correct, that the amount is justly due, that no payments have been made thereon, and that there are no offsets to the same.

4. REMARKS.—If claim rejected, suit must be brought within 30 days after notice or claim will be barred.

WEST VIRGINIA

1. TIME FOR FILING.—Commissioner appointed by court must publish notice to file which time will not be more than 30 days after the date of the first publication of notice which shall not be less than two months nor more than three months from date of first publication of notice. Claimant who had no actual knowledge of notice and presented his claim after such time limit, may participate only in surplus, if any, remaining after payment of claims presented in time.

2. WHERE FILED.—At place designated in notice.

3. MUST CLAIM BE SWORN TO?—No particular form is prescribed except that claims must be itemized and accompanied by proper vouchers with statement of character of claim in full detail.

WISCONSIN

1. TIME FOR FILING.—Not less than three months and not more than four months from the date of the court order that sets the three-month time limit. Creditor who was out of state and proves by affidavit he did not receive notice may be allowed to present his claim up to entry of decree of distribution.

2. WHERE FILED.—In Court of County of defendant's domicile or if nonresident, in any county in which property is located.

3. MUST CLAIM BE SWORN TO?—Yes.

4. REMARKS.—Time to file claims may be extended for good cause, but not beyond two years from date of appointment of executor or administrator.

WYOMING

1. TIME FOR FILING.—Claims must be filed within three months after first publication of notice or within 30 days after mailing of notice to owner, whichever date is later.

2. WHERE FILED.—In duplicate with Clerk of Court.

3. MUST CLAIM BE SWORN TO?—Yes.

CHAPTER 4
APPENDIX II

EXCERPT FROM NEW YORK LAW
EXEMPT PROPERTY

SECTION 5205. PERSONAL PROPERTY EXEMPT FROM APPLICATION TO THE SATISFACTION OF MONEY JUDGMENTS

(a) **Exemption for personal property.** The following personal property when owned by any person is exempt from application to the satisfaction of a money judgment except where the judgment is for the purchase price of the exempt property or was recovered by a domestic, laboring person or mechanic for work performed by that person in such capacity:

1. all stoves kept for use in the judgment debtor's dwelling house and necessary fuel therefor for sixty days; one sewing machine with its appurtenances;

2. the family bible, family pictures, and school books used by the judgment debtor or in the family; and other books, not exceeding fifty dollars in value, kept and used as part of the family or judgment debtor's library;

3. a seat or pew occupied by the judgment debtor or the family in a place of public worship;

4. domestic animals with the necessary food for those animals for sixty days, provided that the total value of such animals and food does not exceed four hundred fifty dollars; all necessary food actually provided for the use of the judgment debtor or his family for sixty days;

5. all wearing apparel, household furniture, one mechanical, gas or electric refrigerator, one radio receiver, one television set, crockery, tableware and cooking utensils necessary for the judgment debtor and the family.

6. a wedding ring; a watch not exceeding thirty-five dollars in value; and

7. necessary working tools and implements, including those of a mechanic, farm machinery, team, professional instruments, furniture and library, not exceeding six hundred dollars in value, together with the necessary food for the team for sixty days, provided, however, that the articles specified in paragraph are necessary to the carrying on of the judgment debtor's profession or calling.

(b) **Exemption of cause of action and damages for taking or injuring exempt personal property.** A cause of action, to recover damages for taking or injuring personal property. A cause of action, to recover damages for taking or injuring personal property exempt from application to the satisfaction o f a money judgment, is exempt from application to the satisfaction of a money judgment. A money judgment and its proceeds arising out of such a cause of action is exempt, for one year after the collection thereof, from application to the satisfaction of a money judgment.

(c) **Trust exemption.** Any property while held in trust for a judgment debtor, where the trust has been created by, or the fund so held in trust has proceeded from, a person other than the judgment debtor, is exempt from application to the satisfaction of a money judgment.

(d) **Income exemptions.** The following personal property is exempt from application to the satisfaction of a money judgment, except such part as a court determines to be unnecessary for the reasonable requirements of the judgment debtor and his dependents.

    1. ninety percent of the income or other payments from a trust the principal of which is exempt under subdivision (d);

    2. ninety percent of the earnings of the judgment debtor for his personal services rendered within sixty days before, and at any time after, an income execution is delivered to the sheriff or a motion is made to secure the application of the judgment debtor's earnings to the satisfaction of the judgment; and

    3. payments pursuant to an award in a matrimonial action, for the support of a wife, where the wife is the judgment debtor, or for the support of a child, where the child is the judgment debtor; where the award was made by a court of the state, determination of the extent to which it is unnecessary shall be made by that court.

(e) **Exemptions to members of armed forces.** The pay and bounty of a non-commissioned officer, musician or private in the armed forces of the United States or the state of New York; a land warrant, pension or other reward granted by the United States, or by a state, for services in the armed forces; a sword, horse, medal, emblem or device of any kind presented as a testimonial for services rendered in the armed forces of the United States or a state; and the uniform, arms and equipment which were used by a person in the service, are exempt from application to the satisfaction of a money judgment; provided, however, that the provisions of this subdivision shall not apply to the satisfaction of any order or money judgment for the support of a person's child, spouse, or former spouse.

(f) **Exemptions for unpaid milk proceeds.** Ninety percent of any money or debt due or to become due to the judgment debtor for the sale of milk produced on a farm operated by him and delivered for his account to a milk dealer licensed pursuant to article twenty-one of the agriculture and markets law is exempt from application to the satisfaction of a money judgment.

SECTION 5206. REAL PROPERTY EXEMPT FROM APPLICATION TO THE SATISFACTION OF MONEY JUDGMENTS

(a) **Exemption of homestead.** Property of one of the following types, not exceeding ten thousand dollars in value above liens and encumbrances, owned and occupied as a principal residence, is exempt from application to the satisfaction of a money judgment, unless the judgment was recovered wholly for the purchase price thereof;

1. a lot of land with a dwelling thereon,

2. shares of stock in a cooperative apartment corporation, or

3. units of a condominium apartment.

But no exempt homestead shall be exempt from taxation or from sale for non-payment of taxes or assessments.

(b) **Homestead exemption after owner's death.** The homestead exemption continues after the death of the person in whose favor the property was exempted for the benefit of the surviving spouse and surviving children until the majority of the youngest surviving child and until the death of the surviving spouse.

(c) **Suspension of occupation as affecting homestead.** The homestead exemption ceases if the property ceases to be occupied as a residence by a person for whose benefit it may so continue, except where the suspension of occupation is for a period not exceeding one year, and occurs in consequence of injury to, or destruction of, the dwelling house upon the premises.

(d) **Exemption of homestead exceeding ten thousand dollars in value.** The exemption of a homestead is not void because the value of the property exceeds ten thousand dollars but the lien of a judgment attaches to the surplus.

(e) **Sale of homestead exceeding ten thousand dollars in value.** A judgment creditor may commence a special proceeding in the county in which the homestead is located against the judgment debtor for the sale, by a sheriff or receiver, of a homestead exceeding ten thousand dollars in value. The court may direct that the notice of petition be served upon any other person. The court, if it directs such a sale, shall so marshal the proceeds of the sale that the right and interest of each person in the proceeds shall correspond as nearly as may be to his right and interest in the property sold. Money, not exceeding ten thousand dollars, paid to a judgment debtor, as representing his interest in the proceeds, is exempt for one year after the payment, unless, before the expiration of the year, he acquires an exempt homestead, in which case, the exemption ceases with respect to so much of the money as was not expended for the purchase of that property; and the exemption of the property so acquired extends to every debt against which the property sold was exempt. Where the exemption of property sold as prescribed in this subdivision has been continued after the judgment debtor's death, or where he dies after the sale and before payment to him of his portion of the proceeds of the sale, the court may direct that portion of the proceeds to which represents his interest be invested for the benefit of the person or persons entitled to the benefit of the exemption, or be otherwise disposed of as justice requires.

(f) **Exemption of burying ground.** Land, set apart as a family or private burying ground, is exempt from application to the satisfaction of a money judgment, upon the following conditions only:

1. a portion of it must have been actually used for that purpose;

2. it must not exceed in extent one-fourth of an acre; and

3. it must not contain any building or structure, except one or more vaults or other places of deposit for the dead, or mortuary monuments.

CHAPTER 4
APPENDIX III

CREDIT PRACTICES AMENDMENT

PART 444—CREDIT PRACTICES FEDERAL TRADE COMMISSION

Sec.
444.1 Definitions
444.2 Unfair credit practices
444.3 Unfair or deceptive cosigner practices
444.4 Late charges
444.5 State exemptions
AUTHORITY: Sec. 18(a), 88 Stat. 2193, as amended 93 Stat. 95 (15 U.S.C. 57a); 80 Stat. 383, as amended, 81 Stat. 54 (5 U.S.C. 552).

SOURCE: 49 FR 7789, Mar. 1, 1984, unless otherwise noted.

444.1 DEFINITIONS.

(a) Lender. A person who engages in the business of lending money to consumers within the jurisdiction of the Federal Trade Commission.

(b) Retail installment seller. A person who sells goods or services to consumers on a deferred payment basis or pursuant to a lease-purchase arrangement within the jurisdiction of the Federal Trade Commission.

(c) Person. An individual, corporation, or other business organization.

(d) Consumer. A natural person who seeks or acquires goods, services, or money for personal, family or household use.

(e) Obligation. An agreement between a consumer and a lender or retail installment seller.

(f) Creditor. A lender or a retail installment seller.

(g) Debt. Money that is due or alleged to be due from one to another.

(h) Earnings. Compensation paid or payable to an individual or for his or her account for personal services rendered or to be rendered by him or her, whether denominated as wages, salary, commission, bonus, or otherwise, including periodic payments pursuant to a pension, retirement, or disability program.

(i) Household goods. Clothing, furniture, appliances, one radio and one television, linens, china, crockery, kitchenware, and personal effects (including wedding rings) of the consumer and his or her dependents, provided that the following are not included within the scope of the term "household goods":

(1) Works of art;

(2) Electronic entertainment equipment (except one television and one radio);

(3) Items acquired as antiques; and

(4) Jewelry (except wedding rings).

(j) Antique. Any item over one hundred years of age, including such items that have been repaired or renovated without changing their original form or character.

(k) Cosigner. A natural person who renders himself or herself liable for the obligation of another person without compensation. The term shall include any person whose signature is requested as a condition to granting credit to another person, or as a condition for forbearance on collection of another person's obligation that is in default. The term shall not include a spouse whose signature is required on a credit obligation to perfect a security interest pursuant to State law. A person who does not receive goods, services, or money in return for a credit obligation does not receive compensation within the meaning of this definition. A person is a cosigner within the meaning of this definition whether or not he or she is designated as such on a credit obligation.

444.2 UNFAIR CREDIT PRACTICES.

(a) In connection with the extension of credit to consumers in or affecting commerce, as commerce is defined in the Federal Trade Commission Act, it is an unfair act or practice within the meaning of Section 5 of that Act for a lender or retail installment seller directly or indirectly to take or receive from a consumer an obligation that:

(1) Constitutes or contains a cognovit or confession of judgment (for purposes other than executory process in the State of Louisiana), warrant of attorney, or other waiver of the right to notice and the opportunity to be heard in the event of suit or process thereon.

(2) Constitutes or contains an executory waiver or a limitation of exemption from attachment, execution, or other process on real or personal property held, owned by, or due to the consumer, unless the waiver applies solely to property subject to a security interest executed in connection with the obligation.

(3) Constitutes or contains an assignment of wages or other earnings unless:
    (i) The assignment by its terms is revocable at the will of the debtor, or
    (ii) The assignment is a payroll deduction plan or preauthorized payment plan, commencing at the time of the transaction, in which the consumer authorizes a series of wage deductions as a method of making each payment, or
    (iii) The assignment applies only to wages or other earnings already earned at the time of the assignment.

(4) Constitutes or contains a nonpossessory security interest in household goods other than a purchase money security interest.

444.3 Unfair or deceptive cosigner practices.

(a) In connection with the extension of credit to consumers in or affecting commerce, as commerce is defined in the Federal Trade Commission Act, it is:

   (1) A deceptive act or practice within the meaning of section 5 of that Act for a lender or retail installment seller, directly or indirectly, to misrepresent the nature or extent of cosigner liability to any person.

   (2) An unfair act or practice within the meaning of section 5 of that Act for a lender or retail installment seller, directly or indirectly, to obligate a cosigner unless the cosigner is informed prior to becoming obligated, which in the case of open end credit shall mean prior to the time that the agreement creating the cosigner's liability for future charges is executed, of the nature of his or her liability as cosigner.

(b) Any lender or retail installment seller who complies with the preventive requirements in paragraph (c) of this section does not violate paragraph (a) of this section.

(c) To prevent these unfair or deceptive acts or practices, a disclosure, consisting of a separate document that shall contain the following statement and no other, shall be given to the cosigner prior to becoming obligated, which in the case of open end credit shall mean prior to the time that the agreement creating the cosigner's liability for future charges is executed:

NOTICE TO COSIGNER

You are being asked to guarantee this debt. Think carefully before you do. If the borrower doesn't pay the debt, you will have to. Be sure you can afford to pay if you have to, and that you want to accept this responsibility.

You may have to pay up to the full amount of the debt if the borrower does not pay. You may also have to pay late fees or collection costs, which increase this amount.

The creditor can collect this debt from you without first trying to collect from the borrower. The creditor can use the same collection methods against you that can be used against the borrower, such as suing you, garnishing your wages, etc. If this debt is ever in default, that fact may become a part of *your* credit record.

This notice is not the contract that makes you liable for the debt.

444.4 Late charges.

(a) In connection with collecting a debt arising out of an extension of credit to a consumer in or affecting commerce, as commerce is defined in the Federal Trade Commission Act, it is an unfair act or practice within the meaning of section 5 of that Act for a creditor, directly or indirectly, to levy or collect any delinquency charge on a payment, which payment is otherwise a full payment for the applicable period and is paid on its due date or within an applicable grace period and is paid on its due date or within an applicable grace period, when the only delinquency is attributable to late fee(s) or delinquency charge(s) assessed on earlier installment(s).

(b) For purposes of this section, "collecting a debt" means any activity other than the use of judicial process that is intended to bring about or does bring about repayment of all or part of a consumer debt.

444.5 STATE EXEMPTIONS.

(a) If, upon application to the Federal Trade Commission by an appropriate State agency, the Federal Trade Commission determines that:

   (1) There is a State requirement or prohibition in effect that applies to any transaction to which a provision of this rule applies; and

   (2) The State requirement or prohibition affords a level of protection to consumers that is substantially equivalent to, or greater than, the protection afforded by this rule;

Then that provision of the rule will not be in effect in that State to the extent specified by the Federal Trade Commission in its determination, for as long as the State administers and enforces the State requirement or prohibition effectively.

CHAPTER 4
APPENDIX IV

EXCERPTS FROM EXEMPTION LAW OF STATE OF FLORIDA

4. HOMESTEAD; EXEMPTIONS

(a) There shall be exempt from forced sale under process of any court, and no judgment, decree or execution shall be a lien thereon, except for the payment of taxes and assessments thereon, obligations contracted for the purchase, improvement or repair thereof, or obligations contracted for house, field or other labor performed on the realty, the following property owned by a natural person:

    (1) a homestead, if located outside a municipality, to the extent of one hundred sixty acres of contiguous land and improvements thereon, which shall not be reduced without the owner's consent by reason of subsequent inclusion in a municipality; or if located within a municipality, to the extent of one-half acre of contiguous land, upon which the exemption shall be limited to the residence of the owner or the owner's family;

    (2) personal property to the value of one thousand dollars.

(b) These exemptions shall inure to the surviving spouse or heirs of the owner.

(c) The homestead shall not be subject to devise if the owner is survived by spouse or minor child, except the homestead may be devised to the owner's spouse if there be no minor child. The owner of homestead real estate, joined by the spouse if married, may alienate the homestead by mortgage, sale or gift and, if married, may be deed transfer the title to an estate by the entirety with the spouse. If the owner or spouse is incompetent, the method of alienation or encumbrance shall be as provided by law.

CHAPTER 5

Bankruptcy

The Bankruptcy Law of 1898 was the first law to allow a business to file a petition in bankruptcy to discharge debts. Consumers were not included since credit was rarely extended to them. The law was modified over the years to expand the relief (some might contend too much relief) of the bankruptcy law to consumers. The Bankruptcy Reform Act became effective October 1, 1979. This act is extensive, and has been amended. This discussion presents the basics on bankruptcy from a creditor's point of view.

WHO MAY FILE

There are two types of petitions which may be filed:

a. A *voluntary petition* may be filed by a debtor whether the debtor is a consumer or a business. The business may be a corporation, partnership or association.

b. An *involuntary petition* may be filed by creditors of an individual or a business. An involuntary petition may not be filed in a wage earner bankruptcy since the consumer debtor agrees to pay the debts over a period of time.

VOLUNTARY PETITION

The debtor may file a petition at any time by alleging the inability to pay debts as they mature. A filing fee is required, and upon acceptance by the clerk, all proceedings against the debtor must cease and desist. This right is also afforded to businesses, but most businesses do not file a bankruptcy petition if they are going out of business. On the other hand, if the business wishes to reorganize and continue to operate, the debtor will take advantage of the bankruptcy laws.

INVOLUNTARY PETITION

To file an involuntary petition, the creditor must show that the debtor is not paying debts as they mature. The key is not whether the debtor is insolvent or the liabilities exceed the assets, but whether the debtor is able to meet the debts as the bills are presented to the debtor. An involuntary petition may be filed by three or more creditors who hold noncontingent undisputed claims (indebtedness) totaling at least $10,000 in debts due from the bankrupt debtor. If the creditor or creditors hold security for the debt, such as an automobile or a mortgage on the residence, the indebtedness must be $5000 more than the value of the security (auto or real property). The claims must be subject to simple calculations which value the claims over $10,000 and must not be subject to offset or setoff which may reduce the amount owing to less than $10,000.[1]

The bankrupt may contest an Involuntary Petition and both parties may seek discovery prior to the trial on the issue of the Involuntary Petition. If the petitioning creditors are successful, the cost and attorney's fees and expenses will be paid from the debtor's estate. If the debtor is successful, a judgment may be granted against the petitioning creditors for reasonable attorney's fees as well as any damages caused to the debtor by such filing. The petitioners' exposure is limited to the costs and attorney's fees providing the petitioners acted in good faith. If the petitioning creditors have acted in bad faith, and the petition was dismissed and the debtor's reputation was damaged or suffered other damages, the creditors may be exposed to liability for compensatory damages as well as punitive damages.

A major risk lies when there is a single creditor who files an Involuntary Petition. The courts seem to feel that this creditor should make a reasonable inquiry to consider the prevailing facts. The courts suspect an ulterior motive on behalf of a single petitioning creditor, if the petition ultimately is dismissed. The petitioning creditor must understand that the courts examine these situations carefully. Consultation with counsel is absolutely recommended before any Involuntary Petition is filed.

The debtor may contest the filing of an involuntary petition and may operate the business. However, the court may appoint a trustee to run the business during the pendency of the proceeding to contest the filing of the involuntary petition.

A business debtor may be placed in involuntary bankruptcy either under chapter 7 or chapter 11.

---

[1] 11 U.S.C. 303(b).

Consultation with an attorney is recommended when you consider filing an involuntary petition.

CREDIT AND COLLECTION TIP: *Contacting other creditors of a consumer may violate the provisions of the Fair Debt Collection Practices Act and, prior to the filing, may create liability due to an invasion of privacy in that the creditor is distributing information to other creditors about the credit reputation of a debtor — another reason to consult with counsel.*

U.S. TRUSTEE

A trustee in a bankruptcy proceeding under chapter 7, 11, or 13 is appointed to collect the assets of the bankrupt, convert them to cash, and distribute the monies to the creditors.[2] The trustee acts as a fiduciary for the benefit of all creditors, secured or unsecured. The trustee has the right to employ attorneys, accountants, and other professionals and do whatever is needed to preserve and protect the assets of the estate. The trustee is empowered to sue on behalf of the bankrupt estate or to avoid certain liens or preferences which affect the debtor estate. In addition, the trustee may accept or reject contracts, such as leases, which bind the debtor. The trustee may continue to operate the business if appointed by the court to succeed a debtor in possession. Normally, a trustee does not actively run a business on a day-to-day basis, but supervises the running of a business through the debtor in possession or, if a large corporation, through the board of directors.

CHAPTERS OF THE BANKRUPTCY ACT

There are four principal chapters (7, 9, 11, and 13) under which a person or business may file a bankruptcy petition. Chapter 9 deals with municipalities and will not be discussed.

CHAPTER 7—LIQUIDATION. Most cases that are filed in court are usually filed under Chapter 7, known as straight bankruptcy. These are asset or no-asset cases. Chapter 7 may be used by individuals, corporations, partnerships, and associations. An individual may only file this type of bankruptcy every six years. The purpose of Chapter 7 is to collect all the assets of the debtor, sell these assets, and convert them into cash. The filing of a sworn petition in bankruptcy listing the assets and liabilities of the debtor commences the Chapter 7. After the trustee deducts the expenses of selling the assets, the fees to the trustees and other professional administrative expenses, the remaining money is distributed to the creditors.

---

[2]11 U.S.C. 704.

The original notice to creditors advising them of Chapter 7 bankruptcy sets forth a date for a first meeting of creditors. This meeting may be adjourned by the trustee upon application of the debtor or the creditors. In the event the debtor fails to appear at the meeting, the trustee may move the court to dismiss the bankruptcy.

At the first meeting of creditors, the debtor must bring all financial records and submit to an examination under oath by the trustee, or any other interested party, as to the particulars of the petition. The inquiry is usually cursory unless the trustee has been put on notice by a creditor of some discrepancy between the listed assets or liabilities of the debtor. The trustee, if notified of some problem, i.e., the existence of a home that is not listed, will request the debtor to furnish documentation prior to the hearing. A creditor should immediately communicate with the trustee any suspicions concerning the activities of the debtor.

Once the trustee finishes the examination of the debtor, which may continue through several adjournments (continuations), any interested party may examine the debtor. During the examination, if the debtor is not responsive to a question, the trustee may order the debtor to produce additional documentation to answer the question at a subsequent hearing. This examination, if properly conducted, can be the basis of an objection by the trustee or a creditor to the bankruptcy petition.

CHAPTER 11—REORGANIZATION. A corporation or person can file a Chapter 11 bankruptcy, known as a reorganization. Reorganization can either be commenced voluntarily or involuntarily.[3] The debtor continues to operate the business as a "debtor in possession" as long as: 1. the debtor runs the business in good faith, and 2. the debtor accounts to the court for all business transactions. Failure to do either of the above may result in the court appointing a trustee to operate the business, or in the alternative, a possible dismissal of the action.

During the reorganization, the debtor may sell assets "in the ordinary course of business" and need not obtain approval from the court.[4] If assets are not sold in the ordinary course of business, or if a large portion of or substantially all the assets are sold, whether or not in the ordinary course of business, approval of the court must be obtained. The debtor must keep adequate financial records, which are to be submitted to the trustee on a monthly basis.

While it is axiomatic to remind a creditor to read a plan of reorganization, most creditors who receive a Chapter 11 plan of reorganization normally do not pay attention to the plan if the obligation is not significant. To motivate a creditor to read the plan, one has only to read two cases. In both cases, the court held that the liability of another party for a debt is not affected by the discharge of the debtor, but at the same time a guarantor could be discharged voluntarily as an integral part of any reorganization plan.[5]

---

[3]11 U.S.C. 301; 11 U.S.C. 303.

[4]11 U.S.C. 363(c)(1).

[5]*Michigan National Bank v. Laskowski,* 580 N.W. 2nd 8 (Mich. Ct. App. 1998); *Republic Supply Company v. Shoaf,* 815 F. 2nd 1046 (5th Cir. 1987).

CREDIT AND COLLECTION TIP: *Accordingly, it is possible for a plan of reorganization to contain a provision discharging a guarantor.*

Thus if the bankrupt debtor failed in his plan of reorganization and ultimately had to be liquidated under Chapter 7, the creditor still would not be able to proceed against the guarantor if the bankrupt debtor was discharged under the plan of reorganization. Consult an attorney.

PLAN OF PAYMENT. The debtor is required to offer a plan of payment to the creditors. This plan will apply separately to each classification of claimants (creditors), such as administrative (priority) claimants, secured creditors, or unsecured creditors.

Priority creditors are those who sell or service the bankrupt after the filing. When the debtor continues to do business after the bankruptcy filing and vendors continue to sell goods or render services to the bankrupt business, these creditors are treated as priority administrative claims. If no priority existed, no vendor would sell to a business operating under the bankruptcy act.

Secured creditors are usually financial institutions and banks which have mortgages on real estate and security agreements on automobiles, boats, machinery, and equipment or accounts receivable and inventory. Secured creditors may seek a removal of the stay of proceedings so that they can take possession of their collateral. (See Automatic Stay.)

Unsecured creditors are those claimants which became creditors prior to the filing of the petition but have no security, such as merchandise suppliers and those who render services such as programmers, consultants, or brokers.

Each class of creditor must vote on the approval of the payment plan to the extent that the plan affects those creditors. The plan will be approved by the court if each classification of creditor receives an amount similar or equal to what the creditor would have received in a Chapter 7 proceeding. Accordingly, the bankruptcy court is protecting each creditor to the extent of money that a creditor would receive if the bankrupt were liquidated and all assets were sold at an auction proceeding. Thus, the total amount of the payment plan in reorganization must equal or exceed the amount that could be realized in liquidation (Chapter 7). The bankruptcy judge has the authority to override a negative vote of any particular class of creditors upon showing the totality of the plan is fair to the majority of creditors. This mechanism is known as a "cramdown."

CRAMDOWN

The code allows the Bankruptcy Court to "cramdown" approval of the plan as to a rejecting class of creditors.[6] The provisions affecting the process of cramdown

---

[6]11 U.S.C. 1126.

are distinct for each class of secured creditors, unsecured creditors, and share-holders. The most common case of cramdown occurs where a secured class is oversecured—where the security (automobile or real estate) is more than ade-quate to cover the indebtedness and objects to the plan; and the debtor's interest in the secured property is vital to the conduct of the debtor's business. The court may allow a payment plan for the secured debt. The amount of the secured claim also may be reduced by the court, in the best interest of the estate to the value of the security and thereafter the secured creditor would become an unsecured cred-itor as to the amount reduced.

In the case of unsecured creditors the court must wrestle with the question of valuation in deciding what the estate is worth in a Chapter 7 liquidation. The court in allowing a cramdown in these classes must determine that the class will receive more under the plan than would be received under a liquidation of the assets of the estate. The court uses a test of what a willing buyer would pay for a going concern. This concept may stretch reality, since the fact that the business is in bankruptcy is often forgotten by the creditor and stressed by the proponents of the cramdown. A valuation battle can be costly and the losing party may be ordered to pay the cost.

In a major revision of the cramdown, a class of creditors who are paid in full, but without post-petition interest, may still have an opportunity to vote against the plan. Thus, the bankrupt will be unable to force a cramdown against a class of unsecured creditors unless that particular class is paid interest.

Consult with counsel before any attempt is made to oppose a cramdown.

RESIDENCE MORTGAGES

While the rights of creditors are subject to modification under the bankruptcy act, this privilege of the bankrupt is severely curtailed as it affects the personal home residence. Under the new Bankruptcy Reform Act, while the debtor may have the option to cure defaults, different terms and conditions (such as a new interest rate or a reduction in the balance of the amount due under the mortgage by asserting that the value of the property is less than the amount due under the mortgage) will not be permitted. The purpose of the change is to protect the mortgagee bank from having the loan reduced to the value of the property.

CREDITOR COMMITTEE

The United States trustee is required to create a creditor's committee consisting of the seven largest unsecured creditors.[7] The trustee contacts the 20 largest unse-cured creditors from the list filed in the petition for bankruptcy. If the largest cred-

---

[7] 11 U.S.C. 1102(b)(1).

itors do not serve, other creditors will be selected. A large creditor located geographically convenient to court should consider serving on the creditor's committee if economically feasible. The committee represents all creditors rather than any particular class of creditors and sets its own schedule as to meetings and procedures for voting. The Bankruptcy Act allows the committee to retain professionals such as attorneys, accountants, appraisers, and other types of industry experts needed to achieve their objectives. The creditor's committee will receive the reports concerning the debtors operation when they are filed. The reports and its experience in the industry enable the committee to review the operation of the business as to salaries, shipments of goods, payments of liabilities, purchases of inventory, payments to insiders, and salaries for relatives; and to embark on any appropriate action.

The individual members of the Creditors' Committee usually are not liable for payment of the professional fees since these fees come from the debtor in possession. In some instances, the Creditors' Committee may guarantee to the professionals the payment of their fees.

The Creditors' Committee will designate certain duties of investigation to specific members, so that all devote an equal amount of time to learning about the operation of the debtor's business. The members of the committee will have available the periodical reports furnished to the trustee and will be able to monitor the progress of the debtor in possession in fulfilling a plan of reorganization and, ultimately, coming out of a Chapter 11 bankruptcy.

If the creditor is one of the seven largest unsecured creditors, it probably is advisable to serve on the Creditors' Committee since this creditor has a substantial amount at stake. The proposed plans may offer from 10% to 20% to 50% payment of debts over a period of time, significant dollars to a large creditor. By serving on the Creditors' Committee, the creditor is receiving information as to the operation of the debtor and may be offering input with regard to a proposed plan to be made by the Creditors' Committee. The committee, if necessary, may make an appropriate request to the court for the appointment of a trustee to operate the business in the event it fears that the debtor in possession is not properly conducting the business. The committee may also pursue fraudulent or preferential transfers and furnish this information to the trustee to act upon or actively defend against an improperly filed security interest.

The creditor's committee and the bankrupt become partners in the quest for salvage of the debtor's business. Suggestions as to financing become an all-important function of the committee. Members of the creditor's committee monitor the pulse of the Chapter 11 bankruptcy and must consider the probability of any plan being viable. A good creditor's committee is of invaluable assistance to the debtor.

The creditor's committee works closely with the members of the secured class to reassure them as to the viability of a reorganization to avoid the dismantling of the business.

Separate committees for other holders of claims such as secured parties and pension claimants may also be formed under the Bankruptcy Act pursuant to the discretion of the court.

The most potent weapon of the creditor's committee is to gather organized support or opposition to the Chapter 11 plan. Thus the debtor is careful to cultivate the committee and be as cooperative as possible.

CONVERSIONS. After notice and hearing, any creditor may request that the Chapter 11 reorganization be converted to a Chapter 7 liquidation for the following reasons.[8]

1. The creditor operates the business with continuing losses and no likelihood of rehabilitation is evident.
2. An inability to effectuate a plan.
3. An unreasonable delay takes place in effectuating a plan, which may prejudice creditors.

Of course, the debtor at any time may voluntarily convert the Chapter 11 reorganization to a Chapter 7 liquidation.

CHAPTER 13—WAGE EARNER

Any individual who is a non-corporate business, with regular income whose unsecured debt does not exceed $250,000 and secured debt does not exceed $350,000, may use chapter 13 to file a voluntary bankruptcy petition. This section covers sole proprietors as well as partnerships but is known as a "wage earner" bankruptcy. (The advantages are somewhere between a Chapter 7 liquidation and Chapter 11 reorganization.)

FILING THE PETITION. Filing can be either individual or joint with a spouse.[9] The filing of a Chapter 13 petition operates as a stay of action not only against the debtor who files the petition but also against co-debtors or guarantors on consumer loans during the pendency of the bankruptcy so long as the debt is to be paid in full.[10] A trustee is appointed to collect the funds from the debtor and to file a plan for repayment of the debts within fifteen days after the filing of the petition or such extension as the court allows. Only the Chapter 13 debtor, not the creditors, has a right to file this plan. The plan must provide for all future earnings to be subject to the supervision and control of the trustee and must provide for full payment of all secured claims.

CREDITORS. The plan may provide cash payments for unsecured creditors for periods no longer than three years unless the court allows a longer period

---

[8]11 U.S.C. 1112(b).

[9]11 U.S.C. 302(a).

[10]11 U.S.C. 1301.

upon good cause (but no longer than five years). Unsecured creditors are only required to be paid an amount equal to or exceeding the amount the creditor would have received if a Chapter 7 bankruptcy had been filed. Upon completion of payments, where less than the full amount of debts is paid, the debtor receives a discharge as to the balance not paid under the plan. If the debtor fails to make the payments, the trustee or the creditors may apply to court for an order to convert the bankruptcy to a Chapter 7 or Chapter 11.

A Chapter 13 plan is voluntary, for a debtor cannot be forced into a repayment plan by creditors. In Chapter 13, the real and personal property of the bankrupt is protected from being sold for the benefit of the creditors by the debtor paying the debts or a portion of them over a period of time.

The secured creditor must accept the plan, but retains a lien subject to the automatic stay which prevents the secured creditor from reclaiming or selling the property. The secured creditor recovers the full value of the claim by virtue of the plan. The debtor may surrender the property securing the debt to the secured creditor. The secured creditor then may sell the security after receiving relief from the automatic stay to discharge the secured claim, and become an unsecured creditor as to any balance due.

PAYMENT. Payment under the plan must begin within 30 days after the initial filing unless that time is extended by the court. To share in any distribution, the creditor, whether secured or unsecured, must file a proof of claim before the specified deadline which is set forth in the original notice of bankruptcy.

The new Bankruptcy Reform Act now allows the debtor to protect the personal residence by filing a Chapter 13 up until an actual foreclosure sale (even though a judgment of foreclosure was already entered).

BANKRUPTCY NOTICE

The first notification of a bankruptcy to a creditor is in the form of a computer-generated printed notice from the bankruptcy court. This notice provides the following information:

a. Name and the location of the bankruptcy court, and the case number.

b. The name and address of the debtor.

c. The date that the petition was filed and whether it has been filed under Chapter 7, 11 or 13.

d. The date and time of the first meeting of creditors.

e. A statement that suits and proceedings against the bankrupt are stayed preventing creditors from commencing or continuing suits in state or federal courts and compelling creditors to assert their claims in the bankruptcy court, a more favorable arena for the bankrupt.

f.   The last date for filing of objections is usually set forth in the notice, or in a Chapter 7 proceeding within 60 days after the date set for the first meeting of creditors.

g.   The names, addresses, and telephone numbers of the attorney for the debtor and of the trustee as well as the name of the bankruptcy judge.

h.   Some notices specify that the bankruptcy is listed as a "no assets" case and a proof of claim need not be filed. If assets are located by the trustee, a new notice will be sent enabling the creditor to file a proof of claim.

i.   The total amount of assets and liabilities may be listed.

RESPONSE TO NOTICE. When a creditor receives the bankruptcy notice, the avenues to be considered are the following:

a.   If the claim of the creditor is too small to justify spending the time and effort to file a proof-of-claim, the creditor may ignore the notice of bankruptcy.

b.   The creditor may prepare and file a proof-of-claim with the bankruptcy court.

c.   Consultation with an attorney is recommended if:

1.   the creditor is a secured creditor and wishes to remove the stay of pro-ceedings to enable the creditor to repossess and reclaim the property cov-ered by a secured lien, or seek from the bankrupt a reaffirmation (see Reaffirmation) of the indebtedness

2.   the claim is large

3.   the claim is complicated

4.   the creditor suspects fraud or preferences (see Preferences) and is con-sidering objecting to the discharge

5.   the security that the creditor holds is subject to rapid devaluation

6.   the creditor is uncertain as to which way to proceed

The question of notification of the filing of a bankruptcy petition is gov-erned by certain rules of which many creditors are unaware. The automatic stay is effective even if the creditor is not aware of the filing of the bankruptcy and the creditor may be liable for damages if the creditor proceeds to recover collateral under a lien after receiving notification of the bankruptcy.

If an employee or agent of the creditor has received notice, notice to one office is sufficient notice to the creditor even if the creditor has a multitude of offices. Many courts have stated that the creditor has a duty to inquire before pro-ceeding if the creditor has reason to believe that the debtor may have filed a peti-tion in bankruptcy or even contemplates filing a petition in bankruptcy.

CREDIT AND COLLECTION TIP: *If a creditor hires an outside attorney or collection agency, notice to that attorney or the agency may in fact be notice to the creditor even where the agency or attorney failed to notify the creditor that they received the bankruptcy notice. If a creditor directs an agency to return a case, the creditor should notify the debtor that the case has been returned. Otherwise, the bankruptcy notice may notify the agency or the attorney and the agency or attorney may fail to notify the creditor because they are no longer actively handling the case. A letter to the agency advising them to forward all bankruptcy notices would be helpful.*

COMPLETING A PROOF OF CLAIM

A proof-of-claim form is sometimes furnished by the court, or it may be obtained in a stationery store that stocks legal forms. (A sample form is in the Appendix.) A summary of the basic information that a bankruptcy proof of claim requires is furnished. We recommend that if you complete a proof of claim, the document should be reviewed by competent counsel.

1. At the top of the form insert the proper bankruptcy court, corresponding to the name appearing on the notice of bankruptcy.
2. The case number (or the index number) must correspond to the case number on the notice of bankruptcy. (The number appears with the year '99-0000 or 0000-99).
3. The debtor's name, which corresponds to the name on the notice of bankruptcy, is usually inserted in the rectangular outlined box.
4. The first blank is the identification of whether an individual, a partnership, or a corporation is filing a proof of claim.
5. If a corporation is filing a proof of claim, list the name and the title of the officer. If a partnership, list the name of the partner.
6. Under certain circumstances, an agent may file a proof of claim. (Consult with counsel.)
7. The total amount of the claim must be inserted.
8. The basis of the claim is described by answering the question which asks for the "consideration of the debt." "Merchandise shipped," "monies loaned," or "services rendered" are appropriate responses. Attach invoices, the note or check evidencing the monies loaned, or a bill describing the services rendered.
9. If the claim is based on a written agreement, attach a copy of the agreement.
10. If the claim is founded on an open account, set forth the invoices or the bill for services rendered as specified above.

11. A statement must be made that a judgment has been rendered for the amount due or that no judgment has been rendered for the amount due.

12. An allegation must be set forth as to any payments made and credited and deducted from the amount due.

13. A statement must be made that the claim is not subject to any set-off, offset, or counter claim, and if so, describe the nature of the claim, i.e., the debtor is claiming defective merchandise or claiming fifty-four cartons were never received.

14. A secured claim must be designated as a secured claim and a copy of the documents supporting the secured claim must be attached, including evidence of perfection of the lien, i.e., UCC financing statement and the security agreement or the real estate mortgage.

15. A general unsecured claim must be designated. If priority or secured claims are filed, consult with an attorney. *In the event your claim is not listed as secured, its secured status may be lost and the claim will be treated as unsecured.*

16. Whenever a proof of claim is forwarded to the bankruptcy court, use certified mail or a post card should be enclosed identifying the case by name and case number to be acknowledged by the bankruptcy clerk and thereafter retained as evidence the proof the claim was properly filed on a specific date.

We are attaching in the appendix an example of a notice of a bankruptcy petition issued by the United States Bankruptcy Court, District of Ohio Eastern Division. On the reverse side of this notice of bankruptcy, the provisions of the automatic stay and a Chapter 13 proof of claim form is printed. In addition to the form, the court provides an explanation of the terms used, together with instructions for filing the proof of claim form. While all the bankruptcy courts across the nation do not provide such information, reviewing this particular form should be helpful.

CHAPTER 7. A proof of claim must be filed within 90 days after the first meeting of creditors. Emphasis is on the *first* meeting of creditors and not the last meeting of creditors (which is the marker for objections to discharge).[11] All proofs of claim are deemed valid unless the trustee or debtor files an objection to the claim.[12]

CHAPTER 11. In all Chapter 11 reorganization cases, creditors should file proofs of claim.[13] The time within which a proof of claim must be filed (bar-date) is set by the court and is printed on the notice of bankruptcy. If a claim is properly listed in the schedule by the debtor and is not disputed, the claim will be rec-

---

[11]Bankruptcy Rule 3002(c).

[12]Bankruptcy Rule 3077.

[13]11 U.S.C. 501.

ognized and will receive a full distribution, even if the creditor does not file a proof of claim. Some creditors examine the schedules, and if the schedules list the creditor, no proof of claim is filed. The possibility is always present that the claim is listed improperly, is not recognized, will become lost, or, for any number of reasons, will not be paid. *We recommend that every creditor should file a proof of claim in a Chapter 11 proceeding even if the creditor is properly listed in the schedules.*

CHAPTER 13. Under a Chapter 13 proceeding, a creditor must file a proof of claim to share in any distribution. The notice of bankruptcy provides a "bar-date" by which time the proof of claim must be filed. Under certain circumstances, both in Chapter 11 and Chapter 13 proceedings, the bar-date may be modified by court order in response to an application to court to permit a creditor to file a late proof of claim. These circumstances are extremely rare especially with consumers, for the court rarely grants leave to extend the time.

LATE PROOF OF CLAIM

A considerable amount of case law has developed regarding the efforts of those creditors who fail to file a timely proof of claim to correct and cure this failure and ultimately file a valid proof of claim. The main ingredient that creditors use is excusable neglect and sometimes the neglect of the attorney, and the main reason is that the proof of claim was lost in the mail.

The usual procedure is that the creditor alleges that an "informal proof of claim" was filed within the specified time limits and that the informal "proof of claim" was later amended with a conventional filing and that this conventional filing in turn relates back to the date of the "informal proof of claim." The question is whether the informal proof of claim could possibly qualify as a proof of claim under the bankruptcy code.

Such informal proofs of claim may include letters to the attorney for the estate, letters to the trustee, participation in the proceedings, seeking a relief from stay without making any effort to file a proof of claim, participating in some particular proceeding in the bankruptcy court, or any other activity which falls within the activities mentioned. This method of curing a failure to file a proof of claim is somewhat different from the basic application to court to file a late proof of claim due to excusable neglect. Consult with counsel.

FIRST MEETING OF CREDITORS

Once it has been determined that a petition of bankruptcy was filed, a creditor must be concerned with the following:

A. Filing a proof of claim.

B. Deciding whether to attend the first meeting of creditors (341 Hearing).

C. Retaining an attorney to handle the proceedings before the bankruptcy court.

D. Deciding whether you as a creditor are going to take an active interest in the bankruptcy proceeding whether by objection, removal of automatic stay or merely attending the 341 Hearing.

E. Whether to serve on the creditors committee.

The first meeting of creditors is usually scheduled about four to five weeks after the petition is filed. The first notice of meeting to each creditor that is listed in the schedules contains the date when the first meeting of creditors will be held. The purpose of the first meeting of creditors is to question and examine the debtor with regard to any information that the creditor wishes to obtain which deals with the filing of the petition in bankruptcy.

An individual who is not a partnership or a corporation may appear without an attorney and ask the bankrupt questions. Partnerships and corporations are required to have an attorney represent them before the bankruptcy court.

The Bankruptcy Act permits any party in interest to examine the bankrupt. The examination may relate to any acts, conduct or property that affect the liabilities and financial conditions of the debtor or to any matter which may affect the administration of the debtor's estate or the debtor's right to a discharge. The examination may relate to the operation of any business and the desirability of its continuance, the source of any money or property acquired or to be acquired by the debtor for purposes of consummating a plan and the consideration offered.

But what is more important, the examination may concern any matter relevant to the filing of the petition, the operation of the business or to the formulation of the plan. This is a broad stroke to enable a creditor to examine the debtor. The first meeting of creditors is an important meeting in a bankruptcy proceeding and if a creditor has any reservations or suspicions, this is the meeting where the creditor should be present to question the debtor.

The clerk of the bankruptcy court as well as the attorney for the bankrupt must provide notice to the creditors of any significant occurrence that develops in a bankruptcy hearing. The bankrupt must also notify the creditors in the event the bankrupt is objecting to their claims or attacking the question of whether they have a properly secured lien on property. For this reason all bankruptcy notices should be read carefully and the creditor should be careful to peruse the notice to be certain of the time frames within which responses must be given.

It is recommended that you use an attorney if any proceedings are to be conducted before the bankruptcy court. The proceedings are complicated and are not the same type of proceedings that take place in other courts. Failure to meet time periods can cause a creditor to lose fundamental rights.

BANKRUPTCY SCHEDULES

When a business files a bankruptcy petition, the bankruptcy code requires them to submit a schedule of all their assets and liabilities and also a complete statement of their financial condition. They also must file a listing of both their contingent and their fixed liabilities. On the asset side they must list all the real estate they own as well as their machinery, equipment and vehicles and they must indicate whether any of these fixed assets have been furnished as security for loans. The schedules are detailed and are organized as responses to twenty searching questions involving the bankrupt's past and present financial operation.

A creditor may secure a copy of these schedules for a nominal fee by contacting the Clerk at the Bankruptcy Court. The simplest way to do this is to mail a request for the schedule to the clerk (call first to inquire about the fee). Within a short time you will receive the information. If the court is nearby, you can go there and usually obtain a copy right away or you can have your attorney obtain a copy of the schedules for you. Some of the bankruptcy courts are online.

> **CREDIT AND COLLECTION TIP:** *If you wish to know whether a petition has been filed, you may call the court and ask the clerk.*

EXEMPTIONS

Under the federal bankruptcy law certain assets in bankruptcy, which are deemed to be necessary for sustenance and living, may be exempt from the reach of creditors:

a. A homestead exemption of $15,000 of the equity in real property which is the principal residence. Some states allow larger homestead exemptions. Florida's exemption is the value of the residence and can exceed one million dollars.

b. An amount not to exceed $7,500 in cash or personal property, if the debtor is not using the homestead exemption. In a joint petition this amount doubles where both spouses own the property.

c. A motor vehicle whose equity does not exceed $2,400.

d. A grub stake consisting of any property or cash value which does not exceed $400.

e. Any number of household items, each of whose value does not exceed $400. Some states limit the total amount claimed, i.e., Texas has a $30,000 limit.

f. Jewelry not exceeding $1,000 in value.

g. Other specific exemptions, such as tools of trade for carpenters, electricians, or plumbers, professional books, etc., up to $1,500 in value.

h.   Life insurance up to $8,000 in value.

i.   Personal injury exemption $15,000 (recovery for injuries sustained in an accident).

j.   Certain pension payments and government payments.

In most instances, the exemptions allowed under state law are more generous than those under federal law. The bankrupt debtor may select the more generous exemptions provided under state law. A review of the state law where the bankrupt resides is recommended.

JURISDICTION

The Bankruptcy Court retains original jurisdiction over all matters which directly affect the bankrupt's estate. Filing a proof of claim constitutes submission to the jurisdiction of the Bankruptcy Court. Thus, a trustee acquires authority to sue a New York creditor in a California Bankruptcy Court.

Counsel for bankrupt estates operate under the assumption that the Bankruptcy Court is "debtor friendly." Thus, the bankrupt will usually request the Bankruptcy Court to retain jurisdiction and handle the claim of the distant creditor. Jurisdiction is discretional, so counsel should be consulted as to whether a specific controversy, such as a landlord/tenant matter, may be litigated in a state court more friendly to a creditor.

AUTOMATIC STAY

Upon the filing of a petition, an automatic stay prevents a creditor from taking any further action in any court except in the Bankruptcy Court.[14] A creditor is prohibited from:

a.   Commencing or continuing a lawsuit against the debtor.

b.   Enforcing a judgment against the debtor.

c.   Creating or enforcing liens.

Thus all suits and proceedings against the debtor must cease. The claim against the debtor is made by filing a proof of claim. The trustee may accept the proof of claim, move to reduce the claim, or expunge it entirely. These matters will be resolved by the Bankruptcy Court.

A secured creditor may apply to the court to remove a stay of proceedings with regard to the creditor's security. If the security is not necessary to the oper-

---

[14] 11 U.S.C. 362.

ation of the business, the Bankruptcy Court may grant an order removing the stay and permit the creditor to recover the property.

Although the Bankruptcy Court has jurisdiction over the property of the bankrupt estate, the court does not have to exercise jurisdiction, and may allow a creditor to foreclose its mortgage in State Court once the automatic stay is removed.

Violations of the automatic stay will usually result in attorney's fees and costs being awarded to the bankrupt. In some cases, punitive damages are awarded and can approach five and six figures, depending upon the extent of the violation and whether the violation is blatant.[15]

REAFFIRMATION

Reaffirmation of a debt permits a debtor to repay an obligation even after a discharge in bankruptcy. By reaffirming the debt to the creditor, the debtor agrees to continue to pay the debt according to the terms of the agreement entered into when the debt was granted. While relatively easy under the prior bankruptcy law, the Bankruptcy Reform Act now requires the agreement to contain a clause that specifically states that reaffirmation agreements may be declined, because the debtor does not have to reaffirm the debt. An additional provision states that the attorney for the debtor has advised the bankrupt of the effect of the agreement and the consequences of a default. If the bankrupt has no attorney representing him/her, the bankrupt must appear in court for a hearing to be certain the agreement is understood. Notice of reaffirmation is provided to all creditors.

A recent case in the 9th District has added some further restrictions to the recent amendments to the Bankruptcy Code. The court noted that the agreement contained language that the debtor had a right to rescind the reaffirmation agreement, but found that the statement was in the same typeface, size, and format as the bulk of the agreement. The court stated that for the "clear and conspicuous" requirement to be met, it must be made prominent in some fashion. Using the same typewriter print as the rest of the agreement is apparently insufficient. Review your reaffirmation agreements and be certain that the requirements set forth in the amendments either be underlined, set forth in bold type or separated from the rest of the agreement and be clear and conspicuous—either outlined with a box or in some other manner. While this is only one decision in the 9th district, it will certainly be utilized by consumers' attorneys in other districts.[16]

In the early 1990s, Sears suffered significant media attention concerning its auto repair operation which had charged numerous customers for unnecessary repairs. In 1997, the media again had a field day with the so-called "debt collec-

---

[15]In re Bush, 166 B.R. 69 (Bankr. W.D. Va. 1994), *rev'd,* 166 B.R. 34 (W.D. Va. 1994).

[16]In re Noble, 182 B.R. 854 (Bankr. W.D. Wash. 1995).

tion" scandal whereby Sears violated the bankruptcy rules regarding the obtaining and filing reaffirmation agreements and at the same time threatened discharged bankruptcy debtors with collection of debts that were improperly reaffirmed and thus were discharged in bankruptcy.

Shortly thereafter, the scandal hit the May Department Stores and Montgomery Ward. Federated Department Stores was not far behind, admitting that they may have a problem similar to Sears. Sears alone estimated that since 1992 it had improperly collected over $160 million dollars. The numbers for the other department stores were not as severe but were significant.

The problem started with a letter from a bankrupt addressed to a bankruptcy judge in Massachusetts, complaining that he was still paying Sears on a debt listed in bankruptcy and that he would like to reopen the bankruptcy case so he could discharge all of his debts including the Sears debt. The bankruptcy judge was curious as to why Sears was still collecting on this debt which was discharged in bankruptcy. Sears countered with the point that the debtor had signed a reaffirmation agreement. However, Sears did not file the reaffirmation agreement in the court before the date of discharge as required by the bankruptcy rules.

It appears that Sears had abandoned the filing of the reaffirmation agreements since it had been criticized in past years by some governmental authorities who said that the reaffirmation agreements were improperly drawn. Sears continued to use the reaffirmation agreements, but did not file. If the reaffirmation agreement was received after discharge, to file the agreement Sears would have to reopen the bankruptcy.

Sears apparently also pursued some of the debtors for collection of the debt. As to the secured debt that was reaffirmed, its only recourse upon default was to obtain recovery of the collateral.

The violations by Sears were twofold. Whereas some agreements were filed, most were not. Secondly, Sears threatened to repossess certain items that were sold to bankrupts when it knew that had no intention of repossessing the items because it was economically prohibitive to repossess. As a result, it was threatening to take certain actions which in fact it had no intention of taking and also was trying to collect discharged debts. This activity was a violation of certain consumer practice laws in the various states and probably of the FDCPA.

One might wonder why Sears was successful in obtaining so many reaffirmation agreements. Perhaps the answer to this question was that it offered the bankrupt the continued use of the Sears charge account in the event the bankrupt reaffirmed the debt. The reaffirmation agreements not only applied to secured debts, such as appliances and other significant items under which retailers are allowed to retain a secured interest, but also to unsecured debt in which the bankrupt was induced to reaffirm because of the offer of the continued use of the charge card.

In Massachusetts, a settlement order apparently was approved by the court to refund a sum of money running into millions of dollars to be distributed to the various bankrupt debtors who executed the reaffirmation agreements.

Interestingly, suit was instituted by the attorney general and consumers. Sears capitulated and did not litigate the class certification or the merits of the case.

Reaffirmation agreements must be filed with the court before discharge. In addition, the attorney for the debtor must sign an affidavit alleging that the bankrupt was advised of the effect of the agreement and the consequences of a default. If the debtor does not have an attorney, the bankrupt must appear in court for a hearing to confirm that the reaffirmation agreement is understood. Notice of reaffirmation is provided to all creditors.

The Bankruptcy Reform Act now offers additional protection to secured creditors and lessors of vessels, rolling stock, and aircraft. The creditor may recover the assets in spite of the automatic stay or a plan of reorganization, unless within 60 days after filing the petition, the bankrupt agrees to reaffirm the obligation and cure any defaults that occurred either before or after the petition was filed. Secured creditors will find the details of this section significantly helpful.

VOLUNTARY PAYMENTS

If the debtor is current on his payments at the time the petition was filed and wants to retain the vehicle, payments continue to be made by the debtor and the account remains current with the creditor. The debtor must meet all contract conditions such as carrying insurance, etc. Attorneys for the bankrupt often recommend this procedure to their clients rather than using the device of a reaffirmation agreement because there are some distinct advantages for the debtor.

When a debtor merely continues payments without any written reaffirmation, the creditor has a right to receive the payments and continues to have the right to repossess the collateral if the debtor defaults in the payments. Nevertheless, the creditor loses all rights to sue the debtor for a deficiency if the collateral cannot be sold for a sufficient amount to discharge the debt. Little motivation exists for the debtor to keep the collateral in good condition since if he defaults in payment and the collateral is repossessed, he will not be liable for any deficiency. The debtor is effectively converting his secured debt in bankruptcy from a recourse obligation to a non-recourse obligation with no liability for failing to maintain or insure the lender's collateral.

The U.S. Bankruptcy Code 521(2) does not permit a debtor to retain the collateral without either redeeming the property or reaffirming the debt. Two circuits have held that a debtor who is current in the payments may retain the collateral without redemption or reaffirmation (2nd Circuit and 9th Circuit). On the other hand, three circuits have held that the debtor, to retain collateral, must either redeem or reaffirm the debt and they do not allow the option of the debtor to continue to make current payments without reaffirming the debt (1st Circuit, 7th Circuit, 11th Circuit).

A split between the circuit courts is fairly apparent and the option to the debtor is only available in certain bankruptcy courts. At some time in the future, the Supreme Court will resolve the question. In the meanwhile, it is important for you to consult with counsel to determine whether the debtor has this option to make current payments without reaffirming the debt and whether you as a creditor wish to take steps to see whether you could oppose this option in those circuits that allow the debtor to use the device.[17]

REAFFIRMATION—LETTER TO THE DEBTOR

An attorney for a debtor argued strenuously that mailing a copy of a letter seeking reaffirmation to a debtor who is represented by an attorney in a bankruptcy proceeding is prohibited. The court relied on Section 524 (c)(3)(A) which requires an attorney to declare in an affidavit that the debtors consent to a reaffirmation agreement was "fully informed and voluntary" and in this case the Illinois Rule of Professional Conduct requires an attorney to keep her client reasonably informed about the status of the matter. The court felt that sending a copy of a letter directly to the debtor was not improper as long as it was not inherently coercive or threatening. The court left open the possibility that if the party writing the letter was a debt collector, there might be a violation of the Fair Debt Collection Practices Act since the debt collector may not communicate with the consumer without the consumers permission if the debt collector knows the consumer is represented by an attorney with respect to such debt and has knowledge of, or can readily ascertain such an attorney's name and address. In this particular case Sears was not a debt collector in the sense that they were collecting debts of others. As a result, the letter was held not to violate the automatic stay provisions nor does the bankruptcy code require as a matter of law that the creditor refrain from copying the debtor on correspondence to the debtor's attorney.[18]

On the other hand, a bankruptcy court held that Ohio which prohibits *direct* solicitation in an attempt to collect debts of debtors known to be represented by attorneys does prevent creditors from seeking reaffirmation agreements under the bankruptcy code by communicating directly with the debtor. The determination was that seeking a reaffirmation agreement was the equivalent of an attempt to collect the debt and thus did fall within the Ohio code. Whether this preemption would be recognized by the federal courts has not been tested, but it points out a sound reason why a review of the particular state law must be made in all instances.[19]

---

[17]In re Burr, 218 B.R. 267 (1st Cir. 1998); *Bank of Boston v. James E. and Katherine A. Burr,* 160 F.3d 843 (1st Cir. 1998)

[18]In the matter of Duke, 7 F.3d 43 (7th Cir. 1996).

[19]*Greenwood Trust v. Smith,* 212 B.R. 599 (B.A.P. 8th Cir. 1997).

A letter offering the debtor an opportunity to reaffirm a debt has been accepted by the courts, as long as the letter is non-threatening and does not appear to coerce the debtor into executing the reaffirmation agreement.[20]

The concept that an offer of reaffirmation violates the automatic stay has been generally rejected by the courts. If this proposition was considered, the whole concept of offering debtors reaffirmation agreements would be undermined; for the opportunity to communicate with the debtor would be terminated. If such was the case, no purpose would exist for Congress to enact the particular sections of the bankruptcy law which enable debtors to reaffirm their debt.

In a recent amendment to the bankruptcy code, the procedure is as follows:

1. Offers the debtor an opportunity to rescind the reaffirmation agreement.
2. Requires an attorney's affidavit that the debtor is fully informed about all rights concerning the reaffirmation agreement.
3. The debtor must be told that there is no obligation to reaffirm.
4. The debtor must execute the reaffirmation voluntarily.
5. The agreement must not impose upon the debtor no undue burden or hardship. In general, the attorneys will not allow their clients to reaffirm a debt unless they have a job or some other obvious source of income which will enable the debtor to make the required payments.

All of these protections being afforded to the debtor would be useless if at the same time the courts interfered with the communication between the creditor and the debtor. The purpose is to require creditors to clearly disclose that the debtor has the option to exercise the right to reaffirm voluntarily and that no language is contained in the letter which might coerce the debtor or mislead the debtor into entering the reaffirmation agreement.

DISMISSAL OF A BANKRUPTCY

After a petition is filed in bankruptcy, the debtor trustee or the creditor may apply to court to dismiss the petition. One reason for dismissal is that the bankrupt has not qualified as a bankrupt. Upon a showing of bad faith by the debtor, the court also may dismiss the petition as "a substantial abuse" of the bankruptcy code. This remedy of substantial abuse is only available to the court and an application based on these grounds is not available to the trustee or a creditor. While arguments may be made that this is unreasonable, the language in the bankruptcy code is specific.

---

[20]In re Hazzard, No. 94 B 18893, 1995 WL 110588, (Bankr. N.D. Ill. Feb. 10, 1995); *In re Jefferson,* 144 B.R. 620 (Bankr. D.R.I. 1992).

PREFERENCES

Nothing prohibits a debtor from preferring one of its creditors over another. For instance, I can pay my Visa Card and ignore American Express. This preference changes once a bankruptcy petition is filed. A preference is a transfer of property by the debtor within 90 days prior to filing of the petition to a creditor for an antecedent debt, defined as an obligation due from the bankrupt which arose prior to the time payment is made, and not incurred at the same time payment is made. The transaction must take place while the debtor is insolvent.[21]

The debtor is considered insolvent for a ninety-day period prior to the filing of the bankruptcy petition. The transfer of property is defined broadly and encompasses direct, indirect, conditional, voluntary, and involuntary transfers.[22] Furnishing property as security would also constitute a preference.

The transfer is a preference only if the creditor receives more than he or she would have received in a Chapter 7 bankruptcy. For instance, payment made to creditor from the sale of a secured property within the ninety-day period is not a preference if the creditor would have received the same amount by virtue of its secured status in the bankruptcy proceedings.

An example of a preference is as follows: A creditor anticipates that a debtor will be filing a petition in bankruptcy and the creditor and debtor are friendly. The debtor ships to the creditor a portion of the inventory in payment of an old debt incurred a year ago. In the next 30 or 60 days a petition in bankruptcy is filed. The trustee could recover from the creditor the inventory returned or its equivalent value providing the creditor meets the criteria for a preference.

Certain exceptions exist with regard to a preference.

1. Where the transaction between the creditor and debtor was a contemporaneous exchange of goods or services for new value, it is not a preference.

2. Payments that are made in the ordinary course of business are not preferences even if for an antecedent debt. The criteria are that the debt must be incurred in the ordinary course of business, payment must be made in the ordinary course of business and in the customary manner of conducting normal business. For example, if the custom was to pay bills on terms of 90 days, then the bill would not be considered an antecedent debt and the payment is not a preference.

3. Security liens granted to creditors for new advances, extensions of credit, or loans are not considered preferences. This exception is targeted at sellers of goods or banks that extend credit to purchase property that then becomes the security for the extension of credit.

4. Statutory liens, such as those of garagemen, mechanics, landlords, and artisans are liens created under state law to provide protection for certain types

---

[21]11 U.S.C. 547

[22]11 U.S.C. 101(54)

of creditors and may only be avoided in bankruptcy under unusual circumstances by the trustee. Normally the liens cannot be attacked as a preference.

5. With regard to a consumer, if the total value of the property involved in the transfer is less than $600, the trustee cannot avoid the transfer.

6. Returning merchandise to a creditor is not a preference.

Several other exceptions to the preference criteria are available, and consultation with counsel is recommended.

INSIDER PREFERENCES

An "insider" is defined as a spouse, child, parent, relative, or partner of the debtor. Transfers to insiders up to a year prior to filing a petition may be set aside. The "insider preference" extends to insiders who guarantee corporate debts, and in anticipation of bankruptcy, cause the corporation to pay the corporate debt to the bank. The guarantor wants the corporation to pay the debt since the personal liability of the guarantor is being reduced with each payment to the bank. The insider's liability on the guarantee is reduced to the detriment of the other general creditors who have not received a personal guarantee. The trustee may proceed to recover the payments to the banks, who are usually the beneficiaries of such an arrangement. This right of recapture by the trustee was modified by the Bankruptcy Reform Act. Where the loan repayment to the bank is made by one other than an insider, the payments may not be subject to recapture. Consult with counsel.

OBJECTION TO DISCHARGE

A creditor or the trustee may file an objection to the bankruptcy or to bar a discharge of a particular debt on the following grounds:[23]

1. Debtor is shown to have concealed assets or transferred assets without consideration prior to bankruptcy or for less than fair consideration.[24]

2. Failure to keep proper records.[25]

3. Perjury by the debtor.[26]

4. Failure to explain disposition of assets to the satisfaction of the court.[27]

5. A false financial statement or fraud in obtaining credit.[28]

---

[23]11 U.S.C. 727.
[24]11 U.S.C. 727(a)(2).
[25]11 U.S.C. 727(a)(3).
[26]11 U.S.C. 727(a)(4).
[27]11 U.S.C. 727(a)(5).
[28]11 U.S.C. 523(a)(2).

If a bank relied, in granting credit, on two pieces of real estate allegedly owned by the debtor and the representation was false, in that only one parcel of real estate was owned, the debt will not be discharged. The creditor must prove that the loan would not have been made if the representation was known to be false. Providing an inflated value of the property or a false financial statement is not sufficient evidence of misrepresentation unless the creditor can prove that the credit would not have been extended. Where the assets disclosed are sufficient to support the granting of the credit notwithstanding the false statement as to other assets, the discharge will be allowed.

TIME LIMITATION TO FILE OBJECTION

Section 523 (C) (1) provides that the debtor shall be discharged from any non-dischargeable debts unless on request of a creditor to whom the debt is owed and after notice and a hearing, the court determines such debt to be excepted from discharge. Accordingly, a debtor will be discharged from certain debts unless the creditor takes **affirmative action** to have the debt declared non-dischargeable. Rule 4007 (C) states that any complaint to determine the dischargeability of any debt shall be filed not later than 60 days following the first date set for the meeting of creditors held pursuant to a 341 pursuant to Section 341(A).

In plain terminology it means that the creditor has *60 days* after the *first date* set for the meeting of creditors to assert a claim that a debt is non-dischargeable. The creditor also has the right to move for an extension of time before the expiration of the original deadline. Nevertheless, the time period is relatively short and a creditor must act quickly to assert a claim that a debt is non-dischargeable. If the creditor fails to meet the time limitation, the debt will probably be discharged since the courts are reluctant to allow a creditor to cure this default. Immediate consultation with counsel is recommended. The time period is not changed by the mere fact that the trustee adjourned the first 341 meeting.[29]

NONDISCHARGEABLE DEBTS

The Bankruptcy Code provides for certain types of debts to be nondischargeable in bankruptcy. These debts are not affected by the bankruptcy, and survive.

1. Most taxes.
2. Debts which were created by the debtor practicing fraud or misrepresentation by use of a false financial statement upon which the creditor relied.
3. Unscheduled debts are not discharged. If the bankrupt did not list the debt in the bankruptcy petition, the debt will not be discharged. The courts have

---

[29]In re Glover, 212 B.R. 860 (Bankr. S.D. Ohio 1997).

held that if the creditor knew about the bankruptcy, or received some notice of the bankruptcy in sufficient time to file a proof of claim, the debt may be discharged (but there are exceptions).

4. Any debt which is a result of embezzlement or larceny.

5. Alimony, maintenance, and support are excluded.

6. Obligations to pay fines (such as traffic fines) are not dischargeable.

7. Student loans.

8. Debts as a result of drunk driving.

9. Debts due to willful, intentional, and malicious injury.

10. Funds which have been borrowed for the purpose of paying nondischargeable federal tax liabilities (added by the Bankruptcy Reform Act). The practice of borrowing money to pay back taxes, and then listing the debt in bankruptcy and discharging the debt to the lender, while not that common, was frequent enough for the Internal Revenue Bureau to persuade Congress to close the loophole. The benefit is to the lender, and now the debt will not be discharged.

Under Section 523 (a) (2) (A) of the Bankruptcy Code, a debt for money, credit, property or services will not be discharged in bankruptcy if it is obtained by false pretenses, false representation, or actual fraud by means of a statement respecting the debtor's financial condition. The question before the court was whether the debt fell under this section of the statute when he charged against his credit card, was unable to pay the credit card bill and was seeking a discharge in bankruptcy of the credit card debt. The creditor, of course, was claiming that the debtor was charging a debt fraudulently knowing that he would be unable to pay it. The court held that the creditor must show actual fraud, i.e., the debtor did not intend to repay the charges at the time the charges were made. The debtor relied on a test *In re Dougherty*[30] which consisted of various factors of circumstantial evidence which are considered in determining the debtor's intent. These factors are as follows:

(1) The length of time between the charges made and the filing of the bankruptcy.

(2) Whether or not an attorney has been consulted concerning the filing of the bankruptcy before the charges were made.

(3) The number of charges made.

(4) The amount of the charges.

(5) Financial condition of the debtor at the time the charges were made.

(6) Whether the charges were above the credit limit.

(7) Whether the debtor made multiple charges on the same day.

---

[30]*In re Dougherty,* 84 B.R. 653 (B.A.P. 9th Cir. 1988).

(8) Whether or not the debtor was employed.

(9) The debtor's prospects for employment.

(10) The financial sophistication of the debtor.

(11) Whether there was a sudden change in the debtor's buying habits.

(12) Whether the purchases were made for luxuries or necessaries.

The court found this test was the preferable approach to determining whether a debt will be non-dischargeable under Section 523 (a) (2) (A) and the court applied this analysis.[31]

A major classification of debts that are non-dischargeable includes debt acquired by a false financial statement in writing with regard to the financial condition of the debtor used to induce the creditor to extend credit and upon which the creditor relied.

The courts are somewhat uncomfortable with this question of reliance and since the bankruptcy judges' major duty is to discharge a debtor, they seek reasons to have a debt discharged notwithstanding the claim that the creditor relied on the misrepresentation. If the misrepresentation was with regard to a minor asset of the debtor, the court might say that the creditor relied on the major assets of the debtor, and that the misrepresentation was immaterial.

Actual fraud by the debtor may be committed by a false representation, by a false pretense, or by some other act of conduct which constitutes the fraud, even without a written statement. The fraud category rests on the fact that a creditor is extending credit based upon misrepresentation of the debtor, whether in a credit application or in any other form of communication. The false representation may be oral as opposed to the use of a written financial statement.

The one area where credit card companies have run into severe problems is where they have issued unsolicited pre-approved credit cards. The credit is extended based on some credit scoring system or other type of screening but with no investigation of the financial status of the debtor. The courts do not look favorably upon the creditor who cannot provide information about the debtors assets and liabilities to justify reliance upon the representations made by the debtor on the credit card application.[32]

Interestingly, one case seemed to show evidence that the debtor had received a preapproved credit card while the debtor's bankruptcy was actually proceeding.[33]

Increasing the limit of the debtor on a credit card without making an investigation regarding the financial condition of the debtor may also be considered by the court when proceeding with a non-dischargeability action.[34]

---

[31]*Matter of Janecek*, 183 B.R. 571, (Bankr. D. Neb. 1995).

[32]Household Credit Services, Inc. v. Walters, 208 B.R. 651 (Bankr. W.D. La. 1997).

[33]In re Hunter, 210 B.R. 212 (Bankr. M.D. Fla. 1997).

[34]In re Sziel, 206 B.R. 490 (Bankr. N.D. Ill. 1997).

The 2nd Circuit is becoming more cognizant of the substantial abuse that sometimes takes place in the bankruptcy courts when they allowed both the trustee and the creditor to participate in the process of objecting to the discharge of a debtor who was a living example of abuse of the statute. The lifestyle of the debtor included over $50,000 a year to send children to private school, but at the same time the debtor was filing a petition in bankruptcy. They had an income of over $400,000. Eventually, the pendulum does swing.[35]

Consultation with counsel is advised as to other nondischargeable debts.

STUDENT LOANS

A student loan may be discharged in bankruptcy through use of a Chapter 13 plan which specifically states the terms under which the student loan will be paid, and contains the magic language that allows a student loan to be discharged pursuant to Section 5-23 (A)(8).

Student loans as a rule may not be discharged unless the court determines that payment of the loan will impose "undue hardship" on the debtor or the debtor's dependents.

Courts have exercised wide discretion in determining on a case-by-case basis when repayment of the loan will impose an undue hardship. Different standards and factors have been used in making these determinations and, as a general rule, the standards are expressed in general terms. Some bankruptcy courts will state that a filing of undue hardship requires the presence of unique or extraordinary circumstances which render it unlikely that the debtor would ever be able to honor his obligations. Other courts have used a four-point test in determining whether there is undue hardship by considering:

1. the accumulated wealth of the debtor
2. the debtor's chance of retaining steady employment
3. the amount the debtor will need to maintain a minimum living standard
4. whether there would be anything left to make payments on the student loan without reducing what is needed for living expenses.

Other courts require good faith for a finding of undue hardship. Still other bankruptcy courts have used a test of two factors:

1. if the dominant purpose of the bankruptcy was to escape a student loan
2. whether the education obtained through the loan had enhanced the debtor's earning capacity.

---

[35]In re Robert N. and Karen E. Cornfeld 164 F. 3d 778 (2nd Cir. 1999).

Unfortunately, the courts accept that they must make a yes or no decision whereas in many instances, the debtor can pay some of the student loan, but not necessarily all of the student loan. This is predicated on the fact that usually the debtor can make some monthly payments and the court is examining some way to recover monies on the student loan and at the same time permit the debtor to carry on with his life. Thus, a solution presented by the 10th Circuit in this matter is not unusual and may be adopted by other courts.[36]

The 3rd Circuit has now joined the 2nd, 6th, and 7th Circuits in stating that a student loan cannot be discharged in a Chapter 7 proceeding unless repaying it will cause "undue hardship." In the instant case the debtor was seeking a discharge of a student loan of $30,000 because he was only making $27,000 a year. Mere financial sacrifice was not sufficient and apparently the only way the court might discharge the loan is if the burden of paying the loan would cause the bankrupt to fall below the minimum standard of living. The end result is that it is probably more difficult than before to obtain a discharge utilizing the hardship route.

The Statute of Limitations on government-insured student loans was removed in 1998. The new law became effective on October 7, 1998.

RETURN OF GOODS

The Bankruptcy Reform Act now allows the bankrupt, after the petition has been filed, to return goods to the seller and allow the seller to assert a setoff against its claim against the bankrupt.[37]

MONITORING LIEN IN BANKRUPTCY

The well known statement that "liens pass through bankruptcy unaffected" is far too broad for creditors to rely on, for there are many ways in which liens may be affected by the bankruptcy proceeding, especially where creditors participate in the bankruptcy proceedings. The normal rule, where a debtor plan under Chapter 13 does not expressly preserve a secured creditors lien, is that the confirmation of the plan acts to extinguish the lien provided that:

1. The secured creditor participated in the debtor's case by filing a proof of claim.
2. The property was either dealt with or provided for by the plan.

---

[36] *Andersen vs. HEAF* (In re Doreen & Anderson) 215 B.R. 792 (KS, 1998).

[37] 11 U.S.C. 546(g).

It is necessary for a creditor to file a proof of claim. The problem is that once a creditor files a proof of claim, most creditors do not follow the bankruptcy if the amount involved is not significant upon the premise that the bankruptcy court will protect the creditor and that their lien will pass through the bankruptcy court proceeding.

It is necessary that the creditor's property be dealt with or provided for in the Chapter 13 plan itself. If the plan does not provide for the secured status, the lien is lost. Before a plan can be confirmed, the bankruptcy court normally holds a hearing on the confirmation of the debtor's plan and the creditor has an opportunity to object to the confirmation. If the creditor does not object, the plan will be confirmed.[38]

VALUATION OF SECURITY

Chapter 13 of the Bankruptcy Court permits a debtor to retain the use and possession of property while paying creditors out of future earnings. The property that most consumers want to retain is their automobile or their home, which are usually subject to a security agreement or mortgage. The Chapter 13 plan may state that the creditor retains the lien on the automobile and the debtor continues to make payments equal to the "present value" of the automobile.

The courts have variously considered the "present value" to be retail value, the replacement value, the fair market value or the wholesale value. Some courts have used the replacement value on the theory that the debtor is continuing to use the car, whereas other courts have emphasized the wholesale value. If the creditor recovered the car, the car would be sold and the wholesale value would be the closest to what the creditor would recover. The Fifth Circuit has chosen the foreclosure value of the car, which probably is somewhat less than the wholesale value of the car (which was adopted by the Sixth Circuit Court of Appeals).[39]

The differences between the circuits were partially resolved by the Supreme Court identifying the proper value to be applied to secured property which the debtor retains in a Chapter 13 case. The appropriate value to use when a Chapter 13 debtor elects to retain the property is the "replacement" value. The definition of replacement value offered by the Supreme Court was "the price a willing buyer in the debtor's trade, business or situation would pay a willing seller to obtain a property of like age and condition." Section 506 Sub. (A) of the Bankruptcy Code was the basis of this decision,

> "such value shall be determined in light of the purpose of the valuation and of the proposed disposition or use of such property."

---

[38]In re Siemers, 205 B.R. 583 (Bankr. D. Minn. 1997).

[39]In re Trimble, 50 F.3d 530 (9th Cir. 1995); *Matter of Rash,* 90 F.3d 1036 (5th Cir. 1996); In re Hoskins, 102 F.3d 311 (7th Cir. 1996); *General Motors Acceptance Corp. v. Jones, 999 F.2d 63 (3d Cir. 1993).*

The Court decided that if the debtor retained the property, the creditor could not possibly foreclose on the property and sell it in a commercially reasonable sale. Therefore, the foreclosure value of the property would certainly be inappropriate. Since the debtor intended to use the property to generate a stream of income, the actual use, rather than a foreclosure sale that will never take place, is the proper guide under a prescription hinged to the property's "disposition or use." The theory of some of the circuits to allow a different valuation based on the facts and circumstances of each case was also rejected. The Court also rejected the idea of averaging a replacement value and a foreclosure value and arriving at some figure in between. Unfortunately, the Court did not identify exactly what "the replacement value" actually is and it appears that this will be left to further litigation. The replacement value could mean the retail value or wholesale value or even some other value depending upon the type of the debtor, the nature of the property and the use to which the property will ultimately be applied.

This particular theory probably will be applied to Chapter 11 as well as Chapter 7 bankruptcies. Unfortunately, litigation over a more refined definition of "replacement value" will probably continue.[40]

RIGHT OF SET-OFF

The question of whether a bank can set off a deposit made by a bankrupt prior to bankruptcy against a loan incurred by the bankrupt has created conflict among the district courts leading to the Supreme Court of the United States finally resolving the question.

The right of set-off entitles persons who owe each other money to apply their mutual debts against each other, thereby avoiding the absurdity of making A pay B when B also owes A. In simpler terms, if Smith owed Jones money and Jones owed Smith money, they offset the money against each other rather than have Smith pay Jones and then Jones pay Smith. Under the bankruptcy code, no specific provision governs whether a creditor has a right of set-off. Section 553(a) provides that whatever rights to a set-off exist under state law are preserved under the federal law in bankruptcy.

Monies on deposit in a bank account are technically a loan by the depositor to the bank, and the bank must repay this loan on demand less any expenses assessed by the bank. The bank occasionally seeks to offset these monies in the bank account against an actual loan made by the bank to the depositor. If no right of set-off by the bank existed, and the monies on deposit were turned over to the Trustee in bankruptcy, the bankrupt depositor might repay the loan over a 3-year period of time under Chapter 13. On the other hand if the proceeding was in Chapter 7 with no right of set-off, the bank will pay the monies on deposit to the Trustee and will receive only whatever distribution the other unsecured creditors

---

[40]*Associates Commercial Corp. vs. Rash*, 117 S. Ct. 1879, 138 L. Ed. 2d 694 (1997).

receive (usually 10 cents or less on the dollar). In many consumer bankruptcies, no distribution is made and even where assets are available, the distribution is usually minimal. Therefore, the right of set-off is a significant advantage to the bank where money is on deposit in the checking account of the bankrupt and an outstanding loan of the bankrupt is in default. But the question arises as to whether this right of set-off violates the automatic stay of all proceedings which affects every creditor after bankruptcy is filed.

In the case that came before the Supreme Court, the results were diametrically opposite each step of the way. The bankruptcy court originally ruled that the bank's "administrative hold" (where the bank put a hold on the bank account but did not transfer any monies to the bank) on the monies on deposit in the bankrupt's account amounted to a set-off and violated the automatic stay. The bank was then sanctioned. After this sanctioning, the bank released the "administrative hold" and immediately made an application for removal of the stay in the bankruptcy court. The bankruptcy court authorized the bank to set off the respondent's remaining checking account balance against the unpaid loan since the court took the position that the creditor was proceeding in the bankruptcy court and therefore was entitled to a removal of the stay, whereas before, the creditor moved unilaterally without the approval of the bankruptcy court.

The problem with this favorable decision by the bankruptcy court was that the respondent had reduced the checking account balance to zero, so at this point there was nothing to set off. The horse had left the barn.

The district court then rendered a decision diametrically opposed to the bankruptcy court and reversed the judgment by holding that the original administrative hold was not a violation. Unfortunately, this decision did not help. The matter then went to the Court of Appeals, which reversed and agreed with the bankruptcy court and stated that the administrative hold was an exercise of the right of set-off and violated the automatic stay. From the Circuit Court of Appeals, the matter went directly to the Supreme Court of the United States.

The Supreme Court held that the action of the bank was not a set-off because the bank did not purport permanently to reduce respondent's account balance by the amount of the defaulted loan. The bank only put an administrative hold on the account so that the monies could be later withdrawn from the bank account and, therefore, the monies still remained on deposit to the credit of the bankrupt. The court identified a requirement of intent with regard to a set-off that is followed by the majority of jurisdictions, and held that a set-off has not occurred until three steps have been taken:

1. A decision to effectuate a set-off.
2. Some action accomplishing the set-off.
3. A recording of the set-off.

The court held that by using an administrative hold, the bank did not meet this test and therefore, the automatic stay was not violated.

It appears that this reasoning might be applied to any monies on deposit with a creditor, such as a lease of equipment, or a lease of real estate, office space or residential apartment space, or any type of storage situation, or circumstances where a deposit of money is left with the creditor for a specific purpose. Creditors should consult with counsel.[41]

A recent case in the 2nd Circuit clarified the above ruling of the Supreme Court. In this instance a credit union placed an administrative hold on the account of a bankrupt. Neither the bankrupt nor the credit union took any action for almost four months. The bankruptcy judge held that this freeze was a willful violation and awarded the bankrupt $500 for attorneys' fees. The credit union appealed and shortly thereafter the Supreme Court handed down the decision on Strumpf dealing with setoffs. Finally, the district court agreed with the bankruptcy court and rejected the credit union's position finding a distinct difference between the Strumpf case and the instance case.[42]

In Strumpf, the administrative hold was on the bank account for only five days whereas here it was maintained for almost two months, not exactly a freeze of a temporary nature as happened in the Supreme Court decision. Actually, the court emphasized the fact that nothing probably would have happened and the freeze would have remained indefinitely unless the bankrupt made the motion to remove the automatic stay.

USING CREDIT CARDS FOR LUXURY GOODS

Under the Bankruptcy Reform Act, Congress extended from 40 to 50 days the period within which a consumer debtor acquired "luxury goods or services" and which debt is presumed non-dischargeable. In the event there was a cash advance, the period was extended from 20 to 60 days under an open-end credit plan in order for the debt to be presumed non-dischargeable.[43] Accordingly, creditors can now reach back almost two months to invoke a presumption of fraud when the credit card is used to purchase luxury goods. With regard to a cash advance, it must be an extension of consumer credit under an open-end credit plan. In the instant case, the debtor apparently had been using the extension of credit from the credit cards to conduct his business transactions and the court reemphasized the fact that this section only applies to consumer debt.[44] The court stated that the advances of credit extended for the consumer debt must be for personal, family, or household purposes. The debt was therefore business and did not fall within Section 523(a) (2) (c).

---

[41]*Citizens Bankof Maryland vs. Strumpf*, 116 S. Ct. 286, 33 L. Ed.2d 258 (1995).

[42]Town of Hempstead Employees F.C.U. v. Wicks, 215 B.R. 316 (Bankr. E.D.N.Y. 1997).

[43]11 U.S.C. ß523(a)(2)(c).

[44]In re Hinshaw, 1995 WL874779 (Bankr. N.D. Fla. 1995).

SUBSTANTIAL ABUSE

Often creditors claim that the debtor is abusing the provisions of the bankruptcy law and taking advantage of creditors. As a matter of fact, Chapter 707(b) of the Bankruptcy Code allows the trustee to move to dismiss a bankruptcy for cause if there is a substantial abuse. The pertinent section follows:

> "After notice and a hearing, the court, on its own motion, or on a motion by the United States Trustee, but not at the request or suggestion of any party in interest, may dismiss a case filed by an individual debtor under this chapter whose debts are primarily consumer debts if it finds that the granting of relief would be a substantial abuse of the provisions of this chapter. There shall be a presumption in favor of granting the relief requested by the debtor."

This section was added by the 1984 Bankruptcy Amendments, and under the 1986 Bankruptcy Act, it was made clear that only the court or the United States Trustee has standing to move to dismiss the bankruptcy. The Act states that a creditor may not submit such a motion and only a trustee may act. Nevertheless, the courts have been clear that the party in interest, i.e., a creditor, may furnish information to the trustee so that the trustee may further investigate to determine whether such a motion to dismiss should be made for abuse of the bankruptcy act.

The court itself on its own motion may move to dismiss the bankruptcy on the grounds of substantial abuse. The motion to dismiss should be filed by the trustee within 60 days after the first day set for the first meeting of creditors, and the debtor must be served with notice no later than 60 days following the first date set for the first meeting of creditors. Therefore, a creditor must act quickly to make this information available to the U.S. Trustee. If the creditor waits, the time for the trustee to move may have passed.

A major requirement is that the debts be primarily consumer in nature. The courts will search for the purpose of the debt as opposed to what the creditor intended. If half of the dollar amount of the debt is consumer debt, some bankruptcy courts will say it is sufficient to meet the statutory requirements of consumer debt. A judgment against a bankrupt resulting from a vehicle accident is not a consumer debt. Consumer debt is usually classified as primarily for personal family or household purposes, and the courts are generous in determining what are personal family or household purposes.[45]

The presumption in favor of granting relief to the debtor will often produce a finding that the debts were not primarily consumer. But the creditor should not try to answer the question of whether it is a consumer debt. Communicate with the Trustee, and let the Trustee do what is necessary.

---

[45]In re Bell 65 B.R. 575 (Bankr. E.D. Mich. 1986); In re Marshalek, 158 B.R. 704, (Bankr. N.D. Ohio 1993).

EXTENDING CREDIT TO THE BANKRUPT

Under Section 364 of the United States Bankruptcy Code, lending institutions may offer to finance debtors who are operating under Chapter 11. With post-petition financing, the lending institution arranges to have its claims treated as administrative expenses, or to receive priority over any and all administrative expenses, or to have its claims secured by a super priority or equal lien on the property. This priority can only be granted to a lending institution or a credit grantor after a notice and hearing before the court.

The presumption is that this particular credit is being extended outside the ordinary course of business and all interested parties must have notice. A formal hearing must be held as to the rights that are to be afforded the lending institution.

The bankruptcy court allows the debtor in possession, after notice and a hearing before the court, to do the following:

(a) obtain unsecured credit as an administrative expense;
(b) obtain secured credit which will have priority over any and all administrative expenses;
(c) obtain credit or incur debt secured by a lien on the property.

In some instances, this type of lending will have priority, under what is called "super priority," over other expenses and other claims and, in effect, will change the order of priorities. With regard to any change of priorities or any super priority liens, court approval is absolutely necessary.

On the other hand, where unsecured credit is extended to a Chapter 11 debtor "in the ordinary course of business," court approval is usually not necessary for the debt to be treated as an administrative expense. Whether a transaction is in the ordinary course of business depends upon the nature of the relationship between the creditor and the bankrupt. Before one extends credit to a Chapter 11 bankrupt, consultation with counsel should be made in order to be certain that the transaction meets the criteria of credit extended in the ordinary course of business. Consideration should be given to whether other creditors feel that the transaction is made within the ordinary course of business and also whether other businesses enter into this same type of transaction and consider same in the ordinary course of business. If significant credit is being extended to the Chapter 11 bankrupt, and the creditor wishes to adequately protect itself, there is no substitute for consulting with counsel before the extension of credit.

While certain transactions clearly are or are not in the ordinary course of business, the gray area may present problems. The question of whether the transaction is in the "ordinary course of the business" has perplexed the courts and leave two types of definitions of the "ordinary course of business." The first test is the most simplistic in that the transaction is an ordinary one and is performed in the operation of the debtor's business. The creditors normally will not expect to receive any notice and will not expect to have an opportunity to object because the creditors recognize that the debtor in possession has been authorized to operate its business.

If the transaction is unusual or out of the ordinary, the creditors will expect to receive notice of the particular transaction. The courts will compare what transactions the debtor entered into before the bankruptcy and what transactions are taking place after the bankruptcy. The criteria of the general test might be the "creditors' expectations" as to what ordinary business normally will be.

The second test requires the transaction be ordinary for the particular business and be the type of transaction engaged in by other similar businesses.

If the creditor meets either one of the above tests and satisfies the court that the financing is in the ordinary course of business, the creditor is entitled to treat the debt as an administrative expense. If the debt was incurred in the ordinary course of business, no notice or hearing is necessary to treat the claim as an administrative expense.

Nevertheless, any post-petition financing that produces any doubt as to whether the creditor is operating in the ordinary course of business with the debtor in possession should be examined carefully before the transaction is completed. Consult with counsel to be assured that you are operating within the ordinary course of business. Otherwise, your claim may not be treated as an administrative expense and the creditor will not have the protection afforded by the Bankruptcy Code.

CREDIT AND COLLECTION TIP: *The creditor usually learns about a super priority financing in a notice from the Bankruptcy Court. Do not discard the notice seeking approval of post-petition financing. Such financing could destroy a valid secured claim. Consult with counsel.*

CHAPTER 5
APPENDIX I

FORM B10 (Official Form 10)(9/97)

INSTRUCTIONS FOR PROOF OF CLAIM FORM

The instructions and definitions below are general explanations of the law. In particular types of cases or circumstances, such as bankruptcy cases that are not filed voluntarily by a debtor, there may be exceptions to these general rules.

DEFINITIONS

Debtor

The person, corporation, or other entity that has filed bankruptcy case is called the debtor.

Creditor

A creditor is any person, corporation, or other entity to whom the debtor owed a debt on the date that the bankruptcy was filed.

Proof of Claim

A form of telling the bankruptcy court how much the debtor owed a creditor at the time the bankruptcy case was filed (the amount of the creditor's claim). This form must be filed with the clerk of the bankruptcy court where the bankruptcy case was filed.

Secured Claim

A claim is a secured claim to the extent that the creditor has a lien on property of the debtor (collateral) that gives the creditor the right to be paid from that property before creditors who do not have liens on the property. Examples of liens are a mortgage on real estate and security interest in a car, truck, boat, television set, or other item of property. A lien may have been obtained through a court proceeding before the bankruptcy case began; in some states a court judgment is a lien. In addition, to the extent a creditor also owes money to the debtor (has a right of setoff), the creditor's claim may be secured claim. (see also Unsecured Claim).

Unsecured Claim

If a claim is not a secured claim it is an unsecured claim. A claim may be partly secured and partly unsecured if the property on which a creditor has a lien is not worth enough to pay the creditor in full.

Unsecured Priority Claim

priority, so they are to be paid in bankruptcy cases before most other unsecured claims (if there is sufficient money or property available to pay these claims). The most common types of priority claims are listed on the proof of claim form. Unsecured claims that are not specifically given priority status by the bankruptcy laws are classified as Unsecured Nonpriority Claims.

Items to be completed in Proof of Claim form (if not already filled in)

Court, Name of Debtor, and Case Number:
Fill in the name of the debtor in the bankruptcy case, and the bankruptcy case number. If you received a notice of the case from the court, all of this information is near the top of the notice.

Information about Creditor:

Complete the section giving the name, address, and telephone number of the creditor to whom the debtor owes money or property, and the debtor's account number, if any. If anyone else has already filed a proof of claim relating to this debt, if you never received notices from the bankruptcy court about this case, if your address differs from that to which the court sent notice, or if this proof of claim replaces or changes a proof of claim that was already filed, check the appropriate box on the form.

1. Basis for Claim:
Check the type of debt for which the proof of claim is being filed. If the type of debt is not listed, check "Other" and

5. Secured Claim
Check the appropriate place if the claim is a secured claim. You must state the type and value of property that is collateral for the claim, attach copies of the documentation of your lien, and state the amount past due on the claim as of the date the bankruptcy case was filed. A claim may be partly secured and partly unsecured (See DEFINITIONS, above).

6. Unsecured Priority Claim:
Check the appropriate place if you have an unsecured priority claim, and the state the amount entitled to priority. (See DEFINITIONS, above). A claim may be partly priority and partly nonpriority if, for example, the claim is far more than the amount given priority by the law. Check the appropriate place to specify the type of priority claim.

7. Credits:
By signing this proof of claim, you are stating under oath that in calculating the amount of your claim you have given the debtor credit for all payments received from the debtor.

8. Supporting Documents:
You must attach to this proof of claim form copies of documents that show the debtor owes the debt claimed or, if the documents are too

briefly describe the type of debt. If you were an employee of the debtor, fill in your social security number and the dates of work for which you were not paid.

2. Date Debt Incurred:
Fill in the date when the debt first was owed by the debtor.

3. Court Judgments:
If you have a court judgment for this debt, state the date the court entered the judgment.

4. Total Amount of Claim at Time Case Filed":
Fill in the total amount of the entire claim. If interest or other charges in addition to the principal amount of the claim are included, check the appropriate place on the form and attach an itemization of the interest and charges.

lengthy, a summary of those documents. If documents are not available, you must attach an explanation of why they are not available

9. When filing all Proof of Claims:
File original and one copy of the Proof of Claim,
Each attachments, at:
  U.S. BANKRUPTCY COURT
  170 N. HIGH STREET
  COLUMBUS, OH 43215-2403

10. Chapter 13 Trustee
  Frank M. Pees 614-436-6700
  130 E. Wilson Bridge Rd., Ste 200
  Worthington, OH43085-6300

APPENDIX II

EXCERPTS FROM BANKRUPTCY CODE PROOF OF CLAIM

UNITED STATES BANKRUPTCY COURT
EASTERN DISTRICT OF CALIFORNIA
SACRAMENTO DIVISION

Proof of Claim

NOTE: This form should not be used to make a claim for an administrative expense arising after the commencement of the case. A "request" for payment of an administrative expense may be filed pursuant to 11 U.S.C. Section 503.

CREDITOR NO.:   INDICATE ANY CHANGE OF NAME OR ADDRESS BELOW:

THIS SPACE FOR COURT USE ONLY

Please provide your telephone number: _____

☐ Check box if you are aware that anyone else has filed a proof of claim relating to your claim. Attach copy of statement giving particulars.

☐ Check box if you have never received any notices from the bankruptcy court in this case.

☐ Check box if the address differs from the address on the envelope sent to you by the Court.

ACCOUNT OR OTHER NUMBER BY WHICH CREDITOR IDENTIFIES DEBTOR

CHECK HERE IF THIS CLAIM EITHER ☐ REPLACES OR ☐ AMENDS
A PREVIOUSLY FILED CLAIM, DATED:

1. BASIS FOR CLAIM
☐ Goods Sold
☐ Services Performed
☐ Money Loaned
☐ Retiree benefits as defined in 11 U.S.C. Section 1114(a)

☐ Personal Injury/Wrongful Death
☐ Taxes
☐ Other (Describe Briefly)

☐ Wages, Salaries and Compensations (Fill out below)
Your Social Security Number _____
Unpaid compensations for services performed
From (date) _____ To (date) _____

2. DATE DEBT WAS INCURRED:

3. IF COURT JUDGMENT, DATE OBTAINED:

4. CLASSIFICATION OF CLAIM. Under the Bankruptcy Code all claims are classified as one or more of the following: (1) Unsecured Nonpriority, (2) Unsecured Priority, (3) Secured. It is possible for part of a claim to be in one category and part in another. CHECK THE APPROPRIATE BOX OR BOXES that best describe your claim and STATE THE AMOUNT OF THE CLAIM AT THE TIME THE CASE WAS FILED.

☐ SECURED CLAIM $ _____
Attach evidence of perfection of security interest.
Brief description of collateral:
☐ Real Estate ☐ Motor Vehicle ☐ Other (Describe)
Amount of arrearage and other charges
at the time the case was filed included
in the secured claim above, if any. $ _____

☐ UNSECURED NONPRIORITY CLAIM $ _____
A claim is unsecured if there is no collateral or lien on
property of the debtor securing the claim or to the extent that
the value of such property is less than the amount of the claim.

☐ UNSECURED PRIORITY CLAIM $ _____
Specify the priority of the claim.

☐ Wages, salaries or commissions (up to $2,000), earned not more than 90
days before filing of the bankruptcy petition or cessation of the debtor's
business, (whichever is earlier). 11 U.S.C. Section 507(a)(3)

☐ Contributions to an employee benefit plan. 11 U.S.C. Section 507(a)(4).

☐ Up to $900 of deposits toward purchase, lease or rental of property or
services for personal, family or household use. 11 U.S.C. Section 507(a)(6)

☐ Taxes or penalties of governmental units. 11 U.S.C. Section 507(a)(7)

☐ Other - Specify applicable paragraph of 11 U.S.C. Section 507(a) _____

5. TOTAL AMOUNT OF
CLAIM AT TIME $ _____ + $ _____ + $ _____ = $ _____
CASE FILED   (Unsecured)   (Secured)   (Priority)   (Total)
☐ Check this box if claim includes charges in addition to the principal amount of the claim. Attach an itemized statement of all
additional charges.

THIS SPACE FOR COURT USE ONLY

$ _____

_____ (Total)

6. CREDITS AND SETOFFS: The amount of all payments on this claim has been credited and deducted for the
purpose of making this proof of claim. In filing this claim, claimant has deducted all amounts that claimant owes
to the debtor.

7. SUPPORTING DOCUMENTS: Attach copies of supporting documents to each copy of your proof of claim, such
as court judgments, purchase orders, invoices, itemized statements of running accounts, contracts, promissory
notes or evidence of security interests. If the documents are unavailable, explain. If documents are voluminous,
attach a summary.

8. TIME-STAMPED COPY: To receive an acknowledgment of the filing of your claim, enclose a stamped, self-
addressed envelope and THREE copies of this proof of claim.

Date	Sign and Print the name and title, if any, of the creditor or other persons authorized to file this claim. (ATTACH COPY OF POWER OF ATTORNEY, IF ANY.)

Penalty for presenting fraudulent claims: Fine of up to $500,000 or imprisonment for up to 5 years, or both. (18 U.S.C. Sections 152 and 3571)   (Trustee Form Rev-8/27/93)

235

CHAPTER 5
APPENDIX III

EXCERPTS FROM BANKRUPTCY REFORM ACT

STAY OF ACTION AGAINST CO-DEBTOR (UNDER CHAPTER XIII)

(a) Except as provided in subsection (b) and (c) of this section, after the order for relief under this chapter, a creditor may not act, or commence or continue any civil action, to collect all or any part of a consumer debt of the debtor from any individual that is liable on such debt with the debtor, or that secure such debt, unless—

    (1) such individual became liable on or secure such debt in the ordinary course of such individual's business; or

    (2) the case is closed, dismissed, or converted to a case under chapter 7 or 11 of this title.

(b) A creditor may present a negotiable instrument, and may give notice of dishonor of such an instrument.

(c) On request of a party in interest and after notice and a hearing, the court shall grant relief from the stay provided by subsection (a) of this section with respect to a creditor, to the extent that—

    (1) as between the debtor and the individual protected under subsection (a) of this section, such individual received the consideration for the claim held by such creditor;

    (2) the plan filed by the debtor proposes not to pay such claim; or

    (3) such creditor's interest would be irreparably harmed by continuation of such stay.

(d) Twenty days after the filing of a request under subsection (c)(2) of this section for relief from the stay provided by subsection (a) of this section, such stay is terminated with respect to the party in interest making such request, unless the debtor or any individual that is liable on such debt with the debtor files and serves upon such party of interest a written obligation to the taking of the proposed action.

CHAPTER 5
APPENDIX IV

EXCERPTS FROM BANKRUPTCY CODE

362. AUTOMATIC STAY

(a) Except as provided in subsection (b) of this section, a petition filed under section 301, 302, or 303 of this title, or an application filed under section 5(a)(3) of the Securities Investor Protection Act of 1970, operates as a stay, applicable to all entities, of—

    (1) the commencement or continuation, including the issuance or employment of process, of a judicial, administrative, or other action or proceeding against the debtor that was or could have been commenced before the commencement of the case under this title, or to recover a claim against the debtor that arose before the commencement of the case under this title;

    (2) the enforcement, against the debtor or against property of the estate, of a judgment obtained before the commencement of the case under this title;

    (3) any act to obtain possession of property of the estate or of property from the estate or to exercise control over property of the estate;

    (4) any act to create, perfect, or enforce any lien against property of the estate;

    (5) any act to create, perfect, or enforce against property of the debtor any lien to the extent that such lien secures a claim that arose before the commencement of the case under this title;

    (6) any act to collect, assess, or recover a claim against the debtor that arose before the commencement of the case under this title;

    (7) the setoff of any debt owing to the debtor that arose before the commencement of the case under this title against any claim against the debtor; and

    (8) the commencement or continuation of a proceeding before the United States Tax Court concerning the debtor.

(b) The filing of a petition under section 301, 302, or 303 of this title, or of an application under section 5(a)(3) of the Securities Investor Protection Act of 1970, does not operate as a stay—

    (1) under subsection (a) of this section, of the commencement or continuation of a criminal action or proceeding against the debtor;

    (2) under subsection (a) of this section—

        (A) of the commencement or continuation of an action or proceeding for—

(i) the establishment of paternity; or

(ii) the establishment or modification of an order for alimony, maintenance, or support; or

(B) of the collection of alimony, maintenance, or support from property that is
not property of the estate;

(3) under subsection (a) of this section, of any act to perfect, or to maintain or continue the perfection of, an interest in property to the extent that the trustee's
rights and powers are subject to such perfection under section 546(b) of this title
or to the extent that such act is accomplished within the period under section
547(e)(2)(A) of this title;

(4) under subsection (a)(1) of this section, of the commencement or continuation of
an action or proceeding by a governmental unit to enforce such governmental
unit's police or regulatory power.

(5) under subsection (a)(2) of this section, of the enforcement of a judgment, other
than a money judgment, obtained in an action or proceeding by a governmental unit to enforce such governmental unit's police or regulatory power.

(6) under subsection (a) of this section, of the set off by a commodity broker, forward contract merchant, stockbroker, financial institutions, or securities clearing
agency of any mutual debt and claim under or in connection with commodity
contracts, as defined in section 761 of this title, forward contracts, or securities
contracts, as defined in section 741 of this title, that constitutes the setoff of a
claim against the debtor for a margin payment, as defined in section 101, 741, or
761 of this title, or settlement payment, as defined in section 101 or 741 of this
title, arising out of commodity contracts, forward contracts, or securities contracts against cash, securities, or other property held by due from such commodity broker, forward contract merchant, stockbroker, financial institutions, or
securities clearing agency to margin, guarantee, secure, or settle commodity
contracts, forward contracts, or securities contracts.

(7) under subsection (a) of this section, of the setoff by a repo participant, of any
mutual debt and claim under or in connection with repurchase agreements that
constitutes the setoff of a claim against the debtor for a margin payment, as
defined in section 741 or 761 of this title, or settlement payment, as defined in
section 741 of this title, arising out of repurchase agreements against cash, securities, or other property held by or due from such repo participant to margin,
guarantee, secure or settle repurchase agreements;

(8) under subsection (a) of this section, of the commencement of any action by the
Secretary of Housing and Urban Development to foreclose a mortgage or deed
of trust in any case in which the mortgage or deed of trust held by the Secretary
is insured or was formerly insured under the National Housing Act and covers
property, or combinations of property, consisting of five or more living units;

(9) under subsection (a), of—

(A) an audit by a governmental unit to determine tax liability;

(B) the issuance tot he debtor by a governmental unit of a notice of tax deficiency.

(C) a demand for tax returns; or

(D) the making of an assessment for any tax and issuance of a notice and demand for payment of such assessment (but any tax lien would otherwise attach to property to the estate by reason of such an assessment shall not take effect unless such tax is a debt of the debtor that will not be discharged in the case and such property or its proceeds are transferred out of the estate to, or otherwise revested in, the debtor).

(10) under subsection (a) of this section, of any act by a lessor to the debtor under a lease of nonresidential real property that has terminated by the expiration of the stated term of the lease before the commencement of or during a case under this title to obtain possession of such property;

(11) under subsection (a) of this section, of the presentment of a negotiable instrument and the giving of notice of an protesting dishonor of such an instrument.

(12) under subsection (a) of this section, after the date which is 90 days after the filing of such petition, of the commencement or continuation, and conclusion to the entry of final judgment, of an action which involves a debtor subject to reorganization pursuant to chapter 11 of this title and which was brought by the Secretary of Transportation under section 31325 of title 46 (including distribution of any proceeds of sale) to foreclose a preferred ship or fleet mortgage, or a security interest in or relating to a vessel or vessel under construction, held by the Secretary of Transportation under section 207 or title XI of the Merchant Marine Act, 1936, or under applicable State law;

(13) under subsection (a) of this section, after the date which is 90 days after the filing of such petition, of the commencement or continuation, and conclusion to the entry of final judgment, of an action which involves a debtor subject to reorganization pursuant to chapter 11 of this title and which was brought by the Secretary of Commerce under section 31325 of title 46 (including distribution of any proceeds of sale) to foreclose a preferred ship or fleet mortgage in a vessel or a mortgage, deed of trust, or other security interest in a fishing facility held by the Secretary of Commerce under section 207 or title XI of the Merchant Marine Act, 1936;

(14) under subsection (a) of this section, of any action by an accrediting agency regarding the accreditation status of the debtor as an educational institution;

(15) under subsection (a) of this section, of any action by a State licensing body regarding the licensure of the debtor as an education institution;

(16) under subsection (a) of this section, of any action by a guaranty agency, as defined in section 435(j) of the Higher Education Act of 1965 or the Secretary of Education regarding the eligibility of the debtor to participate in programs authorized under such Act;

(17) under subsection (a) of this section, of the setoff by a swap participant, of any mutual debt and claim under or in connection with any swap agreement that constitutes the setoff of a claim against the debtor for any payment due from the debtor under or in connection with any swap agreement against any payment due to the debtor from the swap participant under or in connection with any swap agreement or against cash, securities, or other property of the debtor held

by or due from such swap participant to guarantee, secure or settle any swap agreement; or

(18) under subsection (a) of the creation or perfection of a statutory lien for an ad valorem property tax imposed by the District of Columbia, or a political subdivision of a State, if such tax comes due after the filing of the petition.

The provisions of paragraphs (12) and (13) of this subsection shall apply with respect to any such petition filed on or before December 31, 1989.

(c) Except as provided in subsections (d), (e), and (f) of this section—

(1) the stay of an act against property of the estate under subsection (a) of this section continues until such property is no longer property of the estate; and

(2) the stay of any other act under subsection (a) of this section continues until the earliest of—

(A) the time the case is closed;

(B) the time the case is dismissed; or

(C) if the case is a case under chapter 7 of this title concerning an individual or a case under chapter 9, 11, 12, or 13 of this title, the time a discharge is granted or denied.

(D) on request of a party in interest and after notice and a hearing, the court shall grant relief from the stay provided under subsection (a) of this section, such as by terminating, annulling, modifying, or conditioning such stay—

(1) for cause, including the lack of adequate protection of an interest in property of such party in interest;

(2) with respect to a stay of an act against property under subsection (a) of this section, if-

(A) the debtor does not have an equity in such property; and

(B) such property is not necessary to an effective reorganization; or

(3) with respect to a stay of an act against single asset real estate under subsection (a), by a creditor whose claim is secured by an interest in such real estate, unless, not later than the date that is 90 days after the entry of the order for relief (or such later date as the court may determine the cause by order entered within that 90-day period)—

(A) the debtor has filed a plan or reorganization that has a reasonable possibility of being confirmed within a reasonable time; or

(B) the debtor has commenced monthly payments to each creditor whose claim is secured by such real estate (other than a claim secured by a judgment lien or by an unmatured statutory lien), which payments are in an amount equal to interest at a current fair market rate on the value of the creditor's interest in the real estate.

(d) Thirty days after a request under subsection (d) of this section for relief from the stay of any act against property of the estate under subsection (a) of this section, such stay is terminated with respect to the party in interest making such request, unless the court, after notice and a hearing, orders such stay continued in effect pending the conclusion of, or as a result of, a final hearing and determination under subsection

(d) of this section. A hearing under this subsection may be a preliminary hearing, or may be consolidated with the final hearing under subsection (d) of this section. The court shall order such stay continued in effect pending the conclusion of the final hearing under subsection (d) of this section if there is a reasonable likelihood that the party opposing relief from such stay will prevail at the conclusion of such final hearing. If the hearing under this subsection is a preliminary hearing, then such final hearing shall be concluded not later than thirty days after the conclusion of such preliminary hearing, unless the 30-day period is extended with the consent of the parties in interest or for a specific time which the court finds is required by compelling circumstances.

(e) Upon request of a party in interest, the court, with or without a hearing, shall grant such relief from the stay provided under subsection (a) of this section as is necessary to prevent irreparable damage to the interest of an entity in property, if such interest will suffer such damage before there is an opportunity for notice and a hearing under subsection (d) or (e) of this section.

(f) In any hearing under subsection (d) or (e) of this section concerning relief from the stay of any act under subsection (a) of this section—

(1) the party requesting such relief has the burden of proof on the issue of the debtor's equity in property; and

(2) the party opposing such relief has the burden of proof on all other issues.

(g) An individual injured by any willful violation of a stay provided by this section shall recover actual damages, including costs and attorney's fees, and, in appropriate circumstances, may recover punitive damages.

APPENDIX V

EXCERPTS FROM BANKRUPTCY CODE

727. DISCHARGE

(a) The court shall grant the debtor a discharge, unless—

  (1) the debtor is not a individual;

  (2) the debtor, with intent to hinder, delay, or defraud a creditor or an officer of the estate charged with custody of property under this title, has transferred, removed, destroyed, mutilated, or concealed, or has permitted to be transferred, removed, destroyed, mutilated, or concealed—

  (A) property of the debtor, within one year before the date of the filing of the petition; or

  (B) property of the estate, after the date of the filing of the petition;

  (3) the debtor has concealed, destroyed, mutilated, falsified, or failed to keep or preserve any recorded information, including books, documents, records, and papers, from which the debtor's financial condition or business transactions might be ascertained, unless such act or failure to act was justified under all of the circumstances of the case;

  (4) the debtor knowingly and fraudulently, in or in connection with the case—

  (A) made a false oath or account;

  (B) presented or used a false claim;

  (C) gave, offered, received, or attempted to obtain money, property, or advantage, or a promise of money, property, or advantage, for acting or forbearing to act; or

  (D) withheld from an officer of the estate entitled to possession under this title, any recorded information, including books, documents, records, and papers, relating to the debtor's property or financial affairs;

  (5) the debtor has failed to explain satisfactorily, before determination of denial or discharge under this paragraph, any loss of assets or deficiency of assets to meet the debtor's liabilities;

  (6) the debtor has refused, in the case—

    (A) to obey any lawful order of the court, other than an order to respond to a material question or to testify;

    (B) on the ground of privilege against self-incrimination, to respond to a material question approved by the court or to testify, after the debtor has been granted immunity with respect to the matter concerning which such privilege was invoked; or

    (C) on a ground other than the properly invoked privilege against self-incrimination, to respond to a material question approved by the court to testify;

  (7) the debtor has committed any act specified in paragraph (2), (3), (4), (5), or (6) of this subsection, on or within one year before the date of the filing of the petition, or during the case, in connection with another case, under this title or under the Bankruptcy Act, concerning an insider;

  (8) the debtor has been granted a discharge under this section, under section 1141 of this title, or under section 14, 371, or 476 of the Bankruptcy Act, in a case commenced within six years before the date of the filing of the petition;

  (9) the debtor has been granted a discharge under section 1228 or 1328 of this title, or under section 660 or 661 of the Bankruptcy Act, in a case commenced within six years before the date of the filing of the petition, unless payments under the plan in such case totaled at least—

    (A) 100 percent of the allowed unsecured claims in such case; or

    (B) (i) 70 percent of such claims; and
        (ii) the plan was proposed by the debtor in good faith, and was the debtor's best effort; or

 (10) the court approves a written waiver of discharge executed by the debtor after the order for relief under this chapter

(b) Except as provided in section 523 of this title, a discharge under subsection (a) of this section discharges the debtor from all debts that arose before the date of the order for relief under this chapter, and any liability on a claim that is determined under section 502 of this title as if such claim had arisen before the commencement of the case, whether or not a proof of claim based on any such debt or liability is filed under section 501 of this title, and whether or not a claim based on any such debt or liability is allowed under section 502 of this title.

(c) (1) The trustee, a creditor, or the United States trustee may object to the granting of a discharge under subsection (a) of this section.

    (2) On request of a party in interest, the court may order the trustee to examine the acts and conduct of the debtor to determine whether a ground exists for denial of discharge.

(d) On request of the trustee, a creditor, or the United States trustee, and after notice and a hearing, the court shall revoke a discharge granted under subsection (a) of this section if—

    (1) such discharge was obtained through the fraud of the debtor, and the requesting party did not know of such fraud until after the granting of such discharge;

    (2) the debtor acquired property that is property of the estate, or became entitled to acquire property that would be property of the estate, and knowingly and

fraudulently failed to report the acquisition of or entitlement to such property, or to deliver or surrender such property to the trustee; or

   (3) the debtor committed an act specified in subsection (a)(6) of this section.

(e) The trustee, a creditor, or the United States trustee may request a revocation of a discharge—

   (1) under subsection (d)(1) of this section within one year after such discharge is granted; or

   (2) under subsection (d)(2) or (d)(3) of this section before the later off—

      (A) one year after the granting of such discharge; and

      (B) the date the case is closed.

CHAPTER 5
APPENDIX VI

EXCERPTS FROM BANKRUPTCY CODE

547. PREFERENCES

(a) In this section—

    (1) "inventory" means personal property leased or furnished, held for sale or lease, or to be furnished under a contract for service, raw materials, work in process, or materials used or consumed in a business, including farm products such as crops or livestock, held for sale or lease;

    (2) "new value" means money or money's worth in goods, services, or new credit, or release by a transferee of property previously transferred to such transferee in a transaction that is neither void nor voidable by the debtor or the trustee under any applicable law, including proceeds of such property, but does not include an obligation substituted for an existing obligation;

    (3) "receivable" means right to payment, whether or not such right has been earned by performance; and

    (4) a debt for a tax is incurred on the day when such tax is last payable without penalty, including any extension.

(b) Except as provided in subsection (c) of this section, the trustee may avoid any transfer of an interest of the debtor in property—

    (1) to or for the benefit of a creditor;

    (2) for or on account of an antecedent debt owed by the debtor before such transfer was made;

    (3) made while the debtor was insolvent;

    (4) made—

        (A) on or within 90 days before the date of the filing of the petition; or

        (B) between ninety days and one year before the date of the filing of the petition, if such creditor at the time of such transfer was an insider; and

    (5) that enables such creditor to receive more than such creditor would receive if—

        (A) the case were a case under chapter 7 of this title;

        (B) the transfer had not been made; and

(C) such creditor received payment of such debt to the extent provided by the provisions of this title.

(c) The trustee may not avoid under this section a transfer—

   (1) to the extent that such transfer was—

      (A) intended by the debtor and the creditor to or for whose benefit such transfer was made to be a contemporaneous exchange for new value given to the debtor; and

      (B) in fact a substantially contemporaneous exchange;

   (2) to the extent that such transfer was—

      (A) in payment of a debt incurred by the debtor in the ordinary course of business or financial affairs of the debtor and the transferee;

      (B) made in the ordinary course of business or financial affairs of the debtor and the transferee; and

      (C) made according to ordinary business terms;

   (3) that creates a security interest in property acquired by the debtor—

      (A) to the extent such security interest secures new value that was—

         (i) given at or after the signing of a security agreement that contains description of such property as collateral;

         (ii) given by or on behalf of the secured party under such agreement;

         (iii) given to enable the debtor to acquire such property; and

         (iv) in fact used by the debtor to acquire such property; and

      (B) that is perfected on or before 20 days after the debtor receives possession of such property;

   (4) to or for the benefit of a creditor, to the extent that, after such transfer, such creditor gave new value to or for the benefit of the debtor—

      (A) not secured by an otherwise unavoidable security interest; and

      (B) on account of which new value the debtor did not make an otherwise unavoidable transfer to or for the benefit of such creditor;

   (5) that creates a perfected security interest in inventory or a receivable or the proceeds of either, except to the extent that the aggregate of all such transfers to the transferee caused a reduction, as of the date of the filing of the petition and to the prejudice of other's creditors holding unsecured claims, of any amount by which the debt secured by such security interest exceeded the value of all security interests for such debt on the later of—

      (A) (i) with respect to a transfer to which subsection (b)(4)(A) of this section applies, 90 days before the date of the filing of the petition; or

         (ii) with respect to a transfer to which subsection (b)(4)(B) of this section applies, one year before the date of the filing of the petition; or

      (B) the date on which new value was first given under the security agreement creating such security interest;

   (6) that is the fixing of a statutory lien that is not avoidable under section 545 of this title;

(7) to the extent such transfer was a bona fide payment of a debt to a spouse, former spouse, or child of the debtor, for alimony to, maintenance for, or support of such spouse or child, in connection with a separation agreement, divorce decree or other order of a court of record, determination made in accordance with State or territorial law by a governmental unit, or properly settlement agreement, but not to the extent that such debt—

    (A) is assigned to another entity, voluntarily, by operation of law, or otherwise; or

    (B) includes a liability designated as alimony, maintenance, or support, unless such liability is actually in the nature of alimony, maintenance or support; or

(8) if, in a case filed by an individual debtor whose debts are primarily consumer debts, the aggregate value of all property that constitutes or is affected by such transfer is less than $600.

(d) The trustee may avoid a transfer of an interest in property of the debtor transferred to or for the benefit of a surety reimbursement of such a surety that furnished a bond or other obligation to dissolve a judicial lien that would have been avoidable by the trustee under subsection (b) of this section. The liability of such surety under such bond or obligation shall be discharged to the extent of the value of such property recovered by the trustee of the amount paid to the trustee.

(e) (1) For the purposes of this section—

    (A) a transfer of real property other than fixtures, but including the interest of a seller or purchaser under a contract for the sale of real property, is perfect when a bona fide purchase of such property from the debtor against whom applicable law permits such transfer to be perfected cannot acquire an interest that is superior to the interest of the transferee; and

    (B) a transfer of a fixture or property other than real property is perfected when a creditor on a simple contract cannot acquire a judicial lien that is superior to the interest of the transferee.

  (2) For the purposes of this section, except as provided in paragraph (2) of this subsection, a transfer is made—

    (A) at the time such transfer takes effect between the transferor and the transferee, if such transfer is perfected at, or within 10 days after, such time, except as provided in subsection (c)(3)(B);

    (B) at the time such transfer is perfected, if such transfer is perfected after such 10 days; or

    (C) immediately before the date of the filing of the petition, if such transfer is not perfected at the later of—

      (i) the commencement of the case or;

      (ii) 10 days after such transfer takes effect between the transferor and the transferee.

  (3) For the purposes of this section, a transfer is not made until the debtor has acquired rights in the property transferred.

(f) For the purposes of this section, the debtor is presumed to have been insolvent on and during the 90 days immediately preceding the date of the filing of the petition.

(g) For the purposes of this section, the trustee has the burden of proving the avoidability of a transfer under subsection (b) of this section, and the creditor or party in interest against whom recovery or avoidance is sought has the burden of proving the nonavoidability of a transfer under subsection (c) of this section.

APPENDIX VII

EXCERPTS FROM BANKRUPTCY CODE REAFFIRMATION AGREEMENT

B 240
(1/88)

REAFFIRMATION AGREEMENT

Debtor's Name   Bankruptcy Case No.

INSTRUCTIONS:
1) Write debtor's name and bankruptcy case number above.
2) Part-A—Must be signed by both the debtor and the creditor.
3) Part-B—Must be signed by the attorney who represents the debtor in this bankruptcy case.
4) Part-C—Must be completed by the debtor if the debtor is not represented by an attorney in this bankruptcy case.
5) File the completed form by mailing or delivering to the   COURT
   Bankruptcy Clerk.   USE
6) Attach written agreement, if any.   ONLY

PART A—AGREEMENT

Creditor's Name and Address   Summary of Terms of the New Agreement

                                   a) Principal Amount $_____
                                      Interest Rate (APR)_____
                                   b) Description of Security: _____
                                      _____

Date Set for Discharge Hearing   Present Market Value $_____
(if any)

The parties understand that this agreement is purely voluntary and that the debtor may rescind the agreement at any time prior to discharge or within 60 days after such agreement is filed with the court, whichever occurs later, by giving notice of recission to the creditor.

_____   _____
Date   Signature of Debtor

_____   _____
Signature of Creditor   Signature of Joint Debtor

PART B—ATTORNEY'S DECLARATION

This agreement represents a fully informed and voluntary agreement that does not impose an undue hardship on the debtor or any dependent of the debtor.

_____   _____
Date   Signature of Debtor's Attorney

PART C—MOTION FOR COURT APPROVAL OF AGREEMENT
(Complete only where debtor is not represented by an attorney.)

I (we), the debtor, affirm the following to be true and correct:
1) I am not represented by an attorney in connection with this bankruptcy case.
2) My current monthly net income is $_____
3) My current monthly expenses total $_____, including any payment due under this agreement.
4) I believe that this agreement is in my best interest because _____

_____

_____

Therefore, I ask the court for an order approving this reaffirmation agreement.

_____   _____
Date   Signature of Debtor

                                   _____
                                   Signature of Joint Debtor

PART D—COURT ORDER

The court grants the debtor's motion and approves the voluntary agreement upon the terms specified above.

_____   _____
Date   Bankruptcy Judge

CHAPTER 5

APPENDIX VIII

UNITES STATES BANKRUPTCY COURT

EASTERN DISTRICT OF CALIFORNIA
SACRAMENTO DIVISION

NOTICE OF COMMENCEMENT OF CASE UNDER CHAPTER 13 OF THE BANKRUPTCY CODE
MEETING OF CREDITORS AND FIXING OF DATES

CASE NUMBER: _____   Date Filed or Converted: _____

IN RE: _____   Social Security/Tax ID No.: _____

Debtor's Attorney: _____   Telephone No.: _____

Chapter 13 Trustee: _____   Telephone No.: _____

MEETING OF CREDITORS (A SUMMARY OF DEBTOR'S PLAN WILL BE MAILED SEPARATELY.)

Date: _____   Place: _____

Time: _____

DEADLINE TO FILE A PROOF OF CLAIM;
Proofs of claim for a secured, priority or unsecured debt not filed on or before the deadline may be disallowed
for payment through the plan.

COMMENCEMENT OF CASE. An individual's debt adjustment case under Chapter 13 of the Bankruptcy Code has been filed in this Court by the debtor or debtors named above and an Order for Relief has been entered. You will not receive notice of all documents filed in this case. All documents filed with this Court, including lists of the debtor's property and debts, are available for inspection at the office of the Clerk of the Bankruptcy Court, 650 Capitol Mall, Room 8308, Sacramento, CA 95814.

CREDITORS MAY NOT TAKE CERTAIN ACTIONS. A creditor is anyone to whom the debtor owes money. Under the Bankruptcy Code, the debtor is granted certain protection against creditors. Common examples of prohibited actions by creditors are contacting the debtor to demand repayment, taking action against the debtor to collect money owed creditors or to take property of the debtor, and starting or continuing foreclosure or judgment actions, repossessions or wage deductions. Some protection is also given to certain codebtors of consumer debts. If unauthorized actions are taken by a creditor against a debtor or a protected codebtor, the Court may punish that creditor. A creditor who is considering taking action against the debtor, the property of the debtor or any codebtor, should review Section 361 and Section 1301 of the Bankruptcy Code and may wish to seek legal advice. The staffs of the Clerk of the Bankruptcy Court and the Chapter 13 Trustee are not permitted to give legal advice.

MEETING OF CREDITORS. The debtor (both husband and wife in a joint case) is required to appear at the meeting of creditors on the date and at the place set forth above for the purpose of being examined under oath. Attendance by creditors at the meeting is welcome, but not required. At the meeting, the creditors may examine the debtor and transact such other business as may properly come before the meeting. The meeting may be continued or adjourned by notice at the meeting without further written notice to the creditors.

CONFIRMATION. If no written objection to confirmation of the Chapter 13 plan is filed by a party in interest within fourteen (14) days of the conclusion of the meeting of creditors, the plan will be approved and confirmed by the Court without a hearing. A notice of hearing must accompany the objection to confirmation. If confirmation is denied, the debtor will have ten (10) days in which to file an amended plan or notice of conversion to another Chapter of the Bankruptcy Code. If the debtor does not file an amended plan or notice of conversion within the time prescribed, the case may be dismissed pursuant to Section 1307.

PROOF OF CLAIM. Except as otherwise provided by law, in order to share in any payment from the estate, a creditor must timely file a proof of claim. The place to file the proof of claim, either in person or by mail, is the Office of the Clerk of the Bankruptcy Court. A PROOF OF CLAIM FORM WITH YOUR CREDITOR NUMBER IS ON THE BACK OF THIS NOTICE. Proof of claim forms are also available in the Clerk's Office of any Bankruptcy Court. File all claims and attachments in DUPLICATE. If an acknowledgment is requested, file the claim in TRIPLICATE accompanied by a self-addressed stamped envelope.

PURPOSE OF A CHAPTER 13 FILING. Chapter 13 of the Bankruptcy Code is designed to enable a debtor to pay debts in full or in part over a period of time pursuant to a plan. A plan is not effective unless it has been approved and confirmed by the Court. Creditors will be given notice in the event the case is dismissed or converted to another Chapter of the Bankruptcy Code.

Dated:

CHAPTER 6

Law Firms and Collection Agencies

Every credit or collection manager at some point must deal with an outside attorney or a collection agency. To my knowledge, there are no "How to" books on the accepted way to engage a collection agency or attorney. Therefore, this chapter is devoted to the legal problems that are encountered, as well as the criteria for selecting and the methods of monitoring an outside collection agency or attorney.

For purposes of this chapter, we will use the word "attorney" for a law firm and we will use the designation of "agency" for both a regional collection agency or a multi-office national collection agency.

SELECTION OF AN ATTORNEY OR AGENCY

There are three good reasons for using an attorney or collection agency after the creditor has exhausted the collection effort. First, statistics have demonstrated that engaging a new entity involved in the collection of a debt often dramatically improves the results. This is known as "transferring" the collection effort to a third party. Second, the collection agency and attorney provide trained and sophisticated collectors to continue the collection activity. Third, the attorney, in addition to engaging in the activities of a collection agency, is empowered to institute suit against the debtor. However, the major reason is that the creditor cannot collect the debt, and will have to absorb the loss by charging off the indebtedness as a bad debt. This reduces profits.

REPUTATION. The principal reason to engage a particular attorney or agency is reputation. The best source of such information is a personal recommendation from another firm that has been exposed to the agency or attorney. A recommendation that a business has utilized the services over a long period of time and obtained good results both from collection and reporting aspects should be considered. Nevertheless, a creditor should not act without inquiry. The fact that the agency or attorney has satisfied one creditor does not man it will satisfy you, and the fact it has performed well for one year is no assurance it will perform well next year. The attorney or agency not only must collect money and furnish reports, but must meet the following qualifications:

(1) it must belong to trade associations that provide the current laws and court cases to enable the attorney or collection agency to comply with same.

(2) at least as to collection agencies, it must be licensed in the states which require licensing (32 states).

(3) it must have procedures in place to protect the creditor from exposure to suits for violation of the Fair Debt Collection Practices Act.

A recommendation is an excellent place to start, but only the first step in a multi-step process.

THE FIRST REFERRAL. Whether a creditor continues to use an agency or attorney will often depend upon the first referral of a claim or claims. Many creditors decide that if the first claim is not immediately collected, they will seek another firm. Often the money is not collected immediately, and the creditor terminates referring business.

Sometimes the creditor will forward old accounts that have been worked on by another firm to determine whether the new agency or attorney can produce results. This philosophy is not fair. A collector may do an excellent job and still collect no money because the accounts were worked on by a prior firm. Even when new accounts are referred, the possibility exists that the first few will not be collected.

When the first few accounts are collected, the creditor is impressed and often will forward more work. This approach is also flawed, since a combination of fresh accounts and a little luck may have prevailed. The attorney or agency should be monitored to confirm the necessary number of letters and the contacts by telephone, and a reasonable test should cover a period of three to six months. If only a few accounts are referred each year, the creditor should examine the reports carefully to be certain the accounts are processed quickly and thoroughly. If the job is being done right, the collectible money will be collected.

REPORTS. Agencies and attorneys provide a wide variety of reports to their clients. Some of these are statistical reports which show the number of cases referred, the amount referred and the total collected. Others will be detailed case histories of exactly what the collection activity produced on a particular individual case. The former is usually provided for a large number of cases of relatively small amounts, while the latter is provided for an individual case of a large amount, usually commercial matters. Initially, after retaining an agency or attorney, the client should insist upon reports within the first thirty to sixty days and monthly or bimonthly thereafter. Some creditors do not pay attention to the reports, arguing that their only interest is the amount collected, but reports are essential to monitor the progress and the fact that the agency or attorney is devoting attention to the collection effort.

The type of report furnished is significant if it provides information not already available. A descriptive report of procedures is helpful. A statistical report as to the amount collected has little meaning, because a creditor should maintain its own percentages of performance. The creditor must maintain records as to the number of accounts turned over, the dollar amount turned over, the amount recovered, and these records should be compared with the collection agency's record for accuracy. Reports of what the collector has done are meaningless unless you can also monitor the performance and confirm that the collector has made the required number of phone calls, the required number of contacts with the debtor, and sent the required number of letters.

Statistical reports are easily manipulated to show favorable results. One report may deduct bankrupt debtors or out-of-business debtors from the total amount referred, thereby increasing the percentage collected. Another report may not include in the total amount referred those debtors who returned the goods or who were issued a credit because goods were defective or undelivered. Some reports treat returned merchandise as a paid account, while others do not. You must use your own figures, and apply them equally to all outside attorneys and agencies.

MONITORING. One method of monitoring the performance of an attorney or agency is the use of what is known as "dummy names." The client identifies the name of a debtor on a referral with a standardized name of one of the parties in the credit or collection department. For example, if the party employed by the creditor is John Smith at 14 Main Street, Centerville, IN, the referral is made under the name of James Smythe at Main Street, Centerville, IN, and the phone number of John Smith is utilized. The attorney and agency will write James Smythe at that address and the employee of the creditor will be able to identify the date the first letter arrived and the number of days between the second, third and fourth letter. When telephone calls are made, John Smith will identify himself as James Smythe and use some type of excuse to avoid payment. The use of this type of "dummy" enables the creditor to determine if the performance is in accordance with the agreement between the parties.

Where the debtors are businesses and a commercial transaction is involved, the use of a dummy is more difficult, but the same methods may be utilized. Vendors or other businesses may be used as dummies. The creditors merely adds the name of the vendor or closely associated business to the list of debtors referred to the attorney or agency. The vendor or the other closely associated business reports upon the efforts of the agency in collecting the debt.

FINANCIAL RESPONSIBILITY. A request to furnish a financial statement should be standard procedure in the selection of an attorney or collection agency. A careful review of their procedure for handling escrow funds also should be made.

Certified financial statements are prepared primarily to obtain loans from banks or financial institutions. Companies which do not borrow usually do not require their accountants to provide certified financial statements due to the expensive fees and costs. A financial statement, even if uncertified, should disclose whether the firm is solvent and profitable. A representation should be obtained that no judgments are outstanding against the attorney or agency. Inquiry may be made as to whether any suits for violation of the FDCPA were instituted; and if successful, has the problem been corrected.

Most collection agencies and attorneys do not borrow from lending institutions, and their assets consist primarily of cash in the bank and office equipment. The liabilities should be nominal. Unfortunately, attorneys and collection agencies sometimes fail to remit escrow money to the client. Caution by the creditor in this area may avoid grief in the future.

The creditor should periodically audit the agency or law firm by reviewing the checkbooks, deposit dates, remittance dates, expense bills supported by documentation in files and other audit procedures. The remittance and bills should be compared to the files, deposit records, check books and statements.

INSURANCE. You should ask both a law firm and a collection agency about the type of insurance carried and the extent of coverage. In today's litigious environment, insurance is a necessity.

ATTORNEYS. Attorneys are covered by malpractice insurance, which insures them primarily against negligent acts performed in the course of representing clients. The coverage normally ranges from a hundred thousand dollars to one million dollars and substantially more for a large firm which engages many attorneys. Many law firms operate "naked," i.e., without insurance. In some states, the percentage "naked" is substantial. A request for a copy of the malpractice policy is common, and is recommended. The policy will provide the coverage, deductible and the premium and expiration date. Copies of new policies should be requested each year.

Some states (for example, New York) maintain a fund which is specifically earmarked to protect against an attorney stealing monies that were entrusted to the attorney on behalf of the client. In some states, attorneys pay an annual fee to support this fund. Accordingly, if monies are not remitted to the client, the client may have a claim upon this fund for reimbursement. Consult with an attorney.

COLLECTION AGENCIES. Collection agencies carry errors-and-omission policies which are similar to that carried by a business. These policies cover the collection agency if an error or omission is made and the agency becomes liable to one of its customers, or to one of its delinquent debtors. Some of these policies insure the agency against violation of the Fair Debt Collection Practices Act.

A large number of states require agencies to be licensed to conduct business within the state. As part of the licensing process, the state requires the agency to post a bond and have an office in the state. The amount of the bond varies from state to state and may be a fixed amount, or a fixed amount per office in the state, or an amount that is a function either of the number of employees or of the gross billing. The purpose of the bond is to ensure that the agency remits to the client the monies collected from the debtors and, upon a failure to remit, the client may proceed against the insurance company that issued the bond.

REFERENCES. Requesting five to ten references is appropriate. You should avoid those references which have a close personal relationship to the collector, because the reference will be biased. Select references in the same field and choose at least three from the ten provided. The location of the reference should also be considered. One located across the street from the agency may have a different perspective than the one located several hundred miles away.

While contacting the individual named is a reasonable starting point, contacting the clerical staff or other staff members of the reference may produce an unbiased and different perspective. Remember that the firm is providing the ten best clients as references and the likelihood is that the principal of the agency or the partner of the law firm has a personal relationship with the individual furnished as a reference. While this is not meant to imply that information provided will be inaccurate, the reference will probably be biased. The following are suggested inquiries:

1. How often is a report furnished?
2. What is the content of the report furnished?
3. Are monies remitted each month at the same time?
4. Are telephone calls returned promptly?
5. Is the client communication with one party or several parties?
6. In the event the party designated to deal with your firm is absent, is there an alternate who is knowledgeable?
7. Have complaints from customers about the law firm or agency been made to the reference?
8. Are dummy names included in the referral to the agency or attorney to monitor performance, and if so, has the dummy received a collection telephone call, and what was experienced?
9. Are the letters monitored with dummy names?

Such inquiries may lead to other questions, and the creditor will undoubtedly think of additional inquiries. The more communication, the more information will be provided.

LICENSING

All states require attorneys to be licensed and a large number of states require collection agencies to be licensed.

COLLECTION AGENCIES. In the January 1997 issue of the ACA Advocate, published by the American Collectors Association, the trade association reported that forty-one states have laws that affect collection agencies and thirty-one states currently have specific laws requiring out-of-state collection agencies to be licensed, registered, or bonded if the agency should do business in that state. Ten states impose specific requirements for licensing and do not provide exemptions: Alaska, Arizona, Arkansas, Connecticut, Hawaii, Louisiana, Maine, Maryland, Massachusetts, and Minnesota. Seventeen states are "open" to out-of-state collectors as they impose no licensing requirements: Alabama, California, Georgia, Iowa (if collections exceed $25,000), Kansas, Kentucky, Missouri, Montana, New Hampshire, Ohio, Oklahoma, Pennsylvania, Rhode Island, South Carolina, South Dakota, Vermont, and Virginia. Nevertheless, other provisions of the laws in these states may prohibit certain practices. The remaining twenty-three states require collection agencies to be licensed if they are collecting for an in-state creditor or soliciting business. These states may have no specific licensing requirements, but may have a bond and registration requirement.

The U.S. Postal Service does forward letters addressed to a consumer from one state to another state. In the event the agency is not licensed in the other state, the collection agency may be faced with specific problems. It is recommended to include on the envelope underneath the agency's return address, "ADDRESS CORRECTION REQUESTED. DO NOT FORWARD." In such a case, the post office will return the letter to the sender and avoid any potential problems with state licensing laws in the event the letter should be forwarded to a state where the agency is not licensed.

Because most collection agencies conduct business across the entire country in this fluid economy, many collection agencies do conduct business without licenses in states requiring them. Most national agencies are licensed, but some regional agencies do not wish to absorb the licensing expense in a state where little business is conducted. Inquire whether the agency is licensed in the states requiring licenses, and ask for proof.

The collection laws in the various states impose certain burdens upon collection agencies with regard to a large variety of their activities. Some state laws require the collection agency to have an actual office within the state, while other states require that any monies collected from a consumer within the state must be kept in bank accounts in the state. Other states require that the agency keep books and records in the state where the debtor resides and maintain all their records with regard to the collection of the debts in that state. These types of requirements are burdensome and oppressive to small agencies with but one office. The agency may collect only one or two debts in another state in a period of six months or a year. Considerable litigation concerning this particular problem has taken place. The national association of collection agencies, the American Collectors Association (ACA), has been active in trying to modify and reduce the burdensome requirements of these particular laws.

ATTORNEYS. Attorneys have to be licensed in the state where their practice is conducted. The attorney must meet the qualifications of the state bar association, and is formally admitted to practice by a court of the state. Attorneys do not have to qualify in other states to engage in collection activities in those states, except in Connecticut which requires attorneys engaged in collecting consumer accounts to register in the same manner as collection agencies. Texas has licensing laws but does not actively enforce compliance whereas Connecticut is active.

All other states feel that regulation by the state bar association where the attorney is located is adequate. An attorney is permitted to engage in collection activities by writing letters and making telephone calls to a debtor located in a different state.

An attorney cannot practice in the courts of another state and should not consult or advise a client concerning the laws of the other state unless admitted to practice in that state. When a client forwards a claim for suit in another state, a local attorney is retained to institute suit.

TRADE ASSOCIATIONS

A key question to ask is if the collection agency or the attorney belongs to a trade association. In today's legal environment, keeping abreast of the current laws is essential to the operation of a collection agency or a law firm engaged in collection. Aside from policy statements released by the Federal Trade Commission and changes in federal and state laws, both state and federal courts are rendering decisions daily which affect the collection process. Many collection agencies and law firms do not have the staff or the funds to monitor the changing legal atmosphere. The alternative is a trade association which maintains a legal staff whose sole function is to oversee the legal environment and to communicate to its members any changes affecting the collection process.

Inquiry may be made to the association to determine whether the collection agency or attorney is a member in good standing. Of the six thousand collection agencies in the United States, many belong to regional or national associations, but a large number do not belong to any trade association.

There are two major trade associations for collection agencies: The American Collectors Association (ACA), 4040 West 70th Street, Minneapolis, Minnesota 55435, and The Associated Credit Bureau, P.O. Box 21300, Houston, Texas 77218.

The National Association of Credit Management, 8815 Centre Park Dr. Columbia, MO 21045, a large association of creditors, publishes a Credit Manual of Commercial Laws annually which provides a summary of the commercial laws that affect business-to-business transactions.

Law firms belong to state bar associations and/or to the American Bar Association, 750 No. Lake Shore Dr., Chicago, Illinois 60611. In addition, the law firm may be a member of city-wide associations in the major cities, such as Association of the Bar of the City of New York, 42 W. 44th St. New York, NY 10036.

Attorneys and collection agencies belong to the Commercial Law League of America at 222 West Adam Street, Chicago, Illinois, 60606-5278. This association is devoted to commercial matters only, and the association subscribes to the philosophy that the collection agency represents the client and retains the attorney. The Commercial Law League provides guidelines for the relationship between forwarder and receiver of a claim.

The National Association of Retail Collection Attorneys (NARCA), 10832 1515 North Warson Road, St. Louis, MO 63132, provides a listing of attorneys who engage in the collection of consumer accounts. Naturally, this association subscribes to the philosophy that attorneys may deal directly with the client. They provide several compilations of laws that affect collection attorneys.

All of these associations arrange conferences to update their members on the current law, to train their members, and to encourage networking. Most associations issue a magazine or newsletter to inform the members as to new laws, court decisions, administrative agency decisions and other events which affect the industry.

ADVANTAGES OF ATTORNEYS AND COLLECTION AGENCIES

Over the years, many of the large credit card companies expanded, absorbed small credit card issuers, or merged with other credit card issuers. Also, Visa and Mastercard entered the arena. Now a significant number of companies which issue credit cards operate on a national basis. Furthermore, some major credit unions, such as the Navy Federal Credit Union, also operate on a national basis (although a recent decision may affect the national scope of the credit union). These institutions were referring claims to either regional or national collection agencies across the country, and the collection agencies, in turn, were referring these matters to attorneys locally to institute suit.

Collection agencies promoted the idea that creditors should refer all accounts to collection agencies and that if the agency was unable to collect the delinquent account, the collection agency would refer the matter to an attorney. Several law list firms published national lists of attorneys and provided these lists to the collection agencies. The collection agencies selected attorneys from these national lists and forwarded the claims to the attorney operating an office closest to where the debtor's business or the consumer was located. (Examples of these lists of attorneys appear in Appendix II.) The three-way arrangement consisted of permitting the collection agencies to deal directly with the creditors, the law lists publishing the list of attorneys to be selected for referrals, and the attorneys receiving the claims from the collection agencies. While this arrangement was originally applied almost totally to commercial claims, as the credit card industry grew the majority of collection agencies also engaged in collecting debts from consumers.

The target of the membership promotion of NARCA were law firms engaged in consumer collection. The major purpose of NARCA was to promote the concept that creditors could deal directly with attorneys without using the collection agency as an intermediary, and that attorneys could write dunning letters and make telephone calls as effectively as, if not better than, the collection agencies. Creditors understood that the collection agencies could only do two things: write letters and make telephone calls. Collection agencies could not institute suit without retaining an attorney. On the other hand if a claim was referred to an attorney directly, the law firm could write letters, make telephone calls, and furthermore institute suit.

Of course, the effective collection of debts is dependent upon many factors and the collection agencies had several points in their favor. First, many large collection agencies across the country had staffs in excess of 100 people, in some instances as many as 1,000 employees, and could service the large credit grantor. Second, many collection agencies have sophisticated computer programs to enable them to monitor a large volume of accounts. Third, the major weapon of the collection agencies and their clients as to consumer debtors is reporting the consumer to a credit reporting agency, which impacts the consumer's ability to obtain credit. While consumers may be wary of suits by attorneys, they are also apprehensive about their credit profile.

One prime advantage of using an attorney is the availability of legal consultation on problems in the collection effort. Prevention in today's environment may avoid a costly law suit.

The law firms involved in collections are mostly small; only a few have a support staff of over 100 persons. One of the major elements that limited the use of attorneys was the fact that attorneys could only institute suit in the state in which they were admitted to the bar. Since most attorneys were only admitted to the bar in the state in which their office was located, they could not cross state lines to institute suit, but were forced to retain attorneys in the state in which the debtor resided.

From this creation of the new trade association developed the idea of an attorney network for consumer and credit card claims. In essence, a network of attorneys consisted of attorneys located in each state banding together in a loosely knit affiliation which promoted their services to the large credit card grantors in the country. To my knowledge, there are approximately three or four operating networks across the country, and each one of them uses one or more attorneys in each state. Separate and distinct requirements are set forth for each network for law firms to become members. The attorneys may pay initiation dues, annual dues, transmission fees, dues per case received, or a percentage of each fee that is collected. Some of the networks transmit claims electronically and some charge the member attorneys for each electronic transmission. The idea is that the network centralizes the distribution of the cases as well as the status reporting from each member law firm. The network combines the status reports from all the member attorney firms into one combined report. Whereas the networks are suitable for national credit grantors, some regional credit grantors are also using the networks in their regional area.

AGREEMENTS WITH LAW FIRMS OR AGENCIES

Most financial institutions and large corporations require the agency or law firm to execute a written agreement setting forth the terms and conditions under which the accounts are being referred. These agreements range from a few pages to as many as forty pages in length. The agreements cover:

- the fees paid to the agency or law firm
- the procedure of account referral
- the requirement to hold monies in escrow in special trust accounts
- the procedures for remitting money to the client
- the conditions of termination
- the terms of withdrawal of an account
- indemnification of the client
- insurance coverage
- licensing compliance
- status reporting
- reporting payments
- compliance with laws
- right to audit
- fees
- other boilerplate clauses indigenous to all contracts.

A skeleton outline of such a contract is attached in the Appendix.

Most contracts provide that the agency or law firm comply with the Fair Debt Collection Practices Act. The agency or law firm must maintain a record of every payment received and the amount of the fees deducted. The right to audit and inspect records with or without notice should also be included.

Collection agencies cannot start lawsuits, but agreements with law firms should cover, in addition, the criteria under which a suit may be initiated, the payment of costs, disbursements and the control over the conduct of the litigation. For appeals, separate provisions allow the attorney to perform services on a specified hourly rate rather than on a contingency basis. Contracts provide for termination upon thirty-day written notice and for the return of all cases to the client. Copies of judgments are furnished to the client. An optional clause is whether the attorney should file proof of claim in all bankruptcies or only in those exceeding certain amounts. If counterclaims are asserted in a litigation matter, the client must be notified immediately, and furnished with a copy of the papers served upon the attorney. Where counterclaims are interposed, the attorney charges an hourly fee (as opposed to a contingency fee under which the claim is being handled) to defend the counterclaim unless it is frivolous and will be dismissed in the normal course of the action.

The procedures in settlements should include the discretion of the attorney to settle and the procedure for oral or written approval from the client. At the time of signing the contract, attorneys usually submit copies of their malpractice insurance, and collection agencies provide evidence of the bonding by the various states, as well as copies of the errors-and-omissions policies.

A key clause in all contracts is an agreement by the collection agency or law firm indemnifying the creditor against negligent acts. Accordingly, if a suit is instituted against the creditor by reason of the negligent conduct of the agency or law firm, the agreement indemnifies the creditor for costs and expenses in defending the suit and the amount of any judgment awarded against the creditor.

WITHDRAWAL OF CLAIM

A claim may always be withdrawn from a collection agency or a law firm. If the withdrawal is for breach of contract or malpractice, no problem arises. But if the withdrawal is because the agency or law firms did not collect enough money or did not collect it quickly enough, the creditor may be liable for fees for services. Work and effort has been expended in the collection of this account, and the agency or attorney is entitled to be paid for these services, since the creditor is abrogating the right to continue the collection effort. If the account is referred to another collection agency and the claim is collected, the first collector is entitled to a portion of the fee. Collection agencies often refuse to return an account unless the creditor agrees to pay a fee in the event the account is ultimately collected. The same situation applies to a law firm acting on a contingency basis if the claim is withdrawn and referred to another law firm.

This problem is solved by a written agreement enabling the creditor to withdraw the account at any time. The contract provides that if the account is not collected at that time, the agency or law firm will not be entitled to a fee if a secondary law firm or agency should collect the debt. Many large corporations and financial institutions retain a collection agency or law firm for primary work, when the account is referred for the first time for outside collection. After a period of time, the creditor withdraws the account and refers it to a secondary agency or law firm. The theory behind this transfer is that debtors respond positively when a new collector is involved, and perhaps the new collector uses an initial extra effort. Statistics show that secondary firms often collect money that primary agencies were unable to collect. The creditor should not transfer the account unless a written agreement is executed by the primary firm waiving any further fees. Accounts that are paying currently usually are not recalled since the agency or attorney would be entitled to a fee.

If no written agreement exists, the creditor and the agency or law firm may agree on a fixed amount as a full settlement for the withdrawal of one or more claims. This is a negotiable figure and the amount is a function of past and future business and other circumstances prevailing at the time of the withdrawal.

REFERRAL TO ATTORNEYS

After letters and telephone calls are made, collection agencies often refer claims to outside attorneys locally and across the country. (Some large collection agencies employ full-time attorneys on their staff.)

Collection agencies seem to acknowledge that outside attorneys may collect monies by dunning or suit that the agencies themselves are unable to collect. Agencies use their own staff attorneys or outside affiliated attorneys to write letters and contact the debtor by telephone. Statistics show that attorneys' letters and phone calls are successful in generating more collections; for this reason attorneys often argue that creditors should use an attorney initially instead of a collection agency.

Law firms will institute suit after unsuccessful letters and telephone calls and will refer matters to local attorneys across the country to institute suit if the debtor is out of state. As noted before, several organizations provide national lists of collection attorneys. These law firms will accept claims from collection agencies as well as from other attorneys, and from creditors. A creditor may require a written suit authorization setting forth the anticipated costs to start suit before suit is instituted.

SUIT FEES

A suit fee is a fee the local attorney requests in advance of the institution of a suit in addition to the contingency fee. The fee enables the attorney to institute the suit, prosecute the claim, and, if necessary, conduct a trial without any additional payment. Suit must be started to earn a suit fee. If suit is not started, the local attorney must return the suit fee. Preparation of a summons and complaint and delivering same to the sheriff or process server for service is commencement of the suit even if the sheriff or process server does not serve the summons and complaint.

Over the past several years, the fees to institute suit that are paid by out-of-state attorneys have significantly changed. The normal suit fee that most local attorneys charged was approximately 10% of the face amount of the claim. The percentage usually declines to 7% as the amount increases and to as little as 5% on claims over $20,000. The minimum suit fee that almost all local attorneys requested was approximately $100 and, in some instances, the suit fees on large claims ranged as high as $1,000 to $2,500.

If there is no known defense to the case, most attorneys will not request a suit fee in excess of $1,000, even if the claim is as large as $25,000 or $30,000. Exceptions to these estimates depend upon the nature of the claim and whether the local attorney expects the claim to be contested.

The local attorney contemplates that only a small portion of the collection suits will be contested. If the local attorney collects suit fees on every case, the one case that becomes complex will be paid for by the other suit fees. The suit fee is usually non-contingent and will not be returned.

Some attorneys request an additional contingent suit fee payable in the event the attorney is successful in collecting after suit. The contingent suit fee may range from 5% to 10% in addition to the non-contingent suit fee, both of which are in addition to the contingent fees.

In recent years many creditors have taken the position that they do not want to pay a suit fee in advance to institute suit. The forwarders prefer a straight contingent fee payable on collection of the claim by the attorney. This contingent fee covers the entire collection process from initiation of suit through trial. The pressure is on the attorney to produce collection. The creditor only pays a fee if collection is effected.

Where no suit fee is advanced, the normal fee the out-of-state attorneys prefer is a net fee to the local attorney of 15% to 33% of all amounts collected. The fees depend upon whether it is a business or consumer claim and other considerations. Some attorneys will not handle claims at a net fee of lower than 25% without a suit fee, whereas many local attorneys will handle claims at 25% or 30% net fees without a suit fee. Local attorneys charge significantly different fees for business claims and consumer claims, with the fees for consumer claims being higher.

A general trend in the industry today is that claims are being forwarded on a straight contingent basis. The drawback in this arrangement is that the fee charged by the local attorney is more than would be charged with an advance suit fee. The local attorney is earning significantly more, but only if collection is made.

Costs must be advanced to the local attorney whether on a contingent basis or on a suit fee plus contingent basis. If a counterclaim is asserted, the local attorney usually requests an hourly fee to defend the counterclaim.

COURT COSTS

Court costs usually range from $35 to $350 depending upon the amount of the claim. The average filing fee in court is around $100. However, in recent years the filing fees in many of the large cities have increased substantially, approaching $200 in some instances. The attorney must also pay the process server or sheriff to serve the summons and complaint, usually from $15 to $50 depending on the location of the defendant. Unfortunately, some attorneys request court costs not only to cover the minimum costs, but the maximum costs that may be needed which include "anticipated costs:" i.e., costs that may or may not be needed. Necessary costs include service and filing a summons and complaint. Anticipated costs include skip tracing, property executions, garnishees and other expenses of enforcing the judgment. In these cases, court costs are negotiable where "anticipated costs" are requested.

In most states the sheriff serves the summons and complaint and fees are fixed by law. These expenses are the primary reason for the court costs, although the attorney may use the advance costs to engage a service bureau to conduct a search to determine the proper name of the corporation to locate a debtor or to skip trace, if authorized. The court costs and disbursements may also include the use of faxes, messenger services, or other office expenses. Always ask for an accounting of these costs from the local attorney whether or not suit is started. Court costs must be returned if not used.

CONTINGENT FEES

Contingent fees that collection agencies charge may range from as low as 10 to 15 percent to as high as 50 percent. In general, commercial claims warrant fees between 15 and 33 percent and retail claims warrant fees between 25 and 50 percent.

At one time, attorneys used Commercial Law League rates for commercial collections, but these rates were abolished for anti-trust reasons. Nevertheless, today many attorneys use the same rates, since they appear to be fair and equitable.

If a commercial claim is sent to an attorney by a collection agency or law firm (because the debtor is located in another part of the country), the fees for the receiving attorney may be as follows:

- 33 1/3% of the first $75.
- 25% of excess over $75 to $300.
- 18% of excess over $300 to $2000.
- 13% of excess over $2000.

The forwarder (the collection agency or law firm) adds "approximately" 50% or less to the receiver's fee (33 1/3% plus 16 2/3% = 50%) so that the client pays as follows:

- 50% of first $75.
- 33% of excess over $75 to $300.
- 27% of excess over $300 to $2000.
- 20% of excess over $2000.

In addition to the above fees, the client pays a 5% to 10% suit fee to commence suit plus the courts costs. Shopping for fees will usually produce one law firm which will provide a cheaper fee than another.

> **CREDIT AND COLLECTION TIP:** *The cheapest is not always the best; the quality, effort, and experience of the attorney to produce the best result should be the prime consideration.*

COLLECTION OF DEBT BY CREDITOR

The collection of a debt is due to the joint effort of both the client and the agency or attorney. The agency or attorney earns a contingent fee even if the settlement is made with the client. The fact that the client is the last person to contact the debtor, or that payment is made directly to the client, is not material. Whether a client expends more time than the attorney to negotiate a settlement is also not material.

> **CREDIT AND COLLECTION TIP:** *The client is still liable for the contingent fee once the agency or the attorney has been retained and contact with the debtor by the agency or law firm by mail or telephone has been consummated.*

DEPOSITING OR MAILING CHECKS

The agency or law firm must maintain a separate trust account for the monies collected from the debtor. If the checks are deposited, as is generally the case, the contingency fee is deducted before the monies are transmitted to the client. The creditor should obtain a listing each week of the checks deposited in the escrow account.

An alternative is to send the debtor checks directly to the creditor. When the checks are mailed to the creditor, the agency or law firm bills the creditor at the end of the month for the contingency fees. The drawback in mailing checks is that if the checks are lost in the mail, a second effort to collect from the debtor is necessary. If the checks are deposited and the remittance check is lost in the mail, the collection agency or law firm will stop payment and replace the lost check.

ESCROW ACCOUNTS

Both the agency and attorney must maintain a separate trust account for the monies collected from the debtor. The banking system provides that checks clear between two and six business days depending upon whether the check is within the immediate zone or crosses state lines, or other geographical limitations. Nevertheless, agencies and law firms prefer to allow an additional two to three weeks for clearance since the bank must notify the depositor that the check was returned unpaid and the bank uses regular mail. Sometimes a day or two or more may pass at the bank before the notice is mailed to the depositor. Normally, the monies will be remitted once a month, but large amounts may be requested by the creditor to be remitted as soon as the check clears.

ASSIGNMENT OF CLAIM

In some states a non-resident cannot sue; in other states a non-resident individual or corporation may be required to pay in advance to the court the costs that may be awarded to the defendant-debtor in the event the debtor wins the case (costs may amount from a few dollars up to several hundred dollars, depending upon the amount of the suit). In addition, some collection agencies wish to proceed in their own name to facilitate the prosecution of the case. The device used is "an assignment of claim" by the creditor to the collection agency.

The assignment is a short agreement between the creditor and the collection agency assigning the debt to the collection agency for prosecution or for suit. The agency proceeds in its name against the debtor, identifying itself as the assignee of the creditor.

Most claims are not assigned to collection agencies since the relevant problems are encountered in only a few states.

UNMATCHED PAYMENTS

Inquiries should be made as to the procedures for identification of payments received by the agency or law firm. Most collection agencies and attorneys are meticulous about identifying to which creditor the payment belongs. Yet, it is unrealistic to believe that the collection agency or law firm dealing in thousands of small balance accounts can identify and apply each and every payment that it receives.

Every creditor usually has a special bank account for checks which are received, but which cannot be identified or applied to any account. For example, Mary's ex-husband sends in the check for Mary without setting forth any information to help the creditor identify the payment, or Aunt Millie uses her personal check to pay an outstanding bill for her beloved niece. If a creditor maintains an account for unmatched payments, so should the collection agency or law firm. Some agencies and law firms will remit to their clients a listing of all unmatched payments to enable the creditor to match the payments against their customers. Notwithstanding these efforts by the agency or law firm, a certain number of collections will remain unidentified. These monies should be transferred under the abandoned property laws of the various states.

ONE OR TWO COLLECTION AGENCIES OR ATTORNEYS?

Many creditors, if they are large enough, believe that they should always utilize at least two collection agencies or law firms to encourage competition. Other creditors conclude it is difficult enough to find one good collection agency or law firm, and would rather use only one. Both arguments have merit and each creditor has to decide which road to travel.

TESTING

The important consideration is to test the collection agency or law firm fairly, covering a sufficient period of time to fully evaluate performance. Two qualifying firms should receive an equal number of accounts over a given period of time with the same type of account, with same average balances, same aging, same geographical area, and from the same department or source. If the debtors are businesses as opposed to retailers, the business debtors should be in the same industry and should have other similarities such as size, product line, etc. With regard to business accounts, a random selection probably will satisfy these criteria.

When considering the performance of two firms, the reporting qualities should be integrated as well as the communication and support between the firm and the creditor. In general, the agency or law firm which performs better will usually provide the better communication, the better reporting, the better support, the better performance, and generate the fewest complaints.

Until recently, collection agencies were much more successful than attorneys in marketing their services to credit grantors primarily because attorneys were prohibited from advertising or soliciting. Only in the past decade have the barriers to advertising by lawyers been eliminated, and now law firms actively advertise and compete with the collection agencies. Six years ago the National Association of Retail Collection Attorneys (NARCA) was organized for the purpose of presenting to credit grantors the concept that law firms were able to collect debts, and the creditors could use attorneys for initial collection efforts of letters and telephone calls.

PORTFOLIO PURCHASES

While this may not necessarily come under the heading of Credit and Collection Law, it certainly will have an impact on the credit and collection industry. In recent years, a firm known as Commercial Financial Services Inc. became one of the powerhouses in purchasing debt portfolios being offered by the major financial institutions such as Fleet, Chase, MBNA, Discover, etc. An organization of over 3,000 employees was built in Dallas, Texas with connections to more than half of the nation's 25 largest credit card issuers.

This firm was instrumental in driving up the price that credit card companies charge for portfolios from eight to nine cents on the dollar to as high as thirteen and in some instances as much as fourteen cents on the dollar. The firm was also instrumental in the securitization of debts by using them to secure bonds in order to raise additional monies to purchase new debt. Another driving force in the company was their contracts with the major credit card issuers on a forward-flow basis, wherein they were able to continually purchase the debt from the issuers on a continuing ongoing arrangement.

The media has reported that Commercial Financial Services misrepresented its recovery rates and apparently sold credit card loans that were used as collateral for bonds to a company in which close business associates of the principals were president and owner. It appears that there are substantial loans outstanding to the principal owners of the company.

The company in early 1999 filed a Chapter 11 proceeding. Commercial Financial Services has now closed its doors. It is not clear yet whether the reason for the problems was that the operation was not as profitable as it should have been or the fact that the principals had diverted monies to their own pockets from the operation.

The fallout in early 1999 from this Chapter 11 proceeding was that the price of debt portfolios probably dropped two to four cents and is back to where it was several years ago. The net result may be that some of the major players may return to utilizing attorneys and collection agencies rather than selling all of their portfolios. Perhaps some of the sellers of debt portfolios will recognize that reliance on one source for recovery of bad debts is not the wisest course. The major players may decide to continue to sell debt portfolios, but at the same time retain a significant volume in house and continue relationships with agencies and law firms.

The Attorney General of Tennessee issued an opinion letter which will significantly discourage the purchasers of portfolios from operating in the State of Tennessee. The Attorney General ruled that the purchasers of delinquent accounts are subject to the state's licensing requirement since it is a collection service which requires licensing in the event you collect an account for a fee, commission or other compensation. It would appear that any one who purchases portfolio accounts who intends to locate in Tennessee should investigate whether they fall within the definitions set forth by the office of the Attorney General and if appropriate, obtain a license.

INTERNATIONAL COLLECTIONS

Doing business outside the United States presents a mixed bag when retaining attorneys. Our office handles a significant number of claims that are referred overseas and results depend upon not only the attorneys that we retain, but also upon the country in which the debtor resides.

Canada

In Canada outside of Quebec, most attorneys do not work on a contingency basis. But when a relationship is built up with the attorney, the flat fees or hourly charges will be close to what the contingency fee might be. On the other hand, the attorneys do require fees up front to institute suit. Quebec attorneys are permitted to handle matters on a contingency, although some attorneys will ask for an hourly fee. The major problem in Quebec is the language because documents have to be translated into French, although a witness may testify in English.

France

Notwithstanding that Quebec follows the French law, in France the attorneys do not work on a contingency basis, but developing a relationship with the law firm is recommended. The system recognizes that lawyers must have a fee to institute suit which must not be contingent on collection. This might be compared to the suit fee that we use in the United States, with some of the fee contingent on actual collection. In France there are different type of lawyers with different legal qualifications and the fees for the more qualified attorneys are much higher than for the less qualified attorneys.

Germany

Germany is one of the countries where contingency fees are totally prohibited. They have special fees for special procedures and, in general, the fees are constructed in such a way that they escalate with the amount of the indebtedness.

Italy

In Italy, contingency fees are also prohibited, but fees are usually set by the system or by the court which bear some relationship to the amount involved and the quantity of the work.

England

In England, contingency fees are not permitted, but the fees charged usually bear a strong relationship to the amount involved and the work that is necessary to collect the debt. A distinction in British law is that the loser pays the costs and normally the successful party may recover 40-60% of the attorney's fees in addition to the costs and damages awarded.

Russia

The most difficult European country is Russia. Our attorney in Russia advises that the main means of collecting a judgment in Russia is by extortion and threat. A Russian attorney will usually not take a case before they review all the papers and they determine who the party is that they are suing. The amount of money that they require to institute a suit is usually substantial and there is no assurance of collection. No organization is in place to collect a judgment, but hopefully this will improve.

Brazil

In Brazil, you must furnish a power of attorney and you have to have an official certified translation of your documents before any proceeding can be started. The fees are more or less negotiated, although you can work out a combination of fees plus a contingency.

Mexico and Central America

Mexico allows the attorneys to charge either a contingency or an hourly rate. The problem in Mexico is that the legal system operates well in the major cities, but in the smaller cities, towns or villages, it depends a great deal on the extent of the attorney's relationship with the persons in the governmental structure. With regard to some of the countries in Central America, the results depend upon the attorney that you retain. The legal systems leave much to be desired and the enforcement and collection of judgments is speculative at best.

Letters of credit or collect bills of lading are the common means of protection from pursuing debtors or shippers in foreign countries, but latent defects in goods and other breaches of contract may create a claim in a foreign country. In those instances, it is important for you to retain counsel who have relationships with law firms in this country.

CHAMPERTY AND MAINTENANCE

Attorneys cannot pay costs and fees to institute suits in most states. The bar associations feel that this only promotes litigation, and that the attorney should not be the moving force. Attorneys can advance costs, but the client must remain responsible. Even in personal injury cases, the client is responsible for costs even though the attorney advances the monies and is reimbursed from the recovery. In collection suits, the attorney also is reimbursed from the recovery. In some states advancing monies to institute suit is a criminal violation. (In New York, it is a misdemeanor).

CHAPTER 6
APPENDIX I

NEW JERSEY COLLECTION AGENCY LAW

45:18-1. COLLECTION AGENCIES TO FILE BOND

No person shall conduct a collection agency, collection bureau or collection office in this state, or engage therein in the business of collecting or receiving payment for others of any account, bill or other indebtedness, or engage therein in the business of soliciting the right to collect or receive payment for another of any account, bill or other indebtedness, or advertise for or solicit in print the right to collect or receive payment for another of any account, bill or other indebtedness, unless such person, or the person for whom he may be acting as agent has on file with the secretary of state sufficient bond as hereinafter specified.

45:18-2. AMOUNT, TERM AND PROVISIONS OF BOND; RENEWAL; LIMITATION OF ACTIONS

The bond shall be in the sum of five thousand dollars and shall provide that the person giving the same shall, upon written demand, pay and turn over to or for the person for whom any account, bill or other indebtedness is taken for collection the proceeds thereof in accordance with the terms of the agreement upon which such account, bill or other indebtedness was received for collection. The bond shall be in such form and shall contain such further provisions and conditions as the secretary of state deems necessary or proper for the protection of the persons for whom the accounts, bills or other indebtedness are taken for collection, and shall be for the term of one year from its date and must be renewed annually. No action on the bond shall be begun after two years from the expiration thereof.

45:18-3. EXECUTION AND APPROVAL OF BOND; SURETIES

The bond mentioned in sections 45:18-1 and 45:18-2 of this Title shall be executed by the person filing the same with the State of New Jersey for the use of any party aggrieved with sufficient surety, to be furnished by any company or corporation authorized to transact such business in this State. The said bond shall be examined and approved by the Attorney-General and thereafter accepted and filed with the Secretary of State; *provided, however,* that cash may be accepted in lieu of sureties; *and provided, further,* that no such bond with individual sureties thereon may be approved, accepted or filed.

Amended by L.1946, c. 293, p. 988, 1.

45:18-4. RECORD OF BONDS; FILING FEE

The Secretary of State shall keep a record of such bonds, with the names, places of residence and places of business of the principals and sureties, and the name of the officer before whom the bond was executed or acknowledged, and the record shall be open to public inspection. There shall be paid a filing fee of $25.00 to the Secretary of State for the filing of each bond.

Amended by L.1971, C. 169, 1, eff. June 1, 1971.

45:18-5. PENALTY

Any person, member of a partnership or officer of an association or corporation who fails to comply with any of the provisions of this chapter shall be subject to a fine of not more than five hundred dollars or to imprisonment for not more than three months, or both.

45:18-6. EXEMPTIONS

This chapter shall not apply to an attorney at law duly authorized to practice in this state, a national bank, or any bank or trust company duly incorporated under the laws of this state.

45:18-6.1. DISCONTINUANCE OF OPERATION; FILING OF NOTICE

Any person who shall discontinue the operation of a collection agency, collection bureau or collection office in this State pursuant to the chapter hereby supplemented shall file with the Secretary of State a notice of such discontinuance.

CHAPTER 6
APPENDIX II

EXAMPLES OF REFERRAL LISTS OF ATTORNEYS HANDLING COMMERCIAL AND CONSUMER CLAIMS

THE COLUMBIA LIST
2029 JERICHO TPKE
NEW HYDE PARK, NY 11040
516-352-8822
800-645-8288
FAX: 516-328-7712

THE AMERICAN LAWYERS QUARTERLY
853 WESTPOINT PARKWAY SUITE 710
CLEVELAND, OHIO 44145-1532
TELE: 216-871-8700
FAX: 216-871-9997
TOLL FREE: 800-843-4000

WRIGHT-HOLMES LAW LIST
852 1ST AVENUE, SOUTH, SUITE A
NAPLES, FL 33940
800-882-5478
813-434-8880
FAX: 813-434-5983

FORWARDERS LIST OF ATTORNEYS
424 WEST 33RD STREET
11TH FLOOR
NEW YORK, NY 10001
212-714-3115
800-638-9200
FAX: 212-714-3176

THE COMMERCIAL BAR
20 WEST DOVER STREET
EASTON, MD 21601
800-824-9911

THE NATIONAL ASSOCIATION OF
RETAIL COLLECTION ATTORNEYS
8201 GREENSBORO DRIVE
SUITE 300
MCLEAN, VA 22102
800-633-6069

CHAPTER 6
Appendix III

Attorney/Client Agreement

AGREEMENT dated _____ day of _____, 2000 between _____[the firm]_____ located at _____[address]_____ , _____[town]_____ _____[zip code]____ (hereinafter after referred to as the attorney), and _____ referred to as the client.

The parties hereunto agree as follows:

1. REFERRAL OF ACCOUNTS—The client from time to time may refer to the attorney delinquent accounts for collection and the attorney shall attempt to collect those accounts in accordance with the terms of this agreement.

2. CONFLICT OF INTEREST—The attorney shall not accept any accounts which by so doing my create a conflict of interest under the rules of ethics of the Bar Association of the State of New York.

3. WARRANTY OF THE ATTORNEY—The attorney represents and warrants that it has a license to practice law under the State of New York and Connecticut and our network attorney has a license to practice in the state where the network attorney is located. Our firm and our network attorneys have complied with all laws to enable them to perform the obligations which they undertake in this agreement.

   A. The attorney agrees that during the terms of this agreement, the attorney will strictly comply with all applicable, federal, state and all local statutes, rules, regulations and ordinances, including without limitation, the Federal Fair Debt Collection Practices Act, the Federal Credit Reporting Act, Equal Credit Opportunity Act, and any other laws directly or indirectly affecting the collection process.

   B. The attorney will use its best efforts to collect any and all amounts due with regard to the accounts herein referred.

   C. The attorney shall not threaten suit or institute suit on any of the accounts unless expressly authorized by the client in writing.

4. PAYMENTS—The attorney shall place in its special trust account any and all funds collected by the attorney. The attorney shall remit to the client the amount collected less any fees or expenses incurred in the collection effort.

   A. The attorney shall maintain complete records of all payments, disbursements and fees charged to the client.

   B. During the last week of the month following the month in which payment is received, all funds collected by the attorney shall be remitted to the client.

   C. Each remittance hereunder shall be accompanied by a detailed statement setting forth the fees, expenses, and disbursements.

5. INDEMNIFICATION—The attorney shall indemnify and hold harmless the client from and against any and all claims, suits, actions, debts, damages, costs, charges and expenses, including court costs and reasonable attorney's fees and against all liabilities, loss and

damages of any nature, that the client shall or may at any time sustain which arise solely from the failure of the attorneys to perform its obligation under these agreements due to negligence. The client indemnifies the attorney in the same manner.

6. MALPRACTICE INSURANCE—The attorney shall carry a policy of malpractice insurance with a recognized carrier in the amount of one million dollars. The attorney upon request shall furnish the client a copy of the current cover page setting forth the amount of coverage of the insurance policy and other information concerning the insurance coverage upon request.

7. OBLIGATIONS OF THE CLIENT—The client shall provide copies of all documentation and information relating to the accounts referred to the attorney. This information and documentation shall be sufficient for the attorney to validate the debt and to provide information as required under the Fair Debt Collection Practices Act.

   A. Client shall advise attorney whether such an account has been previously placed for collection with another collection agency or attorney.

   B. Client shall promptly furnish written notice to the attorney of any payments that they receive on any account which has been referred to the attorney.

8. TERMINATION—This agreement may be terminated by either party on 30 days prior written notice by either party giving written notice of same to other party. At such time, the attorney shall continue to pursue collection efforts on those accounts that were heretofore referred to him. Nevertheless, in the event that the attorney fails to perform his obligation under this contract by failure to vigorously and diligently perform collection efforts on those accounts, the client shall have a right to immediately demand that the attorney return all the accounts to the client and the attorney shall waive all of his rights to receive compensation on the accounts returned to the client. Before the files are returned to the client, the client shall pay all outstanding fees and expenses to the attorney.

9. FEES—The fee arrangement between the attorney and the client is as follows:

_____

_____

10. INDEPENDENT CONTRACTOR—This agreement creates no relationship such as a joint venture, partnership, association, or employment between the client and the attorney, but rather the attorney shall at all times act as and be an independent contractor. Nothing in this agreement constitutes or authorizes the attorney to bind the client to any obligation or assume or create any responsibility for or on behalf of the client for or to any third party except upon the client's prior approval. Attorney is an independent contractor and shall not represent any third party that is an agent of the client.

11. MODIFICATION AND MERGER—This agreement constitutes the entire agreement of the parties and all other oral representations or agreements are hereby merged herein. This agreement may only be amended in writing executed by both parties.

12. NOTICES—Any written notices or writings concerning this agreement may be delivered either personally or by certified mail to the address at the beginning of this agreement or to such other address as may be given by written notice to the other party.

13. LAWS—This agreement shall be construed or interpreted in accordance with the laws of the State of [name]. If any part of this agreement shall be held void or unenforceable, the remaining portions of this agreement shall remain valid and enforceable.

14. BINDING—This agreement is binding upon the successors and assigns of the respective parties.

   IN WITNESS WHEREOF, the parties have hereunto set their hand and seal the day and year written above.

BY: _____ [THE FIRM] _____

BY: BY:

_____   _____

CHAPTER 6

APPENDIX IV

SUMMARY OF COLLECTION LAWS

THE SUMMARY OF COLLECTION LAWS IS REPRINTED WITH CONSENT FROM OTHER PUBLICATIONS, WITHOUT ANY INDEPENDENT RESEARCH FOR ACCURACY OR LEGAL STATUS, AND THE AMERICAN LAWYERS QUARTERLY DISCLAIMS ANY LIABILITY FOR DIRECT, INCIDENTAL OR CONSEQUENTIAL DAMAGES RESULTING FROM RELIANCE BY ANY PARTY WHATSOEVER UPON THE LEGALITY AND ACCURACY OF THE CONTENTS THEREOF.

Location	Statute of Limitations				Collection Agency Bond and License			General Garnishment Exemption
	Open Accounts Years	Contracts in Writing Years	Domestic Judgments Years	Foreign Judgments Years	Bond	License	Fee	
UNITED STATES								Federal law exempts from garnishment 75% of disposable earnings per work wk. or an amount equal to 30 × fed. min. hourly wage, whichever is greater. State laws are listed below, but where fed. law provides larger exemption, it supersedes state law.
ALABAMA	3	6	20	20	No	Yes* (privilege license, state & county)	$150 (pop. over 20,000) $38 (pop. under 20,000)	See federal law.
ALASKA	6	6	10	10	$5,000	Yes	$20 initial lic. app. $100 initial opr. lic. $100 opr. lic. ren. $100 agy. lic. $100 agy. lic. ren. $20 br. offc. lic. $20 br. offc. ren. All non-res. opr & agency fees are double except for br. offc. fees.	$192.20/wk., or $302.50/wk. if earnings are sole household support

*Out-of-state collectors may be able to obtain limited license or may bypass license requirement. Call collection agency administrator.

Location	Statute of Limitations				Collection Agency Bond and License			General Garnishment Exemption
	Open Accounts Years	Contracts in Writing Years	Domestic Judgments Years	Foreign Judgments Years	Bond	License	Fee	
UNITED STATES								disposable earnings per work wk. or an amount equal to 30 × fed. min. hourly wage, whichever is greater. State laws are listed below, but where fed. law provides larger exemption, it supersedes state law.
ARIZONA	3	6	5 Add'l 5 on request	4 or period in foreign state if less	$10,000-$35,000	Yes	$1,500 orig. lic. $600 lic. ren $500 br. $200 br. ren.	See fed. law. Judge may limit amount available for garnishment of earnings to 15% of take home pay. $150 exemption for garnishment of bank accounts of individuals only.
ARKANSAS	3	5	10 (renewable)	10 (renewable)	$5,000-$25,000 $1,500 br.	Yes	$125 $15 ea. collector	See fed. law. $200/wk. single person, $500/wk. head of household if greater than federal exemption.
CALIFORNIA	4	4	10	10	No	No	No	See fed. law, except 100% earnings necessary for support of debtor or family unless used for personal services.
COLORADO	6	6	20	6	$12,000-$20,000	Yes*	$250 invest $300 orig. lic. $100 ren. $35 collr. $25 colln. mgr.	Greater of 75% of disposable earnings per work wk., or amount equal to 30 × fed. min. hourly wage.
CONNECTICUT	6	6	20	No prov.	$5,000	Yes	$400 $100 invest. $250 ren.	The greater of 75% of disposable earnings for the wk., or 40 x the fed. min. hourly wage.
DELAWARE	3	3	No prov.	No prov.	No	Merc. lic.	$50	85% of wages
DISTRICT OF COLUMBIA	3	3	3	No prov.	No	No	No	See fed. law, except 90% of 1st $200 gross wages per month, 80% on excess of $200 & under $500.
FLORIDA	4	5	20	7	No (Consumer Collns.) Yes (Commercial Collns.)	Regis.*	$200 regis. $50 invest. $200 ren.	See fed. law, except $500 per wk. head of household.
GEORGIA	4	6	7	5	No	No	N/A	See federal law.
HAWAII	6	6	10	6	$25,000 $15,000 ea. br.	Yes	$25 app. $40 regis.	95% of 1st $100, 90% of next $100 and 80% of wages in excess of $200 per mo., or equivalent per wk.

*Out-of-state collectors may be able to obtain limited license or may bypass license requirement. Call collection agency administrator.

281

Location	Statute of Limitations				Collection Agency Bond and License			General Garnishment Exemption
	Open Accounts Years	Contracts in Writing Years	Domestic Judgments Years	Foreign Judgments Years	Bond	License	Fee	
UNITED STATES								disposable earnings per work wk. or an amount equal to 30 × fed. min. hourly wage, whichever is greater. State laws are listed below, but where fed. law provides larger exemption, it supersedes state law.
IDAHO	4	5	6	6	$2,000 initial bond; up to $100,000 ren., depending on net collns. + $2,000 to indemnify state costs	Yes*	$100 / $100 foreign / $50 ren. / $20 app. / $20 solicitor/colltr.	Greater of 75% of disposable earnings for wk., or 30 × fed. min. hourly wage.
ILLINOIS	5	10	20	5	$25,000	Yes*	$75 orig. / $60 ren.	Greater of 85% of gross wages weekly, or 45 × fed. min. hourly wage.
INDIANA	6	10 Executed before 9/1/82 / 6—Executed after 8/31/82	20	20	$5,000	Yes*	$50 +$5 ea. unlic. emp. $15 br. offc.	See federal law.
IOWA	5	10	20	20	No	If collns. exceed $25,000, must notify state and pay $10 fee	No	See fed. law. For consumer cred. transaction, 75% of disposable earnings for wk. or 30 × fed. min. hourly wage, whichever is greater. Consumer may apply to court for greater exemption on basis that it is necessary for the maintenance of the consumer or a family supported wholly or partly by the earnings of the consumer.
KANSAS	3	5	5 (renewable)	5 (renewable)	No	No	No	See federal law.
KENTUCKY	5	15	15	15	No	No	No	See federal law.
LOUISIANA	3	10	10	10	$10,000	Yes	Up to $200 orig./ren. Up to $100 br. offc.	See federal law.
MAINE	6	6	20	20	$20,000 $50,000	Yes*	$400 (2 yrs.)	Greater of 75% disposable earnings for wk., or disposable earnings over 40 × fed. min. hourly wage. Wages due for wife's or child's personal service. In trustee process, 100%.
MARYLAND	3	3	12	12	$5,000	Yes	$200 ea. location	Greater of 75% or amount equal to $145 × no. of wks. in which wages due were earned, except in Carolina, Worcester, Kent and Queen Arne's Counties, see fed. law.

282

*Out-of-state collectors may be able to obtain limited license or may bypass license requirement. Call collection agency administrator.

Location	Statute of Limitations				Collection Agency Bond and License			General Garnishment Exemption
	Open Accounts Years	Contracts in Writing Years	Domestic Judgments Years	Foreign Judgments Years	Bond	License	Fee	
UNITED STATES								disposable earnings per work wk. or an amount equal to 30 × fed. min. hourly wage, whichever is greater. State laws are listed below, but where fed. law provides larger exemption, it supersedes state law.
MASSACHUSETTS	6 (UCC 4)	6 (UCC 4)	20	20	$10,000-$25,000	Yes	$500	See federal law.
MICHIGAN	6	6	10 (renewable)	10	$5,000-$50,000	Yes*	$225 $125 ren. $125 mgr. (non-owner) $50 mgr. (owner)	See federal law.
MINNESOTA	6	6 (UCC 4)	10 (renewable)	10 (renewable)	$5,000-$20,000	Yes	$500 invest. $500 ren. $400 ren. $10 ea. collr.	Greater of 75% disposable earnings or 40 × fed. min hourly wages. For debtor who has been on relief, 100% for 1st six months after return to private employment.
MISSISSIPPI	3	3	7	7 (3 if MS resident)	No	Cert. of Authority	$15- $50	After 30-day grace period, see fed. law. Exemptions not applicable to taxes/pensions.
MISSOURI	5	10	10	10	No	No	No	See fed. law, except 90% of week's net pay, head of household.
MONTANA	5	8	10	10	No	No	No	Maximum subject to garnishment is the lesser of the amount by which his disposal earnings exceed 30% of fed. min. wage or 25% disposable earnings.
NEBRASKA	4	5	5 (renewable)	5	$5,000 for less than 5 lic. solic. $10,000 for 5 to 5 $15,000 for 16+	Yes*	$200 $200 invest. $75 br. $50 br. $35 br. ren. $6 solic.	Greater of 75% disposable earnings (85% if head of household) or 30 × fed. min. hourly wage.
NEVADA	4	6	6	6	$25,000-$50,000	Yes*	$250 app. & survey $100-300 orig. $200 ren. $125 br. $100 ren. br.	See federal law.
NEW HAMPSHIRE	3	3	20	20	No	No	No	50 × fed. min. hourly wage.

*Out-of-state collectors may be able to obtain limited license or may bypass license requirement. Call collection agency administrator.

Location	Statute of Limitations				Collection Agency Bond and License			General Garnishment Exemption
	Open Accounts Years	Contracts in Writing Years	Domestic Judgments Years	Foreign Judgments Years	Bond	License	Fee	
UNITED STATES								disposable earnings per work wk. or an amount equal to 30 × fed. min. hourly wage, whichever is greater. State laws are listed below, but where fed. law provides larger exemption, it supersedes state law.
NEW JERSEY	6	6	20	20 or period in foreign state if less.	$5,000 Surety only	Cert. of Authority	$25 filing fee	Min. $48 pr wk. 90% if earnings are $7,500/yr. or less, court may reduce exemption if earnings are greater. Subject to changes under cost of living index.
NEW MEXICO	4	6	14	14	$5,000-$25,000	Yes*	$200 orig. $200 br. $200 ren.	Greater of 75% or amount ea. wk. equal to 40 × fed. min. hourly wages.
NEW YORK	6	6	20	20	NYC: No Buffalo: $5,000	Yes Yes	$75 Determined by admin.	90% of earnings for services within 60 days before income execution and any time after. Court may reduce as related to federal garnishment exemptions.
NORTH CAROLINA	3	3 (UCC 4)	10	10	$5,000-$50,000	Yes*	$500	100% of last 60 days' earnings for family support. Garnishment not available as remedy in collection of commercial accounts.
NORTH DAKOTA	6	6	10 (renewable)	10	$20,000	Yes*	$300 invest. $200 lic.	75% disposable earnings for work wk., or amt. equal to 40 × fed. min. hourly wage, whichever is greater, plus $20 ea. dependent in household.
OHIO	15	15	21 (Judgment lien must be refiled every 5 yrs)	15	No	No	No	Of earnings for preceding 30 days, 30 × fed. min. hourly wage if paid weekly; 60 × if paid bi-weekly; 65 × if paid semi-monthly; 130 × if paid monthly, or 75% of disposable earnings. See fed. law.
OKLAHOMA	3 (UCC 5)	5	5 (renewable)	5	No	No	No	75% of earnings during 90 days before execution 100% of earnings for personal services prior to trial court judgment. Can extend to 50% to satisfy child support order.
OREGON	6	6	10	10	$10,000 (or irrevocable letters of credit)	Regis.*	$350 orig. $75 ren.	75% of disposable earnings per wk., or $170 of disposable earnings per wk., whichever is greater.
PENNSYLVANIA	6	6	4	4	Yes	Yes	% of sales	100% plus marital property.
RHODE ISLAND	10	10	20	20	No	No	No	First $50 of wages. Social welfare payments and see federal law.
SOUTH CAROLINA	3	3	10	10	No	Yes (Gen. business)	No	100% exemption.

*Out-of-state collectors may be able to obtain limited license or may bypass license requirement. Call collection agency administrator.

Location	Statute of Limitations				Collection Agency Bond and License			General Garnishment Exemption
UNITED STATES	Open Accounts Years	Contracts in Writing Years	Domestic Judgments Years	Foreign Judgments Years	Bond	License	Fee	disposable earnings per work wk. or an amount equal to 30 × fed. min. hourly wage, whichever is greater. State laws are listed below, but where fed. law provides larger exemption, it supersedes state law.
SOUTH DAKOTA	6	3	20	10	No	No	No	80% and 40 × fed. min. hourly wage, plus $25 per wk. for ea. dependent in debtor's household.
TENNESSEE	6	6	10	10	$15,000 1-4 emp. $20,000 5-9 emp. $25,000 10+ emp.	Yes*	$150 app. fee $600 orig. $350 ren. $100 br. $100 loc. mgr. app. $50 mgr. ren. $25 ea. sol.	See federal law. Add $2.50 per wk. for dependent child under 16.
TEXAS	4	4	10	10	$10,000	No	N/A	100% of wages.
UTAH	4	6	8	8	$10,000	Regis.	N/A	See federal law, or $134/wk.
VERMONT	6	6	8	8	No	No	No	75% of disposable earnings for wk., or 30 × fed. min. hourly wage, whichever is greater. If consumer credit transaction, 85% or 40 × fed. min. wage, whichever is greater.
VIRGINIA	3	5	20	10	No	No	No	75% of disposable earnings for wk., or excess of 30 × fed. min. hourly wage, whichever is greater. Varies for support situations. Debtor must be sent notice of how to claim exemption.
WASHINGTON	6	6	10	10	$5,000	Yes*	$375 orig. app. $375 invest. $600 ren. $300 br. & ren.	75% of disposable earnings, or 30 × fed. min. hourly wages, whichever is greater. If consumer cred. transaction, 85% or 40 × fed. min. wage, whichever is greater.
WEST VIRGINIA	5	10	10	10	$5,000	Yes*	$15	80% of wages due or to be due within one year of issuance of execution, or 30 × fed. min. hourly wages. For consumer cred. debts, 80% of disposable earnings a wk., 30 × fed. min. hourly wage.

*Out-of-state collectors may be able to obtain limited license or may bypass license requirement. Call collection agency administrator.

Location	Statute of Limitations				Collection Agency Bond and License			General Garnishment Exemption
	Open Accounts Years	Contracts in Writing Years	Domestic Judgments Years	Foreign Judgments Years	Bond	License	Fee	
UNITED STATES								disposable earnings per work wk. or an amount equal to 30 × fed. min. hourly wage, whichever is greater. State laws are listed below, but where fed. law provides larger exemption, it supersedes state law.
WISCONSIN	6	6	20	20 (for foreign if less)	Net worth $15,000 and up; $25,000 bond	Yes*	$100 invest. (min) $100 license $2 ea solicitor	80% of net pay; affects earnings for all pay periods beginning within 13 weeks of service of garnishment on garnishee; also: earnings exempt for families below federal poverty level, eligible for AFDC, general relief etc.
WYOMING	8	10	5	5	$10,000	Yes*	$200 orig. $100 ren. $100 br.	See federal law.
PUERTO RICO	15	N/A	15	15	$5,000	Yes*	$500 orig. $500 ren.	75% of last 30 days' earnings for family support.

*Out-of-state collectors may be able to obtain limited license or may bypass license requirement. Call collection agency administrator.

STATES HAVING COMMUNITY PROPERTY LAWS

Arizona	California	Idaho	Louisiana	Washington
Nevada	New Mexico	Texas	Wisconsin

Location	Statute of Limitations				Collection Agency Bond and License			Garnishment Exemption	Other
	Open Accounts Years	Contracts in Writing Years	Domestic Judgments Years	Foreign Judgments Years	Bond	License	Fee		
CANADA									
ALBERTA	6	6	10	10	$5,000-$50,000	Yes	$100 orig. $100 br. $25 collr.	Married $400 + $30 ea. child Single parent $300 Single $300	Furniture & appl. $4,000 One car/truck for work $8,000 Tools/equip for work $7,500. Occupied house $40,000. Occupied mobile home $20,000.
BRITISH COLUMBIA	6	6	20	20	10% annual clients' funds handled or $2,500 which-ever is greater.	Yes	$100 $100 br. $25 collr.	70% but no less than $200 per mo. head of household $100 single	N/A
MANITOBA	6	6	10 (renewable)	6	$5,000	Yes	$250	70% of wages, but no less than $250/mo. single, $350/no. with dependents	N/A
NEW BRUNSWICK	6	20	20 (renewable)	N/A (renewable)	$10,000	Yes	$200 main. off $25 e. br. $5 ea. collr.	Wages and salaries. Negotiable bill, draft, note, etc. not overdue. Money due contingently, not absolutely. Money due as officer of crown.	
NEWFOUNDLAND	6	20 (Seal for rent/land)	20	N/A	$20,000	Yes	$200	Married $94.25/wk. + $30 ea. child, single $70.	
NORTHWEST TERRITORIES	N/A	N/A	N/A	N/A	$5,000	Yes	N/A	N/A	
NOVA SCOTIA	6	6	20	N/A	$20,000	Yes	$200 main. offc. $50 ea. br. $20 ea. collr.	Married $225 Single $150	
ONTARIO	6	N/A	20	20	$5,000-$25,000 + up to $20,000 for per-paid colln.	Yes	$200 main offc. $200 br. off. $100 employee	80% gross wages. $1,000 on chattels execution	No exemption on bank accnts. or contracts. Garnishments continue 6 mos. in Provincial Court (small claims), 6 yrs. in higher courts. $500 assets.

*Out-of-state collectors may be able to obtain limited license or may bypass license requirement. Call collection agency administrator.

Location	Statute of Limitations				Collection Agency Bond and License			Garnishment Exemption	Other
	Open Accounts Years	Contracts in Writing Years	Domestic Judgments Years	Foreign Judgments Years	Bond	License	Fee		
CANADA									
PRINCE EDWARD ISLAND	6	6 (Seal, 20)	10 (Renewable)	N/A	$5,000	Yes	$400 orig. $200 ren.	50% single, 50% married, but min. allowance $10/wk.	
QUEBEC	5	30	30	Foreign law applies	$10,000-$25,000	Yes	$175 (2 yrs.)		
SASKATCHEWAN	6	6	10	6	$10,000	Yes	$50 $5 ea. colr.	$200 with 1-3 dep. $225 with 4 or more dep. $100 all others	No exemptions for alimony, separate maintenance, board or lodging, hospital or recoverable by government

*Out-of-state collectors may be able to obtain limited license or may bypass license requirement. Call collection agency administrator.

CHAPTER 7

Checks, Notes and Guarantees

BOUNCED CHECKS—CRIMINAL INTENT

"Issuing a check that bounces is a crime." This statement is partially true. Some background is necessary.

In the 1930s the con artist would enter a small town and issue checks to many of the merchants. Before the checks were cashed, the con man had crossed the state border, leaving the helpless merchants holding the worthless checks. The criminal "bad checks" laws were born.

These laws generally provide that a party who issues a check, knowing that the check will not be paid, may be subject to a fine and imprisonment. The key ingredient of all crimes is the element of "intent" and this crime is no different. The party must know that the check will not be paid. Nevertheless, when creditors receive bad checks, "reasonable" explanations are offered to show the debtor did not know that the check would not be paid.

a. There was a mistake in addition. The calculator the bank gave me for opening the account was broken.

b. My dog chewed up the bank statement, and I thought there was money in the account.

c. My spouse switched the account without telling me.

d. The bank should have called me and told me I didn't have money.

e. I pay the bills, my wife deposits the money. Unfortunately, she left, took the car, the money and the children, and left me with the mortgage and the bills.

f.   The president of the corporation opened a new account without telling the bookkeeper, his wife.

g.   A check was returned unpaid because the chickens fell off the truck.

h.   The computer shows a balance in the account. We are doing it manually now.

i.   The bookkeeper left on vacation, but it doesn't look like she will return. We are reviewing our bank statements now.

j.   I do not know how to add!

The explanations are infinite, depending only on the creativity and resourcefulness of the debtor. Therefore, proving that a consumer or business debtor issued a check knowing the check would not be paid is difficult, if not impossible—with certain exceptions.

Threatening a debtor with criminal prosecution would be unwise unless you are certain that the consumer is committing a fraud. When a check has been returned, don't use innuendoes or inferences, such as:

1.   "There are serious consequences for issuing a bad check."

2.   "I am sure you are aware that issuing a check which is returned is much more serious than just owing money."

3.   "I intend to review this with my counsel to see if we can pursue remedies other than just a civil suit for collection of the debt."

4.   "If I present this to the district attorney, you may have more problems than you anticipate."

Certainly, do not use any flagrant or obvious threats such as:

A.   "If you don't pay the balance on the check, you're going to end up in jail."

B.   "I'm going to see the district attorney and have you arrested."

C.   "I will prosecute you unless you pay this check in ten days."

If you have evidence from information obtained from other sources that the debtor had no intention of paying the check and that the debtor intended a fraud at the time the check was issued, review with counsel whether this debtor may be prosecuted criminally. If the debtor had issued returned checks to other creditors and is engaging in a pattern of fraud, the matter should be reviewed with counsel.

Creditors attempt to enlist the aid of a county, district, or city attorney to help on the theory that the bad-check issuer may be guilty of a crime pursuant to the state laws. In most instances the creditor withdraws the charges after an offer of payment (see Malicious Prosecution, Chapter 9). For this reason, county or city attorneys do not assist the creditor who is referring the check for the sole purpose of collecting the monies and not for prosecuting a crime. A few states and jurisdictions do allow government attorneys to engage in the collection of checks and debts for creditors, although many bar associations and debt collectors oppose this activity.

On the other hand, an issuer of many bad checks to many creditors, or someone with an unsavory reputation issuing a bad check for a large amount may persuade the county, district, or city attorney to actively prosecute. In the course of the prosecution, restitution may be made, and the creditor will have the best of both worlds. If the check was sent through the mail, consulting with the postal inspector is recommended.

LIABILITY FOR ISSUING A BAD CHECK

Many states allow the holder of a returned check to recover the costs and expenses incurred in collecting the check and to recover double and treble damages if the terms and conditions of the statute are met. In recovering double and treble damages, the statutes provide specific notice requirements, forms, and procedures to provide an opportunity for the issuer to pay the check. A review of the state law where the check is enforced is essential before any proceeding is commenced. These statutes are to be distinguished from those authorizing the collection of bank charges for returning bad checks.

COLLECTING BAD CHECK CHARGES

The commentary to the Debt Collection Practices Act allows a creditor to charge a fee for the returned check if the right to collect is set forth in the agreement creating the debt or, in the alternative, if it is permitted by law. In many states, some provision is made for charging a debtor in the event a check is returned. The statutes vary from state to state. Some are extremely burdensome, whereas others do allow a creditor to charge a reasonable charge for a bad check merely by making a demand on the debtor and thereafter suing for the amount.

Some states allow a creditor to charge at least ten dollars for a returned check without any notice or other requirement. Many states allow the creditor to pass on to the debtor the actual charge that the creditor incurs with the proviso that the charge doesn't exceed a specific amount.

Other states have set the maximum amount that may be charged, while other states require a specific type of notice to the debtor. In most states, a specific notice mailed to the debtor within a specified time is usually required and, in many instances, the notice must be mailed by certified or registered mail. Certified or registered mail adds a prohibitive cost if the check is for a small amount.

Some of these states permit a fixed fee of $15 to $20, or 5% of the face amount of the check, as a charge. Others permit charges of up to $100 and some provide for treble damages. Many states have separate provisions applying specifically to retail stores. If the retail outlet clearly and conspicuously displays the charge in the store, the creditor may collect fees ranging from a few dollars to treble damages on each check. A current examination of the state law must be conducted by counsel.

Collecting bad check charges where the debtors are within one state is feasible, since the creditor is regulated only by that state's statute. To collect bad check charges on a national basis would require familiarity with the law of each state and would require the collection procedure to conform with the statute in the debtor's resident state. A national program by the creditor to collect bad check charges in every state would be difficult to institute and would probably not be cost effective because the average fees recovered on the returned check would be approximately $15 to $20. The cost of certified mail decreases the net return on collecting bad check fees. The cost of preparing the specific notices required for each state, and maintaining an up-to-date library of the notices together with secretarial or computer time to prepare each notice would be prohibitive and would decrease the return.

Some collection agencies market their services on the grounds that they can collect the fees for a returned check on a national basis. The theory offered is that the agency is complying with the laws in the state where the agency or creditor is located, and that is sufficient. The flaw in this reasoning is that the Fair Debt Collection Practices Act prohibits any charge unless permitted by law. But suit must be started in the county where the debtor resides. If the bad check charge is not permitted by law in the county where the debtor resides, the debtor is not liable. Thus, threatening to collect the charge is threatening that which cannot be legally collected by suit, which constitutes a violation of the Act. A special review of their procedures should be made to be certain that the agency is complying with the laws of the states and using the proper notices, forms, and certified mail where required. If a national collection program to collect bad checks is difficult for a creditor to institute, a national program for a collection agency would be just as difficult.

The Fair Debt Collection Practices Act prohibits the creditor from collecting the fee that was charged to the creditor for a returned check unless the collection of said fee is expressly authorized by the agreement creating the debt or permitted by law. The actual wording is as follows:

> "A debt collector may not use unfair or unconscionable means to collect or attempt to collect the debt. Without limiting the general application of the foregoing, the following conduct is a violation of this section. 1) The collection of any amount (including any interest, fee, charge or expense incidental to the principal obligation) unless such amount is expressly authorized by the agreement creating the debt or permitted by law. ..."

The commentary to the Debt Collection Practices Act expressly states that "bad checks handling charges" come within the purview of this section.

Accordingly, the collection of a "bad check handling charge" must be expressly authorized by the agreement creating the debt. Appropriate terminology must appear in the order form, or the agreement between the consumer and the creditor, authorizing the collection of a fee in the event that the check is returned, or a clear and conspicuous display must appear at a retail store.

A California case recently addressed the question of whether a state must expressly authorize bad check fees or whether the burden is on the plaintiff to demonstrate that state law prohibits the particular claims. The court did not adopt the defendant's theory that any charges not prohibited by law are necessarily permitted. Accordingly, an express statute must specifically authorize bad check charges in order for a creditor to assess said charges. The other alternative is that the obligation to pay bad check charges is contained in the agreement creating the debt, as specified in the Fair Debt Collection Practices Act.

In the case, there was also the question of whether the posting of notices in the store created an agreement between the creditor and the check-writing consumer. The retail store alleged that it was the intention of the merchant that the notice affixed to the cash register would alert customers to the fees that would be charged if the check did not clear. The store stated that the notice of the fee for a bad check was intended to make the sale subject to these terms.[1]

The court stated that there was absolutely no evidence that the customer saw the signs or intended to accept the offer. Nevertheless, rather than deny summary judgment, the court stated that it would be a question of fact to be decided at a trial to determine whether a contract actually had been entered into between the customers and the retail store.

In its MAP (Member's Attorney Program) bulletin in 1996, the American Collectors Association cited the following states which do not have a provision for a service charge on a returned check:

Arizona	Missouri	Oklahoma
Delaware	Nebraska	Pennsylvania
Hawaii	New Hampshire	Rhode Island
Kentucky	New Jersey	Vermont
Maine	New Mexico	
Massachusetts	Ohio	
Michigan		

California and Connecticut each recently passed a law providing for a service fee which may be charged on any check that is returned unpaid. The law in both states also includes a treble damage clause in the event the check is returned for insufficient funds. Before treble damages can be claimed, the debtor must receive a 30-day written demand for payment in accordance with the provisions

---

[1] *Newman v. Checkwrite California, Inc.,* 912 F.Supp. 1354 (E.D. Cal. 1995).

of the statute. Only a third of the states provide for fixed charges in the event checks are returned. Hopefully, with this passage of the law by California and Connecticut (effective January 1, 1997), creditors in other states that do not allow this type of charge will prevail upon their legislatures to follow suit.

While this was not an important expense in the past, the recent efforts of banks to charge for all services has resulted in bank charges for returned checks ranging from $5 to $15 or more. At least California has recognized this is a significant expense.

POST-DATED CHECKS

A post-dated check is a promise to pay an amount of money on a specified day in the future. Issuing a post-dated check which is returned unpaid creates no presumption of fraud or intent to defraud the creditor. A post-dated check is a reasonable expectation that the maker will have funds available on a specified future date. Since the event is in the future, the maker of the check cannot know at the time of issuance that the check will or will not be paid.

California has held that a post-dated check that is returned unpaid is within the operation of the fraud statute and that "it is, nevertheless a check."[2] Illinois allows no distinction between a check and a check that is post-dated.[3]

Conflict exists between the states as to whether a post-dated check can be the subject of a criminal statute. The general theory is that any criminal statute usually requires an intent on the part of the perpetrator and relates back to a false pretense, and a false pretense under a criminal statute relates to a past existing fact. Even though a promisor has at the time no intention of keeping the promise, such a pretense requires intent to come within the criminal statute, principally because it is a promise of a future act. Certainly, a post-dated check is a promise of a future act.

In most of the early rubber check statutes, the legislatures required the element of intent in order to support a criminal prosecution. For example, the New Jersey statute does not require intent to defraud. Even though the defendant did not intend to actively defraud the party to whom he issued the check, the fact that he had knowledge that the check would not be honored at the time that it was presented is apparently sufficient and may be described as the equivalent of the "intent" to defraud to support a criminal prosecution, at least in New Jersey.[4]

Another case treated the question of whether a post-dated check could be the basis for a criminal prosecution. The court again held that a post-dated check is not a "check" within the contemplation of the bad check law. The court stated

---

[2]*People v. Percuwitz*, 163 California 636; *Wright v. The Bank of America*, 176 Cal. App, 2d 176, 1 Cal. Rptr. 202 (1959).

[3]82 Business Law Journal 347.

[4]*State v. Kelm*, 289 N.J. Super. 55, 672 A.2d 1261 (N.J. Super. Ct. App. Div. 1996), *cert. denied*, 146 N.J. 68, 679 A.2d 655 (N.J. 1996).

that the statute under which the defendant was convicted does not criminalize the passing of a post-dated check which is dishonored for insufficient funds. The offense is not the failure to pay the check, but passing the instrument with the present intent to defraud. Again, the court emphasized that you must prove intent to defraud when passing a check in order to support any type of criminal prosecution.[5]

In a Connecticut case, the court relied upon provisions of the particular statute and stated that this statute did apply to post-dated checks. One of the ingredients was the fact that the defendant resorted to a pretext by passing the check as cash when delivery of the shipment expressly required a cash payment. The defendant resorted to a pretense to operate on the capital of the supplier, expecting to remit after he had been paid by his customer. Unfortunately, the deal with the customer fell through and the court decided that by delivery of a worthless check, falsely representing it to be cash was sufficient intent when the property was obtained by the means used by the defendant and was not purged by the subsequent restoration of the property. Interestingly, the court zeroed in on the fact that there were five other occasions when checks on the same account had been dishonored. Whether other courts in other states, even with similar statutes, would follow this decision is questionable.

The conflict between the various states ends with many state courts holding that a post dated check cannot be the subject of any criminal statute, and other state courts taking a great deal of effort to spell out a situation where the intent of the debtor was sufficient to meet the criteria of the criminal statute. In some instances, the courts rely on the fact that the statutes themselves are worded differently, and therefore provide different avenues for the courts to follow. Needless to say, a reading of the state's statute and a review of the court decisions is not only recommended, but absolutely necessary before any step is taken with regard to prosecuting a debtor for issuing a post-dated check that has not been paid.

STOP PAYMENT

The issuer of a check may direct a bank not to pay a check. Verbal communications to a bank are valid, but written communications are a better means of notifying the bank. Generally, oral communication to a bank to stop payment on a check obligates the bank to keep the stop payment in effect for a period of a week, unless properly followed by a written communication which usually compels the bank to keep the stop payment in effect for 6 months as provided in the Uniform Commercial Code. After the six-month period, it appears that the bank would not be liable if the check was presented for payment. The maker of the check may argue that the bank was negligent for paying the check due to the stale date on the check.[6]

---

[5]*State v. Stooksberry*, 872 S.W.2d 906 (Tenn. 1994).

[6]*RPM Pizza Inc. v. Bank One Cambridge*, 869 F. Supp. 517 (E.D. Mich. 1994).

You should use certified mail, or deliver the notice personally and obtain an initialed receipt of said notice. The written communication should be clear and definitive as to the identification of the exact check, which should include a notation of the dates of both the notice and the check, the check number, the amount, the name of the drawer, and the name of the payee, as well as any other pertinent information.

Some states, such as Arizona, California, Florida, Nevada, and Utah, have special laws affecting stop orders.

The liability of the bank to follow instructions is a function of the banking law of the particular state. If the bank should pay the check despite the stop payment instructions, consultation with an attorney is recommended.

STALE CHECK

In a recent Ohio case, the court was faced with a situation where a stale check was paid after the debtor had delivered a stop payment order to the bank. A stop payment order is valid for six months. The check was paid three weeks after the six-month period ended. Section 4-404 of the Uniform Commercial Code provides as follows:

> "A bank is under no obligation to a customer having a checking account to pay a check, other than a certified check, which is presented more than six months after its date, but it may charge its customer's account for a payment made thereafter in good faith."

The court pointed out that the Uniform Commercial Code expressly permits payment of stale checks if payment is made in good faith. In this particular instance, the check was stale only by three weeks. The term "good faith" is defined as "honesty in fact in the conduct or transaction." Good faith is a subjective test requiring an evaluation of the honesty of the bank's intent, rather than its diligence. Indeed, a bank could act in good faith and still not follow accepted banking procedures.

In the particular case, the court pointed out that the plaintiff was unable to produce any evidence to demonstrate that the bank had noted the stale date or the existence of an expired stop payment order. Furthermore, plaintiff has been unable to raise a question of fact disputing the bank's allegation that its review of the check was limited to a signature verification because of its practices of signature verifications on all checks over $50,000.

The general posture of the courts when dealing with payment of stale checks probably follows this particular case, for the courts seem to feel imposing an obligation on the banks to review the date on each check would be an insurmountable and unfair burden. The plaintiff has to go far beyond the mere fact that a stale check was paid to hold the bank liable. Sometimes, a separate claim for negligence or failure to use normal banking procedures may be asserted.[7]

---

[7]*R.P.M. Pizza, Inc. v. Bank One Cambridge*, 869 F. Supp 517 (B.D. Mich. 1994).

CERTIFIED CHECKS AND CASHIER'S CHECKS

Certified checks and money orders are types of instruments which are used frequently in purchasing homes or securities, and in other business transactions where the payee of the check wants assurance that the check will not be returned unpaid. At a real estate closing, the seller requires certified checks or bank checks. The perception is that a certified check or a bank check is as good as cash. Unfortunately, this is not true. A certified check can be stopped by the maker of the check if a bond is obtained to indemnify the bank against any claim that may be made against the bank. The premium may be substantial, since the amount of the bond may be double the amount or more of the check.

Money orders are checks issued by private institutions after receiving a cash payment in person. The money order is made payable to the person designated by the party paying for the money order, and it is used to send money through the mail rather than cash. The same scenario would apply to stopping payment of a money order issued by American Express or any company which issues money orders, although arguments may be offered that it is closer to a bank check than a certified check.

A cashier's check is a check issued by the bank and signed by a bank officer drawn on the capital assets of the bank. If the bank refuses to pay the check, the payee of the check would look to the assets of the bank for payment. If the bank issues a check on behalf of a depositor after receiving payment from the depositor, the bank would consider the check similar to a certified check and would not stop payment unless the depositor produced a sufficient indemnification bond. Several court decisions have held that a cashier's check is the equivalent of cash and thus cannot be stopped, even with an indemnification bond.

The payee must realize that certified checks, cashier's checks, and money orders are rarely returned unpaid, and only in unusual circumstances would someone incur the expense to arrange for an indemnification bond. On the other hand, while deposits are guaranteed by the Federal Deposit Insurance Corporation, certified checks and cashier's checks are not.

A recent Tennessee Supreme Court case provided an in-depth discussion of the right of banks to stop payment on cashier's checks. The court stated that there were essentially two types of checks in general use: "ordinary checks" and "bank checks," which is a general term used to refer to certified checks and cashier's checks.

A minority of courts have concluded that cashier's checks should be treated as ordinary negotiable instruments (Maryland, Nebraska, Connecticut, Delaware, and Louisiana). In these instances, the reliance is on the Uniform Commercial Code provision governing the liability of obligors on most ordinary checks. On the other hand, the majority of the courts have adopted the "cash equivalent," whereby cashier's checks are treated as equivalent to cash. The bank becomes the guarantor of the value of the check and budgets its resources for the payment of the amount. To allow the bank to stop payment on such an instrument would be inconsistent with a representation it made when issuing the check. Accordingly, the court adopted a theory that the bank may refuse to honor a stop payment on a cashier's check because the check itself is accepted by the bank upon the issuance of the check. The case provides an in-depth analysis of this topic, with many citations.[8]

UNSIGNED CHECK

A check that is unsigned may be deposited by the recipient by endorsing on the reverse side of the check the payee's signature and guaranteeing to the bank the signature of the maker of the check. When the check is presented to the maker's bank, the bank accepts the check and transfers the funds. The maker who receives the debit on the bank statement will not contact the bank since he or she believed the check was signed. The maker who did not sign the check deliberately will contact the bank which, in turn, will contact the depositor's bank and assert no signature. The bank will charge the depositor's account and the depositor will be in no worse or better position than if the check was returned to the maker for signature. The only expense incurred is the charge of the bank for returning the check.

If the unsigned check is returned by mail to the debtor for signature, the debtor may never sign the check and send it back to the creditor. Sometimes the debtor does not sign the check intentionally as a ploy to stall for time. For this reason, we recommend guaranteeing the signature and depositing the check, as described above.

INTEREST AND USURY

Many federal institutions are governed by federal laws which regulate the amount of interest they can charge. The Small Business Investment Act describes a specific criteria under which the Small Business Administration lends money and sets forth certain maximum rates that are allowed to be charged by the Small Business Administration.

Most states have a maximum rate of interest which may be charged on loans. Different maximum rates may be set for individuals and corporations. In addition, the law provides for a lower legal rate of interest after a judgment is obtained. For example, in New York the legal rate allowed to be charged to a corporation is 25%. After a judgment is entered against the corporation, the legal rate

---

[8]*Weldon v. Trust Co. Bank of Columbus* 499 S.E. 2nd 393 (Ga. App. 1998).

which the creditor may charge the corporate debtor is only 9%. Under this set of circumstances, a debtor who has no defense to a suit may find it useful to permit a creditor to enter judgment quickly to reduce the rate of interest that the creditor may charge, rather than delay the suit by interposing frivolous defenses.

Several years ago, the banks were successful in establishing that they can export interest rates from their home state to those credit card customers who are living in different states, even though the interest rate in their home state was prohibited by law in the state in which the credit card customer resided. Late charges also were treated as interest. For this reason, many of the banks position their credit card operations in states which are favorable to the banks and enable them to charge higher rates than are allowed in the other states of the country.

The Monetary Control Act sets forth certain provisions which remove some federal institutions from regulation by the state. Under certain circumstances, the states may override this insulation. State-chartered banks and federal banks also may be insulated against the usury statute of the state, due to the application of federal laws to banks. In most states, laws are specifically applied to the rates of interest and other charges that a state bank may impose.

When one charges a rate in excess of the amount allowed by state law, the rate is deemed to be usurious. Nevertheless, determining whether a rate is usurious or is not usurious is complex and confusing. The rates of interest allowed by the various states vary so substantially that one cannot begin to speak about these rates until the law of each state is examined and a table is constructed as to what restrictions are set forth in each state. The penalties for violations of a statute also differ significantly from state to state:

1. In some states the creditor loses the difference of the interest rate charge which is in excess of the rate allowed.

2. Many states provide that the creditor not only loses the interest in excess of the rate allowed but loses the entire interest.

3. In certain states the creditor may forfeit a sum of money double the amount of the interest charge.

4. In some states the lender may be unable to enforce the entire debt merely because interest in excess of the permitted rate was charged.

5. In some states the charging of usurious rate of interest may actually be a criminal offense ranging from a misdemeanor to a felony.

When the rate of interest is the maximum rate allowed under a particular statute, and then other charges are added by virtue of other transactions or other activities by the debtor, the lender always runs the risk of being targeted with a charge of usury. The other charges may be treated as interest.[9]

---

[9]*Sunburst Bank v. Keith*, 648 So.2d 1147 (Miss. 1995).

Many contracts contain what is commonly known as a "usury savings clause." These clauses basically state something along the following terms:

> Notwithstanding anything contained herein in the contract, in no event shall the aggregate of any interest charged plus any other amounts charged which are deemed interest, exceed the maximum amount of interest which could lawfully be charged. If any amount of interest taken or received by the creditor shall be in excess of the maximum amount of interest which could lawfully be collected, then the excess shall be deemed to have been a result of a mathematical error and shall be refunded promptly to the debtor.

A clause such as this normally will not help if the creditor intended to charge usurious rates, such as where the allowable legal rate of interest was 9% and the promissory note provided for an interest rate of 14%.

A different result follows when the claim of the debtor rests upon the fact that the interest or other charges become usurious after a default in the terms of payment. The note provides for late charges per diem together with an interest rate, which together are in excess of a usurious rate. If there is a default in payment, this is not necessarily a usurious rate of interest providing there is a usury savings clause present.

A usury savings clause may not rescue a transaction that is necessarily usurious by its explicit terms, but on the other hand, it may rescue the collection of usurious interest that is contingent solely on making late payments and the extent of the tardiness of those payments. The court in this case pointed out that the late charges would not necessarily create a usurious rate of interest unless the delinquency was significant. The court did conclude that the occurrence of the contingency, the late payments, would not necessarily have resulted in usurious interest. The debtor would have to be late on numerous monthly payments before the interest generated by the late charges would have been usurious. Under those circumstances, at least in this case, the court held that the late payment provisions were not usurious and were saved by the usury savings clause.[10]

Another problem in usurious contracts is determining whether or not the particular transaction constitutes a loan or constitutes some other type of transaction. If the transaction is not a loan, then the question of usury does not come into play. A loan is a contract whereby one party transfers to the other a sum of money which the other agrees to pay absolutely together with such additional sums as may be agreed upon for the use of the money. The furnishing of merchandise or services does not impact the usury laws.

In the instant case, a late penalty charge imposed on a condominium association was considered to be neither a loan nor a forbearance or any kind of detention of money and accordingly, there was no "lending relationship" as contemplated by the statute in Connecticut. The court concluded that the late charge did not fall within any of the statutory definitions of interest and was not interest as

---

[10]*Parhms v. B&B Ventures, Inc.*, 938 S.W.2d 199 (Tex. Ct. App. 14th Dist. 1997).

a matter of law. The assessments under various fees and charges claimed to be excessive were not subject to the provisions of the state usury laws.[11]

In New York it was common to form a corporation purely for the purposes of avoiding the usury rate. The lending institution would advance the money to the corporation and then would require the individual to guarantee the debt. The court looked through this structure to see whether the purpose of forming the corporation was to take advantage of the higher rate available to corporations as opposed to the lower rates for individuals. If such was the case, the court allowed the defendant to assert the defense of usury.

Many businesses charge 18% per annum or $1^1/_2$% per month on delinquent accounts and often this additional charge for delinquent accounts could exceed the usurious rate either in the state in which the business resides in the state where the customer resides. The problem arises as to which state law would apply, which is a function of whether you are attempting to enforce the debt in the state where the customer resides or in the state where the seller resides. Where the provisions for interest are included in the original agreement, the seller should not be faced with this problem unless the state statute provides for a limitation on the interest charged to corporations or businesses.

The best place for such a provision is in a clear and conspicuous format in the credit application and the guarantee. The good news is that the majority of the states, although not an overwhelming majority, seem to take the position that an increased rate of interest which may be usurious is really not usurious because it basically is avoidable by the borrower paying on time. The minority states do not follow this theory, with some cases depending upon whether the judge feels the increased rate of interest is fair or unfair. It is recommended that your credit applications and the charging of interest be reviewed by counsel.

NEGOTIABLE INSTRUMENTS

We start with a promise to pay a debt which reads as follows:

> I, Mary Jones, hereby acknowledge that I owe John Smith One thousand dollars and promise to pay to John Smith One thousand dollars by June 1, 1996. Signature *Mary Jones*

John Smith decides to sell that obligation of Mary Jones to his uncle (Harry Adams) for $900, because he cannot wait until June 1st for payment. Mary Jones does not pay the debt by June 1st and, ultimately, the uncle sues Mary Jones in court. Mary Jones asserts the defense that John Smith coerced her under duress to sign her signature since she only received $750 and not $1,000.

---

[11]*Mountain View Condominium Ass'n of Vernon, Conn., Inc. v. Rumford Assoc., IV,* No. CV 94556935, 1997 WL 120254 (Conn. Super. Ct. Mar. 4, 1997).

This type of agreement is described as an "IOU" or a "Marker." The defense of duress that Mary Jones is asserting is a valid defense against both John Smith (the assignor), who did the actual coercion, and his uncle (the assignee), who purchased the note from John Smith, but was not aware of the coercion and duress. The purchaser of the note (the uncle) is subject to the defenses to which John Smith is subject. This fair result preserves the defenses of Mary Jones against the person to whom John Smith transferred the note. This is identified as a non-negotiable agreement to pay a payee (Smith), and the note was assigned by the assignor (payee) to an assignee (uncle).

On the other hand, a negotiable instrument would produce an entirely different result. A negotiable instrument states:

I agree to *pay to the order* of John Smith One thousand dollars on the 1st day of June, 1996. *MARY JONES*

The magic words are "pay to the order of," which means that the maker agrees to pay $1,000 to John Smith, or to anyone that John Smith should "order" or designate as the person to receive a negotiation (purchase or transfer) of the note. The purchase of the note for $900 by the uncle from John Smith is defined as a negotiation; and because of those magic words, the legal consequences change radically. When the uncle tries to enforce the note, the defense of duress would not be available to Mary Jones. The third party (uncle) purchases the note for the $900 free of any defenses that the maker of the note (Mary Jones) may assert against the payee (John Smith). This purchase is accomplished by John Smith writing his name on the reverse side of the note. To continue the negotiable characteristics of the note, in favor of the uncle, the magic words "pay to the order" of the "uncle" would precede the signature of John Smith.

The inscription on the reverse side would appear as follows:

Pay to the order of Harry Adams.

Signature *John Smith*

The uncle is described as a "holder in due course" which means he owns the note and is not concerned with the defenses of the maker.

The reason for this result is to promote the negotiability (sale or transfer) of notes so that the purchaser of the note will not be concerned with any defenses of the maker of the note. The Uniform Commercial Code states that not only must words "pay to the order" be used, but the following requirements must also be met:

1. The party to whom the note is negotiated (sold) must have good title to the instrument in that the prior selling party had good title (the note was not stolen by John Smith, the payee).

2. The signature on the note must be genuine. If the signature was forged, Mary Jones would not be liable.

3. No material alteration of the note has occurred (no erasures or alterations of amounts or other material terms).

4. The party to whom the note is negotiated (the uncle) does not have any knowledge of any defect in the note in that the knew of any material alteration, forgery, fraud, duress, or any other defense. If the uncle knows of Mary's defense at the time the note was sold to him, the uncle is not "a holder in due course."

Other circumstances must be met to support a negotiable instrument:

*   The note or check must be in writing.

*   The note or check must be payable either on demand or on some fixed day or time.

*   The note or check may be payable to the order of a named person (John Smith), but may also be payable to the order of the "bearer." Instead of inserting the name of John Smith, the word "bearer" is inserted. A "bearer" instrument is freely transferable, and anyone who comes into possession is the owner of the note (except if stolen).

PROMISSORY NOTES

A promissory note (a negotiable instrument) is often used in business transactions when a business debtor wishes to pay the debt over a period of time. The use of post-dated checks is not desirable since suit cannot be instituted on all post-dated checks until each check is presented for payment and is returned unpaid. If six post-dated checks were delivered to the creditor, and the first check was returned unpaid, suit would lie on that one check, not the remaining five checks. A second suit may be instituted after the next check is returned unpaid. The solution is a series of six promissory notes containing a provision enabling the creditor to accelerate all six notes in the event one of the notes is returned unpaid.

Although promissory notes and checks are both negotiable instruments, substantial distinctions exist between them:

A. Promissory notes may provide for acceleration so that the entire balance will be due upon a default in payment of one note.

B. Promissory notes may provide for reasonable attorney fees or a fixed amount of attorney fees if the note is referred to an attorney for collection.

C. Promissory notes can be drafted in some states with a power of attorney permitting the holder of the note to enter a judgment in a commercial transaction in the event of the default of one note. This is the equivalent of a confession of judgment and is known as a "Cognovit" note (under the Credit Practice Act, not enforceable as to consumers).

D. Promissory notes may contain a variety of terms and conditions which may consume several pages, such as a note prepared by a bank or a financial institution. The note may provide for payment of interest calculated in a number of different ways, the requirement of security to ensure the payment of the note, provisions covering bankruptcy as a default, creating a default by failing to meet other obligations to the creditor, efforts by other creditors against the borrower creating a default, and other acts constituting a default under the note other than non-payment. The note may allow recovery if in the judgment of the creditor the collateral is deemed inadequate to secure the bank. The note may provide for reimbursement to the creditor of all costs and expenses incurred in the granting of the loan or the recovery of the loan, including the cost of attorney fees. The note allows the creditor to assign and transfer the debt. The terms and conditions of the note are unlimited and usually drafted with precision to protect the creditor.

E. Promissory notes are negotiable instruments and may provide for a waiver of defenses and rights in certain circumstances. An example is a waiver of a jury trial and an agreement that the laws of a specific state will control the transaction (usually the state where the lender is located).

TRADE ACCEPTANCE

A trade acceptance is the equivalent of a promissory note drawn by one business person upon another business person and issued for the payment of goods. While there is no prescribed form, the trade acceptance is similar to and operates generally as a promissory note.

GUARANTEES

An individual or a corporation may guarantee the debt of another party. A guarantee must be in writing, since an oral guarantee is unenforceable. The written guarantee must be clear and must specify exactly what is being guaranteed, i.e., the payment of a debt, the performance of a contract. The more specific a guarantee is, the better chance that it will be enforceable. Guarantees can cover many pages, and may provide for the waiver of defenses, a provision that the guarantee continues indefinitely to cover future advances to the corporation, the conditions under which the guarantee may be enforced, and a wide variety of clauses favorable to the person enforcing the guarantee.

CREDIT AND COLLECTION TIP: *Be certain that the guarantee is dated, and that it identifies the place where the guarantee is being executed, the amount being guaranteed, the party's debt that is being guaranteed, and when the guarantee begins to operate.*

CORPORATE GUARANTEE. Guarantees by corporations should be reviewed carefully since the by-laws of many corporations do not permit the execution of guarantees. Corporations in certain states need some form of consideration or benefit or payment to the corporation to be liable on a guarantee. A resolution of the board of directors is usually requested by the lender, stating that the board of directors has authorized this guarantee and, if possible, designating specifically the benefit or the consideration the corporation receives. Even in those states where a consideration is not required, obtaining a corporate resolution of the board of directors is still the best practice.

CREDIT APPLICATION. Guarantees are frequently used in conjunction with credit applications by printing a guarantee on the reverse side or on the bottom of a credit application for execution by the individual officer of the corporation, the principal owner of the stock of the corporation, or a partner of the partnership. If properly drawn and clearly and conspicuously labeled, the guarantee is enforceable.

HUSBAND AND WIFE. A financial institution seeks the guarantee of the husband and wife as a condition of extending credit to the husband's business. If the financial institution is not relying upon the credit of the spouse, under the Equal Credit Opportunity Act, the guarantee of the spouse may be unenforceable (See Chapter 13). A review of that law and the relevant court decisions is recommended.

ELEMENTS OF GUARANTEES

How often have credit grantors heard the following pleas of lack of knowledge or understanding: "I was not aware that I signed a guarantee." "I did not understand what I was signing." "I cannot read English." "I was told that it was only a credit application."

A classic example of a problem with a guarantee occurred in a case in Nevada. The president in his corporate capacity signed a document entitled "Credit Application and Renewal." The document listed the corporation as the customer and the president as owner/president. On the reverse side of this credit application was a document entitled "guarantee," which stated that the president unconditionally guaranteed current or future indebtedness for which the customer was obligated to the plaintiff. The guarantee included terms which allowed the plaintiff to release or surrender the security without the consent of a guarantor. The president admitted signing the guarantee although there were a few blank spaces in the guarantee for the date and the name of the customer.

The president contended no relationship was formed because the plaintiff used a credit application rather than an application for an open account and no underlying contractual relationship existed. The president was not even aware that he signed as a guarantor. The plaintiff said that the president was told that his signature on the guarantee would expedite the approval of credit (and the guarantee probably did expedite approval).

The above set of circumstances is a classic example of what often happens in the business environment.

Parties may be held liable for contracts they did not read. Since the president was a merchant and the one-page guarantee was conspicuously labeled, his failure to read the guarantee is not relevant.

The court held that certain essential elements make a guarantee binding and enforceable:

(1) the name of the guarantor
(2) the name of the party whose debts are being guaranteed
(3) the terms and conditions of the guarantee
(4) the interest of property affected
(5) the consideration to be paid

The court found that since the name of the party whose debts were being guaranteed was omitted, the guarantee is indefinite and non-binding without any other evidence.

Several writings together may supply an essential term which may be missing and may be construed together to supply the essential terms if there is a reference in one document to another document. Where more than one writing is used, there may be a nexus between the writings or an "internal reference" to describe the requisite nexus between the writings. Oral evidence may be admissible to fill in the blank spaces. The credit application and the guarantee construed together clearly refer to the same transaction and the customer's name on the credit application is the same customer referenced in the guarantee. The blank spaces in the guarantee did not render it indefinite, as long as the intent of the parties was readily ascertainable. The court held that oral evidence will be allowed to serve to explain the information that should have been entered in the blank spaces.

While this is a classic example of a guarantor claiming that he didn't read the guarantee and that blank spaces should void the guarantee, the lesson learned is that a guarantee should be carefully completed and reviewed so that the lender has the proper documentation in the event of a problem at a later date. As to the defense that the guarantor did not read or understand the guarantee or thought it was a different type of agreement, a risk is always present where the guarantor is representing himself and no attorney is present. Nevertheless, the guarantee should be conspicuously labeled a guarantee of the debt of a corporation and the print setting forth the guarantee should be readable and understandable by the guarantor. Including the five requirements listed in this Nevada case is also helpful.[12]

FRAUD

Usually a fraudulent act to induce an individual to execute a guarantee will allow a guarantor to avoid his obligation under the guarantee because the courts will allow an agreement to be rendered unenforceable where the party can assert that he was fraudulently induced by the other party to enter into this agreement. Nevertheless, in the case of a guarantee, where the guarantee is absolute, unconditional and irrevocable, a court may take the position that fraud in the inducement of a guarantee of the corporate officer of a corporation's indebtedness is not a defense to an action on the guarantee (when the guarantee recites that it is absolute and unconditional).[13]

BANK GUARANTEES

While many credit applications provide for a guarantee by principal owners of a corporation, these guarantees are usually simple, direct and primarily state that the principal guarantees all the debts of the corporation to the seller. On the other hand, the situation is quite different where the principal owners or officers execute a written guarantee in favor of a lending institution.

Depending upon the policy of the institution extending the credit, the written guarantee may consist of only a few lines, but in most instances the guarantee consists of several paragraphs that primarily provide for waivers of defenses that could be asserted by the guarantor. Guarantees provided by the large financial institutions and banks sometimes run one and two pages of small print and cover every conceivable waiver of defense that may be asserted by the guarantor. The guarantee allows the lender to enter into any type or form of modification or agreement with the primary borrower without affecting the liability of the guarantor.

---

[12]*Pentax Corp. v. Boyd*, 111 Nev. 1296, 904 P.2d 1024 (Nev. 1995).

[13]*Citibank, N.A. v. Plapinger*, 66 N.Y.2d 90, 485 N.E.2d 974, 495 N.Y.S.2d 309 (1985); *Infinity U.S.A., Inc. v. E.I. Dupont DeNemours*.

The comprehensive guarantee of all liability drafted by the major financial institutions set forth virtually everything you can possibly squeeze into a guarantee. The guarantee provides for an "absolute and unconditional guarantee" for the prompt payment of all claims of every nature and description that the lender may have against a corporate borrower. The key words to which a guarantor must be alert are the time frames that affect the guarantee. The most comprehensive terminology is "debts now existing or thereafter incurred" by the corporation. This terminology covers the situation where the guarantor has left the services of the corporation either by retirement, buy out, or otherwise, and is still liable for future loans or advances to the corporation that are unpaid.

Lending institutions also provide for a right to set off monies on deposit or any assets in the possession of the bank against any liabilities of the borrower. Usually this can be done without any notice to the guarantor.

The ability of the lender to continue to finance the borrower without being restricted by the state laws that afford protection to the guarantor is essential to these types of agreement. The lender is most concerned with any activity the borrower may engage in which renews, extends, modifies, accelerates, compromises, or settles any of the obligations of the borrower and the lender does not want to be concerned with notifying the guarantor each time.

Many state laws require a lender to notify the guarantor if any collateral is sold. Court decisions provide that when there are modifications of agreements, guarantors are usually released unless they are notified of the modification. As a result, these comprehensive guarantee agreements provide a waiver by the guarantor of these defenses that he may assert under the law. Some states do provide that certain waivers are ineffective: for example, an obligation on the part of the lender to use reasonable care in the custody and preservation of any collateral. State laws usually do not permit the guarantor to waive notice of sale of the collateral.

The default provisions of guarantees may be extremely comprehensive. A default in any obligation by the corporation to the bank would constitute a default of the primary obligation. If a business happens to be a partnership, the death of the partner usually constitutes a default. Insolvency, assignment for the benefit to creditors, or a bankruptcy may terminate the agreement. Some agreements provide that even the failure to furnish financial information or to permit inspection of the books would constitute a default under the borrower's agreement with the bank. If such a default occurs by virtue of any of these activities, the guarantor would still become liable.

A default might also occur in the event there are enforcement proceedings under any judgment that had been entered against the borrower. Interestingly, some guarantees provide that in the event of default, the financial institution can call upon the guarantor to assemble the collateral and make it available to the bank. The bank may then proceed with the sale. State laws may prohibit, regulate, or otherwise affect many of these obligations in the guarantee.

Sometimes there is more than one guarantor, and the lending institution provides that it may terminate or revoke the other guarantee without terminating and revoking the guarantee of the party against whom it is proceeding. While this may seem unfair, the guarantor against whom the bank proceeds still has a right against the co-guarantor since it is the bank that has released and terminated the obligation to the bank, but the bank cannot release the obligation of its co-guarantors. I have even seen one instance where an agreement provided that a new instrument of guarantee executed in favor of a financial institution would not necessarily terminate the old instrument of guarantee unless it was expressly provided for in the new instrument of guarantee. This could be misleading to a guarantor asked to execute a new guarantee, since it would be reasonable to assume the new guarantee is in place and instead of the old guarantee. Nevertheless, this type of clause in the old guarantee would have to be considered by the courts.

Guarantees may be terminated by the guarantor, and most agreements provide that the termination agreement must be in writing. The guarantor should send a notice of termination by certified mail. The notice of termination would not apply retroactively to any obligations that exist as of the date of termination, but would apply to any new obligations incurred by the corporation after the date of notice of termination. The notice should be worded carefully and reviewed by counsel.

Guarantees provide for the jurisdiction in which a suit must be started and the guarantor waives any defenses as to jurisdiction. The agreement provides that the guarantor waives a jury trial and in some instances the guarantor agrees to service by mail of process (service of a summons of complaint) rather than by personal service, the accepted method — a dangerous clause from a guarantor's point of view, especially if the summons of complaint is lost in the mail.

Attorney fees are also usually provided if the matter is referred to an attorney for collection and range anywhere from 15-25% depending upon the state where the transaction took place. Waiving any defense of the Statute of Limitations is also included, as well as an agreement that a particular state law will govern the interpretation of the guarantee.

The above are some of the highlights of a financial institution instrument of guarantee and no effort is made to cover each and every sentence in the guarantee since many of these guarantees can run several pages of fine print. If a guarantee is executed, read carefully and consult with an experienced counsel.

Since the guarantees are usually executed when the financial institution is advancing monies and since the same financial institution usually states up front that it will not make any changes in its printed forms, one might ask, why review the guarantee or consult with counsel, since the bank will not make changes. All of these so-called printed forms are drafted by other attorneys. Furthermore, banks do make changes in their printed form if a good reason is furnished. Having been house counsel for a major bank in my earlier years, I can testify to the fact that banks will make changes in their printed forms. There is nothing sacred about a printed form other than the fact that the bank took the effort to have the agreement drafted by their counsel and printed because it is used so many times. Since many guarantors execute personal guarantees for corporate debts which far exceed their personal liabilities, I still recommend that counsel review the guarantee carefully to be certain that the client understands all the terms.

DEFENSES AVAILABLE TO GUARANTOR

A recent case reiterated the principle that a guarantor in some states is treated just as a debtor and stands in the shoes of a debtor. Where notice to the debtor is required before collateral is sold, the courts will often take the position that notice to the guarantor must also be furnished.

The bank had a perfected security interest in the assets of a corporation, in which debt was guaranteed by the defendants. The corporation thereafter executed a subordinate security interest on the same property to a third party. The bank failed to file a continuation statement. The corporation filed a petition in bankruptcy and the third party asserted that its subordinate lien had become the primary lien. The defendants executed new guarantees after the fact without being told by the bank that the collateral had been "impaired" by the failure of the bank to file the continuation statement.

The Court of Appeals of Indiana applied the Indiana common law rule. When a creditor unjustifiably impairs collateral securing a debt, the independent, absolute, continuing guarantors should be discharged to the extent the creditor has impaired the right to the collateral.[14] The case was appealed to the Supreme Court of Indiana on the question that the guarantee was not a negotiable instrument, and thus not covered by the Uniform Commercial Code.

Nevertheless, the court held that a guarantor who satisfies the principal debtor's obligation to a creditor generally *steps into the shoes of the debtor,* becoming subjugated to the creditor's claim and entitled to have the collateral as security for the debt. When a creditor unjustifiably impairs the right to the collateral securing a guaranteed loan, it impairs the guarantor's collateral, which recourse the guarantor would have understood itself to have at the time of contracting to guarantee the principal's debt.

Whenever you are dealing with guarantors and you wish to preserve your rights against the guarantor, a creditor should be certain that the guarantor is treated as the equivalent of the debtor with regard to notice, protection of collateral, and any other requirements under the law, and review the law of the particular state as to the status of the guarantor.[15]

---

[14]*Farmers Loan and Trust Co. v. Letsinger,* 635 N.E. 2d 194 (Ind. Ct. App. 1994).

[15]Ibid.

IMPAIRMENT OF CAPITAL

A secured party has an obligation to the guarantor not to impair the collateral. The secured party must be certain that a proper lien is filed so that the collateral can be repossessed and the collateral will maintain the value, reasonable wear and tear excepted. Since the collateral at most times is in the possession of the debtor, these obligations on the behalf of the secured party come into play only with regard to perfecting the lien and after a repossession covering the time period necessary to effectuate a sale of the property.

Section 3-605(e) of the Uniform Commercial Code states as follows:

"if the obligation of a party to pay an instrument is secured by an interest in collateral and a person entitled to enforce the instrument impairs the value of the interest in the collateral, the obligation of an endorser or accommodation party having a right of recourse against the obligor is discharged to the extent of the impairment".

The theory is that if the lender obtains payment from the guarantor, the guarantor becomes subjugated to the lenders security interest in the collateral. If the value of the collateral is impaired because of the conduct of the secured party, the guarantor is discharged to the extent of the impairment. If the impairment is total, the discharge of the guarantor may be total.

This situation arises in the event that the secured party does not properly perfect the security interest and induces the guarantor to execute the instrument of guarantee relying on the fact that the collateral will discharge the indebtedness or most of the indebtedness. If a third party intervenes and exercises his right to the collateral so that the secured party cannot repossess the collateral and sell it and use the proceeds to discharge the indebtedness, the guarantor would be discharged to the extent of the value of the collateral. If the secured party took possession of the collateral and did not promptly arrange a sale and the collateral deteriorated or was placed in an unsecure location where it was easily stolen or removed, the same result would follow. Examples of impairment of capital would be:

1. Where a lender fails to file a continuation statement after five years with the County Clerk's Office and the lien of the lender becomes subordinate to some third parties.
2. In the event the lender fails to properly maintain the security in a warehouse.
3. After repossession allows the security to be damaged through negligence.

Because of this, many agreements provide for a waiver of the defense of impairment of capital and substantially will state as follows:

"the obligation of the undersigned shall not be released or discharged by reason of the fact that a valid lien on the collateral may not be conveyed or created by reason of the fact that the collateral may be subject to equities or defenses or claims in favor of others or may be invalid or defective or may have deteriorated etc.".

Some states have statutes prohibiting the waiver of a guarantor's right to challenge the commercial reasonableness of a sale, but most states do not prohibit a guarantor from waiving the impairment of collateral defense. The original debtor and the original secured party must act prudently with regard to collateral since the destruction of the collateral will certainly impact the obligation of the guarantor.

UNCLAIMED PROPERTY

Abandoned property laws are present in all states. If a business or person has no legal right to property or cash and the property has effectively been abandoned by the owner, the statute requires each business or person that has possession of property or cash belonging to a third party to transfer the property to the state. Most states have laws which provide that certain types of property must be transferred to the state if the property is unclaimed by the owner after a specified period of time.

In many instances, merchants maintain accounts known as "unmatched payments," in which are deposited checks that cannot be matched with corresponding open accounts receivable. Many direct marketers and retailers have unclaimed refunds, credit balances, credit vouchers, and bonus certificates. Gift certificates that are not cashed for many years may also qualify. Consult with your attorney concerning the laws of the particular state in which you are located.

LIABILITY ON SIGNING CHECKS

In the corporate environment, owners, officers, managers and authorized parties execute checks. On the signature line, the title of the party signing the checks should be clearly printed. The corporate name should be printed immediately above the signature, although printing the name at the top of the check is usually sufficient. The reason the title of the party should be printed on the check is because case law has indicated that if an individual signs a check without a proper corporate identification, a possibility exists in certain states that the individual could be liable personally, even though the check was executed in the corporate capacity. In most states either the title or the corporate name on the check should be sufficient, but for adequate protection, both the title and the corporate name should be clear and conspicuous.

ATTACHMENT OF CHECKING ACCOUNTS

In the event a judgment is entered against a corporation, a partnership, or an individual, the creditor has the right to issue a restraining notice or "garnishment," which will attach a bank account up to or double the amount of the judgment. In today's computerized environment, restraining notices are easy to prepare and serve on a bank. In the major metropolitan areas, the money center banks or the large regional banks maintain numerous branches. The restraining notice may be served on only one branch and it will affect all the branches. For example, if half a dozen restraining notices are issued in a major city such as New York, Los Angeles, or Chicago, to the major banks in the city, they may cover hundreds of branches. Thus, the restraining notice is effective and the businessperson, as well as the individual, must be aware that once a judgment is entered, the bank account is vulnerable to execution by the creditor.

PAID-IN-FULL CHECKS

A debtor disputes a debt with a creditor and offers a check for a lesser amount in full settlement of the debt. The creditor receives the check and, at that point, must make a decision whether to deposit the check and accept the settlement, or to return the check and continue to prosecute a claim for the full balance due. If the claim is a bona fide disputed claim and the creditor accepts the check, then the creditor is precluded from instituting any further suit for the balance.

The legal terminology for the above transaction would be "an accord and satisfaction," i.e., a compromise which pays the debt in full. Until recently, this doctrine was almost universally accepted as the majority position throughout the United States. Nevertheless, the "common law" doctrine ("common law" means the law inherited from England, which was not written into statute law but resulted from court decisions and common sense) is no longer the majority view.

Under the common law, the creditor has two options: reject the offer or cash the check. The full settlement check constitutes an offer and when the creditor cashes the "full payment" check concerning a bona fide dispute of an unliquidated or disputed claim, the debtor is released from any further legal obligation under the common law. A creditor cannot avoid an accord and satisfaction by reciting a reservation of rights on the reverse side of the check, or by crossing out the "paid-in-full" language on the check.

Nevertheless, a number of states, including New York, Ohio, South Dakota and West Virginia, had rejected this position. These courts hold that the common law rule places the creditor in a disadvantageous position and permits the debtor to practice extortion. Offering a check for less than the contract amount, but "in full settlement," allegedly inflicts an exquisite form of commercial torture on the creditor. Thus these state courts have held that Section 1-207 of the Uniform Commercial Code (U.C.C.) permits the creditor to cash a check and avoid an accord of satisfaction, if the creditor makes an explicit reservation of rights by writing on the reverse side of the check such words as "without prejudice," "under protest" or words of similar import. The courts adopted this theory based upon a literal interpretation of U.C.C. Section 1–207. No meeting of the minds takes place and the result appears to be unfair when the debtor intends merely to offer the check on condition that the creditor accept it as full payment for the disputed debt. In summary, these states allow a creditor to accept the check as part payment of the debt and to proceed with suit for the balance due, notwithstanding the fact that this is not the intent or wish of the debtor. If a letter accompanies the check spelling out the conditions of the offer of settlement, the creditor may still deposit the check and sue for the balance (New York).

When a check for a lesser amount marked "paid-in-full" is submitted to a creditor and the debt is not disputed, deposit of the check by the creditor will not discharge the debt. But what happens if the debtor claims that the account was disputed and someone else in the corporation knew about the dispute? This situation often arises where a debtor mails a check to a large corporation and the department receiving the check is different from the department which charged the debtor.

This dilemma is addressed by U.C.C. section 3-311, which clearly states that a debtor cannot use a paid-in-full check to discharge a claim if:

1.   the payee is an organization.
2.   if the organization has communicated to the other party that an offer of full payment is to be sent to a particular person, office, or place.
3.   the check was not received by the designated person, office, or place.

The "paid-in-full" check is treated as a partial payment and not an offer to settle unless it meets the above requirements. Unfortunately this rule is not absolute, because the debt will be settled if the recipient of the check had knowledge of the dispute.

The purpose of the section is to prevent an accord and satisfaction from taking place when a check is sent to an automated collection center or a large corporation and is cashed without inspection. In the commercial world, hundreds of thousands of checks are processed daily by merchants and corporations. These parties are neither equipped nor is it economical to inspect every check for the purpose of avoiding an inadvertent accord and satisfaction. The section thus prevents a clever debtor from pulling a fast one by slipping a full settlement check through the system to pay less than the full amount on a disputed debt.

One may revoke an accord and satisfaction within 90 days by fully repaying the amount received. A summary of the state laws is contained in Appendix IV. Nevertheless, some of the states have modified section 3–311 and have either excluded certain parts of the statute or have included additional wording.

Section 3-311, a compromise of the common law and the interpretation of UCC 1-207 (subdivision 2), has been adopted in Arkansas, California, Colorado,

Connecticut, Florida, Georgia, Idaho, Indiana, Kansas, Louisiana, Massachusetts, Missouri, Nebraska, New Jersey, Pennsylvania, Texas, Utah, Virginia, Wisconsin, and Wyoming. (Other states now may have also adopted section 3-311 since we went to print on this book.) In most of the states, section 3-311 has been proposed as a compromise and is working its way through the legislatures. We do know that New York still follows UCC 1-207 which allows the recipient to deposit a check marked "paid-in-full," utilizing the magic words in the UCC, and receiving the money and thereafter suing for the balance. For an in-depth article on the subject written in 1992, see "Evolution of Accord and Satisfaction", 28 New England Law Review 189, Jay Winston.

STATUTE OF LIMITATIONS

When does the Statute of Limitations begin to run when a promissory note contains an acceleration clause that is exercised at the creditor's discretion: at the time of the first default or at the note's maturity date? A provision in a note and mortgage to allow acceleration at the discretion of creditor in the event of default in the payment of interest does not of itself cause the notes to mature and trigger the running of the Statute of Limitations. The exercise of the acceleration provision does not also accelerate the maturity date of the note. The Statute of Limitations does not begin to run until the note becomes mature regardless of the acceleration clause.

The Statute of Limitations in most states are suspended if service cannot be affected upon the defendant within the state. Some states even allow the tolling of the statute if the plaintiff is an infant or incompetent, or is in prison. In addition, many claims are not discovered due to fraud, misrepresentation, or concealment until a period of time after the actual transaction. In those instance, the statute usually runs from the time of the discovery of the claim.

In most states the statute distinguishes between promissory notes and similar obligations in contract. In Georgia, Connecticut, Delaware and Alaska for example, the Statute of Limitations on a promissory note is usually six years. In Idaho, Kansas and Oklahoma the statute is only five years and on the other hand in North Carolina and the District of Columbia just three years.

On open accounts, the statute can range from as little as three to as long as eight years. For example the three year statute on a sales contract is applicable in Arkansas, Arizona, Mississippi, Virginia, Washington and South Carolina and there is a four year statute in Georgia, Florida and California and a six year statute in Massachusetts, Michigan and New Jersey.

In most states time frames for ordinary contracts are different from those for judgments in courts of record. The statute in ordinary contracts can range from three to ten years while judgments in courts of records can range from four to twenty years. You must review the state law to determine the time period that applies to the transaction, not only as to how long the period is but also for what restrictions and requirements must be met in order for a defendant to assert the statute of limitations.

Usually the defense of the Statute of Limitations must be pleaded by the defendant affirmatively (expressly setting forth the defense in the answer to the complaint) and if it is not pleaded affirmatively, the statute is considered to be waived and the plaintiff may then proceed to obtain a judgment notwithstanding the fact that the statute has run. For this reason, many suits are started even though the statute has already run, for defendants sometimes fail to assert the defense in their answer.

With regard to suits against consumers for personal family or household use, one court has held that if the plaintiff had full knowledge that the statute had expired, proceeding with the suit would constitute a violation of the Fair Debt Collection Practices Act. Not enough decision law exists on this point to determine that this is the law since the concept flies in the face of the fact that the Statute of Limitations in most states must be pleaded affirmatively.

CHAPTER 7
Appendix I

New York Dishonored Check—Demand for Payment and Liquidated Damages

General Obligation Law Section 11-104

Section 1. The general obligations law is amended by adding a new section 11-104 to read as follows:

11-104. Additional liability of drawer.

1. Notwithstanding any contrary provision of law, a drawer negotiating a check who knows or should know that payment of such check will be refused by the drawee bank either because the drawer has no account with such bank or because the drawer has insufficient funds on deposit with such bank shall be liable, except as provided in subdivision four of this section, to the payee who has presented such check for payment, not only for the face amount of the check but also for additional, liquidated damages, where the check is dishonored and the drawer fails to pay the face amount of such check within thirty days following the date of mailing by the payee of the second written demand for payment as provided in this section.

2. In the case of a drawer negotiating a check who knows or should know that payment of such check will be refused by the drawee bank because the drawer has no account with such bank, such additional, liquidated damages shall be in an amount to be determined by the court in light of the circumstances, but in no event shall such amount be greater than twice the face amount of the check or seven hundred fifty dollars, whichever is less.

3. In the case of a drawer negotiating a check who knows or should know that payment of such check will be refused by the drawee bank because the drawer has insufficient funds on deposit with such bank, such additional, liquidated damages shall be in an amount to be determined by the court in light of the circumstances, but in no event shall such amount be greater than twice the face amount of the check or four hundred dollars, whichever is less.

4. The drawer shall not be liable to the payee for the additional, liquidated damages provided for by this section if:

   (a) The drawer gave such check as payment for the rental of residential premises; or

(b) The drawer gave such check as payment for residential service supplied by a gas, electric, steam, telephone or water corporation; or

(c) The drawer gave such check as repayment of all, or a portion of, a debt secured by collateral which the payee has repossessed.

5. Defenses which may be asserted against any person not having the rights of a holder in due course, as specified in sections 3-306 and 3-408 of the uniform commercial code, shall be available to a defendant in any action or proceeding in which additional liability is claimed under this section.

6. The additional liquidated damages provided for in this section shall be available only to those persons or entities which post or otherwise give conspicuous notice to the public of the additional, liquidated damages which may be imposed pursuant to this section. Such notice shall set forth the additional liquidated damages that may be imposed if a check is dishonored and the section of law authorizing imposition of such damages, and provide notice that criminal penalties also may apply.

7. The first written demand for payment on the dishonored check shall be in the form prescribed by subdivision eight of this section and shall be sent to the drawer's last known residence address or last known place of business by first class mail and by certified mail return receipt requested with delivery restricted to the drawer, on or after the date the payee received notice that such check had been dishonored. The second written demand for payment on the dishonored check shall be in the form provided in subdivision eight of this section and shall be sent to the drawer at the drawer's last known residence address or last known place of business by first class mail on or after the fifteenth day following the date of receipt of the first written demand for payment.

8. The written demands for payment required by subdivision seven of this section, shall be in the following form and shall be printed in at least ten point type in both the English and Spanish languages:

DEMAND FOR PAYMENT OF DISHONORED CHECK

DATE: 1ST NOTICE

                                                               2ND AND FINAL NOTICE
TO: _____   WARNING: YOU MAY BE
                NAME OF DRAWER   SUED 30 DAYS AFTER
                                                               THE DATE OF THIS
                                                               NOTICE IF YOU DO
                                                               NOT MAKE PAYMENT

        LAST KNOWN RESIDENCE ADDRESS
        OR PLACE OF BUSINESS

YOUR CHECK IN THE AMOUNT OF $_____ DATED _____

PAYABLE TO THE ORDER OF _____ HAS BEEN DISHONORED
BY THE BANK UPON WHICH IT WAS DRAWN, BECAUSE;

    _____ YOU HAD NO ACCOUNT WITH THAT BANK.

    _____ YOU HAD INSUFFICIENT FUNDS ON DEPOSIT WITH THAT BANK.

    IF YOU DO NOT MAKE PAYMENT, YOU MAY BE SUED UNDER SECTION 11-104
OF THE GENERAL OBLIGATIONS LAW TO RECOVER PAYMENT. IF A JUDGMENT IS
RENDERED AGAINST YOU IN COURT, IT MAY INCLUDE NOT ONLY THE ORIGINAL
FACE AMOUNT OF THE CHECK, BUT ALSO ADDITIONAL LIQUIDATED DAMAGES,
AS FOLLOWS: —IF YOU HAD NO ACCOUNT WITH THE BANK UPON WHICH THE
CHECK WAS DRAWN, AN ADDITIONAL SUM WHICH MAY BE EQUIVALENT TO
TWICE THE FACE AMOUNT OF THE CHECK OR SEVEN HUNDRED FIFTY DOLLARS,
WHICHEVER IS LESS; OR

    —IF YOU HAD INSUFFICIENT FUNDS ON DEPOSIT WITH THE BANK UPON
WHICH THE CHECK WAS DRAWN, AN ADDITIONAL SUM WHICH MAY BE EQUIV-
ALENT TO TWICE THE FACE AMOUNT OF THE CHECK OR FOUR HUNDRED DOL-
LARS, WHICHEVER IS LESS.

PLEASE MAKE PAYMENT IN THE AMOUNT OF _____ TO:

_____

NAME OF PAYEE

_____

ADDRESS TO WHICH PAYMENT
SHOULD BE DELIVERED

    IF YOU DISPUTE ANY OF THE FACTS LISTED ABOVE, CONTACT THE PAYEE
IMMEDIATELY.

9. The public service commission shall study the extent to which checks given in payment for residential service supplied by a gas, electric, steam, telephone or water
   corporation are dishonored either because the drawer had no account with the bank
   on which the check was written or because the drawer had insufficient funds on
   deposit with such bank, including the extent of chronic payment with checks that are
   dishonored and the impact of such dishonored checks on the operating costs of these
   corporations and their requests for rate increases, and whether any penalty for dishonored checks, in addition to recovery of the utilities' administrative costs, is necessary. The commission shall report to the governor and the legislature no later than
   one year after the effective date of this section.

   Section 2. This act shall take effect on the sixtieth day after it shall have become a law
   and shall apply to checks drawn on or after such effective date.

CHAPTER 7
APPENDIX II

VARIABLE INTEREST TIME NOTE UNSECURED

is _____   _____. N.Y. _____ 20 ____

On the _____ day of _____ 20____, for value received, the undersigned hereby promises to pay to the order of _____ at its office at _____ N.Y. ("the holder") _____ DOLLARS

With interest payable on _____ and the last day of each _____ thereafter at a variable per annum rate as follows: _____% above the rate of _____ announced to be in effect from time to time for prime domestic commercial loans of 90-day maturities, adjusted as of the date of each such change, but in no event higher than the maximum permitted under applicable law. Interest on any past due amount, whether at the due date thereof or by acceleration, shall be paid at a rate of one percent per annum in excess of the above-stated interest rate but in no event in excess of the maximum legal rate of interest permitted under applicable law for individuals or above the maximum rate a corporation may assert as a defense of usury.

In the event of default in payment of any liability (direct or contingent) to the holder hereof (however acquired), complete and partial suspension or liquidation of business, calling of a meeting of creditors, assignment for the benefit of creditors, dissolution, bulk sale or notice thereof, any mortgage, pledge of or creation of a security interest in any assets without consent of the holder of this note, insolvency of any kind, attachment, distraint, levy, execution, judgment, death, dissolution, merger, consolidation or reorganization of Obligor, tax assessment by the United States or any sate, application for or appointment of a receiver, filing of a voluntary or involuntary petition under any provision of the Bankruptcy Act or amendments thereto, of, by or against any Obligor, (which term shall include each of the undersigned and each endorser or guarantor hereof) or any property or rights of any Obligor, failure of any Obligor, on request, to furnish any financial information, or to permit inspection of any books or records, if any warranty, representation of statement of any Obligor in any application, statement to or agreement with the holder in connection with this note or to induce the holder to make a loan to the Obligor proves to have been false in any material respect when made or furnished, any change in, or discovery with regard to, the condition or affairs of any Obligor which, in the holder's opinion, increases its credit risk, or if the holder for any other reasons deems itself insecure, this note and all other liabilities (direct or contingent) of any Obligor to the holder (however acquired), shall become absolute, due and payable, without demand or notice notwithstanding anything to the contrary contained herein or in any other instrument. In addition to any other rights of holder, under applicable law, the holder shall have a lien on, and a security interest in, the deposit balances of any Obligor, and may at any time, without notice, apply the same to this note or such other liabilities, whether due or not. If an attorney is used to enforce or collect this note, Obligor shall be obligated to pay, in addition, reasonable attorney's fees. Each Obligor waives trial by jury and the right to interpose any counterclaims or setoffs of any kind in any litigation relating to this note or any of such other liabilities. The undersigned shall be jointly and severally liable hereon.

Failure or delay of the holder to enforce any provisions of this note shall not be deemed a waiver of any such provision, nor shall the holder be estopped from enforcing any such provision at a later time. Any waiver of any provision hereof must be in writing. Acceptance of any payments shall not waive or affect prior demand or acceleration of liabilities, and each such payment shall be applied first to the payment of accrued interest and interest.

The provisions of this note shall be construed and interpreted and all rights and obligations hereunder determined in accordance with the laws of the State of New York.

X _____

Note No. _____   Address _____

(VARIABLE INTEREST TIME   _____
NOTE UNSECURED)
                                    Address _____
03 1170* (1-82)

CHAPTER 7
Appendix III

GUARANTY

(insert Date)

_____, New York,   20 _____
Location

WHEREAS_____

(insert name, place of business and, if a corporation, State of incorporation)

_____, (hereinafter called the "Borrower"), desires to transact business with and to obtain credit or a continuation of credit or other financial accommodations from

_____

WHEREAS, the Bank is unwilling to extend or continue credit to or other financial accommodations to the Borrower, unless it receives the following guaranty of the undersigned;

NOW, THEREFORE, in consideration of the premises and of other good and valuable consideration and in order to induce the Bank from time to time, in its discretion, to extend or continue credit or other financial accommodations to the Borrower, the undersigned hereby guarantees, absolutely and unconditionally, to the Bank the payment of all liabilities of the Borrower to the Bank of whatever nature, whether now existing or hereafter incurred, whether created directly or acquired by the Bank by assignment or otherwise, whether matured or unmatured and whether absolute or contingent (all of which are hereinafter collectively referred to as the "Liabilities of the Borrower").

In order to further secure the payment of the Liabilities of the Borrower, the undersigned does hereby give Bank a continuing lien and right of setoff for the amount of the Liabilities of the Borrower upon any and all moneys, securities and any and all other property of the undersigned and the proceeds thereof, now or hereafter actually or constructively held or received by or in transit in any manner to or from the Bank, _____, or any other affiliate of the Bank from or for the undersigned, whether for safekeeping, custody, pledge, transmission, collection or otherwise or coming into the possession of the Bank,

or any other affiliate of the Bank in any way, or placed in any safe deposit box leased by the Bank,

or any other affiliate of the Bank to the undersigned. The Bank is also given a continuing lien and right of setoff for the amount of said Liabilities of the Borrower upon any and all deposits (general and special) and credits of, or for the benefit of the undersigned with, and any and all claims of the undersigned against, the Bank, or any other affiliate of the Bank at any time existing, and the Bank is hereby authorized at any time or times, without prior notice, to apply such deposits or credits, or any part thereof, to such Liabilities of the Borrower, and although said Liabilities of the Borrower may be contingent or unmatured, and whether the collateral security therefore is deemed adequate or not. The undersigned authorizes Bank to deliver a copy of this Guaranty to others as written notification of the undersigned's transfer of a security interest in the collateral described herein to the Bank.

The undersigned agrees that, with or without notice or demand, the undersigned shall reimburse the Bank for all the Bank's expenses (including reasonable fees of counsel for the Bank, who may be employees thereof) incurred in connection with any of the Liabilities of the Borrower or the collection thereof.

This guaranty is a continuing guaranty and shall remain in full force and effect irrespective of any interruptions in the business relations of the Borrower with the Bank; provided, however, that the undersigned may by notice in writing, delivered personally or received by certified mail, return receipt requested, addressed to the Bank's office at _____, terminate this guaranty with respect to all Liabilities of the Borrower incurred or contracted by the Borrower or acquired by the Bank after the date on which such notice is so delivered or received.

All moneys available to the Bank for application in payment or reduction of the Liabilities of the Borrower may be applied by the Bank in such manner and in such amounts and at such time or times as it may see fit to the payment or reduction of such of the Liabilities of the Borrower as the Bank may elect.

The undersigned hereby waives (a) notice of appearance of this guaranty and of extensions of credit or other financial accommodations by the Bank to the Borrower; (b) presentment and demand for payment of any of the Liabilities of the Borrower; (c) protest and notice of dishonor or default to the undersigned or to any other party with respect to any of the Liabilities of the Borrower; (d) all other notices to which the undersigned may otherwise be entitled; and (e) any demand for payment hereunder.

All liabilities of the undersigned to the Bank hereunder or otherwise, whether or not then due or absolute or contingent, shall without notice or demand become due and payable immediately upon the occurrence of any default or event of default with respect to any Liabilities of the Borrower (or the occurrence of any other event which results in acceleration of the maturity of any thereof) or the occurrence of any default hereunder. This is a guaranty of payment and not of collection and the undersigned further waives any right to require that any action be brought against the Borrower or any other person or to require that resort be had to any security or to any balance of any deposit account or credit on the books of the Bank in favor of the Borrower or any other person.

The undersigned hereby consents that from time to time, before or after any default by the Borrower or any notice of termination hereof, with or without further notice to or assent from the undersigned, any security at any time held by or available to the Bank for any obligation of the Borrower, or any security at any time held by or available to the Bank for any obligation of any other person secondarily or otherwise liable for any of the Liabilities of the Borrower, may be exchanged, surrendered or released and any obligation of the Borrower, or of any such other person, may be changed, altered, renewed, extended, continued, surrendered, compromised, waived, discharged or released in whole or in part (including without limitation any such event resulting from any insolvency, bankruptcy, reorganization or other similar proceeding affecting the Borrower or its assets) or any default with respect thereto waived, and the Bank may fail to set off and may release, in whole or in part, any balance of any deposit account or credit on its books in favor of the Borrower, or of any such other person, and may extend further credit in any manner whatsoever to the Borrower, and generally deal or take action or no action with regard to the Borrower or any such security or other person as the Bank may see fit; and the undersigned shall remain bound under this guaranty notwithstanding any such exchange, surrender, release, change, alteration, renewal, extension, continuance, compromise, waiver, discharge, inaction, extension of further credit or other dealing.

The obligations of the undersigned are absolute and unconditional and are valid irrespective of any other agreement or circumstance which might otherwise constitute a defense to the obligations hereunder or to the obligations of others related thereto and the undersigned irrevocably waives the right to assert defenses, setoffs and counterclaims in any litigation relating to this guaranty and the Liabilities of the Borrower. This guaranty sets forth the entire understanding of the parties, and the undersigned acknowledges that no oral or other agreements, conditions, promises, understandings, representations or warranties exist in regard to the obligations hereunder, except those specifically set forth herein.

The undersigned irrevocably waives and shall not seek to enforce or collect upon any rights which it now has or may acquire against the Borrower, either by way of subrogation, indemnity, reimbursement or contribution, or any other similar right, for any amount paid under this guaranty or by way of any other obligations whatsoever of the Borrower to the undersigned. In the event either a petition is filed under the Bankruptcy Code in regard to the Borrower or an action or proceeding is commenced for the benefit of the creditors of the Borrower, this agreement shall at all times thereafter remain effective in regard to any payments or other transfers of assets to the Bank received from or on behalf of the Borrower prior to notice of termination of this guaranty and which are or may be held voidable or otherwise subject to recission or return on the grounds of preference, fraudulent conveyance or otherwise, whether or not the Liabilities of the Borrower have been paid in full.

Each reference herein to the Bank shall be deemed to include its successors and assigns, in whose favor the provisions of this guaranty shall also insure. Each reference herein to the undersigned shall be deemed to include the heirs, executors, administrators, legal representatives, successors and assigns of the undersigned, all of whom shall be bound by the provisions of this guaranty.

The term "undersigned" as used herein shall, if this instrument is signed by more than one party, mean the "undersigned and each of them" and each undertaking herein contained shall be their joint and several undertaking, provided, however, that in the next succeeding paragraph hereof the term "undersigned" shall mean the "undersigned or any of them." If any party hereto shall be a partnership, the agreements and obligations on the part of the undersigned herein contained shall remain in force and applicable against the partnership and all of its partners notwithstanding any changes in the individuals composing the partnership (or any release of one or more partners) and the term "undersigned" shall include any altered or successive partnership but the predecessor partnerships and their partners shall not thereby be released from any obligation or liability.

No delay on the part of the Bank in exercising any rights hereunder or failure to exercise the same shall operate as a waiver of such rights; no notice to or demand on the undersigned shall be deemed to be a waiver of the obligation of the undersigned or of the right of the Bank to take further action without notice or demand as provided herein; nor in any event shall any modification or waiver of the provisions of this guaranty be effective unless in writing signed by an authorized officer of the Bank nor shall any such waiver be applicable except in the specific instance for which given.

This guaranty is, and shall be deemed to be, a contract entered into under and pursuant to the laws of the _____ and shall be in all respects governed, construed, applied and enforced in accordance with the laws of said State; and no defense given or allowed by the laws of any other State or Country shall be interposed in any action hereon unless such defense is also given or allowed by the laws of the

_____.

The undersigned hereby unconditionally WAIVES ANY RIGHT TO JURY TRIAL in connection with actions by or against the Bank arising out of or in connection with the Liabilities of the Borrower and this guaranty.

(If partnership, name of partnership and signature of general partner(s) must appear.)	Individual or Partnership	Corporation
	_____	_____
	Name of Guarantor (Type or Print)	Name of Guarantor (Type or Print)
	_____	_____
	_____	By: _____
	_____	_____
	Address	
	_____	_____
		Title
		CORPORATE SEAL

Individual Acknowledgment

STATE OF
  SS:
COUNTY OF
On the ____ day of _____, 20 ____, before me personally came
_____, to me known to be the individual described in and who executed the foregoing instrument and he/she acknowledged to me that he/she executed the same.

_____, Notary Public
  My commission expires:

Corporate Acknowledgment

STATE OF
  SS:
COUNTY OF
On the ____ day of _____, 20 ____, before me personally came
_____, to me known, who, being by me duly sworn, did depose and say that he/she is _____

of _____, the corporation described in and which executed the above instrument, that he/she knows the seal of said corporation; that the seal affixed to said instrument is such corporate seal; that it was so affixed by order of the board of directors of said corporation, and that he/she signed his name thereto by like order.

_____, Notary Public

My commission expires:

Partnership Acknowledgment

STATE OF

                SS:

COUNTY OF

On the _____ day of _____, 20 ____, before me personally came _____, to me known to be the individual described in and who executed the foregoing instrument and he/she a Partnership, as his/her act and deed.

_____, Notary Public

My commission expires:

CHAPTER 8

Repossession of Property

While the general law of repossession is covered under the Uniform Commercial Code (UCC), Article IX, the repossession of property is primarily restricted and controlled by the written installment contracts and consumer credit contracts which are entered into by the consumer. Since most repossessions involve consumers, consumer protection laws must be considered, including the Bankruptcy Code, Truth in Lending Act, Equal Credit Opportunity Act, and the Fair Debt Collection Practices Act, in addition to the replevin laws of the respective states. Compliance with the laws that affect the extension of credit is required, as well as elimination of deceptive and abusive collection practices in the repossession of a vehicle or boat.

UNIFORM COMMERCIAL CODE

Every state has adopted the Uniform Commercial Code. Most states have made changes but they have little impact on the general provisions, with a few exceptions. A review of the state law with counsel is recommended.

The Uniform Commercial Code is being revised section by section. Article IX, which covers repossession of property, was revised in 1998 and the states are now in the process of adopting the revisions. Consultation with counsel is recommended to determine whether your state has adopted the revised section and in what form (see Chapter 10). Some of the changes in the new Article IX are radical, including significant filing changes.

The Uniform Commercial Code applies to liens created with the consent of both parties. Liens also may be created by statute such as mechanics liens, and garagemen liens (third parties who improve property). The security agreement is identified as "the agreement between the consumer and the lender which creates the lien under the "Uniform Commercial Code." In the security agreement presented to consumers by financial institutions, the consumer identifies the property securing the lien, the terms of repayment, charges and other expenses. The agreement also defines the conditions under which the consumer will maintain the vehicle or boat, what constitutes a default under the agreement, what happens when the default takes place under the agreement, the rights of the secured party with regard to repossessing the vehicle, the terms of crediting the payments, the conditions of the sale of the vehicle, and the allocation of the proceeds from the sale of the vehicle.

If the agreement covers both real and personal property, the secured party may proceed under the Uniform Commercial Code as to the personal property, i.e., automobile or boat, or may proceed under the state law to foreclose the mortgage as to both the real and personal property.

LEASES AND SECURITY INTERESTS

Because of the price of boats and vehicles in today's market, leases are becoming as common as installment security agreements. If the secured party is claiming ownership of the property by virtue of a lease, the Uniform Commercial Code may treat this interest as a "security interest" in the same manner as any installment security agreement depending upon the terms and the intent of the parties. If it is treated as a security interest, the Uniform Commercial Code will provide the rights and remedies to repossess or dispose of the property. Whether the interest is a security interest is determined by whether it is "intended to be a security interest." If at the end of the lease the consumer has an option to buy the property for a nominal consideration, the agreement is probably a security agreement. Nevertheless, the fact that the consumer pays more than a nominal consideration does not insure that the agreement is a lease. Many factors determine whether the arrangement is a lease or a security interest, including whether the consumer is obligated to repair and insure the vehicle and whether the terms are so constructed that the consumer will exercise the option to own the vehicle. If the lease is intended as a security agreement but identified as a lease, the rights and remedies of the respective parties may be controlled by the Uniform Commercial Code and the respective state laws.[1]

---

[1] UCC 9-504(4).

REPOSSESSION AND TERMINATION OF LEASE

One day after the vehicle was repossessed, the debtor filed a petition in bank-ruptcy under Chapter 13. Under the Chapter 13 proceeding the debtor sought to voluntarily pay any arrearages, to assume the lease and to continue to make pay-ments outside of the plan of the Chapter 13 proceeding. The case relied on (General Motors Acceptance Corp. v. D. Lawrence 11 B.R. 44 (Bankr. N.D., Ga. 1981) allowed the debtor to pay pre-petition arrearages during a bankruptcy pro-ceeding. Nevertheless, the court distinguished this case and held that the lease terminated at the time of repossession because the terms of the lease explicitly set forth "this lease will terminate upon the return of the vehicle to the lessor." The lease also set forth that "if you are in default, Ford Credit may cancel the lease, take back the vehicle ...."

Upon the lawful repossession of the vehicle, the lease terminated and the debtor no longer had any interest in the vehicle and thus the lease cannot be assumed because it is not the property of the bankrupt estate. The key fact is that the debtor lease terminated by the repossession *prior to the filing of the petition.* In the other cases where the bankruptcy court allowed the assumption of pre-peti-tion arrearages, the vehicle was still in the possession of the debtor and not in the possession of the creditor.[2]

> CREDIT AND COLLECTION TIP: *Agreements should be carefully prepared for they are usually strictly construed by the courts.*

SECURITY DEPOSITS

Leases on automobiles require security deposits and there has been considerable litigation over whether interest or profits on the security deposits should be earned and turned over to the borrower at the conclusion of the lease. A signifi-cant amount of litigation has taken place over this issue and the courts do not agree on the exact nature of a security deposit. As a result, there is confusion as to whether interest must be paid on a security deposit. The majority seems to favor the fact that a security deposit on an automobile lease is not covered by the UCC or Federal Consumer Leasing Act. In a recent case, there was a thorough analysis of this entire problem and the judge in the 2nd Circuit, substantiating his opinion with a listing of cases across the country, finally held that a security deposit on a lease did not create a security interest, but merely was a debt and accordingly the

---

[2]*In the Matter of Mayhall*, 200 B.R. 241 (Bankr. N.D. Ala. 1996).

borrower is not entitled to interest or profits on that security deposit. The judge engaged in a thorough analysis of the situation and provided a clear picture of the conflicting views concerning the particular issue.[3]

The court relied on a 1997 case which stated basically that neither the Uniform Commercial Code nor the Consumer Leasing Act is applicable to security deposits.[4]

Section 7-101 was also considered in the decision and the argument of the plaintiff was that the security deposit was not immediately placed in a special account. This particular argument was rejected primarily because the plaintiff was not damaged and Section 7-101 was interpreted by other sections as not requiring deposit funds to be put in interest-bearing accounts.

Whenever a deposit is given as security in a transaction, the question arises whether the holder of the security deposit must pay interest to the depositor for the time that the security deposit is held. In most of the states, there are a wide variety of statutory provisions which require parties who receive monies in escrow to pay the parties who deposit the monies' interest on the escrow deposit. For example, in New York, landlords are required to pay interest when a tenant deposits one or two months rent as a security deposit in commercial space. Nevertheless, there are state laws which seem to supersede the UCC and a careful review of the state law should be determined with regard to obligations to pay interest on any deposit.

LATE PAYMENTS—REPOSSESSION

Section 9-503 provides as follows:

> "Unless otherwise agreed, a secured party has on default the right to take possession of the collateral. In taking possession a secured party may proceed without judicial process if this can be done without breach of the peace or may proceed by action ...."

Despite the fact that the statute is clear that whenever the debtor is in default, the creditor has a right to take possession of the collateral as long as the taking of possession is done without a breach of the peace, the creditor must examine the words introducing the paragraph, "unless otherwise agreed." Many courts have held that where a secured creditor routinely accepts the debtor's delinquent payments, the creditor is waiving strict compliance with the parties' contractual requirement to make payments on time (the parties have otherwise agreed as to a payment schedule).

---

[3]*In re Ford Motor Credit Company Motor Vehicle Lease Litigation. Eleanor Werbowsky v. Ford Motor Credit Company* 1998 WL 159051 (SDNY).

[4]*Stinmetz v. Toyota Motor Credit Company* 963 F. Supp. 1294 (E.D.N.Y. 1997).

The courts have held that acceptance of late payments constitutes a waiver of strict compliance with the contract terms specifying when payment should be made. In most of these instances, the cases have dealt with individual consumers who have purchased cars on an installment basis and the debtor is no more than one, two, or maybe three months in arrears and the arrears usually have been continuous.

A secured party, not insisting upon strict compliance in the past, and before embarking upon a course of action to declare a default and effect a repossession, should deliver notice to the debtor that strict compliance with the terms of contract will be demanded henceforth if repossession is to be avoided.

In a particular Arkansas case,[5] the debtor made only one timely payment of the fourteen monthly payments required; thirteen late payments were made ranging from a few days to more than 30 days delinquent from the due date required under the agreement. The debtor was contacted several times about delinquent payments, but no one ever informed him that the bank intended to commence strict enforcement. The court did not summarily decide for the bank, but stated that a jury might decide that by the bank's course of dealing with the debtor, the bank had waived its right to repossession by repeatedly accepting the late payments. The court emphasized that the bank could reinstate its right to repossess by delivering written notice to the debtor stating that thereafter strict compliance was to be expected.

It is recommended that certified or registered mail be used when sending such a written notice, for it will be necessary to prove notice. Failure to prove notice to the debtor may expose the creditor to significant damages for repossessing the secured property, since such repossession may constitute a conversion of property.

CREDIT AND COLLECTION TIP: *Fill out receipt for certified mailing. Do not merely staple it to default letter. By completing the form, it becomes a business record and is admissible as evidence. A blank form stamped as a receipt is susceptible to attack as unreliable.*

RIGHT TO CURE DEFAULT

The right to accelerate the loan is a serious hardship for the consumer, and many statutes and the courts find reasons to shelter the consumer from this acceleration clause, which declares the entire debt due if there is a default in one payment. Some federal statutes, and many states have "right to cure" provisions which provide that the secured party must send a notice to the consumer to allow the con-

---

[5]*Mercedes-Benz Credit Corp. v. Morgan*, 850 S.W.2d. 297 (1993).

sumer time within which to cure the default of one payment so that the loan will not accelerate. Depending upon the type of loan, the secured party should review the appropriate law.

WAIVER

The provisions of most security agreements contain a waiver of notice by the debtor that the creditor will accelerate the debt and a waiver of notice that the creditor will repossess the automobile or boat. While some courts enforce this waiver,[6] other courts find these waiver provisions against public policy and refuse to enforce them.[7]

VIOLATION BY SECURED PARTY

If a secured party violates the provisions of UCC Article 9 and sells the collateral when no right to sell the collateral exists, the secured party is liable for damages.[8] The debtor and a party with a lien on the property may have the right to recover the property from the secured party. If the collateral is consumer goods, the debtor has the right to recover an amount not less than the credit service charge plus ten percent of the principal amount of the debt on the amount originally financed (not the balance due).

STATUTE OF LIMITATIONS

UCC Article 9 does not provide for any statute of limitations, although UCC 2-725 does provide for a four-year limitation. As a general rule the courts look to state legislation for purposes of determining which statute of limitations applies to the repossession of vehicles. It may be shortened by agreement, but no shorter than one year.

PEACEFUL POSSESSION

Most security agreements provide that the secured party may acquire peaceful possession of property. The consumer often voluntarily surrenders the property.

---

[6]*ACE Parts & Distributors v. First Nat. Bank*, 245 S.E. 2d 314 (1978).

[7]*Fontaine v. Industrial National Bank of Rhode Island*, 298 A.2d 521 (1973).

[8]UCC 9-507(1).

Voluntary surrender does not afford the secured party a right to violate the terms of the security agreement. The consumer has the right to require strict compliance with the terms of the security agreement.

BREACH OF PEACE

A repossession must not constitute a breach of peace. Deceptive practices and threats to take security sometimes may constitute a breach of the peace. Certainly physical force is prohibited. Any type of contact with the debtor would probably fall into that category while intimidation by use of threatening instruments, etc., would definitely constitute physical force.[9]

Damaging the person's property during the act of repossession is physical force if the property damaged is not the property sought to be repossessed. Any activity indicating the consumer objects to the repossession, whether this activity is engaged in by the consumer, members of the family, or even neighbors, is evidence that the repossession is not proceeding peacefully. The best repossession is when neither the consumer nor anyone who knows the consumer, such as a friend or relative, is present during the act of repossession. A breach of peace is rare where a car is repossessed on the street or in a public parking lot.

The question of consent arose where the creditor repossessed a computer system by entering the office of the debtor. The plaintiff entered the business premises and handed the employee, who was the only party present on the premises, a set of papers representing a law suit, that she was the guarantor of the obligation, that certain equipment was security for the obligation and that she was removing that equipment. There was conflicting testimony as to whether the employee told her not to take the equipment or whether the employee told her that she doesn't blame her and that the employee would do the same thing.

The defendant asserts that no matter what the employee said, the employee had no authority to consent to the removal because he is not a management employee and that the plaintiff should have been aware of this because she had been his supervisor before she was discharged. The plaintiff on the other hand argues that the employee had apparent authority.

The court concluded that a breach of peace did not occur because the consent of the debtor is not required for repossession of the collateral by the creditor nor is a debtor entitled to a hearing before the creditor repossesses the collateral. Nevertheless, a creditor should not enter or attempt to enter any private structure to repossess the collateral without the express consent of the person in charge or a court order . The consent of the debtor to enter the premises to repossess must be voluntarily and freely given. The court held that it was clear and undisputed that the plaintiff used no force or threats to take the computer system and other

---

[9]*Harris Truck & Trailer v. Foote*, 436 S.W.2d 460 (1968) and *Griffith v. Valley of Sun*, 613 P2d 1283 (1980).

records out of the office. Consent to the repossession is not necessary. All that is necessary is consent by the person in charge for the plaintiff to enter the offices to repossess the collateral. The front door was open and not locked and only one employee was present which automatically made him the person in charge. At no point did the employee of the defendant object to the presence of the plaintiff on the premises.

This seems to stretch the requirements for a peaceful possession. While it is true that the plaintiff did peacefully enter onto the premises, the courts usually tend to believe where the debtor objects to the repossession, the repossession should stop. In this case there was conflicting testimony and apparently the court chose to believe the plaintiff. If a person entered a house with the consent of the owner of the house and then proceeded to engage in a repossession of a lawnmower or a snow blower, and the owner verbally objected to the repossession, it is doubtful whether the court would follow this case. Nevertheless, this was unusual in that the only party present on the premises was an employee and the conflicting testimony seemed to indicate that he consented to the party entering the premises and did not object, or at least did not strenuously object, to the removal of the computer system. It is my opinion that a different result might take place if the same type of conduct was performed in a private residential house where the actual owner was present.[10]

THREAT TO REPOSSESS

Threatening to repossess a vehicle from a consumer where no immediate intention to repossess is present is a violation of the Fair Debt Collection Practices Act, which requires that a creditor must do whatever is threatened.[11] A threat to repossess should only be used where the immediate intent is to retain a repossession firm to repossess the vehicle. Threatening to repossess when only one payment is past due, and the normal custom is to repossess if three or four payments are late, may expose the creditor to liability under the Fair Debt Collection Practices Act.

POLICE OFFICER

Sometimes the repossessing party will ask for the assistance of a police officer whose presence, carrying a weapon, may be considered the use of force because the consumer is not likely to resist. If the officer is a sheriff pursuant to a court order, there is no problem.

---

[10]*Rainwater v. Rx Medical Services Corp.*, 30 UCC Rep Serv.2d 983, 1995 WL 907888 (E.D. Cal. 1995).

[11]15 U.S.C. 1692e(5).

As long as no police officer or court office is present, and no deception is used that a court officer is enforcing the law, the secured party is permitted to use deceptive practices in some jurisdictions,[12] but violation of the Fair Debt Collection Practices Act must be considered.

NOTICE

Most states do not interfere with the terms of the security agreement enabling the secured party to repossess the car peacefully without notice to the debtor. Connecticut and Massachusetts, under certain circumstances, require creditors to notify the debtors before repossession.[13] Louisiana and Wisconsin prohibit peaceful repossession.[14]

SOLDIERS AND SAILORS ACT

Under the U.S. Soldiers and Sailors Civil Relief Act, significant protection is afforded military personnel from peaceful repossession. The act expressly refers to debts that are incurred prior to the time that the consumer entered military service. If the individual is stationed permanently on a post, a court proceeding should be used instead of peaceful repossession.

REPLEVIN

In the event that the secured party cannot obtain peaceful possession of the vehicle, the right to use the remedy of replevin, known as "claim and delivery" and "sequestration" in other states, is available. An application to court must be supported by an affidavit stating that peaceful possession is unavailable and the consumer has not surrendered the vehicle and is still in possession of the property. This application is processed usually after notice to the debtor to allow opposition to the application and to set forth why the secured party should not be entitled to repossess the vehicle. In most states the secured party is required to state in the affidavit the value of the vehicle and to post a bond in an amount double the value of the vehicle.

---

[12]*Ford Motor Credit Company v. Cole*, 503 S.W.2d 853 (1973).

[13]Connecticut General Statute Section 42-98B, Massachusetts General Law chapter 255B, Section 20A(b).

[14]Wis. Stat. 425.206; LSA-C.C.P. art. 34501.

Replevin actions should be pursued to a final judgment. Most secured creditors use public auctions where many lenders sell the automobiles at one centralized location and dispose of the collateral quickly, before obtaining a final judgment. If the replevin action is pursued to final judgment, the final judgment ratifies and approves the sale of the vehicle. If a final judgment is not obtained, the consumer's attorney may be entitled to actual or punitive damages in a conversion action or a similar proceeding for selling the vehicle without a judgment.

Replevin should be used only when the creditor knows where the property is, such as an auto in a repair shop, a boat docked at a marina or a car in a garage. The creditor must recognize that debtors may, and often do, move the property before the sheriff arrives. If the property is in one state/county and debtor in another, action should be in location where property is located. The sheriff may only enforce an order in its own jurisdiction.

PROPERTY TAKEN WITH REPOSSESSION

Any personal property contained in the repossessed vehicle should be returned forthwith to the consumer. A problem arises when the consumer alleges that property was left in the vehicle, but the property is no longer there. Among those who are involved in repossession of vehicles, the frequency within which golf clubs, sporting equipment, and carpenter tools are left in the trunk of the car bears no relationship to the number of golfers or carpenters.

Since the secured party is responsible for the activities of the party who repossesses, careful and exacting procedures have been orchestrated to take inventory of the personal property contained in the repossessed vehicle, especially a boat or a motor home. If the property is damaged or lost by reason of the repossession, the debtor is entitled to damages, including damages for loss of use in the case of tools used in a trade. Such procedures include the use of independent witnesses, videotapes, and photographs.

BANKRUPTCY

Once the bankruptcy petition is filed, the automatic stay provisions freeze all action and prohibit commencing or proceeding with a suit against the bankrupt, continuing any repossession or replevin proceedings and/or sale of secured property. The stay freezes the debtor's assets at the time of the bankruptcy and confines to the Bankruptcy Court the resolution of disputes between creditor and debtor (see Chapter 5).

The stay continues in operation:[15]

---

[15]U.S.C. Section 362(c).

1. until the property is sold by the estate, or is abandoned;
2. until the date the bankruptcy is dismissed, or discharge is approved;
3. until the date on which the stay is terminated by an order of the court; or
4. if the court fails to take any action when an application for a removal of the stay is made.

Several options are offered:

a. The debtor may reaffirm the debt and agree to continue to make payments under the terms of the security agreement until the outstanding deficiency balance is discharged. The same option applies to a lease of a vehicle or boat (see Chapter 5).
b. The debtor may voluntarily surrender security under the security agreement and enter a stipulation with the secured party consenting to the surrender of the vehicle and the removal of the stay.
c. The secured party makes an application by motion to court for a removal of the stay. A stay is not an adversary proceeding under the Bankruptcy Court, but does require notice to the bankrupt and a hearing. If the bankrupt defaults after this notice, the stay should be removed by the court. Both the bankrupt and the trustee must be named in the proceeding. The bankrupt is not entitled to raise counterclaims against the creditor on unrelated matters at the hearing, although valid defenses may be raised to the stay removal.
d. A complaint to reclaim the property or an application to court may be made to request that the trustee abandon any interest in the property.

None of these proceedings should be commenced without careful review and consultation with counsel.

In straight Chapter 7 bankruptcy cases, consumers may purchase any property covered by a security agreement for a price no more than the value of the property. The purpose is to prevent creditors from retaining the property and forcing the debtor to pay a price to redeem the property in excess of the actual value of the property. The consumer may elect to exempt certain property under both the federal or state laws.

The Bankruptcy Act requires the debtor, within 30 days of filing the petition, to file a statement of intention with respect to any secured property. This statement of intention sets forth whether the bankrupt will claim the property as exempt, will surrender the property, or redeem the property. This information will inform the creditor whether the debtor intends to voluntarily surrender the property or whether an application for a removal of the stay is necessary. Some states allow the debtor to continue voluntary payments without surrendering, redeeming or reaffirming the debt (see Chapter 10).

REAFFIRMATION

The debtor's reaffirmation of the agreement with the creditor removes the agreement from the jurisdiction of the Bankruptcy Court. The debtor is obligated to continue any obligation after discharge. Reaffirmation agreements must be made in writing and filed *prior to discharge* and may need to be submitted for approval to the bankruptcy court (see Chapter 5).

In some states if the secured party continues to accept payments beyond the date of discharge of the bankrupt, *without a reaffirmation* of the debt, the secured party is abandoning all rights to obtain a deficiency and may only resort to the vehicle or boat in the event of a default. To protect the right to collect a deficiency from the bankrupt even where the debtor continues to pay currently, the creditor has two options: reaffirmation or application for removal of stay. Failure to obtain reaffirmation, but continuing the acceptance of payments during and after the bankruptcy discharge, will effectively discharge the bankrupt from any liability for a deficiency balance. However, if the Chapter 13 plan provides for 100% repayment, the court may not grant relief of stay if debtor is current. Thus, the court is rewriting the lease.

THIRD-PARTY LIENS

GARAGEMEN'S LIENS—Most states provide that a party who has enhanced the value of the property by expending labor and materials in repairing the property or in some way improving the property is entitled to a lien. This type of lien is asserted by mechanics, repairmen, garagemen, towing firms, or wrecking firms. The lien takes priority over the lien of a secured party. The prime example is a garagemen's lien for repairs on an automobile. Often when the secured party seeks to repossess a vehicle, the vehicle is located at the repair shop with the repair bill unpaid. The towing and storage charges are added to the repair bill and the secured party is faced with substantial bills.

STORAGE CHARGES—The towing and storage charges may or may not be added to the repair bill depending upon the state statute, or depending upon how the courts in the state treat them. Storage and towing charges, because they do not enhance the value of the property, should not be entitled to protection unless specified by statute.[16] A lien is not created if the repair facility initially provided a warranty on the vehicle.

---

[16]*Central Trust v. Dan's Marina*, 858 S.W.2d. 211 (1993).

CONSENT OF OWNER—The consent of the owner of the vehicle is necessary for the repairmen to assert the lien. In a security agreement, the lender loans money in return for a security interest in the boat or vehicle, and the borrower is the owner. In a lease agreement, the owner of the vehicle is the financial institution (bank) and not the party who is leasing and operating the vehicle. The party operating the vehicle has the apparent authority of ownership, and thus when the vehicle is delivered to the repair shop, the repair shop has the right to rely upon this "apparent authority" that the party who delivered the vehicle is the owner. Some cases have held however, that the financial institution is not liable for repairs where consent has not been obtained. Whether all courts will agree with this conclusion is questionable since an unfair and unjust result is produced with respect to repair shops. Under this ruling, the repair shop has the added obligation to determine whether the party is leasing the car and then to obtain the consent of the financial institution.[17]

EXCESSIVE CHARGES—Where the repair shop charges an excessive amount, the lien may be forfeited under certain special circumstances. Nevertheless, this is a minority decision and there is little support that an unreasonable charge can cancel the lien. If the repairman acts in good faith, the lien usually survives.

REDEMPTION

At any time before the secured party has sold or disposed of the collateral or entered into a contract for its disposition, the debtor or any other secured party has an unqualified right to redeem the collateral. This can be done by fulfilling all the obligations of the lease or security agreement, and by paying the balance due as well as the expenses reasonably incurred by the secured party in retaking, holding, and preparing the security for resale.[18] This is an unqualified right of the consumer to redeem prior to the sale of the vehicle. No notice to the consumer of this right to redeem is necessary, but if an improper notice is sent to the consumer contradicting this unqualified right to redeem before the sale of the property, the secured party may be exposed to liability for damages.

SALE OF PROPERTY

The secured party after default may sell, lease, or otherwise dispose of any or all of the collateral in its then condition. The proceeds are applied to the reasonable

---

[17]*Lacomini v. Liberty Mutual Insurance Company*, 497 A 2d. 854 (1985); *Joy Oil Company v. Freuhauf Trailer*, 29 N.W. 2d. 691 (1947).

[18]UCC 9-506.

expenses of retaking, holding, and preparing the collateral for sale or lease, and the satisfaction of any indebtedness secured by a subordinate security interest in the collateral. Disposition may be by public or private sale. Most financial institutions sell the property at public auction or private auction of dealers, in a commercially reasonable manner and properly advertise the sale of the vehicle. Special auctions are conducted in which the financial institutions participate. The cars are sold at these auctions periodically and the wholesale dealers and consumers do not have a chance to buy.[19] Before a private sale is made, consultation with counsel is recommended to be certain you have complied with state law. Since the law varies from state to state, failure to comply will expose the creditor to damages as well as the sale being set aside.

STRICT FORECLOSURE

Strict foreclosure occurs when the secured party retains the vehicle in full satisfaction of the obligation. This is seldom done in today's economic environment, since the vehicle is usually worth less than the balance due. Careful review of the statutory requirements and the court decisions is recommended in the event the secured party engages in this type of foreclosure.

COMMERCIALLY REASONABLE SALE

When disposing of collateral, a few uneducated creditors may overlook their duty to engage in a commercially reasonable sale under UCC 9-504 (1). This section states that a creditor "may sell, lease, or otherwise dispose of any or all of the collateral in its then condition or following any commercially reasonable preparation or processing."

While this section appears to make the preparation of a collateral for disposition optional, a number of courts have held that failure to do so was commercially unreasonable. These courts justified their position on the grounds of a cost-benefit analysis. If minor preparation substantially increases market value, it is commercially reasonable to perform this preparation. Thus, the secured party must act in good faith and in a commercially reasonable manner.

While there is no specific time limit within which an item must be disposed, a prolonged interval between repossession and sale raises the inference of commercial unreasonableness. The burden of proof shifts to the second party to establish that its actions were commercially reasonable. If the delay is excessive, some courts bar the creditor from recovering a deficiency. This result is especially true when the creditor accrues excessive storage charges. The courts feel that the

---

[19]UCC 9-504.

debtor should not be penalized if the loss of value of the property is due to the negligence of the creditor. Commercial reasonableness can be established through comparisons with industry standards and with prior sales conducted by the creditor. The code sets forth three standards for courts to determine whether the sale was performed in a commercially reasonable manner (U.C.C. 9-507(2)):

1. A sale in the usual manner in a recognized market is commercially reasonable.

2. A sale at a price current in a recognized market at the time of sale, regardless of how the sale was completed, is commercially reasonable.

3. Disposing of a collateral in conformity with reasonable commercial practices among dealers in the type of property sold is commercially reasonable.

The fact that the creditor may have obtained a higher price by selling the collateral at a different time or by using a different method is not sufficient by itself to establish that the sale was defective.

Creditors must use common sense to minimize the deficiency. Laziness and negligence by the creditors are primary grounds for a court to hold a sale commercially unreasonable. The following are examples of what may be deemed commercially unreasonable:

1. If creditors in the industry utilize public sale to dispose of collateral, a private sale at a below-average price may be improper.

2. Selling the collateral to a friend at an arbitrary price would be unreasonable.

3. After attempting to sell the collateral privately, failing to notify previous bidders of a future public auction is unreasonable.

4. Choosing an inconvenient location or an unusual time to sell property may be unreasonable.

CREDIT AND COLLECTION TIP: *If the first sale was called off, or delayed, always invite the bidders from the first auction to the second auction. Failure to do so is damaging to the creditor's case, especially if the bids at the original sale were higher than at the second sale.*

DEFICIENCY ACTIONS

If the sale of the vehicle does not produce sufficient monies to cover the balance due under the security agreement and all expenses, the secured party may sue the consumer for the deficiency. Some states place restrictions on this type of proceeding and a review of the state law is necessary to determine whether the full deficiency can be recovered under the security agreement. A secured party who has complied with the UCC and state laws should be entitled to recover the full deficiency. If there has been noncompliance with the laws, the consumer will probably assert this noncompliance as a defense to a suit for a deficiency.

SHIP MORTGAGE ACT

The Ship Mortgage Act was a Federal Act designed for a speedy and uniform practice of foreclosure on boats and ships in the Federal Court, instead of leaving the mortgagee to the distinct and different procedures of the courts of the various states. The purpose of the Act was to encourage institutions to extend credit to owners of boats and ships. The Ship Mortgage Act sets forth certain restrictions and conditions for the boats and ships to qualify for filing under the Act.

Several courts have interpreted the Act to mean that in the event the mortgage on a boat is filed under the Ship Mortgage Act, the Act is the sole and exclusive remedy available to foreclose a mortgage on a boat or ship. If the mortgage is within the Act, the position is that no suit to foreclose may be maintained in a state court.[20] Several other cases support this concept that the Ship Mortgage Act is the exclusive remedy to foreclose a mortgage, and the Act forms a comprehensive scheme for ship foreclosures "leaving no room for the operation of *state law*."

However, the weight seems to be shifting to the concept that the Ship Mortgage Act and the Judicial Sales Act are mere alternatives to the procedures afforded by the state to foreclose on a boat. Where the secured lender has not only obtained a preferred mortgage under the Ship Mortgage Act, but in addition, has obtained an installment security agreement under the state law, at least New York has followed the majority view and stated that the financial institution can proceed under state law to foreclose.[21]

The majority view contradicts this exclusive jurisdiction of the Ship Mortgage Act and holds that a defaulted ship mortgagee may either utilize the Ship Mortgage Act or resort to state law to repossess and sell the vessel either with or without the aid of court. The mortgagee may thus resort to the guidelines of state law to privately foreclose on mortgages under the Act.[22]

Consultation with experienced counsel is recommended.

LIABILITY OF CREDITORS

In a case in Mississippi, a judge stated that where the service performed entails the commission of some illegal, dangerous or tortuous act (wrongful act), the principal and the independent contractor both play an integral part and are thus

---

[20]*Bank of American National Trust & Savings v. Fogle*, 637 F.Supp. 305 (N.D., Col. 1985).

[21]*Chemical Bank v. Barkan* 8841-91 (Supreme Court N.Y., July 23, 1992, unreported).

[22]*First Federal Savings F.S.B. v. M/Y Sweet Retreat*, 844 F.Supp. 99 (D.R.I. 1994).

proximate causes of whatever harm ensues. Where some serious harm can be reasonably anticipated, such as in the performance of a repossession, the creditor cannot allege a defense that the act causing the harm was solely committed by the repossession firm. Repossessing an automobile is considered a dangerous and tortuous act. A violation of the law by the repossession firm may place liability for said tortuous act upon the creditor who authorized the repossession.

The repossession firm was hitching a van to the wrecker and starting to remove it when the plaintiff awakened and went outside to see what was going on. The plaintiff observed a man attaching the van to a truck by way of a "quick snap harness" and the plaintiff began to yell. In pursuing the truck and the van, the plaintiff fell into a ditch and was injured and taken to the hospital. The plaintiff served a complaint upon the repossession firm and the defendant, who authorized the repossession, predicated upon the use of unnecessary force and a breach of peace.

The decision to repossess the van in the early morning hours by use of a "quick snatch harness" and get away without the knowledge of the plaintiff was deliberate and intentional; and was guaranteed to generate fright or anger in the event it was discovered. The action was fraught with the peril of provoking a breach of peace of the most serious kind. The moment the repossession was discovered and the plaintiff attempted to resist the repossession, this terminated the repossession firm's right to continue because in so doing they were causing a breach of peace. Since they did not cease the repossession, they had no legal authority and a tort was committed in continuing over the protest of the plaintiff.

Where the work or service to be performed entails the possibility of the commission of some illegal, dangerous or tortuous act, both the lender and the independent contractor (repossession firm) play an integral part and are both causes of whatever harm ensues. Holding the lender liable for the work of an independent contractor is usually only applicable to work which of itself involves risk of harm to others. If a crime or some tort can be reasonably anticipated in its performance, it is no defense to say that the act causing the harm was committed by the repossession firm and not the firm that employed the repossession firm.[23]

DUTY TO REPOSSESS

The debtor offered to surrender the car and the bank said it would retrieve the vehicle itself with its own internal procedures and that the debtor was not to deliver the car to them. The bank never recovered the vehicle and the vehicle sat for thirteen months. The debtor moved away and the bank merged with another institution. The successor bank repossessed the car.

---

[23]*Rainwater v. Rx Medical Services Corp.*, 30 UCC Rep. Serv.2d. 983, 1995 WL 907888 (E.D. Cal. 1995).

A secured creditor is not required to repossess on default. The creditor may refuse surrender and sue for the debt. However, if the creditor chooses to repossess, the provisions of the statutes prevail and the creditor is required both before and after default to use reasonable care in the custody and preservation of the collateral. The determination of who has possession of the collateral is a question of fact and strict physical possession is not required. The secured party must merely have constructive possession of the collateral which includes the right to control the goods and the physical possession of another.

Whereas the UCC does not state time limits for a secured party to take possession of collateral or to proceed with the sale following the taking of possession, in this particular instance the creditor allowed the car to sit idly for over 13 months after default. The policy of the code is to protect the rights of both the debtor and the creditor while maximizing the recovery. The court held that the secured party cannot wait an inordinate period and then elect to repossess and thereafter sue for deficiency which partially may have been caused by the creditor. The court held that this was an unreasonable disposition of the collateral.[24]

---

[24]*Nationsbank v. Clegg*, 29 UCC Rep. Serv.2d 1366, 1996 WL 165513 (Tenn. Ct. App. 1996).

CHAPTER 8
APPENDIX I

SHIP MORTGAGE ACT

911. WORDS AND TERMS USED IN CHAPTER

When used in this chapter—

(1) The term "document" includes registry and enrollment and license;

(2) The term "documented" means registered or enrolled or licensed under the laws of the United States, whether permanently or temporarily;

(3) Except as provided in section 1011 of this title, the term "port of documentation" means the port at which the vessel is documented, in accordance with law;

(4) The term "vessel of the United States" means any vessel documented under the laws of the United States and such vessel shall be held to continue to be so documented until its documents are surrendered with the approval of the Secretary of Transportation; and

(5) The term "mortgagee," in the case of a mortgage involving a trust deed and a bond issue thereunder, means the trustee designated in such deed.

RECORDING OF SALES, CONVEYANCES, AND MORTGAGES OF VESSELS OF THE UNITED STATES

921. SALE, CONVEYANCE, OR MORTGAGE OF VESSEL OF UNITED STATES; RECORD

(a) No sale, conveyance, or mortgage which, at the time such sale, conveyance, or mortgage is made, includes a vessel of the United States, or any portion thereof, as the whole or any part of the property sold, conveyed, or mortgaged shall be valid, in respect to such vessel, against any person other than the grantor or mortgagor, his heir or devisee, and a person having actual notice thereof, until such bill of sale, conveyance, or mortgage is recorded in the office of the collector of customs of the port of documentation of such vessel, as provided in subsection (b) of this section.

(b) Such collector of customs shall record bills of sale, conveyances, and mortgages delivered to him, in the order of their reception, in books to be kept for that purpose and indexed to show—

(1) The name of the vessel;

(2) The names of the parties to the sale, conveyance, or mortgage;

(3) The time and date of reception of the instrument;

(4) The interest in the vessel so sold, conveyed, or mortgaged; and

(5) The amount and date of maturity of the mortgage.

922. PREFERRED MORTGAGES

(a) A valid mortgage which at the time it is made, includes the whole of any vessel of the United States (other than a towboat, barge, scow, lighter, car float, canal boat, or tank vessel, of less than twenty-five gross tons), shall, in addition, have, in respect to such vessel and as of the date of the compliance with all the provisions of this subsection, the preferred status given by the provisions of section 953 of this title, if—

(1) The mortgage is endorsed upon the vessel's documents in accordance with the provisions of this section;

(2) The mortgage is recorded as provided in section 921 of this title, together with the time and date when the mortgage is so endorsed;

(3) An affidavit is filed with the record of such mortgage to the effect that the mortgage is made in good faith and without any design to hinder, delay, or defraud any existing or future creditor of the mortgagor or any lienor of the mortgaged vessel;

(4) The mortgage does not stipulate that the mortgagee waives the preferred status thereof; and

(5) The mortgagee is a citizen of the United States and for the purposes of this section the Reconstruction Finance Corporation shall, in addition to those designated in sections 888 and 802 of this title, be deemed a citizen of the United States.

(b) Any mortgage which complies in respect to any vessel with the conditions enumerated in this section is hereafter in this chapter called a "preferred mortgage" as to such vessel.

(c) There shall be indorsed upon the documents of a vessel covered by a preferred mortgage—

(1) The names of the mortgagor and mortgagee;

(2) The time and date the indorsement is made;

(3) The amount and date of maturity of the mortgage; and

(4) Any amount required to be indorsed by the provisions of subsection (e) or (f) of this section.

(d) Such indorsement shall be made (1) by the collector of customs of the port of documentation of the mortgaged vessel, or (2) by the collector of customs of any port in which the vessel is found, if such collector is directed to make the indorsement by the collector of customs of the port of documentation; and no clearance shall be issued to the vessel until such indorsement is made. The collector of customs of the port of documentation shall give such direction by wire or letter at the request of the mortgagee and upon the tender of the cost of communication of such direction. Whenever any new document is issued for the vessel, such indorsement shall be transferred to and indorsed upon the new document by the collector of customs.

(e) A mortgage which includes property other than a vessel shall not be held a preferred mortgage unless the mortgage provides for the separate discharge of such property by the payment of a specified portion of the mortgage indebtedness. If a preferred mortgage so provides for the separate discharge, the amount of the portion of such payment shall be indorsed upon the documents of the vessel.

(f) If a preferred mortgage includes more than one vessel and provides for the separate discharge of each vessel by the payment of a portion of the mortgage indebtedness, the amount of such portion of such payment shall be indorsed upon the documents of the vessel. In case such mortgage does not provide for the separate discharge of a vessel and the vessel is to be sold upon the order of a district court of the United States in a suit in rem in admiralty, the court shall determine the portion of the mortgage indebtedness increased by 20 per centum (1) which, in the opinion of the court, the approximate value of the vessel bears to the approximately value of all the vessels covered by the mortgage, and (2) upon the payment of which the vessel shall be discharged from the mortgage.

923. CERTIFIED COPIES OF MORTGAGE; EXHIBITION

The collection of customs upon the recording of a preferred mortgage shall deliver two certified copies thereof to the mortgagor who shall place, and use due diligence to retain, one copy on board the mortgaged vessel and cause such copy and the documents of the vessel to be exhibited by the master to any person having business with the vessel, which may give rise to a maritime lien upon the vessel or to the sale, conveyance, or mortgage thereof. The master of the vessel shall, upon the request of any such person, exhibit to him the documents of the vessel and the copy of any preferred mortgage of the vessel placed on board thereof. The requirement of this section that a copy of a preferred mortgage be placed and retained on board the mortgaged vessel shall not apply in the case of mortgaged vessel which is not self-propelled (including but not limited to, barges, scows, lighters, and car floats).

924. PRIOR AND SUBSEQUENT MARITIME LIENS ON MORTGAGED VESSEL

The mortgagor (1) shall, upon request of the mortgagee, disclose in writing to him prior to the execution of any preferred mortgage, the existence of any maritime lien, prior mortgage, or other obligation or liability upon the vessel to be mortgaged, that is known to the mortgagor, and (2), without the consent of the mortgagee, shall not incur, after the execution of such mortgage and before the mortgagee has had a reasonable time in which to record the mortgage and have indorsements in respect thereto made upon the documents of the vessel, any contractual obligation creating a lien upon the vessel other than a lien for wages of stevedores when employed directly by the owner, operator, master, ship's husband, or agent of the vessel, for wages of the crew of the vessel, for general average, or for salvage, including contract salvage, in respect to the vessel.

925. RECORD OF NOTICE OF CLAIM OF LIEN ON MORTGAGED VESSEL; DISCHARGE OF LIEN

(a) The collector of customs of the port of documentation shall upon the request of any person, record notice of his claim of a lien upon a vessel covered by a preferred mortgage, together with the nature, date of creation, and amount of the lien, and the name and address of the person. Any person who has caused notice of his claim of lien to be so recorded shall, upon a discharge in whole or in part of the indebtedness, forthwith file with the collector of customs a certificate of such discharge. The collector of customs shall thereupon record the certificate.

(b) The mortgagor upon a discharge in whole or in part of the mortgage indebtedness shall forthwith file with the collector of customs for the port of documentation of the vessel, a certificate of such discharge. Such collector of customs shall thereupon record the certificate. In case of a vessel covered by a preferred mortgage, the collector of customs at the port of documentation shall (1) indorse upon the documents of the vessel, or direct the collector of customs at any port in which the vessel is found, to so indorse, the fact of such discharge, and (2) shall deny clearance to the vessel until such indorsement is made.

926. CONDITIONS PRECEDENT TO RECORD; INTEREST ON PREFERRED MORTGAGE

(a) No bill of sale, conveyance, or mortgage shall be recorded unless it states the interest of the grantor or mortgagor in the vessel, and the interest so sold, conveyed, or mortgaged.

(b) No bill of sale, conveyance, mortgage, notice of claim of lien, or certificate of discharge thereof, shall be recorded unless previously acknowledged before a notary public or other officer authorized by a law of the United States, or of a State, Territory, District, or possession thereof, to take acknowledgment of deeds.

(c) In case of a change in the port of documentation of a vessel of the United States, no bill of sale, conveyance, or mortgage shall be recorded at the new port of documentation unless there is furnished to the collector of customs of such port, together with the copy of the bill of sale, conveyance, or mortgage to be recorded, a certified copy of the record of the vessel at the former port of documentation furnished by the collector of such port. The collector of customs at the new port of documentation is authorized and directed to record such certified copy.

(d) A preferred mortgage may bear such rate of interest as is agreed by the parties thereto.

927. INSPECTION OF AND COPIES FROM RECORDS; FEES

Each collector of customs shall permit records made under the provisions of this chapter to be inspected during officer hours, under such reasonable regulations as the collector may establish. Upon the request of any person the collector of customs shall furnish him from the records of the collector's office (1) a certification setting forth the names of the owners of any vessel, the interest held by each owner, and the material facts as to any bill of sale or conveyance of, any mortgage covering, or any lien or other encumbrance upon, a specified vessel, (2) a certified copy of any bill of sale, conveyance, mortgage, notice of claim of lien, or certification of discharge in respect to such vessel, or (3) a certified copy as required by subsection (c) of section 926 of this title. The collector of customs shall collect a fee for any bill of sale, conveyance, or mortgage recorded, or any certificate or certified copy furnished by him, in the amount of 20 cents a folio with a minimum charge of $1, except that if a person requesting certification of more than ten copies of a mortgage which includes more than one vessel, furnishes such copies to the collector, the fee for certification of each copy in excess of ten shall be $1 per copy. All such fees shall be covered into the Treasury of the United States as miscellaneous receipts.

941. FAILURE OF MASTER TO EXHIBIT DOCUMENTS; UNLAWFUL ACTS BY MORTGAGOR; LIABILITY OF COLLECTOR OF CUSTOMS

(a) If the master of the vessel willfully fails to exhibit the documents of the vessel or the copy of any preferred mortgage thereof, as required under section 923 of this title, the Coast Guard may suspend or cancel the master's license.

(b) A mortgagor who, with intent to defraud, violates any provision of section 924 of this title, and if the mortgagor is a corporation or association, the president or other principal executive officer of the corporation or association, shall upon conviction thereof be held guilty of a misdemeanor and shall be fined not more than $1,000 or imprisoned not more than two years, or both. The mortgaged indebtedness shall thereupon become immediately due and payable at the election of the mortgagee.

(c) If any person enters into any contract secured by, or upon the credit of, a vessel of the United States covered by a preferred mortgage, and suffers pecuniary loss by reason of the failure of the collector of customs, or any officer, employee, or agent thereof, properly to perform any duty required of the collector under the provisions of this chapter, the collector of customs shall be liable to such person for damages in the amount of such loss. If any such person is caused any such loss by reason of the failure of the mortgagor, or master of the mortgaged vessel, or any officer, employee, or agent thereof, to comply with any provision of section 923 or 924 of this title, or to file an affidavit as required by subsection (a) of section 922 of this title, correct in each particular thereof, the mortgagor shall be liable to such person for damages in the amount of such loss. The district courts of the United States are given jurisdiction (but not to the exclusion of the courts of the several States, Territories, Districts, or possessions) of suits for the recovery of such damages, irrespective of the amount involved in the suit or the citizenship of the parties thereto. Such suit shall be begun by personal service upon the defendant within the limits of the district. Upon judgment for the plaintiff in any such suit, the court shall include in the judgment an additional amount for costs of the action and a reasonable counsel's fee, to be fixed by the court.

951. LIEN OF PREFERRED MORTGAGE; FORECLOSURE; JURISDICTION; PROCEDURE; FOREIGN SHIP MORTGAGES

A preferred mortgage shall constitute a lien upon the mortgaged vessel in the amount of the outstanding mortgage indebtedness secured by such vessel. Upon the default of any term or condition of the mortgage, such lien may be enforced by the mortgagee by suit in rem in admiralty. Original jurisdiction of all such suits is granted to the district courts of the United States exclusively. In addition to any notice by publication, actual notice of the commencement of any such suit shall be given by the libellant, in such manner as the court shall direct, to (1) the master, other ranking officer, or caretaker of the vessel, and (2) any person who has recorded a notice of claim of an undischarged lien upon the vessel, as provided in section 925 of this title, unless after search by the libellant satisfactory to the court, such mortgagor, aster, other ranking officer, caretaker, or claimant is not found within the United States. Failure to give notice to any such person, as required by this section, shall not constitute a jurisdictional defect; but the libellant shall be liable to such person for damages in the amount of his interest in the vessel terminated by the suit. Suit in personam for the recovery of such damages may be brought in accordance with the provisions of subsection (c) of section 941 of this title.

Foreign ship mortgages: As used in section 951 to 954 of this title, the term "preferred mortgage" shall include, in addition to a preferred mortgage made pursuant to the provisions of this chapter, any mortgage, hypothecation, or similar charge created as security upon any documented foreign vessel (other than a towboat, barge scow, lighter, car float, canal boat, or tank vessel, of less than two hundred gross tons) if such mortgage, hypothecation, or similar charge has been duly and validly executed in accordance with the laws of the foreign nation under the laws of which the vessel is documented and has been duly registered in accordance with such laws in a public register either at the port of registry of the vessel or at a central office; and the term "preferred mortgage lien" shall also include the lien of such mortgage, hypothecation, or similar charge: Provided, however, That such "preferred mortgage lien" in the case of a foreign vessel shall also be subordinate to maritime liens for repairs, supplies towage, use of dry dock or marine railway, or other necessaries, performed or supplied in the United States.

RECEIVER IN FORECLOSURE; POSSESSION BY MARSHAL

In any suit in rem in admiralty for the enforcement of the preferred mortgage lien, the court may appoint a receiver and, in its discretion, authorize the receiver to operate the mortgaged vessel. The marshal may be authorized and directed by the court to take possession of the mortgaged vessel notwithstanding the fact that the vessel is in the possession or under the control of any person claiming a possessory common-law lien.

953. PREFERRED MARITIME LIEN; PRIORITIES; OTHER LIENS

(a) When used hereinafter in this chapter, the term "preferred maritime lien" means (1) a lien arising prior in time to the recording and indorsement of a preferred mortgage in accordance with the provisions of this chapter; or (2) a lien for damages arising out of tort, for wages of a stevedore when employed directly by the owner, operator, master, ship's husband, or agent of the vessel, for wages of the crew of the vessel, for general average, and for salvage, including contract salvage.

(b) Upon the sale of any mortgaged vessel by order of a district court of the United States in any suit in rem in admiralty for the enforcement of a preferred mortgage lien thereon, all preexisting claims in the vessel, including any possessory common-law lien of which a lienor is deprived under the provisions of section 952 of this title, shall be held terminated and shall thereafter attach, in like amount and in accordance with their respective priorities, to the proceeds of the sale; except that the preferred mortgage lien shall have priority over all claims against the vessel, except (1) preferred maritime liens, and (2) expenses and fees allowed and costs taxed, by the court.

954. SUITS IN PERSONAM IN ADMIRALTY ON DEFAULT

(a) Upon the default of any term or condition of a preferred mortgage upon a vessel, the mortgagee may, in addition to all other remedies granted by this chapter, bring suit in personam in admiralty in a district court of the United States, against a mortgagor for the amount of the outstanding mortgage indebtedness secured by such vessel or any deficiency in the full payment thereof.

(b) This chapter shall be construed, in the case of a mortgage covering, in addition to vessels, realty or personalty other than vessels, or both, to authorize the enforcement by suit in rem in admiralty of the rights of the mortgagee in respect to such realty or personalty other than vessels.

961. SURRENDER OF DOCUMENTS; TERMINATION OF MORTGAGEE'S INTEREST; SALE OF MORTGAGED VESSEL

(a) The documents of a vessel of the United States covered by a preferred mortgage may not be surrendered (except in the case of the forfeiture of the vessel or its sale by the order of any court of the United States or any foreign country) without the approval of the Secretary of Transportation. The Secretary shall refuse such approval unless the mortgagee consents to such surrender.

(b) The interest of the mortgagee in a vessel of the United States covered by a mortgage, shall not be terminated by the forfeiture of the vessel for a violation of any law of the United States, unless the mortgagee authorized, consented, or conspired to effect the illegal act, failure, or omission which constituted such violation.

(c) Upon the sale of any vessel of the United States covered by a preferred mortgage, by order of a district court of the United States in any suit in rem in admiralty for the enforcement of a maritime lien other than a preferred maritime lien, the vessel shall be sold free from all preexisting claims thereon; but the court shall, upon the request of the mortgagee, the libellant, or any intervenor, require the purchaser at such sale to give and the mortgagor to accept a new mortgage of the vessel for the balance of the term of the original mortgage. The conditions of such new mortgage shall be the same, so far as practicable, as those of the original mortgage and shall be subject to the approval of the court. If such new mortgage is given, the mortgagee shall not be paid from the proceeds of the sale and the amount payable as the purchase price shall be held diminished in the amount of the new mortgage indebtedness.

(d) No rights under a mortgage of a vessel of the United States shall be assigned to any person not a citizen of the United States without the approval of the Secretary of Commerce. Any assignment in violation of any provision of this chapter shall be void.

(e) No bond, note, or other evidence of indebtedness which is secured by a mortgage of a vessel to a trustee may be issued, transferred, or assigned to a person not a citizen of the United States, without the approval of the Secretary of Commerce, unless the trustee or substitute trustee of such mortgage is approved by the Secretary of Commerce. The Secretary of Commerce shall grant his approval if such trustee or substitute trustee is a bank or trust company which (1) is organized as a corporation, and is doing business, under the laws of the United States or any State thereof, (2) is authorized under such laws to exercise corporate trust powers, (3) is a citizen of the United States, (4) is subject to supervision or examination by Federal or State authority, and (5) has a combined capital and surplus (as set forth in its most recent published report of condition) of at least $3,000,000. If such trustee or a substitute trustee at any time ceases to meet the foregoing qualifications, the Secretary of Commerce shall disapprove such trustee or substitute trustee, and after such disapproval the transfer or assignment of such bond, note, or other evidence of indebtedness to a person not a citizen of the United States, without the approval of the Secretary of Commerce, shall be unlawful. If a bond, note, or other evidence of indebtedness which is secured by a mortgage of a vessel to a trustee is issued, transferred, or assigned to a person not a citizen of the United States in violation of this paragraph, the issuance, transfer, or assignment shall be void.

(f) No vessel of the United States shall be sold by order of a district court of the United States in any suit in rem in admiralty to any person not a citizen of the United States.

971. Persons entitled to lien

Any person furnishing repairs, supplies, towage, use of dry dock or marine railway, or other necessaries, to any vessel, whether foreign or domestic, upon the order of the owner of such vessel, or of a person authorized by the owner, shall have a maritime lien on the vessel, which may be enforced by suit in rem, and it shall not be necessary to allege or prove that credit was given to the vessel.

972. Persons authorized to procure repairs, supplies, and necessaries

The following persons shall be presumed to have authority from the owner to procure repairs, supplies, towage, use of dry dock or marine railway, and other necessaries for the vessel: The managing owner, ship's husband, master, or any person to whom the management of the vessel at the port of supply is intrusted. No person tortuously or unlawfully in possession or charge of a vessel shall have authority to bind the vessel.

973. Notice to person furnishing, repairs, supplies, and necessaries

The officers and agents of a vessel specified in section 972 of this title shall be taken to include such officers and agents when appointed by a charterer, by an owner pro hac vice, or by an agreed purchaser in possession of the vessel.

974. Waiver of right to lien

Nothing in this chapter shall be construed to prevent the furnisher of repairs, supplies, towage, use of dry dock or marine railway, or other necessaries, or the mortgagee, from waiving his right to a lien, or in the case of a preferred mortgage lien, to the preferred status of such lien, at any time by agreement or otherwise; and this chapter shall not be construed to affect the rules of law existing on June 5, 1920, in regard to (1) the right to proceed against the vessel for advances, (2) laches in the enforcement of liens upon vessels, (3) the right to proceed in personam, (4) the rank of preferred maritime liens among themselves, or (5) priorities between maritime liens and mortgages, other than preferred mortgages, upon vessels of the United States.

975. STATE STATUTES SUPERSEDED

This chapter shall supersede the provisions of all State statutes conferring liens on vessel, insofar as such statutes purport to create rights of action to be enforced by suits in rem in admiralty against vessels for repairs, supplies, towage, use of dry dock or marine railway, and other necessaries.

MISCELLANEOUS PROVISIONS

981. EXISTING MORTGAGES NOT AFFECTED

This chapter shall not apply (1) to any existing mortgage, or (2) to any mortgage hereafter placed on a vessel under an existing mortgage, on June 5, 1920, so long as such existing mortgage remains undischarged.

982. BOOKS FOR COLLECTORS OF CUSTOMS

The Commissioner of Customs is authorized and directed to furnish collectors of customs with all necessary books and records, and with certifications of registry and of enrollment and license in such form as provides for the making of all indorsements, thereon required by this chapter.

983. RULES AND REGULATIONS BY COMMISSIONER OF CUSTOMS

The Commissioner of Customs is authorized to make such regulations in respect to the recording and indorsing of mortgages covering vessels of the United States, as he deems necessary to the efficient execution of the provisions of this chapter.

984. SHORT TITLE

This chapter may be cited as the "Ship Mortgage Act, 1920."

CHAPTER 8
APPENDIX II

EXCERPTS FROM OHIO REVISED CODE
CHAPTER 1317. RETAIL INSTALLMENT SALES REPOSSESSION; DEFENSES

1317.16 DISPOSITION OF COLLATERAL BY SECURED PARTY; NOTICE

(A) A secured party whose security interest is taken pursuant to section 1317.071 of the Revised Code may, after default, dispose of any or all of the collateral only as authorized by this section.

(B) Disposition of the collateral shall be by public sale only. Such sale may be as a unit or in parcels and the method, manner, time, place, and terms thereof shall be commercially reasonable. At least ten days prior to sale the secured party shall send notification of the time and place of such sale and of the minimum price for which such collateral will be sold, together with a statement that the debtor may be held liable for any deficiency resulting from such sale, by certified mail, return receipt requested, to the debtor at his last address known to the secured party, and to any persons known by the secured party to have an interest in the collateral. In addition, the secured party shall cause to be published, at least ten days prior to the sale, a notice of such sale listing the items to be sold, in a newspaper of general circulation in the county where the sale is to be held.

(C) Except as modified by this section, section 1309.47 of the Revised Code governs disposition of collateral by the secured party.

CHAPTER 9

Harassment, Intimidation and Invasion of Privacy

The invasion of privacy concept has breathed life into new legal remedies for the consumer. The impact of the word "abuse" on our society is not lost on the sophisticated debtor. If we add to this brew the fact that the courts award damages for emotional stress, a dormant area of the law has now gained the attention of credit and collection managers, for harassment, intimidation, abuse of process, and defamation practiced by the collectors may expose the creditor, collection agency, or law firm to liability.

The courts award damages for mental anguish, emotional suffering, and what may be called "general personal distress." If a physical injury is committed, the general personal distress is usually a result of the physical injury. Nevertheless, even where no personal injury is sustained, such as in cases of fraud or coercion, the court may award damages for emotional distress.

The word "harassment" is defined as "distress," "torment," "irritation," "depression," etc. The words used to define "intimidation" are "scare," "fright," "terror" and "fear." Harassment and intimidation together, usually presumed to be intentional by the very nature of the act, will produce a situation where the debtor may be substantially damaged.

No set definition can determine whether an act constitutes harassment or intimidation. The definitions of both terms as they apply to the collection process are more a question of degree than a question of a finite act. In many instances,

355

harassment and intimidation are self-fulfilling: if the debtor suffers emotional distress or some measurable damages, then the activity must "per se" constitute harassment or intimidation. The courts employ self-serving terms such as "unreasonable" and "abusive," which are subject to diverse interpretations by different courts. Numerous telephone calls to the debtor may be oppressive under one set of circumstances and be totally warranted under another. A telephone call at night may be reasonable in one case and unreasonable in another.

HARASSMENT UNDER THE DEBT COLLECTION PRACTICES ACT

The Fair Debt Collection Practices Act has devoted one section specifically to harassment and abuse. The Act states that "a debt collector may not engage in any conduct the natural consequence of which is to harass, oppress, or abuse any person in connection with the collection of the debt." This sentence lends credibility to the fact that if the debtor can prove abuse, the activity was intimidating and did constitute harassment. The added word "oppress" seems to signify that the government wants to protect the consumer from the overbearing debt collector. The result of the activity is important, not the nature of the activity. Many courts apply the Fair Debt Collection Practices Act as a guideline to determine whether a creditor has committed an abusive or unconscionable collection practice, and sometimes the courts interpret the guidelines liberally. The act delineates six examples of harassment and abuse, but specifically states that these are examples and not the only conduct constituting harassment and abuse:

1. The first example deals with the threat to use violence to harm the person or property of the debtor. A threat to injure the debtor if the debt is not paid is the classic example of harassment or abuse. A threat to damage property of the debtor may be intimidation.

    The example prohibits the injuring of the "reputation" of the debtor, and this concept has been incorporated in several places in the Fair Debt Collection Practices Act. The section of the Fair Debt Collection Practices Act dealing with acquisition of location information is specifically designed to prevent a collection agency from revealing that the debtor is delinquent during efforts to locate the debtor. The commission had difficulty balancing disclosure of the identity of the collection agency as opposed to the injury to the reputation of the debtor. The compromise allows the collection agency to reveal its identity only when asked, but not to reveal any details concerning the debt, or even the fact that a debt exists. In the section dealing with communications the collection agency may only communicate about the debt with the debtor or spouse. No communication is allowed with any other party.

The inclusion of the word "reputation" in subsection 1 develops the theory of invasion of privacy so that any activity which impacts on the reputation of the debtor, whether the communication is true or false, may expose the debt collector to liability. A disparaging statement about the credit reputation of a business or consumer may be actionable, even if true.

2. Abusive language, including religious slurs, profanity, calling the consumer a liar or deadbeat, or the use of racial or sexual language, is prohibited. The creditor or debt collector must recognize that today's technology allows for easy recording of telephone conversations. The courts have awarded damages based solely on what was said, and accepted that the debtor suffered anguish.

3. Publishing a list of consumers who refuse to pay their debts is prohibited unless the creditor complies with the Fair Credit Reporting Act. Reporting delinquents to a credit reporting agency is allowed.

4. Advertising the debt to embarrass the debtor is expressly prohibited under this section. Publicizing the debt in a newspaper, exchanging lists with other members of the industry, or distributing a list of delinquent debtors are the activities targeted.

5. Using the telephone to abuse a debtor is expressly prohibited. Repeated personal contact with the consumer is prohibited. While the commission does not state how many calls constitute harassment, the American Collectors Association has taken the position that in commercial matters two calls a week to the debtor is appropriate. Posing a series of questions or comments to the consumer without allowing the consumer a chance to reply may be abusive. Whether the series of questions constitutes harassment is a function of how harshly the questions are propounded, the nature of the questions, the tone and attitude of the telephone collector, and other circumstances.

6. The debt collector must identify himself or herself meaningfully. The Act does permit the use of aliases, providing the employer is able to identify which collector made the telephone call. Of course, using a false business name, as distinguished from a false "employee" name, in a telephone call is definitely a violation of the Act. Abusive and threatening calls, numerous telephone calls, or calls late at night or at inconvenient times may be violations. An unreasonable number of letters may be harassment and abuse. What the Act doesn't answer is to what degree and to what extent telephone calls and letters become excessive or unreasonable.

Threatening to take an action that cannot be taken or will not be taken is an abusive practice. Threatening to garnishee a salary when a judgment hasn't been obtained or threatening to repossess a car when no valid security agreement exists are other examples of abuse. The definition of excessive or unreasonable as applied by the courts is supposedly a function of the perception of the average ordinary consumer; but most courts tend to protect the "least sophisticated consumer," which means a lower threshold of "excessive" or "unreasonable."

WILLFUL ACT

The courts sometimes distinguish between the action being intentional and willful, as opposed to being negligent. If the act is negligent, the court will not afford relief to the consumer. A debt collector is not liable if there is a preponderance of evidence that the violation was not intentional and resulted solely from a bona-fide error, and the debt collector maintained procedures reasonably adopted to avoid such error. Negligence by itself may be a good defense to a harassment and abuse charge, providing proper procedures and a compliance manual are in place and the incident was solely isolated. Nevertheless, the courts may state that if the negligence is so reckless that a reasonable person should have anticipated the result, the negligent action becomes a willful and intentional act. At what point the negligent act becomes an intentional act is difficult to identify. If the court can find that the offender knew or, with reasonable care, should have known that the actions harass, oppress, and abuse a debtor, a strong likelihood exists that the court will find that harassment existed.

CONTACT WITH THIRD PARTY

The Fair Debt Collection Practices Act prohibits contact with third parties concerning the debt of a consumer (except for location information). This restriction covers contact with the mother or children of the consumer, any brother, sister or close relatives, and also includes contact with an employer, neighbor, or third party. Contacting the spouse is expressly permitted.

Contacting neighbors in person, by telephone, or by letter and advising them that the consumer is unable to pay exposes a debt collector or a creditor to liability. Contacting a neighbor for the sole purpose of leaving a message for the debtor where the creditor has full knowledge of the telephone number of the consumer may constitute harassment since the creditor should have contacted the consumer in the first place. Any statement of a disparaging or derogatory nature to a third party constitutes harassment and advising any third party that the consumer has no money, is dishonest, or has a criminal record, is also harassment.

Probably the most dangerous of all contacts is with the employer of the debtor. Contacting the debtor's employer for the purpose of obtaining assistance from the employer in collecting the debt is "per se" a violation of the Fair Debt Collection Practices Act. Any type of contact with the employer is dangerous, for the debtor is now in a position to blame the creditor for any failure encountered in progress or promotion on the job.

Many collection books recommend that creditors or debt collectors contact the commanding officer of military personnel who are in debt to urge the soldier to pay the outstanding debt. The commanding officer is under no obligation and has no legal authority to require a member of the armed services to pay a debt. The question of contacting a third party may be a violation of the Fair Debt Collection Practices Act prohibiting such communication as to collection agencies and attorneys. Certainly advising the commanding officer that the debtor is delinquent in the payment of the debt may affect a decision of the commanding officer in granting promotions. While many creditors and debt collectors still engage in this practice, we do not recommend its use.[1] Creditors may continue this procedure on the theory they are not subject to the Act, but the danger is self-evident.

INVASION OF PRIVACY

The founding fathers made no provision for "privacy" under the Constitution. The right to privacy began with an article published in 1890 in the Harvard Law Review by Samuel D. Warren and Louis D. Brandeis (who later became a Supreme Court Justice) in which they set forth that a person has a right to be left alone and to conduct activities without outside interference by other persons unless the outside interference is necessary in the interest of public welfare.[2] A broad definition of the invasion of privacy is the unreasonable intrusion into one's personal life either by exploiting the person's name and background or using one's personal affairs for the purpose of humiliation, coercion, or shame. If the ultimate purpose is to cause the debtor to pay the debt, the creditor will find it difficult to argue a reasonable intrusion. In fact, today's society does not provide aid and assistance to the debt collector.

Truth is not a defense in an action for the invasion of privacy. Whereas it may be a defense in defamation or libel, truthful statements about the personal life may be actionable if the said truthful statements are improperly used. While the debtor may be a "deadbeat" and owe many creditors, using the term to a neighbor may be an invasion of privacy. Truthful statements used purely for the purpose of humiliating, coercing, or shaming a party may support a suit for invasion of privacy. If the information disseminated is false, then there may be grounds for a suit for libel and slander in addition to one for invasion of privacy.

RECKLESS NEGLIGENCE

Malice is not an ingredient that must be established to prove an invasion of privacy. At the same time, negligence is not a defense to an invasion of privacy. Where a defendant alleges the defense of negligence, the defendant may be faced

---

[1]*Holloway v. Davis*, 208 So. 2d. 794 44 Al. A. 346 (1967), *La Salle Extension University v. Fogerty*, 253 N.W. 424 (1934) and *Keating v. Conviser*, 246 N.Y. 632 (1922).

[2]Harvard Law Review 193 (1890).

with the same problems that appear in a harassment and abuse case. If the negligence is so reckless and wanton that the creditor should have anticipated the results, or if the creditor knew or should have known that the activity would constitute an invasion of privacy, the courts will state that the reckless negligent act was tantamount to an intentional and willful act.[3]

ABUSE OF PROCESS

Abuse of Process consists of a wrongful initiation of a lawsuit, whether a criminal suit or a civil suit. The main ingredient of an abuse of process lawsuit is that an ulterior purpose is alleged other than the purpose set forth in the lawsuit. A willful and intentional act is an essential ingredient to support the suit. In the alternative a negligent, reckless, or wanton act may be considered willful where the defendant knew or should have anticipated the results of the action. The aggrieved party must have suffered mental anguish or mental distress.

MALICIOUS PROSECUTION

Malicious prosecution requires a suit to be started in either a civil or criminal court which is terminated in favor of the aggrieved party. The suit may be willful, intentional, or malicious. Reckless negligence is also equal to an intentional suit, but the aggrieved party must suffer mental distress or mental anguish or actual damages.

A consumer and consumer attorney was sued for malicious prosecution. In this particular action, the attorney and the consumer abandoned the action for a violation of the FDCPA against an attorney after it was started. The attorney that was being sued then commenced a suit for malicious prosecution against the consumer and her attorney. The case was dismissed in the lower court on the grounds that the FDCPA basically preempted a malicious prosecution suit under state law. The consumer and her attorney were relying on the preemption clauses contained in the FDCPA. The appellate court pointed out that this preemption clause only applies if the state court laws are less restrictive than the federal laws. The court then ruled:

> "We cannot conclude that Congress intended to pre-empt the state law claim seeking compensation for malicious prosecution under the FDCPA."

The court also went on to address the attorney for the consumer and stated:

---

[3]*Mason v. Williams Discount Center, Inc.*, 639 S.W.2d. 836 (1982). Posting a list of debtors' names in view of customers stating that the plaintiff was a bad credit risk. *Santiesteban v. Goodyear Tire and Rubber Co.*, 306 F.2d.9 (1962)—Repossessing a set of tires in view of third parties.

"It is inappropriate to bring an action for a technical violation of the act for the purpose of obtaining the mandatory award of attorney's fees as provided under the act."

The case illustrates that the defendants in FDCPA claims are becoming more aggressive in prosecuting the growing number of attorneys who bring these suits for technical violations. Judges often refer to claims as purely "technical violations" and are becoming less and less favorable to the consumer when the consumer has suffered no damages. If malicious prosecution suits become more prevalent, this alone may become a deterrent to consumer attorneys so that future suits will be brought only for violations that cause injury and harm to the consumer.[4]

In another case Avco purchased retail installment contracts, and attempted to collect the balance due on the account. The debtor told Avco that the signature had been forged. The credit grantor reviewed the information and informed the debtor that the forgery claim was not sufficient to remove his name from the account. Avco subsequently sued the defendant to collect the amount due on the contract. The trial court found in favor of the defendant. Thereafter, the defendant sued Avco for malicious prosecution and alleged that Avco should have known that the debtor had not signed the account documents. Even with that knowledge, the defendant alleged that Avco continued the action against the defendant.

The court stated that the defendant was required to present substantial evidence that Avco instituted a judicial proceeding without probable cause and with malice. The mere fact that the trial ended in his favor and that the debtor suffered some damages was insufficient.

Probable cause in the criminal context is to find "a reasonable ground for suspicion, supported by circumstances sufficiently strong in themselves to warrant a cautious man to believe that the person accused is guilty of the offense charge." In a civil proceeding all that is necessary for probable cause is that the claimant reasonably believe that there is a chance that the claim may be held valid upon adjudication. The court granted summary judgment to Avco.

While this case was favorable to the credit grantor, circumstances could exist which would support a suit for malicious prosecution. If the debtor voluntarily furnished an affidavit of forgery to the creditor, the creditor should seek to obtain the specimen signature and engage in a diligent effort to determine whether the signatures are similar. Wives do sign signatures of husbands and husbands do sign signatures of wives.

Any suit started after a claim of forgery (even without an affidavit of forgery by the debtor) without a handwriting expert's opinion or an in-depth investigation places the creditor at risk in the event the creditor loses the suit.[5]

---

[4]*Ziobron v. Crawford*, 667 N.E.2d (Ind. Ct. App. 1996).

[5]*Leak v. Avco Financial Services*, 646 So.2d 642 (Ala. 1994).

DISTINCTION BETWEEN ABUSE OF PROCESS AND MALICIOUS PROSECUTION

Actions based on abuse of process and malicious prosecution are often joined in the same suit. The distinction between them is shadowy. The major area of concern is using a criminal process in an effort to collect a civil debt. This will often support an action for an abuse of process since an ulterior motive existed, especially if the criminal proceeding is discontinued immediately upon payment of the debt. Whether the debt is collected is not important. The key ingredient is that the criminal process is used for an ulterior purpose. A prosecution on a bad check where the creditor does not appear to testify is strong evidence that the purpose of the prosecution was to collect the debt, not to press criminal charges.

Attachment is available in various states prior to suit. If the attachment is obtained and the suit is continued, no problem exists. If the purpose of the attachment is to coerce the debtor to continue to make payments, to furnish security for the debt, or to guarantee the liability of a corporate debt, the creditor is exposed to an abuse of process suit if the attachment is released after the creditor's goal is achieved.

Another area of danger is starting suit against a party with no liability. An example is where a suit is instituted against a corporation and the directors of the corporation. The debt is obviously a corporate debt, and the directors are not liable. The directors are joined as co-conspirators for the purpose of intimidating and coercing the Board of Directors to vote to settle the claim which will terminate the personal suit against the directors. This type of suit is a prime example of an ulterior purpose.

A malicious prosecution requires more elements than an abuse of process suit. The process of a malicious prosecution suit is where a creditor brings action to collect a debt, but no real foundation exists for the suit. Negligence is not available as a defense against a malicious prosecution suit. A suit to collect a debt already discharged in bankruptcy is malicious prosecution, just as is a suit against a person who has already paid the debt. Sometimes a suit is instituted carelessly against a party with the same name as the true debtor, who never executed a note or had any business relationship at all with the creditor. This type of suit still may constitute malicious prosecution even though the creditor was only negligent. The question is whether the negligence was so reckless as to amount to a willful act.

The classic example of malicious prosecution is issuing a criminal process without justifiable reasons for the sole purpose of coercing a debtor into paying a debt. The issuance of a check returned unpaid due to uncollected or insufficient funds may support a criminal process under some of the state laws. If the criminal process is withdrawn immediately upon payment of the debt, the foundation of a suit for malicious prosecution may be laid.[6]

---

[6]*Zablonsky v. Perkins*, 187 A.2d 314, 230 Md. 365 (1962)—Criminal process issued but money not received. *Gore v. Gorman's Incorporated*, 143 F.Supp. 9 (1956)—Suit to collect a debt discharged in bankruptcy.

DEFAMATION

Defamation is a false statement about a person's reputation and is of two types. Slander is oral defamation with publication to some third party (a third party hears the slanderous statement). Libel is written or printed defamation and includes publication in all media of a permanent nature such as drawings, printings, newspapers, magazines, advertisements, etc. Truth is a defense to defamation.

Certain types of defamations are treated as libel or slander "per se" which means the words themselves are so defamatory that the plaintiff does not have to suffer damages to recover. If a defamation is not "per se," the plaintiff must prove damages. A letter to a third party characterizing one as the "worse kind of crook" is libel "per se." Falsely charging someone in business with being insolvent or bankrupt may be libel "per se" since the credit of a person in business is essential to its operation.

STANDARDS

Pressured by Congress the individual reference services group which includes TransUnion, Equifax, Lexis-Nexis and some other credit reporting agencies have set certain privacy standards in response to the concern over privacy. By 1999, its members will not sell social security numbers, mother's maiden names, birthdates, credit histories, unlisted phone numbers, or information on people's children to the public ... only to "qualified subscribers." Unfortunately, there is no definition of what a qualified subscriber is and there also appears to be no penalties for non-compliance. Whether the government will accept this industry standard as satisfactory is questionable in view of the privacy concerns that continually appear in the newspapers and media.

CHAPTER 9
APPENDIX I

ROBERT F. MASON, ET UX., V. WILLIAMS DISCOUNT CENTER, INC., 639 S.W. 2d836 (1982)

1) That defendant is, and was at all times herein mentioned, a duly organized and existing corporation authorized to do business in Missouri.

2) That said defendant, at all times herein mentioned, operated a retail store in Hermann, Missouri.

3) That plaintiff, Robert F. Mason, also used the name Colonel R.F. Mason.

4) That for a period of time during the year 1980 the defendant in its store, in an area in plain view of its customers, placed a list of names, among which were the name Col. and Linda Mason, under the title "no checks" in large print.

5) That said list was of such size and so placed that it was in the direct view of customers passing through the checkout lane of the store and the lettering was of such size as to be easily readable by such persons.

6) That from the size of the lettering and the placement of the aforesaid list the defendant published to its customers passing through its checkout lane that defendant believed plaintiffs were a bad risk for check cashing purposes and were likely to dishonor payment of any such check.

7) That the publication of the aforesaid list caused plaintiff, Robert F. Mason, mental and physical suffering and shame and humiliation all to his damage in the sum of Seven Thousand Five Hundred Dollars ($7,500.00) and the publication of such list was done willfully, wantonly and maliciously so that said plaintiff is entitled to punitive damages in the sum of Fifty Thousand Dollars ($50,000.00).

WHEREFORE, plaintiff Robert F. Mason prays for judgment against defendant for the sum of Seven Thousand Five Hundred Dollars ($7,500.00) actual damages and the sum of Fifty Thousand Dollars ($50,000.00) as punitive damages and for the costs of this action.

Count II of the petition alleged essentially the same facts as they related to appellant Linda Mason, appellant Robert F. Mason's wife.

The trial court granted respondent's motion to dismiss the petition for failure to state a claim upon which relief could be granted.

[5] Appellants do not mention invasion of privacy in their petition, but they assert in their brief that their petition, as drafted, sufficiently states a cause of action for inva-

sion of privacy, specifically publication of a private matter. This is a recognized action in Missouri. *Biederman's of Springfield Inc. v. Wright*, 322 S.W.2d 892, 895[1] (Mo. 1959); *McNally v. Pulitzer Publishing Co.*, 532 F.2d 69, 78[15-21] (8th Cir. 1976), *cert. denied* 429 U.S. 855, 97 S.Ct. 150, 50 L.Ed.2d 131 (1976).

[6]   The elements of an action for publication of a private matter are (1) publication, (2) absent any waiver or privilege, (3) of private matters in which the public has no legitimate concern, (4) so as to bring shame or humiliation to a person of ordinary sensibilities. *McNally v. Pulitzer Publishing Co., supra*; Restatement 2d of Torts 652D (1977).

[7]   Appellant sufficiently alleged publication. The sign was posted in plain view of all the customers of the store with the effect of publicizing the matter to those customers. This meets the publication standard of *Biederman's of Springfield, Inc. v. Wright, supra*.

Waiver and privilege generally must be pleaded as affirmative defenses. Rule 55.-08; *Ehrle v. Bank Building & Equipment Corporation of America*, 530 S.W.2d 482, 491[8] (Mo.App. 1975). Appellants' petition therefore was not required to include the element of no waiver or privilege in order to state a claim.

[8]   Appellants also sufficiently pleaded that the publication caused shame and humiliation to them. Respondent claims appellants pleaded only a legal conclusion and no facts on this element. This court disagrees. Appellants pleaded that respondent put their names on a list headed "no checks"; that respondent intended to communicate to the community that respondent believed that appellants wrote bad checks; and that appellants suffered shame and humiliation from this publication. These pleadings are statements of ultimate face and not legal conclusions.

The first real issue is whether appellants adequately pleaded that respondent made a statement about a private matter. The pleading alleges that respondent intended the statement "no checks" to communicate a belief of respondent. Respondent argues that the published statement must be of a private fact and the petition only alleges a statement of opinion.

Appellants do not allege respondent put up a sign that simply said, "I believe Colonel and Mrs. Mason are dishonest." This kind of general statement would not be an invasion of privacy. Such a sign does not publicize a specific detail of appellants' lives.

Rather, appellants allege respondent's "no checks" sign made a statement about the quality of appellant's checks. Regardless of whether appellants pleaded that the "no checks" sign was a statement of fact or respondent's opinion, the petition alleged respondent through its sign made a public derogatory statement about a detail of appellants' lives. The sign interfered with appellants' right to be let alone. In light of the liberal interpretation to be given pleadings, appellants' petition sufficiently alleges publication about a private detail of appellants' lives.

CHAPTER 9
APPENDIX II

EXCERPTS FROM MITCHELL V. SURETY ACCEPTANCE CORPORATION 838 F.SUPP. 497 (1993)

[7][8] In Colorado, liability for the tort of intentional infliction of emotional distress may be found only where "the conduct has been so outrageous in character, and so extreme in degree as to go beyond all possible bounds of decency, and to be regarded as atrocious, and utterly intolerable in a civilized community." *Grandchamp v. United Air Lines, Inc.,* 854 F.2d 381, 383 (10th Cir. 1988) (quoting *Rugg v. McCarty,* 173 Colo. 170, 476 P.2d 753, 756 (1970)). The "defendant's conduct must be more than unreasonable, unkind or unfair; it must truly offend community notions of acceptable conduct." Grandchamp, 854 F.2d at 383. While the jury determines the ultimate question whether conduct is outrageous, the court must decide whether reasonable persons could differ on the conduct being outrageous. *Rugg v. McCarty,* 173 Colo. 170, 476 P.2d 753, 754 (1970).

[9] In Rugg, actions to collect a debt on a one-year membership to a health studio was found to state a claim for outrageous conduct. There, plaintiff sought to rescind her contract with the health studio when she was injured during her first exercise class, was forced to quit her employment and was hospitalized. The conduct found by the court to be sufficient to state a claim included repeated harassment with numerous telephone calls and letters demanding payment, notwithstanding the plaintiff's explanation of her distressed condition and her promise to pay as soon as possible; and, sending a letter to plaintiff's employer stating she was not living up to her obligations in a satisfactory manner and inquiring concerning how many garnishments would be tolerated when the defendant did not have a judgment against the plaintiff. Rugg, 476 P.2d at 754.

As I find nothing outrageous in the letter sent to plaintiff on June 14, 1991, her claim for outrageous conduct must rest, if at all, on the phone call initiated by plaintiff to Surety on June 27, 1991. In response to interrogatories, the plaintiff sets forth the nature of this phone conversation:

I have documentation that I spoke to Surety representatives personally in 1991. First, I received a letter of June 14, 1991 from Surety Acceptance Corporation addressed to "Sherrie L. McWilliams, a.k.a. Sherri L. Mitchell" (Exhibit 9). On June 27, 1991, I called Tim West, the person who signed the letter. I told Mr. West that I was not "Sherrie L. McWilliams," I told him that she had been using my social security number, that I had been diagnosed with MS, that the stress caused by these credit problems was aggravating my condition, that the incorrect information on my report had cost me the chance to buy a house and a job in which I had returned to school and that the continued misidentification was making me feel like my life was no longer worth living.

He did not believe a word I said. He only implied that I was lying by laughing and telling me that "according to our source, you are responsible to pay this debt. So you might as well pay it!" He obviously thought I had made up the entire story. I told him of my letters to TRW and that TRW has said they would forward the letters I had sent. I pleaded with him to read the letters; he advised me to send a copy of my driver's license as proof that I had a different social security number than McWilliams'; I repeated that she had been using my social security number; thus, the number they had for her was in fact mine. He just repeated his previous comment about his source and to pay the debt, because that would be the only way that you could get the collection account off your report. (I found out later, according to their read-out of McWilliams' account, that TRW was the "source.")

I asked to speak with a supervisor, he laughed and said, "O.K., but she'll just tell you the same thing." Then, Mary Steven got on the phone. She did also tell me the same thing. Both obviously did not believe me and were unconcerned about my physical and mental state. Thus, they did not take the time to check out my story nor would they taken the numbers of Officer Mark Angelo and Kris Shoemaker, who had investigated this incident and could verify my story.

(Plaintiff's Response to Surety's Interrogatories, pp.8-9).

In conclude that an issue of fact exists as to whether reasonable jurors could find Surety's conduct atrocious or utterly intolerable in a civilized community. Summary judgment will be denied on plaintiff's claim for intentional infliction of emotional distress.

CHAPTER 10

Secured Lending: Mortgages and Security Interests

A lending institution may use a wide variety of methods to secure a loan, including real estate mortgages, accounts receivable financing, advances on inventory, warehousing receipts, or security agreements covering vehicles, boats, machinery, equipment, etc. The use of these devices may be supervised by an attorney or, in some instances, by the lending officer completing form agreements in accordance with the instruction of the attorneys. The legal proceedings to enforce the mortgage or the security agreement are left entirely to the attorney. Rarely does a credit and collection manager become involved in this process.

Nevertheless, the credit and collection manager is deeply involved in negotiating with the debtor when the debtor is in default, and is continually communicating with the attorney in the enforcement process of the mortgage and the security agreement. In this chapter, the basic rights and obligations under a mortgage and security agreement will be explained in order to assist a credit and collection manager in communicating with counsel regarding the enforcement of mortgages and security agreements.

New York State Law will be primarily utilized in this chapter since that is where we practice. Nevertheless, the principles enunciated are substantially similar in most other states. Consultation with your attorney and the use of the services of an attorney are required for the legal enforcement of these agreements.

MORTGAGES

In most states a mortgage is a lien on real estate, land and/or building, furnished by one party to another party to be used as security for the repayment of money. The mortgagee, (the lending institution) holds a mortgage lien on the property, but does not own the property nor does the mortgagee have any right to immediate possession of the property until such time as the mortgage is foreclosed. In some states, the borrower transfers the property in trust to the lender, and the instrument is designated a *deed of trust*. In title states, a mortgage is executed in favor of the lending party, creating a lien on the property while the title remains with the mortgagor. The differences between a "deed of trust" and a "mortgage" are not significant. For our purposes we will consider only the mortgage.

A mortgage is treated as a conveyance of property and, as such, it must meet the criteria set forth in the Statute of Frauds (the state laws requiring certain transactions to be in writing to be enforceable). A mortgage must be in writing and must be signed by the mortgagor or his/her agent, acting pursuant to written authority. A mortgage recites the amount of the indebtedness for which the property is being offered as security, a detailed description of the property, usually by a "metes and bounds" description (describing the property by terminal points, angles, distances, and compass directions), and the terms and conditions under which the parties are to operate under the terms of the mortgage. The mortgage also recites the obligation of the mortgagor (debtor) to pay the mortgage, the taxes and other charges against the property, as well as to maintain the property, and its operation. In addition, the mortgage recites the rights of the mortgagee (lending institution), including the right to act in the event of a default, the right to take possession of the property upon default, the right to make an application to the court for the appointment of a receiver (one who preserves the property during a foreclosure proceeding), and the right to pay taxes and insurance for the benefit of the mortgagor and to operate the property in the event of a foreclosure.

A "mortgage note" is a separate instrument and is essential to enforce the mortgage. The note recites the indebtedness, the terms of payment, the interest rate, the place of payment, and the terms and conditions under which the note must be paid. If the terms of the note and mortgage conflict, the terms of the note control. A mortgage without a note may be unenforceable.

RECORDING

Mortgages are recorded immediately after execution in the office of the county clerk, the register, the recorder of deeds, or a similar county office where the property is located. The recording of the mortgage acts as constructive notice to the entire world that the owner has a lien on the property. The owner of the property may execute a number of mortgages whose priority is established by chronological date when the mortgage is recorded in the county clerk's office. The date of the recording establishes priority, with the mortgage first recorded having priority over a mortgage or lien recorded after that date. A mortgage recorded on the first of January, 1994 would be subordinate to a mortgage recorded on the first of January, 1993. Thus, the importance of filing the mortgage instrument immediately is paramount. At the time of the mortgage closing, the mortgage is immediately delivered to a representative of the title company or attorney who, either on the same day or the next day, will deliver it to the proper office for recording.

TITLE SEARCH

After the mortgage commitment is delivered, but before the mortgage documents are executed, a title search is conducted, either by a title company or by an attorney, depending upon the state. A title search is a summary of the "chain of title" (transfer of property from one person to another), as well as liens, taxes, mortgages, and covenants (agreements restricting or affecting use) that affect the property, listed in chronological order. The purpose of the title search is to determine that the seller has good title to sell, the number of liens against the property, the number of claims against the property, and whether the property is encumbered by any restrictions in prior deeds. The title search will reveal prior mortgages that the debtor has executed. The date of the mortgage and the original amount of the mortgage will be revealed, but the present balance due will not be disclosed by a title search; for this information contacting the mortgagee (usually the bank) is necessary.

The title search reveals whether the debtor has paid the taxes and whether any are unpaid and open. Unpaid taxes become liens against the property after a certain period of time, depending upon the state or county. Once this happens, the lien becomes the equivalent of a mortgage in the same manner as the mortgage becomes a lien against the property.

In addition to determining the number of claims against the property, the lender also wants to find out whether the owner has a clear title to the property as described in the mortgage. Prior deeds may have been recorded which set forth restrictive covenants, restrictions, or easements on the property. An easement is a right of an adjourning property owner to pass over the property of the debtor under certain terms and conditions, or to have a right of way over the property either by use of a road or pathway or even the use of the property itself. Covenants which pass with the land may affect the use of the land, the type of buildings which may be built on the land, or other restrictions as to use of the land, which may have been set forth by the prior owner of the property (such as limiting housing to one-family homes, restrictions on height of building, or use as a slaughterhouse). The lender will have to make a decision on whether the particular covenant or easement affects the value of the property sufficiently to refuse to extend credit. Toxic waste and environmental considerations may also be indirectly revealed by title searches when, for example, a prior owner was a gas station or chemical plant.

ASSIGNMENT OF MORTGAGE

A mortgage may be transferred from one lending institution to another by use of an assignment: an agreement between two parties transferring the ownership of a mortgage from one mortgagee to a new mortgagee. The assignment of mortgage identifies the mortgage and the property covered under the mortgage as well as the name and address of the mortgagor and enough information to leave no doubt as to which mortgage is being assigned. The assignment is recorded in the same manner as a mortgage by filing the assignment in the county where the property is located.

The purchaser of a mortgage by assignment takes the assignment subject to any existing defenses or claims in favor of the mortgagor. In some instances, the mortgagor will execute an "estoppel certificate" which asserts that the mortgagor has no defense or offsets to the mortgage.

JUDGMENT

A judgment creditor who has entered a judgment against the mortgagor and docketed (filed) the judgment with the county clerk where the property is located (see Chapter 1) has the same rights as a mortgagee and will have priority over any subsequent mortgages, whether or not they are recorded. The docketing of the judgment in the county clerk's office where the debtor resides is important, but the creditor may not know where property owned by the debtor is located. Sometimes the debtor cannot be located, and the creditor will docket the judgment with the county clerks of several surrounding counties. When the debtor attempts to sell a residence, the docketed judgment appears in the title search conducted by the buyer. Any purchaser of the property will usually require that the judgment be satisfied. If the judgment is not satisfied, it remains a lien on the property. Consult with counsel.

SALE BY MORTGAGOR

When a mortgagor sells the property to a new owner, the new owner must purchase the property subject to the terms of the mortgage. The original owner of the property remains liable on the mortgage. The new owner will usually agree to assume the payment of the mortgage, and in that instance the new owner becomes the primary obligor and the original owner of the property is liable secondarily.

When interest rates were high, banks provided that any transfer of property matured the mortgage so that the new owner would have to pay the mortgage and obtain a new mortgage at a higher interest rate (or modify the existing mortgage at a higher interest rate). In today's low interest market, the acceleration clause, known as "due on sale," is less frequently used.

MORTGAGOR'S OBLIGATIONS

The mortgagor has an obligation not to impair the value of the property during the term of the mortgage and, in general, to maintain the property. However, in many cases the mortgagor does not maintain and repair the property during foreclosure proceedings. Often, by the time the foreclosure is completed, the amount of money necessary to repair the home or building may be substantial.

USURY

Usury is a defense available to the mortgagor in a foreclosure action. Usury is the charging of interest in excess of that allowed by law. The penalties for usury will vary from the loss of the interest to the loss of the principal in some states. In a few states, usury is a criminal offense.

FUTURE ADVANCES

A mortgage may be used to secure future advances of money. Such a mortgage is valid and may be enforced according to its terms. A mortgage also may be used to secure the debts of another party or to secure a guarantee of another party.

EQUITABLE MORTGAGE

If a security transaction concerning real property does not satisfy the formal requirement of a mortgage (such as not being in writing or not being a proper mortgage or deed in trust) "an equitable mortgage" may be created. An equitable mortgage may or may not have rights with regard to the property, depending upon the circumstances and conditions prevailing at the time it was created, and depending upon the intent of the parties. If the written instrument lacks the essential features of a mortgage, the courts may find that an equitable mortgage exists when the circumstances and other transactions reflect the intent of the parties to create a mortgage.

REAL ESTATE SETTLEMENT PROCEDURES ACT

The Real Estate Settlement Procedures Act, commonly referred to as RESPA, became effective June 20, 1975 to provide consumers with more information as to the settlement costs when purchasing or transferring a residence as a result of a loan from a bank and, at the same time, to prohibit excessive settlement charges. Regulation X defined the settlement process of a transfer of a residential home from one consumer to another.

The law was amended the same year it took effect (1975), in response to an enormous number of complaints about the vague and inflexible provisions causing significant delays in the settlement procedure. Regulation X was modified substantially as to the restrictions on the closing process, but the provisions affecting abusive settlement charges were not altered. The amendment took effect January 2, 1976.

RESPA covers the normal real estate transaction involving a federal mortgage loan. The federal mortgage loan covers almost all mortgage loans since not only are loans from federal agencies covered but any loan from a bank which is insured by the Federal Deposit Insurance Corporation (FDIC) or the Federal Savings and Loan Insurance Corporation.[1] The loan must be secured by a first lien on the residence, and must be used to finance the purchase or transfer of the residence.[2] A home improvement loan, construction loan, permanent loan, or refinancing made after the acquisition of the property is not covered by the Act.[3]

Not later than three days after the lender receives an application for credit from a consumer, the lender must furnish to the consumer a Special Information Booklet[4] prepared by the Housing and Urban Development Corporation (HUD). It sets forth the consumer's rights and obligations when the consumer is obtaining a mortgage loan from a bank.

The lending bank at this point must provide a "good faith estimate" of the charges that will be incurred by the consumer, based on the bank's past experience, who the providers of the services are if the bank requires these providers (such as law firms, title companies), the fact that the estimate is based on the charges of the provider of the service, and the business relationship between the provider and the bank.

The charges for which a "good faith estimate" must be furnished include fees for origination, appraisal, inspection, insurance premium, title search, attorney, recording, transfer tax, and others set forth in the regulation.[5]

---

[1] Reg. X. Sec. 3500.5(c) (1).

[2] Reg. X. Sec. 3500.5(b) (2).

[3] Reg. X. Sec. 3500.5(d) (2) (5).

[4] Reg. X. Sec. 3500.6.

[5] Reg. X. Sec. 3500.7(c).

At the closing, HUD Form 1 must be used by the attorney, title company or other person conducting the closing process. This statement recites a summary of the transaction, including the price, taxes, deposit, adjustments in price, payments, advances, reserves, charges for services, recording and transfer fees, and a detailed breakdown of exactly what took place at the closing.

FORECLOSURE

A foreclosure action is the right of the mortgagee, after the debtor fails to pay as agreed, to exercise the right under the mortgage to recover the property to satisfy the debt. Each state has detailed statutes governing the foreclosure procedure, and a thorough knowledge of the law by an attorney is necessary to undertake a foreclosure.

Judicial foreclosure is a procedure available in all states where the mortgagor commences a suit to foreclose a real estate mortgage. In most states you have a choice of a judicial foreclosure as distinguished from a non-judicial foreclosure.

A judicial foreclosure suit has to be commenced against the debtor in the same manner as any suit is instituted. The procedure varies from state to state but before a judgment can be entered, procedures have to be undertaken by the court to determine that no hardship will be inflicted upon the debtor. In some instances, a person appointed by the court has to review the entire foreclosure proceeding to determine that it was properly performed and that the amount claimed is accurate. If the judgment of foreclosure is finally granted by the court, the creditor can hold a public sale after publication in a newspaper and thereafter proceed against the debtor for a deficiency, if there is a deficiency. The procedures are carefully enumerated in the statute in the various states and require meticulous compliance. In a few states this procedure can be accomplished within sixty or ninety days and in some states the procedure takes six to eight months, but in most states the procedure runs from six months to two years.

The non-judicial foreclosure is available in thirty-five states and is also heavily regulated. The procedure encompasses sending out notices of a proposed sale by service upon any person who has an interest in the property, serving them personally with this information, and publishing notice of the sale in a newspaper over a period of weeks prior to the public sale. In most states, a deficiency judgment can be obtained against the debtor if the property does not bring sufficient monies to pay off the mortgage. In California, a foreclosing party is not entitled to a deficiency judgment. The advantages of a non-judicial sale is that it can be accomplished in a much speedier time frame. The time frame can run from sixty to a hundred-twenty days on average although some states still require up to a year.

CREDIT AND COLLECTION TIP: *In most states the time to apply to court for a deficiency judgment is relatively short, so proceed promptly.*

Another option is for the debtor to offer to surrender the property by transferring the property by means of a deed to the mortgagee or the lender. The benefit to the borrower is that he is relieved of any personal liability. In addition the borrower does not wish to subject himself to the stigma of the publicity associated with the foreclosure. Sometimes the debtor may feel the property is worth more than the mortgage and may offer to sell the property to the mortgagee in consideration of an amount in excess of the balance due on the mortgage.

The lender must understand that offering a deed in lieu of foreclosure is not a defense to the lender's foreclosure action. If the lender believes the property is worth less than the mortgage and the borrower possesses assets in addition to the property in question, the lender would be well advised to institute the foreclosure action and obtain a deficiency judgment.

Another problem with the deed in lieu of foreclosure is that courts sometimes frown upon the transaction because they feel the lender is somehow coercing the debtor. If that is the case, the court may conclude that it was a fraudulent transfer without adequate consideration.

The borrower then may move to set aside the transfer. If the debtor files a petition in bankruptcy, the lender is faced with the additional problem as to the date when the deed is transferred in lieu of foreclosure, for he may be subject to a preferential transfer if it is made within ninety days of the filing of the bankruptcy. If there was not sufficient consideration, such as a transfer to a relative who has a mortgage on the property and the property is worth more than the mortgage, the transfer may be set aside within a year prior to the filing of a bankruptcy as a fraudulent transfer.

In accepting a deed in lieu of foreclosure, the most important consideration is to obtain an independent appraisal of the property to establish that the fair market of the value of the property is equal to or less than the amount of the mortgage debt. Most problems arise because an appraisal has not been made and a claim is asserted that the value of the property was far greater than the amount of the mortgage and thus the debtor was coerced or unduly influenced into executing a deed. The appraisal will also help in the event that the debtor files a petition in bankruptcy.

A lender should not permit the borrower to retain any interest in the property, such as an option to purchase, a right of first refusal when the lender sells, or any other type of lease. The risk is that the court might interpret such relationship as creating a mortgage in lieu of a transfer of property. The lender should usually set forth in the agreement with the debtor that the mortgage shall remain alive and the mortgagee will maintain its priority over any other liens that were filed after the date of the mortgage. The debt must be kept alive in the same manner and the settlement agreement between the parties must establish that the debt is to remain to support the fact that the mortgage will remain. This is usually solved by the lender agreeing not to sue the debtor on the debt in exchange for the deed in lieu of foreclosure, providing the transfer is never set aside and providing that the debtor does not file a petition in bankruptcy.

These are some of the highlights of using a deed in lieu of foreclosure, but recognize that it requires a balancing of various choices and consultation with an experienced attorney is recommended.

ACCELERATION

Acceleration of the mortgage is the right of the mortgagee to declare the entire balance due after a default by the debtor in paying the agreed-upon monthly payment. In most cases, because a foreclosure proceeding is expensive, acceleration is only used against a chronic defaulter, where the value of the property reasonably exceeds the balance due on the mortgage plus the legal fees and expenses of foreclosure and sale. The right to accelerate is usually provided in the mortgage agreement.

NOTICE

After a lending institution decides to foreclose, the matter is referred to inside or outside counsel to commence the foreclosure proceedings and to comply with any notice requirements in the mortgage and to comply with the Fair Debt Collection Practices Act. If the debtor is a consumer, the first step is usually a letter from counsel advising the debtor that if payment is not made, a foreclosure proceeding will be started. The purpose of the foreclosure is to enable the mortgagee to sell the property free and clear of all liens and encumbrances.

SUBORDINATE CLAIMANTS

The method of eliminating all encumbrances subordinate to the mortgage is to join all these claimants as defendants in the law suit. A title search is performed to identify subordinate mortgages, judgments docketed in the county clerk's office, tax liens both state and federal, and any other persons who may have a claim against the property. The title search identifies to counsel the names of those parties to be joined as defendants to bar those claimants from asserting any claim against the property. If those parties who have a claim against the property are not joined, the interest of the claimant is not cut off and the claimant still has a claim against the property even after a foreclosure sale, and transfer to a purchaser.

TENANTS

Counsel joins "John Doe" as defendant(s) to cover those parties who may be occupying the said property by virtue of leases, other agreements, or by being trespassers. This "John Doe" covers the situation where the mortgagee does not know whether tenants exist or who they are. Most leases provide that the lease is subject to the mortgage. The purchaser at the foreclosure sale has the option to evict the tenants or the owner at the end of the foreclosure. On the other hand, the purchaser may deem it economical to continue the leases.

SUIT ON DEBT

The mortgagee has a right to either sue on the mortgage debt or commence a foreclosure proceeding. Once a suit is brought on the debt, the mortgagee cannot start a foreclosure proceeding until a judgment is obtained on the debt and the judgment remains unpaid. For this reason, lenders choose to foreclose the mortgage and not sue on the debt. In addition, a docketed judgment takes its place in priority at the date when the judgment is filed. A foreclosure proceeding relies on the date when the mortgage was recorded, which was probably 5 to 30 years prior to the foreclosure. The mortgage takes its place in the chain of title on the date it is recorded, whereas the judgment does not take its place until it is docketed in the proper office.

PERSONAL SERVICE

Serving the Summons and complaint for foreclosure by "personal" service on the mortgagor is important in foreclosure actions. The lender is concerned that the title company will issue a clean title after the sale without any exceptions. Where service of the Summons and Complaint has been made by means other than personal delivery on the owner of the property, the title companies review the situation, because the mortgagor served by substituted service is more likely to claim he or she was not properly served with the Summons and Complaint and will question the jurisdictional grounds of the foreclosure action. Defective service on the mortgagor (owner) could invalidate the foreclosure.

　　If the owner does not occupy the residence, a greater likelihood exists for improper service. For this reason, counsel will attempt to effectuate personal service of the Summons and Complaint on the debtor even though this is more difficult and may delay commencement of suit.

ANSWER

Most foreclosure proceedings proceed to judgment without the owner or any of the defendants interposing an answer. If they do interpose an answer, the case, as with any other lawsuit, will proceed with discovery, including interrogatories and depositions, and will be disposed of by a summary judgment or will reach a trial.

REFEREE'S REPORT

If no answer is interposed, and the defendants default or a trial results in a decision for the mortgagee, the next step in the proceeding in some states, such as New York, is to request the court to appoint a referee to compute the amount due and to submit a report on the foreclosure. The report usually encompasses a review of all the papers on file, a summary of what transpired during the proceeding and the amount due.

JUDGMENT

After the report is submitted by the referee to the court, the plaintiff finally submits judgment to the court ordering a judicial sale of the property. The judgment requires the plaintiff to advertise the sale in a newspaper pursuant to the requirements of the state statute.

SALE

At a time and place set forth in the newspaper advertisement, the sheriff will conduct the sale and open the bidding at a public auction. The mortgagee is entitled to bid at the sale for the property being foreclosed and thus become the owner of the property.

TITLE AT SALE

The purchaser acquires title to the property at the foreclosure sale free of the claims of the subordinate mortgages, liens, judgments, and claimants and the title reverts to the date of the mortgage. A prior mortgage lien or judgment lien recorded prior to the foreclosed mortgage will survive the sale and remain a lien on the property. Furthermore, the payments of the prior mortgage must be kept up-to-date or the prior mortgagee may commence a separate foreclosure action.

SURPLUS MONEY PROCEEDINGS

If the sale is for a price in excess of the balance due on the mortgage, surplus money proceedings follow. The surplus money is paid into court, and the monies are paid to the other creditors who file claims. Payment is made in order of priority. If monies are left after payment of lien creditors, they are paid to the mortgagor (owner).

DEFICIENCY

If the amount accepted by the sheriff at the sale is insufficient to pay off the mortgage, the balance due is the deficiency amount for which the mortgagor (owner) of the property, and anyone who assumes the mortgage, may still be liable. Many times, no one appears at the auction sale to bid for the foreclosed property, and the lending institution purchases the property at the sale for a nominal amount. In this instance, the deficiency is substantial, since the nominal amount bid by the lender is credited to the balance due on the lender's mortgage. (Actually the amount bid is deducted from the mortgage balance.) Some states prohibit the lender from bidding a nominal amount and require that the fair market value of the property be credited to the balance due on the mortgage, whereas other states allow the lender to credit the actual bid at the sale.

The question of recovering a deficiency judgment against the debtor is controlled by the statutes of the respective states and strict compliance is essential to insure the right to proceed against the debtor for the deficiency amount. In some states the procedure is complex, and consultation with experienced counsel is recommended.

RIGHT OF REDEMPTION

In some states, the debtor enjoys a right of redemption prior to the sale or even as long as two years after the sale. The debtor may redeem the property by payment of the sale price established at the foreclosure sale within a certain period of time, as set forth in the respective state's statute. The redemption right was designed to deter low bids at a foreclosure sale. In those states where a right of redemption is allowed, some statutes allow the mortgagee to extinguish this right of redemption by agreement in the mortgage document.

FORECLOSURE FACT SHEET

The American College of Mortgage Attorneys has provided us with a foreclosure fact sheet which provides information as to the type of mortgages used in the various states, the time to complete the foreclosure and the period to redeem the mortgage. You will find this fact sheet in Appendix IV.

UNIFORM COMMERCIAL CODE

Although we are unable to include the full Uniform Commercial Code (UCC) in this book, in Appendix I you will find the official text of Section 9 of the UCC, issued by the American Law Institute and the National Conference of Commissioners on Uniform State Laws (1990).

Most states adopted the Uniform Commercial Code in somewhat similar form as set forth in Appendix I, but the UCC of each state is distinct and different from the UCC adopted in another state, since the legislatures of each state at the time of adoption made many changes and modifications. These changes and modifications are only minor in some cases, but in other instances are major to the extent that they can produce different results in one state from another state based upon the same set of facts and circumstances. Accordingly, it is absolutely necessary to review the UCC with respect to the state in which the creditor attempts to enforce the terms and conditions of the Code.

UCC 9 has been significantly revised and is now in the process of being adopted by the states. The law as passed does not take effect for 2 years (after 2001). Consultation with counsel is recommended to review the new law if your state has adopted it. The remainder of this chapter deals with the old UCC 9, except for the summary of the new law at the end of the chapter, which delineates the key changes.

FINANCING STATEMENT

The secured party who receives a security interest in equipment or machinery must be concerned that the debtor will not take the same machinery and equipment and grant a security interest to another party. A filing system is in place which provides that the secured party can "perfect" this security interest by filing a "financing statement" in the county in which the property is located, or in which the debtor resides, or in an office designated by the state. In most instances, filing must be done in both the county office and the state office.

The "financing statement" includes the name and address of the secured party, the debtor, the date, description of the personal property, and what type of agreement is being filed: security agreement, assignment, termination, continuation, etc. This instrument is filed in the county office or the state office and is notice to all third parties of the existence of the lien of the secured party. In the event the lien is filed against fixtures, the lien should be filed in the county in which the real estate is located. As a rule, the security agreement need not be filed with the financing statement, although it may be filed.

Certain states use a certificate of title for automobiles, and liens are recited on the title. Filing a financing statement is unnecessary in those states that use the title system, which requires separate procedures for filing and protecting the lien.

Several states have dual filing requirements which require the creditor to file the financing statement in the county in which the debtor resides and with the secretary of state of the state in which the debtor is located. Reviewing the laws of those states is appropriate to determine the requirements. As a general rule, dual-filing states require "dual" or "proper" filing in complete and literal compliance with the statute. An improper filing does not provide constructive notice to anyone and, under a few state laws, does not even bind someone who accidentally finds the financing statement in the state records and has actual notice.

Where there is a multiple filing requirement, a question often raised is whether the creditor obtains some protection for making a proper filing in one place. Under the new Section 9, dual filing problems and multiple offices problems are eliminated. A recent case decided that the creditor received no protection at all. Two creditors made filings against the debtor in a dual-filing state and properly filed in both the county and the state. Nevertheless, when it came time to file the continuation statements, both creditors, for whatever reason, filed only in the county and failed to file in the state offices. The court held that both creditors failed to continue the perfection of their security interest in the collateral and both of them therefore held unperfected security interests. Since the debtor had filed a bankruptcy, the collateral became the property of the estate of the bankrupt and neither of the creditors could assert any type of claim. The moral of the story is that in dual states, you should file both in the county and with the secretary of state or other state offices as required.

A problem may arise where the debtor has two places of business in different counties. As an attorney advising a client, I recommend that you file in each county in which the debtor has a place of business, as well as with the secretary of state. Some difficulty may lie in determining the definition of a "place of business." The courts seem to evaluate the amount of business conducted at the place of business, how much revenue is recovered there, how long it has been located there, etc. Another test that is used is what is known as the "Notoriety Test" which specifies the degree and the extent to which creditors and other third parties are aware of the debtor's place of business and the fact that the debtor is conducting a type of business at that location. The majority of the courts follow the "Notoriety Test." Many of these problems have been solved by the new UCC 9.

CONTENTS OF FINANCING STATEMENT

A filed financing statement is sufficient for most types of collateral if it:

1. Gives the names of the debtor and secured party.
2. Is signed by the debtor.
3. Gives an address of the secured party from which information concerning the security interest may be obtained.

4. Gives a mailing address for the debtor.
5. Contains a statement indicating the types or describing the items of collateral.

A security agreement may be sufficient as a financing statement if it contains all the information required for a financing statement.

The UCC allows for minor errors as provided in section 9-402:

> "A financing statement substantially complying with the requirements of this section is effective even though it contains minor errors which are not seriously misleading."

The question of what is and what is not a minor error varies from state to state as much as from country to country. Sometimes minor errors in one state are major errors in other states. The words used to justify the decision are "seriously misleading" and the interpretation of seriously misleading can also be "misleading."

One thing certain is that the financing statement must contain a signature. Nevertheless, the question of a signature written in pen and ink has been eroded to some degree allowing for stamping the signatures, facsimiles, and other types of reproduction in certain states.

The name of the debtor has to be correct. If the name is wrong, the financing statement will be indexed incorrectly and may "seriously mislead" other parties. A debtor's trade name is required instead of the actual individual name since the framers of the code felt that a third party is looking for the trade name, not the individual's name. This would apply also to the trade name of a partnership, rather than a partner's name.

The debtor's name usually appears on two places in the financing statement, first with the address and a second time for the signature. Where the name in one place is correct and the name in the other place is incorrect, courts have gone both ways in enforcing the financing statement. Some of them hold that one misspelling is sufficient to invalidate the financing statement, whereas other courts seem to feel that if one is correct, it is sufficient to validate the financing statement, at least if it's indexed in the proper place.

DURATION

A financing statement is usually effective for a period of five years. A continuation statement can be filed to extend the period for an additional five years, providing the continuation is filed not less than six months prior to the expiration of the first period. The interplay of the old UCC 9 and the new UCC 9 must be reviewed.

CONTINUATION STATEMENT

Section 9-403 of the Uniform Commercial Code provides as follows:

> "A continuation statement may be filed by the secured party (i) Within six months before and sixty days after a stated maturity date of five years or less (ii) Otherwise within six months before the expiration of the five year period specified in Subsection (2)... Upon timely filing of the continuation statement, the effectiveness of the financing statement is continued for five years after the last date to which the filing was effective whereupon it lapses in the same manner as provided in Section (2) unless another continuation statement is filed before the lapse. Succeeding continuation statements may be filed in the same manner to continue the effect of the financing statement."

A continuation statement filed before the six-month period is not timely and cannot have the continuing effectiveness of the original financing statement. Filing a few days before the six-month period is not substantial compliance and does not cure an untimely filing. Thus it is most important that the continuation statement be filed within that six-month period before the financing statement expires and not one day prior to it.[6] The new UCC 9 must be considered.

SECURITY INTERESTS

The Uniform Commercial Code, Article 9, sets forth the statutory basis and terminology for secured lending with regard to personal property. The term "Security Interest" means the right of the creditor to particular personal property of the debtor to secure payment of the debtor's obligation; the term "Security Agreement" is the instrument which creates this right. The collateral is the personal property offered by the debtor to secure the payment of a debt to a creditor. Article 9 applies to all different types of security interests, covering tangible and intangible personal property, machinery, equipment, fixtures, automobiles, boats, accounts receivable, inventory, stocks, bonds, notes, contract rights, and copyrights. Article 9 expressly excludes any transfer of an interest in real estate or real property.

Under Section 9-203 there are generally four requirements which must be met to create an enforceable security agreement.

1. The parties must intend that there should be a security interest. If the intention of the parties is to create a lease, then naming the document a security interest would be to no avail.

---

[6]*NBD Bank, N.A. v. Timberjack, Inc.*, 208 Mich. App. 153, 527 N.W.2d 50 (Mich. Ct. App. 1995).

2. There are certain requirements with regard to reducing the agreement to a writing. The debtor must sign the agreement, the secured party must be named and the works of art which create the security interest must be set forth. Many of these requirements have been more carefully defined by the courts and if the court feels that these requirements have not been met, the agreement may not be an enforceable security agreement.

3. Value must be furnished by the secured party which may be any form of consideration sufficient to support an enforceable agreement. Value can also take the form of a pre-existing debt if the security interest is intended as security for the pre-existing debt.

4. The debtor must have a right to possession or ownership rights in the property subject to the secured party's right to repossess and to sell the goods at public or private sale if the debtor should default.

The courts have held that a security agreement must contain granting language such as "the property is being delivered to secure the loan" or "furnished as security for the loan." Without such language indicating that the collateral will act as security for the loan, the document may fail as an enforceable security agreement. In essence, the writing must set forth the intent of the parties to create a security interest.

SECURITY AGREEMENT

The security agreement is the basic agreement creating the secured interest of the creditor in the property. It identifies the personal property which is covered and is being used as collateral for the loan, the amount of the loan, the terms of the loan, the interest charged, the terms of the repayment, any late charges, and attorney's fees. The agreement also will include obligations of the debtor to maintain the personal property, to obtain insurance, or to otherwise protect the property. Provisions in favor of the creditor generally deal with the acts of default which accelerate the balance due, the terms and conditions under which the creditor can repossess the collateral, the notices which have to be given, the charges that the debtor must pay, and any other waivers of rights by the debtor, such as a waiver to a jury trial. If the collateral should be crops or fixtures, a description of the real estate where the crops or fixtures are located will be included.

The description is sufficient if it reasonably identifies the collateral intended by the parties. After-acquired property (property acquired after the date of execution of the security agreement) may be covered, except with regard to consumer goods, unless they are acquired within 10 days.

One of the questions often raised is whether a financing statement alone is sufficient to create a security agreement. Most states hold that the execution of a financing statement is not the execution of a security agreement. Perhaps this goes to the ancient theory that a mortgage without a note is insufficient since a mortgage alone is not an obligation, but merely the collateral for the obligation. In this particular instance, the financing statement will merely be the recording device and the security interest will be the obligation. The great majority of the courts adhere to the rule that a financing statement alone is not sufficient to create a security agreement without an accompanying security agreement.

Creditors continually litigate the question of whether a financing statement can act as a security agreement without the magic words that indicate that there is a grant of a security interest. A financing statement alone does not have these magic words. A recent case decided that financing statements with a description of collateral together with invoices from the creditor without a security agreement did not create a valid security interest in goods.[7]

Most security agreements require blank spaces to be completed. The collateral must be identified with model and serial numbers and a description of the property mortgaged. The security agreements are drafted by the lenders (banks) with attention to the rights of the secured party, since the security agreement is designed to benefit the secured party and is used repeatedly. For this reason, secured parties will rarely change the printed portions of the agreement without consulting with counsel. Nevertheless, a printed agreement may be changed if the circumstances so warrant. Sometimes, under unique circumstances, the secured party should consult with counsel to determine if a change sought by the borrowing party is warranted. If the agreement should have an ambiguity, the law will interpret the ambiguity least favorably to the drafter of the agreement (the bank).

WRITING REQUIREMENT

There must be a writing to create a security interest. This is necessary to satisfy the Statute of Frauds, which requires a writing for certain types of transactions, such as real estate transactions, an individual guaranty, or a sale of goods in excess of $500.

The writing must show some intent to create a security interest. On the other hand, if the writing does not really meet the test of whether or not the parties intend to grant a security interest, the courts may refer the matter to a factual inquiry as to whether or not this is what the parties intended. Oral testimony by each party will be admissible to determine the intent of the parties.

When an agreement does not meet the criteria for a security interest, the creditor often tries to utilize all kinds of documents to create the security agreement since the Uniform Commercial Code does not require any particular language to create a security interest. Creditors alleging that a bill of sale, a promissory note or collateral papers are sufficient to establish security interests face the courts on a continual basis. Minutes of meetings of the Board of Directors have

---

[7]*In re Arctic Air, Inc.*, 202 B.R. 533 (Bankr. D.R.I. 1996).

been used in conjunction with bills of sale and notes to create a security interest. Needless to say, the states go different ways.

Some state courts want a clear intent set forth in the security agreement, evidencing a right to create a security interest, and will pay little attention to collateral documents. A review of the particular state law is absolutely necessary when confronted with this issue.

DESCRIPTION OF PROPERTY

A security agreement must "reasonably identify what is described." A copy of a security agreement should be sufficient as a financing statement if it contains the same information that a financing statement is required to contain and is also signed by the debtor. On the other hand a copy of a financing statement will not suffice to be a security agreement.

Any description is sufficient, whether or not it is specific, if it reasonably identifies what is described. This definition should be compared with the description necessary in the financing statement which recites that the financing statement must only contain a statement indicating the type or describing the items of collateral. Where there is no description of the collateral, the security agreement fails since no collateral is identified. In some instances the security agreement may refer to other documentation to identify the collateral.

Major problems can develop when lenders try to protect themselves by using such terms as "All the equipment as set forth in Schedule A" and Schedule A is missing or Schedule A is blank, or Schedule A doesn't list the debtor's equipment. Such a situation would be litigated as to whether there was an intent to furnish all debtor's equipment as collateral, only a part thereof, or perhaps just two machines. The question of identification may be left to oral evidence where no description was set forth.

The major question is whether to use a broad description to include as much property as possible or a narrow specific description and identify each item of property. The latter is probably the better option.

Another problem arises with the phrase "All the debtor's equipment located at 15 Main Street," a specific address which happens to be the defendant's only store. The debtor may subsequently open a new store and move some of the equipment to that store.

The use of the phrase "after-acquired equipment" also presents problems and is the subject of considerable litigation. The purpose of this clause is to have the security agreement cover property which is acquired after the execution of the security agreement. Section 9-108 of the Uniform Commercial Code (see Appendix I) generally validates such after-acquired property interest although it may be subordinate to a purchase money security interest under Section 9-312(3 and 4).

After-acquired property interest is not, by virtue of that fact alone, security for a pre-existing claim (a prior debt secured by the security agreement). The problem arises often in the bankruptcy code, which makes certain transfers for antecedent debts voidable as preferences. If the secured party pays new value and the after-acquired property is given as security in the ordinary course of the debtor's business, the after-acquired property may avoid the problem of the preference. Meeting the two tests will give the secured party full protection as to the collateral named in the security agreement. Despite the considerable litigation over the use of this terminology, lawyers and creditors continue to use it as often as possible, for it is an added protection if enforceable.

The creditor must realize that the description of the property in the security agreement is not the most simple clause to prepare. Consult with counsel before the preparation and drafting of a security agreement.

SIGNATURES

The code requires the debtor to sign the security agreement. It has been held that a typewritten name is sufficient if oral testimony is received, showing the intent of the parties. With regard to who signs the security agreement, the principal debtor should sign the agreement or an officer of the debtor corporation.

Courts have held that in certain states it is not necessary that the corporate name or the proper partnership name of the debtor be on the agreement as long as it was the principal who signed. Other courts disagree and require the proper business name, as well as the individual's name.

ERRORS IN FILING

The Code specifically allows for human error in filing a financing statement, stating under section 9-401 subdivision (2) that

> "A filing that is made in good faith in an improper place or not in all the places required is nevertheless effective with regard to any collateral as to which of the filing complied with the requirements, and is also effective with regard to collateral covered by the financing statement against any person who has knowledge of the contents of such financing statement."

Therefore, if the filing is correct as to one item of security and incorrect as to another item of security, the proper filing as to one item of security will be sustained.

As to filing in the wrong place, the statute seems to say that if the third party has knowledge of the financing statement, that will be sufficient. But, unfortunately, the question as to when a third party acquires this knowledge, or when the searcher, who is acting on behalf of the third party, acquires the knowledge is a difficult one for the courts to answer. The proper approach is that a misfiled security agreement will have priority against someone who actually knew about the misfiled statement. The fact that the party should have known, or with due diligence should have seen the mistake, is not sufficient to constitute actual knowledge. When a searcher sees the misfiling, difficult questions arise. Will the searcher tell the client about the misfiling? Is the searcher obligated to tell the client about the misfiling? Litigation continues in this area without a firm resolution. A review of the new UCC 9 is indicated.

AFTER-ACQUIRED AND EXCHANGED PROPERTY

Article 9 of the Uniform Commercial Code and some state laws prohibit after-acquired property clauses in security agreements to enable a creditor to obtain a lien on property which is later acquired by the consumer. On the other hand, if the consumer exchanges or sells the secured property to a purchaser (whether or not the financing statement is properly or improperly filed), the secured party has a right to the proceeds of the sale. If an exchange of property (with a perfected lien) took place, the secured party may have a right to repossess the property which was exchanged.

PLEDGE

A pledge of security is where the collateral or personal property is actually transferred physically to the creditor and retained by the creditor until the debtor repays the loan. (For example, pawning a watch at a pawn shop.) In this case, no filing is necessary.

ASSIGNMENT OF SECURITY AGREEMENT

A secured lender may assign his or her rights in the security agreement to a purchaser. A financing statement should be filed indicating that an assignment has been made. At the same time, a secured party may release a part or portion of the collateral from the security agreement by executing a partial release of collateral and filing the agreement with the financing statement.

PRIORITIES

The filing of financing statements is similar to the filing of mortgages in that the financing statement which is filed first in time is prior to a second financing statement which is executed later and filed at a later date. The second financing statement filed would have an interest in the personal property subordinate to the first financing statement. However, exceptions exist for a purchase money security interest in inventory and equipment.

AUTOMATIC PERFECTION

Certain types of financing arrangements are perfected "automatically" and no financing statement is necessary. Where consumer goods are involved, where the retailer advances credit to the consumer, and where the consumer executes a retail installment contract, the security interest is perfected automatically and a financing statement need not be filed. The burden on retailers would be excessive, and the likelihood of the same consumer goods being used as collateral a second time is unusual. The other type of "automatic" perfection covers a "purchase money" conditional sale. The seller-lender advances money to the borrower to buy the collateral. The seller-lender security agreement covers the goods purchased, and a financing statement need not be filed.

The question of who has priority where there are conflicting interests concerning personal property may turn on what the nature of the collateral is, whether it is consumer goods or otherwise, and how the security was perfected: by filing, by a purchase money security interest, or by a pledge (possession).

"Perfection" is a word used by the Uniform Commercial Code to describe how a secured creditor acquires priority over other subsequent secured creditors who extend credit to the debtor and receive the same property as collateral. While a creditor may assume that the debtor would not embark on a course of action to collateralize the same security as first liens to different lenders, the major reason for perfecting a security interest is to protect a lien against the Trustee in a bankruptcy, and other creditors who may attack the lien. A secured party who perfects a lien prior to bankruptcy will have the right to recover the collateral by applying to the bankruptcy court to remove the automatic stay in bankruptcy and obtain possession of the collateral. If the security interest is not perfected, the Trustee will utilize the collateral in the bankruptcy, sell the collateral and distribute the proceeds to the creditors of the bankrupt; then the unperfected secured creditor will become a general unsecured creditor.

The Code provides several ways to perfect a security interest. One way is by obtaining possession of the collateral and retaining possession (pledge). Under the Code, several methods provide automatic perfection, including the most common one which is the security interest in consumer goods.

> CREDIT AND COLLECTION TIP: *Nevertheless, the most important way of perfecting is by properly filing a financing statement under the laws of the state in which the debtor is located.*

In most instances the financing statement should be filed in the office designated by the state. A small minority of states (such as New York) provide two places to file a financing statement, 1) the place or office designated by the state; 2) usually the County Clerk's office in the County in which the debtor is located or resides (abolished by the new UCC 9).

If the secured interest was not perfected, a secured party's interest is subordinate to any third party who acquires the property for value. Whether the purchaser of the vehicle knew of the security interest and whether the purchase is a consumer or a business that buys and sells vehicles are immaterial. The key ingredient is that the purchaser transferred the vehicle for value. If the consumer failed to transfer value and made a gift of the vehicle, the secured party should consult with counsel.

GOODS IN TRANSIT

Section 2-705 of the Uniform Commercial Code (UCC) states:

(1) The seller may stop delivery of goods in the possession of a carrier or other bailee when he discovers the buyer to be insolvent (Section 2-702) and may stop delivery of carload, truckload, planeload or larger shipments of express or freight when the buyer repudiates or fails to make a payment due before delivery or if for any other reason the seller has a right to withhold or reclaim the goods.

(2) As against such buyer the seller may stop delivery until

    (a) receipt of the goods by the buyer; or

    (b) acknowledgment to the buyer by any bailee of the goods except a carrier that the bailee holds the goods for the buyer; or

    (c) such acknowledgment to the buyer by a carrier by reshipment or as warehouseman; or

    (d) negotiation to the buyer of any negotiable document of title covering the goods.

(3) (a) To stop delivery the seller must so notify as to enable the bailee by reasonable diligence to prevent delivery of goods.

    (b) After such notification the bailee must hold and deliver the goods according to the directions of the seller but the seller is liable to the bailee for any ensuing charges or damages.

    (c) If a negotiable document of title has been issued for goods, the bailee is not obliged to obey a notification to stop until surrender of the document.

    (d) A carrier who has issued a non-negotiable bill of lading is not obliged to obey a notification to stop goods received from a person other than the consignor.

A recent case considered a situation where the plaintiff shipped natural gas liquids and used a pipeline as an interstate common carrier to transport the liquid. The purchaser filed a petition in bankruptcy and the oil company demanded that the carrier stop the transfer and delivery of the natural gas liquids. Some of the liquids had been delivered to the bankrupt, but the carrier agreed to return a portion still in the carrier's possession. The carrier said they would only return the gas liquids upon receipt from the oil company of an indemnity and a hold harmless agreement plus an irrevocable letter of credit to insure payment of any damages and expenses resulting from the stoppage of delivery.

The court held that the carrier must deliver the goods according to the seller's directions and that the seller is always liable to the bailee (carrier) for any damages that the carrier may thereafter incur. The bailee (carrier) had no right to ask for indemnity for damages by requiring the seller to get a letter of credit to secure their indemnity. The courts made it clear that "the seller automatically undertakes the duty to indemnify when it stops delivery."[8]

In another case, the seller attempted to hold up the delivery of certain goods but in this instance the Bill of Lading was already delivered to the purchaser in a negotiable form. The court held that because it was a negotiable document in the hands of the purchaser, the carrier was under no obligation to stop the transit and must surrender the goods to the purchaser.[9]

LEASES

Any financing transaction may be a security interest if the purpose was to create one. If the parties intended to have a security agreement but labeled the transaction a lease, the lease will be treated as a security agreement subject to the provisions of Article 9. Some states, under a new section in the Uniform Commercial Code, provide that: 1) if the lessee can return the goods and end the lease, or 2) if the goods have some economic life at the end of the lease, the arrangement is a true lease. A lease of personal property which provides that the lessee may purchase the property at the end of the lease for a nominal consideration may convert that lease to a security agreement to be governed by Article 9. Other circumstances are considered by the courts to determine whether the lease was intended as a security agreement.

The code under Section 9-102(1) covers any transaction which is intended to create a security interest in personal property or fixtures. The commentary to the UCC adds that the main purpose of the Section was to bring all "consensual secu-

---

[8]*Siderpali, S.P.A. v. Judal Industries, Inc.,* 833 F.Supp. 1023 (S.D.N.Y. 1993); *Petroleum Products, Inc., v. Mid-America Pipeline Co.,* 815 F.Supp. 1421 (D. Kan. 1993).

[9]*Petroleum Products v. Mid-America Pipeline Co.,* 815 F.Supp. 1421 (D. Kan. 1993).

rity interests" in personal property and fixtures under the terms of this Section of the Code. The intent was to cover almost all situations where a security interest is granted on personal property and fixtures. The definition was intended to be broad enough to include any distinctive claim to assets of a debtor that a creditor may have by reason of any claim or agreement.

A lease is not intended to be a security interest. The case law covering the question of whether a transaction is a lease or a security interest is substantial. If the transaction is truly a lease, no financing statement need be filed and, therefore, no notice need be delivered to third parties. If the transaction is not a lease but a security interest, and the lessor did not file a financing statement, third parties take priority over this creditor when the creditor attempts to assert a claim to the collateral.

By failing to file the financing statement, the creditor has what is known as an "unperfected security interest" and may lose priority to other creditors, such as trustees in bankruptcy or creditors who have perfected security interests.

Creditors often attempt to formulate a lease instead of a security interest to avoid the filing requirements under the Code. Tax reasons and considerations in marketing the product may also dictate why a lease may be more advantageous than a security interest.

The main danger in treating a transaction as a lease when it is a security interest is that if the debtor seeks bankruptcy protection, the trustee may have a prior claim to the collateral because of failure to file a financing statement. The other danger is that the debtor may use the leased property as collateral in another transaction and the new creditor perfects a security interest by filing a financing statement. In either instance, the initial creditor may lose any claim to the leased property, if in fact it was a security interest.

The courts continually refer to what is known as "A True Lease" as opposed to a security agreement. The judicial system has devoted pages and pages of criteria describing what is and what is not a true lease. Each time parties fashion a new plan to evade the law, the courts are put to the test of creating new criteria.

The basic section of the Uniform Commercial Code defining a lease is Section 1-201(37) which sets forth in a page and a half twelve criteria as to whether a transaction creates a lease or security interest. A new proposed Section 1-201(37) is presently being developed that will add more criteria. In addition, under Section 2A of the code which deals directly with consumer leases, one might find some additional distinctions set forth with regard to leases and security interests.

When drafting, perhaps the best advice is to file a financing statement whether the creditor believes it is a lease or a security interest. Unfortunately, strong reasons sometimes are present to avoid filing a financing statement and to construct the transaction as a lease. The creditor's attorney usually will advise the creditor of the calculated risk when embarking on a course of casting a transaction as a lease when in fact it is not a true lease, but really a security interest. The risk is simple, i.e., loss of collateral and treatment as an unsecured creditor in bankruptcy or a legal battle with other creditors who have perfected their security interests in the same collateral.

LIABILITY OF LESSOR

The efforts of the lessee to assert claims against the leasing company continue and in some instances they become successful. In a New Jersey case, the warranty was clearly for manufacturing defects but the court held that the warranty claim may be raised if there is sufficiently close relationship between the car dealer, the manufacturer and the lessor which was the case in this particular instance. What happened here was the leasing company created the lease form and authorized personnel with the dealership to execute the leases. The leasing company was very much involved in the operations of the dealership in closing the leases and its knowledge of the terms of the leases was fairly extensive.[10]

LEASING LEGISLATION

In September of 1996 the Federal Reserve Board issued new rules aimed at simplifying car leasing transactions and clarifying the actual charges to consumers. The agency prepared a form for consumers to take to their dealers which requires the dealers to break out 20 separate costs of leasing, including the car's gross capitalized cost, the security deposits, the insurance premiums, taxes and what is most important, the residual value, being the estimated value of the car at the end of the lease. The forms can be obtained by writing to the Federal Reserve Board Publication Services, 20th & C Streets, N.W., Washington, D.C. 20551, requesting the Federal Consumer Leasing Act disclosure form. The obligation is upon the consumer to obtain the form and the necessary information. Notwithstanding this burden on the consumer, it's an indication of the direction the Federal Reserve Board is moving and one can probably assume that down the road such disclosures may become mandatory. Certainly, many of the states are now adopting leasing laws which do require certain mandatory disclosures to the consumer. Many of the large leasing firms are already beginning to disclose much of the information.

In most instances, these leasing laws are more restrictive than the federal laws and a review of each state's leasing law is absolutely necessary. The New York law and the other state laws are principally designed to supplement the provisions of the Federal Consumer Leasing Act (Appendix III). For example, the New York law includes a provision similar to that contained in the trade regula-

---

[10]*Mercedes Benz Credit Corp. v. Lotito*, 306 N.J. Super. 25, 703 A.2d 288 (N.J. Super. Ct. App. Div. 1997).

tion rule concerning the preservation of consumer's claims and defenses wherein the consumer's rights are not cut off in the event the loans are negotiated to a third party. The New York law also provides certain reinstatement rights to cure defaults solely caused by failure to make a timely payment. Nevertheless, the holder has certain remedies during this period in which the borrower can cure the default. The holder must also deliver a notice of intention to sell the vehicle at early termination and there are certain specific requirements that the vehicle be sold under a commercially reasonable sale. A careful review of the leasing law of New York is necessary in the event vehicles are to be leased to consumers in New York.

> **CREDIT AND COLLECTION TIP:** *The same careful review should be applied to the leasing law of each state where the lessor is leasing vehicles.*

COOPERATIVE AND CONDOMINIUM

The distinction between cooperatives and condominiums is significant. A condominium is an estate in real property consisting of an undivided ownership interest in a portion of a parcel of real property together with a separate ownership interest in another portion of the same parcel. Condominium ownership is a merger of two estates in land into one: the ownership of an apartment or unit in a condominium project and a tenancy in common ownership interest with other co-owners in the common elements of that unit.[11] The condominium is real property and a creditor to recover this property must conduct a foreclosure proceeding under the state law that covers real property. The owner of the condominium is entitled to all the notices and all the provisions that protect the owner of a private residence with regard to the commencement and the prosecution of a foreclosure action.

A cooperative apartment is quite different from a condominium. A cooperative is organized for the purpose of rendering some type of service to shareholders or members who own and control it. Cooperative apartments are usually dwelling units in a multi-dwelling complex. Each member has an interest in the entire complex and a lease of its own property (apartment), although members do not own the apartments as is the case with a condominium. The ownership of the co-op is organized in corporate form and is treated as a corporation and the members of the co-op only receive certificates of stock as indicia of their ownership as well as a lease on the apartment. The relationship between the tenant-shareholder and the co-op owner is largely determined by reviewing the lease, the certificate of incorporation, the stock offering prospectus, the stock subscrip-

---

[11]*UE'C 757* (6th ed. 1990).

tion agreement, financial statements, bylaws, rules and regulations and all the other documents that pertain to the occupation of an apartment.[12]

To recover a cooperative apartment, a creditor must proceed, unless the state law indicates otherwise, under Section 9 of the Uniform Commercial Code which deals with personal property. The owner of the co-op apartment is entitled to all the notices and protection afforded under this particular section of the Uniform Commercial Code. Cooperative ownership is considered personal property because the interest is represented by a lease and a stock certificate; whereas condominium ownership is considered an estate in real property, and is the owner of the property in the same way that a party owns a private residence.[13]

SECURITY INTEREST COPYRIGHT

Computer programs, articles, books, or any other item which are a subject for copyright may be offered as security for an extension of credit. Intellectual property such as trademarks or patents would fall under this category.

Several courts have taken the position that the proper place to file a secured interest is in the copyright office because the federal government has provided a national registration and specifies the place of filing for perfecting a security interest in a copyright. Not all of the federal courts agree with this position and some of them take the position that a security interest may be recorded in the United States copyright office but does not have to be recorded in the United States Copyright Office if the creditor properly filed the security interest in the appropriate state office in accordance with state laws. The recommendation of most attorneys is to file in the United States Copyright Office and in the proper offices in the state depending upon whether it is a dual filing state or only a single filing state. If you have a security interest and you want protection, file in both places.[14]

GENERAL INTANGIBLES

Sometimes a consumer will offer to assign the proceeds of a negligence action as security for a particular indebtedness or to prevent the creditor from proceeding with the collection of the account. The assignment of an expected recovery from a cause of action is treated as a general intangible. A general intangible is a catch-all category defined by Article 9 of any personal property other than goods,

---

[12]Ibid.

[13]*In re Pandeff,* 201 B.R. 865 (Bankr. S.D.N.Y. 1996).

[14]*Peregrine Entertainment, Ltd. v. Capital Federal S & L Assoc. of Denver,* 116 B.R. 194 (C.D. Cal. 1990).

accounts, chattel paper, documents, instruments and money. To accept a general intangible as security for a debt, the UCC provides that a financing statement must be filed and to support the financing statement, the creditor must obtain a security agreement.[15]

WHEN TITLE PASSES

Prior to the Uniform Commercial Code, the common law set forth that when property was repossessed by a creditor, title normally passed directly to the creditor. The common law was radically changed by the Uniform Commercial Code and now when collateral is repossessed, title still remains in the debtor's name until there is some formal disposition by the creditor such as a sale of the property in accordance with the provisions of the Uniform Commercial Code.

The UCC Section 9-207 states as follows:

1. A secured party must use reasonable care in the custody and preservation of collateral in his possession.
2. In the case of an instrument or chattel paper, reasonable care includes taking the necessary steps to preserve rights against prior parties unless otherwise agreed.
3. A secured party is liable for any loss caused by his failure to meet any obligations imposed by the preceding subsection but does not lose his security interest.

This section is an example of several other sections in the Code which state that the creditor has certain obligations after he repossesses the property, including the obligation to exercise reasonable care (UCC Section 1-102(3)). UCC Section 9-501 also provides that a secured party in possession of collateral has the rights and remedies and duties provided in UCC Section 9-207.

A creditor cannot at the same time be the owner and have obligations to the debtor after he repossesses the property. If the creditor is the owner of the property, then he has no obligations at all to the debtor and the only obligations are owed to himself. The creditor would have no right to increase the amount of the debt if he was the owner of the property, even though the security agreement has now become history by virtue of the fact that the creditor has become the owner of the property.

If the secured party was the owner of the property, he is not liable for any losses by virtue of his failure to exercise reasonable care in the custody of the property. The debtor also has the right to redeem the property under Section 9-504 of the UCC and Section 9-505 and 9-506. This right to redeem is certainly

---

[15]*In re Lampiris,* 194 B.R. 3 (Bankr. D.N.H. 1996).

inconsistent with the right of ownership once the creditor has repossessed the property.

> **CREDIT AND COLLECTION TIP:** *Any activity by the creditor which is not consistent with the concept that the secured party is merely a caretaker and a custodian for the property until the property is finally placed at public or private sale may expose the creditor to liability.*

REVISION OF UCC ARTICLE 9

In 1998, the National Conference of Commissioners on Uniform State Laws and the American Law Institute approved a revision of UCC 9. Article 9 of the UCC Code deals primarily with security agreements, security interests on personal property and fixtures, and sets forth the procedures for preparing a security agreement and preparing and filing a financing statement. The final draft that was approved in 1998 provides for a transition period of two years so that all the provisions of UCC 9 will not be effective until 2001. Although your author does not know the exact number, the estimate is that some states have already enacted the revision and in the remaining states the revision is presently before the state legislatures and has reached different stages in the process. The advantage is that the law will become somewhat uniform in all 50 states and one of the goals of the drafters was to have one type of a financing statement and one procedure for filing—so that when we move from state to state, the law is substantially the same.

The rules for the financing statement have been radically changed. Under the existing Rule 9, there are about 10 states which still require dual filing: 1) filing with the secretary of state and 2) where the goods are located or where the debtor is located. Under the new rule we have a one single filing rule that requires the filing of only one financing statement in a state office, such as the secretary of state or a designated clerk of the state. The creditor does not have to concern himself with the location of the collateral nor does he have to file in the county where the collateral or debtor is located. The obligation is to file the financing statement in the state where the debtor is incorporated, registered, or organized; or if the debtor is an individual, where the debtor has a legal residence. There are no dual filings. Nevertheless, if it is a real estate related transaction, the perfection of the filing is where the mortgage is properly filed, indexed, or recorded. The revised law provides that a filing against a foreign debtor is to be done in Washington, D.C. The advantage of this unified rule is that where a security interest covers goods located in many jurisdictions, only one filing is necessary.

A corporation is a registered organization of a state, if it is organized under the laws of the state and thus is treated as being located in that state. Where the corporation is organized can be determined with certainty and will eliminate a determination of which law applies where a corporation has many offices across many states. Accordingly, financing statements will be filed in the state where the corporation is organized or where the debtor resides, notwithstanding where the collateral is located. Where the corporation has more than one office in the same state, the creditor need not determine which is the chief executive office, but merely has to file in the state in which the debtor is registered (organized).

The rules for transition to the new provisions provide that a financing statement perfected prior to the enactment of the new law will remain effective at least for an additional year.

One obligation of a creditor will be to conduct searches in possibly two states. Because the revision provides for a possibly different place to file the financing statement, the creditor, during this period of transition, will have to search in the jurisdictions where the financing statement would be filed under the old UCC 9, as well as in the jurisdictions in which the financing statement would be filed under the new UCC 9. The creditor will have to furnish the necessary information concerning the debtor so that the searching organization will be able to conduct the searches in the proper states to identify any prior liens on the collateral.

If a creditor desires to file a continuation statement during the transition period, the continuation statement has to be filed under the revised UCC 9 as if it was an initial financing statement together with certain information concerning the old financing. The old six-month window to file the continuation statement before the expiration of the five-year period for filing a financing statement disappears and the new continuation statement can be filed at any time before the expiration of the old financing statement as a new financing statement in the proper jurisdiction under the new law. This may be done before the revised UCC 9 becomes effective, although not before it is passed by the respective state legislatures to be effective law. Taking action before the revised law becomes effective in your respective state should only be done after consultation with counsel and filing a continuation statement should be carefully considered to be certain that they are properly filed.

A debtor need not sign the financing statement. The creditor must have the authority to file the financing statement on behalf of the debtor, but this does not have to appear on the financing statement itself. National forms of financing statement will be accepted in every state and no longer will we have separate forms for each state. The revised article permits generic descriptions in the financing statement such as "all assets," but at the same time, the security agreement has to be more specific than "all assets" or "all personal property."

The law permits the filing of the financing statement and has taken away the powers of the clerks to reject the financing statement in the event that they feel, in their opinion, there is a legal deficiency in the information contained in the financing statement. For example, a filing officer may not refuse to file a financing statement if the collateral is missing. The amendment specifically states the limited grounds that the filing officer can use to reject a financing statement.

Article 9 expands the definitions of accounts and adds a new item called "payment intangibles," which includes such items as insurance policies, licensed property, premiums for secondary obligations, and lottery winnings. Article 9 also will now be able to cover such items as letters of credit, guarantees, commercial tort claims, promissory notes, and non-assignable general intangibles.

One interesting aspect of Article 9 is that it will allow partial strict foreclosure which means that a debtor can return the collateral in partial satisfaction of the debt rather than in full satisfaction of the debt and still pay off the balance. This is limited to businesses. A creditor must notify other secured creditors in the event of a foreclosure, which means that the creditor will have to conduct a lien search before he forecloses.

The above is just a summary of some of the highlights of the law of the revised UCC 9 as adopted by the National Conference of Commissioners on Uniform State Laws. As the laws get adopted by each state, there is a possibility that there may be minor changes in each state law. Careful review of the law by your counsel is recommended. In the Appendix, there is a comparison of the current Article 9 and the new Article 9 prepared by Steven O. Weise of Heller, Ehrman, White and McAuliffe, Los Angeles, California which specifically points out the changes between the old Article 9 and the new Article 9. One of the main purposes of the revised Article 9 is to provide for the electronic filing across the states and to provide for uniform procedures and forms across the states. You will also find in the appendix an example of the new forms that will be used.

In view of the dramatic changes in the procedures to prepare a security interest and to prepare and file a financing statement as well as the additional opportunities and changes in the availability of collateral, after the law is passed in your particular state, consult with experienced counsel to review the changes and consider the options that are available under the new law.

CHAPTER 10
APPENDIX I

UNIFORM COMMERCIAL CODE: SECTION 9

TWELFTH EDITION

THE AMERICAN LAW INSTITUTE AND
THE NATIONAL CONFERENCE OF COMMISSIONERS
ON UNIFORM STATE LAWS

OFFICIAL TEXT-1990

S 9-101. SHORT TITLE.

This Article shall be known and may be cited as Uniform Commercial Code-Secured Transactions.

S 9-102. POLICY AND SUBJECT MATTER OF ARTICLE.

(1) Except as otherwise provided in Section 9-104 on excluded transactions, this Article applies

    (a) to any transaction (regardless of its form) which is intended to create a security interest in personal property or fixtures including goods, documents, instruments, general intangibles, chattel paper or accounts; and also

    (b) to any sale of accounts or chattel paper.

(2) This Article applies to security interests created by contract including pledge, assignment, chattel mortgage, chattel trust, trust deed, factor's lien, equipment trust, conditional sale, trust receipt, other lien or title retention contract and lease or consignment intended as security. This Article does not apply to statutory liens except as provided in Section 9-310.

(3) The application of this Article to a security interest in a secured obligation is not affected by the fact that the obligation is itself secured by a transaction or interest to which this Article does not apply.

S 9-103. PERFECTION OF SECURITY INTEREST
IN MULTIPLE STATE TRANSACTIONS.

(1) Documents, instruments and ordinary goods.

  (a) This subsection applies to documents and instruments and to goods other than those described in subsection (3), and minerals described in subsection (5).

  (b) Except as otherwise provided in this subsection, perfection and the effect of perfection or non-perfection of a security interest in collateral are governed by the law of the jurisdiction where the collateral is when the last event occurs on which is based the assertion that the security interest is perfected or unperfected.

  (c) If the parties to a transaction creating a purchase money security interest in goods in one jurisdiction understand at the time that the security interest attaches that the goods will be kept in another jurisdiction, then the law of the other jurisdiction governs the perfection and the effect of perfection or non-perfection of the security interest from the time it attaches until thirty days after the debtor receives possession of the goods and thereafter if the goods are taken to the other jurisdiction before the end of the thirty-day period.

  (d) When collateral is brought into and kept in this state while subject to a security interest perfected under the law of the jurisdiction from which the collateral was removed, the security interest remains perfected, but if action is required by Part 3 of this Article to perfect the security interest,

    (i) if the action is not taken before the expiration of the period of perfection in the other jurisdiction or the end of four months after the collateral is brought into this state, whichever period first expires, the security interest becomes unperfected at the end of that period and is thereafter deemed to have been unperfected as against a person who became a purchaser after removal;

    (ii) if the action is taken before the expiration of the period specified in subparagraph (i), the security interest continues perfected thereafter;

    (iii) for the purpose of priority over a buyer of consumer goods (subsection (2) of Section 9-307), the period of the effectiveness of a filing in the jurisdiction from which the collateral is removed is governed by the rules with respect to perfection in subparagraphs (i) and (ii).

(2) Certificate of title.

  (a) This subsection applies to goods covered by a certificate of title issued under a statute of this state or of another jurisdiction under the law of which indication of a security interest on the certificate is required as a condition of perfection.

  (b) Except as otherwise provided in this subsection, perfection and the effect of perfection or non-perfection of the security interest are governed by the law (including the conflict of laws rules) of the jurisdiction issuing the certificate until four months after the goods are removed from that jurisdiction and thereafter until the goods are registered in another jurisdiction, but in any event not beyond surrender of the certificate. After the expiration of that period, the goods are not covered by the certificate of title within the meaning of this section.

(c)   Except with respect to the rights of a buyer described in the next paragraph, a security interest, perfected in another jurisdiction otherwise than by notation on a certificate of title, in goods brought into this state and thereafter covered by a certificate of title issued by this state is subject to the rules stated in paragraph (d) of subsection (1).

(d)   If goods are brought into this state while a security interest therein is perfected in any manner under the law of the jurisdiction from which the goods are removed and a certificate of title is issued by this state and the certificate does not show that the goods are subject to the security interest or that they may be subject to security interests not shown on the certificate, the security interest is subordinate to the rights of a buyer of the goods who is not in the business of selling goods of that kind to the extent that he gives value and receives delivery of the goods after issuance of the certificate and without knowledge of the security interest.

(3)   Accounts, general intangibles and mobile goods.

(a)   This subsection applies to accounts (other than an account described in subsection (5) minerals) and general intangibles (other than uncertificated securities) and to goods which are mobile and which are of a type normally used in more than one jurisdiction, such as motor vehicles, trailers, rolling stock, airplanes, shipping containers, road building and construction machinery and commercial harvesting machinery and the like, if the goods are equipment or are inventory leased or held for lease by the debtor to others, and are not covered by a certificate of title described in subsection (2).

(b)   The law (including the conflict of laws rules) of the jurisdiction in which the debtor is located governs the perfection and the effect of perfection or non-perfection of the security interest.

(c)   If, however, the debtor is located in a jurisdiction which is not a part of the United States, and which does not provide for perfection of the security interest by filing or recording in that jurisdiction, the law of the jurisdiction in the United States in which the debtor has its major executive office in the United States governs the perfection and the effect of perfection or non-perfection of the security interest through filing. In the alternative, if the debtor is located in a jurisdiction which is not a part of the United States or Canada and the collateral is accounts or general intangibles for money due or to become due, the security interest may be perfected by notification to the account debtor. As used in this paragraph, "United States" includes its territories and possessions and the Commonwealth of Puerto Rico.

(d)   A debtor shall be deemed located at his place of business if he has one, at his chief executive office if he has more than one place of business, otherwise at his residence. If, however, the debtor is a foreign air carrier under the Federal Aviation Act of 1958, as amended, it shall be deemed located at the designated office of the agent upon whom service of process may be made on behalf of the foreign air carrier.

(e)   A security interest perfected under the law of the jurisdiction of the location of the debtor is perfected until the expiration of four months after a change of the debtor's location to another jurisdiction, or until perfection would have ceased by the law of the first jurisdiction, whichever period first expires. Unless perfected in the new jurisdiction before the end of that period, it becomes unperfected as against a person who became a purchaser after the change.

(4) Chattel paper.

The rules stated for goods in subsection (1) apply to a possessory security interest in chattel paper. The rules stated for accounts in subsection (3) apply to a non-possessor security interest in chattel paper, but the security interest may not be perfected by notification to the account debtor.

(5) Minerals.

Perfection and the effect of perfection or non-perfection of a security interest which is created by a debtor who has an interest in minerals or the like (including oil and gas) before extraction and which attaches thereto as extracted, or which attaches to an account resulting from the sale thereof at the wellhead or minehead are governed by the law (including the conflict of laws rules) of the jurisdiction wherein the wellhead or minehead is located.

(6) Uncertificated securities.

The law (including the conflict of laws rules) of the jurisdiction of organization of the issuer governs the perfection and the effect of perfection or non-perfection of a security interest in uncertificated securities.

As amended in 1972 and 1977.

S 9-104. TRANSACTIONS EXCLUDED FROM ARTICLE.

This Article does not apply

(a)   to a security interest subject to any statute of the United States, to the extent that such statute governs the rights of parties to and third parties affected by transactions in particular types of property; or

(b)   to a landlord's lien; or

(c)   to a lien given by statute or other rule of law for services or materials except as provided in Section 9-310 on priority of such liens; or

(d)   to a transfer of a claim for wages, salary or other compensation of an employee; or

(e)   to a transfer by a government or governmental subdivision or agency; or

(f)   to a sale of accounts or chattel paper as part of a sale of the business out of which they arose, or an assignment of accounts or chattel paper which is for the purpose of collection only, or a transfer of a right to payment under a contract to an assignee who is also to do the performance under the contract or a transfer of a single account to an assignee in whole or partial satisfaction of a preexisting indebtedness; or

(g)   to a transfer of an interest in or claim in or under any policy of insurance, except as provided with respect to proceeds (Section 9-306) and priorities in proceeds (Section 9-312); or

(h)   to a right represented by a judgment (other than a judgment taken on a right to pay-ment which was collateral); or

(i)   to any right of setoff; or

(j)   except to the extent that provision is made for fixtures in Section 9-313, to the cre-ation or transfer of an interest in or lien on real estate, including a lease or rents there-under; or

(k)   to a transfer in whole or in part of any claim arising out of tort; or

(l)   to a transfer of an interest in any deposit account (subsection (1) of Section 9-105), except as provided with respect to proceeds (Section 9-306) and priorities in pro-ceeds (Section 9-312).

S 9-105. DEFINITIONS AND INDEX OF DEFINITIONS.

(1)   In this Article unless the context otherwise requires:

   (a)   "Account debtor" means the person who is obligated on an account, chattel paper or general intangible;

   (b)   "Chattel Paper" means a writing or writings which evidence both a mone-tary obligation and a security interest in or a lease of specific goods, but a charter or other contract involving the use or hire of a vessel is not chattel paper. When a transaction is evidenced both by such a security agreement or a lease and by an instrument or a series of instruments, the group of writings taken together constitutes chattel paper;

   (c)   "Collateral" means the property subject to a security interest, and includes accounts and chattel paper which have been sold;

   (d)   "Debtor" means the person who owes payment or other performance of the obligation secured, whether or not he owns or has rights in the collateral, and includes the seller of accounts or chattel paper. Where the debtor and the owner of the collateral are not the same person, the term "debtor" means the owner of the collateral in any provision of the Article dealing with the collat-eral, the obligor in any provision dealing with the obligation, and may include both where the context so requires;

   (e)   "Deposit account" means a demand, time, savings, passbook or like account maintained with a bank, savings and loan association, credit union or like organization, other than an account evidenced by a certificate of deposit;

   (f)   "Document" means document of title as defined in the general definitions of Article 1 (Section 1-201), and a receipt of the kind described in subsection (2) of Section 7-201;

   (g)   "Encumbrance" includes real estate mortgages and other liens on real estate and all other rights in real estate that are not ownership interests;

   (h)   "Goods" includes all things which are movable at the time the security inter-est attaches or which are fixtures (Section 9-313), but does not include money, documents, instruments, accounts, chattel paper, general intangibles, or min-erals or the like (including oil and gas) before extraction. "Goods" also includes standing timber which is to be cut and removed under a conveyance or contract for sale, the unborn young of animals, and growing crops;

(i) "Instrument" means a negotiable instrument (defined in Section 3-104), or a certificated security (defined in Section 8-102) or any other writing which evidences a right to the payment of money and is not itself a security agreement or lease and is of a type which is in ordinary course of business transferred by delivery with any necessary indorsement or assignment;

(j) "Mortgage" means a consensual interest created by a real estate mortgage, a trust deed on real estate, or the like;

(k) An advance is made "pursuant to commitment" if the secured party has bound himself to make it, whether or not a subsequent event of default or other event not within his control has relieved or may relieve him from his obligation;

(l) "Security agreement:" means an agreement which creates or provides for a security interest;

(m) "Secured party" means a lender, seller or other person in whose favor there is a security interest, including a person to whom accounts or chattel paper have been sold. When the holders of obligations issued under an indenture of trust, equipment trust agreement or the like are represented by a trustee or other person, the representative is the secured party;

(n) "Transmitting utility" means any person primarily engaged in the railroad, street railway or trolley bus business, the electric or electronics communications transmission business, the transmission of goods by pipeline, or the transmission or the production and transmission of electricity, steam, gas or water, or the provision of sewer service.

(2) Other definitions applying to this Article and the sections in which they appear are:

"Account".	Section 9-106.
"Attach".	Section 9-203.
"Construction mortgage".	Section 9-313(1).
"Consumer goods".	Section 9-109(1).
"Equipment".	Section 9-109(2).
"Farm products".	Section 9-109(3).
"Fixture".	Section 9-313(1).
"Fixture Filing".	Section 9-313(1).
"General intangibles".	Section 9-106.
"Inventory".	Section 9-109(4).
"Lien creditor".	Section 9-301(3).
"Proceeds".	Section 9-306(1).
"Purchase money security interest".	Section 9-107.
"United States".	Section 9-103.

(3) The following definitions in other Articles apply to this Article:

"Check".	Section 3-104.
"Contract for Sale".	Section 2-106.
"Holder in due course".	Section 3-302.

"Note".   Section 3-104.
"Sale".   Section 2-106.

S 9-106. Definitions: "Account"; "General Intangibles".

"Account" means any right to payment for goods sold or leased or for services rendered which is not evidenced by an instrument or chattel paper, whether or not it has been earned by performance. "General intangibles" means any personal property (including things in action) other than goods, accounts, chattel paper, documents, instruments, and money. All rights to payment earned or unearned under a charter or other contract involving the use or hire of a vessel and all rights incident to the charter or contract are accounts.

S 9-107. Definitions: "Purchase Money Security Interest".

A security interest is a "purchase money security interest" to the extent that it is

(a) taken or retained by the seller of the collateral to secure all or part of its price; or

(b) taken by a person who by making advances or incurring an obligation gives value to enable the debtor to acquire rights in or the use of collateral if such value is in fact so used.

S 9-108. When After-Acquired Collateral Not Security for Antecedent Debt.

Where a secured party makes an advance, incurs an obligation, releases a perfected security interest, or otherwise gives new value which is to be secured in whole or in part by after-acquired property his security interest in the after-acquired collateral shall be deemed to be taken for new value and not as security for an antecedent debt if the debtor acquires his rights in such collateral either in the ordinary course of his business or under a contract of purchase made pursuant to the security agreement within a reasonable time after new value is given.

S 9-109. Classification of Goods: "Consumer Goods"; "Equipment" "Farm Products"; "Inventory".

Goods are

(1) "consumer goods" if they are used or bought for use primarily for personal, family or household purposes;

(2) "equipment" if they are used or bought for use primarily in business (including farming or a profession) or by a debtor who is a non-profit organization or a governmental subdivision or agency or if the goods are not included in the definitions of inventory, farm products or consumer goods;

(3) "farm products" if they are crops or livestock or supplies used or produced in farming operations or if they are products of crops or livestock in their unmanufactured states (such as ginned cotton, wool-clip, maple syrup, milk and eggs), and if they are in the possession of a debtor engaged in raising, fattening, grazing or other farming operations.

If goods are farm products they are neither equipment nor inventory;

(4) "inventory" if they are held by a person who holds them for sale or lease or to be furnished under contracts of service or if he has so furnished them, or if they are raw materials, work in process or materials used or consumed in a business. Inventory of a person is not to be classified as his equipment.

S 9-110. SUFFICIENCY OF DESCRIPTION.

For the purposes of this Article any description of personal property or real estate is sufficient whether or not it is specific if it reasonably identifies what is described.

S 9-111. APPLICABILITY OF BULK TRANSFER LAWS.

The creation of a security interest is not a bulk transfer under Article 6 (see Section 6-103).

S 9-112. WHERE COLLATERAL IS NOT OWNED BY DEBTOR.

Unless otherwise agreed, when a secured party knows that collateral is owned by a person who is not the debtor, the owner of the collateral is entitled to receive from the secured party any surplus under Section 9-502(2) or under Section 9-504(1), and is not liable for the debt or for any deficiency after resale, and he has the same right as the debtor

(a) to receive statements under Section 9-203;

(b) to receive notice of and to object to a secured party's proposal to retain the collateral in satisfaction of the indebtedness under Section 9-505;

(c) to redeem the collateral under Section 9-506;

(d) to obtain injunctive or other relief under Section 9-507(1); and

(e) to recover losses caused to him under Section 9-208(2).

S 9-113. SECURITY INTERESTS ARISING UNDER ARTICLE ON SALES OR UNDER ARTICLE ON LEASES.

A security interest arising solely under the Article on Sales (Article 2) or the Article on Leases (Article 2A) is subject to the provisions of this Article except that to the extent that and so long as the debtor does not have or does not lawfully obtain possession of the goods

(a) no security agreement is necessary to make the security interest enforceable; and

(b) no filing is required to perfect the security interest; and

(c)   the rights of the secured party on default by the debtor are governed

   (i)   by the Article on Sales (Article 2) in the case of a security interest arising sole-
           ly under such Article or (ii) by the Article on Leases (Article 2A) in the case of
           a security interest arising solely under such Article.

S 9-114. CONSIGNMENT.

(1)   A person who delivers goods under a consignment which is not a security interest
      and who would be required to file under this Article by paragraph (3)(c) of Section
      2-326 has priority over a secured party who is or becomes a creditor of the consignee
      and who would have a perfected security interest in the goods if they were the prop-
      erty of the consignee, and also has priority with respect to identifiable cash proceeds
      received on or before delivery of the goods to a buyer, if

   (a)   the consignor complies with the filing provision of the Article on Sales with
         respect to consignments (paragraph (3)(c) of Section 2-326) before the con-
         signee receives possession of the goods; and

   (b)   the consignor gives notification in writing to the holder of the security interest
         if the holder has filed a financing statement covering the same types of goods
         before the date of the filing made by the consignor; and

   (c)   the holder of the security interest receives the notification within five years
         before the consignee receives possession of the goods; and

   (d)   the notification states that the consignor expects to deliver goods on consign-
         ment to the consignee, describing the goods by item or type.

(2)   In the case of a consignment which is not a security interest and in which the require-
      ments of the preceding subsection have not been met, a person who delivers goods
      to another is subordinate to a person who would have a perfected security interest
      in the goods if they were the property of the debtor.

S 9-201. GENERAL VALIDITY OF SECURITY AGREEMENT.

Except as otherwise provided by this Act a security agreement is effective according to its
terms between the parties, against purchases of the collateral and against creditors.
Nothing in this Article validates any charge or practice illegal under any statute or regulation thereunder governing usury, small loans, retail installment sales, or the like, or
extends the application of any such statute or regulation to any transaction not otherwise
subject thereto.

S 9-203. ATTACHMENT AND ENFORCEABILITY
OF SECURITY INTEREST; PROCEEDS; FORMAL REQUISITES.

(1)   Subject to the provisions of Section 4-208 on the security interest of a collecting bank,
      Section 8-321 on security interests in securities and Section 9-113 on a security inter-
      est arising under the Article on Sales, a security interest is not enforceable against the
      debtor or third parties with respect to the collateral and does not attach unless:

   (a)   the collateral is in the possession of the secured party pursuant to agreement,
         or the debtor has signed a security agreement which contains a description of
         the collateral and in addition, when the security interest covers crops growing
         or to be grown or timber to be cut, a description of the land concerned;

    (b)   value has been given; and

    (c)   the debtor has rights in the collateral.

(2)   A security interest attaches when it becomes enforceable against the debtor with respect to the collateral. Attachment occurs as soon as all of the events specified in subsection (1) have taken place unless explicit agreement postpones the time of attaching.

(3)   Unless otherwise agreed a security agreement gives the secured party the rights to proceeds provided by Section 9-306.

(4)   A transaction, although subject to this Article, is also subject to_____*, and in the case of conflict between the provisions of this Article and any such statute, the provisions of such statute control. Failure to comply with any applicable statute has only the effect which is specified therein.

S 9-204. AFTER-ACQUIRED PROPERTY; FUTURE ADVANCES.

(1)   Except as provided in subsection (2), a security agreement may provide that any or all obligations covered by the security agreement are to be secured by after-acquired collateral.

(2)   No security interest attaches under an after-acquired property clause to consumer goods other than accessions (Section 9-314) when given as additional security unless the debtor acquires rights in them within ten days after the secured party gives value.

(3)   Obligations covered by a security agreement may include future advances or other value whether or not the advances or value are given pursuant to commitment (subsection (1) of Section 9-105).

S 9-205. USE OR DISPOSITION OF COLLATERAL WITHOUT ACCOUNTING PERMISSIBLE.

A security interest is not invalid or fraudulent against creditors by reason of liberty in the debtor to use, commingle or dispose of all or part of the collateral (including returned or repossessed goods) or to collect or compromise accounts or chattel paper, or to accept the return of goods or make repossessions, or to use, commingle or dispose of proceeds, or by reason of the failure of the secured party to require the debtor to account for proceeds or replace collateral. This section does not relax the requirements of possession where perfection of a security interest depends upon possession of the collateral by the secured party or by a bailee.

S 9-206. AGREEMENT NOT TO ASSERT DEFENSES AGAINST ASSIGNEE; MODIFICATION OF SALES WARRANTIES WHERE SECURITY AGREEMENT EXISTS.

(1)   Subject to any statute or decision which establishes a different rule for buyers or lessees of consumer goods, an agreement that a buyer or lessee may have against the seller or lessor is enforceable by an assignee who takes his assignment for value, in

good faith and without notice of a claim or defense, except as to defenses of a type which may be asserted against a holder in due course of a negotiable instrument under the Article on Commercial Paper (Article 3). A buyer who as part of one transaction signs both a negotiable instrument and a security agreement makes such an agreement.

(2) When a seller retains a purchase money security interest in goods the Article on Sales (Article 2) governs the sale and any disclaimer, limitation or modification of the seller's warranties.

S 9-207. RIGHTS AND DUTIES WHEN COLLATERAL IS IN SECURED PARTY'S POSSESSION.

(1) A secured party must use reasonable care in the custody and preservation of collateral in his possession. In the case of an instrument or chattel paper reasonable care includes taking necessary steps to preserve rights against prior parties unless otherwise agreed.

(2) Unless otherwise agreed, when collateral is in the secured party's possession

    (a) reasonable expenses (including the cost of any insurance and payment of taxes or other charges) incurred in the custody, preservation, use or operation of the collateral are chargeable to the debtor and are secured by the collateral;

    (b) the risk of accidental loss or damage is on the debtor to the extent of any deficiency in any effective insurance coverage;

    (c) the secured party may hold as additional security any increase or profits (except money) received from the collateral, but money so received, unless remitted to the debtor, shall be applied in reduction of the secured obligation;

    (d) the secured party must keep the collateral identifiable but fungible collateral may be commingled;

    (e) the secured party may repledge the collateral upon terms which do not impair the debtor's right to redeem it.

(3) A secured party is liable for any loss caused by his failure to meet any obligation imposed by the preceding subsections but does not lose his security interest.

(4) A secured party may use or operate the collateral for the purpose of preserving the collateral or its value or pursuant to the order of a court of appropriate jurisdiction or, except in the case of consumer goods, in the manner and to the extent provided in the security agreement.

S 9-208. REQUEST FOR STATEMENT OF ACCOUNT OR LIST OF COLLATERAL.

(1) A debtor may sign a statement indicating what he believes to be the aggregate amount of unpaid indebtedness as of a specified date and may send it to the secured party with a request that the statement be approved or corrected and returned to the debtor. When the security agreement or any other record kept by the secured party identifies the collateral a debtor may similarly request the secured party to approve or correct a list of the collateral.

(2) The secured party must comply with such a request within two weeks after receipt by sending a written correction or approval. If the secured party claims a security interest in all of a particular type of collateral owned by the debtor he may indicate that fact in his reply and need not approve or correct an itemized list of such collateral. If the secured party without reasonable excuse fails to comply he is liable for any loss caused to the debtor thereby; and if the debtor has properly included in his request a good faith statement of the obligation or a list of the collateral or both the secured party may claim a security interest only as shown in the statement against persons misled by his failure to comply. If he no longer has an interest in the obligation or collateral at the time the request is received he must disclose the name and address of any successor in interest known to him and he is liable for any loss caused to the debtor as a result of failure to disclose. A successor in interest is not subject to this section until a request is received by him.

(3) A debtor is entitled to such a statement once every six months without charge. The secured party may require payment of a charge not exceeding $10 for each additional statement furnished.

S 9-301. PERSONS WHO TAKE PRIORITY OVER UNPERFECTED SECURITY INTERESTS; RIGHTS OF "LIEN CREDITOR".

(1) Except as otherwise provided in subsection (2), an unperfected security interest is subordinate to the rights of

   (a)   persons entitled to priority under Section 9-312;

   (b)   a person who becomes a lien creditor before the security interest is perfected;

   (c)   in the case of goods, instruments, documents, and chattel paper, a person who is not a secured party and who is a transferee in bulk or other buyer not in ordinary course of business or is a buyer of farm products in ordinary course of business, to the extent that he gives value and receives delivery of the collateral without knowledge of the security interest and before it is perfected;

   (d)   in the case of accounts and general intangibles, a person who is not a secured party and who is a transferee to the extent that he gives value without knowledge of the security interest and before it is perfected.

(2) If the secured party files with respect to a purchase money security interest before or within ten days after the debtor receives possession of the collateral, he takes priority over the rights of a transferee in bulk or of a lien creditor which arise between the time the security interest attaches and the time of filing.

(3) A "lien creditor" means a creditor who has acquired a lien on the property involved by attachment, levy or the like and includes an assignee for benefit of creditors from the time of assignment, and a trustee in bankruptcy from the date of the filing of the petition or a receiver in equity from the time of appointment.

(4) A person who becomes a lien creditor while a security interest is perfected takes subject to the security interest only to the extent that it secures advances made before he becomes a lien creditor or within 45 days thereafter or made without knowledge of the lien or pursuant to a commitment entered into without knowledge of the lien.

S 9-302. When Filing Is Required to Perfect Security Interest; Security Interests to Which Filing Provisions of This Article Do Not Apply.

(1) A financing statement must be filed to perfect all security interests except the following:

    (a) a security interest in collateral in possession of the secured party under Section 9-305;

    (b) a security interest temporarily perfected in instruments or documents without delivery under Section 9-304 or in proceeds for a 10 day period under Section 9-306;

    (c) a security interest created by an assignment of a beneficial interest in a trust or a decedent's estate;

    (d) a purchase money security interest in consumer goods; but filing is required for a motor vehicle required to be registered; and fixture filing is required for priority over conflicting interests in fixtures to the extent provided in Section 9-313;

    (e) an assignment of accounts which does not alone or in conjunction with other assignments to the same assignee transfer a significant part of the outstanding accounts of the assignor;

    (f) a security interest of a collecting bank (Section 4-208) or in securities (Section 8-321) or arising under the Article on Sales (see Section 9-113) or covered in subsection (3) of this section;

    (g) an assignment for the benefit of all the creditors of the transferor, and subsequent transfers by the assignee thereunder.

(2) If a secured party assigns a perfected security interest, no filing under this Article is required in order to continue the perfected status of the security interest against creditors of and transferees from the original debtor.

(3) The filing of a financing statement otherwise required by this Article is not necessary or effective to perfect a security interest in property subject to

    (a) a statute or treaty of the United States which provides for a national or international registration or a national or international certificate of title or which specifies a place of filing different from that specified in this Article for filing of the security interest; or

    (b) the following statutes of this state; (list any certificate of title statute covering automobiles, trailers, mobile homes, boats, farm tractors, or the like, and any central filing statute*); but during any period in which collateral is inventory held for sale by a person who is in the business of selling goods of that kind, the filing provisions of this Article (Part 4) apply to a security interest in that collateral created by him as debtor; or

    (c) a certificate of title statute of another jurisdiction under the law of which indication of a security interest on the certificate is required as a condition of perfection (subsection (2) of Section 9-103).

(4) Compliance with a statute or treaty described in subsection (3) is equivalent to the filing of a financing statement under this Article, and a security interest in property subject to the statute or treaty can be perfected only by compliance therewith except as

provided in Section 9-103 on multiple state transactions. Duration and renewal of perfection of a security interest perfected by compliance with the statute or treaty are governed by the provisions of the statute or treaty; in other respects the security interest is subject to this Article.

S 9-303. WHEN SECURITY INTEREST IS PERFECTED; CONTINUITY OF PERFECTION.

(1) A security interest is perfected when it has attached and when all of the applicable steps required for perfection have been taken. Such steps are specified in Sections 9-302, 9-304, 9-305 and 9-306. If such steps are taken before the security interest attaches, it is perfected at the time when it attaches.

(2) If a security interest is originally perfected in any way permitted under this Article and is subsequently perfected in some other way under this Article, without an intermediate period when it was unperfected, the security interest shall be deemed to be perfected continuously for the purposes of this Article.

S 9-304. PERFECTION OF SECURITY INTEREST IN INSTRUMENTS, DOCUMENTS, AND GOODS COVERED BY DOCUMENTS; PERFECTION BY PERMISSIVE FILING; TEMPORARY PERFECTION WITHOUT FILING OR TRANSFER OF POSSESSION.

(1) A security interest in chattel paper or negotiable documents may be perfected by filing. A security interest in money or instruments (other than certificated securities or instruments which constitute part of chattel paper) can be perfected only by the secured party's taking possession, except as provided in subsections (4) and (5) of this section and subsections (2) and (3) of Section 9-306 on proceeds.

(2) During the period that goods are in the possession of the issuer of a negotiable document therefor, a security interest in the goods is perfected by perfecting a security interest in the document, and any security interest in the goods otherwise perfected during such period is subject thereto.

(3) A security interest in goods in the possession of a bailee other than one who has issued a negotiable document therefor is perfected by issuance of a document in the name of the secured party or by the bailee's receipt of notification of the secured party's interest or by filing as to the goods.

(4) A security interest in instruments (other than certified securities) or negotiable documents is perfected without filing or the taking of possession for a period of 21 days from the time it attaches to the extent that it arises for new value given under a written security agreement.

(5) A security interest remains perfected for a period of 21 days without filing where a secured party having a perfected security interest in an instrument (other than a certificated security), a negotiable document or goods in possession of a bailee other than one who has issued a negotiable document therefor

    (a) makes available to the debtor the goods or documents representing the goods for the purpose of ultimate sale or exchange or for the purpose of loading, unloading, storing, shipping, transshipping, manufacturing, processing or otherwise dealing with them in a manner preliminary to their sale or exchange, but priority between conflicting security interests in the goods is subject to subsection (3) of Section 9-312; or

(b) delivers the instrument to the debtor for the purpose of ultimate sale or exchange or of presentation, collection, renewal or registration of transfer.

(6) After the 21 day period in subsections (4) and (5) perfection depends upon compliance with applicable provisions of this Article.

S 9-305. WHEN POSSESSION BY SECURED PARTY PERFECTS SECURITY INTEREST WITHOUT FILING.

A security interest in letters of credit and advices of credit (subsection (2)(a) of Section 5-116), goods, instruments (other than certificated securities), money, negotiable documents, or chattel paper may be perfected by the secured party's taking possession of the collateral. If such collateral other than goods covered by a negotiable document is held by a bailee, the secured party is deemed to have possession from the time the bailee receives notification of the secured party's interest. A security interest is perfected by possession from the time possession is taken without a relation back and continues only so long as possession is retained, unless otherwise specified in this Article. The security interest may be otherwise perfected as provided in this Article before or after the period of possession by the secured party.

S 9-306. "PROCEEDS", SECURED PARTY'S RIGHTS ON DISPOSITION OF COLLATERAL.

(1) "Proceeds" includes whatever is received upon the sale, exchange, collection or other disposition of collateral or process. Insurance payable by reason of loss or damage to the collateral is proceeds, except to the extent that it is payable to a person other than a party to the security agreement. Money, checks, deposit accounts, and the like are "cash proceeds". All other proceeds are "non-cash proceeds".

(2) Except where this Article otherwise provides, a security interest continues in collateral notwithstanding sale, exchange or other disposition thereof unless the disposition was authorized by the secured party in the security agreement or otherwise, and also continues in any identifiable proceeds including collections received by the debtor.

(3) The security interest in proceeds is a continuously perfected security interest if the interest in the original collateral was perfected but it ceases to be a perfected security interest and becomes unperfected ten days after receipt of the proceeds by the debtor unless

(a) a filed financing statement covers the original collateral and the proceeds are collateral in which a security interest may be perfected by filing in the office or offices where the financing statement has been filed and, if the proceeds are acquired with cash proceeds, the description of collateral in the financing statement indicates the types of property constituting the proceeds; or

(b)   a filed financing statement covers the original collateral and the proceeds are identifiable cash proceeds; or

(c)   the security interest in the proceeds is perfected before the expiration of the ten day period.

Except as provided in this section, a security interest in proceeds can be perfected only by the methods or under the circumstances permitted in this Article for original collateral of the same type.

(4)   In the event of insolvency proceedings instituted by or against a debtor, a secured party with a perfected security interest in proceeds has a perfected security interest only in the following proceeds:

(a)   in identifiable non-cash proceeds and in separate deposit accounts containing only proceeds;

(b)   in identifiable cash proceeds in the form of money which is neither commingled with other money nor deposited in a deposit account prior to the insolvency proceedings;

(c)   in identifiable cash proceeds in the form of checks and the like which are not deposited in a deposit account prior to the insolvency proceedings; and

(d)   in all cash and deposit accounts of the debtor in which proceeds have been commingled with other funds, but the perfected security interest under this paragraph (d) is

     (i)   subject to any right to setoff; and

     (ii)   limited to an amount not greater than the amount of any cash proceeds received by the debtor within ten days before the institution of the insolvency proceedings less the sum of (I) the payments to the secured party on account of cash proceeds received by the debtor during such period and (II) the cash proceeds received by the debtor during such period to which the secured party is entitled under paragraphs (a) through (c) of this subsection (4).

(5)   If a sale of goods results in an account or chattel paper which is transferred by the seller to a secured party, and if the goods are returned to or are repossessed by the seller or the secured party, the following rules determine priorities:

(a)   If the goods were collateral at the time of sale, for an indebtedness of the seller which is still unpaid, the original security interest attaches again to the goods and continues as a perfected security interest if it was perfected at the time when the goods were sold. If the security interest was originally perfected by a filing which is still effective, nothing further is required to continue the perfected status; in any other case, the secured party must take possession of the returned or repossessed goods or must file.

(b)   An unpaid transferee of the chattel paper has a security interest in the goods against the transferor. Such security interest is prior to a security interest asserted under paragraph (a) to the extent that the transferee of the chattel paper was entitled to priority under Section 9-308.

(c)   An unpaid transferee of the account has a security interest in the goods against the transferor such security interest is subordinate to a security interest asserted under paragraph (a).

(d)   A security interest of an unpaid transferee asserted under paragraph (b) or (c) must be perfected for protection against creditors of the transferor and purchasers of the returned or repossessed goods.

S 9-307. PROTECTION OF BUYERS OF GOODS.

(1)   A buyer in ordinary course of business (subsection (9) of Section 1-201) other than a person buying farm products from a person engaged in farming operations takes free of a security interest created by his seller even though the security interest is perfected and even though the buyer knows of its existence.

(2)   In the case of consumer goods, a buyer takes free of a security interest even though perfected if he buys without knowledge of the security interest, for value and for his own personal, family or household purposes unless prior to the purchase the secured party has filed a financing statement covering such goods.

(3)   A buyer other than a buyer in ordinary course of business (subsection (1) of this section) takes free of a security interest to the extent that it secures future advances made after the secured party acquires knowledge of the purchase, or more than 45 days after the purchase, whichever first occurs, unless made pursuant to a commitment entered into without knowledge of the purchase and before the expiration of the 45 day period.

S 9-308. PURCHASE OF CHATTEL PAPER AND INSTRUMENTS.

A purchaser of chattel paper or an instrument who gives new value and takes possession of it in the ordinary course of his business has priority over a security interest in the chattel paper or instrument

(a)   which is perfected under Section 9-304 (permissive filing and temporary perfection) or under Section 9-306 (perfection as to proceeds) if he acts without knowledge that the specific paper or instrument is subject to a security interest; or

(b)   which is claimed merely as proceeds of inventory subject to a security interest (Section 9-306) even though he knows that the specific paper or instrument is subject to the security interest.

S 9-309. PROTECTION OF PURCHASERS OF INSTRUMENTS, DOCUMENTS, AND SECURITIES.

Nothing in this Article limits the rights of a holder in due course of a negotiable instrument (Section 3-302) or a holder to whom a negotiable document of title has been duly negotiated (Section 7-501) or a bona fide purchaser of a security (Section 8-302) and the holders or purchasers take priority over an earlier security interest even though perfected. Filing under this Article does not constitute notice of the security interest to such holders or purchasers.

S 9-310. PRIORITY OF CERTAIN LIENS ARISING BY OPERATION OF LAW.

When a person in the ordinary course of his business furnishes services or materials with respect to goods subject to a security interest, a lien upon goods in the possession of such person given by statute or rule of law for such materials or services takes priority over a perfected security interest unless the lien is statutory and the statute expressly provides otherwise.

S 9-311. ALIENABILITY OF DEBTOR'S RIGHTS: JUDICIAL PROCESS.

The debtor's rights in collateral may be voluntarily or involuntarily transferred (by way of sale, creation of a security interest, attachment, levy, garnishment or other judicial process) notwithstanding a provision in the security agreement prohibiting any transfer or making the transfer constitute a default.

S 9-312. PRIORITIES AMONG CONFLICTING SECURITY INTERESTS IN THE SAME COLLATERAL.

(1) The rules of priority stated in other sections of this Part and in the following sections shall govern when applicable: Section 4-208 with respect to the security interests of collecting banks in items being collected, accompanying documents and proceeds; Section 9-103 on security interests related to other jurisdictions; Section 9-114 on consignments.

(2) A perfected security interest in crops for new value given to enable the debtor to produce the crops during the production season and given not more than three months before the crops become growing crops by planting or otherwise takes priority over an earlier perfected security interest to the extent that such earlier interest secures obligations due more than six months before the crops become growing crops by planting or otherwise, even though the person giving new value had knowledge of the earlier security interest.

(3) A perfected purchase money security interest in inventory has priority over a conflicting security interest in the same inventory and also has priority in identifiable cash proceeds received on or before the delivery of the inventory to a buyer if

   (a) the purchase money security interest is perfected at the time the debtor receives possession of the inventory; and

   (b) the purchase money secured party gives notification in writing to the holder of the conflicting security interest if the holder had filed a financing statement covering the same types of inventory (i) before the date of the filing made by the purchase money secured party, or (ii) before the beginning of the 21 day period where the purchase money security interest is temporarily perfected without filing or possession (subsection (5) of Section 9-304); and

   (c) the holder of the conflicting security interest receives the notification within five years before the debtor receives possession of the inventory; and

   (d) the notification states that the person giving the notice has or expects to acquire a purchase money security interest in inventory of the debtor, describing such inventory by item or type.

(4) A purchase money security interest in collateral other than inventory has priority over a conflicting security interest in the same collateral or its proceeds if the pur-

chase money security interest is perfected at the time the debtor receives possession of the collateral or within ten days thereafter.

(5) In all cases not governed by other rules stated in this section (including cases of purchase money security interests which do not qualify for the special priorities set forth in subsections (3) and (4) of this section), priority between conflicting security interests in the same collateral shall be determined according to the following rules:

   (a) Conflicting security interests rank according to priority in time of filing or perfection. Priority dates from the time a filing is first made covering the collateral or the time the security interest is first perfected, whichever is earlier, provided that there is no period thereafter when there is neither filing nor perfection.

   (b) So long as conflicting security interests are unperfected, the first to attach has priority.

(6) For the purposes of subsection (5) a date of filing or perfection as to collateral is also a date of filing or perfection as to proceeds.

(7) If future advances are made while a security interest is perfected by filing, the taking of possession, or under Section 8-321 on securities, the security interest has the same priority for the purposes of subsection (5) with respect to the future advances as it does with respect to the first advance. If a commitment is made before or while the security interest is so perfected, the security interest has the same priority with respect to advances made pursuant thereto. In other cases a perfected security interest has priority from the date the advance is made.

S 9-313. PRIORITY OF SECURITY INTERESTS IN FIXTURES.

(1) In this section and in the provisions of Part 4 of this Article referring to fixture filing, unless the context otherwise requires:

   (a) goods are "fixtures" when they become so related to particular real estate that an interest in them arises under real estate law;

   (b) a "fixture filing" is the filing in the office where a mortgage on the real estate would be filed or recorded of a financing statement covering goods which are or are to become fixtures and conforming to the requirements of subsection (5) of Section 9-402;

   (c) a mortgage is a "construction mortgage" to the extent that it secures an obligation incurred for the construction of an improvement on land including the acquisition cost of the land, if the recorded writing so indicates.

(2) A security interest under this Article may be created in goods which are fixtures or may continue in goods which become fixtures, but no security interest exists under this Article in ordinary building materials incorporated into an improvement on land.

(3) This Article does not prevent creation of an encumbrance upon fixtures pursuant to real estate law.

(4) A perfected security interest in fixtures has priority over the conflicting interest of an encumbrancer or owner of the real estate where

(a)   the security interest is a purchase money security interest, the interest of the encumbrancer or owner arises before the goods become fixtures, the security interest is perfected by a fixture filing before the goods become fixtures or within ten days thereafter, and the debtor has an interest of record in the real estate or is in possession of the real estate; or

(b)   the security interest is perfected by a fixture filing before the interest of the encumbrancer or owner is of record, the security interest has priority over any conflicting interest of a predecessor in title of the encumbrancer or owner, and the debtor has an interest of record in the real estate or is in possession of the real estate; or

(c)   the fixtures are readily removable factory or office machines or readily removable replacements of domestic appliances which are consumer goods, and before the goods become fixtures the security interest is perfected by any method permitted by this Article; or

(d)   the conflicting interest is a lien on the real estate obtained by legal or equitable proceedings after the security interest was perfected by any method permitted by this Article.

(5) A security interest in fixtures, whether or not perfected, has priority over the conflicting interest of an encumbrancer or owner of the real estate where

(a)   the encumbrancer or owner has consented in writing to the security interest or has disclaimed an interest in the goods as fixtures; or

(b)   the debtor has a right to remove the goods as against the encumbrancer or owner. If the debtor's right terminates, the priority of the security interest continues for a reasonable time.

(6) Notwithstanding paragraph (a) of subsection (4) but otherwise subject to subsections (4) and (5), a security interest in fixtures is subordinate to a construction mortgage recorded before the goods become fixtures if the goods become fixtures before the completion of the construction. To the extent that it is given to refinance a construction mortgage a mortgage has this priority to the same extent as the construction mortgage.

(7) In cases not within the preceding subsections, a security interest in fixtures is subordinate to the conflicting interest of an encumbrancer or owner of the related real estate who is not the debtor.

(8) When the secured party has priority over all owners and encumbrancers of the real estate, he may, on default, subject to the provisions of Part 5, remove his collateral from the real estate but he must reimburse any encumbrancer or owner of the real estate who is not the debtor and who has not otherwise agreed for the cost of repair of any physical injury, but not for any diminution in value of the real estate caused by the absence of the goods removed or by any necessity of replacing them. A person entitled to reimbursement may refuse permission to remove until the secured party gives adequate security for the performance of this obligation.

S 9-314. ACCESSIONS.

(1) A security interest in goods which attaches before they are installed in or affixed to other goods takes priority as to the goods installed or affixed (called in this section "accessions") over the claims of all persons to the whole except as stated in subsection (3) and subject to Section 9-315(1).

(2) A security interest which attaches to goods after they become part of a whole is valid against all persons subsequently acquiring interests in the whole except as stated in subsection (3) but is invalid against any person with an interest in the whole at the time the security interest attaches to the goods who has not in writing consented to the security interest or disclaimed an interest in the goods as part of the whole.

(3) The security interest described in subsections (1) and (2) do not take priority over

    (a)   a subsequent purchaser for value of any interest in the whole; or

    (b)   a creditor with a lien on the whole subsequently obtained by judicial proceedings; or

    (c)   a creditor with a prior perfected security interest in the whole to the extent that he makes subsequent advances if the subsequent purchase is made, the lien by judicial proceedings obtained or the subsequent advance under the prior perfected security interest is made or contracted for without knowledge of the security interest and before it is perfected. A purchaser of the whole at a foreclosure sale other than the holder of a perfected security interest purchasing at his own foreclosure sale is a subsequent purchaser within this section.

(4) When under subsections (1) or (2) and (3) a secured party has an interest in accessions which has priority over the claims of all persons who have interests in the whole, he may on default subject to the provisions of Part 5 remove his collateral from the whole but he must reimburse any encumbrancer or owner of the whole who is not the debtor and who has not otherwise agreed for the cost of repair of any physical injury but not for any diminution in value of the whole caused by the absence of the goods removed or by any necessity for replacing them. A person entitled to reimbursement may refuse permission to remove until the secured party gives adequate security for the performance of this obligation.

S 9-315. PRIORITY WHEN GOODS ARE COMMINGLED OR PROCESSED.

(1) If a security interest in goods was perfected and subsequently the goods or a part thereof have become part of a product or mass, the security interest continues in the product or mass if

    (a)   the goods are so manufactured, processed, assembled or commingled that their identity is lost in the product or mass; or

    (b)   a financing statement covering the original goods also covers the product into which the goods have been manufactured, processed or assembled. In a case to which paragraph (b) applies, no separate security interest in that part of the original goods which has been manufactured, processed or assembled into the product may be claimed under Section 9-314.

(2) When under subsection (1) more than one security interest attaches to the product or mass, they rank equally according to the ratio that the cost of the goods to which each interest originally attached bears to the cost of the total product or mass.

S 9-316. PRIORITY SUBJECT TO SUBORDINATION.

Nothing in this Article prevents subordination by agreement by any person entitled to priority.

S 9-317. SECURED PARTY NOT OBLIGATED ON CONTRACT OF DEBTOR.

The mere existence of a security interest or authority given to the debtor to dispose of or use collateral does not impose contract or tort liability upon the secured party for the debtor's acts or omissions.

S 9-318. DEFENSES AGAINST ASSIGNEE; MODIFICATION OF CONTRACT AFTER NOTIFICATION OF ASSIGNMENT; TERM PROHIBITING ASSIGNMENT INEFFECTIVE; IDENTIFICATION AND PROOF OF ASSIGNMENT.

(1) Unless an account debtor has made an enforceable agreement not to assert defenses or claims arising out of a sale as provided in Section 9-206 the rights of an assignee are subject to

    (a) all the terms of the contract between the account debtor and assignor and any defense or claim arising therefrom; and

    (b) any other defense or claim of the account debtor against the assignor which accrues before the account debtor receives notification of the assignment.

(2) So far as the right to payment or a part thereof under an assigned contract has not been fully earned by performance, and notwithstanding notification of the assignment, any modification of or substitution for the contract made in good faith and in accordance with reasonable commercial standards is effective against an assignee unless the account debtor has otherwise agreed but the assignee acquires corresponding rights under the modified or substituted contract. The assignment may provide that such modification or substitution is a breach by the assignor.

(3) The account debtor is authorized to pay the assignor until the account debtor receives notification that the amount due or to become due has been assigned and that payment is to be made to the assignee. A notification which does not reasonably identify the rights assigned is ineffective. If requested by the account debtor, the assignee must seasonably furnish reasonable proof that the assignment has been made and unless he does so the account debtor may pay the assignor.

(4) A term in any contract between an account debtor and an assignor is ineffective if it prohibits assignment of an account or prohibits creation of a security interest in a gen-

eral intangible for money due or to become due or requires the account debtor's consent to such assignment or security interest.

FILING

S 9-401. PLACE OF FILING; ERRONEOUS FILING; REMOVAL OF COLLATERAL.

FIRST ALTERNATIVE SUBSECTION (1)

(1)   The proper place to file in order to perfect a security interest is as follows:

   (a)   when the collateral is equipment used in farming operations, or farm products, or accounts or general intangibles arising from or relating to the sale of farm products by a farmer, or consumer goods, then in the office of the _____ in the county of the debtor's residence or if the debtor is not a resident of this state then in the office of the _____ in the county where the goods are kept, and in addition when the collateral is crops growing or to be grown in the office of the _____ in the county where the land is located.

   (b)   when the collateral is timber to be cut or is minerals or the like (including oil and gas) or accounts subject to subsection (5) of Section 9-103, or when the financing statement is filed as a fixture filing (Section 9-313) and the collateral is goods which are or are to become fixtures, then in the office where a mortgage on the real estate would be filed or recorded;

   (c)   in all other cases, in the office of the (Secretary of State) and in addition, if the debtor has a place of business in only one county of this state, also in the office of _____ of such county, or, if the debtor has no place of business in this state, but resides in the state, also in the office of _____ of the county in which he resides.

   Note: *One of the three alternatives should be selected as subsection (1).*

(2)   A filing which is made in good faith in an improper place or not in all of the places required by this section is nevertheless effective with regard to any collateral as to which the filing complied with the requirements of this Article and is also effective with regard to collateral covered by the financing statement against any person who has knowledge of the contents of such financing statement.

(3)   A filing which is made in the proper place in this state continues effective even though the debtor's residence or place of business or the location of the collateral or its use, whichever controlled the original filing, is thereafter changed.

ALTERNATIVE SUBSECTION (3)

(3)   A filing which is made in the proper county continues effective for four months after a change to another county of the debtor's residence or place of business or the location of the collateral, whichever controlled the original filing. It becomes ineffective thereafter unless a copy of the financing statement signed by the secured party is filed in the new county within said period. The security interest may also be perfected in the new county after the expiration of the four-month period; in such case

perfection dates from the time of perfection in the new county. (A change in the use of the collateral does not impair the effectiveness of the original filing.)

(4) The rules stated in Section 9-103 determine whether filing is necessary in this state.

(5) Notwithstanding the preceding subsections, and subject to subsection (3) of Section 9-302, the proper place to file in order to perfect a security interest in collateral, including fixtures, of a transmitting utility is the office of the (Secretary of State). This filing constitutes a fixture filing (Section 9-313) as to the collateral described therein which is or is to become fixtures.

(6) For the purposes of this section, the residence of an organization is its place of business if it has one or its chief executive office if it has more than one place of business.

S 9-402. FORMAL REQUISITES OF FINANCING STATEMENT; AMENDMENTS; MORTGAGE AS FINANCING STATEMENT.

(1) A financing statement is sufficient if it gives the names of the debtor and the secured party, is signed by the debtor, gives an address of the secured party from which information concerning the security interest may be obtained, gives a mailing address of the debtor and contains a statement indicating the types, or describing the items, of collateral. A financing statement may be filed before a security agreement is made or a security interest otherwise attaches. When the financing statement covers crops growing or to be grown, the statement must also contain a description of the real estate concerned. When the financing statement covers timber to be cut or covers minerals or the like (including oil and gas) or accounts subject to subsection (5) of Section 9-103, or when the financing statement is filed as a fixture filing (Section 9-313) and the collateral is goods which are or are to become fixtures, the statement must also comply with subsection (5).

A copy of the security agreement is sufficient as a financing statement if it contains the above information and is signed by the debtor. A carbon, photographic or other reproduction of a security agreement or a financing statement is sufficient as a financing statement if the security agreement so provides or if the original has been filed in this state.

(2) A financing statement which otherwise complies with subsection (1) is sufficient when it is signed by the secured party instead of the debtor if it is filed to perfect a security interest in

(a) collateral already subject to a security interest in another jurisdiction when it is brought into this state, or when the debtor's location is changed to this state. Such a financing statement must state that the collateral was brought into this state or that the debtor's location was changed to this state under such circumstances; or

(b) proceeds under Section 9-306 if the security interest in the original collateral was perfected. Such a financing statement must describe the original collateral; or

(c) collateral as to which the filing has lapsed; or

(d) collateral acquired after a change of name, identity or corporate structure of the debtor (subsection (7)).

(3) A form substantially as follows is sufficient to comply with subsection (1):

Name of debtor (or assignor)_____

Address_____

Name of secured party (or assignee)_____

Address_____

    1.   This financing statement covers the following types (or items) of property:

       (Describe) _____

    2.   (If collateral is crops) The above described crops are growing or are to be grown on:

       (Describe Real Estate) _____

    3.   (If applicable) The above goods are to become fixtures on:*

       (Describe Real Estate)_____and this financing statement is to be filed (for record) in the real estate records. (If the debtor does not have an interest of record) The name of a record owner is

       _____

    4.   (If products of collateral are claimed) Products of the collateral are also covered.

       (use   ) . . . .

       whichever   ) Signature of Debtor (or Assignor)

       is   ) . . . .

       applicable)) Signature of Secured Party (or Assignee)

(4) A financing statement may be amended by filing a writing signed by both the debtor and the secured party. An amendment does not extend the period of effectiveness of a financing statement. If any amendment adds collateral, it is effective as to the added collateral only from the filing date of the amendment. In this Article, unless the context otherwise requires, the term "financing statement" means the original financing statement and any amendments.

(5) A financing statement covering timber to be cut or covering minerals or the like (including oil and gas) or accounts subject to subsection (5) of Section 9-103, or a financing statement filed as a fixture filing (Section 9-313) where the debtor is not a transmitting utility, must show that it covers this type of collateral and must recite that it is to be filed (for record) in the real estate records, and the financing statement must contain a description of the real estate (sufficient if it were contained in a mortgage under the law of this state). If the debtor does not have an interest of record in the real estate, the financing statement must show the name of a record owner.

(6) A mortgage is effective as a financing statement filed as a fixture filing from the date of its recording if

(a)   the goods are described in the mortgage by item or type; and

(b)   the goods are or are to become fixtures related to the real estate described in the mortgage; and

(c)   the mortgage complies with the requirements for a financing statement in this section other than a recital that it is to be filed in the real estate records; and

(d)   the mortgage is duly recorded.

No fee with reference to the financing statement is required other than the regular recording and satisfaction fees with respect to the mortgage.

(7)   A financing statement sufficiently shows the name of the debtor if it gives the individual, partnership or corporate name of the debtor, whether or not it adds other trade names or names of partners. Where the debtor so changes his name or in the case of an organization its name, identity or corporate structure that a filed financing statement becomes seriously misleading, the filing is not effective to perfect a security interest in collateral acquired by the debtor more than four months after the change, unless a new appropriate financing statement is filed before the expiration of that time. A filed financing statement remains effective with respect to collateral transferred by the debtor even though the secured party knows of or consents to the transfer.

(8)   A financing statement substantially complying with the requirements of this section is effective even though it contains minor errors which are not seriously misleading.

S 9-403. WHAT CONSTITUTES FILING; DURATION OF FILING; EFFECT OF LAPSED FILING; DUTIES OF FILING OFFICER.

(1)   Presentation for filing of a financing statement and tender of the filing fee or acceptance of the statement by the filing officer constitutes filing under this Article.

(2)   Except as provided in subsection (6) a filed financing statement is effective for a period of five years from the date of filing. The effectiveness of a filed financing statement lapses on the expiration of the five year period unless a continuation statement is filed prior to the lapse. If a security interest perfected by filing exists at the time insolvency proceedings are commenced by or against the debtor, the security interest remains perfected until termination of the insolvency proceedings and thereafter for a period of sixty days or until expiration of the five year period, whichever occurs later. Upon lapse the security interest becomes unperfected, unless it is perfected without filing. If the security interest becomes unperfected upon lapse, it is deemed to have been unperfected as against a person who became a purchaser or lien creditor before lapse.

(3)   A continuation statement may be filed by the secured party within six months prior to the expiration of the five year period specified in subsection (2). Any such continuation statement must be signed by the secured party, identify the original statement by file number and state that the original statement is still effective. A continuation statement signed by a person other than the secured party of record must be accompanied by a separate written statement of assignment signed by the secured party of record and complying with subsection (2) of Section 9-405, including payment of the required fee. Upon timely filing of the continuation statement, the effectiveness of the original statement is continued for five years after the last date to which the filing was effective whereupon it lapses in the same manner as provided in subsection (2) unless another continuation statement is filed prior to such lapse. Succeeding continuation statements may be filed in the same manner to continue the effectiveness of the original statement. Unless a statute on disposition of public records provides otherwise, the filing officer may remove a lapsed statement from the files and destroy it immediately if he has retained a microfilm or other photographic record,

or in other cases after one year after the lapse. The filing officer shall so arrange matters by physical annexation of financing statements to continuation statements or other related filings, or by other means, that if he physically destroys the financing statements of a period more than five years past, those which have been continued by a continuation statement or which are still effective under subsection (6) shall be retained.

(4) Except as provided in subsection (7) a filing officer shall mark each statement with a file number and with the date and hour of filing and shall hold the statement or a microfilm or other photographic copy thereof for public inspection. In addition the filing officer shall index the statement according to the name of the debtor and shall note in the index the file number and the address of the debtor given in the statement.

(5) The uniform fee for filing and indexing and for stamping a copy furnished by the secured party to show the date and place of filing for an original financing statement or for a continuation statement shall be $_____ if the statement is in the standard form prescribed by the (Secretary of State) and otherwise shall be $_____, plus in each case, if the financing statement is subject to subsection (5) of Section 9-402, $_____. The uniform fee for each name more than one required to be indexed shall be $_____. The secured party may at his option show a trade name for any person and an extra uniform indexing fee of $_____ shall be paid with respect thereto.

(6) If the debtor is a transmitting utility (subsection (5) of Section 9-401) and a filed financing statement so states, it is effective until a termination statement is filed. A real estate mortgage which is effective as a fixture filing under subsection (6) of Section 9-402 remains effective as a fixture filing until the mortgage is released or satisfied of record or its effectiveness otherwise terminates as to the real estate.

(7) When a financing statement covers timber to be cut or covers minerals or the like (including oil and gas) or accounts subject to subsection (5) of Section 9-103, or is filed as a fixture filing, (it shall be filed for record and) the filing officer shall index it under the names of the debtor and any owner of record shown on the financing statement in the same fashion as if they were the mortgagors in a mortgage of the real estate described, and, to the extent that the law of this state provides for indexing of mortgages under the name of the mortgagee, under the name of the secured party as if he were the mortgagee thereunder, or where indexing is by description in the same fashion as if the financing statement were a mortgage of the real estate described.

S 9-404. TERMINATION STATEMENT.

(1) If a financing statement covering consumer goods is filed on or after_____, then within one month or within ten days following written demand by the debtor after there is no outstanding secured obligation and no commitment to make advances, incur obligations or otherwise give value, the secured party must file with each filing officer with whom the financing statement was filed, a termination statement to the effect that he no longer claims a security interest under the financing statement, which shall be identified by file number. In other cases whenever there is no outstanding secured obligation and no commitment to make advances, incur obligations or otherwise give value, the secured party must on written demand by the debtor send the debtor, for each filing officer with whom the financing state-

ment was filed, a termination statement to the effect that he no longer claims a security interest under the financing statement, which shall be identified by file number. A termination statement signed by a person other than the secured party of record must be accompanied by a separate written statement of assignment signed by the secured party of record complying with subsection (2) of Section 9-405, including payment of the required fee. If the affected secured party fails to file such a termination statement as required by this subsection, or to send such a termination statement within ten days after proper demand therefor, he shall be liable to the debtor for one hundred dollars, and in addition for any loss caused to the debtor by such failure.

(2) On presentation to the filing officer of such a termination statement he must note it in the index. If he has received the termination statement in duplicate, he shall return one copy of the termination statement to the secured party stamped to show the time of receipt thereof. If the filing officer has a microfilm or other photographic record of the financing statement, and of any related continuation statement, statement of assignment and statement of release, he may remove the originals from the files at any time after receipt of the termination statement, or if he has no such record, he may remove them from the files at any time after one year after receipt of the termination statement.

(3) If the termination statement is in the standard form prescribed by the (Secretary of State), the uniform fee for filing and indexing the termination statement shall be $_____, and otherwise shall be $_____, plus in each case an additional fee of $_____for each name more than one against which the termination statement is required to be indexed.

S 9-405. ASSIGNMENT OF SECURITY INTEREST; DUTIES OF FILING OFFICER; FEES.

(1) A financing statement may disclose an assignment of a security interest in the collateral described in the financing statement by indication in the financing statement of the name and address of the assignee or by an assignment itself or a copy thereof on the face or back of the statement. On presentation to the filing officer of such a financing statement the filing officer shall mark the same as provided in Section 9-403(4). The uniform fee for filing, indexing and furnishing filing data for a financing statement so indicating an assignment shall be $_____if the statement is in the standard form prescribed by the (Secretary of State) and otherwise shall be $_____, plus in each case an additional fee of $_____for each name more than one against which the financing statement is required to be indexed.

(2) A secured party may assign of record all or part of his rights under a financing statement by the filing in the place where the original financing statement was filed of a separate written statement of assignment signed by the secured party of record and setting forth the name of the secured party of record and the debtor, the file number and the date of filing of the financing statement and the name and address of the assignee and containing a description of the collateral assigned. A copy of the assignment is sufficient as a separate statement if it complies with the preceding sentence. On presentation to the filing officer of such a separate statement, the filing officer shall mark such separate statement with the date and hour of the filing. He shall note the assignment on the index of the financing statement, or in the case of a fixture fil-

ing, or a filing covering timber to be cut, or covering mineral or the like (including oil and gas) or accounts subject to subsection (5) of Section 9-103, he shall index the assignment under the name of the assignor as grantor and, to the extent that the law of this state provides for indexing the assignment of a mortgage under the name of the assignee, he shall index the assignment of the financing statement under the name of the assignee. The uniform fee for filing, indexing and furnishing filing data about such a separate statement of assignment shall be $_____if the statement is in the standard form prescribed by the (Secretary of State) and otherwise shall be $_____, plus in each case an additional fee of $_____for each name more than one against which the statement of assignment is required to be indexed. Notwithstanding the provisions of this subsection, an assignment of record of a security interest in a fixture contained in a mortgage effective as a fixture filing (subsection (6) of Section 9-402) may be made only by an assignment of the mortgage in the manner provided by the law of this state other than this Act.

(3) After the disclosure or filing of an assignment under this section, the assignee is the secured party of record.

S 9-406. RELEASE OF COLLATERAL; DUTIES OF FILING OFFICER; FEES.

A secured party of record may by his signed statement release all or a part of any collateral described in a filed financing statement. The statement of release is sufficient if it contains a description of the collateral being released, the name and address of the secured party, and the file number of the financing statement. A statement of release signed by a person other than the secured party of record must be accompanied by a separate written statement of assignment signed by the secured party of record and complying with subsection (2) of Section 9-405, including payment of the required fee. Upon presentation of such a statement of release to the filing officer he shall mark the statement with the hour and date of filing and shall note the same upon the margin of the index of the filing of the financing statement. The uniform fee for filing and noting such a statement of release shall be $_____if the statement is in the standard form prescribed by the (Secretary of State) and otherwise shall be $_____, plus in each case an additional fee of $_____for each name more than one against which the statement of release is required to be indexed.

S 9-407. INFORMATION FROM FILING OFFICER.

(1) If the person filing any financing statement, termination statement, statement of assignment, or statement of release, furnishes the filing officer a copy thereof, the filing officer shall upon request note upon the copy the file number and date and hour of the filing of the original and deliver or send the copy to such person.

(2) Upon request of any person, the filing officer shall issue his certificate showing whether there is on file on the date and hour stated therein, any presently effective financing statement naming a particular debtor and any statement of assignment thereof and if there is, giving the date and hour of filing of each such statement and the names and addresses of each secured party therein. The uniform fee for such a certificate shall be $_____if the request for the certificate is in the standard form prescribed by the (Secretary of State) and otherwise shall be $_____. Upon request the filing officer shall furnish a copy of any filed financing statement or statement of assignment for a uniform fee of $_____per page.

S 9-408. FINANCING STATEMENTS COVERING CONSIGNED OR LEASED GOODS.

A consignor or lessor of goods may file a financing statement using the terms "consignor," "consignee," "lessor," "lessee" or the like instead of the terms specified in Section 9-402. The provisions of this Part shall apply as appropriate to such a financing statement but its filing shall not of itself be a factor in determining whether or not the consignment or lease is intended as security (Section 1-207(37)). However, if it is determined for other reasons that the consignment or lease is so intended, a security interest of the consignor or lessor which attaches to the consigned or leased goods is perfected by such filing.

DEFAULT

S 9-501. DEFAULT; PROCEDURE WHEN SECURITY AGREEMENT COVERS BOTH REAL AND PERSONAL PROPERTY.

(1) When a debtor is in default under a security agreement, a secured party has the right and remedies provided in this Part and except as limited by subsection (3) those provided in the security agreement. He may reduce his claim to judgment, foreclose or otherwise enforce the security interest by any available judicial procedure. If the collateral is documents the secured party may proceed either as to the documents or as to the goods covered thereby. A secured party in possession has the rights, remedies and duties provided in Section 9-207. The rights and remedies referred to in this subsection are cumulative.

(2) After default, the debtor has the rights and remedies provided in this Part, those provided in the security agreement and those provided in Section 9-207.

(3) To the extent that they give rights to the debtor and impose duties on the secured party, the rules stated in the subsections referred to below may not be waived or varied except as provided with respect to compulsory disposition of collateral (subsection (3) of Section 9-504 and Section 9-505) and with respect to redemption of collateral (Section 9-506) but the parties may by agreement determine the standards by which the fulfillment of these rights and duties is to be measured if such standards are not manifestly unreasonable:

   (a) subsection (2) of Section 9-502 and subsection (2) of Section 9-504 insofar as they require accounting for surplus proceeds of collateral;

   (b) subsection (3) of section 9-504 and subsection (1) of Section 9-505 which deal with disposition of collateral;

   (c) subsection (2) of Section 9-505 which deals with acceptance of collateral as discharge of obligation;

   (d) Section 9-506 which deals with redemption of collateral; and

   (e) subsection (1) of Section 9-507 which deals with the secured party's liability for failure to comply with this Part.

(4) If the security agreement covers both real and personal property, the secured party may proceed under this Part as to the personal property or he may proceed as to

both the real and the personal property in accordance with his rights and remedies in respect of the real property in which case the provisions of this Part do not apply.

(5) When a secured party has reduced his claim to judgment the lien of any levy which may be made upon his collateral by virtue of any execution based upon the judgment shall relate back to the date of the perfection of the security interest in such collateral. A judicial sale, pursuant to such execution, is a foreclosure of the security interest by judicial procedure within the meaning of this section, and the secured party may purchase at the sale and thereafter hold the collateral free of any other requirements of this Article.

As amended in 1972.

S 9-502. COLLECTION RIGHTS OF SECURED PARTY.

(1) When so agreed and in any event on default the secured party is entitled to notify an account debtor or the obligor on an instrument to make payment to him whether or not the assignor was theretofore making collections on the collateral, and also to take control of any proceeds to which he is entitled under Section 9-306.

(2) A secured party who by agreement is entitled to charge back uncollected collateral or otherwise to full or limited recourse against the debtor and who undertakes to collect from the account debtors or obligors must proceed in a commercially reasonable manner and may deduct his reasonable expenses of realization from the collections. If the security agreement secures an indebtedness, the secured party must account to the debtor for any surplus, and unless otherwise agreed, the debtor is liable for any deficiency. But, if the underlying transaction was a sale of accounts or chattel paper, the debtor is entitled to any surplus or is liable for any deficiency only if the security agreement so provides.

S 9-503. SECURED PARTY'S RIGHT TO TAKE POSSESSION AFTER DEFAULT.

Unless otherwise agreed a secured party has on default the right to take possession of the collateral. In taking possession a secured party may proceed without judicial process if this can be done without breach of the peace or may proceed by action. If the security agreement so provides the secured party may require the debtor to assemble the collateral and make it available to the secured party at a place to be designated by the secured party which is reasonably convenient to both parties. Without removal a secured party may render equipment unusable, and may dispose of collateral on the debtor's premises under Section 9-504.

S 9-504. SECURED PARTY'S RIGHT TO DISPOSE OF COLLATERAL AFTER DEFAULT; EFFECT OF DISPOSITION.

(1) A secured party after default may sell, lease or otherwise dispose of any or all of the collateral in its then condition or following any commercially reasonable preparation or processing. Any sale of goods is subject to the Article on Sales (Article 2). The proceeds of disposition shall be applied in the order following to

(a) the reasonable expenses of retaking, holding, preparing for sale or lease, selling, leasing and the like and, to the extent provided for in the agreement and not prohibited by law, the reasonable attorneys' fees and legal expenses incurred by the secured party;

(b) the satisfaction of indebtedness secured by the security interest under which the disposition is made;

(c) the satisfaction of indebtedness secured by any subordinate security interest in the collateral if written notification of demand therefor is received before distribution of the proceeds is completed. If requested by the secured party, the holder of a subordinate security interest must seasonably furnish reasonable proof of his interest, and unless he does so, the secured party need not comply with his demand.

(2) If the security interest secures an indebtedness, the secured party must account to the debtor for any surplus, and, unless otherwise agreed, the debtor is liable for any deficiency. But if the underlying transaction was a sale of accounts or chattel paper, the debtor is entitled to any surplus or is liable for any deficiency only if the security agreement so provides.

(3) Disposition of the collateral may be by public or private proceedings and may be made by way of one or more contracts. Sale or other disposition may be as a unit or in parcels and at any time and place and on any terms but every aspect of the disposition including the method, manner, time, place and terms must be commercially reasonable. Unless collateral is perishable or threatens to decline speedily in value or is of a type customarily sold on a recognized market, reasonable notification of the time and place of any public sale or reasonable notification of the time after which any private sale or other intended disposition is to be made shall be sent by the secured party to the debtor, if he has not signed after default a statement renouncing or modifying his right to notification of sale. In the case of consumer goods no other notification need be sent. In other cases notification shall be sent to any other secured party from whom the secured party has received (before sending his notification to the debtor or before the debtor's renunciation of his rights) written notice of a claim of an interest in the collateral. The secured party may buy at any public sale and if the collateral is of a type customarily sold in a recognized market or is of a type which is the subject of widely distributed standard price quotations he may buy at private sale.

(4) When collateral is disposed of by a secured party after default, the disposition transfers to a purchaser for value all of the debtor's rights therein, discharges the security interest under which it is made and any security interest or lien subordinate thereto. The purchaser takes free of all such rights and interests even though the secured party fails to comply with the requirements of this Part or of any judicial proceedings

(a) in the case of a public sale, if the purchaser has no knowledge of any defects in the sale and if he does not buy in collusion with the secured party, other bidders or the person conducting the sale; or

(b) in any other case, if the purchaser acts in good faith.

(5) A person who is liable to a secured party under a guaranty, endorsement, repurchase agreement or the like and who receives a transfer of collateral from the secured party

or is subrogated to his rights has thereafter the rights and duties of the secured party. Such a transfer of collateral is not a sale or disposition of the collateral under this Article.

S 9-505. COMPULSORY DISPOSITION OF COLLATERAL; ACCEPTANCE OF THE COLLATERAL AS DISCHARGE OF OBLIGATION.

(1) If the debtor has paid sixty per cent of the cash price in the case of a purchase money security interest in consumer goods or sixty per cent of the loan in the case of another security interest in consumer goods, and has not signed after default a statement renouncing or modifying his rights under this Part a secured party who has taken possession of collateral must dispose of it under Section 9-504 and if he fails to do so within ninety days after he takes possession the debtor at his option may recover in conversion or under Section 9-507(1) on secured party's liability.

(2) In any other case involving consumer goods or any other collateral a secured party in possession may, after default, propose to retain the collateral in satisfaction of the obligation. Written notice of such proposal shall be sent to the debtor if he has not signed after default a statement renouncing or modifying his rights under this subsection. In the case of consumer goods no other notice need be given. In other cases notice shall be sent to any other secured party from whom the secured party has received (before sending his notice to the debtor or before the debtor's renunciation of his rights) written notice of a claim of an interest in the collateral. If the secured party receives objection in writing from a person entitled to receive notification within twenty-one days after the notice was sent, the secured party must dispose of the collateral under Section 9-504. In the absence of such written objection the secured party may retain the collateral in satisfaction of the debtor's obligation.

S 9-506. DEBTOR'S RIGHT TO REDEEM COLLATERAL.

At any time before the secured party has disposed of collateral or entered into a contract for its disposition under Section 9-504 or before the obligation has been discharged under Section 9-505(2) the debtor or any other secured party may unless otherwise agreed in writing after default redeem the collateral by tendering fulfillment of all obligations secured by the collateral as well as the expenses reasonably incurred by the secured party in retaking, holding and preparing the collateral for disposition, in arranging for the sale, and to the extent provided in the agreement and not prohibited by law, his reasonable attorney's fees and legal expenses.

S 9-507. SECURED PARTY'S LIABILITY FOR FAILURE TO COMPLY WITH THIS PART.

(1) If it is established that the secured party is not proceeding in accordance with the provisions of this Part disposition may be ordered or restrained on appropriate terms and conditions. If the disposition has occurred the debtor or any person entitled to notification or whose security interest has been made known to the secured party prior to the disposition has a right to recover from the secured party any loss

caused by a failure to comply with the provisions of the Part. If the collateral is consumer goods, the debtor has a right to recover in any event an amount not less than the credit service charge plus ten per cent of the principal amount of the debt or the time price differential plus 10 per cent of the cash price.

(2) The fact that a better price could have been obtained by a sale at a different time or in a different method from that selected by the secured party is not of itself sufficient to establish that the sale was not made in a commercially reasonable manner. If the secured party either sells the collateral in the usual manner in any recognized market therefor or if he sells at the price current in such market at the time of his sale or if he has otherwise sold in conformity with reasonable commercial practices among dealers in the type of property sold he has sold in a commercially reasonable manner. The principles stated in the two preceding sentences with respect to sales also apply as may be appropriate to other types of disposition. A disposition which has been approved in any judicial proceeding or by any bona fide creditors, committee or representative of creditors shall conclusively be deemed to be commercially reasonable, but this sentence does not indicate that any such approval must be obtained in any case nor does it indicate that any disposition not so approved is not commercially reasonable.

CHAPTER 10
APPENDIX II

TITLE 15. COMMERCE AND TRADE
CHAPTER 41. CONSUMER CREDIT PROTECTION CONSUMER CREDIT COST DISCLOSURE CONSUMER LEASES

1667A. CONSUMER LEASE DISCLOSURES

Each lessor shall give a lessee prior to the consummation of the lease a dated written statement on which the lessor and lessee are identified setting out accurately and in a clear and conspicuous manner the following information with respect to that lease, as applicable:

(1) A brief description or identification of the leased property;

(2) The amount of any payment by the lessee required at the inception of the lease;

(3) The amount paid or payable by the lessee for official fees, registration, certificate of title, or license fees or taxes;

(4) The amount of other charges payable by the lessee not included in the periodic payments, a description of the charges and that the lessee shall be liable for the differential, if any, between the anticipated fair market value of the leased property and its appraised actual value at the termination of the lease, if the lessee has such liability;

(5) A statement of the amount or method of determining the amount of any liabilities the lease imposed upon the lessee at the end of the term and whether or not the lessee has the option to purchase the leased property and at what price and time;

(6) A statement identifying all express warranties and guarantees made by the manufacturer or lessor with respect to the leased property, and identifying the party responsible for maintaining or servicing the leased property together with a description of the responsibility;

(7) A brief description of insurance provided or paid for by the lessor or required of the lessee, including the types and amounts of the coverages and costs;

(8) A description of any security interest held or to be retained by the lessor in connection with the lease and a clear identification of the property to which the security interest relates;

(9) The number, amount, and due dates or periods of payments under the lease and the total amount of such periodic payments;

(10) Where the lease provides that the lessee shall be liable for the anticipated fair market value of the property on expiration of the lease, the first market value of the property at the inception of the lease, the aggregate cost of the lease on expiration, and the differential between them; and

(11) A statement of the conditions under which the lessee or lessor may terminate the lease prior to the end of the term and the amount or method of determining any penalty or other charge for delinquency, default, late payments, or early termination.

The disclosures required under this section may be made in the lease contract to be signed by the lessee. The Board may provide by regulation that any portion of the information required to be disclosed under this section may be given in the form of estimates where the lessor is not in a position to know exact information.

1667B. LESSEE'S LIABILITY OF EXPIRATION OR TERMINATION OF LEASE

(a) Estimated residual value of property as basis; presumptions; action by lessor for excess liability; mutually agreeable final adjustment. Where the lessee's liability on expiration of a consumer lease is based on the estimated residual value of the property such estimated residual value shall be a reasonable approximation of the anticipated actual fair market value of the property on lease expiration. There shall be a rebuttable presumption that the estimated residual value is unreasonable to the extent that the estimated residual value exceeds the actual residual value by more than three times the average payment allocable to a monthly period under the lease. In addition, where the lessee has such liability on expiration of a consumer lease there shall be a rebuttable presumption that the lessor's estimated residual value is not in good faith to the extent that the estimate residual value exceeds the actual residual value by more than three times the average payment allocable to a monthly period under the lease and such lessor shall not collect from the lessee the amount of such excess liability on expiration of a consumer lease unless the lessor brings a successful action with respect to such excess liability. In all actions, the lessor shall pay the lessee's reasonable attorney's fees. The presumptions stated in this section shall not apply to the extent the excess of estimated over actual residual value is due to physical damage to the property beyond reasonable wear and use, or to excessive use, and the lease may set standards for such wear and use if such standards are not unreasonable. Nothing in this subsection shall preclude the right of a willing lessee to make any mutually agreeable final adjustment with respect to such excess residual liability, providing such an agreement is reached after termination of the lease.

(b) Penalties and charges for delinquency, default, or early termination. Penalties or other charges for delinquency, default, or early termination may be specified in the lease only at an amount which is reasonable in the light of the anticipated or actual harm caused by the delinquency, default, or early termination, the difficulties of proof of loss, and the inconvenience or nonfeasibility of otherwise obtaining an adequate remedy.

(c) Independent professional appraisal of residual value of property at termination of lease; finality. If a lease has a residual value provision at the termination of the lease, the lessee may obtain at his expense, a professional appraisal of the leased property by an independent third party agreed to by both parties. Such appraisal shall be final and binding on the parties.

1667C. CONSUMER LEASE ADVERTISING; LIABILITY OF ADVERTISING MEDIA

(a) Contents of lease advertisements. No advertisements to aid, promoted, or assist directly or indirectly any consumer lease shall state the amount of any payment, the number of required payments, or that any or no downpayment or other payment is required at inception of the lease unless the advertisement also states clearly and conspicuously and in accordance with regulations issued by the Board each of the following items of information which is applicable:

   (1)   That the transaction advertised is a lease.

   (2)   The amount of any payment required at the inception of the lease or that no such payment is required if that is the case.

   (3)   The number, accounts, due dates or periods of scheduled payments, and the total of payments under the lease.

   (4)   That the lessee shall be liable for the differential, if any, between the anticipated fair market value of the leased property and its appraised actual value at the termination of the lease, if the lessee has such liability.

   (5)   A statement of the amount or method of determining the amount of any liabilities the lease imposes upon the lessee at the end of the term and whether or not the lessee has the option to purchase the leased property and at what price and time.

(b) Radio advertisements.

   (1)   In general. An advertisement by radio broadcast to aid, promote, or assist, directly or indirectly, any consumer lease shall be deemed to be in compliance with the requirements of subsection (a) if such advertisement clearly and conspicuously-

      (A)   states the information required by paragraphs (1) and (2) of the subsection (a);

      (B)   states the number, amounts, due dates or periods of scheduled payments and the total of such payment under the lease;

      (C)   includes—

         (i)   a referral to-

            (I)   a toll-free telephone number established in accordance with paragraph (2) that may be used by consumers to obtain the information required under subsection (a); or

            (II)   a written advertisement that—

               (aa)   appears in a publication in general circulation in the community served by the radio station on which such advertisement is broadcast during the period beginning 3 days before any such broadcast and ending 10 days after such broadcast; and

               (bb)   includes the information required to be disclosed under subsection (a); and

         (ii)   the name and dates of any publication referred to in clause (i) (II); and

(D)   includes any other information which the Board determines necessary to carry out this chapter.

(2)   Establishment of toll-free number.

(A)   In general. In the case of a radio broadcast advertisement described in paragraph (1) that includes referral to a toll-free telephone number, the lessor who offers the consumer lease shall-

(i)   establish such a toll-free telephone number not later than the date on which the advertisement including the referral is broadcast;

(ii)   maintain such telephone number for a period of not less than 10 days, beginning on the date of any such broadcast; and

(iii)   provide the information required under subsection (a) with respect to the lease to any person who calls such number.

(B)   Form of information. The information required to be provided under subparagraph (A) (iii) shall be provided verbally or, if requested by the consumer, in written form.

(3)   No effect on other law. Nothing in this subsection shall affect the requirements of the Federal law as such requirements apply to advertisement by any medium other than radio broadcast.

(C)   Liability of advertising media. There is no liability under this section on the part of any owner or personnel, as such, of any medium in which an advertisement appears or through which it is disseminated.

1667D. CIVIL LIABILITY OF LESSORS

(a)   Ground for maintenance of action. Any lessor who fails to comply with any requirement imposed under section 182 or 183 of this chapter with respect to any person is liable to such person as provided in section 130.

(b)   Additional grounds for maintenance of action; "creditor" defined. Any lessor who fails to comply with any requirement imposed under section 184 of this chapter with respect to any person who suffers actual damage from the violation is liable to such person as provided in section 130. For the purposes of this section, the term "creditor" as used in sections 130 and 131 shall include a lessor as defined in this chapter.

(c)   Jurisdiction of courts; time limitation. Notwithstanding section 130(e), any action under this section may be brought in any United States district court or in any other court of competent jurisdiction. Such actions alleging a failure to disclose or otherwise comply with the requirements of this chapter shall be brought within one year of the termination of the lease agreement.

1667E. APPLICABILITY OF STATE LAWS; EXEMPTIONS BY BOARD FROM LEASING REQUIREMENTS

(a)   This chapter does not annul, alter, or affect, or exempt any person subject to the provisions of this chapter from complying with the laws of any State with respect to consumer leases, except to the extent that those laws are inconsistent with any provision of this chapter, and then only to the extent of the inconsistency. The Board is authorized to determine whether such inconsistencies exist. The Board may not determine that any State law is inconsistent with any provision of this chapter if the Board determines that such law gives greater protection and benefit to the consumer.

(b) The Board shall by regulation exempt from the requirements of this chapter any class of lease transactions within any State if is determines that under the law of that State that class of transactions is subject to requirements substantially similar to those imposed under this chapter or that such law gives greater protection and benefit to the consumer, and that there is adequate provision for enforcement.

CHAPTER 10
APPENDIX III

REGULATION M—CONSUMER LEASING

PART 213-CONSUMER LEASING (REGULATION M)

Sec.
213.1 General provisions.
213.2 Definitions and rules of construction.
213.3 Exempted transaction.
213.4 Disclosures
213.5 Advertising
213.6 Preservation and inspection of evidence of compliance.
213.7 Inconsistent state requirements.
213.8 Exemption of certain state regulated transactions.
APPENDIX A TO PART 213-PROCEDURES AND CRITERIA FOR STATE EXEMPTIONS FROM THE CONSUMER LEASING ACT
APPENDIX B TO PART 213-PROCEDURES AND CRITERIA FOR BOARD DETERMINATION REGARDING PREEMPTION
APPENDIX C TO PART 213-MODEL FORMS
APPENDIX D TO PART 213-FEDERAL ENFORCEMENT AGENCIES
SUPPLEMENT I-CL-1 TO PART 213-OFFICIAL STAFF COMMENTARY TO REGULATION M
AUTHORITY: 15 U.S.C. 1604.
SOURCE: Reg. M, 46 FR 20951, Apr. 7, 1981, unless otherwise noted.

213.1 GENERAL PROVISIONS.

(a) *Authority.* This regulation, known as Regulation M, is issued by the Board of Governors of the Federal Reserve System to implement the consumer leasing portions of the Truth in Lending Act, which is title I of the consumer Credit Protection Act, as amended (15 U.S.C. 1601 et seq.).

(b) *Purpose.* The purpose of this regulation is to assure that lessees of personal property are given meaningful disclosures of lease terms, to delimit the ultimate liability of lessees in leasing personal property and to require meaningful and accurate disclosures of lease terms in advertising.

(c) *Enforcement and liability.* Section 108 of the Act contains the administrative enforcement provisions. Sections 112, 130, 131, and 185 of the Act contain the liability provisions for failing to comply with the requirements of the act and this regulation.

(d) *Issuance of staff interpretations.* (1) Officials in the Board's Division of consumer and Community Affairs are authorized to issue official staff interpretations of this regulation. Official staff interpretations provide the formal protection afforded under section 130(f) of the Act.

   (2) A request for an official staff interpretation shall be in writing and addressed to the Director, Division of Consumer and Community Affairs, Board of Governors of the Federal Reserve System, Washington, DC 20551. The request shall contain a complete statement of all relevant facts concerning the issue, including copies of all pertinent documents.

   (3) No staff interpretations will be issued approving lessor's forms, statements, calculation tools, or methods. This restriction does not apply to forms, statements, tools, or methods whose use is required or sanctioned by a government agency.

213.2 DEFINITIONS AND RULES OF CONSTRUCTION.

(a) *Definitions.* For the purposes of this regulation, unless the context indicates otherwise, the following definitions apply:

   (1) *Act* means the Truth in Lending Act (15 U.S.C. 1601 et seq.).

   (2) *Advertisement* means any commercial message in any newspaper, magazine, leaflet, flyer or catalog, on radio, television or public address system, in direct mail literature or other printed material on any interior or exterior sign or display, in any window display, in any point-of, transaction literature or price tag which is delivered or made available to a lessee or prospective lessee in any manner whatsoever.

   (3) *Agricultural purpose* means a purpose related to the production, harvest, exhibition, marketing, transportation, processing, or manufacture of agricultural products by a natural person who cultivates, plants, propagates, or nurtures those agricultural products, including but not limited to the acquisition of personal property and services used primarily in farming. *Agricultural products* include agricultural, horticultural, viticultural, and dairy products, livestock, wildlife, poultry, bees, forest products, fish and shellfish, and any products thereof, including processed and manufactured products, and any and all products raised or produced on farms and any processed or manufactured products thereof.

   (4) *Arrange for lease of personal property* means to provide or offer to provide a lease which is or will be extended by another person under a business or other relationship pursuant to which the person arranging such lease:

      (i) Receives or will receive a fee, compensation, or other consideration for such service; or

      (ii) Has knowledge of the lease terms and participates in the preparation of the contract documents required in connection with the lease.

(5)   *Board* refers to the Board of Governors of the Federal Reserve System.

(6)   *Consumer* lease means a contract in the form of a bailment or lease for the use of personal property by a natural person primarily for personal, family or household purposes, for a period of time exceeding four months, for a total contractual obligation not exceeding $25,000, whether or not the lessee has the option to purchase or otherwise become the owner of the property at the expiration of the lease. It does not include a lease which meets the definition of a credit sale in Regulation Z, 12 CFR 226.2(a) nor does it include a lease for agricultural, business or commercial purposes or one made to an organization.

(7)   *Lessee* means a natural person who leases under, or who is offered a consumer lease.

(8)   *Lessor* means a person who in the ordinary course of business regularly leases, offers to lease, or arranges for the leasing of personal property under a consumer lease.

(9)   *Organization* means a corporation, trust, estate, partnership, cooperative, association, government, or governmental subdivision, agency, or instrumentality.

(10)   *Period* means a day, week, month, or other subdivision of a year.

(11)   *Person* means a natural person or an organization.

(12)   *Personal property* means any property which is not real property under the law of the state where it is located at the time it is offered or made available for lease.

(13)   *Real property* means property which is real property under the law of the state in which it is located.

(14)   *Realized value* means (i) the price received by the lessor for the leased property at disposition, (ii) the highest offer for disposition, or (iii) the fair market value at the end of the lease term.

(15)   *Security interest* and *security* means any interest in property which secures payment or performance of an obligation. The terms include, but are not limited to, security interests under the Uniform Commercial Code, real property mortgages, deeds of trust, and other consensual or confessed liens whether or not recorded, mechanic's, materialman's, artisan's, and other similar liens, vendor's liens in both real and personal property, any lien on property arising by operation of law, and any interest in a lease when used to secure payment or performance of an obligation.

(16)   *State* means any state, the District of Columbia, the Commonwealth of Puerto Rico, and any territory or possession of the United States.

(17)   *Total lease obligation* equals the total of (i) the scheduled periodic payments under the lease, (ii) any non-refundable cash payment required of the lessee or agreed upon by the lessor and lessee or any trade-in allowance made at consummation, and (iii) the estimated value of the leased property at the end of the lease term.

(18)   *Value at consummation* equals the cost to the lessor of the leased property including, if applicable, any increase or markup by the lessor prior to consummation.

(b) *Rules of construction.* For purposes of this regulation, the following rules of construction apply:

    (1)   Unless the context indicates otherwise, lease shall be construed to mean consumer lease.

    (2)   A transaction shall be considered consummated at the time a contractual relationship is created between the lessor and lessee, irrespective of the time of the performance of either party.

    (3)   Captions and catchlines are intended solely as aids to convenient reference, and no inference as to the intent of any provisions may be drawn from them. [46 FR 20951, Apr. 7, 1981; 46 FR 29245, June 1, 1981]

213.3 EXEMPTED TRANSACTIONS.

This regulation does not apply to lease transactions of personal property which are incident to the lease of real property and which provide that (a) the lessee has no liability for the value of the property at the end of the lease term except for abnormal wear and tear, and (b) the lessee has no option to purchase the leased property.

213.4 DISCLOSURES.

(a) *General requirements.* (1) Any lessor shall, in accordance with this regulation and to the extent applicable, make the disclosures required by paragraph (g) of this section with respect to any consumer lease. Such disclosures shall be made clearly, conspicuously, in meaningful sequence, and in accordance with the further requirements of this section. All numerical amounts and percentages shall be stated in figures and shall be printed in not less than the equivalent of 10-point type, .075 inch computer type, or elite size typewritten numerals, or shall be legibly handwritten.

    (2)   Disclosures shall be made prior to the consummation of the lease on a dated written statement which identifies the lessor and the lessee, and a copy of the statement shall be given to the lessee at the time. All of the disclosures shall be made together on either (i) the contract or other instrument evidencing the lease on the same page and above the place for the lessee's signature; or (ii) a separate statement which identifies the lease transaction.

    (3)   In any lease of multiple items, the description required by paragraph (g)(1) of this section may be provided on a separate statement or statements which are incorporated by reference in the disclosure statement required by paragraph (a) of this section.

    (4)   All disclosures required to be given by this regulation shall be made in the English language except in the commonwealth of Puerto Rico, where disclosures may be made in the Spanish language with English language disclosures provided upon the customer's request, either in substitution for the Spanish disclosures or as additional information in accordance with paragraph (b) of this section.

(b) *Additional information.* At the lessor's option, additional information or explanations may be supplied with any disclosure required by this regulation, but none shall be stated, utilized, or placed so as to mislead or confuse the lessee or contradict, obscure, or detract attention from the information required to be disclosed. Any lessor who elects to make disclosures specified in any provision of State law which, under 213.7 of this regulation, is inconsistent with the requirements of the act and this regulation may-

(1) Make such inconsistent disclosures on a separate paper apart from the disclosures made pursuant to this regulation; or

(2) Make such inconsistent disclosures on the same statement on which disclosures required by this regulation are made, provided:

   (i) All disclosures required by this regulation appear separately and above any other disclosures,

   (ii) Disclosures required by this regulation are identified by a clear and conspicuous heading indicating that they are made in compliance with federal law, and

   (iii) All inconsistent disclosures appear separately and below a conspicuous demarcation line, and are identified by a clear and conspicuous heading indicating that the statements made thereafter are inconsistent with the disclosure requirements of the federal Consumer Leasing Act.

(c) *Multiple lessors; multiple lessees.* When a transaction involves more than one lessor, only one lessor need make the disclosures required by this regulation, and the one that discloses shall be the one chosen by the lessors. When a lease involves more than one lessee, the disclosures may be made to any lessee who is primarily liable on the lease.

(d) *Unknown information estimate.* If, at the time disclosures must be made, an amount or other item of information required to be disclosed, or needed to determine a required disclosure, is unknown or not available to the lessor and the lessor has made a reasonable effort to ascertain it, the lessor may use an estimated amount or an approximation of the information, provided the estimate or approximation is clearly identified as such, is reasonable, is based on the best information available to the lessor, and is not used for the purpose of circumventing or evading the disclosure requirements of this regulation. Notwithstanding the requirement of this paragraph that the estimate be based on the best information available, a lessor is not precluded in a purchase option lease from understating the estimated value of the leased property at the end of the term in computing the total lease obligation as required in paragraph (g) (15) (i) of this section.

(e) *Effect of subsequent occurrence.* If information required to be disclosed in accordance with this regulation is subsequently rendered inaccurate as a result of any act, occurrence, or agreement subsequent to the delivery of the required disclosures, the inaccuracy resulting therefrom does not constitute a violation of this regulation.

(f) *Leap Year.* Any variance in any term required under this regulation to be disclosed, or stated in any advertisement, which occurs by reason of the addition of February 29 in each leap year, may be disregarded, and such term may be disclosed or stated without regard to such variance.

(g) *Specific disclosure requirements.* In any lease subject to this section, the following items, as applicable, shall be disclosed:

(1) A brief description of the leased property, sufficient to identify the property to the lessee and lessor.

(2) The total amount of any payment, such as a refundable security deposit paid by cash, check or similar means, advance payment, capitalized cost reduction or any trade-in allowance, appropriately identified, to be paid by the lessee at consummation of the lease.

(3) The number, amount, and due dates or periods of payments scheduled under the lease and the total amount of such periodic payments.

(4) The total amount paid or payable by the lessee during the lease term for official fees, registration, certificate of title, license fees, or taxes.

(5) The total amount of all other charges, individually itemized, payable by the lessee to the lessor, which are not included in the periodic payments. This total includes the amount of any liabilities the lease imposes upon the lessee at the end of the term, but excludes the potential difference between the estimated and realized values, required to be disclosed under paragraph (g) (13) of this section.

(6) A brief identification of insurance in connection with the lease including (i) if provided or paid for by the lessor, the types and amounts of coverages and cost to the lessee, or (ii) if not provided or paid for by the lessor, the types and amounts of coverages required of the lessee.

(7) A statement identifying any express warranties or guarantees available to the lessee made by the lessor or manufacturer with respect to the leased property.

(8) An identification of the party responsible for maintaining or servicing the leased property together with a brief description of the responsibility, and a statement of reasonable standards for wear and use, if the lessor sets such standards.

(9) A description of any security interest, other than a security deposit disclosed under paragraph (g)(2) of this section, held or to be retained by the lessor in connection with the lease and a clear identification of the property to which the security interest relates.

(10) The amount or method of determining the amount of any penalty or other charge for delinquency, default, or late payments.

(11) A statement of whether or not the lessee has the option to purchase the leased property and, if at the end of the lease term, at what price, and, if prior to the end of the lease term, at what time, and the price or method of determining the price.

(12) A statement of the conditions under which the lessee or lessor may terminate the lease prior to the end of the lease term and the amount or method of determining the amount of any penalty or other charge for early termination.

(13) A statement that the lessee shall be liable for the difference between the estimated value of the property and its realized value at early termination or the end of the lease term, if such liability exists.

(14) Where the lessee's liability at early termination or at the end of the lease term is based on the estimated value of the leased property, a statement that the

lessee may obtain at the end of the lease term or at early termination, at the lessee's expense, a professional appraisal of the value which could be realized at sale of the leased property by an independent third party agreed to by the lessee and the lessor, which appraisal shall be final and binding on the parties.

(15) Where the lessee's liability at the end of the lease term is based upon the estimated value of the leased property:

(i) The value of the property at consummation of the lease, the itemized total lease obligation at the end of the lease term, and the difference between them.

(ii) That there is a rebuttable presumption that the estimated value of the leased property at the end of the lease term is unreasonable and not in good faith to the extent that it exceeds the realized value by more than three times the average payment allocable to a monthly period, and that the lessor cannot collect the amount of such excess liability unless the lessor brings a successful action in court in which the lessor pays the lessee's attorney's fees, and that this provision regarding the presumption and attorney's fees does not apply to the extent the excess of estimated value over realized value is due to unreasonable wear or use, or excessive use.

(iii) A statement that the requirements of paragraph (g)(15)(ii) of this section do not preclude the right of a willing lessee to make any mutually agreeable final adjustment regarding such excess liability.

(h) *Renegotiations or extensions.* If any existing lease is renegotiated or extended, such renegotiation or extension shall be considered a new lease subject to the disclosure requirements of this regulation, except that the requirements of this paragraph shall not apply to (1) a lease of multiple items where a new item(s) is provided or a previously leased item(s) is returned, and the average payment allocable to a monthly period is not changed by more than 25 per cent, or (2) a lease which is extended for not more than 6 months on a month-to-month basis or otherwise.

213.5 ADVERTISING.

(a) *General rule.* No advertisement to aid, promote, or assist directly or indirectly any consumer lease may state that a specific lease of any property at specific amounts or terms is available unless the lessor usually and customarily leases or will lease such property at those amounts or terms.

(b) *Catalogs and multi-page advertisements.* If a catalog or other multiple-page advertisement sets forth or gives information in sufficient detail to permit determination of the disclosures required by this section in a table or schedule of lease terms, such catalog or multiple-page advertisement shall be considered a single advertisement provided:

(1) The table or schedule and the disclosures made therein are set forth clearly and conspicuously; and

(2) Any statement of lease terms appearing in any place other than in that table or schedule of lease terms clearly and conspicuously refers to the page or pages on which that table or schedule appears, unless that statement discloses all of the lease terms required to be stated under this section.

(c) *Terms that require additional information.* No advertisement to aid, promote, or assist directly or indirectly any consumer lease shall state the amount of any payment, the number of required payments, or that any or no downpayment or other payment is required at consummation of the lease unless the advertisement also states clearly and conspicuously each of the following items of information as applicable.

    (1)   That the transaction advertised is a lease.

    (2)   The total amount of any payment such as a security deposit or capitalized cost reduction required at the consummation of the lease, or that no such payments are required.

    (3)   The number, amounts, due dates or periods of scheduled payments, and the total of such payments under the lease.

    (4)   A statement of whether or not the lessee has the option to purchase the leased property and at what price and time. The method of determining the price may be substituted for disclosure of the price.

    (5)   A statement of the amount or method of determining the amount of any liabilities the lease imposes upon the lessee at the end of the term and a statement that the lessee shall be liable for the difference, if any, between the estimated value of the leased property and its realized value at the end of the lease term, if the lessee has such liability.

(d) *Multiple item leases; merchandise tags.* If a merchandise tag for an item normally included in a multiple item lease sets forth information which would require additional disclosures under paragraph (c) of this section, such merchandise tag need not contain such additional disclosures, provided it clearly and conspicuously refers to a sign or display which is prominently posted in the lessor's showroom. Such sign or display shall contain a table or schedule of those items of information to be disclosed under paragraph (c) of this section.

213.6 PRESERVATION AND INSPECTION OF EVIDENCE OF COMPLIANCE.

(a) Evidence of compliance with the requirements imposed under this regulation, other than advertising requirements under 213.5, shall be preserved by the lessor for a period of not less than 2 years after the date such disclosure is required to be made.

(b) Each lessor shall, when directed by the appropriate administrative enforcement authority designated in section 108 of the Act, permit that authority or its duly authorized representative to inspect its relevant records and evidence of compliance with this regulation.

213.7 INCONSISTENT STATE REQUIREMENTS.

(a) *Preemption.* A State law which is similar in nature, purpose, scope, intent, effect, or requisites to a section of chapter 5 of the Act is not inconsistent with the Act or this regulation within the meaning of section 186 (a) of the Act if the lessor can comply with the State law without violating this regulation. If a lessor cannot comply with a State law without violating a provision of this regulation which implements a section of chapter 5 of the Act, such State law is inconsistent with the requirements of the Act and this regulation within the meaning of section 186(a) of the Act and is pre-empted.

(b) *Procedures.* A state, through its governor, attorney general, or other appropriate official having primary enforcement or interpretative responsibilities for its consumer leasing law, may apply to the Board for a determination that the State law offers greater protection and benefit to lessees than a comparable provision(s) of chapter 5 of the Act and its implementing provision(s) in this regulation, or is otherwise not inconsistent with chapter 5 of the Act and this regulation, or for a determination with respect to any issues not clearly covered by paragraph (a) of this section as to the consistency or inconsistency of a State law with chapter 5 of the Act or its implementing provisions in this regulation.

213.8 EXEMPTION OF CERTAIN STATE REGULATED TRANSACTIONS.

(a) *Exemption for State regulated transactions.* In accordance with the provisions of appendix A to Regulation M, part 213, any state may make application to the Board for exemption of any class of transactions within the state from the requirements of chapter 5 of the Act and the corresponding provisions of this regulation, provided that:

   (1) The Board determines that under the law of that state, that class of transactions is subject to requirements substantially similar to those imposed under chapter 5 of the Act and the corresponding provisions of this regulation; or the lessee is afforded greater protection and benefit than is afforded under chapter 5 of the Act, and

   (2) There is adequate provision for enforcement.

(b) *Procedures and criteria.* The Procedures and criteria under which a state may apply for the determination provided for in paragraph (a) of this section are set forth in appendix A to Regulation M.

(c) *Civil liability.* In order to assure that the concurrent jurisdiction of Federal and state courts created in sections 130(e) and 185(c) of the Act shall continue to have substantive provisions to which such jurisdiction shall apply, and generally to aid in implementing the Act with respect to any class of transactions exempted pursuant to paragraph (a) of this section and appendix A, the Board pursuant to sections 105 and 186(b) of the Act hereby prescribes that:

   (1) No such exemptions shall be deemed to extend to the civil liability provisions of sections 130, 131, and 185 of the Act; and

   (2) After an exemption has been granted, the disclosure requirements of the applicable state law shall constitute the disclosure requirements of the Act, except to the extent that such state law imposes disclosure requirements not imposed by the Act. Information required under such state law with the exception of those provisions which impose disclosure requirements not imposed by the Act shall, accordingly, constitute a requirement imposed under chapter 5 of the Act for the purpose of section 130(a).

APPENDIX A TO PART 213-PROCEDURES AND CRITERIA FOR STATE EXEMPTIONS FROM THE CONSUMER LEASING ACT

(a) *Application.* Any state may make application to the Board, pursuant to the terms of this appendix and the Board's Rules of Procedure (12 CFR part 262), for a determination that under the laws of the state, consumer lease transactions as provided in section 181(1) of the Act and 213.2 of this regulation, within that state are subject to requirements which are substantially similar to those imposed under chapter 5 of the Act or which provide greater protection and benefit to lessees than those provided under chapter 5, and that there is adequate provision for enforcement of such requirements. Such application shall be made by letter addressed to the Board signed by the governor, the attorney general, or any official of the state having responsibilities under the state laws which are applicable to the relevant class of transactions.

(b) *Supporting documents.* The application shall be accompanied by:

   (1) A copy of the full text of the laws of the state which are claimed by the applicant to impose requirements substantially similar to those imposed under chapter 5 or to provide greater protection and benefit to lessees than does chapter 5 with respect to consumer lease transactions as defined in 213.2 of this regulation.

   (2) A comparison of each requirement of state law with the corresponding requirement of chapter 5, together with reasons to support the claim that the requirements of state law are substantially similar to or provide greater protection and benefit to lessees than requirements of chapter 5 with respect to the class of consumer lease transactions. It shall also demonstrate that any differences are not inconsistent with and do not result in a diminution in the protection and benefit afforded lessees under chapter 5 and state that there are no other state laws which, due to their relations to the state law under consideration, should be considered by the Board in making its determination.

   (3) A copy of the full text of the laws of the state which provide for enforcement of the state laws referred to in paragraph (b)(1) of this appendix.

   (4) A comparison of the provisions of state law with the provisions of sections 108, 112, 130, 131, 183(a), 183(b), and 185 of the Act, together with reasons to support the claim that such state laws provide for

      (i) Administrative enforcement of the state laws referred to in paragraph (b)(1) of this appendix which is equivalent to the enforcement provided under section 108 of the Act;

      (ii) Criminal liability for willful and knowing violation of the state law with penalties substantially similar to those prescribed under section 112 of the Act, except that more severe penalties may be provided;

      (iii) Civil liability for failure to comply with the requirements of the state law, including class action liability, which is substantially similar to that provided under sections 130, 131, 185(b) of the Act, except that more severe penalties may be provided;

(iv) In leases where the lessee's liability at the end of the lease term is based on the estimated value of the leased property, a limitation on the lessee's liability at the end of the lease term substantially similar to that provided by section 183(a) of the Act, except that a stricter limitation may be provided;

(v) A provision prescribing that all penalties and other charges for delinquency, default or early termination specified in the lease must be reasonable substantially similar to that provided in section 183(b) of the Act, except that a stricter provision may be provided; and

(vi) A statute of limitations that prescribes a period in which to institute civil actions of substantially similar duration as that provided under section 185(c) of the Act, except that a longer period may be provided.

(5) A statement identifying the office designated or to be designated to administer the state laws referred to in paragraph (b)(1) of this appendix, together with complete information regarding the fiscal arrangements for administrative enforcement (including the amount of funds available or to be provided), the number and qualifications of personnel engaged therein, and a description of the procedures under which such state laws are to be administratively enforced, including administrative enforcement with respect to federally-chartered elssors. The foregoing statement should include reasons to support the claim that there is adequate provision for enforcement of such state laws.

(c) *Criteria for determination.* The Board will consider the following criteria along with any other relevant information in making a determination whether the laws of a state impose requirements substantially similar to or provide greater protection and benefit to lessees than under chapter 5, and whether there is adequate provision for enforcement of such laws:

(1) In order for provisions of state law to be substantially similar to or provide greater protection and benefit to lessees than the provision of chapter 5, the provisions of state law shall require that

(i) Definitions and rules of construction import the same meaning and have the same application as those prescribed under 213.2 of this regulation;

(ii) Lessors make all of the applicable disclosures required by this regulation and within the same (or more stringent) time periods as are prescribed by this regulation;

(iii) Lessors abide by obligations substantially similar to those prescribed by chapter 5, under conditions substantially similar to (or more stringent than) those prescribed in chapter 5;

(iv) Lessors abide by the same (or more stringent) prohibitions as are provided in chapter 5;

(v) Lessees need comply with no obligations or responsibilities which are more costly or burdensome as a condition of exercising any of the rights or gaining the benefits and protections in the state law which correspond to those afforded by chapter 5, than those obligations or responsibilities imposed upon lessees in chapter 5; and

(vi) Substantially similar or more favorable rights and protections are provided to lessees under conditions substantially similar to or more favorable (to lessees) than those afforded by chapter 5.

(2)   In determining whether the provisions for enforcement of the state law referred to in paragraph (b)(1) of this appendix are adequate, consideration will be given to the extent to which, under the laws of the state, provision is made for

(i)   Administrative enforcement, including necessary facilities, personnel and funding;

(ii) Criminal liability for willful and knowing violation with penalties substantially similar to those prescribed under section 112 of the Act, except that more severe criminal penalties may be prescribed;

(iii) Civil liability for failure to comply with the provisions of the state law substantially similar to that provided under sections 130, 131 and 185(b) of the Act, except that more severe civil liability penalties may be prescribed;

(iv) In leases where the lessee's liability at the end of the lease term is based on the estimated value of the leased property, a limitation on the lessee's liability at the end of the lease term substantially similar to that provided in section 183(a) of the Act, and a provision requiring that penalties be reasonably substantially similar to that provided in section 183(b) of the Act, except that stricter standards on end-term liability and penalty provisions may be prescribed; and

(v)   A statute of limitations with respect to civil liability of substantially similar duration to that provided under section 185(c) of the Act, except that a longer duration may be provided.

(d) *Public notice of filing and proposed rulemaking.* Following initial review of an application filed in accordance with the requirements of paragraphs (a) and (b) of this appendix, notice of such filing and proposed rulemaking will be published by the Board in the FEDERAL REGISTER, and a copy of such application will be made available for examination by interested persons during business hours at the Board and at the Federal Reserve Bank of each Federal Reserve District in which any part of the state of the applicant is situated. A reasonable period of time will be allowed from the date of such publication for the Board to receive written comments from interested persons with respect to that application.

(e) *Exemption from requirements of chapter 5.* If the Board determines that under the law of a state consumer lease transactions are subject to requirements which are substantially similar to or which provide greater protection and benefit to lessees than those imposed under chapter 5 and that there is adequate provision for enforcement, the Board will exempt such class of transactions in that state from the requirements of chapter 5 in the following manner and subject to the following conditions:

(1)   Notice of the exemption will be published in the FEDERAL REGISTER, and the Board will furnish a copy of such notice to the official who made application for such exemption and to each Federal authority responsible for administrative enforcement of the requirements of chapter 5.

(2)   The appropriate official of any state which receives an exemption shall inform the Board within 30 days of the occurrence of any change in its related law

(including regulations). The report of any such change shall contain the full text of that change together with statements setting forth the information and opinions with respect to that change as specified in paragraphs (b)(2) and (4) of this appendix. The official who has received an exemption shall file with the Board from time to time such reports as the Board may require.

(3) The Board will inform the official of any subsequent amendments to chapter 5 (including the implementing provisions of this regulation and the Board's formal interpretations) which might call for amendment of state law, regulations or formal interpretations thereof.

(f) *Adverse determination.* (1) If the Board denies the application for exemption, it will notify the appropriate state official of the facts upon which its decision is based and shall afford that state a reasonable opportunity to demonstrate or achieve compliance.

(2) If, after giving the state an opportunity to demonstrate or achieve compliance, the Board finds that it still cannot grant the exemption, the Board will publish in the FEDERAL REGISTER a notice of its decision and will furnish a copy of such notice to the official who made application for such exemption.

(g) *Revocation of exemption.* (1) The Board reserves the right to revoke any exemption if at anytime it determines that the state law does not, in fact, impose requirements which are substantially similar to or provide greater protection and benefit to lessees than those imposed under chapter 5, or that there is not, in fact, adequate provision for enforcement.

(2) Before revoking any state exemption, the Board will notify the appropriate state official of the facts or conduct which in the opinion of the Board warrants such revocation and shall afford that state such opportunity as the Board deems appropriate to demonstrate or achieve compliance.

(3) If, after having been afforded the opportunity to demonstrate or achieve compliance, the Board determines that the state has not done so, notice of the Board's intention to revoke such exemption shall be published as a notice of proposed rulemaking in the FEDERAL REGISTER. A period of time will be allowed from the date of such publication for the Board to receive written comments from interested persons.

(4) In the event of revocation of such exemption, notice of such revocation shall be published by the Board in the FEDERAL REGISTER, and a copy of such notice shall also be furnished to the appropriate state official and to the federal authorities responsible for enforcement of requirements of chapter 5, and the class of transactions affected within that state shall then be subject to the requirements of chapter 5, to administrative enforcement as provided under section 108, to criminal liability as provided under section 112, and to civil liability as provided under sections 130, 131, and 185(b) of the Act. [46 FR 20951, Apr. 7, 1981; 46 FR 29245, June 1, 1981]

APPENDIX B TO PART 213—PROCEDURES AND CRITERIA FOR BOARD DETERMINATION REGARDING PREEMPTION

Procedures and criteria under which any state may apply for a determination that a state law is not inconsistent with and not preempted by a provision of chapter 5 of the Act pursuant to 213.7 of this regulation.

(a) *Application.* Any state may make application to the Board pursuant to the terms of this appendix and the Board's Rules of Procedure (12 CFR part 262), for a determination that a law of such state is consistent with a provision of chapter 5 of the Act, because such state law provides greater protection and benefit to lessees than does the provision of chapter 5, that such law is consistent with a provision of chapter 5 for any other reason, or for a determination of any issues not clearly covered by 213.7 of this regulation with regard to the relationship of the federal law to the state law. Such application shall be made by letter addressed to the Board signed by the governor, attorney general or any official of the state having responsibilities under the state law.

(b) *Supporting documents.* The application shall be accompanied by:

   (1)   A copy of the full text of the laws of the state which are claimed by the applicant to be consistent with a provision of chapter 5 or whose relationship (with regard to consistency or inconsistency) to a provision of chapter 5 is claimed by the applicant to be not clearly covered by the standards and criteria for comparison set forth in 213.7 of this regulation.

   (2)   A comparison of each requirement of the state law with the corresponding requirement of chapter 5, with reasons to support the claim that the state law is consistent with a provision of chapter 5 or that the relationship (with regard to consistency or inconsistency) between the state law and chapter 5 is not clearly covered by the standards and criteria set forth in 213.7 of this regulation.

   (3)   A copy of the full text of any provisions of state law corresponding to sections 112, 130, 131, 183(a), 183(b), 185(b), and 185(c) of the Act (if applicable), together with reasons for the applicant's claim that such state provisions are not inconsistent (because they provide greater protection and benefit to lessees or for other reasons) with the act.

   (4)   A statement that there are not state laws (including administrative or judicial interpretations) other than those submitted to the Board which have any bearing on whether or not the state law is consistent with a provision of chapter 5.

   (5)   A statement identifying the office designated or to be designated to administer the state laws referred to in paragraph (b)(1) of this appendix. If no such administrative office exists, then a statement identifying the office to which the Board can address any correspondence regarding the request for such determination shall accompany the application.

(c) *Criteria for determination.* The Board will consider the following criteria along with any other relevant information, in addition to the criteria set forth in 213.7 of this regulation, in making a determination of whether or not state law is inconsistent with a provision of chapter 5. In order for provisions of state law to be determined to be consistent with a provision of chapter 5, the provisions of state law shall, to the extent relevant to the determination, require that

   (1)   Definitions and rules of construction import the same meaning and have the same application as those prescribed by this regulation;

   (2)   Lessors make all of the applicable disclosures required by the corresponding provision of chapter 5 and this regulation, and within the same (or more stringent) time periods as those prescribed by this regulation;

(3)   Lessors abide by obligations substantially similar to those prescribed by a provision of chapter 5 under conditions substantially similar (or more stringent) to those in chapter 5;

(4)   Lessors abide by the same (or more stringent) prohibitions as are provided by chapter 5;

(5)   Lessees need comply with no obligations or responsibilities which are more costly or burdensome as a condition of exercising any of the rights or gaining the benefits and protections provided in the state law, which correspond to those afforded by chapter 5, than those obligations or responsibilities imposed on lessees in chapter 5; and

(6)   Lessees are to have rights and protections substantially similar to or more favorable than those provided by the corresponding provisions of chapter 5 under conditions and within time periods which are substantially similar to or more favorable (to lessees) than those prescribed by chapter 5.

(d) *Public notice of filing and proposed rulemaking.* In connection with any application which has been filed in accordance with the requirements of paragraphs (a) and (b) of this appendix, notice of such filing and proposed rulemaking will be published by the Board in the FEDERAL REGISTER, and a copy of such application will be made available for examination by interested persons during business hours at the Board and at the Federal Reserve Bank of each Federal Reserve District in which any part of the state of the applicant is situated. A period of time will be allowed from the date of such publication for the Board to receive written comments from interested persons with respect to the application.

(e) *Determination that a state law is consistent with chapter 5.* If the Board determines on the basis of the information before it that the law of a state is consistent with a provision of chapter 5, notice of such determination shall be published in the following manner and shall be subject to the following conditions:

(1)   Notice of the determination will be published in the FEDERAL REGISTER, and the Board will furnish a copy of such notice to the official who made application for such exemption and to each federal authority responsible for administrative enforcement of the requirements of chapter 5.

(2)   The appropriate official of any state which receives such a determination shall inform the Board within 30 days of the occurrence of any change in its related law (or regulations). The report of any such change shall contain copies of the full text of the law, as changed, together with statements setting forth the information and opinions with respect to that change as specified in paragraphs (b)(2) and (4) of this appendix. The appropriate official of any state which has received such a determination shall file with the Board from time to time such reports as the Board may require.

(3)   The Board will inform the appropriate official of any state which receives such a determination of any subsequent amendments to chapter 5 (including the implementing provisions of this regulation and the Board's formal interpretations) which might call for amendment of state law, regulations, or formal interpretations.

(f) *Adverse determination.* (1) If, after publication of notice in the FEDERAL REGISTER as provided under paragraph (d) of this appendix, the Board finds that such state law is inconsistent with a provision of chapter 5, it will notify the appropriate state official of the facts upon which such finding is based and shall afford that state official a reasonable opportunity to demonstrate further that such state law is not inconsistent with the corresponding provisions of chapter 5, if such state official desires to do so.

(2)   If, after having afforded the state official such further opportunity to demonstrate that the state law is consistent with a provision of chapter 5, the Board finds that the state law is inconsistent, it will publish in the FEDERAL REGISTER a notice of its decision with respect to such application and will furnish a copy of such notice to the official who made application for the determination.

(g) *Reversal of determination.* (1) The Board reserves the right to reverse any determination made under this appendix to the effect that a state law is consistent with a provision of chapter 5 because of subsequently discovered facts, a change in the state or federal law (by amendment or administrative or judicial interpretation or otherwise) or for any other reason bearing on the coverage or impact of the state or federal law.

(2)   Before reversing any such determination, the Board will notify the appropriate state official of the facts or conduct which in the opinion of the Board, warrants such reversal and shall afford that state such opportunity as the Board deems appropriate under the circumstances to demonstrate that the determination should not be reversed.

(3)   If, after having been afforded the opportunity to demonstrate that its law is consistent with a provision of chapter 5, the Board determines that the state has not done so, notice of the Board's intention to reverse such determination shall be published as a notice of proposed rulemaking in the FEDERAL REGISTER. A reasonable period of time will be allowed from the date of such publication for the Board to receive written comments from interested persons.

(4)   In the event of reversal of such determination, notice shall be published by the Board in the FEDERAL REGISTER, and a copy of such notice shall also be furnished to the appropriate state official and to the Federal authorities responsible for enforcement of the requirements of chapter 5, and the state law affected shall then be considered inconsistent with and preempted by chapter 5 within the meaning of section 186(a) of the Act. [46 FR 20951, Apr. 7, 1981; 46 FR 29245-29246, June 1, 1981]

CHAPTER 10
APPENDIX IV

FORECLOSURE FACT SHEET*

State	Procedure Utilized	Time to Complete (approx.)	Period to Redeem
Ala.	*Non-Judicial* Publish for 3 wks., sell during 4th wk.	30 days	1 year
Alaska	Non-Judicial: Notice of Default recorded after Deed of Trust is 30 days in default, NOD must be mailed w/i 10 days, a Notice of Sale must be posted and published for 4 wks. Sale is by auction.	90 days after recdg. NOD	None
	Judicial: Commenced by service of a summons and complaint, continues as a regular lawsuit and ends with a money judgment and a decree of fore-closure and order to sell property. Notice of Sale posted in same manner as for Non-Judicial. Sale must be confirmed by Court.	Varies	1 Yr. by Trustor; 60 days for junior lienors
Ariz.	A *mortgage* (rarely used) may only be foreclosed by an action at law. After entry of Judgment, mortgaged property is sold at sheriff's sale.	6–9 mos.	6 mos.
	A *Deed of Trust* can be foreclosed in the same manner as a mortgage or under a Power of Sale. Trustee records a Notice of Sale in County where property is located. A copy of notice along with a statement of the breach must be sent by certified mail w/i	4 mos.	None

* Source—*National Mortgage Law Summary*, American College of Mortgage Attorneys. Reprinted with permission.

State	Procedure Utilized	Time to Complete (approx.)	Period to Redeem
	5 days to all parties (except Trustee) on Trust Deed as well as to each person who has a record interest in property. Notice is then published for 4 wks. and must be posted. Sale is conducted by Trustee, or by atty. or agent for Trustee.		
Ark.	*Judicial Foreclosure* is most frequently used. Culminates in a final decree and a commissioner's sale.	60–90 days	1 Year
	Statutory Foreclosure used primarily for residential property; may only be used by banks, svgs. and in assoc. and mtge. cos.		
Calif.	*Trustee's Sale* Trustee's Sale is used unless a deficiency judgment is sought. Commenced by filing request with Trustee to commence foreclosure. Trustee records, mails and publishes Notice of Default and Election to Sell. If defaults are not cured w/i 3 mos., lender may request Trustee to file a Notice of Sale. Sale can be conducted 21 days after Notice of Sale is recorded.	4 mos.	3 mos. if a credit bid is made; 12 mos. if a defic is sought
	Judicial Foreclosure Judicial Foreclosure is commenced by filing of Complaint. A Judg. of foreclosure and order of sale is entered following a trial or default by borrower. Sale may take place 21 days after mailing, posting and publication of notice.	9–18 mos.	Same
Colo.	*Trustee's Sale* Foreclosure commenced by filing Notice of Election and Demand for Sale along with evidence of the indebtedness, original Deed and names and addresses of all persons claiming an interest in property with public Trustee. The Trustee must record the notice w/i 10 days and publish for 5 weeks.	50–70 days	75 days

State	Procedure Utilized	Time to Complete (approx.)	Period to Redeem
	During publication period, a summary proceeding is brought in Dist. Ct. to obtain Order Authorizing Sale which is a prerequisite to Trustee's sale.		
Conn.	*Judicial Foreclosure* When Judg. is entered, Ct. can enter a judgment of foreclosure by sale or a judgment of strict foreclosure.	4–16 mos.	None
	In a *foreclosure by sale*, a sale date is set and the property is sold at auction, the proceeds are returned to the Ct. and disbursed to the lien holders based upon their respective priorities.		
	If a *judgment of strict foreclosure* is entered, the Ct. sets "law days" for the owner, the foreclosing party and the holder of each subsequent encumbrance. Law days are assigned in inverse order to their priorities with the owner being first and party foreclosing being last. Each has the right to redeem on its respective law day and, if they fail to do so, that person loses their interest in the property.		
Del.	*Judicial Foreclosure* Must sue out a writ of scire facias sur mortgage in county where property is located. An action is commenced by filing a Praecipe and Complaint with the Protonotary of the Superior Court. The Writ is served with the complaint. At judgment, execution is by a writ of levari facias which is directed to the proper officer, who subjects the mortgaged property to sale.	4–5 mos.	None
D.C.	*Statutory and Judicial Foreclosure* Power of Sale: After default, note is accelerated. Notice is sent to borrower and to office of recorder of deed; Trustee advertises sale.	45-90 days	None

State	Procedure Utilized	Time to Complete (approx.)	Period to Redeem
Fla.	*Judicial Foreclosure* The action is one *in rem* but *quasi in rem* if personal service is obtained and a deficiency is sought. Following judgment, a sale is held by Clerk of Circuit Court one month after the date of judgment, after publication of the notice of sale for two weeks. After sale, there is a 10-day period for objections.	6 mos.	None
Ga.	*Non-Judicial and Judicial Foreclosure* Non-judicial is most common. Power of Sale must be contained in security agreement. After default, notice of sale must be advertised for 4 weeks before sale date. Sale must be held on first Tuesday of month between 10:00 A.M. and 4:00 P.M.	4–6 wks.	None
	Judicial foreclosure can be used by petition to the superior court of the county where property is located. Sale is made by Sheriff.	30 days min.	None
Hi.	*Judicial and Non-Judicial Foreclosure* Judicial: commenced by Complaint, summary judgment, followed by auction and confirmation. If no objections, Ct. will confirm a sale by the commissioner w/o an auction if price is adequate.	10–12 mos.	None
	Non-Judicial: notice of sale published for 3 wks. with last publication not less than 14 days before sale. Posting of notice at premises 21 days before sale.	45 days	None
Idaho	*Judicial and Non-Judicial Foreclosure* Judicial foreclosure used to foreclose mortgages.	150 days	6 mos. or 1 yr.
	Non-judicial foreclosure used for Deeds of Trust. Notice is given, followed by advertisement, then by sale.	120 days	None

State	Procedure Utilized	Time to Complete (approx.)	Period to Redeem
Ill.	*Judicial Foreclosure* Commenced by filing of complaint. Upon entry of a judgment, the property is generally sold via public sale, although method for private sale does exist. Notice of Sale must be published for 3 wks. with last publication at least 7 days before sale. Sale must be confirmed.	6 mos.	Waived
Ind.	*Judicial Foreclosure* Typically combined with a suit to enforce the note. After judgment is obtained, the Sheriff is requested to sell the property but not until statutory moratorium on execution has expired. Sheriff must advertise the sale for at least 30 days prior to sale.	6–8 mos.	None
Iowa	*Judicial and Non-Judicial Foreclosure* Judicial foreclosure requires notice of default to borrower and right to cure. Petition is filed with application for receiver. Sale held by Sheriff.	6–8 mos.	1 yr.
	Non-judicial foreclosure involves agreement between parties to surrender the property and waive deficiency. Agmt. is recorded and notice is given to junior lien holders and parties in possession.		30 days
Kan.	*Judicial Foreclosure* Suit must be filed for establishment of debt and lien priority; judgment authorizes sale at public auction.	6 mos.	3–12 mos
Ken.	*Judicial Foreclosure* Commenced by filing suit. After judgment, property is sold by Master Commissioner who then files report.	90 days	1 yr.

State	Procedure Utilized	Time to Complete (approx.)	Period to Redeem
La.	*Judicial Foreclosure* (two methods) Ordinary Process involves the filing of a suit with citation to the debtor. After judgment, a writ of fieri facias (seizure) is issued and the property is sold at a judicial sale.	Several mos.	None
	Executory process may be invoked where mortgagor has executed mortgage and acknowledged the debt. A petition with original note and a certified copy of mortgage attached is filed in Court. A notice demand is served upon debtor. If payment is not made w/i 3 days, a writ of seizure and sale addressed to Sheriff is issued. A notice of sale is then published once a week for 30 days. Property is then sold at public auction.	8–10 wks.	None
Maine	Eight different methods of which foreclosure by judicial action is most common. Commenced by filing complaint with the Court. Following entry of judgment, there is a 90-day redemption period before a sale is scheduled. A notice of Sale must be published for 3 weeks prior to sale by auction.	9 mos.	1 yr.
Md.	Security Instrument must authorize a power of sale and/or an assent to decree foreclosure. If so, suit can be filed and, for assent to decree foreclosures, an order apptg. Trustee must be signed by Court. Trustee must advertise sale for 3 wks. prior to sale. After sale, Trustee files report with Court. An Order is issued requiring a notice of sale be published for 3 wks. Setting a limit to file objections. If no objections are filed, sale is then ratified.	90 days	None
Ma.	Three methods of foreclosure available… action, entry and sale. Action is rarely used. Entry and Sale are usually used at the same time. Before the entry and foreclosure sale may occur, the federal Soldiers and Sailors Civil Relief Act and the Mass. Implementing	10–13 wks.	3 yrs.

State	Procedure Utilized	Time to Complete (approx.)	Period to Redeem
	statute must be satisfied. This is done by filing a complaint in the Land Court seeking a judgment that no person is entitled to the benefit of the Act. The mortgagee can then proceed with sale pursuant to power of sale. Notice of sale must be published for three weeks. At sale, property is sold by auctioneer.		
Mich.	*Judicial and Non-Judicial Foreclosure* Judicial action: the mortgagee must file suit in the circuit court where the property is located requesting that the court declare a default and order the sale of the property in order to satisfy the debt that is owed.	6 mos.	6 mos.
	Non-judicial foreclosure (foreclosure by advertisement) requires that the property be advertised for sale for 4 wks. The sale is conducted by the county sheriff as an auction. In order to use this procedure, mortgage must be recorded and contain a power of sale.	6 wks.	Varies
Minn.	*Judicial and Non-Judicial Foreclosure* Foreclosure by action is the judicial process which is conducted the same as a civil suit. A judgment is entered for the amount due and the Sheriff is ordered to make the sale pursuant to a certified transcript of the judgment.	1+ yrs.	6 mos./ 12 mos.
	Foreclosure by advertisement is the non-judicial process which is only available when mortgage contains a power of sale, the mortgage must be recorded and no action can be pending on the debt. The Notice of Sale is published for 6–8 wks.	8–15 mos.	
Miss.	Foreclosure is by Power of Sale. A notice of sale is published for 3 wks. Posting of notice required.	4 wks.	None

State	Procedure Utilized	Time to Complete (approx.)	Period to Redeem
Mo.	Non-judicial under a Deed of Trust. Trustee must give at least 20 days notice of the sale. Advertisement must take place at least 20 times.	30–45 days	Applies only if mtgee. purch. at sale
Mont.	*Judicial and Non-Judicial Foreclosure* Judicial foreclosure is an action to enforce the obligation secured with a request for the equitable remedy of foreclosure of the collateral. The holder of an obligation secured by a real estate mortgage must seek enforcement by foreclosure unless the property has become valueless.	60 days	1 year
	Non-judicial foreclosure under a Deed of Trust requires recording and mailing the Notice of Sale 120 days before the sale, publication for 3 wks. With last publication 20 days before sale.	6 mos.	None
Neb.	*Judicial and Non-Judicial Foreclosure* Judicial foreclosure commenced by filing a petition in District Court. After a decree of foreclosure is entered, borrower has 20 days to request a stay. Stay can vary between 3 & 9 mos. Depending on type of property. After stay, lender may file request with clerk of court for an order of sale. Sheriff publishes notice of sale for 4 wks. before sale.	5–6 mos. w/o stay	None
	Non-judicial foreclosure can be used only with Deeds of Trust. Must record and mail notice of default to all necessary parties. Mtgor. has 1 month to cure default. If not cured, Trustee publishes Notice of Sale for 5 wks. prior to sale.	3 mos.	None
Nev.	*Judicial and Non-Judicial Foreclosure* Judicial foreclosure is commenced by filing suit in county where property is located. A judgment of foreclosure and order or sale is entered prior to sale.	Varies	1 year

State	Procedure Utilized	Time to Complete (approx.)	Period to Redeem
	Non-judicial foreclosure under a Deed of Trust requires Trustee to record and mail an executed notice of breach and election to sell. Trustee may proceed with sale if deficiency in payment is not cured w/i 35 days after recdg. and more than 3 mos. has elapsed since recdg. Notice of the sale must be given 20 days before sale. *A one action rule applies in both types of foreclosure which requires the creditor to proceed against the security first.	4 mos.	None
N.H.	*Non-judicial foreclosure* is commenced by publishing notice of sale for 3 wks. A copy of notice must be served on mtgor. or sent by certified mail 25 days before the sale.	60 days	None
N.J.	*Judicial foreclosure* is commenced by filing a complaint in Superior Court. Upon issuance of a Judgment and a writ of execution, the writ is sent to Sheriff, and after publication of notice of sale, the sale is held.	8–24 mos.	10 days
N.M.	*Judicial Foreclosure* After sending mtgor. notice of default and giving an opportunity to cure, foreclosure is commenced by filing a complaint. After judgment is entered, notice of sale must be published for 4 wks. prior to sale.	3–9 mos.	9 mos.
N.Y.	*Judicial and Non-Judicial Foreclosure* Judicial foreclosure (most common) is commenced by filing complaint in Supreme Court. After judgment is secured, notice of sale is published for 3 or 4 wks. Sale must take place w/i 21–28 days (publication 2× wk. for 3 wks.) or 28–35 days (publication 1× wk. for 4 wks.) after 1st publication. Court-apptd. Referee conducts sale.	12–18 mos.	None

State	Procedure Utilized	Time to Complete (approx.)	Period to Redeem
	Foreclosure by Advertisement (Non-judicial foreclosure) is rarely used due to title problems and strict procedural technicalities which, if not followed exactly, could result in procedure being invalidated. Power of Sale must be contained in mtge. No action can be pending on the debt. Notice of sale must be published for 12 wks. prior to sale. Posting required 84 days prior to sale. Other special requirements apply. No deed is given but rather a whole series of affidavits must be recorded with County Clerk to establish ownership.		
N. Car.	*Judicial and Non-Judicial Foreclosure* Foreclosure by action (Judicial) is rarely used. A civil action is commenced. After judgment is secured, publication of notice of sale is required prior to sale.		
	Foreclosure by Power of Sale (Non-judicial) requires that a notice of hearing be filed with Clerk of Court and sent to all proper parties. Certain statutory requirements for producing a notice of sale must be met prior to sale.	3 mos.	None
N. Dak.	*Judicial* Foreclosure by action commenced by filing of complaint in district court. Statutory written notice required to be sent to mtgor. 30 days prior to commencing foreclosure. If default not cured, proceedings can be commenced to foreclose. Sheriff conducts sale.	5–6 mos.	6 mos.
Ohio	*Judicial* Foreclosures must be commenced in county where property is located. Once decree of foreclosure is entered, an order of sale is issued.	6 mos.	None
Okla.	*Judicial* Foreclosed commenced by filing of complaint in county where property is located. Property must be appraised, unless waived, and cannot		None

State	Procedure Utilized	Time to Complete (approx.)	Period to Redeem
	be sold for less than 2/3 of appraised value. Notice of sale must be published for 30 days prior to date of sale and order of sale must conform to judgment. Property is sold by Sheriff.		
Ore.	*Judicial and Non-Judicial Foreclosure* Mortgage can only be foreclosed judicially. Procedure and effect of sale same as that for execution of a judgment for recovery of money.	6–12 mos.	180 days
	Deed of Trust can be foreclosed judicially in the same manner as mortgage or can be foreclosed non-judicially by Trustee under Power of Sale. Notice of Default and Election to Sell is recorded and sale date is set for a Wednesday approx. 4 1/2 months from date of Notice of Default. Notice of Sale is served on all parties, then published for 4 wks. prior to sale.	4 1/2 mos.	None
Pa.	Mortgagee can proceed by action on bond (which is normally accompanied by warrant to confess judgment) or by mortgage foreclosure. After judgment is obtained, a praecipe for a writ of execution is filed with county Sheriff and sale is scheduled.	165 days	None
R.I.	*Judicial and Non-Judicial Foreclosure* Judicial foreclosure can be accomplished by an action for possession or by peaceable and open entry in the presence of 2 witnesses. Procedure is rarely used.	60 days	None
	Non-judicial foreclosure is accomplished through Power of Sale. A Notice of Sale is published for 3 wks. prior to sale.		
S. Car.	Judicial foreclosure is commenced by filing summons and complaint. Notice of Sale must be published for 3 wks. prior to sale.	60–120 days	None

State	Procedure Utilized	Time to Complete (approx.)	Period to Redeem
S. Dak.	*Judicial and Non-Judicial Foreclosure* Judicial foreclosure is by action and is generally used for commercial mortgages.	6 mos.	1 year
	Non-judicial foreclosure is by publishing a notice of sale for 4 wks. prior to sale.	30–45 days	
Tenn.	Non-judicial foreclosure under Power of Sale in Deed of Trust. Notice of Sale must be published 3x prior to sale.	30 days	2 yrs.
Tex.	Non-judicial foreclosure under Power of Sale in Deed of Trust. Notice of Sale must be posted, filed and mailed 21 days before date of sale. Notice must be sent by certified mail to borrower.	21 days	None
Utah	*Judicial and Non-Judicial Foreclosure* Judicial foreclosure follows ordinary requirements for civil action.		6 mos. for mtges.
	Non-judicial foreclosure is accomplished under Power of Sale. Notice of Default must be recorded, followed by three month period to cure default. Sale then conducted by Trustee.	3 mos.	None
Ver.	Judicial foreclosure is commenced by filing action in Superior Ct. Action is considered as a strict foreclosure. Upon recdg. Judg. and a decree of foreclosure and certificate of non-redemption, creditor can sell property.	60–90 days	6 mos.
Va.	*Non-Judicial Foreclosure* Trustee must give written notice of sale to borrower 14 days prior to sale and publish notice of sale in accordance with statute.	14–21 days	None
Wash.	*Judicial and Non-Judicial Foreclosure* Judicial foreclosure follows a normal civil action.	90–120 days	1 year

State	Procedure Utilized	Time to Complete (approx.)	Period to Redeem
	Non-judicial foreclosure under Power of Sale. A 30-day Notice of Default is followed by a 90-day notice of sale. Sale cannot take place sooner than 190 days from date of default.	7 mos.	None
W. Va.	Non-judicial foreclosure under Power of Sale in Deed of Trust. Trustee must publish notice of sale and give notice to borrower.	60 days	None
Wis.	Judicial foreclosure is commenced by filing summons and complaint. After judgment, Notice of Sale must be posted and published 1x wk. for 6 wks. prior to sale.	3–4 mos.	1 year
Wyo.	Mortgage or Deed of Trust can be foreclosed by advertisement and sale based upon Power of Sale. A 10-day written notice of intent to foreclose by advertisement must be sent to record owner. Notice is then published for 4 wks. prior to sale.	45 days	3 mos.

CHAPTER 10

APPENDIX V

A Comparison of a Security Agreement Under The Current Article 9 and the Draft New Article 9

SECURITY AGREEMENT

This Security Agreement ("Security Agreement") is made the ~~30th~~ 1st day of ~~June~~ July, 2001,[1] between Vending Machine Manufacturing Co., a Delaware Corporation ("Debtor") and Finance Company, an Illinois Corporation ("Secured Party"), ~~as Agent for the lenders listed on Exhibit A.~~[2]

This Security Agreement is entered into with respect to:

(i) a loan (the "Loan") to be made by Secured Party to Debtor[3] pursuant to a Loan Agreement (the "Loan Agreement") dated the same date as this Security Agreement;

(ii) the sale by Debtor and the purchase of Secured Party of Accounts[4];

Reprinted with permission of *Steven O. Weise,* Heller Ehrman White & McAuliffe, Los Angeles, California, sweise@hewm.com, *August 1, 1998.*

[1]The Drafting Committee has completed its work and obtained ALI and NCCUSL approval in 1998. This Security Agreement, for discussion purposes, assumes that the new Article 9 becomes effective in the relevant jurisdiction on July 1, 2001, as contemplated by the new Article 9. All statutory references in this document refer to the August 5, 1998 Draft of Article 9.

[2]The "secured party" includes a "representative" of the "secured party." §9-102(a)(72)(E). A financing statement may name a representative of the secured party without indicating that capacity. §§ 9-502(a)(2), 9-503(d). This rule should also apply to the security agreement if the obligations described cover those held by all participants.

[3]Note that if the "debtor" is a guarantor securing its obligations under a guaranty the guarantor will have the rights of a debtor for the collateral that it supplies and also as an "obligor" if the primary obligor has also supplied collateral. §§ 9-102(28) and (59) and 9-602. Either way it cannot waive its rights. § 9-602.

[4]Note the expanded definition of "accounts," described below. Article 9 continues to apply to the sale of accounts. § 9-109(a)(3).

(iii) the sale by Debtor and the purchase by Secured Party of Payment Intangibles[5]; and

(iv) the sale by Debtor and the purchase by Secured Party of Promissory Notes.[6]

Secured Party and Debtor agree as follows:

1. DEFINITIONS.

1.1 *"Collateral."* The Collateral shall consist of all of the ~~following~~ personal property[7] of Debtor, wherever located, and now owned or hereafter acquired,[8] including:

(i) Accounts, [including health-care-insurance receivables][9] ~~all amounts owed to Debtor for the licensing of intellectual property rights;~~

(ii) Chattel paper,[10] ~~including equipment leases and conditional sales agreements;~~

(iii) Inventory,[11] ~~including property held for sale or lease and raw materials;~~

(iv) Equipment,[12] ~~including property used in the Debtor's business, machinery and production machines;~~

(v) Instruments, [including Promissory Notes][13] ~~notes, negotiable instruments, and negotiable certificates of deposit;~~

~~(vi)~~ Securities ~~Investment Property;~~[14]

---

[5]Article 9 applies to the sale of "payment intangibles." § 9-109(a)(3). The definition is discussed below. Sales of payment intangibles are automatically perfected under § 9-309(a)(3). These changes are designed to facilitate securitization transactions without interfering with the sale of loan participations.

[6]Article 9 applies to the sale of "promissory notes." § 9-109(a)(3). The definition is discussed below. Sales of promissory notes are automatically perfected under § 9-309(a((4).

[7]A financing statement may use a "supergeneric" description, such as "all my personal property." § 9-504(2). A security agreement may not. § 9-108(c). Article 9 provides a "safe-harbor" for describing collateral by an Article 9 category in a security agreement or in a financing statement. § 9-108(b)(3).

[8]A security interest cannot apply to after-acquired commercial tort claims. § 9-204(b)(2).

[9]"Accounts" include a wide variety of rights to payment arising out of the transfer of rights in tangible and intangible personal property, including credit card receivables § 9-102(a)(2). Article 9 now covers security interests in rights under an insurance policy if the right is a "health-care-insurance receivable." § 9-102(a)(46) and 9-109(d)(8). A separate reference to "health-care-insurance receivable" is not necessary.

[10]"Chattel paper" includes tangible and intangible chattel paper. § 9-102(a)(11), (31), and (78). This results in some special perfection and priority rules discussed below.

[11]"Goods," and therefore inventory, includes software embedded in goods. § 9-102(a)(44) and (75).

[12]"Equipment" no longer has its own definition, it is the residual category of goods (goods that are not inventory, farm products, or consumer goods). § -102(a)(2). "Goods," and therefore equipment, includes software embedded in goods. § 9-102(a)(44) and (75).

[13]"Instruments" continue to include non-Article 3 payment obligations that are "of a type that in ordinary course of business [are] transferred by delivery with any necessary indorsement or assignment. A reference to "instruments" includes "promissory notes." § 9-102(a)(47). A separate reference to "promissory notes" is not necessary. As noted above, Article 9 applies tot he sale of promissory notes. § 9-109(a)(3). A "promissory note" is an "instrument" that is not "order" paper or a certificate of deposit. § 9-102(a)(65).

[14]"Investment property" is the terminology used to cover what used to be securities. See new Article 8 and current § 9-107. A reference to "general intangibles" (§ 9-102(a)(42)) or "instruments" (§ 9-102(a)(47)) will not include "investment property."

(vii)   Documents, ~~including a documents of title, a warehouse receipt, and a bill of lading;~~

(viii) <u>Deposit accounts;</u>[15]

(ix)   <u>Debtor's claim for interference with contract against Big Soda Pop Company;</u>[16]

(x)   <u>Letter of credit rights;</u>[17]

(xi)   General intangibles, [including payment intangibles][18] ~~licenses, intellectual property, and tax returns;~~

(xii)   [Supporting obligations] ~~Rights ancillary to, or arising in any way in connection with, any of the foregoing, including security agreements securing any of the foregoing, guaranties guarantying any of the foregoing, documents, notes, drafts representing any of the foregoing, the right to returned goods, warranty claims with respect to any of the foregoing, amounts owed in connection with the short term use or licensing of any of the foregoing, government payments in connection with the purchase or agreement not to produce any of the foregoing;~~[19]

(xiii) ~~books and records pertaining to the foregoing and the equipment containing the books and records; and~~

(xiv)   [to the extent not listed above as original collateral, proceeds and products of the foregoing]~~, including money, deposit accounts, goods, insurance proceeds and other tangible or intangible property received upon the sale or other disposition of the foregoing;~~[20]

---

[15]A reference to "general intangibles" will include "payment intangibles," but will not include a "deposit account." § 9-102(a)(42). There are special perfection rules, discussed below.

[16]Article 9 covers a security interest in a tort claim if the claim is a "commercial tort claim." §§ 9-102(a)(13), 9-109 (d)(12). The description of the collateral must refer to a specific tort claim and cannot describe the claim by "type." § 9-108(e)(1). The security interest cannot cover after-acquired tort claims. § 9-204(b)(2). A reference to "general intangibles" will not include a "commercial tort claim." § 9-102(a)(42).

[17]Letter of credit rights are the right to payment under a letter of credit. § 9-102(a)(51). Article 5 controls the right to draw under a letter of credit. § 5-114. A reference to "general intangibles" will not include letter of credit rights. § 9-102 (a) (42). There are special perfection rules discussed below.

[18]A reference to "general intangibles" does not include some types of collateral that may sound like a "general intangible," such as commercial tort claims, deposit accounts, investment property, and letter of credit rights. The term does include payment intangibles and software. § 9-102(a)(42). A separate reference to those types of collateral is not necessary. A "payment intangible" is a general intangible where the account debtor's principal obligation is the payment of money. § 9-102(a)(61).

[19]"Supporting obligations" include guaranties and letters of credit that support payment of another obligation. § 9-102(a)(77). A security interest in an obligation automatically attaches to a related support obligation. § 9-203(f). A security agreement does not need a separate reference to "supporting obligations." The security interest is automatically perfected if the security interest in the underlying collateral is perfected. § 9-308(d).

[20]"Proceeds" is broadly defined to include whatever is acquired upon the sale, lease, license, exchange or other disposition of collateral; rights arising out of collateral; and collections and distributions on collateral. § 9-102(a)(64). This is much broader than under current law. Article 9 will look to non-UCC law for the method of tracing. § 9-315(b)(2). It is expected that for money the courts will use the lowest intermediate balance rule. A security interest in collateral automatically attaches to proceeds (§ 9-203(f)), continues in collateral following its sale (§ 9-315(a)(1)), and initially remains perfected (§ 9-313(c) and (d)). A security agreement does not need a separate reference to "proceeds."

1.2 *"Obligations."* This Security Agreement secures the following:

(i) Debtor's obligations under the Loan, the Loan Agreement, and this Security Agreement;

(ii) all of Debtor's other present and future obligations to Secured Party;[21]

(iii) the repayment of (a) any amounts that Secured Party may advance or spend for the maintenance or preservation of the Collateral[22] and (b) any other expenditures that Secured Party may make under the provisions of this Security Agreement or for the benefit of Debtor;

(iv) all amounts owed under any modifications, renewals or extensions of any of the foregoing obligations; and

(v) any of the foregoing that arises after the filing of a petition by or against Debtor under the Bankruptcy Code, even if the obligations due not accrue because of the automatic stay under Bankruptcy Code § 362 or otherwise.

This Security Agreement does not secure any obligation described above which is secured by a consensual lien on real property.[23]

1.3 *UCC.* Any term used in the Uniform Commercial Code ("UCC") and not defined in this Security Agreement has the meaning given to the term in the UCC.[24]

2. GRANT OF SECURITY INTEREST.

Debtor grants a security interest in the Collateral to Secured Party to secure the payment or performance of the Obligations.[25]

3. PERFECTION OF SECURITY INTERESTS.

3.1 *Filing of financing statement.*

(i) Debtor ~~shall sign~~ authorizes Secured Party to file[26] a financing statement (the "Financing Statement") describing the Collateral.

---

[21]A security agreement may secure future advanced. § 9-204(c).

[22]A security interest automatically secures expenses relating to the foreclosure sale, other than attorneys fees. § 9-615(a)(1).

[23]This is designed to avoid problems under state real property anti-deficiency laws, such as those that exist in California. See generally § 9-604.

[24]Under the current Article 9 there is some risk in using terms defined under the UCC because of the relatively narrow scope of those terms. These include "accounts" and "proceeds." The expansion of the definitions of those terms (as discussed above) considerably reduces the risk of incorporating defined terms by reference. Care should continue to be taken that an incorporated definition has the meaning the parties intend to give to that word.

[25]Article 9 still does not use the word "grant" for the creation of a security interest. § 9-102(a)(73), 9-203. It is likely that practice will continue to use the term "grant."

[26]The debtor's signature not required. § 9-502. Although current law probably permits electronic filings so long as the debtor has "signed" something along the way, this change will facilitate electronic filings. The secured party will need the debtor to authorize the secured party to file a financing statement. The debtor's authentication of the security agreement "authorizes" the secured party to file a financing statement covering the collateral described in the security agreement. § 9-509(b)(1). This affirmative statement is not necessary.

(ii)   Debtor authorizes Secured Party to file a financing statement (the "Financing Statement") describing any agricultural liens or other statutory liens held by Secured Party.[27]

(iii) Secured Party shall receive prior to the Closing an official report from the Secretary of State of ~~each Collateral State and~~ the Debtor State[28] (the "SOS ~~Reports~~ Report") indicating that Secured Party's security interest is prior to all other security interests or other interests reflected in the report.

3.2   *Possession.*

(i)   Debtor shall have possession of the Collateral, except where expressly otherwise provided in this Security Agreement or where Secured Party chooses to perfect its security interest by possession in addition to the filing of a financing statement.[29]

(ii)   Where Collateral is in the possession of a third party, Debtor will join with Secured Party in notifying the third party of Secured Party's security interest and obtaining an acknowledgment from the third party that it is holding the Collateral for the benefit of Secured Party.[30]

3.3   *Control Agreements.* Debtor will cooperate with Secured Party in obtaining a control agreement[31] in form and substance satisfactory to Secured Party with respect to Collateral consisting of:

---

[27]An "agricultural lien" is a lien created by statute, involving agriculture and not dependent on possession. § 9-102(a)(5). It is not a "security interest." Non-UCC law will continue to govern the creation and attachment of agriculture liens and thus govern their enforceability between the holder of the lien and the debtor. A "secured party" includes the holder of an agricultural lien. §§ 9-102(a)(72)(B), 9-109(a)(2). Perfection will occur under Article 9. §§ 9-308(b). Non-UCC law will govern the creation and perfection of other statutory liens. § 9-109(d)(2).

[28]As defined below in the security agreement, the "Debtor State" is the state of the debtor's incorporation. Under new Article 9 a secured party will file a financing statement for all types of collateral in the state of the debtor's "location." § 9-2301(1). For debtors formed by a filing with a state, the debtor's "location" is the state of its organization. § 9-307(e).

[29]For a security interest perfected by possession, the location of the collateral governs the perfection of the security interest. § 9-301(2). A security interest in an instrument may be perfected by filing. § 9-312(a). A security interest in an instrument (and other tangible property) may be perfected by possessions. § 9-313(a). Perfection by possession may confer better protection. Possession of an instrument will eliminate the risk of a holder in due course defeating the rights of the secured interest in an instrument perfected by possession will prevail over one perfected only by filing. § 9-330(d). There are similar rules for chattel paper. § 9-330.

[30]If a third party has possession of the collateral, perfection occurs when the third party "acknowledges" that it holds the collateral for the secured party's benefit. § 9-313(c)(1) and (2). A lessee of collateral in the ordinary course of the debtor's business may not qualify as a third party in possession. The acknowledgment requirement changes current law which requires only that the third party receive notice of the security interest.

[31]Article 9 borrows the concept of using a control agreement as a perfection devices for investment property from current law to use in several circumstances under the new Article 9. See current §§ 8-106 and 9-115.

      (i)   <u>Deposit Accounts;</u>[32] <u>and</u>

      (ii)   <u>Investment Property;</u>[33]

      (iii) <u>Letter of credit rights;</u> and[34]

      (iv) <u>Electronic chattel paper.</u>[35]

3.4 *Marking of Chattel Paper.* <u>Debtor will not create any Chattel Paper without placing a legend on the Chattel Paper acceptable to Secured Party indicating that Secured Party has a security interest in the Chattel Paper.</u>[36]

4. POST-CLOSING COVENANTS AND RIGHTS CONCERNING THE COLLATERAL.

4.1 *Inspection.* The parties to this Security Agreement may inspect any Collateral in the other party's possession, at any time upon reasonable notice.

4.2 *Personal Property.* The Collateral shall remain personal property at all times. Debtor shall not affix any of the Collateral to any real property in any manner which would change its nature from that of personal property to real property or to a fixture.

---

[32]A security interest in deposit account may be perfected only by "control." § 9-312(b). "Control" occurs automatically when the depository institution with respect to the deposit account is the secured party. For third parties, it occurs either (i) when the depository institution has agreed with the secured party that the intermediary will follow directions from the secured party without further consent from the debtor, or (ii) the secured party puts the account in its own name. § 9-104. The existence of control does not of itself prevent the debtor from transferring funds from the account. See § 9-104(b). A transferee of money that does not act in "collusion" with the debtor will take the funds free of any security interest in the funds. § 9-332.

[33]A security interest in investment property may be perfected by filing or control. §§ 9-312(a), 9-313(e), 9-314(a). Generally, "control" of a security entitlement exists when a securities intermediary has agreed with the secured party that the intermediary will follow directions from the secured party without further consent from the debtor. § 9-106. Generally control of a certificated security occurs by delivery with any necessary endorsement. § 9-106. "Delivery" (as defined in § 8-301) without an endorsement will constitute perfection by possession, but not "control." § 9-313. A secured party with control of investment property will generally have priority over a secured party that perfects solely by the filing of a financing statement. § 9-328(1).

[34]"Control" is the only way to perfect a security interest in letter of credit rights. § 9-312(b)(2), except to the extent the letter of credit rights are a supporting obligation for other collateral. § 9-308(d). Control requires the consent of the issuer of the letter of credit or compliance with other practice. §§ 5-114(c), 9-107.

[35]A security interest in electronic chattel paper may be perfected by filing or control. §§ 9-312(a), 9-314(a). "Control" requires compliance with special rules for the electronic identification of the secured party "on" the electronic copy. § 9-105. A secured party that perfects a security interest in electronic chattel paper by control will generally defeat a secured party that has perfected its security interest only by filing. § 9-330(b).

[36]Purchasers of chattel paper will have priority in chattel paper claims "merely" as proceeds of inventory if purchaser (i) purchases in ordinary course of its business, (ii) acts in good faith, (iii) gives new value, and (iv) takes possession. In addition, the inventory secured party must not have marked the chattel paper. § 9-330. Marking tangible chattel paper does not operate to perfect the security interest, as does the electronic identification that a secured party can do to perfect a security interest in electronic chattel paper by obtaining "control" of the chattel paper.

4.3 *Secured Party's Collection Rights.* Secured Party shall have the right at any time to ~~notify any account debtors and any obligors under instruments to make payments directly to Secured Party. Secured Party may at any time judicially~~ enforce Debtor's rights against the account debtors and obligors.[37]

4.4 *Limitations on Obligations Concerning Maintenance of Collateral.*

    (i)   *Risk of Loss.* Debtor has the risk of loss of the Collateral. ~~Secured Party shall not be responsible for any injury to, loss to, or loss in value of, the Collateral, or any part thereof, arising from any act of nature, flood, fire or any other cause beyond the control of Secured Party.~~[38]

    (ii)   *No Collection Obligation.* Secured Party have no duty to collect any income accruing on the Collateral or to preserve any rights relating to the Collateral.

4.5 *No Disposition of Collateral.* <u>Secured Party does not authorize any other sales of any of the Collateral.</u> ~~Except as to inventory held for sale or lease in ordinary course of business,~~ Debtor has no right to sell, lease, or otherwise dispose of any of the Collateral.[39]

4.6 <u>*Purchase Money Security Interests.* To the extent Debtor uses the Loan to purchase Collateral, Debtor's repayment of the Loan shall apply on a "first-in-first-out" basis so that the portion of the Loan used to purchase a particular item of Collateral shall be paid in the chronological order the Debtor purchased the Collateral.</u>[40]

---

[37]A secured party may enforce all of debtor's rights against account debtor, including proceeding against collateral provided by the account debtor. § 9-607(a). The secured party may enforce claims against third persons obligated on the account party's obligation. A junior secured party that collects a check as proceeds of an account or inventory may defeat the senior if the junior qualifies as a holder in due course. § 9-331. The junior would have even greater protection if the common debtor deposited the account debtor's check in the debtor's deposit account and then wrote its own check to the junior secured party. In that case the junior would prevail unless it acted in "collusion" with the debtor to violate the rights of the senior secured party. § 9-332(b).

[38]Revised Article 9 clarifies that the debtor generally bears most risks concerning the collateral. § 9-207.

[39]A transferee takes free of a security interest if the secured party authorizes the disposition "free of the security interest." § 9-315(a). The statute makes clear that the secured party must intend to release its security interest in connection with its approval of the disposition. The express prohibition on transfer has been broadened to cover all types of collateral. Article 9 now protects ordinary course licensees of general intangibles and lessees of goods, as well as buyers of goods. §§ 1-201(a)(0), 9-320 and (-321. This language means that the debtor will "violate" the rights of the secured party if the debtor makes a transfer, thereby giving the secured party greater protection against certain transferees.

[40]For inventory only, a PMSI in inventory remains a PMSI with the extent it secures purchase money obligation for other inventory. § 9-103(b)(2). A secured party may have a PMSI in software to the extent the secured party finances the software n an "integrated" transaction with the goods in which the software will be used. § 9-103(c). "Embedded" software ill constitute part of the "goods' themselves. § 9-102(a)(44) and (75). Article 9 authorized the parties to agree on a "reasonable" method of determining how much of the secured obligation is a "purchase money obligation." § 9-103(e). The PMSI for the price will have priority over an enabling loan. § 9-324(g). Multiple enabling PMSIs will rank in order of filing. § 9-322(a) and 9-324(g)(2).

5. DEBTOR'S REPRESENTATIONS AND WARRANTIES.

Debtor warrants and represents that:

5.1 *Title to and transfer of Collateral.* ~~Its~~ It has rights in or the power to transfer the Collateral and its title to the Collateral is free of all adverse claims, liens, security interests and restrictions on transfer or pledge except as created by this Security Agreement.[41]

5.2 *Location of ~~Collateral. All collateral consisting of goods is located solely in the States (the "collateral States") listed~~ Debtor.* Debtor is incorporated in the State (the "Debtor State") identified in Exhibit ~~C~~ B.[42]

5.3 ~~*Location*~~ *Name of Debtor.* Debtor's ~~chief executive office is located in the State (the "Debtor State") identified in Exhibit C.~~ exact legal name is as set forth in the first paragraph of this Security Agreement.[43]

6. DEBTOR'S COVENANTS.

Until the Obligations are paid in full, Debtor agrees that it will:

6.1 preserve its corporate existence and not, in one transaction or a series of related transactions, merge into or consolidate with any other entity, or sell all or substantially all of its assets;[44]

---

[41]Consignee of goods or seller of accounts or chattel paper does not have to have "rights in" the collateral to grant security interest if consignor or buyer has not perfected its security interest. § 9-203(b)(2). This recognizes that although the consignee or the seller may not "own" the property, those persons still have the "power" to grant an effective security interest in the property. See § 9-318. Generally, §§ 9-406 - 9-409 invalidate contractual and statutory restrictions on transfer the transfer of contractual rights that would impair the creation or perfection of the security interest in those rights or permit the creation or perfection to constitute a breach of the debtor's agreement with the other party to the agreement. For certain contract rights, such as the right to receive money, Article 9 also disregards contractual restrictions on enforcement of the right to enforce the security interest.

[42]All filings are at the "location" of the debtor. § 9-301(1). This replaces the current rule that provides for filing at the location of collateral for goods. "Location" of the debtor means the state of formation for entities that registers to come into existence. § 9-307(e). This replaces the rule that looks to the state of the debtor's chief executive office. For security interest perfected by possession, the location of the collateral remains relevant. § 9-301(2).

[43]The financing statement must use the registered name of debtor if there is one; the use of an incorrect name is seriously misleading if a standard search does not find it. Statute again clarifies that trade names are neither sufficient nor necessary. §§ 9-502(a)(1), 9-503, 9-506(b). A financing statement does not have to indicate the representative capacity of the secured part. § 9-503(d).

[44]Article 9 now contains a set of rules that concern when a "new debtor" becomes bound by the security agreement and financing statement of the original debtor. See §§ 9-102(a)(56), 9-102(a)(60), 9-203(d), 9-326. Generally, under these provisions, the security interest created by the new debtor in favor or its secured party will prevail over that created by the original debtor in favor of its secured party.

6.2 not change the state ~~where any Collateral consisting of goods is located, except to another Collateral State;~~ of its incorporation;[45] and

6.3 ~~not change the state of its chief executive office; and~~[46]

6.4 not change its corporate name without providing Secured Party with 30 days' prior written notice.[47]

7. EVENTS OF DEFAULT.

The occurrence of any of the following shall, at the option of Secured Party, be an Event of Default:

7.1 Any default, Event of Default (as defined) by Debtor under the Loan Agreement or any of the other Obligations;

7.2 Debtor's failure to comply with any of the provisions of, or the incorrectness of any representation or warranty contained in, this Security Agreement, the Note, or in any of the other Obligations;

7.3 Transfer or disposition of any of the Collateral, except as expressly permitted by this Security Agreement;

7.4 Attachment, execution or levy on any of the Collateral;

7.5 Debtor voluntarily or involuntarily becoming subject to any proceeding under (a) the Bankruptcy Code or (b) any similar remedy under state statutory or common law; ~~or~~

7.6 Debtor shall fail to comply with, or become subject to any administrative or judicial proceeding under any federal, state or local (a) hazardous waste or environmental law, (b) asset forfeiture or similar law which can result in the forfeiture of property, or (c) other law, where noncompliance may have any significant effect on the Collateral; or

7.7 Secured Party shall receive at any time following the Closing an SOS Report indicating that Secured Party's security interest is not prior to all other security interests or other interests reflected in the report.[48]

---

[45]Because the secured party must file a financing statement in the state of incorporation, if the debtor reincorporates in another state, the secured party has the usual four months to reperfect or lose its perfection. § 9-316(a).

[46]As noted above, Article 9 no longer requires a filing in the state of the debtor's chief executive office. § 9-301(1).

[47]The secured party has four months to file an amendment to the financing statement if the debtor changes its name to make the financing statement "seriously misleading." § 9-507(b).

[48]The filing office may reject a financing statement for a limited number of reasons (e.g. no filing fee; no debtor name). § 9-516(b). A refusal by filing office to accept a financing statement for any other reason does not prevent the financing statement from being effective (§ 9-516(d)), except that a subsequent purchaser (including a secured party) that gives value in reliance of the absence of the financing statement will have priority § 9-516(d). Current law makes a filing effective if wrongfully refused. However, most decisions under current law protect the first filer against subsequent searchers, even if the subsequent searcher relies on the absence of a filing. The change is based on the view that the first filer is in the best position to determine if the filing office accepted the filing.

8. DEFAULT COSTS.

8.1 Should an Event of Default occur, Debtor will pay to Secured Party all costs reasonably incurred by the Secured Party for the purpose of enforcing its rights hereunder, including:

    (i)   costs of foreclosure;[49]

    (ii)   costs of obtaining money damages; and

    (iii) a reasonable fee for the services of attorneys employed by Secured Party for any purpose related to this Security Agreement or the Obligations, including consultation, drafting documents, sending notices or instituting, prosecuting or defending litigation or arbitration.[50]

9. REMEDIES UPON DEFAULT.

9.1 *General.* Upon any Event of Default, Secured Party may pursue any remedy available at law (including those available under the provisions of the UCC), or in equity to collect, enforce or satisfy any Obligations then owing, whether by acceleration or otherwise.[51]

9.2 *Concurrent Remedies.* Upon any Event of Default, Secured Party shall have the right to pursue any of the following remedies separately, successively or concurrently:

    (i)   File suit and obtain judgment and, in conjunction with any action, Secured Party may seek any ancillary remedies provided by law, including levy of attachment and garnishment.

    (ii)   Take possession of any Collateral if not already in its possession without demand and without legal process. Upon Secured Party's demand, Debtor will assemble and make the Collateral available to Secured Party as they direct. Debtor grants to Secured Party the right, for this purpose, to enter into or on any premises where Collateral may be located.

    (iii) Without taking possession, sell, lease or otherwise dispose of the Collateral at public or private sale in accordance with the UCC.

10. FORECLOSURE PROCEDURES.

10.1 *No Waiver.* No delay or omission by Secured Party to exercise any right or remedy accruing upon any Event of Default shall: (a) impair any right or remedy, (b) waive any default or operate as an acquiescence to the Event of Default, or (c) affect any subsequent default of the same or of a different nature.

---

[49]These are provided for by statute. § 9-615.

[50]Article 9 provides for the recovery foreclosure costs, including attorneys fees (if the parties have so agreed). § 9-615.

[51]The secured party's enforcement rights continue to be cumulative. § 9-601(c).

10.2 *Notices.* Secured Party shall give Debtor such notice of any private or public sale as may be required by the UCC.[52]

10.3 <u>*Condition of Collateral.*</u> Secured Party ~~shall have~~ <u>has</u> no obligation to ~~give a notice to any other person.~~ <u>clean-up or otherwise prepare the Collateral for sale.</u>[53]

10.4 *No Obligation to Pursue Others.* Secured Party have no obligation to attempt to satisfy the Obligations by collecting them from any other person liable for them and Secured Party may release, modify or waive any collateral provided by any other person to secured any of the Obligations, all without affecting Secured Party's rights against Debtor. <u>Debtor waives any right it may have to require Secured Party to pursue any third person for any of the Obligations.</u>[54]

10.5 *Compliance With Other Laws.* <u>Secured Party may comply with any applicable state or federal law requirements in connection with a disposition of the Collateral and compliance will not be considered adversely to affect the commercial reasonableness of any sale of the Collateral.</u> [55]

10.6 *Warranties.* Secured Party may sell the Collateral without giving any warranties as to the Collateral. <u>Secured Party may specifically disclaim any warranties of title or the like.</u>[56] This procedure will not be considered adversely to affect the commercial reasonableness of any sale of the Collateral.

10.6 *Sales on Credit.* <u>If Secured Party sells any of the Collateral upon credit, Debtor will be credited only with payments actually made by the purchaser, received by Secured Party and applied to the indebtedness of the Purchaser. In the event the purchaser</u>

---

[52]Secured party must give notice of sale to other secured parties of record. § 9-611(b). The statute provides practical rules indicating which secured parties of record are entitled to notice. § 9-611(c)(3)(B). The statute provides a "safe harbor" form for giving notice to the debtor of a private or public sale. § 9-613(5).

[53]Secured party "may" dispose of collateral "in its then condition of following any commercially reasonable preparation or processing." § 9-610(a). Although the language of the statue is permissive, a comment will indicate that the secured party should engage in a cost benefit analysis of whether some preparation is appropriate, taking into account the secured party's risk of collection preparation costs from the debtor.

[54]Default rules apply to secondary obligors. § 9-601(b). This continues the rule of current law. Secondary obligor (and other obligors, but not debtor) may waive rights to the extent permitted by the law outside of Article 9. § 9-602(d). This changes the rule of current law, where most decisions hold that a guarantor cannot waive anything the principal debtor could not waive. The debtor may be a "guarantor" to the extent it provides collateral to secure the obligation of another person. See the definition of "Obligations" in this Security Agreement. § 9-12(a)(59) and (71).

[55]An Official Comment to § 9-610 directly addresses this issue. It notes that this would be an appropriate circumstance for the parties to agree on a "standard [] measuring the fulfillment of the ... duties of the secured party" if the standard is "not manifestly unreasonable." § 9-603.

[56]Secured party automatically gives title warranties unless disclaimed, statute provided sample disclaimer language. § 9-610(d), (e) and (f).

fails to pay for the Collateral, Secured Party may resell the Collateral and Debtor shall be credited with the proceeds of the sale.[57]

10.7 *Purchases by Secured Party.* In the event Secured Party purchases any of the Collateral being sold, Secured Party may pay for the Collateral by crediting some or all of the Obligations of the Debtor.[58]

10.8 ~~*Deficiency Judgment.* If it is determined by an authority of competent jurisdiction that a disposition by Secured Party did not occur in a commercially reasonable manner, Secured Party may obtain a deficiency from Debtor for the difference between the amount of the Obligation foreclosed and the amount that a commercially reasonable sale would have yielded.~~[59]

10.9 *No Marshalling.* Secured Party have no obligation to marshal any assets in favor of Debtor, or against or in payment of:

(i)   the Note,

(ii)   any of the other Obligations, or

(iii)   any other obligation owed to Secured Party by Debtor or any other person.

10.10 ~~*Retention of Collateral.* Secured Party will not be considered to have to have offered to retain the Collateral in satisfaction of the Obligations unless Secured Party has entered into a written agreement with Debtor to that effect.~~[60]

11. MISCELLANEOUS.

11.1 *Assignment.*

(i)   *Binds Assignees.* This Security Agreement shall bind and shall inure to the benefit of the heirs, legatees, executors, administrators, successors and assigns of

---

[57]A secured party does not have to apply noncash proceeds unless the failure to do so would be commercially unreasonable. The secured party must apply any noncash proceeds in a commercially reasonable manner. § 9-6015(c). This gives the secured party ability to accept a note from the buyer at a foreclosure sale and establish a commercially reasonable discount value or credit the debtor as the secured party receives payments. This may be an appropriate circumstance for the parties to agree on a "standard [] measuring the fulfillment of the … duties of a secured party" if the standard is "not manifestly unreasonable." § 9-603. See Official Comment to § 9-615.

[58]The calculation of deficiency following a commercially reasonable sale of collateral at an "unreasonably low" price to the secured party, a guarantor or an affiliate of one of these people, will be based on amount that would have been obtained has a third person purchased the collateral. § 9-615(f).

[59]The statute adopts the rebuttable presumption rule for non-consumer transactions. § 9-626(3)(B). This adopts the rule of a majority of jurisdictions under current law.

[60]Secured party may accept collateral in satisfaction of the debt even if the secured party does not have possession of the collateral. Current law allows retention only if the secured party has possession of the collateral. Secured party may accept collateral in partial satisfaction of the debt with the written consent of the debtor. Secured part may not make a "constructive" acceptance of collateral. This rejects decisions under current law that permit an implied acceptance, usually based on an extended retention of possession by the secured party without taking any action. Instead, the duration of any delay by the secured part will go to the question of the commercial reasonableness of the sale. § 9-620.

~~Debtor and~~ Secured Party <u>and shall bind all persons who become bound by this Security Agreement.</u>[61]

(ii) *No Assignments by Debtor.* Secured Party does not consent to any assignment by Debtor except as expressly provided in this Security Agreement.

(iii) *Secured Party Assignments.* Secured Party may assign its rights and interests under this Security Agreement. If an assignment is made, Debtor shall render performance under this Security Agreement to the assignee. Debtor <u>waives and</u>[62] will not assert against any assignee any claims, defenses or setoffs which Debtor could assert against Secured Party except defenses which cannot be waived.

11.2 *Severability.* Should any provision of this Security Agreement be found to be void, invalid or unenforceable by a court or panel of arbitrators of competent jurisdiction, that finding shall only affect the provisions found to be void, invalid or unenforceable and shall not affect the remaining provisions of this Security Agreement.

11.3 *Notices.* Any notices required by this Security Agreement shall be deemed to be delivered when <u>a record</u>[63] <u>has been</u> (a) deposited in any United States postal box if postage is prepaid, and the notice properly addressed to the intended recipient, (b) received by telecopy, (c) received through the Internet, and (d) when personally delivered.

11.4 *Headings.* Section headings used by this Security Agreement are for convenience only. They are not a part of this Security Agreement and shall not be used in construing it.

11.5 *Governing Law.* This Security Agreement is being executed and delivered and is intended to be performed in the State of Illinois and shall be construed and enforced in accordance with the laws of the State of California, except to the extent that the UCC provides for ~~perfection under~~ <u>the application of</u> the law of ~~another state~~ <u>the Debtor States.</u>[64]

11.6 *Rules of Construction.*

(i) No reference to "proceeds" in this Security Agreement authorizes any sale, transfer, or other disposition of the Collateral by the Debtor.

(ii) "Includes" and "including" are not limiting.

(iii) "Or" is not exclusive.

(iv) "All" includes "any" and "any" includes "all."

(v) "All" includes "any" and "any" includes "all."

---

[61]A security agreement is operative with respect to a person that "becomes bound" as a "new debtor" to a security agreement entered into by another person. Under some circumstances, usually in an acquisition context, one person may "become bound" by a security agreement that an acquired person has signed. §§ 9-102(a)(56), 9-203(d) and (e).

[62]Neither the debtor nor a secondary obligor may waive certain rights under Article 9. § 9-602.

[63]Article 9 will adopt the use of the term "record" generally to replace the concept of a "writing." § 9-102(a)(69).

[64]For purposes of perfection and the effect of perfection, Article 9 generally looks the state of the debtor's formation. § 9-301.

11.7 *Integration and Modifications.*

  (i)   This Security Agreement is the entire agreement of the Debtor and Secured Party concerning its subject matter.

  (ii)   Any modification to this Security Agreement must be made in writing and signed by the party adversely affected.

11.8 *Waiver.* Any party to this Security Agreement may waive the enforcement of any provision to the extent the provision is for its benefit.

11.9 *Further Assurances.* Debtor agrees to execute any further documents, and to take any further actions, reasonably requested by Secured Party to evidence or perfect the security interest granted herein or to effectuate the rights granted to Secured Party herein.

The parties have signed this Security Agreement as of the day and year first above written at Los Angeles, California.

"DEBTOR"

Vending Machine Manufacturing Co.
a California corporation

By: _____
       Jane Drink-Soft
       President

By: _____
       Bob Soft-Drink
       Secretary

CHAPTER 11

Fair Debt Collection Practices Act

The Fair Debt Collection Practices Act is the most important federal legislation affecting the credit and collection industry. Prior to its enactment, no federal law on debt collection existed, although several federal agencies regulated isolated activities. For example, the Postal Service relies on the mail fraud extortion statute which requires "intent" and which is difficult to prove for the "garden variety" unethical debt collection practice. The Federal Communications Commission provisions against phone harassment also required intent, making them difficult to enforce. The Federal Trade Commission's powers are limited, covered in the statute creating the agency.

As the extension of credit and the credit card industry grew after World War II, the abuses of the collection industry grew proportionally and became a frequent subject for the media. The complaints against collection agencies grew exponentially as a function of the huge increase in extending credit and issuing credit cards. Calling on Sundays, leaving messages with neighbors, threatening to send "collectors" to the debtor's house, adding charges without notifying the debtor, and being nasty on the telephone are just a few examples of the numerous abuses, which were infinite and only limited by the collector's creativity. The stage was set for federal entry into the area; and the Fair Debt Collection Practices Act was passed in 1977, by an overwhelming majority of one vote, and became effective on March 30, 1978.

At the time of enactment, only 37 states had laws regulating abuses of collection activity. But most of these states provided few remedies for the individual consumer and many of the laws were inadequate to achieve the purpose for which they were designed.[1] States covering 40 million consumers had no collection laws. Furthermore, even if each of the states had a proper law addressing the problem of debt collection, the states could not regulate interstate debt collection practices including letters and the technology available to make interstate collection calls.

The Act only applied to those who collect the debt of another which is aimed primarily at collection agencies, but in 1986, an amendment was passed to include attorneys. Creditors who collect their own debts are exempt from the Act.

CREDITOR COMPLIANCE

Our firm, as well as most attorneys, recommends that creditors comply with the Act wherever applicable, notwithstanding the fact that creditors are not subject to the Act. The Act has established the standard for determining and identifying whether an activity is an abusive collection practice. For example, a creditor in a business-to-business transaction makes the following comments to the owner of another business who owes money:

> CR: Charlie, I know it's midnight, but you've owed me this debt for almost 12 months, so why shouldn't I call you at 12 o'clock? If you had paid the debt, it would not be necessary for me to call you.

> DTR: Look, I've had a bad year. I've told you a dozen times before that I don't have the money, but as soon as I do have it, I will try to send you some money each month. Will you please let me get some sleep so I can get up tomorrow?

> CR: Charlie, be sure to get some sleep because tomorrow night I'm going to call you at 1 o'clock, and the next night I'm going to call you at 2 o'clock, and the night after that I'm going to call you at 3 o'clock until I receive some payment on this debt.

Most state laws prohibit "abusive or unconscionable collection practices" and creditors as well as collection agencies and attorneys are subject to these state laws. The court will examine the Fair Debt Collection Practices Act to determine whether the creditor's practice is identified as a violation. If the activity does qualify as a violation, the court will probably decide that an abusive or unconscionable practice took place under state law. The procedure of the court is to use the Fair Debt Collection Practices Act as the standard to measure the abusive collection activity and then apply the general terms of the state law to the activity. Since the practice described above is a violation under the Act, the court would

---

[1]Alabama, Delaware, Georgia, Kansas, Kentucky, Mississippi, Missouri, Montana, Ohio, Oklahoma, Rhode Island, South Carolina, South Dakota.

determine that the violation must necessarily qualify as an abusive or unconscionable practice under the state law. The suit would be commenced under state law, but the court would apply the standards set by the Fair Debt Collection Practices Act to determine if state law should apply to the creditor. For this reason, creditors should comply with the provisions of the Act. The result is equitable, since creditors should not be allowed to engage in deceptive or abusive collection practices that are clearly violations of the Fair Debt Collection Practices Act.

A listing presented by the American Collection Association highlighted twenty-one states where creditors are subject to some or all of the collection laws that apply to collection agencies and attorneys. The states are as follows:

California	Michigan
Colorado	New Hampshire
Connecticut	New York
District of Columbia	North Carolina
Florida	Oregon
Hawaii	Pennsylvania
Iowa	South Carolina
Louisiana	Texas
Maine	Vermont
Maryland	West Virginia
Massachusetts	Wisconsin

Aside from the liability imposed on creditors by statute, the question of whether creditors may be liable for the violations of the collection agency or their attorney has always interested consumer attorneys. About ten years ago the Federal Trade Commission prosecuted American Family Publishers, (one of the major direct marketing firms that awards ten million dollars in sweepstakes prizes each year) on the theory that they had a pervasive influence over their collection agency. The position of the Federal Trade Commission was that the American Family Publishers was so involved with their collection agency and that their influence over the agency was so pervasive that when the agency violated the law in sending out letters the F.T.C. felt that the American Family Publisher was just as much at fault. American Family Publishers argued logically that the agency was an independent contractor and therefore American Family Publisher should not be liable for the violation of an independent contractor. In short the F.T.C. thought that American Family Publishers was just looking the other way while their agency was engaging in flagrant violations of the F.D.C.P.A.

It was as if the American Family Publishers had told the agency that the bottom line is collection and the creditor does not want to know how you perform the collection.

The F.T.C. issued a public press release describing this and alleging that the American Family Publishers knew or should have known about the practices being engaged in by the agency. Ultimately a consent order was entered into between the F.T.C. and American Family Publishers. While the consent order provided for stringent controls over the collection efforts of American Family Publisher, it did not provide for any fine.

The position of the Federal Trade Commission was difficult since it sought to impose liability upon a creditor for the acts of an independent contractor. The theory is that the creditor should make diligent inquiry into the activities of the collection agency to determine whether the agency was violating the Fair Debt Collection Practice Act. Carried to its illogical conclusion, a shipper would be under an obligation to make diligent inquiry to determine whether its trucking company was properly licensed and complying with all the state and federal regulations dealing with the trucking industry. On inquiry to the Federal Trade Commission as to whether this is what they intend, the commissioner at the time, Barry Cutler, seemed to take the position that this was an unusual case with American Family Publishers and each situation would be considered on a case by case basis.

Since a creditor collects debts for itself, himself, or herself, and not for another party, a creditor is exempt from the Act. The section excludes any officer or employee of a creditor, affiliated corporations, any officer or employee of the United States or any state, process servers, and nonprofit organizations. But in certain circumstances a creditor may become subject to the Act, such as where the creditor uses a name other than his own.

ATTORNEY COVERAGE

In July of 1986, the Act was amended to cover all attorneys who collect debts. Initially, the Commission's position was that only attorneys regularly engaged in collecting a debt were subject to the Act. Now the Act applies to attorneys collecting even isolated debts. While commercial litigation involving business debts is exempt under the Act, commercial attorneys recognize the Act has established the standard for collecting debts and probably will be applied to business collection as well as consumer collection, where applicable.

The Act specifically covers attorneys who engage in the same activities as collection agencies, including such activities as sending demand letters or using the telephone to demand payment from the debtor.

Attorneys thought that a legal practice limited to legal activities such as filing and prosecuting lawsuits is not subject to the Act.[2] Then, one of the federal circuit courts chose to disagree with the prevailing view,[3] and was quickly followed
by another federal court decision which decided there was no attorney exemption
and refused to create an exemption for purely legal activities. These decisions created a split in the federal courts as to whether attorneys practicing only litigation
are covered by the Fair Debt Collection Practices Act.[4] As a result of this conflict
between the federal district courts, the Supreme Court of the United States on
April 18, 1995 held that lawyers engaged in consumer debt collection litigation
must comply with the Fair Debt Collection Practices Act.

The reasoning was that attorneys who institute suit meet the definition of a
"debt collector" as one regularly engaged in the collection of or attempt to collect
consumer debts. The Supreme Court also stated that when Congress repealed the
exemption, no effort was made to confine the repeal to those activities prior to
suit. Ergo, Congress repealed the exemption in its entirety and intended to require
litigation activities to be covered by the Act. The fact that anomalous results are
created fell on deaf ears. For example, since the attorney is the agent of the consumer (client), the attorney for the creditor would have to include the mini-
miranda (see mini-miranda—on page 345) warning in every letter and telephone
call to the attorney for the consumer as well as on the summons and complaint
and all pleadings in a lawsuit. Justice Breyer dismissed these awkward results
because they depend upon "readings that courts seem unlikely to endorse."
Nevertheless, the courts have not rendered decisions yet, and until they do, a cautious attorney will apply the act to litigation.

This decision will have serious implications in the conduct of a law suit.
Some of the more significant problems will be reviewed later in this chapter.

COMMENTARY

The Federal Trade Commission issued a commentary on the Fair Debt Collection
Practices Act on December 13, 1988 which superseded all previously issued staff
interpretations of the Act (see Appendix). The purpose of the commentary was to
clarify and modify these interpretations. Commentaries are not a trade regulation
rule or a formal agency action, and are not binding on the Commission, the public or the courts. A commentary by the Federal Trade Commission is similar to a

---

[2]*National Union Buyer Insurance Co. v. Hartel*, 741 F. Supp. 1139 (S.D. New York 1990); *Fireman's Insurance Co. v. Keating*, 753 F. Supp. 1137 (S.D. New York 1990); *Green vs. Hocking*, 792 F. Supp. 1064 (E.D. Mich. 1992).

[3]*Fox v. Citicorp Credit Services*, 15 F.3rd 1507 (9th Cir. 1994).

[4]*Heintz v. Jenkins*, 25 F. 3rd 536 (7th Cir. 1994).

textbook explanation of its interpretation of law. Even though they are not binding, the commentaries present the position and attitude of the Commission and often determine whether it will prosecute a violation of the Act.

We will now focus on the provisions of the Act.

FINDINGS AND PURPOSE

The findings and the purpose of the Fair Debt Collection Practices Act is to eliminate abusive, deceptive and unfair debt collection practices.

DEFINITIONS

Communication is defined as conveying information regarding a debt to any person through any type of medium, which includes all letters, faxes, telephone conversations and probably modems. It expressly excludes the institution of suit and other contact during the course of the suit which is not a collection activity.

A *debt* is an obligation to pay money arising out of a transaction in which the money, property, insurance, or service is primarily used for personal, family, or household purposes. Under the terms of this Section, a commercial or business transaction is exempt from the Act. This would apply even if an individual is operating the business in his own name, such as "Thomas O'Reilly doing business individually as (d/b/a) O'Reilly's Restaurant."

CONSUMER DEBT

Several court decisions have held whether the loan is for a personal family or household use does not depend upon the intent of the seller, the nature of the product, or for what purpose the product itself was intended. The courts look solely to the purpose for which the consumer uses the product. A product designed for a business and intended to be sold to a business can be used for a personal purpose; and if it is used for a personal, family or household purpose, the transaction is subject to the Fair Debt Collection Practices Act. An example might be the publishing of a book of higher mathematics used solely for nuclear physics. Nevertheless, if this particular book is used by a student to learn nuclear physics, it now becomes a consumer item used for a consumer purpose notwithstanding that the book was published for graduate nuclear scientists and is not sold to universities or schools for educational purposes.

BUSINESS DEBT

A court held that the business was covered under the Fair Debt Collection Practices Act where the collection agency telephoned the individual consumer on a business debt at the home of the consumer. The court reasoned that contacting the individual at his home converted the debt from a business debt to a consumer debt because the call was made to his home residence. The court reasoned that there was a strong inference made to the individual that he was personally liable rather than the business because of the fact that the telephone call was made to his residence. This was a remarkable decision and, in my opinion, the court was merely stretching to find some way to hold the collection agency liable because in this instance flagrant violations occurred. Nevertheless, it is an example of the position of the courts and the efforts of the courts to stretch the act where they think it is appropriate.[5]

ATTORNEYS

Since attorneys became subject to the Fair Debt Collection Practices Act, law firms who are not primarily engaged in debt collections have from time to time alleged that they are not debt collectors since they are not regularly engaged in the collection of debts. Prior to the time that attorneys became subject to the act, this defense carried substantial weight and was successful in many cases where the collection practice was minimum. Since 1987 when attorneys became subject to the act, the attorneys became subject to Section 15 USC, Section 1692, Subdivision A(6)which define debt collectors as:

> "any person who uses any instrumentality of interstate commerce or the mails in any business the principle purpose of which is the collection of any debts, or who regularly collects or attempts to collect, directly or indirectly, debts owed or due or asserted to be owed or due another."

The Supreme Court of the United States held that the act applies to attorneys who "regularly" engage in consumer debt collection activities even when that activity consists of litigation.[6] In determining whether activity constitutes "regular" debt collection, courts have considered different criteria, including the sheer volume of the law firm's practice devoted to debt collections;[7] the number

---

[5]*James Rodney Moore Sr. v. Principal Credit Corporation,* 1998 WL 378387 (N.D. Mass. 1998).

[6]*Heintz v. Jenkins,* 514 U.S. 291 (1995).

[7]*Nance v. Petty Livingston, Dawson and Devenina,* 881 F. Supp. 223 (W.D. Va. 1994).

of debt collection cases filed as a percentage of all cases filed;[8] and the percentage of the practice.[9]

In a Connecticut case, 10% of the defendants new files were direct debt collection cases for one client. A year later new debt collection files were only 3% of total new files. The court noted that these cases did not constitute a large source of revenue since the firm had a gross income of over $500,000 and total receipts for debt collection was only $800. If the new cases opened in a given year were the sole measure of regularity, 10% of the cases is significant to warrant a finding of regularity.

Nevertheless, the court emphasized that other factors may be equally important. The fact that the client and law firms relationship lasted only three years and that the overall volume during the three years was a small portion of the overall case load as well as a small portion of gross receipts led the court to believe that the attorneys activity did not constitute regular debt collection. It seems this court has added an additional criteria i.e. the percentage of gross receipts that the law firms earns. The court seemed generous in using this measurement, but reflects the recent attitude of the courts to favor the debt collector where the violation is minor.[10]

LOCATION INFORMATION

Contacting third parties presented unique problems for the Federal Trade Commission. Certainly debt collectors are interested in locating debtors, but, at the same time, they should not be permitted to disclose to a third party that the consumer is in debt. Debt collectors frequently threaten to reveal to neighbors, local grocery stores, banks, rotary clubs, etc., the financial condition of the consumer. One of the major purposes of the Act was to discourage any such action by the debt collector. Nevertheless, the drafters acknowledged that the debt collector is entitled to contact third parties to locate the debtor.

The result was a compromise. When communicating with a third party to locate a consumer, the debt collector must identify himself and state that "we are confirming or correcting location information" concerning the consumer and only *if expressly requested* identify the debt collector. While this may appear to make no sense, the drafters of the Act finally settled on this procedure to balance the interests of the consumer and the debt collector.

---

[8]*Crossley v. Lieberman*, 868 F. 2nd 566 (3rd Cir. 1989).

[9]*Cacace v. Lucas*, 775 F. Supp. 502 (D. Conn. 1990).

[10]*Von Schmidt v. Kratter*, No 3:95CV1734JBA, 1997 WL 908371 (D. Conn. Sept. 30, 1997).

The debt collector should not refer to the debt and is allowed only a single contact with a particular third party. The debt collector is not to communicate by postcard or indicate by letterhead that the agency is in the collection business. The conversation may be as follows:

TP: Hello.

CR: Good morning. My name is Jerry Ford. And I'm trying to confirm the address of Phillip Johnson. We had him located at 430 Oak Road, Spring Grove, but we are told that he has moved. We are wondering whether you know whether he is still at that address?

TP: Wait a minute. What's your name?

CR: My name is Jerry Ford.

TP: And you want to know about Phil Johnson? Why do you want to know about him? Why are you trying to find out about him?

CR: We're trying to confirm if he's still living in Spring Grove or whether you know where he's moved to.

TP: I want to know why you want to know. Who are you?

CR: My name is Jerry Ford, and I'm just trying to find out where Phil Johnson is living.

TP: Look, what is the purpose of this call? And why do you want to know where Phil Johnson lives? I want to know who you are.

CR: My name is Jerry Ford, and I am employed by the ABC Collection Agency, and we are trying to locate Philip Johnson.

TP: Then you're trying to locate him to collect some money. Is that what the story is?

CR: Can you give me any information about where he is located?

TP: I haven't spoken to Phil Johnson in about three months and even if I did know, I probably wouldn't give you any information. But how did you get my name?

CR: Philip Johnson gave your name and address as a reference on his credit application.

TP: I guess I can't stop him from that, but I don't know where he is. By the way, how much money does he owe you?

CR: I can't tell you anything further.

TP: Then I guess you'll have to try to get some information from someone else. Goodbye.

CR: Goodbye.

The debt collector did furnish the name of the employer, but refused to reveal any further information. A debt collector may not use any name in correspondence with the third party if that name suggests the conducting of a collection business. On the other hand, if the name of the agency does not indicate a collection agency, the debt collector may use the letterhead (Jones Management Corp.) to seek location information. The Act specifically says that the name cannot contain the word "debt," "collector" or "collection." The word "credit" probably also should be classified with these words, even though not specifically mentioned in the Act.

CONTACTING CREDITORS TO FILE BANKRUPTCY

Revealing financial information to another creditor of the consumer is not permitted under the Fair Debt Collection Practices Act. Under the bankruptcy law, three creditors are necessary to file an involuntary petition in bankruptcy against the debtor. If the creditor intends to contact other creditors to form a group to file an involuntary petition in bankruptcy, the conversations with the other creditors may be dangerous since financial information is being exchanged and disclosed to third parties. If the involuntary petition in bankruptcy is actually filed, the risk is minimal; but if no petition in bankruptcy is filed, the risk of violating the Fair Debt Collection Practices Act increases significantly.

The better course is to contact your attorney to speak to the other creditors so that there will be strict compliance with the Fair Debt Collection Practices Act.

COMMUNICATION WITH CONSUMERS AND THIRD PARTIES

CONTACT WITH CONSUMER. The Act limits any communication concerning the debt to the consumer or the spouse of the consumer. Communicating with any third parties about the debt of the consumer is prohibited. Always ask the party what the relationship is to the debtor before leaving a message. Do not speak to children, grandchildren, mother, grandmother, brother, sister, uncle, aunt, cousin, or any other relative. Furthermore, do not communicate with housekeepers, babysitters of the children, nurses caring for the spouse, girl friends or boy friends, significant others, roommates, tenants or subtenants, or any other third party. Certainly, never leave a message with an itinerant who happens to pick up the telephone, such as the plumber, electrician, gardener, paper deliverer, meter reader, painter, TV or appliance repairman, priest or rabbi or any other third party.

Exceptions to this rule include the debtor's attorney, consumer reporting agency (if permitted by the Fair Credit Reporting Act), the creditor, the attorney for the creditor, or the attorney for the debt collector. Accordingly, it is permissible for the creditor to discuss the case with the creditor's attorney or with the debtor's attorney. The matter may be reported to a credit reporting agency.

Consider the following telephone conversation:

TP: Hello.

CR: This is Jerry Ford. Can I please speak to Phil Johnson?

TP: Phillip isn't in right now, but he will be back in several hours. Can I take a message for him?

CR: Who is this?

TP: I'm his mother.

CR: Will you please leave a message for him to call Jerry Ford at this telephone number—(800) 555-1212?

TP: Jerry Ford. Aren't you with the ABC Collection Agency? This is the money that he owes on his Honda Accord, and he's about three months behind?

CR: Ma'am, would you please just leave a message for him.

TP: Look, I know all about this loan because I'm the one who makes the payments. And the reason we're behind is that he's been sick for the last three weeks, and he hasn't received a paycheck. As soon as he receives his next paycheck, we're going to send you the payment.

CR: Ma'am, I really can't talk about the debt.

TP: My son and I live here alone and I take care of all the finances. I pay the rent and the telephone bills and, believe me, I am well aware of this debt and I do want to pay it. I don't want you to take any action because I want you to understand that I intend to pay the debt. Now exactly what was the purpose of this phone call?

CR: Alright. I'm here to tell you that unless we do not get the payment within the next ten days, we will have no alternative but to send it to our repossession firm to repossess the car because we cannot continue to carry this as an open account for more than three months.

TP: I don't know whether I can make it within the next ten days. But I'm certain I'll be able to pick up at least two payments by the end of the month. Could you possibly give me to the end of the month?

CR: The end of the month is almost three weeks away. But, if you make a promise that we will have the check by the 30th of January and not a day later, then I will put this on "hold" until the 30th of January. But we must have the check in our office by the 30th of January, not in the mail by that date.

TP: Please, we need the car very badly, and I will make certain that we will have at least two payments in the mail by the 28th so you will definitely have it on the 30th of the month. Please wait until the 30th of the month.

CR: Alright Ma'am. We'll wait until the 30th of the month.

TP: Thank you very much. I will get the check in by that time. I appreciate your extending the time until the 30th.

CR: Alright Ma'am. Goodbye.

TP: Goodbye.

Despite the mother taking care of all the finances and being familiar with the debt, the debt collector violated the Act by communicating information about the debt to the mother. The debt collector should have terminated the conversation and waited until the consumer returned the call. If the consumer failed to call, the debt collector should have contacted the consumer at a different time.

TIME AND PLACE OF CONTACT. Contact cannot be made at any unusual time or place or at a place known to be inconvenient to the consumer. The usual convenient time for contact is between 8:00 a.m. and 9:00 p.m. If the collector does not have information to the contrary, a call on a Sunday is not illegal per se. However, to support a call on Sunday, several efforts should have been made during the week to contact the consumer.

CONTACTING EMPLOYERS. If the debt collector knows or has reason to know that the consumer's employer prohibits communication, no communication should be attempted. Furthermore, if a call is made at the consumer's place of employment, care should be exercised that the debtor is not being overheard by fellow employees and that it is a suitable time to speak. The telephone conversation might develop as follows:

CR: Can you talk to me now?

DTR: Yeah, I guess so.

CR: Does your boss allow personal calls?

DTR: Yeah.

CR: Are you in a private place where no one can hear what we say?

DTR: Yeah, I guess so.

CR: Do you have the time to speak to me now or are you busy with your job? Do you want me to call you at another time or at home tonight?

DTR: I guess we can talk now.

The questions as to personal calls, privacy, and non-interference with the job are designed to limit exposure. If the debtor requested no further calls at work, comply with the request. Notwithstanding such preparation, in today's environment, contact with the consumer debtor at the place of employment should be made only as a last resort. Such efforts are wrought with danger.

Many states have restrictions imposed upon collection agencies with regard to contacting debtors at their places of business. Some states even have additional restrictions imposed on contacting the debtor in general.

Massachusetts is probably the most burdensome in that it prohibits placing a telephone call to the debtor's place of employment if the debtor has made a written or oral request that such telephone calls not be made, provided that any oral requests shall be valid for only ten days unless the debtor provides a written confirmation postmarked or delivered within seven days of such request. The Massachusetts statute also requires a written notice to be sent to the debtor within thirty days after the first communication to a debtor at a place of employment. In addition, the statute prohibits any debtor communication in excess of two in each seven-day period at a debtor's residence and two calls in each thirty-day period other than at the debtor's residence for each debt.

Washington also states that a communication to a debtor at a place of employment more than one time in a single week may constitute harassment. Maine and Connecticut prohibit contacting the consumer at the place of employment if the collection agency knows or has reason to know that the consumer's employer prohibits the consumer from receiving a communication. Arizona and Arkansas prohibit contact at a place of employment without first attempting to contact the debtor at the place of residence.

Minnesota and Wisconsin prohibit the debt collector from enlisting the aid of a neighbor or third party to request the debtor to contact the collection agency. New Hampshire has rather extensive restrictions including permitting debt collectors to send a single letter to the place of employment if they have been unable to locate the debtor and permitting a phone call to the debtor if they are unable to contact the debtor at the residence. Oregon and Pennsylvania statutes deal with the frequency of contact at the place of employment or at the residence. The following are pertinent sections for some states. Other states may have similar statutes.

Arizona, Administrative Code Banking Department Title 4,

Chapter 4, Section R4-4-1512.

Arkansas, Statute Ann. Section 17-21-307.

Colorado Revised Statute Section 12-14-105.

Connecticut, Rules and Regulations of the Banking

Commissioner Concerning Collection Agencies 42-131d-3a.

Maine Revised Statue Section 11012(1).

Massachusetts, 209 CMR18.15(1).

Minnesota Section 332-37.

New Hampshire, Revised Statute Annotated Section 358-c:3.

Oregon Rev. Stat. Section 646.639.

Pennsylvania, Section 303.4.

Washington, RCW Section 19-16.250.

Wisconsin, Section 74.14.

CONTACTING ATTORNEYS. If a consumer debtor is represented by an attorney, contact must be made with the attorney. Usually, representation by an attorney is learned from the client, a telephone call, or letter from the consumer. The attorney must be representing the consumer with regard to the particular debt.

What can be done if the attorney fails to respond to a letter or telephone call? The commentary to the Debt Collection Practices Act does not seem to answer this question. The American Collectors Association, at least with regard to *commercial* matters, has taken the position that if the attorney does not respond within fourteen days, then the debt collector may once again contact the debtor. It would appear that resumption of contact directly with the consumer should be allowed after a reasonable time has elapsed and after a reasonable effort (two letters or two telephone calls seem appropriate) to contact the attorney. Thus, after at least two efforts (by letter or telephone) and a reasonable wait (two weeks), contacting the consumer again is the next logical step. Be certain that the client knows to notify you that an attorney is representing the debtor.

ANSWERING MACHINES. Communicating with the telephone or telegraph company is not a third party contact since the business purpose of these communication companies is to transmit messages. Leaving a message with an answering service falls under the same category. The commentary states:

"A debt collector may contact the employee of a telephone or telegraph company in order to contact the consumer without violating the prohibition on communication to third parties, if the only information given is that necessary to enable the collector to transmit the message to or make the contact with the consumer."

To what extent this applies to a live telephone answering service, the commentary is not clear. It is suggested that only a name and telephone number be furnished.

Today, there are more answering machines than live telephone operators. Usually, consumers will identify themselves on the answering machines by name or telephone number. Leaving a full message on an answering machine utilized solely by the consumer and identified both by name and telephone number should not be in violation of the Act. The danger is that a message may be left with the wrong party or that the answering machine may be used by more than one party, such as a friend, a roommate, or the whole family. With a name or number corresponding to the dialed number and name, a full message may be left with certain recommendations. A statement that "this message is only for John Smith at 555-1212" would be helpful. The debtor's contention that a third person heard the message, such as a friend or neighbor is not a violation. The debtor installed the machine, and wanted the caller to leave the message. The important ingredient is to be sure the number is correct for the party being called.

> CREDIT AND COLLECTION TIP: *If two parties are identified on the answering machine, do not leave more than a name or telephone number, since the creditor is on notice that a third party may hear the message.*

CEASING COMMUNICATIONS

If the consumer advises the creditor by written notice that he or she does not want to receive any further collection efforts, no further communication with the debtor is allowed except:

1. to advise the consumer that the debt collector's further efforts are being terminated.
2. to notify the consumer that the debt collector or creditor may use specific remedies which are ordinarily invoked (such as institution of suit, repossession of auto).
3. where applicable, to notify the consumer that the debt collector intends to invoke a specific remedy.

The response to a cease communication notice form the consumer must not include a demand for payment but is limited to the three exceptions stated above. Any further communication other than described above violates the Fair Debt Collection Practices Act.

HARASSMENT AND ABUSE

This Section prohibits any conduct which harasses, oppresses, or abuses the debtor in connection with the collection of a debt. Despite considerable progress over the last twenty years, some agencies still engage in these tactics because of lack of knowledge or care. This Section provides that "without limiting the general application of the foregoing, the following conduct is a violation of the Section. ..." Thus, any activity which harasses, oppresses, or abuses a debtor will be a violation of the Act, notwithstanding that the conduct is not expressly included in the six subdivisions of this Section.

THREAT OF VIOLENCE. The use of or threat to use violence or other criminal means to harm the physical person, reputation, or property of any person is prohibited. A lengthy series of questions or comments to the consumer without giving the consumer a chance to reply may constitute an abuse. Such statements as: "We're not playing around here—we can play tough" or "We're going to send somebody to collect for us one way or the other" are classic examples of threats of violence.[11]

OBSCENE LANGUAGE. The use of obscene or profane language, the natural consequence of which is to abuse the hearer or reader, is prohibited. Religious slurs, profanity, obscenity, calling the consumer a liar or a deadbeat, and the use of racial or sexual epithets are examples of this.[12]

PUBLICATION OF LIST OF DEBTORS. Publication of a list of consumers who refuse to pay debts is prohibited. Exchanging lists of "deadbeats" with other creditors would fall within the prohibitions of this Section. To maintain a list of delinquent accounts and distribute that list of accounts to members of an association would require complying with the Fair Credit Reporting Act (see Chapter 14—Fair Credit Reporting). Associations should not maintain lists of delinquent consumers despite the fact their members often suggest the potential benefits of such a list.

ADVERTISING DEBT. The advertisement for sale of a debt to coerce payment of the debt or shaming a consumer by publicizing the debt to neighbors, friends, or local shopkeepers is not permitted.

REPEATING TELEPHONE CALLS. Causing a telephone to ring or engaging any person in telephone conversation repeatedly with the intent to annoy or abuse that person is prohibited. Multiple contacts with the consumer may constitute a violation of the Act. In general, more than two contacts a week may be harassment. How often a creditor may leave a message on an answering service is not clear. If the first contact consists of a telephone message, a second contact the next day is not unreasonable. If two messages were left two days in a row, a third contact on the third day may be harassment depending upon the nature of the message, who is taking the message, and other circumstances.[13]

IDENTIFYING TELEPHONE COLLECTOR. The placement of telephone calls without meaningful disclosure of the caller's identity is prohibited. The debt collector must identify himself or herself to the consumer directly and must comply with the identification requirement (see this chapter—Location information on page 489) if the contact is for the purpose of location information.

---

[11]*Baker v. G.C. Services*, 677 F. 2d 775 (1982).

[12]*Jeter v. Credit Bureau*, 760 F. 2d 1168 (1985).

[13]*Bingham v. Collection Bureau, Inc.*, 505 F. Supp. 864 (1981).

PERSONAL COMMENTS OR INQUIRIES. Warnings of a personal nature, e.g., that the debtor should not have had children if he/she could not afford children, or inquiries about personal possessions, such as jewelry,[14] are prohibited.

FALSE OR MISLEADING REPRESENTATIONS

Prior to the passage of the Fair Debt Collection Practices Act, using the following script to locate a debtor was not uncommon:

THIRD PARTY: Hello?

ATTORNEY: Good morning, sir. This is the firm of Johnson and Ford. To whom am I speaking?

TP: Who is this calling?

ATTY: This is the firm of Johnson and Ford, and my name is Jerry Ford. We are the attorneys for Mary Baker, who is the grandmother of Robert Higgins.

TP: Robert Higgins?

ATTY: Yes, sir, Robert Higgins. We are trying to locate Mr. Higgins. His grandmother died about five months ago and we have a bequest in the will. We can't give you the exact amount, but it's over five figures—at least ten thousand dollars. We have been trying to locate Mr. Higgins, so we could give him this money.

TP: His grandmother left him over ten thousand dollars? I can't believe that.

ATTY: Well, you can believe it, sir. If you want, we'll be glad to give you our name and address, and we'll be glad to verify it to you either in writing or otherwise. All we're trying to do is locate him.

TP: How did you get my name?

ATTY: Your name was furnished to us by one of her nurses who told us that you were a friend of Mr. Higgins. It was difficult locating you, but because there was so much money involved, we made a very determined effort. We have contacted several other people with the same name as you, but none of them knew Mr. Higgins. Do you know Mr. Higgins?

TP: Yes, I know Mr. Higgins.

ATTY: Do you know where we can locate Mr. Higgins?

---

[14]Id.

TP: Yes, I know where you can locate him. I'm not so sure I should tell you because he owes a lot of people a lot of money.

ATTY: We're not trying to collect money from him. We're trying to give money to him.

TP: Actually, he recently moved to Florida and he's living there under one of his relative's names. He's living in a house down there with his relatives.

ATTY: Oh, is that right? Do you know if he's working? Maybe we can reach him at his job.

TP: Yes. He works for the city bus company down there in the repair and maintenance garage.

ATTY: I'm sure he'll be happy to receive this money.

TP: Yes, I'm certain he will.

ATTY: Can you give me his address in Florida?

TP: Yes, he lives on 35 Main Street in Ocala.

ATTY: Do you have his phone number?

TP: It's (305) 555-1212.

ATTY: Thank you very much. We're going to get in touch with him immediately to let him know about the good news.

TP: Okay. I'll call him too and tell him the good news. You want to give me your name and address?

ATTY: Certainly. I'll be glad to give it to you. Johnson and Ford, 5555 Park Avenue, New York City, New York. (212) 555-1212.

TP: Thanks very much. Goodbye.

ATTY: Goodbye.

The result of a juicy carrot at the end of the stick sometimes produces unique results in locating a debtor who has left for parts unknown. Another misleading device used was as follows:

TP: Hello.

DC: Is this Marie Baker?

TP: Who is this?

DC: This is emergency at the Meadowville Hospital. Your mother just got admitted to the hospital, but don't worry, she's okay. She's going to be fine. There's just a little minor thing that has to be taken care of, but we have to get the consent of your father. So could you please tell me quickly where I can reach your father at his work?

TP: At his work?

DC: Do you know where he works?

TP: Are you sure my mother's all right?

DC: Yes, your mother's okay. She's going to be fine. It's nothing serious. The important thing is to let us get in touch with your father.

TP: Okay, my dad works at the ABC Roofing Company on the edge of town on Green Street. I'm not sure of the address.

DC: The ABC Roofing Company.

TP: Yes, that's right.

DC: Do you have the telephone number?

TP: No, I don't have the number. I don't know where the number is.

DC: Okay, we'll find the number. Thanks very much, Marie. And don't worry. Your mother will be in touch with you or get in touch with your father.

The debt collector was able to locate where the consumer worked, but unfortunately the child had an uncomfortable afternoon until the mother or father returned to the house. Few laws regulated this type of deception during the 1950s, 1960s, and 1970s. Sometimes these deceptions were targeted at locating bank accounts, automobiles, or luxury boats, or the names of stock brokers or financial consultants who may have had assets of the debtor.

This section of the Act prohibits any false, deceptive, or misleading representation to collect a debt. The section lists sixteen prohibited activities, but at the same time states that the sixteen prohibitions are merely examples of what cannot be done, and thus a debt collector will not be able to use any type of false, deceptive, or misleading representation to collect a debt.

Most of the prohibitions are standard and obvious, whereas others consist of an effort to evade the intent and purpose of the Act.

DEBT AFFILIATED WITH GOVERNMENT. The false representation that a debt is vouched for, bonded by, or affiliated with the United States or any state, including the use of any badge, uniform, or facsimile, is a violation.

MISREPRESENTATION OF AMOUNT OF DEBT. The false representation of the character, amount, or legal status of any debt is prohibited. It was common to state that $425 was due, when in fact only $25 was due. The idea was to prompt a telephone call from the debtor. The debt collector would acknowledge the mistake and then continue to press the debtor for the collection of the $25.

STATUTE OF LIMITATIONS. Filing a lawsuit on an account barred by the statute of limitations qualifies as deception of the legal status of the debt in one federal court.[15] Whether this case will be followed is questionable, since in most states, the statute of limitations is an affirmative defense that must be asserted by the defendant. Thus, when a suit is filed, the plaintiff does not know whether the defendant will assert the defense. If it is not asserted, the plaintiff may enter a judgment if successful.

USE OF "PLAINTIFF" AND "DEFENDANT." Wording in the collection notice of "plaintiff v. defendant" where no suit has been started constitutes a misrepresentation under the Act, just as a letter threatening to garnishee the salary is a misrepresentation if no judgment has been entered.

MISREPRESENTING USE OF ATTORNEY. Where a party is not an attorney, the representation that an individual is an attorney or that any communication is from an attorney is false. A creditor should not use an attorney's name in a collection effort when the attorney has not authorized the use of the name and is not supervising the collection effort (see Facsimile Signatures).

A recent decision in the Court of Appeals for the Second Circuit involved a collection agency which was mass mailing over one million letters a year under the signature of an attorney as general counsel to the collection agency, but maintained offices with two other attorneys at a law firm at a different address. The Court decided that the use of the attorney's letterhead and signature on the letters did communicate to the consumer that the letters were from the attorney, even though as a practical matter the attorney was not involved in the collection effort. The collection agency prepared the letters, decided who should receive them, decided when the debtor should receive them, decided how many letters should be sent, and made all other decisions concerning the collection effort. The Court also held that the attorney did not review the debtor's file, did not determine which particular letter should be sent, and did not approve the sending of the letter. In fact, the attorney played no day-to-day role in the debt collection practice. The Court further held that the attorney did not receive instruction from the client and did not even talk to the client. Under these circumstances, the Court held that the attorney violated the Debt Collection Practices Act, since the collection agency, and not the attorney, was sending the letter to the debtor and this constituted a misrepresentation both by the collection agency and the attorney. This decision reinforced the attitude of the courts that the collection agency which pays an attorney for the use of the attorney's name and letterhead violates the Act unless the attorney is involved in the day-to-day collection effort.[16]

---

[15]*Kimber v. Federal Financial Corp.* 668 F. Supp. 1480 (1987).

[16]*Clomon v. Jackson,* 988 F.2d 1314 (2nd Cir. 1993).

THREAT OF ARREST. A statement that non-payment of the debt may result in the arrest or imprisonment of any person or the seizure, garnishee, attachment or sale of any property or wages is unlawful and a threat that the debt collector intends to take such action is a false representation.

Threatening to put the debtor in jail if the debt is not paid is expressly prohibited. In the Middle Ages, debtors were imprisoned if they were unable to pay their debts. The only way the debtor could leave prison was to persuade a friend or relative to pay the debt, and then the debtor would pay the debt to the friend or relative (usually by working off the debt over may years). Today, the alternative to debtor's prison is bankruptcy.

CRIMINAL PENALTIES FOR ISSUING A BAD CHECK. Most states provide criminal penalties if an individual *intentionally* issues a check that is returned unpaid. Since many consumers are aware of this law, some debt collectors threaten to arrest a debtor if a check has been returned unpaid (see Chapter 7 on Checks, Notes and Guarantees). The Act expressly prohibits such gross deception unless the debtor committed a crime and the debt collector intends to prosecute that crime.

To be a crime, the debtor must "intend" to defraud the creditor. In most instances, the debtor expected to have money in the bank or deposited checks which were returned unpaid and the account became overdrawn. If the account is closed, a creative debtor can allege that the spouse closed the account without his or her knowledge, or a check was issued on an old account which was closed many years ago, or can use some other excuse which removes the question of intent to defraud. For this reason, most attorney generals and district attorneys do not prosecute consumers for issuing returned checks, because their offices do not wish to assist a collection agency or attorney or creditor in the collection of a debt (see Chapter 7).

THREATENING ACTION THAT IS NOT INTENDED. The threat to take any action that cannot legally be taken or is not intended to be taken is the most important of the sixteen examples of prohibited activities and produces the most problems for creditor and debt collector. The area covered is comprehensive: Every firm must be careful not to be entrapped by the pitfalls of this subdivision.

Threatening to report a returned check to the police department is a violation unless the intent is to prosecute criminally, and the check actually is reported to the police department. The same rules apply to a threat to report a debt to a credit bureau.

The most frequent problem encountered is the threat to start suit. Prior to the enactment of the Fair Debt Collection Practices Act, the Federal Trade Commission took the position that if a threat is made that suit "may" be started, the debt collector must start suit in at least 25% of the cases. A California court disagreed and held that no fixed percentage was required. A certain number of suits had to be started, a procedure to start suit had to be in place, and the client had to approve suit in a "certain number" of cases.[17]

---

[17]*Trans World Accounts v. Federal Trade Commission*, 594 F.2d 212 (1979).

The commentary states that "a debt collector may state that certain action is possible, if it is true that such action is legal and is frequently taken by the collector or creditor with respect to similar debts; however, if the debt collector has reason to know there are facts that make the action unlikely in the particular case, a statement that the action was possible would be misleading." Whether the courts will follow this narrow analysis is yet to be seen.

The same reasoning applies to a threat that legal action has been recommended and will be taken when no such recommendation was made. To support a recommendation for suit, evidence must exist that the creditor will act on the recommendation at least some of the time. Lack of intent may be inferred when the amount of the debt is so small as to that the action is not economical or at least when the debt collector is unable to take the action because the creditor has not authorized the action. Threatening suit within a certain period of time or threatening immediate referral to an outside collection agency is deceptive unless the time frames are met. For example, threatening a referral in two weeks and actually referring it two months later misleads the consumer as to urgency. If the claim is never referred to an agency, a misrepresentation is also committed.

ATTORNEY'S LETTERHEAD

The National Consumer Law Center is supported by the Legal Services Corporation, which is federally funded by the United States Government. The National Consumer Law Center publishes a wide variety of books for consumer attorneys across the nation; one of these publications is entitled The Fair Debt Collection Practices Act. In the book, the National Consumer Law Center teaches a consumer attorney how to institute suit against collection agencies, law firms, and creditors. Besides setting forth their analysis of the law, they also provide example interviews with consumers, forms, and the actual laws.

In the second edition of the publication and in their newsletter, they stated: "Unless another course of conduct is made clear in any lawyer's collection letter, a lawyer's letterhead implicitly threatens suit."

Two cases in the 7th Circuit resulted in decisions that a lawyer's letterhead does not carry an implicit threat of suit. The court categorically stated that

"This argument is equally frivolous. If this statement were true, every collection letter from an attorney would be subject to an FDCPA action in order to determine whether the attorney actually intended to take legal action at the time the initial validation notice was sent. Clearly, this was not the intent of Congress when it enacted FDCPA."[18]

---

[18]*Sturdevant v. Thomas E. Jolas, P.C.*, 942 F. Supp. 426 (W.D. Wis. 1996).

In both cases (the same plaintiff's attorney represented both plaintiffs) the plaintiff argued that the letterhead constituted an implied threat to bring legal action that was false, deceptive, and misleading because neither of the lawyers are admitted to practice law in Wisconsin and, therefore, cannot legally bring a suit to collect on the debt. The court stated:

> "Plaintiff's argument is unpersuasive. Defendant's letter does not refer to or threaten legal action. Plaintiffs have failed to show identification of itself and its agent is synonymous with a 'threat' of legal action under Section 1692E. Defendant is a law firm and Winston a lawyer. Common sense and fairness dictate that defendant identify itself and the agent for which it is acting when attempting to collect a debt. The cases cited by plaintiffs to support their argument all involve direct threats by lawyers to take legal action."[19]

Hopefully, these two decisions put this "position" of the National Consumer Law Center to rest, and your author's firm was pleased to be the defendant in one case.

PRE-LEGAL DEPARTMENT. The Federal Trade Commission frowns on using a "pre-legal department" heading on a letter unless a pre-legal department is organized within the collection agency or law firm. Distinguishing a "pre-legal department" from a "collection department" or a "legal department" is difficult, and special divisions of authority and activity would have to be designated. The suggestion is not to use such terminology.

LEAST SOPHISTICATED CONSUMER. In situations where the courts try to determine whether the consumer is being misled or deceived by a threat of suit or some other action, the courts use the test of "the least sophisticated consumer." The courts try to protect those "debtors on the low side of reasonable capacity who read a given notice or hear a given statement and read into the message oppressiveness, falsehood or threat."[20]

TRANSFER OF DEBT. The false representation that a sale or transfer of a debt shall cause the consumer to lose a defense of payment of the debt is prohibited. Under the Credit Practices Act, and under many state laws, the sale of a debt will not cut off the defenses of the consumer and the consumer may still allege those defenses in a suit by the purchaser of the debt. This section applies to an assignment of the creditor's claim to a collection agency (see Appendix—Chapter 6).

FALSELY IMPLYING A CRIMINAL ACT. The false representation that the consumer has committed any crime is not permitted. Threatening a consumer with

---

[19]*Wallace v. Winston & Morrone, P.C.*, 95-C-354-C USDC, WD Wisc., (October 30, 1996).

[20]*Bingham v. Collection Bureau Inc.*, 505 F. Supp. 864 (1981); *Jeter v. Credit Bureau, 760 F.2d. 1168 (1985).*

arrest or jail for issuing a check that is returned unpaid is a violation unless the creditor knows that the debtor intended to defraud the creditor.

FALSE CREDIT INFORMATION. To communicate or threaten to communicate to any person credit information which is known or which should be known to be false is a violation. Failure to communicate to a credit reporting agency that a debt is disputed may also be a violation. On the other hand, if the debt has been reported to the credit reporting agency and then the debt becomes disputed, the obligation does not rest upon the collection agency or law firm to report the dispute. The creditor (or the consumer) must report the dispute to the credit reporting agency.

SIMULATED LEGAL PROCESS. This section is targeted at simulated legal process where the documents sent to the consumer imply a summons and complaint, or other official document, and is not a summons and complaint.

DECEIT TO COLLECT DEBT. The use of any false representation or deceptive means to collect or attempt to collect any debt, or to obtain any information concerning a consumer, is expressly prohibited. This is the most comprehensive subdivision of the section and is a "catchall" to cover any misrepresentation, the nature and purpose of which is to deceive the debtor. Any deception or misrepresentation not mentioned in this law or commentary is covered by this general section. If a facsimile of a Western Union telegram is used as a collection letter, a misrepresentation occurs because the consumer is deceived into believing a sense of urgency exists. A statement in the letter that "a failure to respond is an admission of liability" is a deception.

MINI-MIRANDA WARNING. This section requires a disclosure in *all communications* of the following phrase: "This is an attempt to collect the debt and any information will be used for that purpose" (mini-Miranda warning). This would apply to both *oral* and *written* communication. The disclosure must be in all letters including balance letters, explanatory letters, or other correspondence between the consumer and the debt collector. The print should be legible and at least as large as the typewritten portion of the letter. There are some state statutes that require the disclosure statement to be in at least 10 point type.

The FTC commentary states that this mini-Miranda phrase must be in the first communication with the debtor, but not in subsequent communications. Nevertheless, several federal courts have disagreed with the Federal Trade commission and require that this warning be in all communications, both oral and written. (One federal court agrees with the Federal Trade Commission.)

On September 30, 1996, an amendment to the FDCPA was passed by Congress which amendment became effective January 1, 1997. The amendment reads as follows:

"The failure to disclose in the initial written communication with the consumer, and, in addition, if the initial communication with the consumer is oral, in that initial oral communication, that the debt collector is attempting to collect a debt and that any further information obtained will be used for that purpose and the failure to disclose in subsequent communications that *the communication is from a debt collector,* except that this paragraph shall not apply to a formal pleading made in connection with a legal action." (Emphasis added.)

After the first communication, whether it be oral or in writing, the mini-Miranda warning is not required. The major advantage for collection agencies is that no mini-Miranda warning is required after the first letter if the letterhead of the collection agency sets forth sufficient wording to indicate that the sender of the letter is a collection agency. If the letterhead of the collection agency refers to the fact that it is a collection agency such as, "ABC Collection Agency," this new statement will not be necessary in subsequent letters since the consumer knows who the sender of the letter is. If the name of the collection agency does not contain the necessary words to indicate to the debtor that the communication is from a debt collector, the collection agency will have to include in the body of the letter or at some other conspicuous place the statement that, "This communication is from a debt collector."

With regard to law firms the Federal Trade Commission has taken the position that the letterhead of an attorney is not sufficient to communicate to a debtor that the communication is from a debt collector. Therefore, on each subsequent written or oral communication, the attorney will have to include either a written statement or an oral statement that, "This communication is from a debt collector."

A problem also arises with omitting the mini-Miranda warning in all subsequent communications since there are several states which still require the mini-Miranda warning in each communication. They include Colorado, Connecticut, District of Columbia, Hawaii, Idaho, Iowa, Maine, Michigan, North Carolina, Oregon, and Texas. Each of the states requires some form of the mini-Miranda warning in either the initial written communication or oral communications, or sets forth other specified requirements. An examination of each state law should be made before the elimination of the mini-Miranda warning. As a result of these requirements by the various states, most law firms and many of the collection agencies are still including the mini-Miranda warning in all communications, both oral and written, until such time as the states begin to repeal the requirement. Continuation of the mini-Miranda warning in communications after the first communication as a substitute for "this communication is from a debt collector" is probably acceptable, but the author at this writing knows of no case addressing the situation. The best approach for communication after the first communication is to use both the mini-Miranda warning and the new statement required by the 1996 amendment.

When addressing correspondence to an attorney for a debtor, cautious attorneys generally include the Mini-Miranda warning, and under the new amendment the additional statement, "This communication is from a debt collector," on the basis that the attorney is the agent of the debtor. If the debt collector is obligated under the act to include these statements when communicating with the debtor, the statement should be included when communicating with an agent of the debtor, such as the attorney for the debtor.

A recent case in the Tenth Circuit has rejected this reasoning and has held that failure to include a Mini-Miranda warning is not a violation of the act when there is no evidence that the collection agency was attempting to mislead the attorney, and when it was fairly clear to the attorney from all the facts of the communication, (and in this case, oral) that the collection agency was trying to collect a debt.[21]

USE OF FORM OF GOVERNMENTAL COMMUNICATIONS. Using return addresses and the form or shape of envelopes indicating that the communication is being mailed from a governmental office, when such is not the case, is prohibited under the Section.

USE OF ANOTHER NAME. A debt collector must use the same name consistently when dealing with the consumer. The use of any business, company, or organization name other than the true name of the debt collector's business, company, or organization is prohibited. This section is not only directed at a debt collector, but is also targeted at the creditor.

A creditor may not use any name that would falsely imply that a third party is involved in the collection. If the creditor creates a collection agency which is a shell with no assets and no employees, but maintains an address different from the creditor, the consumer is misled to believe another firm is collecting other than the creditor.

MISREPRESENTING LEGAL DOCUMENTS.

DR: I just received some papers left at the door. Your name was on them.

CR: You can ignore them. Now, about the debt.

The false representation or implication that documents are *not* legal process or do not require action by the consumer applies where the consumer was led to believe that a summons and complaint was not served (when, in fact, it was served), and therefore no defense or answer was required is prohibited. Thus, the creditor can enter a default judgment.

---

[21]*Dikeman v. National Educators, Inc.,* 81 F.3d 949 (10th Cir. 1996).

FACSIMILE SIGNATURE—MASS MAILINGS

The consumer attorneys obtained a favorable decision on a fact situation similar to *Clomon v. Jackson*, which involved the use of an attorney's facsimile signature by the collection agency where the attorney was not involved with the client or the preparation or mailing of the letters. This particular case was different in that the attorney actually owned the collection agency and was operating a separate office for his law practice adjacent to the collection agency. The court held that the owner-attorney had no real involvement in the mailing of the letters to the debtors. Like the attorney in *Clomon*, the court found a cozy relationship with the "referring" collection agency. The attorney was not personally or directly involved in deciding when or to whom a dunning letter should be sent. Like the attorney in *Clomon*, the attorney did not review the debtor's file and did not determine when the particular letter should be sent nor did he approve the sending of the particular letters based on the recommendation of others. The attorney stated that the letters were only brought to his attention for advice and guidance when there was some unusual problem or something out of the ordinary.

While this situation was somewhat unusual, considering the relationship of the attorney to the collection agency, the court decided the attorney was not the real source of the letters and that the true source of the letters was the collection agent who pushed the button on the agency's computer. Accordingly, the court decided that the attorney violated the FDCPA.[22]

Notwithstanding the *Clomon v. Jackson* and the *Avila v. Rubin* cases, collection agencies are still using the services of an attorney. In a recent case,[23] the Circuit Court of Appeals for the Fourth Circuit found that attorneys have to be involved on a day-to-day basis in the preparation and mailing of letters and must review the information. The court stated at the beginning of the decision as follows:

> The notices were not signed by Lanocha (the attorney involved), nor did he receive or review the information on the AFP computer tapes—either in general or in relation to any particular account. Lanocha did not read or review the letters prepared by the NFS computers under his name. He did not have a list of customers who received his letters. According to AFP's Vice-President of Finance, Stephen F. McCarthy, Lanocha did not confer with AFP regarding the text of the letters, and, in fact, had no contact with AFP regarding any aspect of the collection activities from 1983 until 1990.

The court in this instance was following the *Clomon* and *Avila* decisions where an attorney had no involvement whatsoever in the collection process.

---

[22]*Avila v. Rubin*, 84 F.3d 222 (7th Cir. 1996); *Cloman v. Jackson*, 988 F.2d 1314 (2nd Cir. 1993).

[23]*United States v. National Fin. Serv., Inc.*, 98 F.3d 131 (4th Cir. 1996).

The defendant, National Financial Services, Inc., was handling the collection of thousands of accounts every few weeks averaging approximately $20. This case apparently is an outgrowth of the proceeding that the Federal Trade Commission commenced against American Family Publishers about five years ago, where the American Family Publishers entered into a consent order with the commission that stated that American Family Publishers had a pervasive influence over the agency and that because of this pervasive influence, and knowledge of the fact that the agency was violating the FDCPA, the consent order was entered into, wherein American Family Publishers agreed to restrictions on its collection effort.

Danielson v. Hicks case, which held that letters generated by employees working for an attorney at the attorney's law firm are correspondence from an attorney and therefore, the attorney did not falsely represent that the letters were from an attorney. The court stated that the letters were sent by the employees of the attorney pursuant to the implicit directions of the attorney, which did not violate the Fair Debt Collection Practice Act. A federal court in the 7th District now followed this 8th Circuit decision with the same conclusion, although with different supporting arguments.

In both cases, the plaintiffs relied upon *Clomon v. Jackson* and *Avila v. Rubin* to allege that a facsimile of an attorney's signature appearing on a computer-generated letter constituted mass-produced debt collection letters and the use of the facsimile signature of the attorney falsely represented that the letters were communications from an attorney. Both *Clomon* and *Avila* found violations of Section 1692E-3 of the FDCPA on the grounds the letters falsely implied that they were "actually from the attorneys" who signed them. The court stated that in each case the defendant attorney was acting pursuant to some relationship with a debt collection agency in permitting the use of a facsimile of the signature on the debt collection notices and the defendant attorney was not representing the actual creditor. The attorney did not prepare or review the accounts and had no involvement in the collection procedures. In *Avila*, the defendant attorney was the debt collection agency's chief executive officer and owned 80 percent of the agency's stock. In *Clomon*, the defendant's attorney was employed on a part-time basis as general counsel for the debt collection agency.

A recent case dealt with an attorney receiving the accounts directly from the creditor where attorneys were involved on a day to day basis and supervised the collection effort. After distinguishing the *Clomon & Avila* decisions the court stated:

> "It cannot be disputed that the November 2nd letter contains the facsimile signature of defendant attorney Winston (*your author*). However, the November 2nd letter was from defendant Winston in his capacity as the attorney for plaintiff's creditor, Webster's Unified, Inc.. Defendants were the actual debt collectors rather than representatives of otherwise unidentified debt collector as in Avila & Clomon. The fact that the letter contained a facsimile signature rather than the actual signature of defendant Winston is inconsequential."

The court then dismissed the complaint.[24]

Shortly after the *Kartavich* decision another decision in the 2nd Circuit was handed down on March 25, 1997 which further clarified the *Clomon* and *Avila* decisions. The court acknowledged that the defendant, a law firm, made a mass mailing and that a facsimile signature was used. At the same time it stated that *Clomon v. Jackson* "did not flatly ban such activities."

The fact that the creditor's collection procedures were verified, that the collection letters were created by the attorney, that the attorney decided when and which letters were to be sent and to whom and the attorney reviewed the hard copies provided on each debtor may justify defendant's representation that the letters in question were from an attorney. In a footnote the court discussed the cursory nature of the review in that it was only a brief look at a computer printout of the debtor's relevant information. Nevertheless, the court felt that such behavior could meet the Clomon standard in light of the relatively small size of the debts involved and the fact that the client had "no additional information" on the debtor.

The court also cited a decision which was the same case cited in *Clomon v. Jackson* and offered this case as an example of permissible conduct, i.e., a collection letter was sent directly from an attorney's office after the attorney reviewed information provided by the client and determined independently whether the letter should be sent.[25]

Another case in Florida also clarified *Clomon v. Jackson*. The attorney was employed by a collection agency and the agency supervisor recommended certain accounts for legal review by the attorney. The attorney received the legal review accounts through the computer and printed them out. The attorney then reviewed the printed list of legal review accounts, which included the file number, the consumer's name, the original balance, the current balance, the client code, and the status of account. The attorney performed a random audit of ten percent of the accounts, and after the review of the random audit, the attorney authorized the sending of the letters by manually inputting the codes into the collection agency's computer systems.[26]

The court quoted *Clomon v. Jackson* in recognizing that sometimes mass mailings may be the only feasible means of contacting large numbers of debtors, but stated "no mass mailing technique is permissible regardless of how effective it might be if that technique constitutes a false, deceptive or misleading communication." The Florida court concluded that there was a genuine issue of a material fact as to whether the attorney violated the FDCPA, based on her level of involve-

---

[24]*Kartavich v. Winston & Morrone, P.C.*, 96-C-08930S USDC, W.D. Wisc. (February 19, 1997).

[25]*Anthes v. Transworld Sys., Inc.*, 765 Supp. 162 (D. Del. 1991); *Goldberg v. Winston & Morrone P.C.*, No. 95 Civ. 9282, 1997 WL 139526 (S.D.N.Y. Mar. 26, 1997).

[26]*Dalton v. FMA Enter., Inc.*, No. 95-396-CIV-FTM-17, 1997 WL 48871 (M.D. Fla. Feb. 3, 1997).

ment in the attempted debt collection activity, and left it to a trial to assess the credibility of the evidence as to whether the attorney was involved. At the trial the court held the attorney did not violate the FDCPA.

From the above three cases it seems clear that the 7th Circuit, the 2nd Circuit and the 11th Circuit have now produced decisions that allow attorneys to conduct mass mailings under a facsimile signature providing they are meaningfully involved in the day-to-day operation, control and supervision of the collection effort. The key seems to be that the attorney or the staff must review the file of the debtor, prior to mailing the letter (but not necessarily the letter) and be meaningfully involved. It appears that the statement made in *Cloman v. Jackson* that "few if any attorneys can conduct a mass mailing" seems to be referring to attorneys who represent collection agencies and are not involved in the day-to-day operation—where the collection agency was doing all the work and merely using the attorney's letterhead and signature.

On a rereading of *Newman vs. CheckRite California Inc.* 912 F. Supp. 1354 (1995), the court mentioned that they do not rule out the possibility that legal assistants may review the files to be meaningfully involved as required under Cloman vs. Jackson providing of course that the legal assistants are under the active supervision and control of an attorney.[27]

UNFAIR PRACTICES

A debt collector may not use unfair or unconscionable means to collect or attempt to collect a debt. The Commission has provided eight examples of unfair or unconscionable means to collect a debt, but other acts may qualify for inclusion. The Commission has defined an unfair debt practice as one that causes injury to the consumer that is:

a. substantial,
b. not outweighed by countervailing benefits to consumers or competition; and
c. not reasonably avoidable by the consumer.

The following are some of the examples of unfair or unconscionable methods of collecting a debt.

COLLECTION OF CHARGES. The collection of any incidental charges to the collection of a debt is prohibited unless said amount is expressly authorized by the agreement creating the debt or permitted by law. This prohibition includes the

---

[27]*Waddlington v. Credit Acceptance Corp.*, 76 F.3d 103 (6th Cir. 1996); *Newman v. Checkrite California, Inc.*, 912 F. Supp. 1354 (E.D. Cal. 1995).

collection of late charges, interest charges, finance charges, or service charges, unless they are expressly set forth in the agreement that created a debt. In a loan situation, the agreement creating a debt would be the originating loan document. In the purchase of goods at a retail store, the charges are to be displayed at the point of purchase. If the goods are purchased by direct mail, the charges would have to be displayed in the order form contained in the catalogue or the promotional direct marketing piece. If the purchase is made by telephone, the charges are to be disclosed over the telephone at the same time the purchase is made.

Prior to the enactment of the Fair Debt Collection Practices Act, creditors commonly charged the consumer the fee the bank charged the creditor when the consumer's check was returned unpaid. Such a charge is prohibited under this section, unless it is clearly specified at the time of purchase that there will be a charge in the event that a check is returned unpaid or permitted by law.[28]

In some states bad check charges are allowed by state law. If it is not authorized by state law, the charge cannot be collected unless contained in the agreement creating the debt.

Excessive charges of any type are unconscionable and cannot be collected notwithstanding a written agreement to pay these charges. If "reasonable attorneys' fees" are used, the fees must be reasonable and must be determined by the law of the state in which the contract is entered or is enforced. If bad check charges are allowed, the charges must comply with the law. Shipping and handling charges may not be excessive. Restocking charges must be reasonable.

CREDIT CARD PAYMENTS. Some collection agencies and attorneys have offered the consumer the right to make their payment by use of a credit card rather than the use of a check or cash. Certain risks are present in offering a credit card option to consumers by collection agencies or attorneys.

As a general rule, the banks which are licensed by Visa and MasterCharge are prohibited or discouraged from entering into merchant agreements with firms which collect delinquent accounts. The Visa and MasterCharge agreement generally provides that the bank must enter into an agreement with the party selling the product or offering the service. The collection agency or attorney offers this option and then sends the authorization directly to the client and the client processes the payment through their agreement with the bank. A further option to the collection agency or attorney is to process the payment through one of the third party agencies who process credit card charges for a fee for those businesses which are unable to persuade a bank to enter into an agreement with them because of financial problems or other business reasons. For example, banks are reluctant to enter into merchant agreements with recently organized direct marketing firms who are selling by telemarketing or catalogs.

Consumer attorneys have been somewhat active in this area on the theory that by permitting the consumer to use a credit card, the debt collector is merely

---

[28]*West v. Costen*, 558 F. Supp. 564 (1983).

substituting one debt for another debt and the substituted debt carries interest and other charges which were not incurred in the original sale of the product or service. This additional charge violates the FDCPA section prohibiting any additional charges except in the agreement creating the debt.

The American Collector's Association reported an unpublished decision issued October 6, 1997 in the 6th Circuit Court of Appeals which upheld a collection agency's practice of accepting payment by credit card, even where the collection agency required the consumer to pay the 5% transaction fee associated with such payment, on the theory that the debtor had the option.[29] But the decision leaves some unanswered questions on this uncomfortable practice, which may be tested in the courts again.

Another risk is that the bank, when it becomes aware that these charges are being processed by the collection agency or attorney, will declare it to be a violation of the original agreement between the bank and the merchant. If the merchant is a substantial customer, it is unlikely that the bank will declare the agreement null and void for a breach of contract.

A similar situation occurs where the collection agency uses check-by-phone. Most check-by-phone operators charge a transaction fee. Some collection agencies pass this transaction fee on to the customer and add it to the balance due. In some instances the charge is under a dollar and in other instances it may be several dollars. I have heard of some collection agencies making a profit and adding additional monies to the cost of the transaction. This is similar to the transfer of a balance to a credit card where an additional charge is imposed on the debtor which was not in the original agreement creating the debt. On the other hand with check by phone, the debtor has no choice but to pay the additional transaction charge.

CREDIT AND COLLECTION TIP: *Until there is a definitive decision in this area, any debt collector who is pursuing these types of practices is running the risk of testing the water and having the court decide a case of first impression.*

POST-DATED CHECKS. Creditors sometimes accept post-dated checks, i.e., checks that are dated at some future date, and thus cannot be deposited until said date. An example would be a debtor who owes $400 and offers the creditor 4 checks for $100, each dated one month apart starting on January 1st and ending on April 1st to pay the debt in full. (See Chapter 7—Checks, Notes and Guarantees.)

The acceptance from any person of a check post-dated by more than five days is not allowed unless such person is notified in writing of the intent to deposit such check. If a check is post-dated more than five days, the debt collector must give the consumer notice by mail in writing of the debt collector's inten-

---

[29]*Lee v. Main Accounts,* 125 F. 3d 855 (6th Cir. 1997).

tion to deposit the checks at least three and not more than ten days prior to such deposit.

The solicitation of any post-dated check or other post-dated payment for the purpose of threatening or instituting criminal prosecution would be prohibited under this subdivision. Threatening criminal proceedings where no lawful right exists to make the threat is a rewording of Section 1692(b)4.

Since a bank will refuse to accept a check for deposit prior to its date, threatening to deposit or depositing a post-dated check prior to the date is an unfair practice.

BOUNCED CHECKS. In a case in the 7th Circuit, the court held that there is no authority in the statute for a collection agency to charge a consumer a fee on check upon which payment was stopped. Many states' statutes allow fees for checks that are returned for insufficient funds or uncollected funds but there is no provision for the situation where the check is marked "payment stopped." Since there was no authority for such a fee, charging such a fee violates the FDCPA.[30]

The 10th U.S. Circuit Court of Appeals has now held that the payment obligations arising from bounced checks constitute a debt within the meaning of the Fair Debt Collection Practices Act and any collection effort on a bad check is covered by the Fair Debt Collection Practices Act.[31]

TELEPHONE CHARGES. The true purposes of a communication may not be concealed so that the consumer will incur a telephone or telegram charge. A debt collector may not call the consumer collect or ask a consumer to return the call long distance without first disclosing its identity and the purpose of the call.

TAKING PROPERTY OF DEBTOR. Section 808(b) of the Act states that the following is a violation:

> "Taking or threatening to take any nonjudicial action to effect dispossession or disablement of property is prohibited if:
>
> a.   there is no present right to possession of the property claimed as collateral through an enforceable security interest;
>
> b.   there is no present intention to take possession of the property; or
>
> c.   the property is exempt by law from such dispossession or disablement."

The Fair Debt Collection Practices Act includes secured parties whose principal business is enforcing security interests *only for purposes of this subdivision.* If the secured party does not otherwise fall within this subdivision, the secured party is not subject to the rest of the provisions of the act. The purpose of this sec-

---

[30]*Ozkaya v. Telecheck Services, Inc.,* 982 F. Supp. 578 (N.D. Ill. 1997).

[31]*Snow v. Riddle,* 143 F.3d 1350 (10th Cir. 1998).

tion is to prevent someone from threatening to take possession of the property if there is:

a.   no right to possession;

b.   no present intention to take possession of the property;

c.   the property is exempt by law.

The secured party, such as a bank, who has a lien on a boat or an automobile, cannot threaten to take possession unless it has a legal right to take possession, a present intent to take possession, and a valid security agreement.

POST CARD. Communicating with the debtor by post card is a violation of the Act because a post card can be read by anyone. The use of a fax machine would depend upon whether other parties have access, but since the creditor does not know if a third party has access, its use is not recommended.

ENVELOPES. This subsection prohibits any writing other than the debt collector's name and address on the envelope unless the business name does not indicate a debt collection business. A debt collector may not use "debt" or "collector" or any other word which indicates the debt collection business. A transparent envelope is a violation if the collection notice is seen through the window or the transparency. "Personal or Confidential" on the envelope is permissible if sent to the home address of the consumer.[32] It is not permissible to use an envelope that contains "final demand for payment" in large print.[33]

VALIDATION OF DEBT

Within five days of the first communication, the consumer must be given a written notice, if not provided in the original communication, containing the amount of the debt and the name of the creditor along with a statement that the debt will be assumed to be valid unless the consumer disputes it within thirty days. The debt collector must send a verification of the debt or copy of a judgment if the consumer timely disputes the debt. No requirements are set forth as to the form of the notice providing all the information is furnished. Nevertheless, subdivision b of the Act requires that if the consumer disputes the debt, the collector must cease collection efforts until the debt is verified and a response to the consumer is mailed. Failure by the consumer to dispute the debt may not be interpreted by a court as an admission of liability.

---

[32]*Masuda v. Thomas Richards and Company,* 759 F. Supp. 1456 (1991).

[33]*Kleczy v. First Federal Credit Control Inc.,* 486 N.E. 2d 204 (1984).

The validation notice does not prohibit collection activities during the 30-day period unless the debtor disputes the debt. Even after the debtor disputes the debt, the statute allows the debt collector to continue collection activities after mailing verification of the debt or a copy of the judgment, or the name and address of the original creditor, if the consumer requests it, but the courts seem to say that no or little action should be taken during the 30-day period and the interpretation by the courts seem to be stretched to allowing the debtor a 30-day free grace period.

Nevertheless, while it is not a violation of the Act to institute suit during the 30-day period, the act of "advising" the consumer that suit will be started within the 30-day period may be a violation. The theory is that the "communication" contradicts the 30-day period. The courts feel that a debt collector cannot initially offer the debtor 30 days to dispute the debt and at the same time threaten to sue in 14 days. The threat to sue in 14 days contradicts the offer of the 30 days required by the statute, and thus is a violation. It seems that the more recent decisions are allowing the debtor to dun during the thirty-day period, providing the second letter is more in the nature of a reminder than a contradiction or overshadowing of the 30-day period to dispute the debt. How to carefully word the letter in order not to run abreast of a violation or what is more important not to trigger a law suit is another situation. One case in the 6th Circuit which allowed such a reminder letter may be worth mentioning. The second collection letter read as follows:

> "Fourteen days have passed since Computer Credit's last communication with you and your seriously delinquent balance with the Miami Valley Hospital still remains unpaid. In the absence of a valid reason for nonpayment, this debt must be paid. If we are not notified that your debt has been paid before April 4, 1996 and if this debt is not disputed, we shall advise you of our final position regarding the status of your account."[34]

The Second Circuit reversed a District Court case which held in favor of the collection agency. The collection agency stated in its letter that it would place an account for "immediate collection" and that payment within ten days would prevent "the posting" of unpaid collections to debtor's credit record. A letter mailed twenty days later urged "payment in full" within 5 days.

The District Court was liberal in granting summary judgment in favor of the collection agency, alleging that there was no "threatening contradiction" and that overshadowing did not take place because of the fact that the validation notice was not overshadowed by what was printed on the front side of the letter.

The Second Circuit, notorious for applying the Fair Debt Collections Practices Act on a strict liability basis, reversed and stated that conflicting state-

---

[34]*Smith v. Computer Credit Inc.*, 167 F. 3d 1052 (6th Cir. 1999)

ments existed in the letter and that the threat to "post" the debtor's payments was sufficient overshadowing.[35]

If the attorney actually institutes suit by serving a summons and complaint during the 30-day period, but does not mention the possibility of suit in the letter, the commentary states that the commencement of suit is not a violation. The recommendation at this time followed by most creditors and attorneys, is not to threaten suit or actually institute suit during the 30-day period. As a practical matter, few creditors or attorneys start suit during the 30 day period.

The recent case of *Heintz v. Jenkins*[36] may also resolve this confusion. If litigation is now subject to coverage of the Act, then commencing suit is covered by the Act and clearly violates the 30-day period if suit is commenced within that time. This is another reason not to sue within the 30-day period.

Such phrases in the letter as "immediate full payment," "now" and "phone us today" have been held to flatly contradict the 30-day period to dispute the debt, and thus constitute a violation of the Act.[37] A threat to sue if payment is not received in ten days also was deemed a violation.[38] The common thread in the recent decisions seems to be prohibiting (rather than limiting) the right to demand payment or threatening to sue before the expiration of the 30-day period. As a result, many collection agencies and law firms are conservatively writing a simple non-threatening letter and taking no additional action during the 30-day period.

Some cases have held that the type size of the validation notice must be the same type size as in the typewritten portion of the letter. If the letter should contain only capitalization, and the mini-Miranda warning and the validation are printed in small case print, the court may conclude that no notice existed since the notice was "overshadowed" by the general impression of the letter. Placing the disclosure and the validation notice on the reverse side compels the use of the phrase "see reverse side" on the front side of the letter and may cause overshadowing. Whether using the three words "see reverse side" is clear and conspicuous enough to advise the consumer that the reverse side will set forth the rights under the Fair Debt Collection Practices Act has been questioned by various judges.[39]

Heintz v. Jenkins[40] has had an additional effect on this section of the Act. Sometimes a case is referred to an attorney for immediate institution of suit, such as a replevin action to repossess a boat or automobile, or a foreclosure action on

[35]*Russell v. Equifax, A.R.S.,* 74 F.3d 30 (2nd Cir. 1996).

[36]See supra note 4.

[37]*Miller v. Payco General American Credits, Inc.,* 943 F.2d 482 (1991).

[38]*Graziano v. Harrison,* 950 F.2d 107 (1991).

[39]*Anthes v. Transworld Systems, Inc.,* 765 F. Supp. 162 (1991); *Higgins v. Capitol Credit Services, Inc.,* 762 F. Supp. 1128 (1991); *Riviera v. MAB Collections, Inc.,* 682 F. Supp. 174 (1988).

[40]See supra note 4.

a residence; the debt collector or creditor specifically instructs the attorney not to send a letter to the consumer or contact the consumer by telephone prior to the institution of suit. Prior to this decision, attorneys feel that litigation was not subject to the Fair Debt Collection Practices Act and found no problem in complying with the client's instruction. The *Heintz v. Jenkins* case held that litigation against a consumer to collect a debt is covered by the Act. Accordingly, the validation notice must be attached to the summons and complaint (as well as the mini-Miranda warning) since it is the first communication with the consumer.

What if the summons requires under state or city law that the consumer debtor answer within 20 days? Will the federal courts treat this 20-day period to interpose an answer as a contradiction of the 30-day period allowing the debtor to dispute the debt, or will the courts not endorse such an anomalous result? In the meanwhile, it is still a violation since it contradicts the 30 day period to dispute the debt, and no court up to now has addressed the problem. Some attorneys advise debtors that they have 30 days to answer to avoid overshadowing.

If the debt collector intends to take no further action, it seems that the debt collector may ignore a request for a verification. Accordingly, it appears that if the debt collector receives a written request for a verification, and wishes to continue pursuing the debtor further, it will have to provide the verification. On the other hand, if the debt collector should decide not to engage in any further collection activity, and return the case to the client, the verification request does not have to be honored.[41] Nevertheless, the client cannot merely send the case to another agency or law firm without first providing verification.

Subdivision 3 of the Act clearly does not require any communication in writing. Even if this statement is merely an oral communication, the debt will be assumed to be valid. The paragraph makes no assumption about what happens if the debtor disputes the debt within the 30 days. The only obligations of the debt collector is the assumption that the debt is valid. On the other hand, Subdivision 4 and 5 clearly state that the communication must be in writing or "a written request." Thus, paragraphs 4 and 5 do not begin to operate until there is something in writing. Some letters omitted the requirement in Section 4 that the consumer must notify the debt collector in writing. Strangely, the courts have held this as a technical violation of the Act, even though the consumer is being afforded a broader opportunity to obtain verification of the debt without any communication in writing or without a written request. In one case, the court said that failure to include the writing requirement was a violation because the defendant cannot alter or restructure the statutory provisions. The court went on to state that the contents of the debtor's letter could not override the language in the statute and the debt collector could totally ignore his obligation in the letter to send a verification without a writing and still enforce the terms of the statute. While this seems to be stretching to protect the

---

[41]*Smith v. Transworld Sys., Inc.*, 953 F.2d 1025 (6th Cir. 1992); *Jang v. A.M. Miller and Assoc., Inc.*, No. 95 C 4919, 1996 WL 5435096 (N.D. Ill. July 31, 1996).

consumer, it is another example of what was affectionately referred to as "strict liability" of the Fair Debt Collection Practices Act.

On the other hand in another case, Sections 3 and 4 were properly set forth in the letter but were set forth in reverse order. The plaintiff in this instance argued that the particular provisions be set forth in the same order as they are set forth in Section 809. At least in this case the court took the attitude that this was not a material misrepresentation to the unsophisticated debtor and that the debtor was not mislead by this reversal.[42]

In another case, the collection agency reported the debtor to a credit reporting agency because there was no notification by the consumer in writing. The consumer did notify the collection agency orally over the telephone and the collection agency admitted that they had knowledge because of this oral communication. The judge in this instance held that the true test of determining if the debt collector falsely reported a consumer debt to the credit reporting agency was whether the collection agency knew or should have known that the debt was disputed and did not depend upon when or how the agency acquired the knowledge. Again, the court here ignored the "strict liability" approach to the statute and applied plain and simple common sense.[43] Unfortunately, all the courts do not apply the Act this rationally and when the court decides to hold the collection agency liable, the court will often become technical and apply the act in an exacting manner.

A recent case stated clearly that there was no authority directly supporting the idea that you must use the language of the statute on a word-for-word basis. The important ingredient is to convey the intended message required by the statute.

A creditor has an obligation to report a debt as disputed if it has been reported to a credit reporting agency and the same rules apply to a collection agency. If the debtor disputes the debt orally and does not dispute it in writing, that is sufficient notification to the debt collector to require him to report the debt as disputed to any credit reporting agency to which he had previously reported the debt. Many collection agencies and debt collectors as well as creditors may have operated on the thesis that they did not report the debt as disputed unless they received a notification from the consumer in writing. The Circuit Court of Appeals has clearly stated that an oral dispute requires the debt collector to act.[44]

MULTIPLE DEBTS

This section requires the debt collector to apply payments received in accordance with the consumer's direction. Payment for a new purchase should not be

---

[42]*Goldberg v. Winston*, 1997 WL 139526 (S.D.N.Y. 1997).

[43]*Kartovich v. Winston*, 96-e-0893S USDC, W.D. Wisc. (Feb. 19, 1997). (unpublished decision)

[44]*Brady v. Credit Recovery*, 160 F. 3d 64 (1st Cir., 1998).

applied to an old debt. The debt collector must apply a payment exactly as the debtor directs. Creditors should also comply with this section.

LEGAL ACTION BY DEBT COLLECTORS

A suit that affects an interest in real property must be started in the judicial district in which the property is located. For suits other than those affecting real property (which covers most suits), the action must be brought in the judicial district in which the consumer signed the contract or in which the consumer resides at the commencement of the action.

RIGHT OF ASSIGNMENT

The American Collectors Association has reported that twenty-five states have enacted "right of assignment" laws with more states considering adopting laws to allow assignment. Twelve states have expressly prohibited this practice by either a statute or court decision.

The right of assignment gives that creditor the ability to assign the claim to a collection agency which enables the collection agency to file suit in its own name instead of the client's name. This enables many claims against one debtor to be coordinated into one suit, but unfortunately presents serious problems when a contest develops on a claim. The divisions of funds when collection occurs may also become a problem unless resolved prior to handling.

PRO SE PLAINTIFFS

Often consumer attorneys institute suit for violations of FDCPA in their own names, since the attorneys themselves actually received the letter or telephone call, and included in the complaint is a claim for attorney's fees. Several cases have held that where the plaintiff appears "pro se" (for himself/herself), the plaintiff is not entitled to attorney's fees since the plaintiff is a consumer not represented by an attorney and thus not incurring the cost of an attorney.[45]

DECEPTIVE FORMS

Designing or furnishing forms knowing they are deceptive or will be used to deceive the consumer into believing that someone other than the creditor is par-

---

[45]*Benson v. Hafif,* 114 F.3d 1193 (9the Cir. 1997).

ticipating in the collection of the debt is expressly forbidden. Prior to the Act, the practice of selling to creditors form letters with the letterhead of a collection agency was common where the agency was not involved in the collection process, and was not participating in the collection of the debt.

Some debt collectors will prepare and mail a letter on behalf of a creditor for a fixed fee per letter. An argument may be made that the creditor is attempting to persuade the consumer that the debt collector is participating in the collection of the debt when the only interest of the debt collector is the fixed fee. Is collecting a fixed fee (called flat rating in the industry) sufficient participation? The commentary states that a debt collector is not violating this section if a flat fee is charged per letter providing the performance of other tasks associated with collection, such as handling verification requests, negotiating payment arrangements, and keeping individual records shows evidence *of participation* in the collection of the debt. If the debt collector merely received the mail, and delivered it to the creditor unopened, a violation would exist. To comply with this section, the mail must be opened and reviewed by the debt collector. The debt collector must negotiate payment arrangements, verify the debts, respond where appropriate and keep records.

USE OF INSIDE COUNSEL. A publisher markets recipe books to housewives across the country. The credit manager has been using outside collection agencies both on a contingency basis and by paying a flat rate for each collection letter. The results are average. One day she has lunch with the general counsel and suggests to the attorney that she would probably obtain better results if she could use a letter with the attorney's letterhead. The attorney resists immediately since he does not want to undertake this additional work. The credit manager persists and offers to write the letter, submit it to the attorney for approval, and then print and mail the letters, using a printed signature. The credit manager assures the attorney that she will handle all the correspondence and that the attorney will have absolutely no involvement in the collection process. The credit manager uses an address of a warehouse located several miles from the executive offices of the employer and uses a telephone number in her office. The letters are printed and mailed by the credit manager, and the results are exceptional.

The Act specifically states that if a creditor uses any name other than its own which would indicate that a third person is collecting or attempting to collect a debt, the creditor shall become subject to the Act. This section is thus also targeted at creditors who use their inside counsel to write collection letters to the consumer to indicate an independent attorney is being paid to collect the account. On the other hand, if the letter bore the same address as the creditor and stated at the bottom of the letter that the attorney was employed by the creditor or was house counsel, the creditor would not be using a name other than her own and no deception would be practiced upon the debtor. Of course, the impact of the collection letter would be decreased.

Credit managers know that transferring a debt to an outside collection agency, and especially to an attorney, increases the collection percentages. Creditors in the past created bogus collection agencies with addresses across the street. The creditor would write the letter using the bogus collection agency letterhead. The mail would be picked up and answered by employees of the creditor, and all payments are processed by employees of the creditor. The collection agency would have no employees, no staff, and no life of its own. This section of the Act was designed specifically to address and correct this problem of deceiving the consumer into believing an outside third party is collecting the debt.

Many businesses use their inside house counsel to send collection letters. The following are some guidelines, but reliance on these guidelines is no assurance of compliance since the case law is sparse on this subject. Compliance with "meaningful involvement" as set forth in the Cloman and Ruben case is also necessary:

a. The ethics committees of most state bar associations usually require an attorney to have control over any matter referred to the attorney and to have sufficient information to determine the validity of any claim made by a client. Under those circumstances, the attorney should review a listing of all the debts for which letters are sent and should be able to verify, supervise, and control all the activities which the office conducts on a day-to-day basis, and thus be "meaningfully involved."

b. If the counsel is an inside attorney employed by the creditor full time, the address on the stationery should be the address where the office is, i.e., the same address as the creditor. An attorney who is employed by a creditor is not shielded from liability when acting as a debt collector.[46]

c. Inside counsel should be identified as "house counsel" to be certain the consumer is not led to believe the attorney is outside counsel.

Since attorneys are covered by the Fair Debt Collection Practices Act, they are debt collectors, thus, they may write letters on their letterhead without thereafter instituting suit providing there is no wording in the letter which infers that suit will be started, such as "further action," "legal proceedings," "further steps," etc.

CREDIT AND COLLECTION TIP: *A creditor is exposed to two distinctly different risks by the operation of this section. First, if the creditor violates the law by using letters prepared by a debt collector who is not participating in the debt, the creditor immediately becomes subject to the Fair Debt Collection Practices Act; and second, by virtue of subdivision b, the creditor is in violation of the Act if the creditor deceives the consumer into believing someone other than the creditor is collecting the debt when such is not the case.*

---

[46]*Dorsey v. Morgan,* 760 F. Supp. 509 (1991).

DAMAGES

This section imposes civil liability for actual damages and additional damages up to $1,000. Attorneys' fees are recoverable for the successful party. A recent District court decision held that a debtor may only collect $1,000 in each suit, not for each violation.[47] Most Federal courts have followed this decision. The Act permits actions to be brought in federal or state courts within one year of the violation. Class action status (see Glossary) is available and in such an event the damages will not exceed the lesser of $500,000 or one percent of the net worth of the debt collector.

BONA FIDE ERROR

The debt collector may avoid liability if it can prove that it was an unintentional act and resulted from a bona fide error. Under those circumstances a debt collector can allege that if a violation did occur, it was an isolated violation and an unintentional act over which the debt collector had no control. The key to this defense is maintaining a procedure manual and monitoring the staff. One district court judge said it all: "I find generally that a program of constant on-the-job training, coupled with telephonic monitoring, supervision, and reference to a standardized manual is a procedure reasonably adopted to avoid violation of the Act."[48]

ATTORNEY FEES

A favorable decision to law firms and collection agencies was made by the Court of Appeals for the Fifth Circuit when it considered the question of whether to award attorney's fees after a technical violation of the Fair Debt Collection Practices Act with no award of actual damages. The court zeroed in on the wording in the Fair Debt Collection Practices Act which requires a "successful" action to support an award of attorney's fees.

The court reasoned that a violation is not "successful" if the plaintiff is unable to prove actual damages. This interpretation of the statute requires plaintiffs to seek more than technical violations before bringing suit. The court felt that this will deter suits brought only as a means of generating attorney's fees.

The court went on to state that the FDCPA will still punish errant debt collectors. The law mandates that the debt collector not only compensate the debtor fully for any monetary damages, emotional stress, or other injury that the debtor can prove the debt collector caused, but also allows the courts to assess punitive damages and requires the debt collector to pay the plaintiff's attorney's fees in

---

[47]*Wright v. Finance Service of Norwalk Inc.*, 996 F.2d 820 (6th Cir. 1993).

[48]See supra note 7.

addition to its own. Congress considered the risk of such punishment adequate to deter debt collectors from intentionally violating the Act.[49]

This decision may have an impact on the cottage industry of attorneys who are instituting suits against collection agencies and law firms for technical violations of the FDCPA. The states and districts most favorable to consumers (California, Illinois and New York) may not follow the Fifth Circuit (Louisiana, Texas and Mississippi).

Several decisions have been rendered making it more difficult for the consumer attorneys to obtain large awards for attorney's fees and statutory damages. In a recent California decision, the court identified three factors: "The frequency and persistence of the debt collector's non-compliance, the nature of such non-compliance, and the extent to which non-compliance was intentional." The court awarded only $700 in statutory damages.[50]

In several cases in the Western District of Wisconsin, the court held that the frequency and persistence of non-compliance only applies to the debt collector's actions as to the plaintiff and does not apply to the other persons adversely affected. In this instance the defendant admitted the liability and plaintiff did not even have to prove liability on defendant's part. The violation was also a technical violation and apparently did not include any claim for actual damages.[51]

In another case in West Virginia the judge awarded $200 in statutory damages and substantially reduced the attorney's fees.[52]

In Illinois, the court reduced attorney's fees from $26,857.50 to $7,000 apparently because the number of hours claimed to have been expended was totally unreasonable.[53]

From the above it should be clear that the courts are not being as generous as they used to be in connection with awarding attorney's fees on technical violations or in instances where the defendant has admitted the liability and the only question open is the statutory damages and the attorney's fees. Secondly, it seems that attorneys and collection agencies are becoming more aggressive in contesting the bills submitted by plaintiff's attorney at the conclusion of a case.

Defendants in these types of cases should not be so quick to settle in the $1,000 to $3,000 range after receiving a letter or a summons and complaint from the consumer attorney. Such a settlement only rewards the consumer attorney by paying an hourly rate of somewhere between $750 and $1,000 per hour. This type of settlement encourages the consumer attorney to write more letters and serve more summonses. On the other hand, if more collection agencies and attorneys contest these suits for technical violations, the consumer attorneys may be forced

---

[49]*Johnson v. Eaton*, 80 F.3d 148 (5th Cir. 1996).

[50]*Meszaros v. United Collection Corp.*, No. C 95-4634 THE, 1996 WL 346872 (N.D. Cal. June 14, 1996).

[51]*Beckham v. Midwest Billing Service Inc.* 95-C-915-C (October 29, 1996, W.D. Wisc.).

[52]*Shifflet v. Accelerated Recovery Sys., Inc.*, No. CIV A. 95-00070-C, 1996 WL 335379 (W.D. Va. May 23, 1996).

[53]*Purnell v. Kovitz Shifrin & Watzman*, No. 95 C 2554, 1996 WL 521401 (N.D. Ill. Sept. 11, 1996).

to seek their livelihood from other areas. Where the law firm or collection agency is wrong, money should be offered, but certainly should not exceed the value of the actual time that the consumer's attorney devoted to preparing the letter or complaint. If there is a technical violation, the same reasoning should be used. If the consumer attorney institutes suit on a technical violation, an admission of liability might succeed in significantly limiting the statutory damages and the attorney fees to a figure less than any settlement offer the consumer attorney would accept.

A defendant should not measure the settlement offer against the total exposure to attorney's fees for its own attorney, the attorney's fees for plaintiff's attorney, and the damages under the FDCPA. A defendant can always justify a settlement to the consumer comparing the settlement offer with this contingent liability. But in view of the many decisions rendered in favor of the defendant collection agencies and law firms, measuring a settlement offer on this theory only rewards the consumer attorney and at the same time encourages the attorney to assert more claims. Defendants should realize that the proper approach is to contest FDCPA claims where appropriate and make the consumer attorneys work for their fees. The awards to plaintiffs in many instances are significantly less than $1,000—and the awards for attorney fees are consistently being reduced. In some cases no amount was awarded for technical violations. Unless the violation is clear and is of the type to cause actual damage, consider all the alternatives before embarking on the settlement road.

CLASS ACTIONS

The most disturbing development under the Fair Debt Collections Practice Act is the recent significant increase in the number of class actions. One of the reasons may be a new publication by the National Consumer Law Center, the purpose of which is to teach consumer attorneys how to and when to institute class action suits. The book includes text, forms for complaints and pleadings, and checklists, as well as case citations.

The maximum damages recoverable in a class action under the FDCPA are 1% of the net worth of the debt collector or $500,000, whichever amount is lesser [15 USC 1692G, (a)2(B)] plus the attorney fees of plaintiff's counsel. If there are actual damages in the class action and the number in the class is large, the amount of damages may be significant. For this reason, the plaintiff's attorney will seek to sue the major collection agencies and the major law firms on the theory that 1% of their net worth will be a significant amount. The plaintiff's attorney also attempts to sue the principal of the collection agency or the senior partners of the law firm and join them individually in the law suit on the theory that the owners of the law firm or the collection agency also have significant net worth.

A class action is really composed of two elements: a motion to certify the class and the action to prove a violation of the Fair Debt Collection Practices Act with regard to the class. A separate suit against the defendant is asserted on behalf of the individual plaintiff.

In most instances the defendant collection agency or law firm will seek to involve their insurance company in the defense of the lawsuit. The exposure under a class action suit could be significant, depending upon the number included in the class and the complexity of the lawsuit. The exposure in a class action suit is limited to $500,000 or 1% of the net worth plus attorney fees, but the Act does not limit the amount of attorney's fees that the plaintiff's attorney seeks to recover, which may be substantial. Therefore, almost all defendants in a class action suit will utilize their insurance coverage unless the deductible is substantial.

The same letter containing the same violation sent to a large number of debtors presents an ideal situation for a plaintiff to assert a class action. Nevertheless, consumers' attorneys are faced with certain problems in having a class action certified.

A major defense to class certification is probably the de minimis recovery of the class members in a class action for violation of the Fair Debt Collection Practices Act. In most instances, the amount of recovery available to the class members is limited by the statutory maximum amount of recovery set at 1% of net worth of the debt collector.

For example, assume that the defendant has a net worth of $1,000,000, and the class consists of 1,000. If you multiply the net worth by 1%, the defendant is liable for the sum of $10,000. The defendant may argue that to recover $10 per class member ($10,000 divided by 1,000) is not in the best interest of the class member. If the class member instituted a suit individually under the Fair Debt Collection Practices Act, the individual could recover at least $1,000 in statutory damages (plus actual damages, if any) as opposed to recovering only $10 as a member of the class. The class action statute allows a member of the class to be removed from the class so that it can assert its own private action and the defendant will argue that most of the members of the class would recover more if they remove themselves from the class than if they remain members of the class.

While some courts have taken judicial notice of this argument and have denied class certification, most courts have examined this de minimis argument from an entirely different perspective. The courts acknowledge that members of a class would only receive $10 per individual but the members of the class would probably not institute a suit individually. Furthermore, the purpose of the act is to deter harassment and unconscionable and deceptive activities of the debt collector and the use of a class action achieves that purpose even though each member of the class would only receive $10.

Another element is the fact that the federal courts have been generous in awarding attorney's fees to the attorneys for the plaintiffs. If the plaintiffs are successful in certifying the class and obtaining an award for the members of the class of a de minimis amount, the defendants are still subject to an award for attorney's fees. In most of these cases, considerable discovery involving interrogatories, depositions and motions of both parties is required.

NET WORTH

We finally received a decision which defined the net worth of the defendant. The Fair Debt Collection Practices Act provides for damages in a class action up to 1% of the defendant corporation's net worth. In this particular case, the plaintiff argued that the net worth did not include good will and that the financial statement grossly understated the true value. In most instances, the net worth of collection agencies and law firms usually consist of the office equipment and the computer equipment in the office and often the computers, copy machines, printers, etc. are leased instead of being owned. Furthermore in small businesses, the principals tend to take out the profits either in salary or otherwise. In the particular case at hand, the defendants argued strenuously that the plaintiffs are entitled only to the net worth as measured and computed by the balance sheet. The court decided that Congress offered a simple, expedient process of determining damages by means of examining the financial statements which most businesses maintain. The court decided that to require the parties to spend thousands of dollars in expert fees just to help the court decide the appropriate recovery amount for the plaintiff would not be in the best interest of all parties. Therefore, the financial statement furnished by the defendant was the measurement for determining the net worth.[54]

OFFER OF JUDGMENT

If a suit is commenced by an individual (not a class action), the amount of recovery is limited to actual damages plus additional damages not exceeding $1,000— as determined by the court. If there are no actual damages, the limit of damage is $1,000. After suit is started, the defendant has available the offer of judgment, which is an offer to pay an amount of money.

The major problem for the defendant in an individual suit is that the plaintiff's attorney is generating attorney's fees which the defendant will have to pay; and the longer the defendant contests the case, the greater the attorney's fees of the plaintiff's attorney. An offer of judgment at the beginning of the suit may influence the judge when awarding the attorney's fees at the conclusion of the suit if the plaintiff rejects the offer of judgment and recovers the same or less than the offer of judgment. Thus, an offer of judgment of $1,000 plus enough attorney fees to cover the professional services already performed may stop the incurring of charges for attorney's fees to which the plaintiff's attorney will be entitled.

---

[54]*Sanders vs. Jackson C.A.*, 33 F. Supp. 2d 693 (7th Cir., 1998). *Continental Webb Press Inc. vs. NRLB*, 767 F. 2d 321 (7th Cir. 1984).

TRANSFER OF LOAN PORTFOLIOS

The purchase of loan portfolios is common in today's banking and institutional environment. When the loan portfolio is bought for servicing and collecting and the accounts are not in default, the creditor is collecting for its own account and is not subject to the Fair Debt Collection Practices Act. If the great majority of the loans are in default or if the entire portfolio of loans is in default, the creditor is subject to the provisions of the Act. The question left unanswered is what percentage of default turns the loan portfolio into a defaulted loan portfolio.

The normal loan portfolio at the original lending institution contains 2% to 5% of defaulted loans. Suppose half of that loan portfolio was sold and the remaining half of the loan portfolio included all the defaulted loans, so that the defaulted loans approach 10%. Would that turn the entire loan portfolio into a defaulted loan portfolio, so that the purchaser would be subject to the provisions of the Act? We do not know of any case that has addressed this problem.

A market exists for the sale of accounts that are barred by the Statute of Limitations. But whether efforts to collect on these out of statute debts is a violation of the FDCPA is still an open question. In a recent case in the 7th Circuit, a judge refused to dismiss a FDCPA action in which the main allegation was that the agency had violated the act by attempting to collect time barred debts. In most states, a debtor must assert the fact that the debt is time barred as an affirmative defense. One prior case had held that an agency did violate the FDCPA when it filed suit on a claim that was outside of the Statute of Limitations, despite the agency's argument that the debtor was supposed to assert it as an affirmative defense in his pleadings.

In any event, in the recent case the judge dismissed the motion for summary judgment and did not rule on the question of whether an agency can or cannot send dunning letters on time barred debts. There will be other litigation on this point because of the fact that the debt portfolios of time barred debts continue to be sold.[55]

EVICTION NOTICE

In the United States District Court of the Southern District, a decision was rendered that a three-day eviction notice required under New York State law was a violation of the Fair Debt Collection Practices Act, since it was a communication relating to a debt and failed to conform to the Act because it did not contain a validation notice or the mini-miranda warning. In a subsequent opinion regarding a certification for a interlocutory appeal, the judge acknowledged the fact that there is a conflict between the circuits as to whether an obligation must involve the

---

[55]*Stepney v. Outsourcing Solutions, Inc.*, No. 97C52288, 1997 WL 722972, (N.D. Ill. Nov. 13, 1997).

deferral of a payment to constitute a debt within the meaning of the Fair Debt Collection Practices Act. Rent is payable in advance and to pay rent is not one involving deferral of a payment.

The court took judicial notice of the position of the Federal Trade Commission that a notice "required by law as a prerequisite to enforce the contractual obligation between creditor and debtor, by judicial or non-judicial legal process" is not a communication within the meaning of the FDCPA. The three-day notice at issue was required by Section 711 of the New York Real Property Actions and Procedure Law as a prerequisite to the institution of summary proceedings for non-payment. The judge acknowledged that if the court adopted the FTC's view, the complaint would have been dismissed. After acknowledging that the attorneys would probably not wait thirty days to commence eviction proceedings and acknowledging further that the landlord clients would probably sign the eviction notices themselves, the major concern for prompt review seems to be the that attorneys representing tenants on non-payment proceedings are seeking to use these alleged violations of the FDCPA to seek dismissal of otherwise meritorious petitions.[56]

The judge allowed the appeal, and the Circuit Court of Appeals affirmed.

RECOMMENDED LETTER

In a decision in the 7th Circuit Court of Appeals in 1997, Chief Judge Posner set forth in the opinion a letter which it declared to be "safe" from violation of the FDCPA if used within the jurisdiction of the 7th Circuit (Indiana, Illinois, Wisconsin). The court said that they were "simply trying to provide some guidance on how to comply with it" (FDCPA). The letter reads as follows:

Dear (Consumer),

I have been retained by Medicard Services to collect from you the entire balance which as of September 25, 1995 was $1656.90, that you owe Medicard Services on your MasterCard account #5414701617068749.

If you want to resolve this matter without a lawsuit, you must, within one week of the date of this letter, either pay Medicard $316 against the balance that you owe (unless you paid it since your last statement) or call Medicard at 1-800-221-5920 Ext. 6130 and work out arrangements of payment. If you do neither of these things I will be entitled to file a lawsuit against you, for the collection of this debt when the week is over.

Federal Law gives you thirty days after you receive this letter to dispute the validity of the debt or any part of it. If you don't dispute within that period, I'll assume that it's valid. If you do dispute it - by notifying me in writing to that effect

---

[56]*Romea v. Heilberger & Associates*, 988 F. Supp. 712 (S.D.N.Y. 1997).

- I will, as required by the law, obtain and mail to you proof of the debt. And if, within the same period, you request in writing the name and address of your original creditor, if the original creditor is different from the current creditor (Medicard Services) I will furnish you with that information too.

The law does not require me to wait until the end of the thirty day period before suing you to collect this debt. If, however you request proof of the debt or the name and address of the original creditor within the thirty day period that begins with your receipt of this letter, the law requires me to suspend my efforts (through litigation or otherwise) to collect the debt until I mail the requested information to you.

Sincerely,

(Collection Attorney)

Judge Posner is regarded as one of the more respected members of the Circuit Court of Appeals of the 7th Circuit and the court is terribly frustrated with the suits for technical violations of the FDCPA. Nevertheless, debt collectors may have serious problems in other circuits with the letter he propounded.[57]

Certainly questions of overshadowing appear in the letter because of the suit threat during the thirty day period and there is some confusion in the letter as to the requirement of a notification in writing. The author does not recommend the use of this type of a letter in any of the other circuits other than the 7th and it's not even certain that other judges in the 7th Circuit would feel the same way as Judge Posner in considering the letter "safe."

Some of the other possible violations of the FDCPA include the following:

1. The fact that the letter did not include a mini-miranda warning as required under Section 807 (11).

2. The fact that payment was demanded within one week instead of thirty days.

3. The thirty day validation notice was somewhat confusing and an unsophisticated debtor might be lead to believe that to dispute the validity of the debt adequately under the law, they would be required to dispute in writing.

4. The fact the debtor was to pay the client or contact the client, for the debt collector may not be "meaningfully involved."

REGISTRATION OF ATTORNEYS

Connecticut is fundamentally the only state that enforces a law requiring attorneys to register with the Banking Commissioner and thereafter to be licensed. In

---

[57]*Bartlett v. Heibl,* 128 F.3d 497 (7th Cir. 1997).

addition, it requires you to post a bond and file significant information with the state. Connecticut also requires you to deposit all collections in Connecticut banks. The National Association of Retail Collection Attorneys in one of its recent articles offered that several other states may require attorneys collecting debts across state lines to obtain a license or bond. The main problem with some of these state laws is that the statute refers to a "debt collector" rather than to a collection agency. Thus, wherever the words "debt collector" or words of similar import are mentioned, the statute may or may not be applicable to an attorney who collects debts. On the other hand, most of these state statutes have exemptions for certain types of debts, exemptions for out-of-state attorneys, and other provisions that may exempt the attorney from complying with the requirements of the statute. Furthermore, to the author's knowledge none of the other states are actively enforcing these statutes against out-of-state attorneys.

Out-of-state attorneys must tread lightly in Connecticut because there are two court decisions, one of which stating that an out-of-state attorney must be licensed and the second one stating that if an out-of-state attorney is not licensed, then the out-of-state attorney automatically violates the Fair Debt Collection Practices Act.[58]

On the other hand, we now have several decisions by other circuits that a failure to be licensed is not per se a violation of the Fair Debt Collection Practices Act unless there is some other activity that actually violates the act. (See the later section on *Licensing*). The failure to license alone is not sufficient to constitute a violation of the act. Since these decisions, the consumer attorneys are not so quick to institute suits where there is a failure to be licensed. In Connecticut the story is totally different and the consumer attorneys are alert to an attorney who collects in Connecticut without being registered.

Although the author has not reviewed all of these statutes, the National Association of Retail Collection Attorneys newsletter recommends that attorneys should review:

Colorado	(Colo. Rev. Stat Sec. 12-14-103(e);
Connecticut	(Conn. Gen. Stat. Sec. 42-127a(a);
Conn. Credit Collection Act, 5-36-4851;	
Florida	(Fla. Stat. Ann. Chp. 559.55);
Indiana	(Ind. Code Sec. 26-2201);
Maine	(Me. Rev. Stat. Ann. 32 Sec. 11001);
Massachusetts	(Mass. Gen. L. c. 93 Sec. 24);
Maryland	(Md. Code Ann.BR 7-101);

---

[58]*Gaetano v. Payco,* 774 F. Supp. 1404 (D. Conn. 1990); *Sharinn & Lipshie P.C. et al v. Brian Woolf,* No. 3:95 CV 00265, (U.S.D.C. Conn. May 21, 1995).

Nevada	(Nev. Rev. Stat. Sec. 649.005);
Washington	(Wash. Rev. Code Sec. 19.16);
Wisconsin	(Wis. Stat. Ann. Sec. 218.04);
West Virginia	(W. Va. Code Sec. 46A-2-101);
Wyoming	(Wyo. Stat. Sec. 33-11-101)

LICENSING

In an unpublished opinion, the 9th Circuit Court of Appeals in California decided that the mere fact that a collection agency failed to be licensed in the state is not sufficient to constitute a violation of the Fair Debt Collection Practices Act, unless the particular activities in the complaint actually did violate the FDCPA separate and apart from the licensing statute. The judges considered the Commerce Clause of the U.S. Constitution and discussed the economic protection engaged in by the state of Nevada which was designed to benefit in-state economic interests by burdening out-of-state competition, and cited a Supreme Court case, *New Energy Company v. Linebach,* 486 U.S. 269 (1988). The particular statute even prohibited all contacts by an unlicensed agency even where the defendant made an inquiry concerning a debt reported to a credit reporting agency.[59]

This court seems to follow a prior Circuit Court of Appeals case in California which held that the court must first determine if it was a prohibited activity under the FDCPA and clearly stated that collection practices by an unlicensed agency were not of themselves a violation of the FDCPA.[60] These cases in the Circuit Court of Appeals in California fly in the face of the Connecticut case which was decided in 1990 and held that a violation of the state licensing law does create a violation of the FDCPA.[61]

Whether these California cases will persuade other circuits to follow or whether Connecticut will prevail, only time will tell. Perhaps the Supreme Court will decide the issue.

A recent case out of Virginia produced a startling result in that the court ignored the literal reading of the statute. The statute read that a debt collector shall not engage in conduct deemed to be the practice of law unless he is licensed as an attorney in the State of West Virginia. In short, the statute effectively prevented out-of-state attorneys from sending letters to consumers in the State of West Virginia. The court stated that the statute was not designed to regulate the practice of law nor increase the business for West Virginia attorneys and refused to believe

---

[59]*Codar, Inc. v. State of Ariz.,* 95 F.3d 1156 (9the Cir. 1996).

[60]*Wade v. Regional Credit Ass'n,* 87 F.3d 1098 (9the Cir. 1996).

[61]*Gaetano v. Payco of Wis., Inc.,* 774 F. Supp. 1404 (D. Conn. 1990).

that the legislature intended to limit out-of-state attorneys' ability to mail correspondence on behalf of a client that was directed to a West Virginia consumer.[62]

DON'T KILL THE MESSENGER

Finally, one consumer attorney instituted a suit against the deliverer of a collection message, Western Union, as well as the collection agency that sent the message. The court held that those parties who exercised control of the letters can be considered debt collectors, but not those people who merely deliver the message. The mere the fact that Western Union knew that it was a collection notice was not sufficient to cause Western Union to be a debt collector. At least in this instance, they did not kill the messenger.[63]

AFFILIATED COMPANY LIABILITY

Hospitals have been involved in several suits where they have affiliated collection agencies which are a hundred percent controlled by the hospital. Under the Fair Debt Collection Practices Act, the consumer argues that the hospital controls the agency and this misleads the consumer. A corporation may use a corporate affiliate to collect the corporation's debts using the corporate affiliate's names. In some instances the situation operates in inverse order where the subsidiary refers its accounts to the parent and the parent collects its debts. With regard to the latter situation, a corporation may use a corporate affiliate to collect the corporation's debts using the corporate affiliate's name. Where the parent owned a hundred percent of the subsidiary and was collecting the subsidiary's debt, the parent qualifies for the exception of the definition of debt collector. This is because the subsidiary is related to the parent and the parent was only collecting debts for the subsidiary and other related entities owned by the parent and the parent's principal business was not necessarily debt collection. Nevertheless, if the affiliation is not clearly spelled out, the parent could be liable on the basis of designing, compiling or furnishing forms, knowing such form would be used to create the false belief in a consumer that a person other than a creditor is participating in the collection of the debt as set forth in section 1692J (a).[64]

---

[62]*Chevy Chase Bank v. William C. McCamant*, 512 S.E. 2d 217 (W.Va. 1998).

[63]*Dolores Aquino v. Credit Control Services*, 4 F. Supp. 2d 927 (N.D. Cal. 1998).

[64]*Taylor v. Rollins*, 1998 WL 164890 (N.D. Ill. 1998); *Aubert v. American General Finance*, 137 F.3d 976 (7th Cir. 1998); *Wells v. McDonough NPC*, 1999 WL 162796 (N.D. Ill); *Hannison v. NBD*, 968 F. Supp. 837 (EDNY 1997).

Where the creditor has set up an affiliated collection agency, the question revolves around whether the agency is collecting debts for other third parties or just for the creditor. In all these situations the creditor is also faced with the issue of whether the creditor is maintaining control over the operations of the agency. This is often an issue of fact, although stock ownership of the agency usually is not a factor nor is the fact that individuals from the creditor serve on the board of directors of the agency. Nevertheless, the courts are not in agreement on this particular issue and sometimes the court will look at a violation of the section 1692J(a) of the FDCPA rather than look at the question of affiliation. Citicorp was using a wholly owned subsidiary and sent a letter under the name of the subsidiary. Despite the fact that Citicorp stated in the letter that the subsidiary was a unit of CRS (Citicorp Retail Services), the appellate court held that designation that it was a unit of CRS may not have necessarily been enough to inform an unsophisticated consumer. The facts in the cases are somewhat different, but in this instance the court did not agree with the court in Taylor v. Rollins which stated that if the principal business was not debt collection and it only provided services for related entities, it could not be in violation of the Fair Debt Collection Practices Act.[65]

---

[65]*McQuire v. Citicorp Retail Services*, 147 F.3d 232 (2nd Cir. 1998).

CHAPTER 11
APPENDIX I

The Fair Debt Collection Practices Act As Amended by Public Law 104-208, 110 Stat. 3009 (Sept. 30, 1996)

AN ACT

Sept. 20, 1977
[H.R. 5294]

To amend the Consumer Credit Protection Act to prohibit abusive practices by debt collectors.

Consumer Credit Protection Act, amendments

Be in enacted by the Senate and House of Representatives of the United States of America in Congress assembled, That the Consumer Credit Protection Act (15 U.S.C. 1601 et seq.) is amended by adding at the end thereof the following new title:

Fair Debt Collection Practices Act

TITLE VIII—DEBT COLLECTION PRACTICES

818.   Effective date

15 USC 1601
note

§ 801. Short Title
This title may be cited as the "Fair Debt Collection Practices Act."

15 USC 1692

§ 802. Congressional findings and declaration of purpose

(a) There is abundant evidence of the use of abusive, deceptive, and unfair debt collection practices by many debt collectors. Abusive debt collection practices contribute to the number of personal bankruptcies, to marital instability, to the loss of jobs, and to invasions of individual privacy.

(b) Existing laws and procedures for redressing these injuries are inadequate to protect consumers.

(c) Means other than misrepresentation or other abusive debt collection practices are available for the effective collection of debts.

(d) Abusive debt collection practices are carried on to a substantial extent in interstate commerce and through means and instrumentalities of such commerce. Even where abusive debt collection practices are purely intrastate in character, they nevertheless directly affect interstate commerce.

(e) It is the purpose of this title to eliminate abusive debt collection practices by debt collectors, to insure that those debt collectors who refrain from using abusive debt collection practices are not competitively disadvantaged, and to promote consistent State action to protect consumers against debt collection abuses.

15 USC 1692a

§ 803. Definitions
As used in this title—

(1) The term "Commission" means the Federal Trade Commission.

(2) The term "communication" means the conveying of information regarding a debt directly or indirectly to any person through any medium.

(3) The term "consumer" means any natural person obligated or allegedly obligated to pay any debt.

(4) The term "creditor" means any person who offers or extends credit creating a debt or to whom a debt is owed, but such term does not include any person to the extent that he receives an assignment or transfer of a debt in default solely for the purpose of facilitating collection of such debt for another.

(5) The term "debt" means any obligation or alleged obligation of a consumer to pay money arising out of a transaction in which the money, property, insurance or services which are the subject of the transaction are primarily for personal, family, or household purposes, whether or not such obligation has been reduced to judgment.

(6) The term "debt collector" means any person who uses any instrumentality of interstate commerce or the mails in any business the principal purpose of which is the collection of any debts, or who regularly collects or attempts to collect, directly or indirectly, debts owed or due or asserted to be owed or due another. Notwithstanding the exclusion provided by clause (f) of the last sentence of this paragraph, the term includes any creditor who, in the process of collecting his own debts, uses any name other than his own which would indicate that a third person is collecting or attempting to collect such debts. For the purpose of section 808(6), such term also includes any person who uses any instrumentality of interstate commerce or the mails in any business the principal purpose of which is the enforcement of security interests. The term does not include—

(A) any officer or employee of a creditor while, in the name of the creditor, collecting debts for such creditor;

(B) any person while acting as a debt collector for another person, both of whom are related by common ownership or affiliated by corporate control, if the person acting as a debt collector does so only for persons to whom it is so related or affiliated and if the principal business of such person is not the collection of debts;

(C) any officer or employee of the United States or any State to the extent that collecting or attempting to collect any debt is in the performance of his official duties;

(D) any person while serving or attempting to serve legal process on any other person in connection with the judicial enforcement of any debt;

(E) any nonprofit organization which, at the request of consumers, performs bona fide consumer credit counseling and assists consumers in the liquidation of their debts by receiving payments from such consumers and distributing such amounts to creditors; and

(F) any person collecting or attempting to collect any debt owed or due or asserted to be owed or due another to the extent such activity (i) is incidental to a bona fide fiduciary obligation or a bona fide escrow arrangement; (ii) concerns a debt which was originated by such person; (iii) concerns a debt which was not in default at the time it was obtained by such person; or (iv) concerns a debt obtained by such person as a secured party in a commercial credit transaction involving the creditor.

(7) The term "location information" means a consumer's place of abode and his telephone number at such place, or his place of employment.

(8) The term "State" means any State, territory, or possession of the United States, the District of Columbia, the Commonwealth of Puerto Rico, or any political subdivision of any of the foregoing.

15 USC 1692b

§ 804. Acquisition of location information

Any debt collector communicating with any person other than the consumer for the purpose of acquiring location information about the consumer shall—

(1) identify himself, state that he is confirming or correcting location information concerning the consumer, and only if expressly requested, identify his employer;

(2) not state that such consumer owes any debt;

(3) not communicate with any such person more than once unless the debt collector reasonably believes that the earlier response of such person is erroneous or incomplete and that such person now has correct or complete location information;

(4) not communicate by post card;

(5) not use any language or symbol on any envelope or in the contents of any communication effected by the mails or telegram that indicates that the debt collector is in the debt collection business or that the communication relates to the collection of a debt; and

(6) after the debt collector knows the consumer is represented by an attorney with regard to the subject debt and has knowledge of, or can readily ascertain, such attorney's name and address, not communicate with any person other than that attorney, unless the attorney fails to respond within a reasonable period of time to the communication from the debt collector.

15 USC 1692c

§ 805. Communication in connection with debt collection

(a) COMMUNICATION WITH THE CONSUMER GENERALLY. Without the prior consent of the consumer given directly to the debt collector or the express permission of a court or competent jurisdiction, a debt collector may not communicate with a consumer in connection with the collection of any debt—

(1) at any unusual time or place or a time or place known or which should be known to be inconvenient to the consumer. In the absence of knowledge of circumstances to the contrary, a debt collector shall assume that the convenient time for communicating with a consumer is after 8 o'clock antimeridian and before 9 o'clock postmeridian, local time at the consumer's location;

(2) if the debt collector knows the consumer is represented by an attorney with respect to such debt and has knowledge of, or can readily ascertain, such attorney's name and address, unless the attorney fails to respond within a reasonable period of time to a communication from the debt collector or unless the attorney consents to direct communication with the consumer; or

(3) at the consumer's place of employment if the debt collector knows or has reason to know that the consumer's employer prohibits the consumer from receiving such communication.

(b) COMMUNICATION WITH THIRD PARTIES. Except as provided in section 804, without the prior consent of the consumer given directly to the debt collector, or the express permission of a court of competent jurisdiction, or as reasonably necessary to effectuate a postjudgment judicial remedy, a debt collector may not communicate, in connection with the collection of any debt, with any person other than a consumer, his attorney, a consumer reporting agency if otherwise permitted by law, the creditor, the attorney of the creditor, or the attorney of the debt collector.

(c) CEASING COMMUNICATION. If a consumer notifies a debt collector in writing that the consumer refuses to pay a debt or that the consumer wishes the debt collector to cease further communication with the consumer, the debt collector shall not communicate further with the consumer with respect to such debt, except—

(1) to advise the consumer that the debt collector's further efforts are being terminated;

(2) to notify the consumer that the debt collector or creditor may invoke specified remedies which are ordinarily invoked by such debt collector or creditor; or

(3) where applicable, to notify the consumer that the debt collector or creditor intends to invoke a specified remedy.

If such notice from the consumer is made by mail, notification shall be complete upon receipt.

(d) For the purpose of this section, the term "consumer" includes the consumer's spouse, parent (if the consumer is a minor), guardian, executor, or administrator.

15 USC 1692d

§ 806. Harassment or abuse

A debt collector may not engage in any conduct the natural consequence of which is to harass, oppress, or abuse any person in connection with the collection of a debt. Without limiting the general application of the foregoing, the following conduct is a violation of this section:

(1) The use or threat of use of violence or other criminal means to harm the physical person, reputation, or property of any person.

(2) The use of obscene or profane language or language the natural consequence of which is to abuse the hearer or reader.

(3) The publication of a list of consumers who allegedly refuse to pay debts, except to a consumer reporting agency or to persons meeting the requirements of section 603(f) or 604(3)[1] of this Act.

(4) The advertisement for sale of any debt to coerce payment of the debt.

(5) Causing a telephone to ring or engaging any person in telephone conversation repeatedly or continuously with intent to annoy, abuse, or harass any person at the called number.

(6) Except as provided in section 804, the placement of telephone calls without meaningful disclosure of the caller's identity.

15 USC 1692e

§ 807. False or misleading representations

A debt collector may not use any false, deceptive, or misleading representation or means in connection with the collection of any debt. Without limiting the general application of the foregoing, the following conduct is a violation of this section:

(1) The false representation or implication that the debt collector is vouched for, bonded by, or affiliated with the United States or any State, including the use of any badge, uniform, or facsimile thereof.

(2) The false representation of—

(A) the character, amount, or legal status of any debt; or

(B) any services rendered or compensation which may be lawfully received by any debt collector for the collection of a debt.

(3) The false representation or implication that any individual is an attorney or that any communication is from an attorney.

(4) The representation or implication that nonpayment of any debt will result in the arrest or imprisonment of any person or

---

[1]So in original; however, should read "604(a)(3)."

the seizure, garnishment, attachment, or sale of any property or wages of any person unless such action is lawful and the debt collector or creditor intends to take such action.

(5) The threat to take any action that cannot legally be taken or that is not intended to be taken.

(6) The false representation or implication that a sale, referral, or other transfer of any interest in a debt shall cause the consumer to—

(A) lose any claim or defense to payment of the debt; or

(B) become subject to any practice prohibited by this title.

(7) The false representation or implication that the consumer committed any crime or other conduct in order to disgrace the consumer.

(8) Communicating or threatening to communicate to any person credit information which is known or which should be known to be false, including the failure to communicate that a disputed debt is disputed.

(9) The use or distribution of any written communication which simulates or is falsely represented to be a document authorized, issued, or approved by any court, official, or agency of the United States or any State, or which creates a false impression as to its source, authorization, or approval.

(10) The use of any false representation or deceptive means to collect or attempt to collect any debt or to obtain information concerning a consumer.

(11) The failure to disclose in the initial written communication with the consumer, and in addition, if the initial communication with the consumer is oral, in that initial oral communication, that the debt collector is attempting to collect a debt and that any information obtained will be used for that purpose, and the failure to disclose in subsequent communications that the communication is from a debt collector, except that this paragraph shall not apply to a formal pleading made in connection with a legal action.

(12) The false representation or implication that accounts have been turned over to innocent purchasers for value.

(13) The false representation or implication that documents are legal process.

(14) The use of any business, company, or organization name other than the true name of the debt collector's business, company, or organization.

(15) The false representation or implication that documents are not legal process forms or do not require action by the consumer.

(16) The false representation or implication that a debt collector operates or is employed by a consumer reporting agency as defined by section 603(f) of this Act.

15 USC 1692f

§ 808. Unfair practices

A debt collector may not use unfair or unconscionable means to collect or attempt to collect any debt. Without limiting the general application of the foregoing, the following conduct is a violation of this section:

(1) The collection of any amount (including any interest, fee, charge, or expense incidental to the principal obligation) unless such amount is expressly authorized by the agreement creating the debt or permitted by law.

(2) The acceptance of a debt collector from any person of a check or other payment instrument postdated by more than five days unless such person is notified in writing of the debt collector's intent to deposit such check or instrument not more than ten nor less than three business days prior to such deposit.

(3) The solicitation of a debt collector of any postdated check or other postdated payment instrument for the purpose of threatening or instituting criminal prosecution.

(4) Depositing or threatening to deposit any postdated check or other postdated instrument prior to the date on such check or instrument.

(5) Causing charges to be made to any person for communications by concealment of the true propose of the communication. Such charges include, but are not limited to, collect telephone calls and telegram fees.

(6) Taking or threatening to take any nonjudicial action to effect dispossession or disablement of property if—

(A) there is not present right to possession of the property claimed as collateral through an enforcement security interest;

(B) there is no present intention to take possession of the property; or

(C) the property is exempt by law from such dispossession or disablement.

(7) Communicating with a consumer regarding a debt by post card.

(8) Using any language or symbol, other than the debt collector's address, on any envelope when communicating with a consumer by use of the mails or by telegram, except that a debt collector may use his business name if such name does not indicate that he is in the debt collection business.

15 USC 1692g

§ 809. Validation of debts

(a) Within five days after the initial communication with a consumer in connection with the collection of any debt, a debt collector shall, unless the following information is contained in the initial communication or the consumer has paid the debt, send the consumer a written notice containing—

(1) the amount of the debt;

(2) the name of the creditor to whom the debt is owed;

(3) a statement that unless the consumer, within thirty days after receipt of the notice, disputes the validity of the debt, or any portion thereof, the debt will be assumed to be valid by the debt collector;

(4) a statement that if the consumer notifies the debt collector in writing within the thirty-day period that the debt, or any portion thereof, is disputed, the debt collector will obtain verification of the debt or a copy of a judgment against the consumer and a copy of such verification or judgment will be mailed to the consumer by the debt collector; and

(5) a statement that, upon the consumer's written request within the thirty-day period, the debt collector will provide the consumer with the name and address of the original creditor, if different from the current creditor.

(b) If the consumer notifies the debt collector in writing within the thirty-day period described in subsection (a) that the debt, or any portion thereof, is disputed, or that the consumer requests the name and address of the original creditor, the debt collector shall cease collection of the debt, or any disputed portion thereof, until the debt collector obtains verification of the debt or any copy of a judgment, or the name and address of the original creditor, and a cop of such verification or judgment, or name and address of the original creditor, is mailed to the consumer by the debt collector.

(c) The failure of a consumer to dispute the validity of a debt under this section may not be construed by any court as an admission of liability by the consumer.

15 USC 1692h

§ 810. Multiple debts

If any consumer owes multiple debts and makes any single payment to any debt collector with respect to such debts, such debt collector may not apply such payment to any debt which is disputed by the consumer and, where applicable, shall apply such payment in accordance with the consumer's directions.

§ 811. Legal actions by debt collectors

(a) Any debt collector who brings any legal action on a debt against any consumer shall—

    (1) in the case of an action to enforce an interest in real property securing the consumer's obligation, bring such action only in a judicial district or similar legal entity in which such real property is located; or

    (2) in the case of an action not described in paragraph (1), bring such action only in the judicial district or similar legal entity—

        (A) in which such consumer signed the contract sued upon; or

        (B) in which such consumer resides at the commencement of the action.

(b) Nothing in this title shall be construed to authorize the bringing of legal actions by debt collectors.

§ 812. Furnishing certain deceptive forms

(a) It is unlawful to design, compile, and furnish any form knowing that such form would be used to create the false belief in a consumer that a person other than the creditor of such consumer is participating in the collection of or in an attempt to collect a debt such consumer allegedly owes such creditor, when in fact such person is not so participating.

(b) Any person who violates this section shall be liable to the same extent and in the same manner as a debt collector is liable under section 813 for failure to comply with a provision of this title.

§ 813. Civil liability

(a) Except as otherwise provided by this section, any debt collector who fails to comply with any provision of this title with respect to any person is liable to such person in an amount equal to the sum of—

    (1) any actual damage sustained by such person as a result of such failure;

    (2) (A) in the case of any action by an individual, such additional damages as the court may allow, but not exceeding $1,000; or

        (B) in the case of a class action, (i) such amount for each named plaintiff as could be recovered under subparagraph (A), and (ii) such amount as the court may allow for all other class members, without regard to a minimum individual recovery, not to exceed the lesser of $500,000 or 1 per centum of the net worth of the debt collector; and

(3) in the case of any successful action to enforce the foregoing liability, the costs of the action, together with a reasonable attorney's fee as determined by the court. On a finding by the court that an action under this section was brought in bad faith and for the purpose of harassment, the court may award to the defendant attorney's fees reasonable in relation to the work expended and costs.

(b) In determining the amount of liability in any action under subsection (a), the court shall consider, among other relevant factors—

(1) in any individual action under subsection (a)(2)(A), the frequency and persistence of noncompliance by the debt collector, the nature of such noncompliance, and the extent to which such noncompliance was intentional; or

(2) in any class action under subsection (a)(2)(B), the frequency and persistence of noncompliance by the debt collector, the nature of such noncompliance, the resources of the debt collector, the number of persons adversely affected, and the extent to which the debt collector's noncompliance was intentional.

(c) A debt collector may not be held liable in any action brought under this title if the debt collector shows by a preponderance of evidence that the violation was not intentional and resulted from a bona fide error notwithstanding the maintenance of procedures reasonably adapted to avoid any such error.

(d) An action to enforce any liability created by this title may be brought in any appropriate United States district court without regard to the amount in controversy, or in any other court of competent jurisdiction, within one year from the date on which the violation occurs.

(e) No provision of this section imposing any liability shall apply to any act done or omitted in good faith in conformity with any advisory opinion of the Commission, notwithstanding that after such act or omission has occurred, such opinion is amended, rescinded, or determined by judicial or other authority to be invalid for any reason.

15 USC 1692l

§ 814. Administrative enforcement

(a) Compliance with this title shall be enforced by the Commission, except to the extend that enforcement of the requirements imposed under this title is specifically committed to another agency under subsection (b). For purpose of the exercise by the Commission of its functions and powers under the Federal Trade Commission Act, a violation of this title shall be deemed in unfair or deceptive act or practice in violation of that Act. All of the functions and powers of the Commission under the Federal Trade Commission Act are available to the Commission to enforce compliance by any person with this title, irrespective of whether that person is engaged in commerce or meets any other jurisdictional tests in the Federal Trade Commission Act, including the power to enforce the provisions of this title in the same manner as if the violation had been a violation of a Federal Trade Commission trade regulation rule.

(b) Compliance with any requirements imposed under this title shall be enforced under—

(1) section 8 of the Federal Deposit Insurance Act, in the case of—

(A) national banks, by the Comptroller of the Currency;

(B) member banks of the Federal Reserve System (other than national banks), by the Federal Reserve Board; and

(C) banks the deposits or accounts of which are insured by the Federal Deposit Insurance Corporation (other than members of the Federal Reserve System), by the Board of Directors of the Federal Deposit Insurance Corporations;

(2) section 5(d) of the Home Owners Loan Act of 1933, section 407 of the National Housing Act, and sections 6(i) and 17 of the Federal Home Loan Bank Act, by the Federal Home Loan Bank Board (acting directing or through the Federal Savings and Loan Insurance Corporation), in the case of any institution subject to any of those provisions;

(3) the Federal Credit Union Act, by the Administrator of the National Credit Union Administration with respect to any Federal credit union;

(4) subtitle IV of Title 49, by the Interstate Commerce Commission with respect to any common carrier subject to such subtitle;

(5) the Federal Aviation Act 1958, by the Secretary of Transportation with respect to any air carrier or any foreign carrier subject to that Act; and

(6) the Packers and Stockyards Act, 1921 (except as provided in section 406 of that Act), by the Secretary of Agriculture with respect to any activities subject to that Act.

(c) For the purpose of the exercise by any agency referred to in subsection (b) of its powers under any Act referred to in that subsection, a violation of any requirement imposed under this title shall be deemed to be a violation of a requirement imposed under that Act. In addition to its powers under any provision of law specifically referred to in subsection (b), each of the agencies referred to in that subsection may exercise, for the purpose of enforcing compliance with any requirement imposed under this title any other authority conferred on it by law, except as provided in subsection (d).

(d) Neither the Commission nor any other agency referred to in subsection (b) may promulgate trade regulation rules or other regulations with respect to the collection of debts by debt collectors as defined in this title.

15 USC 1692m

§ 815. Reports to Congress by the Commission

(a) Not later than one year after the effective date of this title and at one-year intervals thereafter, the Commission shall make reports to the Congress concerning the administration of its functions under this title, including such recommendations as the Commission deems necessary or appropriate. In addition, each report of the Commission shall include its assessment of the extent to which compliance with this title is being achieved and a summary of the enforcement actions taken by the Commission under section 814 of this title.

(b) In the exercise of its functions under this title, the Commission may obtain upon request the views of any other Federal agency which exercises enforcement functions under section 814 of this title.

15 USC 1692n

§ 816. Relation to State laws

This title does not annul, alter, or affect, or exempt any person subject to the provisions of this title from complying with the laws of any State with respect to debt collection practices, except to the extent that those laws are inconsistent with any provision of this title, and then only to the extent of the inconsistency. For purposes of this section, a State law is not inconsistent with this title if the protection such law affords any consumer is greater than the protection provided by this title.

15 USC 1692o

§ 817. Exemption for State regulation

The Commission shall by regulation exempt from the requirements of this title any class of debt collection practices within any State if the Commission determines that under the law of that State that class of debt collection practices is subject to requirements substantially similar to those imposed by this title, and that there is adequate provision for enforcement.

15 USC 1692p

§ 818. Effective date

This title takes effect upon the expiration of six months after the date of its enactment, but section 809 shall apply only with respect to debts for which the initial attempt to collect occurs after such effective date.

Approved September 20, 1977.

LEGISLATIVE HISTORY:
Public Law 95-109 [H.R. 5294]
HOUSE REPORT No. 95-131
    (Comm. on Banking, Finance, and Urban Affairs).
SENATE REPORT No. 95-382
    (Comm. on Banking, Housing, and Urban Affairs).
CONGRESSIONAL RECORD, Vol. 123 (1977):
    Apr. 4, considered and passed House.
    Aug. 5, considered and passed Senate, amended.
    Sept. 8, House agreed to Senate amendment.
WEEKLY COMPILATION OF PRESIDENTIAL DOCUMENTS.
    Vol. 13, No. 39:
    Sept. 20, Presidential statement.
AMENDMENTS:
SECTION 621, SUBSECTIONS (b)(3), (b)(4) and (b)(5) were amended to transfer certain administrative enforcement responsibilities, pursuant to Pub. L. 95-473, § 3(b), Oct. 17, 1978. 92 Stat. 166; Pub. L. 95-630, Title V. § 501, November 10, 1978, 92 Stat. 3680; Pub. L. 98-443, § 9(h), Oct. 4, 1984, 98 Stat. 708.
SECTION 803, SUBSECTION (6), defining "debt collector" was amended to repeal the attorney at law exemption at former Section (6)(F) and to redesignate Section 803(6)(G) pursuant to Pub. L. 99-361, July 9, 1986, 100 Stat. 768. For legislative history, *see* H.R. 237, HOUSE REPORT No. 99-405 (Comm. on Banking, Finance, and Urban Affairs). CONGRESSIONAL RECORD: Vol. 131 (1895); Dec. 2, considered and passed House, Vol. 132 (1986): June 26, considered and passed Senate.
SECTION 807, SUBSECTION (11), was amended to affect when debt collectors must state (a) that they are attempting to collect a debt and (b) that information obtained will be used for that purpose, pursuant to Pub. L. 104-208 § 2305, 110 Stat. 3009 (Sept. 30, 1996).

CHAPTER 11
APPENDIX II

Staff Commentary—
Fair Debt Collection Practices Act

FEDERAL TRADE COMMISSION

STATEMENT OF GENERAL POLICY OR INTERPRETATION STAFF COMMENTARY ON THE FAIR DEBT COLLECTION PRACTICES ACT

AGENCY: Federal Trade Commission.

ACTION: Publication of staff commentary.

SUMMARY: The Commission staff is issuing its Commentary on the Fair Debt Collection Practices Act that will supersede all previously issued staff interpretations of the Act. The purpose of the Commentary is to clarify and codify these interpretations.

DATE: December 13, 1988.

ADDRESS: Federal Trade Commission, Washington, DC 20580.

FOR FURTHER INFORMATION CONTACT: Clarke W. Brinckerhoff, Program Advisor, John F. LeFevre, Program Advisor, Division of Credit Practices, Federal Trade Commission, Washington, DC 20580, (202) 326-3206 or (202) 326-3209.

SUPPLEMENTARY INFORMATION: On March 7, 1986, the staff of the Federal Trade Commission ("staff" or "FTC staff") published its proposed Staff Commentary on the Fair Debt Collection Practices Act ("FDCPA") in the Federal Register (51 FR 8019). That notice set forth the text of the proposed Commentary, along with (1) the staff's rationale for issuing the Commentary and (2) a list of the principal areas where it varied in appreciable measure from the informal opinions previously offered by the FTC staff. That notice also briefly described the FDCPA, the Commission's role in enforcing the statute, and the FTC's staff's interest in improving the present method of providing advice by making informal staff letters available to the public. It explained that the staff viewed the publication of the Commentary as an opportunity to provide a more comprehensive vehicle for providing staff opinions concerning the FDCPA, and to revise previous advice that the staff had come to believe was inconsistent or inaccurate. Both the notice dated March 7, 1986, and the introduction to the proposed Commentary specified that it does not have the force of a

549

trade regulation rule or formal agency action, and that it is not binding on the Commission or the public.

The notice in the Federal Register dated march 7, 1986, stated that the FTC staff would accept public comments on the proposed Commentary to aid in preparation of the final product. Three trade associations, six corporations, the consumer protection division of the offices of three state attorney's General, one state regulatory agency, one national consumer organization, two local consumer groups, and two law firms responded to this invitation. Although the notice stated the FTC staff was requesting comments until May 6, 1986, all comments were taken into account in preparing the Commentary, even those received after that date.

On July 9, 1986, four months after publication of the proposed Commentary, the President signed into law a bill (Pub. L. 99-3610 repealing former section 803(6)(F)), which had exempted "any attorney-at-law collecting a debt as an attorney on behalf of and in the name of a client." The FTC staff has responded to a large number of inquiries from attorneys seeking its views on how the FDCPA applies to their practices. Therefore, the staff has added comments in appropriate locations to reflect the advice it has provided to attorneys on these issues.

This notice (1) summarizes comments received from the public in response to the FTC staff's 1986 publication of the Fair Debt Collection Practices Act Commentary in "proposed" form, (2) highlights the major areas where the staff revised the Commentary based on those comments or refused to do so, and (3) outlines the major issues added to the Commentary, reflecting written advice which the staff has provided to attorneys following repeal of the "attorney-at-law collecting a debt" exemption in July 1986.

In this notice, the word "comment" refers to an opinion set forth in the Commentary by the staff, "public commenter" refers to a party that submitted views on the proposed Commentary following its publication in the Federal Register, and "public comments" refers to those views.

PRINCIPAL REVISIONS TO COMMENTARY BASED ON PUBLIC COMMENTS

Generally, the FTC staff found the public comments helpful in preparing the final version of the Commentary, although not all the proposals were adopted. Most of the public comments were aimed at clarifying the staff's intent. The redraft adopted these suggestions where it appeared that they resulted in an appreciable improvement. The overwhelming majority of the revisions the FTC staff made in the Commentary involved only minor changes (adding a word or parenthetical phrase or making some minor editorial change), and were designed to clarify points or to avoid possible unintended inferences. However, besides the addition of comments relating to attorney debt collectors, there were some changes of a substantive nature that were made based on public comments. This section highlights the most significant of the clarifications and revisions that were made based on public comments.

1. Location information (section 804 (1.5))

The FTC staff has made adjustments to two comments to acknowledge that a debt collector who is seeking location information by mail may identify his employer when expressly asked to do so. The staff added parenthetical references to comment #4 to section 804, and to comment #4 to section 807(14), which discusses section 804(1) and (5) under the heading "relation to other sections."

One public commenter pointed out that if the person from whom the location information is sought replies by expressly requesting the name of the employer of the individual debt collector who sent the letter,[1] sections 804(1) and 804(5) may appear to place conflicting obligations on the debt collection firm. On the one hand, section 804(1) requires a debt collector employee, in communications seeking location information, to "identify his employer" if "expressly requested." Yet section 804(5) generally prohibits a debt collector from using "any language or symbol on any envelope or in the contents of any communication effected by the mails or telegram that indicates that the debt collector is in the debt collection business or that the communication relates to the collection of a debt."

The FTC staff believes a proper interpretation of the FDCPA is to read section 804(1) as controlling this situation, because it specifically addresses the situation in which an individual expressly requests the name of the debt collection firm. In that case, we believe that the debt collection firm must reveal its identity in order to acquire location information. The comments bearing on this issue have therefore been changed to reflect that position.

2. Contact limited to consumer's attorney (section 805(a))

Public commenters argued forcefully that comment #3, stating that a debt collector could not communicate with a consumer who stated that an attorney would represent him with respect to all *future* debts, would place an unreasonable burden on the debt collector. They reported that the standard operating procedure for many debt collectors is to close the consumer's file once a debt is collected or efforts to collect it cease. Should a second debt from the same consumer be assigned to the debt collector, therefore, the collector might be unaware of the previous file on that debtor and would not know whether the consumer was represented by an attorney with respect to all future debts. These commenters contend that the only way a debt collector could comply with our proposed interpretation would be to check every new debtor file against the closed files to determine whether (1) the collector had ever previously contacted that debtor, (2) the debtor had previously been represented by an attorney, and (3) the debtor had given the collector a blanket notice of legal representation. They suggested instead that, when contacted about a subsequent debt, the consumer should simply inform the debt collector that he is still represented by an attorney and that the debt collector should contact the attorney.

The FTC staff now believes that the portion of comment #3 in the proposed Commentary regarding future representation is simply not supported by the statute, or envisioned by its legislative history. Furthermore, it could easily be the case that the attorney in fact no longer represents the consumer. Accordingly, the staff has modified the second paragraph of comment #3 to section 805(a) to repeal the broad reference to "all current and future debts" with the more appropriate "other debts."

3. Consumer consent to third party contacts (section 805(b))

The statement in comment #1 that consumers consent to third party contacts "may be presumed from circumstances" has been deleted. One public commenter expressed concern that this formulation might open the door to overreaching by debt collectors. The

---

[1]Such communication would be signed by the individual debt collector, without indicating that the letter is from a debt collection firm.

deleted phrase was not necessary to the point involved—that consent need not necessarily be in writing—which is better made by providing a clear example of such consent.

4. Lists of debtors (Section 806(3))

One public commenter noted that this section of the proposed Commentary did not completely reflect the FDCPA's reference to sections of the Fair Credit Reporting Act. The description has been amended and a comment has been added to reflect that relationship, in accord with a prior staff opinion on the section and a Commission interpretation on the FCRA.

5. Statement by debt collector of possible action (Section 807(5))

A revision was made to correct the Commentary's inadvertent reference to the *creditor,* rather than to the *debt collector,* in comment #3 to this section. Comment #3 concerns statements by the debt collector about action that is unlikely to be taken in a particular case. Obviously, as several public commenters pointed out, the creditor's knowledge that action is unlikely is not automatically imputed to the debt collector.

6. Documents deceptive as to authorship (Section 807(9))

An appropriate clause has been added to the description an to comment #1, to give a more complete discussion of this section than in the proposed Commentary, which focused only on documents that fraudulently appear to be government documents. One public commenter correctly pointed out that the statute covers a much wider range of deceptive practices as to the source of the document.

7. Letters marked "personal" or "confidential" (Section 808(8))

Comment #3 to this section has been expanded to assert that use of the term "Personal" or "Confidential," as well as the word "Telegram" or the like, does not violate this section.

One public commenter stated that debt collectors use designations of this sort to protect the consumer's privacy by attempting to ensure that the envelope is not opened by unauthorized persons, and argued that such terms are essentially part of the letter's address.

The FTC staff agrees that the proposed change is logical. The staff has already recognized that a rigid, literal approach to section 808(8) would lead to absurd results (i.e., taken literally, it would prohibit showing any part of the consumer's address on the envelope). The legislative purpose was to prohibit a debt collector from using symbols or language on envelopes that would reveal that the contents pertain to debt collection—not to totally bar the use of harmless words or symbols on an envelope. Indeed, it was for this reason that comment #3 to this section of the proposed Commentary (in accord with prior informal staff advice) explicitly recognized that the term "Telegram" or similar designation on an envelope does not violate this section.

8. Waiver of venue provision (Section 811)

Numerous public commenters objected to comment #1 to this section, indicating a fear that the staff's interpretation would lead to a flood of waiver provisions hidden in the fine print of consumer credit contracts. Although the FTC staff believes that these parties misread the comment, which clearly stated that any waiver "must be provided to the debt collector," the comment has been expanded to be even more explicit on the point.

SIGNIFICANT PUBLIC COMMENTS NOT ADOPTED

There were several areas in which public commenters suggested changes in the Commentary that were not adopted. This section discusses the most significant of those proposals, and sets forth the staff's principal reasons for maintaining its position.

1. Contacts in which the collector does not mention the debt (Sections 803(2), 805(a), 805(c))

Several public commenters contended that the FTC staff's treatment of certain contacts consumers as violations of the FDCPA was incorrect because the contacts did not involve a "communication" under the definition provided in section 803(2), which refers to "conveying of information regarding a debt directly or indirectly to any person." These commenters argued that contacts that do not explicitly refer to the debt are not "communications" and, hence, do not violate any provision where that term is used.

The FTC staff continues to believe that some contacts with consumers can violate section 805(a) or section 805(c) because they at least "indirectly" refer to the debt, even if the obligation is not specifically mentioned. For example, there is no doubt that a debt collector who has previously contacted a consumer about a debt violates section 805(a) if he calls the consumer at 3 AM and says only "Hi, this is Joe. I haven't forgotten you"—the words may not refer to the debt, but the consumer will know from previous collection efforts by "Joe" what the call is about. The words "or indirectly" in the definition make it clear that Congress intended a common sense approach to this situation. Furthermore, the word "communication" (or variations thereof) is used six times in section 804, which authorizes the seeking of location information from third parties with the general requirement that the debt will *not* be disclosed to such parties, demonstrating that this term was not intended to be limited throughout the statute to acts that specifically refer to the debt, regardless of the definition set forth in section 803(2).

2. Definition of "location information" (section 803(7))

Public commenters made varying suggestions that would effectively amend the section's definition of "location information"—i.e., "a consumer's place of abode and his telephone number at such place, or his place of employment." One public commenter expressed the view that a debt collector was somehow limited by this language to obtaining only one of the three enumerated items (home address or home phone or work address), while others suggested that we interpret the definition to include a fourth item (work phone). Because no public commenter provided a convincing rationale for its position, and because the FTC staff believes that the definition is clear, both suggestions were declined.

3. Use of "copy of a judgment" in notice (section 807(2)(A))

Some public commenters criticized the staff's statement in comment #3 to section 807(2) that the validation notice provided by a debt collector to comply with section 809(a)(4) may use the phrase "copy of a judgment" even where no judgment exists. Staff had previously advised in informal opinion letters that the use of those words violated section 807(2)(A) because they suggested that a judgment existed when it did not. Because the practical effect of these interpretations was to make verbatim use of the statutory language of section 809(a)(4) of violation of section 807(2)(A), they were rejected by the leading court decision[2] and by the staff in the proposed Commentary. The FTC staff continues to believe its reasons for revising prior staff opinions (discussed in item 5 of the notice in the Federal Register dated March 7, 1986) are wellfounded, and thus it has adhered to that position.

One public commenter suggested that we might also permit the phrase "copy of *a* judgment" as well. Because the phrase used in section 809(a)(4) is "copy of *a* judgment" (emphasis added) and this language led to the staff's current interpretation, the Commentary has not been revised on this point.

4. False allegations of fraud (section 807(7))

Some public commenters contended that the language of this section, which outlaws the "false representation or implication that the consumer committed any crime or other conduct *in order to disgrace the consumer*" (emphasis added) demonstrates that specific intent is essential to a violation. The FTC staff agrees that some element of intent is involved, but believes that an intent to disgrace can be inferred from the nature of the acts the consumer is being accused off—fraud (comment 1) or crime (comment 2). Therefore, the comments on this section have not been changed.

5. Disclosure of debt collection purpose (section 807(11))

Several public commenters questioned the staff's refusal to construe section 807(11) as requiring debt collectors to disclose the purpose of each and every written and oral contact, pointing out that court decisions have gone both way son the issue. The staff's position, reflect in the Commission's Sixth and Seventh Annual Reports to Congress—that such disclosures need not be made where they are obvious or have already been made—has not changed, and the comments provide no new argument for revising that view.

Other public commenters asked the staff to retrace the comment stating that a debt collector may not send a note saying only "please call me right away" to a consumer whom the collector has not previously contacted. They argued that such a note could not violate this section because it made no reference to the debt and therefore was not a "communication," as defined in section 803(2). Because the staff believes that (1) the intent of section 807(11) was to require that debt collectors' purposes be known to parties they contact, and (2) the use of the term "communication" in other sections of the FDCPA shows that its construction is not always limited to the definition set forth in section 803(2), this comment was retained.[3]

6. Elements of unfairness (section 808)

Some public commenters criticized comment #2, which concerns general violations of this section of the FDCPA, for construing the term "unfair" in the same way as the Commission has construed it under section 5 of the FTC Act. They argued that the comment would, in effect, repeal some of the subsections of section 808 because the prescribed conduct would not cause the type of injury required, or would not be considered unfair based on a cost/benefit analysis. Because the location of the comment—under section 808

---

[2]*Blackwell v. Professional Business Services of Georgia, Inc.*, 526 F. Supp. 535, 535-39 (N.D. Ga. [1987]).

[3]See discussion of FDCPA section 804 in item 1 of this section of this notice.

generally, as opposed to any of its subsections—makes it clear that the staff did not intend to negate any of the eight types of conduct specified by Congress to be a violation of this provision in subsections (1) through (8), the staff retained this comment.

Other public commenters asked that comment #2 be expanded to state that section 808 does not cover inadvertent acts or any act that was reasonably calculated to collect the debt. Because this comment was meant simply to reflect the FTC staff's view that the Commission's approach to "unfair practices" (as reflected in its treatment of that concept in section 5 of the FTC Act) is applicable in analyzing general violations of section 808, comment #2 has not been substantially revised.

7. Details of validation notices (section 809(a))

Some public commenters objected to the staff's view that section 809(a) imposes no requirements as to form, sequence, location, or type size of the notice (comment 3); to our reasons for reversing prior informal opinions to the contrary (item 10 in the March 7, 1988 notice in the Federal Register); and to our view that the notice may be provided orally (comment 5). However, the public commenters provided no new analysis to change the staff's reading the section. Therefore, the Commentary has not bee changed on this point.

8. Proper forum for suit on an oral contract (section 811(a)(2))

One public commenter suggested deletion of comment 4 to section 811. Section 811(a)(2) clearly states that there are only two districts where suit may be brought by a debt collector on a debt—where the consumer "signed the contract sued upon" and where the consumer "resides at the commencement of the action." The staff decided to retain the comment, which simply notes the obvious fact that if there is only an oral agreement (which by definition can not be "signed"), suit may only be brought where the consumer resides.

9. Miscellaneous requests for added comments.

Some public commentors made a number of suggestions that the FTC staff establish *new* principles in the Commentary.[4] Although not all of the proposals were without merit, the staff believes it is unwise to add major new sections to the final versions of the Commentary to address issues that have never been the subject of staff correspondence.

---

[4]The principal proposals were that the staff add to the Commentary (1) a lengthy new comment in section 803(6) that a party could be a "debt collector" with respect to some accounts but not others, (2) a definition of "default" in connection with section 803(6)(G)(iii) (now section 803(6)(F)(iii)) concerning accounts not in default where received, (3) a statement that section 808(3) does not prohibit a debt collector from responding to a specific credit reference inquiry from a creditor, (4) substantial new material to various comments in section 807(14) to cover a situation where one debt collector provides services as a contractor for another debt collector, (5) a statement that section 808(1) does not prohibit an agreement between a consumer and debt collector, and (6) a statement that the verification required by section 809(b) may be provided by an agent of the debt collector.

New Comments Based on Recent Staff Letters To Attorneys

The staff has added comments to reflect the large volume of written advice it has provided to attorneys following repeal of the "attorney-at-law" exemption in July 1986.[5] This section synthesizes the conclusions reached in the most significant additions made to the Commentary based on this recent correspondence.

1. Coverage (Sections 803(2, 5, 6), 811)

Attorneys or law firms that engage in traditional debt collection activities (sending dunning letters, making collection calls to consumers) are covered by the FDCPA, but those whose practice is limited to legal activities are not covered.[6] Similarly, filing or service of a complaint or other legal paper (or transmission of a notice that is a legal prerequisite to enforcement of a debt) is not a "communication" covered by the FDCPA, but traditional collection efforts are covered.[7]

A student loan is a "debt" covered by the FDCPA;[8] however, alimony, tort claims, and non-pecuniary obligations are not covered.[9]

A salaried attorney who collects debts on behalf of, and in the name of his creditor employer,[10] and a state educational agency that collects student loans[11] are exempt from coverage by the FDCPA.

Debt collectors (including attorney debt collectors) are subject to the venue limitations of the FDCPA.[12]

2. Communications by debt collectors (sections 805(b), 806(3-4))

An attorney debt collector, who represents either (1) a creditor or (2) a debt collector that previously tried to collect an account, may report his collection efforts to the debt collector.[13] An attorney may communicated with a witness in a lawsuit that has been filed.[14]

---

[5]Although most of the issues raised in those letters related to attorneys as debt collectors, a few of them also asked for interpretations on other issues as well. For the sake of completeness, all significant staff opinions included in this correspondence (which has been widely circulated already) have been included in the Commentary.

[6]Section 803(6), comments 1-2.

[7]Section 803(2), comment 2; section 809(a), comments 6-7.

[8]Section 803(5), comment 1.

[9]Section 803(5), comment 2.

[10]Section 803(6)(A), comment 4(a).

[11]Section 803(6)(C), comment 4(c).

[12]Section 811, comment 6.

[13]Section 805(b), comment 6.

[14]Section 805(b), comment 8.

A debt collector may provide a list of consumers, against whom judgments have been entered, to an investigator in order to locate such individuals.[15] A debt collector may place a public notice required by law as a prerequisite to enforcing the debt.[16]

3. Dispute and verification (section 809)

An attorney debt collector must provide the required validation notice, even if a previous debt collector (or the creditor) has given such notice.[17] A debt collector does not comply with this obligation to verify the debt simply by including proof with the first communication to the consumer.[18]

An attorney debt collector may take legal action within 30 days of sending the required validation notice, regardless of whether the consumer disputes the debt; if the consumer disputes the debt, the attorney may still take legal action but must cease other collection efforts (*e.g.*, letters or calls to the consumer) until verification is obtained and mailed to the consumer.[19]

4. Permissible forum to enforce a judgment on a debt (section 811)

If a judgment has been obtained from a forum that satisfies the requirements of this section, a debt collector may bring suit to enforce it in another jurisdiction.[20]

By direction of the Commission.
Donald S. Clark,
Secretary.

FEDERAL TRADE COMMISSION STAFF COMMENTARY ON THE FAIR DEBT COLLECTION PRACTICES ACT

Introduction

This Commentary is the vehicle by which the staff of the Federal Trade Commission publishes its interpretations of the Fair Debt Collection Practices Act (FDCPA). It is a guideline intended to clarify the staff interpretations of the statue, but does not have the force or effect of statutory provisions. It is not a formal trade regulation rule or advisory opinion of the Commission, and thus is not binding on the Commission or the public.

The Commentary is based primarily on issues discussed in informal staff letters responding to public requests for interpretations and on the Commission's enforcement program, subsequent to the FDCPA's enactment. It is intended to synthesize staff views on important issues and to give clear advice where inconsistencies have been discovered among staff letters. In some cases, reflection on the issues posed or relevant court decisions have resulted in a different interpretation from that expressed by the staff in those informal letters. Therefore, the Commentary supersedes the staff views expressed in such correspondence.

---

[15]Section 806(3-4), comment 5.

[16]Section 806(3-4), comment 6.

[17]Section 809(a), comment 7.

[18]Section 809(b), comment 1.

[19]Section 809(a), comment 8.

[20]Section 811, comment 5.

In many cases several different sections or subsections of the FDCPA may apply to a given factual situation. This results from the effort by Congress in drafting the FDCPA to be both explicit and comprehensive, in order to limit the opportunities for debt collectors to evade the underlying legislative intention. Although it may be of only technical interest whether a given act violates one, two, or three sections of the FDCPA, the Commentary frequently provides cross references to other applicable sections so that is may serve as a more comprehensive guide for its users. The Commentary attempts to discuss the more common overlapping references, usually under the heading "Relation to other sections," and deals with issues raised by each factual situation under the section or subsection that the staff deems most directly applicable to it.

The Commentary will be revised and updated by the staff as needed, based on the experience of the Commission in responding to public inquiries about, and enforcing, the FDCPA. The Commission welcomes input from interested industry, consumer, and other public parties on the Commentary and on issues discussed in it.

The staff will continue to respond to requests for informal interpretations. Updates of the Commentary will consider and, where appropriate, incorporate issues raised in correspondence and other public contacts, as well as the Commission's enforcement efforts. Therefore, a party who is interested in raising an issue for inclusion in future editions of the Commentary does not need to make any formal submission or request to that effect.

The Commentary should be used in conjunction with the statute. The abbreviated description of each section or subsection in the Commentary is designed only as a preamble to discussion of issues pertaining to each section and is not intended as a substitute for the statutory text.

The Commentary should not be considered as a reflection of all court rulings under the FDCPA. For example, on some issues judicial interpretations of the statute vary depending on the jurisdiction, with the result that the staff's enforcement position cannot be in accord with all decided cases.

Section 801—Short Title

Section 801 names the statute the "Fair Debt Collection Practices Act."

The Fair Debt Collection Practices Act (FDCPA) is Title VIII of the Consumer Credit Protection Act, which also includes other federal statues relating to consumer credit, such as the Truth in Lending Act (Title I), the Fair Credit Reporting Act (Title VI), and the Equal Credit Opportunity Act (Title VII).

Section 802—Findings and Purpose

Section 802 recites the Congressional findings that serve as the basis for the legislation.

Section 803—Definitions

Section 803(1) defines "Commission" as the Federal Trade Commission.

1. *General.* The definition includes only the Federal Trade Commission, not necessarily the staff acting on its behalf.

Section 803(2) defines "communication" as the "conveying of information regarding a debt directly or indirectly to any person through any medium."

1. *General.* The definition includes oral and written transmission of messages which refer to a debt.

2. *Exclusions.* The term does not include formal legal actions (e.g., filing of a lawsuit or other petition/pleadings with a court; service of a complaint or other legal papers in connection with a lawsuit, or activities directly related to such service). Similarly, it does not include a notice that is required by law as a prerequisite to enforcing a contractual obligation between creditor and debtor, by judicial or nonjudicial legal process.

    The term does not include situations in which the debt collector does not convey information regarding the debt, such as:

    -   A request to a third party for a consume to return a telephone call to the debt collector, if the debt collector does not refer to the debt or the caller's status as (for affiliation with) a debt collector.

    -   A request to a third party for information about the consumer's assets, if the debt collector does not reveal the existence of a debt.

    -   A request to a third party in connection with litigation e.g., requesting a third party to complete a military affidavit that must be filed as a prerequisite to enforcing a default judgment, if the debt collector does not reveal the existence of the debt.

Section 803(3) defines "consumer" as "any natural person obligated or allegedly obligated to pay any debt."

1. *General.* The definition includes only a "natural person" and not an artificial person such as a corporation or other entity created by statute.

Section 803(4) defines "creditor" as "any person who offers or extends credit creating a debt or to whom a debt is owed." However, the definition excludes a party who "receives an assignment or transfer of a debt in default solely for the purpose of facilitating collection of such debt for another."

1. *General.* The definition includes the party that actually extended credit or became the obligee on an account in the normal course of business, and excludes a party that was assigned a delinquent debt only for collection purposes.

Section 803(5) defines "debt" as a consumer's "obligation...to pay money arising out of a transaction in which the money, arising out of a transportation in which the money, property, insurance, or services (being purchased) are primarily for personal, family, or household purposes ..."

1. *Examples.* The term includes:

    Overdue obligations such as medical bills that were originally payable in full within a certain time period (e.g., 30 days).

    A dishonored check that was tendered in payment for goods or services acquired or used primarily for personal, family, or household purposes.

A student loan, because the consumer is purchasing "services" (education) for personal use.

2. *Exclusions.* The term does not include:

- Unpaid taxes, fines, alimony, or tort claims, because they are not debts incurred from a "transportation (involving purchase of) property or services for personal, family or household purposes."

- A credit card that a cardholder retains after the card issuer has demanded its return. The cardholder's account balance is the debt.

- A non-pecuniary obligation of the consumer such as the responsibility to maintain adequate insurance on the collateral, because it does not involve an "obligation to pay money."

Section 803(6) defines "debt collector" as a party "who uses any instrumentality of interstate commerce or the mails in collection of debts owed another."

1. *Examples.* The term includes:

- Employees of a debt collection business, including a corporation, partnership, or other entity whose business is the collection of debts owned another.

- A firm that regularly collects overdue rent on behalf of real estate owners, or periodic assessments on behalf of condominium associations, because it "regularly collects debts owned or due another."

- A party based in the United States who collects debts owned by consumers residing outside the United States, because he "uses the mails: in the collection business. The residence of the debtor is irrelevant.

- A firm that collects debts in its own name for a creditor solely by mechanical techniques, such as (1) placing phone calls with pre-recorded messages and recording consumer responses, or (2) making computer-generated mailings.

- An attorney or law firm whose efforts to collect consumer debts on behalf of its clients regularly include activities traditionally associated with debt collection, such as sending demand letters (dunning notices) or making collection telephone calls to the consumer. However, an attorney is not considered to be a debt collector simply because he responds to an inquiry from the consumer following the filing of a lawsuit.

2. *Exclusions.* The term does not include:

- Any person who collects debts (or attempts to do so) only in isolated instances, because the definition includes only those who "regularly" collect debts.

- A credit card issuer that collects its cardholder's account, even when the account is based upon purchases from participating merchants, because the issuer is collecting its own debts, not those "owed or due another."

- An attorney whose practice is limited to legal activities (e.g., the filing and prosecution of lawsuits to reduce debts to judgment).

3. *Application of definition to creditor using another name.* Creditors are generally excluded from the definition of "debt collector" to the extent that they collect their own debts in their own name. However, the term specifically applies to "any creditor who, in the process of collecting his own debts, uses any name other than his own which would indicate that a third person is" involved in the collection.

    - A creditor is a debt collector for purposes of this act if:

    - He uses a name other than his own to collect his debts, including a fictitious name.

    - His salaried attorney employees who collect debts use stationery that indicates that attorneys are employed by someone other than the creditor or are independent or separate from the creditor (e.g., ABC Corp. sends collection letters on stationery of "John Jones, Attorney-at-Law").

    - He regularly collects debts for another creditor; however, he is a debt collector only for purposes of collecting these debts, not when he collects his own debt in his own name.

    - The creditor's collection division or related corporate collector is not clearly designated as being affiliated with the creditor; however, the creditor is not a debt collector if the creditor's correspondence is clearly labeled as being from the "collection unit of the (creditor's name)," since the creditor is not using a "name other than this own" in that instance.

    Relation to other sections. A creditor who is covered by the FDCPA because he uses a "name other than his own" also may violate section 807(14), which prohibits using a false business name. When he falsely uses an attorney's name, he violates section 807(3).

4. *Specific exemptions from definition of debt collector.*

    (a) *Creditor employees.* Section 803(6)(A) provides that "debt collector" does not include "any officer or employee of a creditor while, in the name of the creditor, collecting debts for such creditor."

    The exemption includes a collection agency employee, who works for a creditor to collect in the creditor's name at the creditor's office under the creditor's supervision, because he has become the *de facto* employee of the creditor.

    The exemption includes a creditor's salaried attorney (or other) employee who collects debts on behalf of, and in the name of, that creditor.

    The exemption does not include a creditor's former employee who continues to collect accounts on the creditor's behalf, if he acts under his own name rather than the creditor's.

    (b) *Creditor-controlled collector.* Section 803(6)(B) provides that "debt collector" does not include a party collecting for another, where they are both "related by common ownership or affiliated by corporate control, if the (party collects) only for persons to whom it is so related or affiliated and if the principal business of such person is not the collection of debts."

    The exemption applies where the collector and creditor have "common ownership or corporate control." For example, a company is exempt when it attempts to collect debts of another company after the two entities have merged.

    The exemption does not apply to a party related to a creditor (if it also collects debts for others in addition to the related creditors).

(c) *State and federal officials.* Section 803(6)(C) provides that "debt collector" does not include any state or federal employee "to the extent that collecting or attempting to collect any debt is in the performance of his official duties."

The exemption applies only to such governmental employees in the performance of their "official duties" and, therefore, does not apply to an attorney employed by a county government who also collected bad checks for local merchants where that activity is outside his official duties.

The exemption includes a state educational agency that is engaged in the collection of student loans.

(d) *Process servers.* Section 803(6)(D) provides that "debt collector" does not include "any person while serving or attempting to serve legal process on any other person in connection with the judicial enforcement of any debt."

The exemption covers marshals, sheriffs, and any other process servers while conducting their normal duties relating to serving legal papers.

(e) *Non-profit counselors.* Section 803(6)(E) provides that "debt collector" does not include "any nonprofit organization which, at the request of consumers, performs bona fide consumer credit counseling and assists consumers in the liquidation of their debts by receiving payments from such consumers and distributing such amounts to creditors."

This exemption applies only to nonprofit organizations; it does not apply to for-profit credit counseling services that accept fees from debtors and regularly transmit such funds to creditors.

(f) *Miscellaneous.* Section 803(6)(F) provides that "debt collector" does not include collection activity by a party about a debt that "(i) is incidental to a bona fide fiduciary obligation or escrow arrangement; (ii) was originated by such person; (iii) was not in default at the time it was obtained by such person; or (iv) (was) obtained by such person as a secured party in a commercial credit transaction involving the creditor."

The exemption (i) for bona fide fiduciary obligations or escrow arrangements applies to entities such as trust departments of banks, and escrow companies. It does not include a party who is named as a debtor's trustee solely for the purpose of conducting a foreclosure sale (i.e., exercising a power of sale in the event of default on a loan).

The exemption (ii) for a party that originated the debt applies to the original creditor collecting his own debts in his own name. It also applies when a creditor assigns a debt originally owed to him, but retains the authority to collect the obligation on behalf of the assignee to whom the debt becomes owed. For example, the exemption applies to a creditor who makes a mortgage or school loan and continues to handle the account after assigning it to a third party. However, it does not apply to a party that takes assignment of retail installment contracts from the original creditor and then reassigns them to another creditor but continues to collect the debt arising from the contracts, because the debt was not "originated by" the collector/first assignee.

The exception (iii) for debts not in default when obtained applies to parties such as mortgage service companies whose business is servicing current accounts.

The exemption (iv) for a secured party in a commercial transaction applies to a commercial lender who acquires a consumer account that was used as collateral, following default on a loan from the commercial lender to the original creditor.

(g) *Attorneys.* A provision of the FDCPA, as enacted in 1977 (former section 803(6)(F), providing that "debt collector" does not include "any attorney-at-law collecting a debt as an attorney on behalf of and in the name of a client," was repealed by Pub. L. 99-361, which became effective in July 1986. Therefore, an attorney who meets the definition set forth in section 803(6) is now covered by the FDCPA.

Section 803(7) defines "location information" as "a consumer's place of abode and his telephone number at such place, or his place of employment."

This definition includes only residence, home phone number, and place of employment. It does not cover work phone numbers, names of supervisors and their telephone numbers, salaries or dates of paydays.

Section 803(8) defines "state" as "any State, territory, or possession of the United States, the District of Columbia, the Commonwealth of Puerto Rico, or any political subdivision of any of the foregoing."

Section 804—Acquisition of Location Information

Section 804 requires a debt collector, when communicating with third parties for the purpose of acquiring information about the consumer's location to "(1) identify himself, state that he is confirming or correcting location information concerning the consumer, and, only if expressly requested, identify his employer, " (2) not refer to the debt, (3) usually make only a single contact with each third party, (4) not communicate by post card, (5) not indicate the collection nature of his business purpose in any written communication, and (6) limit communications to the consumer's attorney, where the collector knows of the attorney, unless the attorney fails to respond to the communication.

1. *General.* Although the FDCPA generally protects the consumer's privacy by limiting debt collector communications about personal affairs to third parties, it recognizes the need for some third party contact by collectors to seek the whereabouts of the consumer.

2. *Identification of debt collector (section 804(1)).* An individual employed by a debt collector seeking location information must identify himself, but must not identify his empower unless asked. When asked, however, he must give the true and full name of the employer, to comply with this provision and avoid a violation of § 807(14).

   An individual debt collector may use an alias if it is used consistently and it is does not interfere with another party's ability to identify him (e.g., the true identity can be ascertained by the employer).

3. *Referral to debt (section 804(2)).* A debt collector may not refer to the consumer's debt in any third party communication seeking location information, including those with other creditors.

4. *Reference to debt collector's business (section 804(5)).* A debt collector may not use his actual name in his letterhead or elsewhere in a written communication seeking location information, if the name indicates collection activity (such as a name containing

the word "debt," "collector," or "collection"), except when the person contacted has expressly requested that the debt collector identify himself.

5. *Communication with consumer's attorney (section 804(6))*. Once a debt collector learns a consumer is represented by an attorney in connection with the debt, he must confine his request for location information to the attorney. (See also comments on section 805(a)(2)).

Section 805—Communication in Connection With Debt Collection.

Section 805(a)—Communication with the consumer. Unless the consumer has consented or a court order permits, a debt collector may not communicate with a consumer to collect a debt (1) at any time or place which is unusual or known to be inconvenient to the consumer (8AM-9PM is presumed to be convenient), (2) where he knows the consumer is represented by an attorney with respect to the debt, unless the attorney fails to respond to the communication in a reasonable time period, or (3) at work if he knows the consumer's employer prohibits such contacts.

1. *Scope*. For purposes of this section, the term "communicate" is given its commonly accepted meaning. Thus, the section applies to contacts with the consumer related to the collection of the debt, whether or not the debt is specifically mentioned.

2. *Inconvenient or unusual times or places (section 805(a)(1))*. A debt collector may not call the consumer at any time, or on any particular day, if he has credible information (from the consumer or elsewhere) that it is inconvenient. If the debt collector does not have such information, a call on Sunday is not *per se* illegal.

3. *Consumer represented by attorney (section 805(a)(2))*. If a debt collector learns that a consumer is represented by an attorney in connection with the debt, even if not formally notified of this fact, the debt collector must contact only the attorney and must not contact the consumer.

   A debt collector who knows a consumer is represented by counsel with respect to a debt is not required to assume similar representation on other debts; however, if a consumer notifies the debt collector that the attorney has been retained to represent him for other debts placed with the debt collector, the debt collector must deal only with that attorney with respect to such debts.

   The creditor's knowledge that he consumer has an attorney is not automatically imputed to the debt collector.

4. *Calls at work (section 805(a)(3))*. A debt collector may not call the consumer at work if he has reason to know the employer forbids such communication (e.g., if the consumer has so informed the debt collector).

Section 805(b)—Communication with third parties. Unless the consumer consents, or a court order or section 804 permits, "or as reasonably necessary to effectuate a postjudgment judicial remedy," a debt collector "may not communicate, in connection with the collection of any debt, with any person other than the consumer, his attorney, a consumer reporting agency if otherwise permitted by law, the creditor, the attorney of the creditor, or the attorney of the debt collector."

1. *Consumer consent to the third party contact.* The consumer's consent need not be in writing. For example, if a third party volunteers that a consumer has authorized him to pay the consumer's account, the debt collector may normally presume the consumer's consent, and may accept the payment and provide a receipt to the party that makes the payment. However, consent may not be inferred only from a consumer's inaction when the debt collector requests such consent.

2. *Location information.* Although a debt collector's search for information concerning the consumer's location (provided in § 804) is expressly excepted from the ban on third party contacts, a debt collector may not call third parties under the pretense of gaining information already in his possession.

3. *Incidental contacts with telephone operator or telegraph clerk.* A debt collector may contact an employee of a telephone or telegraph company in order to contact the consumer, without violating the prohibition on communicating to third parties, if the only information given is that necessary to enable the collector to transmit the message to, or make the contract with, the consumer.

4. *Accessibility by third party.* A debt collector may not send a written message that is easily accessible to third parties. For example, he may not use a computerized billing statement that can be seen on the envelope itself.

    A debt collector may use an "in care of" letter only if the consumer lives at, or accepts mail at, the other party's address.

    A debt collector does not violate this provision when an eavesdropper overhears a conversation with the consumer, unless the debt collector has reason to anticipate the conversation will be overhead.

5. *Non-excepted parties.* A debt collector may discuss the debt only with the parties specified in this section (consumer, creditor, a party's attorney, or credit bureau). For example, unless the consumer has authorized the communication, a collector may not discuss the debt (such as a dishonored check) with a bank, or make a report on a consumer to a non-profit counseling service.

6. *Judicial remedy.* The words "as reasonably necessary to effectuate a postjudgment judicial remedy" mean a communication necessary for execution or enforcement of the remedy. A debt collector may not send a copy of the judgment to an employer, except as part of a formal service of papers to achieve a garnishment or other remedy.

7. *Audits or inquiries.* A debt collector may disclose his files to a government official or an auditor, to respond to an inquiry or conduct an audit, because the disclosure would not be "in connection with the collection of any debt."

8. *Communications by attorney debt collectors.* An attorney who represents either a creditor or debt collector that has previously tried to collect an account may communicate his efforts to collect the account to the debt collector. Because the section permits a debt collector to communicate with "the attorney of the creditor, or the attorney of the debt collector," communications between these parties (even if the attorney is also a debt collector) are not forbidden.

    An attorney may communicated with a potential witness in connection with a lawsuit he has filed (e.g., in order to establish the existence of a debt), because the section was not intended to prohibit communications by attorneys that are necessary to conduct lawsuits on behalf of their clients.

Section 805(c)—Ceasing communication. Once a debt collector receives written notice from a consumer that he or she refuses to pay the debt or wants the collector to stop further collection efforts, the debt collector must cease any further communication with the consumer except "(1) to advise the consumer that the debt collector's further efforts are being terminated; (2) to notify the consumer that the debt collector or creditor may invoke specified remedies which are ordinarily invoked by such debt collector or creditor; or (3) where applicable, to notify the consumer that the debt collector or creditor intends to invoke a specified remedy."

1. *Scope.* For purposes of this section, the term "communicate" is given its commonly accepted meaning. Thus, the section applies to any contact with the consumer related to the collection of the debt, whether or not the debt is specifically mentioned.

2. *Request for payment.* A debt collector's response to a "cease communication" notice from the consumer may not include a demand for payment, but is limited to the three statutory exceptions.

Section 805(d)—"consumer" definition. For section 805 purposes, the term "consumer" includes the "consumer's spouse, parent (if the consumer is a minor), guardian, executor, or administrator."

1. *Broad "consumer" definition.* Because of the broad statutory definition of "consumer" for the purposes of this section, many of its protections extend to parties close to the consumer. For example, the debt collector may not call the consumer's spouse at a time or place known to be inconvenient to the spouse. Conversely, he may call the spouse (guardian, executor, etc.) at any time or place that would be in accord with the limitations of section 805(a).

Section 806—Harassment or Abuse

Section 806 prohibits a debt collector from any conduct that would "Harass, oppress, or abuse any person in connection with the collection of a debt." It provides six examples of harassment or abuse.

1. *Scope.* Prohibited actions are not limited to the six subsections listed as examples of activities that violate this provision.

2. *Unnecessary calls to third parties.* A debt collector may not leave telephone messages with neighbors when the debt collector knows the consumer's name and telephone number and could have reached him directly.

3. *Multiple contacts with consumer.* A debt collector may not engage in repeated personal contacts with a consumer with such frequency as to harass him. Subsection (5) deals specifically with harassment by multiple phone calls.

4. *Abusive conduct.* A debt collector may not pose a lengthy series of questions or comments to the consumer without giving the consumer a chance to reply. Subsection (2) deals specifically with harassment involving obscene, profane, or abusive language.

Section 806(1) prohibits the "use or threat of use of violence or other criminal means to harm any person."

1. *Implied threat.* A debt collector may violate this section by an implied threat of violence. For example, a debt collector may not pressure a consumer with statements such as "We're not playing around here—we can play tough" or "We're going to send somebody to collect for us one way or the other."

Section 806(2) prohibits the use of obscene, profane, or abusive language.

1. *Abusive language.* Abusive language includes religious slurs, profanity, obscenity, calling the consumer a liar or a deadbeat, and the use of racial or sexual epithets.

Sect 806(3) prohibits the "publication of a list of consumers who allegedly refuse to pay debts," except to report the items to a "consumer reporting agency," as defined in the Fair Credit Reporting Act or to a party otherwise authorized to receive it under that Act.
Section 806(4) prohibits the "advertisement for sale of any debt to coerce payment of the debt."

1. *Shaming prohibited.* These provisions are designed to prohibit debt collectors from "shaming" a customer into payment, by publicizing the debt.
2. *Exchange of lists.* Debt collectors may not exchange lists of consumers who allegedly refuse to pay their debts.
3. *Information to creditor subscribers.* A debt collector may not distribute a list of alleged debtors to its creditor subscribers.
4. *Coded lists.* A debt collector that publishes a list of consumers who have had bad debts, coded to avoid generally disclosing the consumer's identity (e.g., showing only the drivers license number and first three letters of each consumer's name) does not violate this provision, because such publication is permitted under the Fair Credit Reporting Act.
5. *List for use by investigator.* A debt collector does not violate these provisions by providing a list of consumers against whom judgments have been entered to a private investigator in order to locate such individuals, because section 805(b) specifically permits contacts "reasonably necessary to effectuate a post-judgment judicial remedy."
6. *Publich notice required by law.* A debt collector does not violate these provisions by providing public notices that are required by law as a prerequisite to enforcement of a security interest in connection with a debt.

Section 806(5) prohibits contacting the consumer by telephone "repeatedly or continuously with intent to annoy, abuse, or harass any person at the called number."

1. *Multiple phone calls.* "Continuously" means making a series of telephone calls, one right after the other. "Repeatedly" means calling with excessive frequency under the circumstances.

Section 806(6) prohibits, except where section 804 applies, "the placement of telephone calls without meaningful disclosure of the caller's identity."

1. *Aliases.* A debt collector employee's use of an alias that permits identification of the debt collector (i.e., where he uses the alias consistently, and his true identity can be ascertained by the employer) constitutes a "meaningful disclosure of the caller's identity."

2. *Identification of caller.* An individual debt collector must disclose his employer's identity, when discussing the debt on the telephone with consumers or third parties permitted by section 805(b).

3. *Relation to other sections.* A debt collector who uses a false business name in a phone call to conceal his identity violates section 807(14), as well as this section.

Section 807—False or Misleading Representations

Section 807 prohibits a debt collector from using any "false, deceptive, or misleading representation or means in connection with the collection of any debt." It provides sixteen examples of false or misleading representations.

1. *Scope.* Prohibited actions are not limited to the sixteen subsections listed as examples of activities that violate this provision. In addition, section 807(1), which prohibits the "use of any false representation or deceptive means" by a debt collector, is particularly broad and encompasses virtually every violation, including those not covered by the other subsections.

Section 807(1) prohibits "the false representation or implication that the debt collector is vouched for, bonded by, or affiliated with the United States or any State."

1. *Symbol on dunning notices.* A debt collector may not use a symbol in correspondence that makes him appear to be a government official. For example, a collection letter depicting a police badge, a judge, or the scales of justice, normally violates this section.

Section 807(2) prohibits falsely representing either "(A) the character, amount, or legal status of any debt; or (B) any services rendered or compensation which may be lawfully received by" the collector.

1. *Legal Status of debt.* A debt collector may not falsely imply that legal action has begun.

2. *Amount of debt.* A debt collector may not claim an amount more than actually owed, or falsely assert that the debt has matured or that it is immediately due and payable, when it is not.

3. *Judgment.* When a debt collector provides the validation notice required by section 809(a)(4), the notice may include the words "copy of a judgment" whether or not a judgment exists, because section 809(a)(4) provides for a statement including these words. Compliance with section 809(a)(4) in this manner will not be considered a violation of section 807(2)(A).

Section 807(3) prohibits falsely representing or implying that "any individual is an attorney or that any communication is from an attorney."

1. *Form of legal correspondence.* A debt collector may not send a collection letter from a "Pre-Legal Department," where no legal department exists. An attorney may use a computer service to send letters on his own behalf, but a debt collector may not send a computer-generated letter deceptively using an attorney's name.

2. *Named individual.* A debt collector may not falsely represent that a person named in a letter is his attorney.

3. *Relation to other sections.* If a creditor falsely uses an attorney's name rather than his own in his collection communications, he both loses his exemption from the FDCPA's definition of "debt collector" (Section 803(6)) and violates this provision.

Section 807(4) prohibits falsely representing or implying to the consumer that non-payment "will result in the arrest or imprisonment of any person or the seizure, garnishment, attachment, or sale of any property or wages of any person."

Section 807(5) prohibits the "threat to take any action that cannot legally by taken or that is not intended to be taken."

1. *Debt collector's statement of his own definite action.* A debt collector may not state that he will take any action unless he intends to take the action when the statement is made, or ordinarily takes the action in similar circumstances.

2. *Debt collector's statement of definite action by third party.* A debt collector may not state that a third party will take any action unless he has reason to believe, at the time the statement is made, that such action will be taken.

3. *Statement of possible action.* A debt collector may not state or imply that he or any third party may take any action unless such action is legal and there is a reasonable likelihood, at the time the statement is made, that such action will be taken. A debt collector may state that certain action is possible, if it is true that such action is legal and is frequently taken by the collector creditor with respect to similar debts; however, if the debt collector has reason to know there are facts that make the action unlikely in the particular case, a statement that the action was possible would be misleading.

4. *Threat of criminal action.* A debt collector may not threaten to report a dishonored check or other fact to the police, unless he actually intends to take this action.

5. *Threat of attachment.* A debt collector may not threaten to attach a consumer's tax refund, when he has no authority to do so.

6. *Threat of legal or other action.* Section 807(5) refers not only to a false threat of legal action, but also a false threat by a debt collector that he will report a debt to a credit bureau, assess a collection fee, or undertaken any other action if the debt is not paid. A debt collector may also not misrepresent the imminence of such action.

A debt collector's implication, as well as a direct statement, of planned legal action may be an unlawful deception. For example, reference to an attorney or to legal proceedings may mislead the debtor as to the likelihood or imminence of legal action.

A debt collector's statement that legal action has been recommended is a representation that legal action may be taken, since such a recommendation implies that the creditor will act on it at least some of the time.

Lack of intent may be inferred when the amount of the debt is so small as to make the action totally unfeasible or when the debt collector is unable to take the action because the creditor has not authorized him to do so.

7. *Illegality of threatened act.* A debt collector may not threaten that he will illegally contact an employer, or other third party, or take some other "action that cannot legally be taken" (such as advising the creditor to sue where such advice would violate state rules governing the unauthorized practice of law). If state law forbids a debt collector from suing in his own name (or from doing so without first obtaining a formal assignment and that has not been done), the debt collector may not represent that he will sue in that state.

Section 807(6) prohibits falsely representing or implying that a transfer of the debt will cause the consumer to (A) lose any claim or defense, or (B) become subject to any practice prohibited by the FDCPA.

1. *Referral to creditor.* A debt collector may not falsely state that the consumer's account will be referred back to the original creditor, who would take action the FDCPA prohibits the debt collector to take.

Section 807(7) prohibits falsely representing or implying that the "consumer committed any crime or other conduct in order to disgrace the consumer."

1. *False allegation of fraud.* A debt collector may not falsely allege that the consumer has committed fraud.

2. *Misrepresentation of criminal law.* A debt collector may not make a misleading statement of law, falsely implying that the consumer has committed a crime, or mischaracterize what constitutes an offense by misstating or omitting significant elements of the offense. From example, a debt collector may not tell the consumer that he has committed a crime by issuing a check that is dishonored, when the statute applies only where there is a "scheme to defraud."

Section 807(8) prohibits "Communicating or threatening to communicate to any person (false) credit information, including the failure to communicate that a disputed debt is disputed.

1. *Disputed debt.* If a debt collector knows that a debt is disputed by the consumer, either from receipt of written notice (section 809) or other means, and reports it to a credit bureau, he must report is as disputed.

2. *Post-report dispute.* When a debt collector learns of a dispute after reporting the debt to a credit bureau, the dispute need not also be reported.

Section 807(9) prohibits the use of any document designed to falsely imply that it issued from a state or federal source, or "which creates a false impression as to its source, authorization, or approval."

1. *Relation to other sections.* Most of the violations of this section involve simulated legal process, which is more specifically covered by section 807(13). However, this subsection is broader in that it also covers documents that fraudulently appear to be official government documents, or otherwise mislead the recipient as to their authorship.

Section 807(10) prohibits the "use of any false representation or deceptive means to collect or attempt to collect any debt or to obtain information concerning a consumer."

1. *Relation to other sections.* The prohibition is so comprehensive that violation of any part of section 807 will usually also violate subsection (10). Actions that violate more specific provisions are discussed in those sections.
2. *Communication format.* A debt collector may not communicate by a format or envelope that misrepresents the nature, purpose, or urgency of the message. It is a violation to send any communication that conveys to the consumer a false sense of urgency. However, it is usually permissible to send a letter generated by a machine, such as a computer or other printing device. A bona fide contest entry from, which provides a clearly optional location to enter employment information, enclosed with request for payment, is not deceptive.
3. *False statement or implications.* A debt collector may not falsely state or imply that a consumer is required to assign his wages to his creditor when he is not, that the debt collector has counseled the creditor to sue when he has not, that adverse credit information has been entered on the consumer's credit record when it has not, that the entire amount is due when it is not, or that he cannot accept partial payments when in fact he is authorized to accept them.
4. *Misrepresentation of law.* A debt collector may not mislead the consumer as to the legal consequences of the consumer's actions (e.g., by falsely implying that a failure to respond is an admission of liability).

    A debt collector may not state that federal law requires a notice of the debt collector's intent to contact third parties.
5. *Misleading letterhead.* A debt collector's employee who is an attorney may not use "attorney-at-law" stationery without referring to his employer, so as to falsely imply tot he consumer that the debt collector had retained a private attorney to bring suit on the account.

Section 807(11) requires the debt collector to "disclose clearly in all communications made to collect a debt or to obtain information about a consumer, that the debt collector is attempting to collect a debt and that any information obtained will be used for that purpose," except where section 804 provides otherwise.

1. *Oral communications.* A debt collector must make the required disclosures in both oral and written communications.
2. *Disclosure to consumers.* When a debt collector contacts a consumer and clearly discloses that he is seeking payment of a debt, he need not state that all information will be used to collect a debt, since that should be apparent to the consumer. The debt collector need not repeat the required disclosure in subsequent contacts.

A debt collector may not send the consumer a note saying only "please call me right away" unless there has been prior contact between the parties and the collector is thus known to the consumer.

3.   *Disclosure to third parties.* Except when seeking location information, the debt collector must state in the first communication with a third party that he is attempting to collect the debt and that information will be used for that purpose, but need not do so in subsequent communications with that party.

Section 807(12) prohibits falsely representing or implying that "accounts have been turned over to innocent purchasers for value."

1.   *Relation to other sections.* Section 807(6)(A) prohibits a false statement or implication that threatening to affect the consumer's rights may be affected by transferring the account; this subsection forbids falsely stating or implying that a transfer to certain parties has occurred.

Section 807(13) prohibits falsely representing or implying that "documents are legal process."

1.   *Simulated legal process.* A debt collector may not send written communications that deceptively resemble legal process forms. He may not send a form or a dunning letter that, taken as a whole, appears to simulate legal process. However, one legal phrase (such as "notice of legal action" or "show just cause why") alone will not result in a violation of this section unless it contributes to an erroneous impression that the document is a legal form.

Section 807(14) prohibits the "use of any business, company, or organization name other than the (collector's) true name."

1.   *Permissible business name.* A debt collector may use a name that does not misrepresent his identity or deceive the consumer. Thus, a collector may use its full business name, the name under which it usually transacts business, or a commonly-used acronym. When the collector uses multiple names in its various affairs, it does not violate this subsection if it consistently uses the same name when dealing with a particular consumer.

2.   *Creditor misrepresentation of identity.* A creditor may not use any name that would falsely imply that a third party is involved in the collection. The in-house collection unit of "ABC Corp." may use the name "ABC Collection Division," but not the name "XYZ Collection Agency" or some other unrelated name.

     A creditor violates this section if he uses the name of a collection bureau as a conduit for a collection process that the creditor controls in collecting his own accounts. Similarly, a creditor may not use a fictitious name or letterhead, or a "post office box address" name that implies someone else is collecting his debts.

     A creditor does not violate this provision where an affiliated (and differently named) debt collector undertakes collection activity, if the debt collector does business separately from the creditor (e.g., where the debt collector in fact has other clients that he treats similarly to the creditor, has his own employees, deals at arms length with the creditor, and controls the process himself).

3. *All collection activities covered.* A debt collector business must use its real business name, commonly-used name, or acronym in both written and oral communications.

4. *Relation to other sections.* If a creditor uses a false business name, he both loses his exemption from the FDCPA's definition of "debt collector" (section 803(6)) and violates this provision. If a debt collector falsely uses the name of an attorney rather than his true business name, he violates section 807(3) as well as this section. When a debt collector uses a false business name in a phone call, he violates section 806(6) as well as this section.

When using the mails to obtain location information, a debt collector may not (unless expressly requested by the recipient to identify the firm) use a name that indicates he is in the debt collector business, or he will violate section 804(5). When a debt collector's employee who is seeking location information replies to an inquiry about him employer's identity under section 804(1), he must give the true name of his employer.

Section 807(15) prohibits falsely representing or implying that documents are not legal process forms or do not required action by the consumer.

1. *Disguised legal process.* A debt collector may not deceive a consumer into failing to respond to legal process by concealing the import of the papers, thereby subjecting the consumer to a default judgment.

Section 807(16) prohibits falsely representing or implying that a debt collector operates or is employed by a "consumer reporting agency" as defined in the Fair Credit Reporting Act.

1. *Dual agencies.* The FDCPA does not prohibit a debt collector from operating a consumer reporting agency.

2. *Misleading names.* Only a bona fide consumer reporting agency may use names such as "Credit Bureau," "Credit Bureau Collection Agency," "General Credit Control," "Credit Bureau Rating, Inc.," or "National Debtors Rating." A debt collector's disclaimer in the text of a letter that the debt collector is not affiliated with (or employed by) a consumer reporting agency, will not necessarily avoid a violation if the collector uses a name that indicates otherwise.

3. *Factual issue.* Whether a debt collector that has called itself a credit bureau actually qualifies as such is a factual issue, to be decided according to the debt collector's actual operation.

Section 808—Unfair Practices

Section 808 prohibits a debt collector from using "unfair or unconscionable means" in his debt collection activity. It provides eight example so unfair practices.

1. *Scope.* Prohibited actions are not limited to the eight subsections listed as examples of activities that violate this provision.

2. *Elements of unfairness.* A debt collector's act in collecting a debt may be "unfair" if it causes injury to the consumer that is (1) substantial, (2) not outweighed by countervailing benefits to consumers or competition, and (3) not reasonably avoidable by the consumer.

Section 808(1) prohibits collecting any amount unless the amount is expressly authorized by the agreement creating the debt or is permitted by law.

1. *Kinds of amounts covered.* For purposes of this section, "amount" includes not only the debt, but also any incidental charges, such as collection charges, interest, service charges, late fees, and bad check handling charges.

2. *Legality of charges.* A debt collector may attempt to collect a fee or charge in addition to the debt if either (a) the charge is expressly provided for in the contract creating the debt and the charge is not prohibited by state law, or (B) the contract is silent but the charge is otherwise expressly permitted by state law. Conversely, a debt collector may not collect an additional amount if either (A) state law expressly prohibits collection of the amount or (B) the contract does not provide for collection of the amount and state law is silent.

3. *Legality of fee under state law.* If state law permits collection of reasonable fees, the reasonableness (and consequential legality) of these fees is determined by state law.

4. *Agreement not in writing.* A debt collector may establish an "agreement" without a written contract. For example, he may collect a service charge on a dishonored check based on a posted sign on the merchant's premises allowing such a charge, if he can demonstrate that the consumer knew of the charge.

Section 808(2) prohibits accepting a check postdated by more than five days unless timely written notice is given to the consumer prior to deposit.
Section 808(3) prohibits soliciting any postdated check for purposes of threatening or instituting criminal prosecution.
Section 808(4) prohibits depositing a postdated check prior to its date.

1. *Postdated checks.* These provisions do not totally prohibit debt collectors from accepting postdated checks from consumers, but rather prohibit debt collectors from misusing such instruments.

Section 808(5) prohibits causing any person to incur telephone or telegram charges by concealing the true purpose of the communication.

1. *Long distance calls to the debt collector.* A debt collector may not call the consumer collect or ask a consumer to call him long distance without disclosing the debt collector's identity and the communication's purpose.

2. *Relation to other section.* A debt collector who conceals his purpose in asking consumers to call long distance may also violate section 807(11), which requires the debt collector to disclose his purpose in some communications.

Section 808(6) prohibits taking nonjudicial action to enforce a security interest on property, or threatening to do so, where (A) there is not present right to the collateral, (B) there is no present intent to exercise such rights, or (C) the property is exempt by law.

1. *Security enforcers.* Because the FDCPA's definition of "debt collection" includes parties whose principal business is enforcing security interests only for section 808(6) purposes, such parties (if they do not otherwise fall within the definition) are subject only to this provision and not to the rest of the FDCPA.

Section 808(7) prohibits "Communicating with a consumer regarding a debt by post card."

1. *Debt.* A debt collector does not violate this section if he sends a post card to a consumer that does not communicate the existence of the debt. However, if he had not previously disclosed that he is attempting to collect a debt, he would violate section 807(11), which requires this disclosure.

Section 808(8) prohibits showing anything other than the debt collector's address, on any envelope in any written communication to the consumer, except that a debt collector may use his business name if it does not indicate that he is in the debt collector business.

1. *Business names prohibited on envelopes.* A debt collector may not put on his envelope any business name with "debt" or "collector" in it, or any other name that indicates he is in the debt collection business. A debt collector may not use the American Collectors Association logo on an envelope.
2. *Collector's name.* Whether a debt collector/consumer reporting agency's use of his own "credit bureau" or other name indicates that he is in the collection business, and thus violates the section, is a factual issue to be determined in each individual case.
3. *Harmless words or symbols.* A debt collector does not violate this section by using an envelope printed with words or notations that do not suggest the purpose of the communication. For example, a collector may communicate via an actual telegram or similar service that uses a Western Union (or other provider) logo and the word "telegram" (or similar word) on the envelope, or a letter with the word "Personal" or "Confidential" on the envelope.
4. *Transparent envelopes.* A debt collector may not use a transparent envelope, which reveals language or symbols indicating his debt collector business, because it is the equivalent of putting information on an envelope.

Section 809—Validation of Debts

Section 809(a) requires a collector, within 5 days of the first communication, to provide the consumer a written notice (if not provided in that communication) containing (1) the amount of the debt and (2) the name of the creditor, along with a statement that he will (3) assume the debt's validity unless the consumer disputes it within 30 days, (4) send a verification or copy of the judgment if the consumer timely disputes the debt, and (5) identify the original creditor upon written request.

1. *Who must provide notice.* If the employer debt collector agency gives the required notice, employee debt collectors need not also provide it. A debt collector's agent may give the notice, as long as it is clear that the information is being provided on behalf of the debt collector

2. *Single notice required.* The debt collector is not required to provide more than one notice for each debt. A notice need not offer to identify the original creditor unless the name and address of the original creditor are different from the current creditor.

3. *Form of notices.* The FDCPA imposes no requirements as to the form, sequence, location, or typesize of the notice. However, an illegible notice does not comply with this provision.

4. *Alternate terminology.* A debt collector may condense and combine the required disclosures, as long as he provides all required information.

5. *Oral notice.* If a debt collector's first communication with the consumer is oral, he may make the disclosures orally at that time in which case he need not send a written notice.

6. *Legal action.* A debt collector's institution of formal legal action against a consumer (including the filing of a complaint or service of legal papers by an attorney in connection with a lawsuit to collect a debt) or transmission of a notice to a consumer that is required by law as a prerequisite to enforcing a contractual obligation is not a "communication in connection with collection of any debt," and thus does not confer section 809 notice-and-validation rights on the consumer.

7. *Collection activities by attorneys.* An attorney who regularly attempts to collect debts by means other than litigation, such as writing the consumer demand letters (dunning notices) or calling the consumer on the phone about the obligation (except in response to a consumer's call to him after suit has been commenced), must provide the required notice, even if a previous debt collector (or creditor) has given such a notice.

8. *Effect of including proof with first notice.* A debt collector must verify a disputed debt even if he has included proof of the debt with the first communication, because the section is intended to assist the consumer when a debt collector inadvertently contacts the wrong consumer at the start of his collection efforts.

Section 809(b) requires that, if the consumer disputes the debt or requests identification of the original creditor in writing, the collector must cease collection efforts until he verifies the debt and mails a response. Section 809(c) states that a consumer's failure to dispute the validity of a debt under this section may not be interpreted by a court as an admission of liability.

1. *Pre-notice collection.* A debt collector need not cease normal collection activities within the consumer's 30-day period to give notice of a dispute until he receives a notice from the consumer. An attorney debt collector may take legal action within 30 days of sending the notice, regardless of whether the consumer disputes the debt. If the consumer disputes the debt, the attorney may still take legal action but must cease collection efforts until verification is obtained and mailed to the consumer.

A debt collector may report a debt to a credit bureau within the 30-day notice period, before he receives a request for validation or a dispute notice from the consumer.

Section 810—Multiple Debts

Section 810 provides: "If any consumer owes multiple debts and makes any single payment to any debt collector with respect to such debts, such debt collector may not apply such payment to any debt which is disputed by the consumer and, where applicable, shall apply such payment in accordance with the consumer's directions."

Section 811-Legal Actions by Debt Collectors

Section 811 provides that a debt collector may sue a consumer only in the judicial district where the consumer resides or signed the contract sued upon, except that an action to enforce a security interest in real property which secures the obligation must be brought where the property is located.

1. *Waiver.* Any waiver by the consumer must be provided directly to the debt collector (not to the creditor in the contract establishing the debt), because the forum restriction applies to actions brought by the debt collector.

2. *Multiple defendants.* Since a debt collector may sue only where the consumer (1) lives or (2) signed the contract, the collector may not join an ex-husband as a defendant to a suit against the ex-wife in the district of her residence, unless he also lives there or signed the contract there. The existence of community property at her residence that is available to pay his debts does not alter the forum limitations on individual consumers.

3. *Real estate security.* A debt collector may sue based on the location of a consumer's real property only when he seeks to enforce an interest in such property that secures the debts.

4. *Services without written contract.* Where services were provided pursuant to an oral agreement, the debt collector may sue only where the consumer resides. He may not sue where services were performed (if that is different from the consumer's residence), because that is not included as permissible forum location by this provision.

5. *Enforcement of judgments.* If a judgment is obtained in a forum that satisfies the requirements of this section, it may be enforced in another jurisdiction, because the consumer previously has had the opportunity to defend the original action in a convenient forum.

6. *Scope.* This provision applies to lawsuits brought by a debt collector, including an attorney debt collector, when the debt collector is acting on his own behalf or on behalf of his client.

Section 812—Furnishing Certain Deceptive Forms

Section 812 prohibits any party from designing and furnishing forms, knowing they are or will be used to deceive a consumer to believe that someone other than his creditor is collecting the debt, and imposes FDCPA civil liability on parties who supply such forms.

1. *Practice prohibited.* This section prohibits the practice of selling to creditors dunning letters that falsely imply that a debt collector is participating in collection of the debt, when in fact only the creditor is collecting.

2. *Coverage.* This section applies to anyone who designs, complies, or furnishes the forms prohibited by this section.

3. *Pre-collection letters.* A form seller may not furnish a creditor with (1) a letter on a collector's letterhead to be used when the collector is not involved in collecting the creditor's debts, or (2) a letter indicating "copy to (the collector)" if the collector is not participating in collecting the creditor's debt. A form seller may not avoid liability by including a statement in the text of a form letter that the sender has not yet been assigned the account for collection, if the communication as a whole, using the collector's letterhead, represents otherwise.

4. *Knowledge required.* A party does not violate this provision unless he knows or should have known that his form letter will be used to mislead consumers into believing that someone other than the creditor is involved in collecting the debt.

5. *Participation by debt collector.* A debt collector that uses letters as his only collection tool does not violate this section, merely because he charges a flat rate per letter, if he is meaningfully "participating in the collection of a debt." The consumer is not misled in such cases, as he would be in the case of a party who supplied the creditor with form letters and provided little or no additional service in the collection process. The performance of other tasks associated with collection (e.g. handling verification requests, negotiating payment arrangements, keeping individual records) is evidence that such party is "participating in the collection."

Section 813—Civil Liability

Section 813(A) imposes civil liability in the form of (1) actual damages, (2) discretionary penalties, and (3) costs and attorney's fees, (B) discusses relevant factors a court should consider in assessing damages, (C) exculpates a collector who maintains reasonable procedures from liability for an unintentional error, (D) permits actions to be brought in federal or state courts within one year from the violation, and (E) shields a defendant who relies on an advisory opinion of the Commission.

1. *Employee liability.* Since the employees of a debt collection agency are "debt collectors," they are liable for violations to the same extent as the agency.

2. *Damages.* The courts have awarded "actual damages" for FDCPA violations that were not just out-of-pocket expenses, but included damages for personal humiliation, embarrassment, mental anguish, or emotional distress.

3. *Application of statute of limitation period.* The section's one year statute of limitations applies only to private lawsuits, not to actions brought by a government agency.

4. *Advisory opinions.* A party may act in reliance on a formal advisory opinion of the Commission pursuant to 16 CFR 1.1-1.4, without risk of civil liability. This protection does not extend to reliance on this Commentary or other informal staff interpretations.

Section 814—Administrative Enforcement

Section 814 provides that the principal federal enforcement agency for the FDCPA is the Federal Trade Commission, but assigns enforcement power to other authorities empowered by certain federal statutes to regulate financial, agricultural, and transportation activities, where FDCPA violations related to acts subject to those laws.

Section 815—Reports to Congress by Commission

Section 815 requires the Commission to submit an annual report to Congress which discusses its enforcement and other activities administering the FDCPA, assesses the degree of compliance, and makes recommendations.

Section 916—Relations to State Laws

Section 816 provides that the FDCPA pre-empts state laws only to the extent that those laws are inconsistent with any provision of the FDCPA, and then only to the extent of the inconsistency. A State law is not inconsistent if it gives consumers greater protection than the FDCPA.

1. *Inconsistent laws.* Where a state law provides protection to the consumer equal to, or greater than, the FDCPA, it is not pre-empted by the federal statute.

Section 817—Exemption For State Regulation

Section 817 orders the Commission to exempt any class of debt collection practices from the FDCPA within any State if it determines that State laws regulating those practices are substantially similar to the FDCPA, and contain adequate provision for enforcement.

1. *State exemptions.* A state with a debt collector law may apply to the Commission for an exemption. The Commission must grant the exemption if the state's law is substantially similar to the FDCPA, and there is adequate provision for enforcement. The Commission has published procedures for processing such applications (16 CFR 901).

Section 818—Effective Date

Section 818 provides that the FDCPA took effect six months from the date of its enactment.

1. *Key dates.* The FDCPA was approved September 20, 1977, and became effective March 20, 1978. [FR Doc. 88-28573 File 12-12-88; 6:45 am]

CHAPTER 12

Truth in Lending Regulation Z

After reading the advertisement, the consumer borrowed the sum of one hundred dollars for one year with interest at nine percent. After the loan was made, the consumer learned that the nine dollars interest was subtracted from the hundred dollar loan and he only received ninety-one dollars. The consumer had to repay the loan in twelve monthly payments over the year. The effective rate of interest on this loan, since only ninety-one dollars was given to the borrower, and the loan was repaid monthly, approached nineteen percent and not the nine percent as advertised.

If the loan was secured by a lien on an automobile, the opportunity for the lender to charge expenses in addition to the interest in the printed form contract was only limited by the creativity of the institution. While most major banks attempt to disclose to consumers the cost of borrowing money, other less scrupulous banks and financial institutions are guilty of some form of deceptive and misleading advertising concerning the true cost of borrowing and the accuracy of the annual interest rate.

The Truth In Lending Act (TIL) was originally signed by President Johnson in 1968 and was intended to induce the consumer to shop for the best price for credit in the same way one shops for the best price for an automobile. The creditor is required to make full disclosure of important credit charges so that the consumer may shop for the most favorable credit terms. The Act, amended several times, basically requires creditors to disclose to the consumer the actual cost of the borrowing. The thrust of the Act is to enable the consumer to compare the various credit terms, to require detailed disclosure of the cost of credit, and to protect the consumer against inaccurate and unfair credit billing and credit card practices. The findings and purposes of the Truth In Lending Act are:

> "to assure a meaningful disclosure of credit terms so that the consumer will be able to compare more readily various credit terms available to him and avoid the uninformed use of credit."

Disclosures must be "clear and conspicuous" and are to be presented to the consumer in a "reasonable understandable form." The Act also deals with the practice of leasing automobiles for consumer use as an alternative to installment credit sales since these leases are offered without adequate cost disclosure.

Three basic documents must be considered. The Truth In Lending Act (of which the Fair Credit Billing Act is a part) consists of 40 pages (double column). Regulation Z are the rules and regulations (covering 80 pages) implementing the Truth In Lending Act. The Official Staff Commentary (another 103 pages) to Regulation Z of the Truth In Lending Act is designed to explain and interpret Regulation Z. An in-depth analysis of these 223 pages obviously is beyond the scope of this book, but this chapter will attempt to present an overview of the highlights. The Truth In Lending Act is included in the Appendix, and Regulation Z and the commentary, not included because of their length, may be ordered free form the Board of Governors of the Federal Reserve Board, Washington D.C.

DEFINITIONS

Creditor—The creditor is the person who has regularly extended credit at least twenty-five times in the preceding year in connection with the loan, sale of property, services or otherwise. A creditor who extends loans secured by homes is covered by the Act merely by extending credit five times in the preceding calendar year providing all the extension of credits were secured by a dwelling.

The extension of credit must be repayable by agreement in more than four installments and a finance charge is or may be required. The creditor must also be the person to whom the obligation is initially payable.[1]

When a loan is transferred and assigned to another institution, the party to whom the loan is initially payable is still covered by the Truth In Lending Act; and the party and the institution which receive the assignment are still subject to certain disclosure requirements under the Act.

Consumer—The consumer is the party to whom credit is offered. The money, property, or services which are the subject of the transaction must be for personal, family, or household purposes.

---

[1] 12 CFR 226.2 (17); *Childs v. Ford Motor Credit Co.*, 470 F. Supp. 708 (1979); *Tom Benson Chevway Rental & Leasing v. Allen*, 571 S.W. 2d 346 cert. denied 442 U.S. 930 (1978).

Credit Card—A credit card is any card or other credit devised for the purpose of obtaining money, property, labor, or services on credit.

EXEMPTIONS

The creditor must make a determination whether the transaction is exempt from the Truth In Lending Act because it is a commercial transaction.[2] As a general rule commercial, business, agricultural or organizational credit are exempt from the TIL.[3]

The commentary sets forth factors to consider to determine whether a transaction is exempt. With regard to the acquisition of antiques, securities, or art, the following factors are important:

1. The business of the borrower in relation to the property to be acquired.
2. The degree to which the borrower can personally manage the acquisition.
3. The ratio of income from the acquisition to the total income of the borrower.
4. The size of the transaction.
5. The borrower's statement as to the purpose of the loan.

The commentary also sets forth three examples of exempt transactions involving business purpose credit:

1. A loan to expand a business even if secured by the borrower's residence or personal property.
2. A loan to improve a principal residence by putting in a business office.
3. A business account used occasionally for consumer purposes.

If a firm loans money to employees for personal purposes, the loan is for a consumer purpose and is covered by the Act. On the other hand, a loan for a child's tuition secured by mechanic's tools is considered consumer credit as is a personal account used occasionally for business purposes.[4] Consultation with experienced counsel is recommended for marginal fact situations.

Any credit card issued for the sole purpose of obtaining business credit is exempt under the Act, as well as any credit extension for agricultural purposes. An extension of credit to a corporation or organization is exempt, regardless of the purpose of the credit. Any extension of credit in excess of $25,000 is exempt, except an extension of credit for a residence which is used as the principal dwelling. Such extensions of credit are covered even if they exceed the $25,000

---

[2] 12 CFR 226.3; *Smith v. Chapman* 436 F. Supp. 58 (1977) Affd 614 F. 2nd 968 (1980).

[3] 12 CFR 226.3.

[4] 12 CFR 226.3.

threshold. An extension of credit involving public utility services such as gas, water, electricity, etc. is not covered under the Act. Transactions in securities or commodities accounts in which credit is extended by a broker dealer registered with the Security and Exchange Commission or Commodity Future Trading Commission are not covered.

FINANCE CHARGES

The finance charge is the cost of consumer credit as a dollar amount and includes any charge payable directly or indirectly by the consumer as a result of the extension of credit.[5]

If the charge is made to the consumer in a comparable cash transaction, the charge is not a finance charge. Nevertheless, if the charge for the credit transaction exceeds the charge in a cash transaction, the difference is a "finance charge." The burden rests with the creditor to compare a cash transaction and a credit transaction to determine if the difference in price is due to the extension of the credit. The regulation offers concrete examples to illustrate the definition.

Examples follow:

1. Interest is the largest ingredient (sometimes the only ingredient) of the finance charge. The difference between the credit price and the cash price is the interest.

2. If the creditor imposes a charge on the consumer to cover a specific cost of doing business (extending credit), the extra charge becomes a finance charge, since it is incurred by the consumer as a result of the extension of credit.

3. All service, transaction, activity, and carrying charges are considered finance charges.

4. A fee to participate in a credit plan is a finance charge.

5. Loan fees, finders fees, and similar charges are considered finance charges, as well as fees for an investigation of a credit report.

6. Premiums or any other charge for any guarantee or insurance protecting the creditor against the consumer's default or other credit loss is a finance charge.

7. Charges for premiums for credit life (insuring the extension of credit), accident or life insurance are also included in the finance charge with certain exceptions.

---

[5]*Bates v. Provident Consumer Discount Co.*, 493 F. Sup. 605 (1979); *Meyers v. Clearview Dodge Sales, Inc.*, 539 F.2d 511 (1976).

8. Premiums for insurance written in connection with a consumer credit transaction against loss or damage to property or liability dealing with property are also included in the finance charges.

   Case law indicates that creditors should include the cost of credit life insurance in the finance charge. If most loans are sold with life insurance, the premium should be included as a finance charge. Court decisions suggest the premium be included as part of the amount when quoting a repayment schedule.[6] On the other hand, if the insurance coverage may be obtained from an insurance company of the consumer's choice and is properly disclosed, the premium need not be included as a finance charge. The consumer must know how much the insurance costs before an election is made as well as the term of the insurance, if the term is less than the term of the transaction. Single interest insurance which protects only the creditor's interest in the property is considered a finance charge.

9. Inspection and handling fees for the disbursement of loan proceeds are considered a finance charge.

10. Fees for preparing a Truth In Lending disclosure statement or charges for a maintenance or service contract are finance charges.

11. Except if imposed in connection with a mortgage on a residence, appraisal, investigation, and credit report fees are finance charges, providing the charge is reasonable in amount and bona fide. They can be excluded as a finance charge in real estate transactions if they are included in the application fee charged to all applicants, even if credit is ultimately denied.

12. Compulsory pre-paid finance charges paid before the consummation of any credit transaction or withheld from the advance are generally a finance charge, although the commentary is not clear on this point and allows exceptions to this general rule.

CHARGES NOT CONSIDERED FINANCE CHARGES

The regulation leads the lender to believe that if the exemption is not specifically listed, it doesn't exist. This is not so, since the regulation explicitly states that the creditor must make the decision as to whether the difference in the cost is due to the extension of credit. If the difference in the cost of credit is not due to the extension of credit, it is not a finance charge. The following are examples not considered finance charges:

1. Taxes, license fees, or registration fees paid by both cash or credit customers.

2. Discounts that are available to both cash and credit customers, such as volume discounts.

---

[6]*US Life Corp. Credit v. FTC*, 599 F.2d 1387 (1979).

3. Charges for service policy, auto club membership, or a policy of insurance against latent defects.

4. Application fees may be excluded if designed to recover the cost associated with processing applications for credit and charged to all applicants, not just approved applicants who receive credit.

5. Late payment charges for an unanticipated late payment, exceeding a credit limit, or for delinquency, default, or similar occurrence.

6. Certain fees in transactions secured by real property in residential mortgage transactions, if bona fide and reasonable in amount, including fees for title examination, abstract of title, fees for preparing deeds, mortgages, notary, appraisal, credit reporting fees, and amounts required to be paid into escrow or trust accounts.

7. Discounts offered to induce payment for the purchase by cash, check, or other means.

8. Any charge passed to the buyer imposed by a creditor for providing credit to the buyer or for providing credit on certain terms.

9. "Seller points" (a charge by creditor to the debtor for providing credit), such as those frequently involved in real estate transactions.

ANNUAL PERCENTAGE RATE (APR)

The annual percentage rate is a measure of credit expressed in a yearly rate.[7] In simple terms, *all the finance charges that are included in the definition of finance charges must be translated into a simple interest rate on the outstanding balance for one year.*[8] The regulation spends several pages setting forth the appropriate mathematical formulas for translating charges. This process is perhaps the most important contribution of the Truth In Lending Act. The ability of the consumer to understand, in simple terms, the cost of borrowing is the main purpose of the Act, and any effort to evade or circumvent its intent and purpose will expose the lender to liability for violating the provisions of the Act.[9]

If a hundred dollar loan at six percent interest is to be repaid in one lump sum at the end of the year with the payment of a hundred and six dollars, the annual interest rate is six percent. If a hundred dollar loan is repaid monthly, the interest rate almost doubles to 11 to 12 percent. If payments are made quarterly, the interest charge is substantially more than six percent, but less than 11 to 12 percent. Labeling a variety of other charges as expenses for a particular procedure or service also misleads the uninformed consumer. The purpose of the Act is to

---

[7]16 CFR Sec. 226.22.

[8]12 CFR Sec. 226.4.

[9]12 CFR Sec. 226.18; TIL 107.

lump together all of these other service and expense charges as interest, since the charge is for the extension of credit. The conversion into an annual simple percentage rate levels the playing field among all the lenders so that the consumer can compare the true rates of interest.

OPEN-END CREDIT

An open-end credit plan is defined under the Truth In Lending Act as one contemplating repeated transactions, such as the Visa or Mastercard credit card or revolving bank credit. Any other plan not contemplating repeated transactions is a closed-end plan. The repeated transaction plan must set forth the terms and conditions of the transaction, including the finance charge or interest charge on the unpaid balance computed in accordance with the terms of the transaction. The open-end credit coverage specifically requires that the creditor have twenty-five open-end accounts in the preceding calendar year, or five open-end accounts if those accounts are secured by a residence. The purpose of identifying an open-end credit plan or a closed-end credit plan is *to determine the extent of the disclosures.* Travel and entertainment cards that do not impose an interest charge are treated as closed-end credit. If the card issuer enters into transactions payable in more than four installments, the card issuer may be subject to the open-end disclosures if twenty-five accounts were opened in the preceding calendar year.

INITIAL DISCLOSURES

The initial disclosure by the creditor occurs before a credit card is issued and before the consumer pays any fees or charges to the creditor. The disclosure must be clear and conspicuous.[10] The finance charge and the annual percentage rates must be more conspicuous than other disclosures, usually by using capital letters or letters in different colors. The creditor is required to describe an open-end credit "finance charge" and "annual percentage rate." The Truth In Lending Act requires specific disclosures under Section 127A for open-end consumer credit plans, including the following where applicable:

1. The annual percentage rate imposed and a statement that such rate does not include costs other than interest.
2. A full description of any variable rate, including the annual percentage rate, the maximum amount being charged, the maximum annual percentage rate, a table disclosing the repayment options, and other details.
3. An itemization of any fees imposed by the creditor, including annual fees, application fees, transaction fees, and closing costs commonly described as

---

[10]12 CFR Sec. 226.6.

"points," and the time such fees are payable, plus a disclosure as to what is charged by outside third parties, such as government authorities, appraisers, and attorneys, in addition to a good faith estimate of those fees.

4. If the credit is to be secured by a residence, disclosure that the residence will be forfeited in the event of a default.

5. A clear and conspicuous statement that if a change in rates, terms or provisions occurs, the consumer may refuse to consummate the agreement and obtain a refund of all fees.

6. A statement of the conditions under which the creditor may terminate the account and require immediate payment of the outstanding balance.

7. The repayment option under the plan.

8. An example of the minimum monthly or periodic payment, and the time needed to repay the entire balance due.

9. A disclosure of the minimum periodic payment the length of the repayment period, the balloon payment at the end, if any, and whether the repayment covers all interest and charges.

10. Any limitation on the amount of any increase in the minimum payments, resulting in negative amortization.

11. Any limitation contained on the number of extensions of credit.

12. The amount of credit which may be obtained during any month of the defined period.

13. A statement that the consumer should consult a tax advisor regarding the deductibility of interest and charges.

14. The maximum interest rate if a variable rate is used. If the interest rate is set and is unchanged during the entire period of the credit, the maximum rate does not have to be disclosed.

Often in the instance where there are two owners of a house and one owner wishes to borrow money, the other owner is required to sign the mortgage even though they have not become obligated under the loan which the mortgage secures. We now have a case in point that states that the co-signer is entitled to all disclosure rights at the time of signing as well as any rights of a primary borrower, where the property is foreclosed.[11]

The Official Staff Commentary of the Truth and Lending Act sets forth that payment deferral is not considered a new credit transaction even though the debtor was offered nine one-month payment deferrals, for which he paid each time. The debtor was claiming that the nine deferrals cost him over $1,000 in interest and that he was entitled to a disclosure of this finance charge because of the payment deferrals. The court properly held that the Truth in Lending Act does not create a duty of disclosure when creditors offer payment holidays.[12]

---

[11]*Soto v. PNC Bank*, 221 B.R. 343 (E.D. Pa. 1998)

[12]*Vegal v. P & C Bank*, Ohio Na. No. 97-3915/4147 (6th Cir. December 20, 1998).

PERIODIC STATEMENTS

Periodic statements must be sent to the consumer at the end of each billing cycle, if a finance charge has been imposed during the cycle, or if an outstanding debit of more than a dollar remains at the end of the cycle. If no amount is owing, no statement need be sent.[13]

The periodic statement must contain the following:[14]

A. Credit balance.

B. Identification of all transactions.

C. Listing of all credit relating to credit extensions together with other types of credits.

D. Disclosure of any periodic rates that may be used to compute the finance charge, whether or not applied during the cycle.

E. Identification of the balance on which the finance charge is computed.

F. Whether any split rates were charged on the balance.

G. The total finance charge amount for the plan is not required, but each type of finance charge imposed during the cycle must be separately itemized.

H. The annual percentage rate.

I. Any other charges actually imposed during the cycle.

J. The closing date of the billing cycle.

K. If applicable, the time within which the new balance shall be paid (a "free ride").

L. The address to send any notice of billing errors.

M. The general purpose address. A telephone number may or may not be included, but the address must be included and must be clear and conspicuous.

The periodic statement must itemize and identify by type the amount of any other finance charges debited to the account and the dollar amount of the finance charge added during the billing cycle. The term "finance charge" must be used. The commentary emphasizes other charges which must be disclosed (not finance charges), such as membership fees, late charges, charges for exceeding credit limit, taxes, and charges in connection with real estate transactions.

SALE CREDIT

Sale credit is defined as using a credit card to buy goods, whereas non-sale credit is defined as using a credit card to obtain cash advances or overdraft checking. The commentary lists separate sale credit rules and non-sale credit rules.

---

[13]12 CFR 226.7.

[14]12 CFR 226.7(a).

BILLING RIGHTS

At least once a year the creditor must send a statement of the statutory protections for billing errors and disclose to the consumer the claims and defenses available to credit card users.[15]

CHANGE IN TERMS

Any change in terms must be communicated to the consumer at least fifteen days before the change or modification takes effect. The commentary sets forth changes that require the fifteen-day notice as well as those which do not. The fifteen-day notice does not have to be provided if the consumer's liability or obligation is not affected.

CREDIT BALANCES

When a credit balance in excess of $1.00 is created in an open-end transaction, it shall be credited to the consumer's account or any part refunded upon request. A good faith effort to refund to the consumer by cash, check, or money order, or credit to a deposit account of the consumer with respect to any part of the credit balance remaining in the account for more than six months, must be made. If the consumer's current location is not known, no further action is required by the creditor.[16]

DISCLOSURE ON RENEWAL

The creditor must provide the card holder with notice of renewal at least thirty days, or one billing cycle, before the renewal date.

RIGHT TO RESCIND

The plaintiff claimed the bank violated the Truth in Lending Act by failing to notify them of their right to rescind for a three-day period. Plaintiff contended the bank's notice was defective because it expired before consummation of the transaction. Section 125 of the Truth in Lending Act provides as follows:

---

[15]12 CFR 226.9.

[16]12 CFR 226.21.

". . . . the obligor (consumer) shall have the right to rescind the transaction until midnight of the third business day following the consummation of the transaction or the delivery of the information and rescission forms required under this section together with a statement containing the material disclosures required under this chapter whichever is later. ..."

If the lender fails to supply the notice of the right to rescind or fails to disclose the regulation, the obligor has three years from the consummation of the loan to rescind.

The regulation defines "consummation" as the time that a consumer becomes contractually obligated on credit transactions. The defendants argued that there was no mutual consent until they signed the property-improvement agreement and addendum. Nevertheless, the court pointed out that the bank offered them a $460,000 loan by the use of a loan-commitment letter and that the plaintiffs expressly accepted the essential terms of that offer. The acceptance of the letter of commitment was sufficient consideration under California contract law. The court thereafter held that the loan agreement actually took place when the loan commitment was signed, and not when the property-improvement agreement was signed five days later.

The court defined consummation as the time the consumer becomes contractually obligated in a credit transaction. It certainly can be argued that accepting a commitment letter does obligate the party to perform the terms of the commitment letter and ultimately to execute the improvement agreement. On the other hand, if the loan-commitment letter was breached, the only liability would be the damages for breach of the loan-commitment letter. The lender would have a cause of action for the damages sustained by not granting the loan and having the debtor execute the property-improvement agreements. Executing a loan commitment letter does not make the debtor liable on the credit transaction, but only liable for damages for breaching the loan-commitment letter. Obviously these arguments were not adopted by the Court of Appeals of the 9th Circuit in California.[17]

EXPIRATION OF RIGHT TO RESCIND. A Florida case which seemed to disagree with several other decisions, held that the statutory right of rescission under the TILA expires three years after the transaction closing date and may not be revived as a defense in recoupment where a creditor commenced a foreclosure action. The debtor asserted that his right to recission in a recoupment action stretched even beyond the three year period set forth in the statute. On appeal, the Appellate Court upheld the lower court and noted that the statute expressly provided that the right and the remedy expires three years after the closing date.[18]

---

[17]*Larson v. California Federal Bank*, 76 F.3d 387 (9th Cir. 1996).

[18]*Beach v. Great Western Bank*, 69 So. 2d 146 (Fla. 1997); *Great Western Bank v. Shoemaker*, 69 So. 2d 805 (Fla. Ct. App., 2d Dist. 1997); *Beach v. Great Western Bank*, 69 So. 2d 146 (Fla. 1997); *Beach v. Ocwen Federal Bank*, 97-5310 U.S. S.

CLOSED-END CREDIT

All consumer credit is treated as closed-end credit unless it meets the definition of open-end credit. In a typical closed-end credit transaction, credit is advanced for a specific time period and the amount financed, finance charge, and scheduled payments are agreed upon between the lender and the customer. Thus, closed-end credit covers almost all credit transactions, except credit cards and other credit extensions which meet the criteria of open-end credit or revolving credit.

The time of disclosure for a closed-end transaction must be before the confirmation of the transaction. The disclosure should reflect the terms of the obligations between the parties. Disclosure statements are to be designed so the consumer can understand any mathematical computation and to provide an easy basis for comparing the cost of credit offered by other competitors. As in open-end credit, finance charges and the annual percentage rate must be displayed in a clear and conspicuous manner.

SEGREGATION OF DISCLOSURE

The disclosure must be segregated from everything else (such as the advertising copy), and must not contain information that is not related to the disclosure. The purpose is so that the consumer will not be confused and will easily absorb the information. The disclosure must be written and copies must be furnished to the consumer who can retain the disclosure. The only specific requirement is that the disclosure is legible. Segregating the disclosure by outlining it in a box, by using bold print or a different color, or by using a different type style is permitted. The disclosure may be placed on the same document as the credit contract, on a separate disclosure statement, on the front and back of the document, or continued to another page.

The creditor must disclose the following information wherever applicable:[19]

A. Identity of the creditor.
B. Amount financed, subtracting any pre-paid finance charge and adding any other amounts to the finance charge.
C. Itemization of the amount financed, including the amount of any proceeds, the amount credited, the amount paid to other persons, and the pre-paid finance charges.
D. Finance charge.
E. Annual percentage rate.
F. Variable rate, where applicable.

---

[19]12 CFR 226.18.

G. The payment schedule, which includes the payments and the timing of the payments.

H. The total of the payments.

I. The demand feature, where applicable.

J. The total sale price, if it is a credit sale.

K. Any pre-payment privileges.

L. Any dollar or percentage charge, if applicable, for late payment.

M. Disclosure of security interest if any property is being pledged as security.

N. Any insurance premiums.

O. Security interest charges.

P. Reference to appropriate contract document for information about non-payment default, right to accelerate, or pre-payment privileges.

Q. With regard to a residential mortgage, a statement as to whether the mortgage may be assumed.

R. Requirement of a deposit, if applicable.

TIMING OF DISCLOSURE

A closed-end disclosure must be made before the credit is granted. The phrase used is "before consummation" of the transaction.[20] Consummation occurs when the consumer becomes obligated, even if the creditor has the right to disapprove of the transaction. With regard to mail or telephone orders for credit sales, the creditor may delay disclosures until the due date of the first payment. Nevertheless, prior to accepting an actual order, the creditor must make available to the consumer the cash price or principal amount, the finance charge, the annual percentage rate or variable rate information, and repayment terms. Any obligations which are payable on demand at any time after consummation must be disclosed.[21]

ENTITLED TO DISCLOSURE

Only one consumer has primary liability on an obligation and this particular consumer is the only one entitled to disclosure, even though guarantors are involved in the credit extension. Guarantors and endorsers are not considered consumers, but have certain other rights if they are obligated on credit card plans. While the consumer is entitled to the disclosure, the Act is not clear as to the extent guaran-

---

[20]*Bryson v. Bank of New York*, 584 F. Supp. 1306 (1984).

[21]12 CFR 226.17(b).

tors and endorsers are entitled to the disclosure provisions, but co-buyers are entitled to notice.

The amount of proceeds paid to the consumer, the amount credited to the consumer's account, and any amounts paid to other persons must be itemized. The pre-paid finance charge is usually a part of the finance charge, even though it may be disclosed as part of the amount financed.

PAYMENT SCHEDULE

The number of payments, the amount of each payment, and the timing of the payment schedule to repay the obligation must be disclosed. Usually the due date for the first payment is disclosed, how often each subsequent payment is due, and the amount of time between the payments, such as monthly or quarterly payments. The total of all the payments must be set forth. The provisions for pre-payment must be disclosed in the event of penalty or other charges.

LATE PAYMENT CHARGES

Late payment charges should include the right to accelerate the debt in favor of the creditor, any fees imposed for collection costs including attorney's fees or repossession charges and, of course, the charge for making a late payment.[22]

SECURITY INTEREST

Although no specific wording is required, a security interest in any property should be identified as a pledge, lien, mortgage or a security interest.

INSURANCE

If the creditor is attempting to sell credit insurance, disability insurance, or property insurance, the premiums should be properly disclosed to exclude them from the finance charge. If the creditor chooses to include the premium in the finance charge, disclosure is not necessary. If the disclosures are not in compliance with the Act, an incomplete disclosure results and the charge then would have to be included in the finance charge.

---

[22] 12 CFR 226.18(e).

ADVERTISEMENT

An advertisement is any commercial method that promotes consumer credit or lease transactions, including newspaper, radio, television, Internet Web sites, display, point-of-sale literature, price tags, or billboards. Advertising applies to both closed-end credit and open-end credit.[23]

Certain triggering terms (see below) and finance rates in advertising copy require disclosure of major terms, including the annual percentage rate. The rule is intended to insure that all important terms of the credit plan, not just the most attractive terms, appear in an advertisement.

The Act identifies certain words and phrases (the triggering terms) used in advertisement to promote credit which will activate the operation of the Truth In Lending Act with which the creditor must comply.

Examples of triggering terms for closed-end credit are as follows:

a. The amount of down payment:
    1. 10% down.
    2. $1000 down.
    3. 90% financing.
    4. Trade-in with $1000 appraised value.
b. The amount of any payment:
    1. Monthly payments of less than $250 on all our loan plans.
    2. Pay $30 per $1000 amount borrowed.
    3. $400 per month.
c. The number of payments or the period of repayment:
    1. Up to four years of pay.
    2. Forty-eight months to pay.
    3. 30-year mortgage available.
d. The amount of any finance charge:
    1. Financing less than $300 per year.
    2. Less than $1200 interest.
    3. $2.00 monthly carrying charge.

An advertisement using a triggering term must include the annual percentage rate, the term of repayment, and the down payment (percentage or amount). The advertisement must state the annual percentage rate, even if it is the same as the interest rate, and this rate must be identified as the APR, as distinguished from the interest rate.[24] Ironically, there is no time requirement for the television

---

[23]12 CFR 226.24.

[24]TIL Sec. 107.

disclosure. Many consumer groups continually argue that the disclosures are meaningless because a consumer does not have enough time to read the entire disclosure on television.

The annual percentage rate must be disclosed accurately and must include any finance charges such as points, mortgage insurance premiums, etc. Where variable rates are used or the rates may change in the future, an annual percentage rate as of a specified date or an estimated annual percentage rate is permissible.[25]

Advertisements of variable rates should state that the rate may increase or is subject to change. Merely identifying a "graduated payment adjustable mortgage" is insufficient without a statement that the rate itself may increase or is subject to change.

RECORD RETENTION

A creditor shall retain records for at least two years after the date of disclosures.[26]

CONSUMER LEASE

A consumer lease is a lease of personal property, such as an automobile or boat, to a private individual. The lease must be for personal, family, or household purposes and must be for a term of more than four months. Renting a car for a weekend is not a consumer lease. The term excludes leases where the customer pays more than $25,000, but includes leases in which the customer has an option to buy at the end of the lease. However, a lease in which the payments equal or exceed the value of the property and which allows the consumer to buy the property at the end of the lease for a nominal payment is actually a closed-end credit sale and not a consumer lease. The advertising requirements under consumer leases follow in general the open-end and closed-end credit disclosures.

ARBITRATION

A recent case in the Ninth Circuit Court (California) reinforces the concept that the use of arbitration provisions in lending agreements is not a violation of the Truth in Lending Act and will be enforced in accordance with federal law. Under federal law an agreement to arbitrate is valid, irrevocable, and enforceable. The Court held that an agreement to arbitrate was not unconscionable despite the fact

---

[25]12 CFR 226.22.

[26]12 CFR 226.25.

the terms were not explained to the plaintiffs. The arbitration agreement was not unfair merely because the agreement shields the defendant from class action suits or suits brought on behalf of the general public.[27]
In one particular case,[28] the court stated,

> "we know of no case holding that parties dealing at arm's length have a duty to explain to each other the terms of a written contract. We decline to impose such an obligation where the language of the contract clearly and explicitly provides for arbitration of disputes arising out of the contractual relationship."

Furthermore, when the defendants alleged the unconscionability of a contract, the court's response was that an arbitration clause is not "per se" unreasonably favorable to one party over another party.

CRIMINAL LIABILITY

The act provides for criminal liability for furnishing false or inaccurate information, for failure to provide information which is required to be disclosed under the provisions of the law, or for using any chart or table in such a manner as to consistently understate the annual percentage rate. The penalty shall be a fine of not more than $5,000, or imprisonment for not more than one year, or both.

STATE LAW

Approximately 30 states have some form of Truth In Lending law which affects interest, usury, credit granting, revolving credit, insurance, banking or motor vehicle installment credit, etc. The state legislation exempts certain businesses and determines the transactions subject to the Truth In Lending Act.[29]
State law requirements are preempted if they are inconsistent with the federal Act. The federal law prevails if the state law is more lenient. State laws may provide rights, responsibilities, and procedures for consumers and creditors different from those required by the federal law. If the state law adds additional obligations, the creditor must comply with the state law. A careful review of the state law should be performed.

---

[27]*Meyers v. United Home Loan Inc.*, 1993 WL 307747 (N.D. Cal. 1993); *Perry v. Thomas*, 482 U.S. 483, 107 S. Ct. 2520 (1987).

[28]*Meyers v. Univest Home Loan, Inc.*, No. C-93-1783 MHP, 1993 WL 307747 (N.D. Cal. Aug. 4, 1993); *Perry v. Thomas*, 482 U.S. 483, 107 S. Ct. 2520, 96 L. Ed. 2d 426 (1987).

[29]12 CFR 226.29.

HOME EQUITY

Throughout the regulations specific divisions apply directly to home equity loans and other types of secured mortgage financing. These sections are only applicable to the situation where security is provided by the consumer to the lender, and are not applicable to open-end or closed-end credit transactions.

INTEREST AND COSTS

The cost of liability insurance paid for by a lender and added to the balance of the loan was not considered interest by the Court of Appeals of the 7th Circuit. There is a distinction between fees which compensate the bank for extending credit and fees which reimburse the bank for the actual costs extended.[30]

In addition, the same 7th Circuit decided that the providers of insurance premium financing are subject to the disclosure requirements of the Truth and Lending Act.[31]

A recent case confirmed that if you offer credit cards with an introductory interest rate and a higher interest rate for cash advances, and that information is disclosed in a solicitation letter and even referred the reader to the back of letter for a comprehensive list of the terms of the agreement, such a solicitation letter provides adequate disclosure.[32]

LEGISLATION

Regulation Z was revised and became effective on March 31, 1998 with mandatory compliance by October 1998. The highlights of the final rule included a determination of whether an extension of credit was open-ended or close-ended, whether deferred payment plans were open-ended, and guidance was offered on a particular type of deferred payment plan. A copy of the Official Staff Commentary on Regulation Z can be obtained from the Federal Trade Commission.

COMMENT

Most lending institutions engage a legal compliance officer to be certain that the provisions and the forms of the Truth In Lending Act and Regulation Z are fully

---

[30]*Doe v. Norwest Bank Minnesota, N.A.* 107 F.3d 1297 (8th Cir. 1997); *Richardson v. National City Bank of Evansville*, 141 F.3d 1228 (7th Cir. 1998).

[31]*Autry v. Northwest Premium Services, Inc.*, 144 F.3d 1037 (7th Cir. 1998).

[32]*Wilson v. First Union Nat'l Bank of Georgia*, No. 2961439, 1998 WL 151646 (Ala. Civ. App. Apr. 3, 1998).

complied with and no firm should embark on this form of lending without a careful review of the law.

BIBLIOGRAPHY

1. "A Functional Analysis of Truth In Lending," 26 *UCLA Law Review* 711 (April, 1979).

2. Open-End Credit Disclosures Requirements under the Truth In Lending, 53 *Southern California Law Review* 1005 (1979).

3. A Primer on the Uniform Guidelines for the Enforcement of Regulation Z, 96 *The Banking Law Journal* 886 (November 1979).

CHAPTER 12
APPENDIX I

TRUTH IN LENDING ACT

15 USC 1601 et seq.; 82 Stat. 146; Pub. L. 90-321 (May 29, 1968)
Public Law 90-321) (as amended), Title I (Chapters 1 through 4)

CHAPTER 1—GENERAL PROVISIONS

SECTION 101—SHORT TITLE

This title may be cited as the Truth in Lending Act.

[15 USC 1601 note.]

SECTION 102—FINDINGS AND DECLARATION OF PURPOSE

(a) The Congress finds that economic stabilization would be enhanced and the competition among the various financial institutions and other firms engaged in the extension of consumer credit would be strengthened by the informed use of credit. The informed use of credit results from an awareness of the cost thereof by consumers. It is the purpose of this title to assure a meaningful disclosure of credit terms so that the consumer will be able to compare more readily the various credit terms available to him and avoid the uninformed use of credit, and to protect the consumer against inaccurate and unfair credit billing and credit card practices.

(b) The Congress also finds that there has been a recent trend toward leasing automobiles and other durable goods for consumer use as an alternative to installment credit sales and that these leases have been offered without adequate cost disclosures. It is the purpose of this title to assure a meaningful disclosure of the terms of leases of personal property for personal, family, or household purposes so as to enable the lessee to compare more readily the various lease terms available to him, limit balloon payments in consumer leasing, enable comparison of lease terms with credit terms where appropriate, and to assure meaningful and accurate disclosures of lease terms in advertisements.

[15 USC 1601. As amended by acts of Oct. 28,1974 (88 Stat. 1511); March 23, 1976 (90 Stat. 257); and Dec. 26, 1981 (95 Stat. 1515).]

SECTION 103—DEFINITIONS AND RULES OF CONSTRUCTION

(a) The definitions and rules of construction set forth in this section are applicable for the purposes of this title.

(b) The term *"Board"* refers to the Board of Governors of the Federal Reserve System.

(c) The term *"organization"* means a corporation, government or governmental subdivision or agency, trust, estate, partnership, cooperative, or association.

(d) The term *"person"* means a natural person or an organization.

(e) The term *"credit"* means the right granted by a creditor to a debtor to defer payment of debt or to incur debt and defer its payment.

(f) The term *"creditor"* refers only to a person who both (1) regularly extends, whether in connection with loans, sales or property or services, or otherwise, consumer credit which is payable by agreement in more than four installments or for which the payment of a finance charge is or may be required, and (2) is the person to whom the debt arising from the consumer credit transaction is initially payable on the face of the evidence of indebtedness or, if there is no such evidence of indebtedness, by agreement. Notwithstanding the preceding sentence, in the case of an open-end credit plan involving a credit card, the card issuer and any person who honors the credit card and offers a discount which is a finance charge are creditors. For the purposes of the requirements imposed under chapter 4 and sections 127(a)(5), 127(a)(6), 127(a)(7), 127(b)(1), 127(b)(2), 127(b)(3), 127(b)(8), and 127(b)(10) of chapter 2 of this title, the term "creditor" shall also include card issuers whether or not the amount due is payable by agreement in more than four installments or the payment of a finance charge is or may be required, and the Board shall, by regulation, apply these requirements to such card issuers, to the extent appropriate, even though the requirements are by their terms applicable only to creditors offering open-end credit plans.

(g) The term *"credit sale"* refers to any sale in which the seller is a creditor. The term includes any contract in the form of a bailment or lease if the bailee or lessee contracts to pay as compensation for use a sum substantially equivalent to or in excess of the aggregate value of the property and services involved and it is agreed that the bailee or lessee will become, or for no other or a nominal consideration has the option to become, the owner of the property upon full compliance with his obligations under the contract.

(h) The adjective *"consumer,"* used with reference to a credit transaction, characterizes the transaction as one in which the party to whom credit is offered or extended is a natural person, and the money, property, or services which are the subject of the transaction are primarily for personal, family, or household purposes.

(i) The term *"open-end credit plan"* means a plan under which the creditor reasonably contemplates repeated transactions, which prescribes the terms of such transactions, and which provides for a finance charge which may be computed from time to time on the outstanding unpaid balance. A credit plan which is an open-end credit plan within the meaning of the preceding sentence is an open-end credit plan even if credit information is verified from time to time.

(j) The term *"adequate notice,"* as used in section 133, means a printed notice to a cardholder which sets forth the pertinent facts clearly and conspicuously so that a person against whom it is to operate could reasonably be expected to have noticed it and understood its meaning. Such notice may be given to a cardholder by printing the notice on any credit card, or on each periodic statement of account, issued to the cardholder, or by any other means reasonably assuring the receipt thereof by the cardholder.

(k) The term *"credit card"* means any card, plate, coupon book or other credit device existing for the purpose of obtaining money, property, labor, or services on credit.

(l) The term *"accepted credit card"* means any credit card which the cardholder has requested and received or has signed or has used, or authorized another to use, for the purpose of obtaining money, property, labor, or services on credit.

(m) The term *"cardholder"* means any person to whom a credit card is issued or any person who has agreed with the card issuer to pay obligations arising from the issuance of a credit card to another person.

(n) The term *"card issuer"* means any person who issues a credit card, or the agent of such person with respect to such card.

(o) The term *"unauthorized use,"* as used in section 133, means a use of a credit card by a person other than the cardholder who does not have actual, implied, or apparent authority for such use and from which the cardholder receives no benefit.

(p) The term *"discount"* as used in section 167 means a reduction made from the regular price. The term "discount" as used in section 167 shall not mean a surcharge.

(q) The term *"surcharge"* as used in section 103 and section 167 means any means of increasing the regular price to a cardholder which is not imposed upon customers paying by cash, check, or similar means.

(r) The term *"State"* refers to any State, the Commonwealth of Puerto Rico, the District of Columbia, and any territory or possession of the United States.

(s) The term *"agricultural purposes"* includes the production, harvest, exhibition, marketing, transportation, processing, or manufacture of agricultural products by a natural person who cultivates, plants, propagates, or nurtures those agricultural products, including but not limited to the acquisition of farmland, real property with a farm residence, and personal property and services used primarily in farming.

(t) The term *"agricultural products"* includes agricultural, horticultural, viticultural, and dairy products, livestock, wildlife, poultry, bees, forest products, fish and shellfish, and any products thereof, including processed and manufactured products, and any and all products raised or produced on farms and any processed or manufactured products thereof.

(u) The term *"material disclosures"* means the disclosure, as required by this title, of the annual percentage rate, the method of determining the finance charge and the balance upon which a finance charge will be imposed, the amount of the finance charge, the amount to be financed, the total of payments, the number and amount of payments, and the due dates or periods of payments scheduled to repay the indebtedness.

(v) The term *"dwelling"* means a residential structure or mobile home which contains one to four family housing units, or individual units of condominiums or cooperatives.

(w) The term *"residential mortgage transaction"* means a transaction in which a mortgage, deed of trust, purchase money security interest arising under an installment sales contract, or equivalent consensual security interest is created or retained against the consumer's dwelling to finance the acquisition or initial construction of such dwelling.

(x) As used in this section and section 167, the term *"regular price"* means the tag or posted price charged for the property or service if a single price is tagged or posted, or the price charged for the property or service when payment is made by use of an open-end credit plan or a credit card if either (1) no price is tagged or posted, or (2) two prices are tagged or posted, one of which is charged when payment is made by use of an open-end credit plan or a credit card and the other when payment is made by use of cash, check, or similar means. For purposes of this definition, payment by check, draft, or other negotiable instrument which may result in the debiting of an open-end credit plan or a credit cardholder's open-end account shall not be considered payment made by use of the plan or the account.

(y) Any reference to any requirement imposed under this title or any provision thereof includes reference to the regulations of the Board under this title or the provision thereof in question.

(z) The disclosure of an amount or percentage which is greater than the amount or percentage required to be disclosed under this title does not in itself constitute a violation of this title.

> [15 USC 1602. As amended by acts of Oct. 26, 1970 (84 Stat. 1126); Oct. 28, 1974 (88 Stat. 1511); Feb. 27, 1976 (90 Stat. 197); July 27, 1981 (95 Stat. 144); and Oct. 15, 1982 (96 Stat. 1538).]

SECTION 104—EXEMPTED TRANSACTIONS

This title does not apply to the following:

(1) Credit transactions involving extensions of credit primarily for business, commercial, or agricultural purposes, or to government or governmental agencies or instrumentalities, or to organizations.

(2) Transactions in securities or commodities accounts by a broker-dealer registered with the Securities and Exchange Commission.

(3) Credit transactions, other than those in which a security interest is or will be acquired in real property, or in personal property used or expected to be used as the principal dwelling of the consumer, in which the total amount financed exceeds $25,000.

(4) Transactions under public utility tariffs, if the Board determines that a State regulatory body regulates the charges for the public utility services involved, the charges for delayed payment, and any discount allowed for early payment.

(5) Loans made, insured, or guaranteed pursuant to a program authorized by title IV of the Higher Education Act of 1965 (20 U.S.C. 1070 et seq.).

[15 USC 1603. As amended by acts of Oct. 28, 1974 (88 Stat. 1517); March 31, 1980 (94 Stat. 169); Dec. 26, 1981 (95 Stat. 1515); and Oct. 15, 1982 (96 Stat. 1538).

Section 701 (b) and (c) of the Garn-St Germain Depository Institutions Act of 1982 (12 USC 1099 and 15 USC 1603 note) provides:

(b) Loans made, insured, or guaranteed pursuant to a program authorized by title IV at the Higher Education Act of 1965 (20 U.S.C. 1070 et seq.) shall not be subject to any disclosure requirements of any State law.

(c) The amendment made by subsection (a) and subsection (b) shall be effective with respect to loans made prior to, on, and after the date at enactment of this Act [October 13, 1982].

Subsection (a) added paragraph (5) to section 104 of the Truth in Lending Act.]

Section 105—Regulations

(a) The Board shall prescribe regulations to carry out the purposes of this title. These regulations may contain such classifications, differentiations, or other provisions, and may provide for such adjustments and exceptions for any class of transactions, as in the judgment of the Board are necessary or proper to effectuate the purposes of this title, to prevent circumvention or evasion thereof, or to facilitate compliance therewith.

(b) The Board shall publish model disclosure forms and clauses for common transactions to facilitate compliance with the disclosure requirements of this title and to aid the borrower or lessee in understanding the transaction by utilizing readily understandable language to simplify the technical nature of the disclosures. In devising such forms, the Board shall consider the use by creditors or lessors of data processing or similar automated equipment. Nothing in this title may be construed to require a creditor or lessor to use any such model form or clause prescribed by the Board under this section. A creditor or lessor shall be deemed to be in compliance with the disclosure provisions of this title with respect to other than numerical disclosures if the creditor or lessor (1) uses any appropriate model form or clause as published by the Board, or (2) uses any such model form or clause and changes it by (A) deleting any information which is not required by this title, or (B) rearranging the format, if in making such deletion or rearranging the format, the creditor or lessor does not affect the substance, clarity, or meaningful sequence of the disclosure.

(c)   Model disclosure forms and clauses shall be adopted by the Board after notice duly given in the Federal Register and an opportunity for public comment in accordance with section 553 of title 5, United States Code.

(d)   Any regulation of the Board, or any amendment or interpretation thereof, requiring any disclosure which differs from the disclosures previously required by this chapter, chapter 4, or chapter 5, or by any regulation of the Board promulgated thereunder shall have an effective date of that October 1 which follows by at least six months the date of promulgation, except that the Board may at its discretion take interim action by regulation, amendment, or interpretation to lengthen the period of time permitted for creditors or lessors to adjust their forms to accommodate new requirements or shorten the length of time for creditors or lessors to make such adjustments when it makes a specific finding that such action is necessary to comply with the findings of a court or to prevent unfair or deceptive disclosure practices. Notwithstanding the previous sentence, any creditor or lessor may comply with any such newly promulgated disclosure requirements prior to the effective date of the requirements.

[15 USC 1604. As amended by acts of March 31, 1980 (94 Stat. 170) and Dec. 26, 1981 (95 Stat. 1515).]

Section 106—Determination of Finance Charge

(a)   Except as otherwise provided in this section, the amount of the finance charge in connection with any consumer credit transaction shall be determined as the sum of all charges, payable directly or indirectly by the person to whom the credit is extended, and imposed directly or indirectly by the creditor as an incident to the extension of credit. The finance charge does not include charges of a type payable in a comparable cash transaction. Examples of charges which are included in the finance charge include any of the following types of charges which are applicable.

   (1)   Interest, time price differential, and any amount payable under a point, discount, or other system of additional charges.

   (2)   Service or carrying charge.

   (3)   Loan fee, finder's fee, or similar charge.

   (4)   Fee for an investigation or credit report.

   (5)   Premium or other charge for any guarantee or insurance protecting the creditor against the obligor's default or other credit loss.

(b)   Charges or premiums for credit life, accident, or health insurance written in connection with any consumer credit transaction shall be included in the finance charge unless

   (1)   the coverage of the debtor by the insurance is not a factor in the approval by the creditor of the extension of credit, and this fact is clearly disclosed in writing to the person applying for or obtaining the extension of credit; and

   (2)   in order to obtain the insurance in connection with the extension of credit, the person to whom the credit is extended must give specific affirmative written indication of his desire to do so after written disclosure to him of the cost thereof.

(c) Charges or premiums for insurance, written in connection with any consumer credit transaction, against loss of or damage to property or against liability arising out of the ownership or use of property, shall be included in the finance charge unless a clear and specific statement in writing is furnished by the creditor to the person to whom the credit is extended, setting forth the cost of the insurance if obtained from or through the creditor, and stating that the person to whom the credit is extended may choose the person through which the insurance is to be obtained.

(d) If any of the following items is itemized and disclosed in accordance with the regulations of the Board in connection with any transaction, then the creditor need not include that item in the computation of the finance charge with respect to that transaction:

   (1) Fees and charges prescribed by law which actually are or will be paid to public officials for determining the existence of or for perfecting or releasing or satisfying any security related to the credit transaction.

   (2) The premium payable for any insurance in lieu of perfecting any security interest otherwise required by the creditor in connection with the transaction, if the premium does not exceed the fees and charges described in paragraph (1) which would otherwise be payable.

(e) The following items, when charged in connection with any extension of credit secured by an interest in real property, shall not be included in the computation of the finance charge with respect to that transaction:

   (1) Fees or premiums for title examination, title insurance, or similar purposes.

   (2) Fees for preparation of a deed, settlement statement, or other documents.

   (3) Escrows for future payments of taxes and insurance.

   (4) Fees for notarizing deeds and other documents.

   (5) Appraisal fees.

   (6) Credit reports.

[15 USC 1605. As amended by acts of March 31, 1980 (94 Stat. 170) and Dec. 26, 1981 (95 Stat. 1515).]

SECTION 107—DETERMINATION OF ANNUAL PERCENTAGE RATE

(a) The annual percentage rate applicable to any extension of consumer credit shall be determined, in accordance with the regulations of the Board,

   (1) in the case of any extension of credit other than under an open-end credit plan, as

      (A) that nominal annual percentage rate which will yield a sum equal to the amount of the finance charge when it is applied to the unpaid balances of the amount financed, calculated according to the actuarial method of allocating payments made on a debt between the amount financed and the amount of the finance charge, pursuant to which a payment is applied first to the accumulated finance charge and the balance is applied to the unpaid amount financed; or

    (B)   the rate determined by any method prescribed by the Board as a method which materially simplifies computation while retaining reasonable accuracy as compared with the rate determined under subparagraph (A).

(2)   in the case of any extension of credit under an open-end credit plan, as the quotient (expressed as a percentage) of the total finance charge for the period to which it relates divided by the amount upon which the finance charge for that period is based, multiplied by the number of such periods in a year

(b)   Where a creditor imposes the same finance charge for balances within a specified range, the annual percentage rate shall be computed on the median balance within the range, except that if the Board determines that a rate so computed would not be meaningful, or would be materially misleading, the annual percentage rate shall be computed on such other basis as the Board may by regulation require.

(c)   The disclosure of an annual percentage rate is accurate for the purpose of this title if the rate disclosed is within a tolerance not greater than one-eighth of 1 per centum more or less than the actual rate or rounded to the nearest one-fourth of 1 per centum. The Board may allow a greater tolerance to simplify compliance where irregular payments are involved.

(d)   The Board may authorize the use of rate tables or charts which may provide for the disclosure of annual percentage rates which vary from the rate determined in accordance with subsection (a)(1)(A) by not more than such tolerances as the Board may allow. The Board may not allow a tolerance greater than 8 per centum of that rate except to simplify compliance where irregular payments are involved.

(e)   In the case of creditors determining the annual percentage rate in a manner other than as described in subsection (d), the Board may authorize other reasonable tolerances.

[15 USC 1606. As amended by acts of March 31, 1980 (94 Stat. 170) and Dec. 26, 1981 (95 Stat. 1515).]

SECTION 108—ADMINISTRATIVE ENFORCEMENT

(a)   Compliance with the requirements imposed under this title shall be enforced under

(1)   section 8 of the Federal Deposit Insurance Act, in the case of

    (A)   national banks, by the Comptroller of the Currency.

    (B)   member banks of the Federal Reserve System (other than national banks), by the Board.

    (C)   banks insured by the Federal Deposit Insurance Corporation (other than members of the Federal Reserve System), by the Board of Directors of the Federal Deposit Insurance Corporation.

(2)   section 5(d) of the Home Owners' Loan Act of 1933, section 407 of the National Housing Act, and sections 6(i) and 17 of the Federal Home Loan Bank Act, by the Federal Home Loan Bank Board (acting directly or through the Federal Savings and Loan Insurance Corporation), in the case of any institution subject to any of those provisions.

(3)   the Federal Credit Union Act, by the Administrator of the National Credit Union Administration with respect to any Federal credit union.

(4)   the Federal Aviation Act of 1958, by the Civil Aeronautics Board with respect to any air carrier or foreign air carrier subject to that Act.

(5)   the Packers and Stockyards Act, 1921 (except as provided in section 406 of that Act), by the Secretary of Agriculture with respect to any activities subject to that Act.

(6)   the Farm Credit Act of 1971, by the Farm Credit Administration with respect to any Federal land bank, Federal land bank association, Federal intermediate credit bank, or production credit association.

(b) For the purpose of the exercise by any agency referred to in subsection (a) of its powers under any Act referred to in that subsection, a violation of any requirement imposed under this title shall be deemed to be a violation of a requirement imposed under that Act. In addition to its powers under any provision of law specifically referred to in subsection (a), each of the agencies referred to in that subsection may exercise, for the purpose of enforcing compliance with any requirement imposed under this title, any other authority conferred on it by law.

(c) Except to the extent that enforcement of the requirements imposed under this title is specifically committed to some other Government agency under subsection (a), the Federal Trade Commission shall enforce such requirements. For the purpose of the exercise by the Federal Trade Commission of its functions and powers under the Federal Trade Commission Act, a violation of any requirement imposed under this title shall be deemed a violation of a requirement imposed under that Act. All of the functions and powers of the Federal Trade Commission under the Federal Trade Commission Act are available to the Commission to enforce compliance by any person with the requirements imposed under this title, irrespective of whether that person is engaged in commerce or meets any other jurisdictional tests in the Federal Trade Commission Act.

(d) The authority of the Board to issue regulations under this title does not impair the authority of any other agency designated in this section to make rules respecting its own procedures in enforcing compliance with requirements imposed under this title.

(e) (1) In carrying out its enforcement activities under this section, each agency referred to in subsection (a) or (c), in cases where an annual percentage rate or finance charge was inaccurately disclosed, shall notify the creditor of such disclosure error and is authorized in accordance with the provisions of this subsection to require the creditor to make an adjustment to the account of the person to whom credit was extended, to assure that such person will not be required to pay a finance charge in excess of the finance charge actually disclosed or the dollar equivalent of the annual percentage rate actually disclosed, whichever is lower. For the purposes of this subsection, except where such disclosure error resulted from a willful violation which was intended to mislead the person to whom credit was extended, in determining whether a disclosure error has occurred and in calculating any adjustment, (A) each agency shall apply (i) with respect to the annual percentage rate, a tolerance of one-quarter of 1 percent more or less than the actual rate, determined without regard to section 107(c) of this title, and (ii) with respect to the finance charge, a corresponding numerical tolerance as generated by the tolerance provided under this subsection for the annual percentage rate; except that (B) with respect to transactions consummated after two years following the effective date of section 608 of the Truth in Lending Simplification and Reform Act, each agency shall apply (i) for transactions that have a scheduled amortization of ten years or less with respect to the annual percentage rate, a tolerance not to exceed one-quarter of 1 percent more or less than the actual rate, determined without regard to section 107(c) of this title, but in no event a tolerance of less than the tolerances allowed under section 107(c), (ii) for transactions that have a scheduled amortization of more than ten years, with respect to the annual percentage rate, only such tolerances as are allowed under section 107(c) of this title, and (iii) for all transactions, with respect to the finance charge, a corresponding numerical tolerance as generated by the tolerances provided under this subsection for the annual percentage rate.

(2)   Each agency shall require such an adjustment when it determines that such disclosure error resulted from (A) a clear and consistent pattern or practice of violations, (B) gross negligence, or (C) a willful violation which was intended to mislead the person to whom the credit was extended. Notwithstanding the preceding sentence, except where such disclosure error resulted from a willful violation which was intended to mislead the person to whom credit was extended, an agency need not require such an adjustment if it determines that such disclosure error—

(A)   resulted from an error involving the disclosure of a fee or charge that would otherwise be excludable in computing the finance charge, including but not limited to violations involving the disclosures described in sections 106(b), (c) and (d) of this title, in which event the agency may require such remedial action as it determines to be equitable, except that for transactions consummated after two years after the effective date of section 608 of the Truth in Lending Simplification and Reform Act, such an adjustment shall be ordered for violations of section 106(b);

(B)   involved a disclosed amount which was 10 per centum or less of the amount that should have been disclosed and (i) in cases where the error involved a disclosed finance charge, the annual percentage rate was disclosed correctly, and (ii) in cases where the error involved a disclosed annual percentage rate, the finance charge was disclosed correctly; in which event the agency may require such adjustment as it determines to be equitable;

(C)   involved a total failure to disclose either the annual percentage rate or the finance charge, in which event the agency may require such adjustment as it determines to be equitable; or

(D)   resulted from any other unique circumstance involving clearly technical and nonsubstantive disclosure violations that do not adversely affect information provided to the consumer and that have not misled or otherwise deceived the consumer.

In the case of other such disclosure errors, each agency may require such an adjustment.

(3)   Notwithstanding paragraph (2), no adjustment shall be ordered (A) if it would have a significantly adverse impact upon the safety or soundness of the creditor, but in any such case, the agency may require a partial adjustment in an amount which does not have such an impact except that with respect to any

transaction consummated after the effective date of section 608 of the Truth in Lending Simplification and Reform Act, the agency shall require the full adjustment, but permit the creditor to make the required adjustment in partial payments over an extended period of time which the agency considers to be reasonable, (B) if the amount of the adjustment would be less than $1, except that if more than one year has elapsed since the date of the violation, the agency may require that such amount be paid into the Treasury of the United States, or (C) except where such disclosure error resulted from a willful violation which was intended to mislead the person to whom credit was extended, in the case of an open-end credit plan, more than two years after the violation, or in the case of any other extension of credit, as follows:

    (i) with respect to creditors that are subject to examination by the agencies referred to in paragraphs (1) through (3) of section 108(a) of this title, except in connection with violations arising from practices identified in the current examination and only in connection with transactions that are consummated after the date of the immediately preceding examination, except that where practices giving rise to violations identified in earlier examinations have not been corrected, adjustments for those violations shall be required in connection with transactions consummated after the date of the examination in which such practices were first identified;

    (ii) with respect to creditors that are not subject to examination by such agencies, except in connection with transactions that are consummated after May 10, 1978; and

    (iii) in no event after the later of (I) the expiration of the life of the credit extension, or (II) two years after the agreement to extend credit was consummated.

(4) (A) Notwithstanding any other provision of this section, an adjustment under this subsection may be required by an agency referred to in subsection (a) or (c) only by an order issued in accordance with cease and desist procedures provided by the provision of law referred to in such subsections.

    (B) in the case of an agency which is not authorized to conduct cease and desist proceedings, such an order may be issued after an agency hearing on the record conducted at least thirty but not more than sixty days after notice of the alleged violation is served on the creditor. Such a hearing shall be deemed to be a hearing which is subject to the provisions of section 8(h) of the Federal Deposit Insurance Act and shall be subject to judicial review as provided therein.

(5) Except as otherwise specifically provided in this subsection and notwithstanding any provision of law referred to in subsection (a) or (c), no agency referred to in subsection (a) or (c) may require a creditor to make dollar adjustments for errors in any requirements under this title, except with regard to the requirements of section 165.

(6) A creditor shall not be subject to an order to make an adjustment, if within sixty days after discovering a disclosure error, whether pursuant to a final written examination report or through the creditor's own procedures, the

creditor notifies the person concerned of the error and adjusts the account so as to assure that such person will not be required to pay a finance charge in excess of the finance charge actually disclosed or the dollar equivalent of the annual percentage rate actually disclosed, whichever is lower.

(7)   Notwithstanding the second sentence of subsection (e)(1), subsection (e)(3)(C)(i), and subsection (e)(3)(C)(ii), each agency referred to in subsection (a) or (c) shall require an adjustment for an annual percentage rate disclosure error that exceeds a tolerance of one quarter of one percent less than the actual rate, determined without regard to section 107(c) of this title, with respect to any transaction consummated between January 1, 1977, and the effective date of section 608 of the Truth in Lending Simplification and Reform Act.

[15 USC 1607. As amended by acts of March 10, 1970 (84 Stat. 49); Oct. 28, 1974 (88 Stat. 1517); March 31, 1980) (94 Stat. 171, 173); and Oct. 4, 1984 (98 Stat. 1708).]

SECTION 109—VIEWS OF OTHER AGENCIES

In the exercise of its functions under this title, the Board may obtain upon request the views of any other Federal agency which, in the judgment of the Board, exercises regulatory or supervisory functions with respect to any class of creditors subject to this title.

[15 USC 1608. As amended by act of Oct. 3, 1984 (98 Stat. 1708).]

SECTION 110—[REPEALED]

SECTION 111—EFFECT ON OTHER LAWS

(a) (1)   Except as provided in subsection (e), chapters 1, 2, and 3 do not annul, alter, or affect the laws of any State relating to the disclosure of information in connection with credit transactions, except to the extent that those laws are inconsistent with the provisions of this title, and then only to the extent of the inconsistency. Upon its own motion or upon the request of any creditor, State, or other interested party which is submitted in accordance with procedures prescribed in regulations of the Board, the Board shall determine whether any such inconsistency exists. If the Board determines that a State-required disclosure is inconsistent, creditors located in that State may not make disclosures using the inconsistent term or form, and shall incur no liability under the law of that State for failure to use such term or form, notwithstanding that such determination is subsequently amended, rescinded, or determined by judicial or other authority to be invalid for any reason.

(2)   Upon its own motion or upon the request of any creditor, State, or other interested party which is submitted in accordance with procedures prescribed in regulations of the Board, the Board shall determine whether any disclosure required under the law of any State is substantially the same in meaning as a disclosure required under this title. If the Board determines that a State-required disclosure is substantially the same in meaning as a disclosure required by this title, then creditors located in that State may make such disclosure in compliance with such State law in lieu of the disclosure required by

this title, except that the animal percentage rate and finance charge shall be disclosed as required by section 122.

(b) This title does not otherwise annul, alter or affect in any manner the meaning, scope or applicability of the laws of any State, including, but not limited to, laws relating to the types, amounts or rates of charges, or any element or elements of charges, permissible under such laws in connection with the extension or use of credit, nor does this title extend the applicability of those laws to any class of persons or transactions to which they would not otherwise apply.

(c) In any action or proceeding in any court involving a consumer credit sale, the disclosure of the annual percentage rate as required under this title in connection with that sale may not be received as evidence that the sale was a loan or any type of transaction other than a credit sale.

(d) Except as specified in sections 125, 130, and 166, this title and the regulations issued thereunder do not affect the validity or enforceability of any contract or obligation under State or Federal law.

(e) The provisions of subsection (c) of section 122 and subsections (c), (d), (e), and (f) of section 127 shall supersede any provision of the law of any State relating to the disclosure of information in any credit or charge card application or solicitation which is subject to the requirements of section 127(c) or any renewal notice which is subject to the requirements of section 127(d), except that any State may employ or establish State laws for the purpose of enforcing the requirements of such sections.

[15 USC 1610. As amended by acts of Oct. 28, 1974 (88 Stat. 1516); March 31, 1980 (94 Stat. 173); Dec. 26, 1981 (95 Stat. 1515); and Nov. 3, 1988 (102 Stat. 2967).]

Section 112—Criminal Liability for Willful and Knowing Violation

Whoever willfully and knowingly

(1) gives false or inaccurate information or fails to provide information which he is required to disclose under the provisions of this title or any regulation issued thereunder,

(2) uses any chart or table authorized by the Board under section 107 in such a manner as to consistently understate the annual percentage rate determined under section 107(a)(l)(A), or

(3) otherwise fails to comply with any requirement imposed under this title, shall be fined not more than $5,000 or imprisoned not more than one year, or both.

[15 USC 1611.]

Section 113—Effect on Governmental Agencies

(a) Any department or agency of the United States which administers a credit program in which it extends, insures, or guarantees consumer credit and in which it provides instruments to a creditor which contain any disclosures required by this title shall, prior to the issuance or continued use of such instruments, consult with the Board to assure that such instruments comply with this title.

(b) No civil or criminal penalty provided under this title for any violation thereof may be imposed upon the United States or any department or agency thereof, or upon any State or political subdivision thereof, or any agency of any State or political subdivision.

(c) A creditor participating in a credit program administered, insured, or guaranteed by any department or agency of the United States shall not be held liable for a civil or criminal penalty under this title in any case in which the violation results from the use of an instrument required by any such department or agency.

(d) A creditor participating in a credit program administered, insured, or guaranteed by any department or agency of the United States shall not he held liable for a civil or criminal penalty under the laws of any State (other than laws determined under section 111 to be inconsistent with this title) for any technical or procedural failure, such as a failure to use a specific form, to make information available at a specific place on an instrument, or to use a specific typeface, as required by State law, which is caused by the use of an instrument required to be used by such department or agency.

[15 USC 1612. As amended by acts of March 31, 1980 (94 Stat. 184) and Dec. 26, 1981 (93 Stat. 1515).]

SECTION 114—REPORTS BY BOARD AND ATTORNEY GENERAL

Each year the Board shall make a report to the Congress concerning the administration of its functions under this title, including such recommendations as the Board deems necessary or appropriate. In addition, each report of the Board shall include its assessment of the extent to which compliance with the requirements imposed under this title is being achieved.

[15 USC 1613. As amended by acts of March 31, 1980 (94 Stat. 174); Dec. 26, 1981 (95 Stat. 1515); and Dec. 21, 1982 (96 Stat. 1825).]

SECTION 115—[REPEALED]

CHAPTER 2—CREDIT TRANSACTIONS

SECTION 121—GENERAL REQUIREMENT OF DISCLOSURE

(a)   Subject to subsection (b), a creditor or lessor shall disclose to the person who is obligated on a consumer lease or a consumer credit transaction the information required under this title. In a transaction involving more than one obligor, a creditor or lessor, except in a transaction under section 125, need not disclose to more than one of such obligors if the obligor given disclosure is a primary obligor

(b)   If a transaction involves one creditor as defined in section 103(f), or one lessor as defined in section 181(3), such creditor or lessor shall make the disclosures. If a transaction involves more than one creditor or lessor, only one creditor or lessor shall be required to make the disclosures. The Board shall by regulation specify which creditor or lessor shall make the disclosures.

(c)   The Board may provide by regulation that any portion of the information required to be disclosed by this title may be given in the form of estimates where the provider of such information is not in a position to know exact information.

(d)   The Board shall determine whether tolerances for numerical disclosures other than the annual percentage rate are necessary to facilitate compliance with this title, and if it determines that such tolerances are necessary to facilitate compliance, it shall by regulation permit disclosures within such tolerances. The Board shall exercise its authority to permit tolerances for numerical disclosures other than the annual percentage rate so that such tolerances are narrow enough to prevent such tolerances from resulting in misleading disclosures or disclosures that circumvent the purposes of this title.

[15 USC 1631. As amended by acts of Oct. 28, 1974 (88 Stat. 1516); Jan. 2, 1976 (89 Stat. 1159); March 31, 1980 (94 Stat. 174); and Dec. 26, 1981 (95 Stat. 1515).l

SECTION 122—FORM OF DISCLOSURE; ADDITIONAL INFORMATION

(a)   Information required by this title shall be disclosed clearly and conspicuously, in accordance with regulations of the Board. The terms 'annual percentage rate' and 'finance charge' shall be disclosed more conspicuously than other terms, data, or information provided in connection with a transaction, except information relating to the identity of the creditor. Except as provided in subsection (c), regulations of the Board need not require that disclosures pursuant to this title be made in the order set forth in this title and, except as otherwise provided, may permit the use of terminology different from that employed in this title if it conveys substantially the same meaning.

(b) Any creditor or lessor may supply additional information or explanation with any disclosures required under chapters 4 and 5 and, except as provided in sections 127A(b)(3) and 128(b)(1), under this chapter.

(c) (1) The information described in paragraphs (1)(A), (3)(B)(i)(I), (4)(A), and (4)(C)(i)(I) of section 127(c) shall be—

   (A) disclosed in the form and manner which the Board shall prescribe by regulations; and

   (B) placed in a conspicuous and prominent location on or with any written application, solicitation, or other document or paper with respect to which such disclosure is required.

(2) (A) In the regulations prescribed under paragraph (1)(A) of this subsection, the Board shall require that the disclosure of such information shall, to the extent the Board determines to be practicable and appropriate, be in the form of a table which—

   (i) contains clear and concise headings for each item of such information; and

   (ii) provides a clear and concise form for stating each item of information required to be disclosed under each heading.

   (B) In prescribing the form of the table under subparagraph (A), the Board may—

   (i) list the items required to be included in the table in a different order than the order in which such items are set forth in paragraph (1)(A) or (4)(A) of section 127(c); and

   (ii) subject to subparagraph (C), employ terminology which is different than the terminology which is employed in section 127(c) if such terminology conveys substantially the same meaning.

   (C) Either the heading or the statement under the heading which relates to the time period referred to in section 127(c)(1)(A)(iii) shall contain the term "grace period."

[15 USC 1632. As amended by acts of Oct. 28, 1974 (88 Stat. 1516); March 31, 1980 (94 Stat. 174); Dec. 26, 1981 (95 Stat. 1515); Nov. 3, 1988 (102 Stat. 2966); and Nov. 23, 1988 (102 Stat. 4731).]

SECTION 123—EXEMPTION FOR STATE-REGULATED TRANSACTIONS

The Board shall by regulation exempt from the requirements of this chapter any class of credit transactions within any State if it determines that under the law of that State that class of transactions is subject to requirements substantially similar to those imposed under this chapter, and that there is adequate provision for enforcement.

[15 USC 1633.]

SECTION 124—EFFECT OF SUBSEQUENT OCCURRENCE

If information disclosed in accordance with this chapter is subsequently rendered inaccurate as the result of any act, occurrence, or agreement subsequent to the delivery of the required disclosures, the inaccuracy resulting therefrom does not constitute a violation of this chapter.

[15 USC 1634.]

SECTION 125—RIGHT OF RESCISSION AS TO CERTAIN TRANSACTIONS

(a) Except as otherwise provided in this section, in the case of any consumer credit transaction (including opening or increasing the credit limit for an open-end credit plan) in which a security interest, including any such interest arising by operation of law, is or will be retained or acquired in any property which is used as the principal dwelling of the person to whom credit is extended, the obligor shall have the right to rescind the transaction until midnight of the third business day following the consummation of the transaction or the delivery of the information and rescission forms required under this section together with a statement containing the material disclosures required under this title, whichever is later, by notifying the creditor, in accordance with regulations of the Board, of his intention to do so. The creditor shall clearly and conspicuously disclose, in accordance with regulations of the Board, to any obligor in a transaction subject to this section the rights of the obligor under this section. The creditor shall also provide, in accordance with regulations of the Board, appropriate forms for the obligor to exercise his right to rescind any transaction subject to this section.

(b) When an obligor exercises his right to rescind under subsection (a), he is not liable for any finance or other charge, and any security interest given by the obligor, including any such interest arising by operation of law, becomes void upon such a rescission. Within 20 days after receipt of a notice of rescission, the creditor shall return to the obligor any money or property given as earnest money, downpayment, or otherwise, and shall take any action necessary or appropriate to reflect the termination of any security interest created under the transaction. If the creditor has delivered any property to the obligor, the obligor may retain possession of it. Upon the performance of the creditor's obligations under this section, the obligor shall tender the property to the creditor, except that if return of the property in kind would be impracticable or inequitable, the obligor shall tender its reasonable value. Tender shall be made at the location of the property or at the residence of the obligor, at the option of the obligor. If the creditor does not take possession of the property within 20 days after tender by the obligor, ownership of the property vests in the obligor without obligation on his part to pay for it. The procedures prescribed by this subsection shall apply except when otherwise ordered by a court.

(c) Notwithstanding any rule of evidence, written acknowledgment of receipt of any disclosures required under this title by a person to whom information, forms, and a statement is required to be given pursuant to this section does no more than create a rebuttable presumption of delivery thereof.

(d) The Board may, if it finds that such action is necessary in order to permit homeowners to meet bona fide personal financial emergencies, prescribe regulations authorizing the modification or waiver of any rights created under this section to the extent and under the circumstances set forth in those regulations.

(e) This section does not apply to—

(1) a residential mortgage transaction as defined in section 103(w);

(2) a transaction which constitutes a refinancing or consolidation (with no new advances) of the principal balance then due and any accrued and unpaid finance charges of an existing extension of credit by the same creditor secured by an interest in the same property;

(3) a transaction in which an agency of a State is the creditor; or

(4) advances under a preexisting open-end credit plan if a security interest has already been retained or acquired and such advances are in accordance with a previously established credit limit for such plan.

(f) An obligor's right of rescission shall expire three years after the date of consummation of the transaction or upon the sale of the property, whichever occurs first, notwithstanding the fact that the information and forms required under this section or any other disclosures required under this chapter have not been delivered to the obligor, except that if (1) any agency empowered to enforce the provisions of this title institutes a proceeding to enforce the provisions of this section within three years after the date of consummation of the transaction, (2) such agency finds a violation of section 125, and (3) the obligor's right to rescind is based in whole or in part on any matter involved in such proceeding, then the obligor's right of rescission shall expire three years after the date of consummation of the transaction or upon the earlier sale of the property, or upon the expiration of one year following the conclusion of the proceeding, or any judicial review or period for judicial review thereof, whichever is later.

(g) In any action in which it is determined that a creditor has violated this section, in addition to rescission the court may award relief under section 130 for violations of this title not relating to the right to rescind.

[15 USC 1635. As amended by acts of Oct. 28, 1974 (88 Stat. 1517, 1519); March 31, 1980 (94 Stat. 175); Dec. 26, 1981 (95 Stat. 1515); and Oct. 17, 1984 (98 Stat. 2234).]

SECTION 126—[REPEALED]

SECTION 127—OPEN-END CONSUMER CREDIT PLANS

(a) Before opening any account under an open-end consumer credit plan, the creditor shall disclose to the person to whom credit is to be extended each of the following items, to the extent applicable:

(1) The conditions under which a finance charge may be imposed, including the time period (if any) within which any credit extended may be repaid without incurring a finance charge, except that the creditor may, at his election and without disclosure, impose no such finance charge if payment is received after the termination of such time period. If no such time period is provided, the creditor shall disclose such fact.

(2) The method of determining the balance upon which a finance charge will be imposed.

(3) The method of determining the amount of the finance charge, including any minimum or fixed amount imposed as a finance charge.

(4)   Where one or more periodic rates may be used to compute the finance charge, each such rate, the range of balances to which it is applicable, and the corresponding nominal annual percentage rate determined by multiplying the periodic rate by the number of periods in a year.

(5)   Identification of other charges which may be imposed as part of the plan, and their method of computation, in accordance with regulations of the Board.

(6)   In cases where the credit is or will be secured, a statement that a security interest has been or will be taken in (A) the property purchased as part of the credit transaction, or (B) property not purchased as part of the credit transaction identified by item or type.

(7)   A statement, in a form prescribed by regulations of the Board of the protection provided by sections 161 and 170 to an obligor and the creditor's responsibilities under sections 162 and 170. With respect to one billing cycle per calendar year, at intervals of not less than six months or more than eighteen months, the creditor shall transmit such statement to each obligor to whom the creditor is required to transmit a statement pursuant to section 127(b) for such billing cycle.

(8)   In the case of any account under an open-end consumer credit plan which provides for any extension of credit which is secured by the consumer's principal dwelling, any information which—

(A)   is required to be disclosed under section 127A(a); and

(B)   the Board determines is not described in any other paragraph of this subsection.

(b) The creditor of any account under an open-end consumer credit plan shall transmit to the obligor, for each billing cycle at the end of which there is an outstanding balance in that account or with respect to which a finance charge is imposed, a statement setting forth each of the following items to the extent applicable:

(1)   The outstanding balance in the account at the beginning of the statement period.

(2)   The amount and date of each extension of credit during the period, and a brief identification, on or accompanying the statement of each extension of credit in a form prescribed by the Board sufficient to enable the obligor either to identify the transaction or to relate it to copies of sales vouchers or similar instruments previously furnished, except that a creditor's failure to disclose such information in accordance with this paragraph shall not be deemed a failure to comply with this chapter or this title if (A) the creditor maintains procedures reasonably adapted to procure and provide such information, and (B) the creditor responds to and treats any inquiry for clarification or documentation as a billing error and an erroneously billed amount under section 161. In lieu of complying with the requirements of the previous sentence, in the case of any transaction in which the creditor and seller are the same person, as defined by the Board, and such person's open-end credit plan has fewer than 15,000 accounts, the creditor may elect to provide only the amount and date of each extension of credit during the period and the seller's name and location where the transaction took place if (A) a brief identification of the transaction has been previously furnished, and (B) the creditor responds to and treats any

inquiry for clarification or documentation as a billing error and an erroneously billed amount under section 161.

(3)   The total amount credited to the account during the period.

(4)   The amount of any finance charge added to the account during the period, itemized to show the amounts, if any, due to the application of percentage rates and the amount, if any, imposed as a minimum or fixed charge.

(5)   Where one or more periodic rates may be used to compute the finance charge, each such rate, the range of balances to which it is applicable, and, unless the annual percentage rate (determined under section 107(a)(2)) is required to be disclosed pursuant to paragraph (6), the corresponding nominal annual percentage rate determined by multiplying the periodic rate by the number of periods in a year.

(6)   Where the total finance charge exceeds 50 cents for a monthly or longer billing cycle, or the pro rata part of 50 cents for a billing cycle shorter than monthly, the total finance charge expressed as an annual percentage rate (determined under section 107(a)(2)), except that if the finance charge is the sum of two or more products of a rate times a portion of the balance, the creditor may, in lieu of disclosing a single rate for the total charge, disclose each such rate expressed as an annual percentage rate, and the part of the balance to which it is applicable.

(7)   The balance on which the finance charge was computed and a statement of how the balance was determined. If the balance is determined without first deducting all credits during the period, that fact and the amount of such payments shall also be disclosed.

(8)   The outstanding balance in the account at the end of the period.

(9)   The date by which or the period (if any) within which payment must be made to avoid additional finance charges, except that the creditor may, at his election and without disclosure, impose no such additional finance charge if payment is received after such date or the termination of such period.

(10) The address to be used by the creditor for the purpose of receiving billing inquiries from the obligor.

(c) (1) (A) Any application to open a credit card account for any person under an open-end consumer credit plan, or a solicitation to open such an account without requiring an application, that is mailed to consumers shall disclose the following information, subject to subsection (e) and section 122(c):

(i) (I) Each annual percentage rate applicable to extensions of credit under such credit plan.

(II) Where an extension of credit is subject to a variable rate, the fact that the rate is variable, the annual percentage rate in effect at the time of the mailing, and how the rate is determined.

(III) Where more than one rate applies, the range of balances to which each rate applies.

(ii) (I) Any annual fee, other periodic fee, or membership fee imposed for the issuance or availability of a credit card, including any account maintenance fee or other charge imposed based on activity or inactivity for the account during the billing cycle.

(II) Any minimum finance charge imposed for each period during which any extension of credit which is subject to a finance charge is outstanding.

(III) Any transaction charge imposed in connection with use of the card to purchase goods or services.

(iii) (I) The date by which or the period within which any credit extended under such credit plan for purchases of goods or services must be repaid to avoid incurring a finance charge, and, if no such period is offered, such fact shall be clearly stated.

(II) If the length of such "grace period" varies, the card issuer may disclose the range of days in the grace period, the minimum number of days in the grace period, or the average number of days in the grace period, if the disclosure is identified as such.

(iv) (I) The name of the balance calculation method used in determining the balance on which the finance charge is computed if the method used has been defined by the Board, or a detailed explanation of the balance calculation method used if the method has not been so defined.

(II) In prescribing regulations to carry out this clause, the Board shall define and name not more than the 5 balance calculation methods determined by the Board to be the most commonly used methods.

(B) In addition to the information required to be disclosed under subparagraph (A), each application or solicitation to which such subparagraph applies shall disclose clearly and conspicuously the following information, subject to subsections (e) and (f):

(i) Any fee imposed for an extension of credit in the form of cash.

(ii) Any fee imposed for a late payment.

(iii) Any fee imposed in connection with an extension of credit in excess of the amount of credit authorized to be extended with respect to such account.

(2) (A) In any telephone solicitation to open a credit card account for any person under an open-end consumer credit plan, the person making the solicitation shall orally disclose the information described in paragraph (1)(A).

(B) Subparagraph (A) shall not apply to any telephone solicitation if-

(i) the credit card issuer—

(I) does not impose any fee described in paragraph (1)(A)(ii)(I); or

(II) does not impose any fee in connection with telephone solicitations unless the consumer signifies acceptance by using the card;

(ii) the card issuer discloses clearly and conspicuously in writing the information described in paragraph (1) within 30 days after the consumer requests the card, but in no event later than the date of delivery of the card; and

(iii) the card issuer discloses clearly and conspicuously that the consumer is not obligated to accept the card or account and the consumer will not be obligated to pay any of the fees or charges disclosed unless the consumer elects to accept the card or account by using the card.

(3) (A) Any application to open a credit card account for any person under an open-end consumer credit plan, and any solicitation to open such an account without requiring an application, that is made available to the public or contained in catalogs, magazines, or other publications shall meet the disclosure requirements of subparagraph (B), (C), or (D).

(B) An application or solicitation described in subparagraph (A) meets the requirement of this subparagraph if such application or solicitation contains—

(i) the information—

(I) described in paragraph (1)(A) in the form required under section 122(c) of this chapter, subject to subsection (e), and

(II) described in paragraph (1)(B) in a clear and conspicuous form, subject to subsections (e) and (f);

(ii) a statement, in a conspicuous and prominent location on the application or solicitation, that—

(I) the information is accurate as of the date the application or solicitation was printed;

(II) the information contained in the application or solicitation is subject to change after such date; and

(III) the applicant should contact the creditor for information on any change in the information contained in the application or solicitation since it was printed;

(iii) a clear and conspicuous disclosure of the date the application or solicitation was printed; and

(iv) a disclosure, in a conspicuous and prominent location on the application or solicitation, of a toll free telephone number or a mailing address at which the applicant may contact the creditor to obtain any change in the information provided in the application or solicitation since it was printed.

(C) An application or solicitation described in subparagraph (A) meets the requirement of this subparagraph if such application or solicitation—

(i) contains a statement, in a conspicuous and prominent location on the application or solicitation, that—

(I) there are costs associated with the use of credit cards; and

   (II) the applicant may contact the creditor to request disclosure of specific information of such costs by calling a toll free telephone number or by writing to an address, specified in the application;

   (ii) contains a disclosure, in a conspicuous and prominent location on the application or solicitation, of a toll free telephone number and a mailing address at which the applicant may contact the creditor to obtain such information; and

   (iii) does not contain any of the items described in paragraph (1).

(D) An application or solicitation meets the requirement of this subparagraph if it contains, or is accompanied by—

   (i) the disclosures required by paragraphs (1) through (6) of subsection (a);

   (ii) the disclosures required by subparagraphs (A) and (B) of paragraph (1) of this subsection included clearly and conspicuously (except that the provisions of section 122(c) shall not apply); and

   (iii) a toll free telephone number or a mailing address at which the applicant may contact the creditor to obtain any change in the information provided.

(F) Upon receipt of a request for any of the information referred to in subparagraph (B), (C), or (D), the card issuer or the agent of such issuer shall promptly disclose all of the information described in paragraph (1).

(4) (A) Any application or solicitation to open a charge card account shall disclose clearly and conspicuously the following information in the form required by section 122(c) of this chapter, subject to subsection (e):

   (i) Any annual fee, other periodic fee, or membership fee imposed for the issuance or availability of the charge card, including any account maintenance fee or other charge imposed based on activity or inactivity for the account during the billing cycle.

   (ii) Any transaction charge imposed in connection with use of the card to purchase goods or services.

   (iii) A statement that charges incurred by use of the charge card are due and payable upon receipt of a periodic statement rendered for such charge card account.

(B) In addition to the information required to be disclosed under subparagraph (A), each written application or solicitation to which such subparagraph applies shall disclose clearly and conspicuously the following information, subject to subsections (e) and (f):

   (i) Any fee imposed for an extension of credit in the form of cash.

   (ii) Any fee imposed for a late payment.

   (iii) Any fee imposed in connection with an extension of credit in excess of the amount of credit authorized to be extended with respect to such account.

(C)   Any application to open a charge card account, and any solicitation to open such an account without requiring an application, that is made available to the public or contained in catalogs, magazines, or other publications shall contain—

    (i)   the information—

        (I)   described in subparagraph (A) in the form required under section 122(c) of this chapter, subject to subsection (e), and

        (II) described in subparagraph (B) in a clear and conspicuous form, subject to subsections (e) and (f);

    (ii) a statement, in a conspicuous and prominent location on the application or solicitation, that—

        (I)   the information is accurate as of the date the application or solicitation was printed;

        (II) the information contained in the application or solicitation is subject to change after such date; and

        (III) the applicant should contact the creditor for information on any change in the information contained in the application or solicitation since it was printed;

    (iii) a clear and conspicuous disclosure of the date the application or solicitation was printed; and

    (iv) a disclosure, in a conspicuous and prominent location on the application or solicitation, of a toll free telephone number or a mailing address at which the applicant may contact the creditor to obtain any change in the information provided in the application or solicitation since it was printed.

(D)   If a charge card permits the card holder to receive an extension of credit under an open-end consumer credit plan, which is not maintained by the charge card issuer, the charge card issuer may provide the information described in subparagraphs (A) and (B) in the form required by such subparagraphs in lieu of the information required to be provided under paragraph (1), (2), or (3) with respect to any credit extended under such plan, if the charge card issuer discloses clearly and conspicuously to the consumer in the application or solicitation that—

    (i)   the charge card issuer will make an independent decision as to whether to issue the card;

    (ii) the charge card may arrive before the decision is made with respect to an extension of credit under an open-end consumer credit plan; and

    (iii) approval by the charge card issuer does not constitute approval by the issuer of the extension of credit.

    The information required to be disclosed under paragraph (1) shall be provided to the charge card holder by the creditor which maintains such open-end consumer credit plan before the first extension of credit under such plan.

    (E)   For the purposes of this subsection, the term "charge card" means a card, plate, or other single credit device that may be used from time to time to obtain credit which is not subject to a finance charge.

  (5)   The Board may, by regulation, require the disclosure of information in addition to that otherwise required by this subsection or subsection (d), and modify any disclosure of information required by this subsection or subsection (d), in any application to open a credit card account for any person under an open-end consumer credit plan or any application to open a charge card account for any person, or a solicitation to open any such account without requiring an application, if the Board determines that such action is necessary to carry out the purposes of, or prevent evasions of, any paragraph of this subsection.

(d) (1)   Except as provided in paragraph (2), a card issuer that imposes any fee described in subsection (c)(1)(A)(ii)(I) or (c)(4)(A)(i) shall transmit to a consumer at least 30 days prior to the scheduled renewal date of the consumer's credit or charge card account a clear and conspicuous disclosure of—

    (A)   the date by which, the month by which, or the billing period at the close of which, the account will expire if not renewed;

    (B)   the information described in subsection (c)(1)(A) or (c)(4)(A) that would apply if the account were renewed, subject to subsection (e); and

    (C)   the method by which the consumer may terminate continued credit availability under the account.

  (2) (A)   The disclosures required by this subsection may be provided—

      (i)   prior to posting a fee described in subsection (c)(1)(A)(ii)(I) or (c)(4)(A)(i) to the account, or

      (ii)   with the periodic billing statement first disclosing that the fee has been posted to the account.

    (B)   Disclosures may be provided under subparagraph (A) only if—

      (i)   the consumer is given a 30-day period to avoid payment of the fee or to have the fee recredited to the account in any case where the consumer does not wish to continue the availability of the credit; and

      (ii)   the consumer is permitted to use the card during such period without incurring an obligation to pay such fee.

  (3)   The Board may by regulation provide for fewer disclosures than are required by paragraph (1) in the case of an account which is renewable for a period of less than 6 months.

(e) (1)   If the amount of any fee required to be disclosed under subsection (c) or (d) is determined on the basis of a percentage of another amount, the percentage used in making such determination and the identification of the amount against which such percentage is applied shall be disclosed in lieu of the amount of such fee.

  (2)   If a credit or charge card issuer does not impose any fee required to be disclosed under any provision of subsection (c) or (d), such provision shall not apply with respect to such issuer.

(f) If the amount of any fee required to be disclosed by a credit or charge card issuer under paragraph (1)(B), (3)(B)(i)(II), (4)(B), or (4)(C)(i)(II) of subsection (c) varies from State to State, the card issuer may disclose the range of such fees for purposes of subsection (c) in lieu of the amount for each applicable State, if such disclosure includes a statement that the amount of such fee varies from State to State.

(g) (1) Whenever a card issuer that offers any guarantee or insurance for repayment of all or part of the outstanding balance of an open-end credit card plan proposes to change the person providing that guarantee or insurance, the card issuer shall send each insured consumer written notice of the proposed change not less than 30 days prior to the change, including notice of any increase in the rate or substantial decrease in coverage or service which will result from such change. Such notice may be included on or with the monthly statement provided to the consumer prior to the month in which the proposed change would take effect.

(2) In any case in which a proposed change described in paragraph (1) occurs, the insured consumer shall be given the name and address of the new guarantor or insurer and a copy of the policy or group certificate containing the basic terms and conditions, including the premium rate to be charged.

(3) The notices required under paragraphs (1) and (2) shall each include a statement that the consumer has the option to discontinue the insurance or guarantee.

(4) No provision of this subsection shall be construed as superseding any provision of State law which is applicable to the regulation of insurance.

(5) The Board shall define, in regulations, what constitutes a "substantial decrease in coverage or service" for purposes of paragraph (1).

[15 USC 1637. As amended by acts of Oct. 28, 1974 (88 Stat. 1511, 1519, 1521); March 31, 1980 (94 Stat. 176); Dec. 26, 1981 (95 Stat. 1515); Nov. 3, 1988 (102 Stat. 2960, 2968; and Nov. 23, 1988 (102 Stat. 4729).]

SECTION 127A—DISCLOSURE REQUIREMENTS FOR OPEN-END CONSUMER CREDIT PLANS SECURED BY THE CONSUMER'S PRINCIPAL DWELLING

(a) In the case of any open-end consumer credit plan which provides for any extension of credit which is secured by the consumer's principal dwelling, the creditor shall make the following disclosures in accordance with subsection (b):

(1) Each annual percentage rate imposed in connection with extensions of credit under the plan and a statement that such rate does not include costs other than interest.

(2) In the case of a plan which provides for variable rates of interest on credit extended under the plan—

(A) a description of the manner in which such rate will be computed and a statement that such rate does not include costs other than interest;

(B) a description of the manner in which any changes in the annual percentage rate will be made, including—

          (i)   any negative amortization and interest rate carryover;

          (ii)   the timing of any such changes;

          (iii) any index or margin to which such changes in the rate are related; and

          (iv) a source of information about any such index;

   (C)   if an initial annual percentage rate is offered which is not based on an index—

          (i)   a statement of such rate and the period of time such initial rate will be in effect; and

          (ii)   a statement that such rate does not include costs other than interest;

   (D)   a statement that the consumer should ask about the current index value and interest rate;

   (E)   a statement of the maximum amount by which the annual percentage rate may change in any 1-year period or a statement that no such limit exists;

   (F)   a statement of the maximum annual percentage rate that may be imposed at any time under the plan;

   (G)   subject to subsection (b)(3), a table, based on a $10,000 extension of credit, showing how the annual percentage rate and the minimum periodic payment amount under each repayment option of the plan would have been affected during the preceding 15-year period by changes in any index used to compute such rate;

   (H)   a statement of—

          (i)   the maximum annual percentage rate which may be imposed under each repayment option of the plan;

          (ii)   the minimum amount of any periodic payment which may be required, based on a $10,000 outstanding balance, under each such option when such maximum annual percentage rate is in effect; and

          (iii) the earliest date by which such maximum annual interest rate may be imposed; and

              (I)   a statement that interest rate information will be provided on or with each periodic statement.

(3)   An itemization of any fees imposed by the creditor in connection with the availability or use of credit under such plan, including annual fees, application fees, transaction fees, and closing costs (including costs commonly described as "points"), and the time when such fees are payable.

(4)   (A)   An estimate, based on the creditor's experience with such plans and stated as a single amount or as a reasonable range, of the aggregate amount of additional fees that may be imposed by third parties (such as governmental authorities, appraisers, and attorneys) in connection with opening an account under the plan.

      (B)   A statement that the consumer may ask the creditor for a good faith estimate by the creditor of the fees that may be imposed by third parties.

(5)   A statement that—

      (A)   any extension of credit under the plan is secured by the consumer's dwelling; and

      (B)   in the event of any default, the consumer risks the loss of the dwelling.

(6)   (A)   A clear and conspicuous statement—

            (i)   of the time by which an application must be submitted to obtain the terms disclosed; or

            (ii)   if applicable, that the terms are subject to change.

      (B)   A statement that—

            (i)   the consumer may elect not to enter into an agreement to open an account under the plan if any term changes (other than a change contemplated by a variable feature of the plan) before any such agreement is final; and

            (ii)   if the consumer makes an election described in clause (i), the consumer is entitled to a refund of all fees paid in connection with the application.

      (C)   A statement that the consumer should make or otherwise retain a copy of information disclosed under this subparagraph.

(7)   A statement that—

      (A)   under certain conditions, the creditor may terminate any account under the plan and require immediate repayment of any outstanding balance, prohibit any additional extension of credit to the account, or reduce the credit limit applicable to the account; and

      (B)   the consumer may receive, upon request, more specific information about the conditions under which the creditor may take any action described in subparagraph (A).

(8)   The repayment options under the plan, including—

      (A)   if applicable, any differences in repayment options with regard to—

            (i)   any period during which additional extensions of credit may be obtained; and

            (ii)   any period during which repayment is required to be made and no additional extensions of credit may be obtained;

      (B)   the length of any repayment period, including any differences in the length of any repayment period with regard to the periods described in clauses (i) and (ii) of subparagraph (A); and

      (C)   an explanation of how the amount of any minimum monthly or periodic payment will be determined under each such option, including any differences in the determination of any such amount with regard to the periods described in clauses (i) and (ii) of subparagraph (A).

(9)   An example, based on a $10,000 outstanding balance and the interest rate (other than a rate not based on the index under the plan) which is, or was

recently, in effect under such plan, showing the minimum monthly or periodic payment, and the time it would take to repay the entire $10,000 if the consumer paid only the minimum periodic payments and obtained no additional extensions of credit.

(10) If, under any repayment option of the plan, the payment of not more than the minimum periodic payments required under such option over the length of the repayment period—

    (A) would not repay any of the principal balance; or

    (B) would repay less than the outstanding balance by the end of such period, as the case may be, a statement of such fact, including an explicit statement that at the end of such repayment period a balloon payment (as defined in section 147(f)) would result which would be required to be paid in full at that time.

(11) If applicable, a statement that—

    (A) any limitation in the plan on the amount of any increase in the minimum payments may result in negative amortization;

    (B) negative amortization increases the outstanding principal balance of the account; and

    (C) negative amortization reduces the consumer's equity in the consumer's dwelling.

(12) (A) Any limitation contained in the plan on the number of extensions of credit and the amount of credit which may be obtained during any month or other defined time period.

    (B) Any requirement which establishes a minimum amount for—

        (i) the initial extension of credit to an account under the plan;

        (ii) any subsequent extension of credit to an account under the plan; or

        (iii) any outstanding balance of an account under the plan.

(13) A statement that the consumer should consult a tax advisor regarding the deductibility of interest and charges under the plan.

(14) Any other term which the Board requires, in regulations, to be disclosed.

(b) (1) (A) The disclosures required under subsection (a) with respect to any open-end consumer credit plan which provides for any extension of credit which is secured by the consumer's principal dwelling and the pamphlet required under subsection (e) shall be provided to any consumer at the time the creditor distributes an application to establish an account under such plan to such consumer.

    (B) In the case of telephone applications, applications contained in magazines or other publications, or applications provided by a third party, the disclosures required under subsection (a) and the pamphlet required under subsection (e) shall be provided by the creditor before the end of the 3-day period beginning on the date the creditor receives a completed application from a consumer.

(2)   (A)   Except as provided in paragraph (1)(B), the disclosures required under subsection (a) shall be provided on or with any application to establish an account under an open-end consumer credit plan which provides for any extension of credit which is secured by the consumer's principal dwelling.

(B)   The disclosures required under subsection (a) shall be conspicuously segregated from all other terms, data, or additional information provided in connection with the application, either by grouping the disclosures separately on the application form or by providing the disclosures on a separate form, in accordance with regulations of the Board.

(C)   The disclosures required by paragraphs (5), (6), and (7) of subsection (a) shall precede all of the other required disclosures.

(D)   Whether or not the disclosures required under subsection (a) are provided on the application form, the variable rate information described in subsection (a)(2) may be provided separately from the other information required to be disclosed.

(3)   In preparing the table required under subsection (a)(2)(G), the creditor shall consistently select one rate of interest for each year and the manner of selecting the rate from year to year shall be consistent with the plan.

(c)   In the case of an application to open an account under any open-end consumer credit plan described in subsection (a) which is provided to a consumer by any person other than the creditor—

(1)   such person shall provide such consumer with—

(A)   the disclosures required under subsection (a) with respect to such plan, in accordance with subsection (b); and

(B)   the pamphlet required under subsection (e); or

(2)   if such person cannot provide specific terms about the plan because specific information about the plan terms is not available, no nonrefundable fee may be imposed in connection with such application before the end of the 3-day period beginning on the date the consumer receives the disclosures required under subsection (a) with respect to the application.

(d)   For purposes, of this section and sections 137 and 147, the term "principal dwelling" includes any second or vacation home of the consumer.

(e)   In addition to the disclosures required under subsection (a) with respect to an application to open an account under any open-end consumer credit plan described in such subsection, the creditor or other person providing such disclosures to the consumer shall provide—

(1)   a pamphlet published by the Board pursuant to section 4 of the Home Equity Consumer Protection Act of 1988; or

(2)   any pamphlet which provides substantially similar information to the information described in such section, as determined by the Board.

[15 USC 1637a. As added by act of Nov. 23, 1988 (102 Stat. 4725).]

SECTION 128—CONSUMER CREDIT NOT UNDER OPEN-END CREDIT PLANS

(a) For each consumer credit transaction other than under an open-end credit plan, the creditor shall disclose each of the following items, to the extent applicable:

(1) The identity of the creditor required to make disclosure.

(2) (A) The "amount financed," using that term, which shall be the amount of credit of which the consumer has actual use. This amount shall be computed as follows, but the computations need not be disclosed and shall not be disclosed with the disclosures conspicuously segregated in accordance with subsection (b)(1):

   (i) take the principal amount of the loan or the cash price less downpayment and trade-in;

   (ii) add any charges which are not part of the finance charge or of the principal amount of the loan and which are financed by the consumer, including the cost of any items excluded from the finance charge pursuant to section 106; and

   (iii) subtract any charges which are part of the finance charge but which will be paid by the consumer before or at the time of the consummation of the transaction, or have been withheld from the proceeds of the credit.

   (B) In conjunction with the disclosure of the amount financed, a creditor shall provide a statement of the consumer's right to obtain, upon a written request, a written itemization of the amount financed. The statement shall include spaces for a "yes" and "no" indication to be initialed by the consumer to indicate whether the consumer wants a written itemization of the amount financed. Upon receiving an affirmative indication, the creditor shall provide, at the time other disclosures are required to be furnished, a written itemization of the amount financed. For the purposes of this subparagraph, 'itemization of the amount financed' means a disclosure of the following items, to the extent applicable:

   (i) the amount that is or will be paid directly to the consumer;

   (ii) the amount that is or will be credited to the consumer's account to discharge obligations owed to the creditor;

   (iii) each amount that is or will be paid to third persons by the creditor on the consumer's behalf, together with an identification of or reference to the third person; and

   (iv) the total amount of any charges described in the preceding subparagraph (A)(iii).

(3) The "finance charge," not itemized, using that term.

(4) The finance charge expressed as an "annual percentage rate," using that term. This shall not be required if the amount financed does not exceed $75 and the finance charge does not exceed $5, or if the amount financed exceeds $75 and the finance charge does not exceed $7.50.

(5)   The sum of the amount financed and the finance charge, which shall be termed the "total of payments."

(6)   The number, amount, and due dates or period of payments scheduled to repay the total of payments.

(7)   In a sale of property or services in which the seller is the creditor required to disclose pursuant to section 121(b), the "total sale price," using that term, which shall be the total of the cash price of the property or services, additional charges, and the finance charge.

(8)   Descriptive explanations of the terms "amount financed," "finance charge," "annual percentage rate," "total of payments," and "total sale price" as specified by the Board. The descriptive explanation of "total sale price" shall include reference to the amount of the downpayment.

(9)   Where the credit is secured, a statement that a security interest has been taken in (A) the property which is purchased as part of the credit transaction, or (B) property not purchased as part of the credit transaction identified by item or type.

(10) Any dollar charge or percentage amount which may be imposed by a creditor solely on account of a late payment, other than a deferral or extension charge.

(11) A statement indicating whether or not the consumer is entitled to a rebate of any finance charge upon refinancing or prepayment in full pursuant to acceleration or otherwise, if the obligation involves a precomputed finance charge. A statement indicating whether or not a penalty will be imposed in those same circumstances if the obligation involves a finance charge computed from time to time by application of a rate to the unpaid principal balance.

(12) A statement that the consumer should refer to the appropriate contract document for any information such document provides about nonpayment, default, the right to accelerate the maturity of the debt, and prepayment rebates and penalties.

(13) In any residential mortgage transaction, a statement indicting whether a subsequent purchaser or assignee of the consumer may assume the debt obligation on its original terms and conditions.

(b) (1)   Except as otherwise provided in this chapter, the disclosures required under subsection (a) shall be made before the credit is extended. Except for the disclosures required by subsection (a)(1) of this section, all disclosures required under subsection (a) and any disclosure provided for in subsection (b), (c), or (d) of section 106 shall be conspicuously segregated from all other terms, data, or information provided in connection with a transaction, including any computations or itemization.

(2)   In the case of a residential mortgage transaction, as defined in section 103(w), which is also subject to the Real Estate Settlement Procedures Act, good faith estimates of the disclosures required under subsection (a) shall be made in accordance with regulations of the Board under section 121(c) before the credit is extended, or shall be delivered or placed in the mail not later than three business days after the creditor receives the consumer's written application, whichever is earlier. If the disclosure statement furnished within three days of

the written application contains an annual percentage rate which is subsequently rendered inaccurate within the meaning of section 107(c), the creditor shall furnish another statement at the time of settlement or consummation.

(c) (1) If a creditor receives a purchase order by mail or telephone without personal solicitation, and the cash price and the total sale price and the terms of financing, including the annual percentage rate, are set forth in the creditor's catalog or other printed material distributed to the public, then the disclosures required under subsection (a) may be made at any time not later than the date the first payment is due.

(2) If a creditor receives a request for a loan by mail or telephone without personal solicitation and the terms of financing, including the annual percentage rate for representative amounts of credit, are set forth in the creditor's printed material distributed to the public, or in the contract of loan or other printed material delivered to the obligor, then the disclosures required under subsection (a) may be made at any time not later than the date the first payment is due.

(d) If a consumer credit sale is one of a series of consumer credit sales transactions made pursuant to an agreement providing for the addition of the deferred payment price of that sale to an existing outstanding balance, and the person to whom the credit is extended has approved in writing both the annual percentage rate or rates and the method of computing the finance charge or charges, and the creditor retains no security interest in any property as to which he has received payments aggregating the amount of the sales price including any finance charges attributable thereto, then the disclosure required under subsection (a) for the particular sale may be made at any time not later than the date the first payment for that sale is due. For the purposes of this subsection, in the case of items purchased on different dates, the first purchased shall be deemed first paid for, and in the case of items purchased on the same date, the lowest priced shall be deemed first paid for.

[15 USC 1638. As amended by acts of March 31, 1980 (94 Stat. 178) and Dec. 26, 1981 (95 Stat. 1515).]

Section 129—[Repealed]

Section 130—Civil Liability*

(a) Except as otherwise provided in this section, any creditor who fails to comply with any requirement imposed under this chapter, including any requirement under section 125, or chapter 4 or 5 of this title with respect to any person is liable to such person in an amount equal to the sum of—

(1) any actual damage sustained by such person as a result of the failure;

(2) (A) (i) in the case of an individual action twice the amount of any finance charge in connection with the transaction, or (ii) in the case of an individual action relating to a consumer lease under chapter 5 of this title, 25 per centum of the total amount of monthly payments under the lease, except that the liability under this subparagraph shall not be less than $100 nor greater than $1,000; or

---

*Creditors choosing to comply with the amended statute and implementing regulations prior to October 1, 1982 are subject to the amended civil liability provisions. (Pub. L. 97-25 § 301).

      (B)   in the case of a class action, such amount as the court may allow, except that as to each member of the class no minimum recovery shall be applicable, and the total recovery under this subparagraph in any class action or series of class actions arising out of the same failure to comply by the same creditor shall not be more than the lesser of $500,000 or 1 per centum of the net worth of the creditor; and

  (3)   in the case of any successful action to enforce the foregoing liability or in any action in which a person is determined to have a right of rescission under section 125, the costs of the action, together with a reasonable attorney's fee as determined by the court. In determining the amount of award in any class action, the court shall consider, among other relevant factors, the amount of any actual damages awarded, the frequency and persistence of failures of compliance by the creditor, the resources of the creditor, the number of persons adversely affected, and the extent to which the creditor's failure of compliance was intentional. In connection with the disclosures referred to in subsections (a) and (b) of section 127, a creditor shall have a liability determined under paragraph (2) only for failing to comply with the requirements of section 125, section 127(a), or of paragraph (4), (5), (6), (7), (8), (9), or (10) of section 127(b) or for failing to comply with disclosure requirements under State law for any term or item which the Board has determined to be substantially the same in meaning under section 111 (a)(2) as any of the terms or items referred to in section 127(a) or any of those paragraphs of section 127(b). In connection with the disclosures referred to in subsection (c) or (d) of section 127, a card issuer shall have a liability under this section only to a cardholder who pays a fee described in section 127(c)(1)(A)(ii)(I) or section 127(c)(4)(A)(i) or who uses the credit card or charge card. In connection with the disclosures referred to in section 128, a creditor shall have a liability determined under paragraph (2) only for failing to comply with the requirements of section 125 or of paragraph (2) (insofar as it requires a disclosure of the 'amount financed'), (3), (4), (5), (6), or (9) of section 128(a), or for failing to comply with disclosure requirements under State law for any term which the Board has determined to be substantially the same in meaning under section 111(a)(2) as any of the terms referred to in any of those paragraphs of section 128(a). With respect to any failure to make disclosures required under this chapter or chapter 4 or 5 of this title, liability shall be imposed only upon the creditor required to make disclosure, except as provided in section 131.

  (b) A creditor or assignee has no liability under this section or section 108 or section 112 for any failure to comply with any requirement imposed under this chapter or chapter 5, if within sixty days after discovering an error, whether pursuant to a final written examination report or notice issued under section 108(e)(1) or through the creditor's or assignee's own procedures, and prior to the institution of an action under this section or the receipt of written notice of the error from the obligor, the creditor or assignee notifies the person concerned of the error and makes whatever adjustments in the appropriate account are necessary to assure that the person will not be required to pay an amount in excess of the charge actually disclosed, or the dollar equivalent of the annual percentage rate actually disclosed, whichever is lower.

(c) A creditor or assignee may not be held liable in any action brought under this section or section 125 for a violation of this title if the creditor or assignee shows by a preponderance of evidence that the violation was not intentional and resulted from a bona fide error notwithstanding the maintenance of procedures reasonably adapted to avoid any such error. Examples of a bona fide error include, but are not limited to, clerical, calculation, computer malfunction and programming, and printing errors, except that an error of legal judgment with respect to a person's obligations under this title is not a bona fide error.

(d) When there are multiple obligors in a consumer credit transaction or consumer lease, there shall be no more than one recovery of damages under subsection (a)(2) for a violation of this title.

(e) Any action under this section may be brought in any United States district court, or in any other court of competent jurisdiction, within one year from the date of the occurrence of the violation. This subsection does not bar a person from asserting a violation of this title in an action to collect the debt which was brought more than one year from the date of the occurrence of the violation as a matter of defense by recoupment or set-off in such action, except as otherwise provided by State law.

(f) No provision of this section, section 108(b), section 108(c), section 108(e), or section 112 imposing any liability shall apply to any act done or omitted in good faith in conformity with any rule, regulation, or interpretation thereof by the Board or in conformity with any interpretation or approval by an official or employee of the Federal Reserve System duly authorized by the Board to issue such interpretations or approvals under such procedures as the Board may prescribe therefor, notwithstanding that after such act or omission has occurred, such rule, regulation, interpretation, or approval is amended, rescinded, or determined by judicial or other authority to be invalid for any reason.

(g) The multiple failure to disclose to any person any information required under this chapter or chapter 4 or 5 of this title to be disclosed in connection with a single account under an open-end consumer credit plan, other single consumer credit sale, consumer loan, consumer lease, or other extension of consumer credit, shall entitle the person to a single recovery under this section but continued failure to disclose after a recovery has been granted shall give rise to rights to additional recoveries. This subsection does not bar any remedy permitted by section 125.

(h) A person may not take any action to offset any amount for which a creditor or assignee is potentially liable to such person under subsection (a)(2) against any amount owed by such person, unless the amount of the creditor's or assignee's liability under this title has been determined by judgment of a court of competent jurisdiction in an action of which such person was a party. This subsection does not bar a consumer then in default on the obligation from asserting a violation of this title as an original action, or as a defense or counterclaim to an action to collect amounts owed by the consumer brought by a person liable under this title.

[15 USC 1640. As amended by acts of Oct. 28, 1974 (88 Stat. 1518); Feb. 27, 1976 (90 Stat. 197); March 23, 1976 (90 Stat. 260); and Nov. 3, 1988 (102 Stat. 2966).]

Section 13—Liability Of Assignees*

(a) Except as otherwise specifically provided in this title, any civil action for a violation of this title or proceeding under section 108 which may be brought against a creditor may be maintained against any assignee of such creditor only if the violation for which such action or proceeding is brought is apparent on the face of the disclosure statement, except where the assignment was involuntary. For the purpose of this section, a violation apparent on the face of the disclosure statement includes, but is not limited to (1) a disclosure which can be determined to be incomplete or inaccurate from the face of the disclosure statement or other documents assigned, or (2) a disclosure which does not use the terms required to be used by this title.

(b) Except as provided in section 125(c), in any action or proceeding by or against any subsequent assignee of the original creditor without knowledge to the contrary by the assignee when he acquires the obligation, written acknowledgment of receipt by a person to whom a statement is required to be given pursuant to this title shall be conclusive proof of the delivery thereof and, except as provided in subsection (a), of compliance with this chapter. This section does not affect the rights of the obligor in any action against the original creditor.

(c) Any consumer who has the right to rescind a transaction under section 125 may rescind the transaction as against any assignee of the obligation.

[15 USC 1641. As amended by acts of March 31, 1980 (94 Stat. 182) and Dec. 26, 1981 (95 Stat. 1515).]

Section 132—Issuance of Credit Cards

No credit card shall be issued except in response to a request or application therefor. This prohibition does not apply to the issuance of a credit card in renewal of, or in substitution for, an accepted credit card.

[15 USC 1641. As amended by act of Oct. 26, 1970 (84 Stat. 1126).]

Section 133—Liability of Holder of Credit Card

(a) (1) A cardholder shall be liable for the unauthorized use of a credit card only if—

    (A) the card is an accepted credit card;

    (B) the liability is not in excess of $50;

    (C) the card issuer gives adequate notice to the cardholder of the potential liability;

    (D) the card issuer has provided the cardholder with a description of a means by which the card issuer may be notified of loss or theft of the card, which description may be provided on the face or reverse side of the statement required by section 127(b) or on a separate notice accompanying such statement;

*Assignees of creditors choosing to comply with the amended statute and implementing regulations prior to October 1, 1982 are subject to the amended civil liability provisions (Pub. L. 97-25 § 301).

(E) the unauthorized use occurs before the card issuer has been notified that an unauthorized use of the credit card has occurred or may occur as the result of loss, theft, or otherwise; and

(F) the card issuer has provided a method whereby the user of such card can be identified as the person authorized to use it.

(2) For purposes of this section, a card issuer has been notified when such steps as may be reasonably required in the ordinary course of business to provide the card issuer with the pertinent information have been taken, whether or not any particular officer, employee, or agent of the card issuer does in fact receive such information.

(b) In any action by a card issuer to enforce liability for the use of a credit card, the burden of proof is upon the card issuer to show that the use was authorized or, if the use was unauthorized, then the burden of proof is upon the card issuer to show that the conditions of liability for the unauthorized use of a credit card, as set forth in subsection (a), have been met.

(c) Nothing in this section imposes liability upon a cardholder for the unauthorized use of a credit card in excess of his liability for such use under other applicable law or under any agreement with the card issuer.

(d) Except as provided in this section, a cardholder incurs no liability from the unauthorized use of a credit card.

[15 USC 1643. As added by act of Oct. 26, 1970 (84 Stat. 1126) and amended by acts of March 31, 1980 (94 Stat. 182) and Dec. 26, 1981 (95 Stat. 1515).]

SECTION 134—FRAUDULENT USE OF CREDIT CARD

(a) Whoever knowingly in a transaction affecting interstate or foreign commerce, uses or attempts or conspires to use any counterfeit, fictitious, altered, forged, lost, stolen, or fraudulently obtained credit card to obtain money, goods, services, or anything else of value which within any one-year period has a value aggregating $1,000 or more; or

(b) Whoever, with unlawful or fraudulent intent, transports or attempts or conspires to transport in interstate or foreign commerce a counterfeit, fictitious, altered, forged, lost, stolen, or fraudulently obtained credit card knowing the same to be counterfeit, fictitious, altered, forged, lost, stolen, or fraudulently obtained; or

(c) Whoever, with unlawful or fraudulent intent, uses any instrumentality of interstate or foreign commerce to sell or transport a counterfeit, fictitious, altered, forged, lost, stolen, or fraudulently obtained credit card knowing the same to be counterfeit, fictitious, altered, forged, lost, stolen, or fraudulently obtained; or

(d) Whoever knowingly receives, conceals, uses, or transports money, goods, services, or anything else of value (except tickets for interstate or foreign transportation) which (1) within any one-year period has a value aggregating $1,000 or more, (2) has moved in or is part of, or which constitutes interstate or foreign commerce, and (3) has been obtained with a counterfeit, fictitious, altered, forged, lost, stolen, or fraudulently obtained credit card; or

(e) Whoever knowingly receives, conceals, uses, sells, or transports in interstate or foreign commerce one or more tickets for interstate or foreign transportation, which (1) within any one-year period have a value aggregating $500 or more, and (2) have been purchased or obtained with one or more counterfeit, fictitious, altered, forged, lost, stolen, or fraudulently obtained credit cards; or

(f) Whoever in a transaction affecting interstate or foreign commerce furnishes money, property, services, or anything else of value, which within any one-year period has a value aggregating $1,000 or more, through the use of any counterfeit, fictitious, altered, forged, lost, stolen, or fraudulently obtained credit card knowing the same to be counterfeit, fictitious, altered, forged, lost, stolen, or fraudulently obtained—shall be fined not more than $10,000 or imprisoned not more than ten years, or both.

[15 USC 1644. As amended by acts of Oct. 26, 1970 (84 Stat. 1127) and Oct. 28, 1974 (88 Stat. 1520).]

Section 135—Business Credit Cards

The exemption provided by section 104(1) does not apply to the provisions of sections 132, 133, and 134, except that a card issuer and a business or other organization which provides credit cards issued by the same card issuer to ten or more of its employees may by contract agree as to liability of the business or other organization with respect to unauthorized use of such credit cards without regard to the provisions of section 133, but in no case may such business or other organization or card issuer impose liability upon any employee with respect to unauthorized use of such a credit card except in accordance with and subject to the limitations of section 133.

[15 USC 1645. As added by act of Oct. 28, 1974 (88 Stat. 1519).]

Section 136—Dissemination of Annual Percentage Rates

(a) The Board shall collect, publish, and disseminate to the public, on a demonstration basis in a number of standard metropolitan statistical areas to be determined by the Board, the annual percentage rates charged for representative types of nonsale credit by creditors in such areas. For the purpose of this section, the Board is authorized to require creditors in such areas to furnish information necessary for the Board to collect, publish, and disseminate such information.

(b) (1) The Board shall collect, on a semiannual basis, credit card price and availability information, including the information required to be disclosed under section 127(c) of this chapter, from a broad sample of financial institutions which offer credit card services.

 (2) The broad sample of financial institutions required under paragraph (1) shall include—

 (A) the 25 largest issuers of credit cards; and

 (B) not less than 125 additional financial institutions selected by the Board in a manner that ensures—

 (i) an equitable geographical distribution within the sample; and

 (ii) the representation of a wide spectrum of institutions within the sample.

(3) Each financial institution in the broad sample established pursuant to paragraph (2) shall report the information to the Board in accordance with such regulations or orders as the Board may prescribe.

(4) The Board shall—

(A) make the information collected pursuant to this subsection available to the public upon request; and

(B) report such information semiannually to Congress.

(c) The Board is authorized to enter into contracts or other arrangements with appropriate persons, organizations, or State agencies to carry out its functions under subsections (a) and (b) and to furnish financial assistance in support thereof.

[15 USC 1646. As amended by acts of March 31, 1980 (94 Stat. 183); Dec. 26, 1981 (95 Stat. 1515); and Nov. 3, 1988 (102 Stat. 2967).]

SECTION 137—HOME EQUITY PLANS

(a) In the case of extensions of credit under an open-end consumer credit plan which are subject to a variable rate and are secured by a consumer's principal dwelling, the index or other rate of interest to which changes in the annual percentage rate are related shall be based on an index or rate of interest which is publicly available and is not under the control of the creditor.

(b) A creditor may not unilaterally terminate any account under an open-end consumer credit plan under which extensions of credit are secured by a consumer's principal dwelling and require the immediate repayment of any outstanding balance at such time, except in the case of—

(1) fraud or material misrepresentation on the part of the consumer in connection with the account;

(2) failure by the consumer to meet the repayment terms of the agreement for any outstanding balance; or

(3) any other action or failure to act by the consumer which adversely affects the creditor's security for the account or any right of the creditor in such security.

(c) (1) No open-end consumer credit plan under which extensions of credit are secured by a consumer's principal dwelling may contain a provision which permits a creditor to change unilaterally any term required to be disclosed under section 127A(a) or any other term, except a change in insignificant terms such as the address of the creditor for billing purposes.

(2) Notwithstanding the provisions of subsection (1), a creditor may make any of the following changes:

(A) Change the index and margin applicable to extensions of credit under such plan if the index used by the creditor is no longer available and the substitute index and margin would result in a substantially similar interest rate.

(B) Prohibit additional extensions of credit or reduce the credit limit applicable to an account under the plan during any period in which the value of the consumer's principal dwelling which secures any outstanding balance is significantly less than the original appraisal value of the dwelling.

(C)   Prohibit additional extensions of credit or reduce the credit limit applicable to the account during any period in which the creditor has reason to believe that the consumer will be unable to comply with the repayment requirements of the account due to a material change in the consumer's financial circumstances.

(D)   Prohibit additional extensions of credit or reduce the credit limit applicable to the account during any period in which the consumer is in default with respect to any material obligation of the consumer under the agreement.

(E)   Prohibit additional extensions of credit or reduce the credit limit applicable to the account during any period in which—

(i)   the creditor is precluded by government action from imposing the annual percentage rate provided for in the account agreement; or

(ii)   any government action is in effect which adversely affects the priority of the creditor's security interest in the account to the extent that the value of the creditor's secured interest in the property is less than 120 percent of the amount of the credit limit applicable to the account.

(F)   Any change that will benefit the consumer

(3)   Upon the request of the consumer and at the time an agreement is entered into by a consumer to open an account under an open-end consumer credit plan under which extensions of credit are secured by the consumer's principal dwelling, the consumer shall be given a list of the categories of contract obligations which are deemed by the creditor to be material obligations of the consumer under the agreement for purposes of paragraph (2)(D).

(4)   (A)   For purposes of paragraph (2)(F), a change shall be deemed to benefit the consumer if the change is unequivocally beneficial to the borrower and the change is beneficial through the entire term of the agreement.

(B)   The Board may, by regulation, determine categories of changes that benefit the consumer.

(d)   If any term or condition described in section 127A(a) which is disclosed to a consumer in connection with an application to open an account under an open-end consumer credit plan described in such section (other than a variable feature of the plan) changes before the account is opened, and if, as a result of such change, the consumer elects not to enter into the plan agreement, the creditor shall refund all fees paid by the consumer in connection with such application.

(e)   (1)   No nonrefundable fee may be imposed by a creditor or any other person in connection with any application by a consumer to establish an account under any open-end consumer credit plan which provides for extensions of credit which are secured by a consumer's principal dwelling before the end of the 3-day period beginning on the date such consumer receives the disclosure required under section 127A(a) and the pamphlet required under section 127A(e) with respect to such application.

(2)   For purposes of determining when a nonrefundable fee may be imposed in accordance with this subsection if the disclosures and pamphlet referred to in paragraph (1) are mailed to the consumer, the date of the receipt of the disclosures by such consumer shall be deemed to be 3 business days after the date of mailing by the creditor.

[15 USC 1647. As added by act of Nov. 23, 1988 (102 Stat. 4731).]

CHAPTER 3—CREDIT ADVERTISING

Section

141   Catalogs and multiple-page advertisements
142   Advertising of downpayments and installments
143   Advertising of open-end credit plans
144   Advertising of credit other than open-end plans
145   Nonliability of media
146   Use of annual percentage rate in oral disclosures
147   Advertising of open-end consumer credit plans secured by the consumer's principal dwelling

SECTION 141—CATALOGS AND MULTIPLE-PAGE ADVERTISEMENTS

For the purposes of this chapter, a catalog or other multiple-page advertisement shall be considered a single advertisement if it clearly and conspicuously displays a credit terms table on which the information required to be stated under this chapter is clearly set forth.

[15 USC 1661.]

SECTION 142—ADVERTISING OF DOWNPAYMENTS AND INSTALLMENTS

No advertisement to aid, promote, or assist directly or indirectly any extension of consumer credit may state

(1)   that a specific periodic consumer credit amount or installment amount can be arranged, unless the creditor usually and customarily arranges credit payments or installments for that period and in that amount.

(2)   that a specified downpayment is required in connection with any extension of consumer credit, unless the creditor usually and customarily arranges downpayments in that amount.

[15 USC 1662.]

SECTION 143—ADVERTISING OF OPEN-END CREDIT PLANS

No advertisement to aid, promote, or assist directly or indirectly the extension of consumer credit under an open-end credit plan may set forth any of the specific terms of that plan unless it also clearly and conspicuously sets forth all of the following items:

(1)   Any minimum or fixed amount which could be imposed.

(2)   In any case in which periodic rates may be used to compute the finance charge, the periodic rates expressed as annual percentage rates.

(3)   Any other term that the Board may by regulation require to be disclosed.

[15 USC 1663. As amended by acts of March 31, 1980 (94 Stat. 177) and Dec. 26, 1981 (95 Stat. 1515).]

SECTION 144—ADVERTISING OF CREDIT OTHER THAN OPEN-END PLANS

(a)   Except as provided in subsection (b), this section applies to any advertisement to aid, promote, or assist directly or indirectly any consumer credit sale, loan, or other extension of credit subject to the provisions of this title, other than an open-end credit plan.

(b)   The provisions of this section do not apply to advertisements of residential real estate except to the extent that the Board may by regulation require.

(c)   If any advertisement to which this section applies states the rate of a finance charge, the advertisement shall state the rate of that charge expressed as an annual percentage rate.

(d)   If any advertisement to which this section applies states the amount of the downpayment, if any, the amount of any installment payment, the dollar amount of any finance charge, or the number of installments or the period of repayment, then the advertisement shall state all of the following items:

(1)   The downpayment, if any.

(2)   The terms of repayment.

(3)   The rate of the finance charge expressed as an annual percentage rate.

[15 USC 1664. As amended by acts of March 31, 1980 (94 Stat. 183) and Dec. 26, 1981 (95 Stat. 1515).]

SECTION 145—NONLIABILITY OF MEDIA

There is no liability under this chapter on the part of any owner or personnel, as such, of any medium in which an advertisement appears or through which it is disseminated.

[15 USC 1665.]

SECTION 146—USE OF ANNUAL PERCENTAGE RATE IN ORAL DISCLOSURES

In responding orally to any inquiry about the cost of credit, a creditor, regardless of the method used to compute finance charges, shall state rates only in terms of the annual percentage rate, except that in the case of an open-end credit plan, the periodic rate also may be stated and, in the case of an other than open-end credit plan where a major component of the finance charge consists of interest computed at a simple annual rate, the simple annual rate also may be stated. The Board may, by regulation, modify the requirements of this section or provide an exception from this section for a transaction or class of transactions for which the creditor cannot determine in advance the applicable annual percentage rate.

[15 USC 1665a. As added by act of Oct. 28, 1974 (88 Stat. 1517) and amended by acts of March 31, 1980 (94 Stat. 185) and Dec. 26, 1981 (95 Stat. 1515).]

SECTION 147—ADVERTISING OF OPEN-END CONSUMER CREDIT PLANS SECURED BY THE CONSUMER'S PRINCIPAL DWELLING

(a) If any advertisement to aid, promote, or assist, directly or in directly, the extension of consumer credit through an open-end consumer credit plan under which extensions of credit are secured by the consumer's principal dwelling states, affirmatively or negatively, any of the specific terms of the plan, including any periodic payment amount required under such plan, such advertisement shall also clearly and conspicuously set forth the following information, in such form and manner as the Board may require:

  (1)   Any loan fee the amount of which is determined as a percentage of the credit limit applicable to an account under the plan and an estimate of the aggregate amount of other fees for opening the account, based on the creditor's experience with the plan and stated as a single amount or as a reasonable range.

  (2)   In any case in which periodic rates may be used to compute the finance charge, the periodic rates expressed as an annual percentage rate.

  (3)   The highest annual percentage rate which may be imposed under the plan.

  (4)   Any other information the Board may by regulation require.

(b) If any advertisement described in subsection (a) contains a statement that any interest expense incurred with respect to the plan is or may be tax deductible, the advertisement shall not be misleading with respect to such deductibility.

(c) No advertisement described in subsection (a) with respect to any home equity account may refer to such loan as "free money" or use other terms determined by the Board by regulation to be misleading.

(d) (1)   If any advertisement described in subsection (a) includes an initial annual percentage rate that is not determined by the index or formula used to make later interest rate adjustments, the advertisement shall also state with equal prominence the current annual percentage rate that would have been applied using the index or formula if such initial rate had not been offered.

  (2)   The annual percentage rate required to be disclosed under the paragraph (1) rate must be current as of a reasonable time given the media involved.

  (3)   Any advertisement to which paragraph (1) applies shall also state the period of time during which the initial annual percentage rate referred to in such paragraph will be in effect.

(e) If any advertisement described in subsection (a) contains a statement regarding the minimum monthly payment under the plan, the advertisement shall also disclose, if applicable, the fact that the plan includes a balloon payment.

(f) For purposes of this section and section 127A, the term "balloon payment" means, with respect to any open-end consumer credit plan under which extensions of credit are secured by the consumer's principal dwelling, any repayment option under which—

(1)   the account holder is required to repay the entire amount of any outstanding balance as of a specified date or at the end of a specified period of time, as determined in accordance with the terms of the agreement pursuant to which such credit is extended, and

(2)   the aggregate amount of the minimum periodic payments required would not fully amortize such outstanding balance by such date or at the end of such period.

[15 USC 1665b. As added by act of Nov. 23, 1988 (102 Stat. 4730).]

CHAPTER 4—CREDIT BILLING

Section

SECTION 161—CORRECTION OF BILLING ERRORS

(a) If a creditor, within sixty days after having transmitted to an obligor a statement of the obligor's account in connection with an extension of consumer credit, receives at the address disclosed under section 127(b)(10) a written notice (other than notice on a payment stub or other payment medium supplied by the creditor if the creditor so stipulates with the disclosure required under section 127(a)(7) from the obligor in which the obligor—

(1)   sets forth or otherwise enables the creditor to identify the name and account number (if any) of the obligor,

(2)   indicates the obligor's belief that the statement contains a billing error, and

(3)   sets forth the reasons for the obligor's belief (to the extent applicable) that the statement contains a billing error, the creditor shall, unless the obligor has, after giving such written notice and before the expiration of the time limits herein specified, agreed that the statement was correct—

(A)   not later than thirty days after the receipt of the notice, send a written acknowledgment thereof to the obligor, unless the action required in subparagraph (B) is taken within such thirty-day period, and

(B)   not later than two complete billing cycles of the creditor (in no event later than ninety days) after the receipt of the notice and prior to taking any action to collect the amount, or any part thereof, indicated by the obligor under paragraph (2) either—

(i) make appropriate corrections in the account of the obligor, including the crediting of any finance charges on amounts erroneously billed, and transmit to the obligor a notification of such corrections and the creditor's explanation of any change in the amount indicated by the obligor under paragraph (2) and, if any such change is made and the obligor so requests, copies of documentary evidence of the obligor's indebtedness; or

(ii) send a written explanation or clarification to the obligor, after having conducted an investigation, setting forth to the extent applicable the reasons why the creditor believes the account of the obligor was correctly shown in the statement and, upon request of the obligor, provide copies of documentary evidence of the obligor's indebtedness. In the case of a billing error where the obligor alleges that the creditor's billing statement reflects goods not delivered to the obligor or his designee in accordance with the agreement made at the time of the transaction, a creditor may not construe such amount to be correctly shown unless he determines that such goods were actually delivered, mailed or otherwise sent to the obligor and provides the obligor with a statement of such determination.

After complying with the provisions of this subsection with respect to an alleged billing error, a creditor has no further responsibility under this section if the obligor continues to make substantially the same allegation with respect to such error

(b) For the purpose of this section, a "billing error" consists of any of the following:

(1) A reflection on a statement of an extension of credit which was not made to the obligor or, if made, was not in the amount reflected on such statement.

(2) A reflection on a statement of an extension of credit for which the obligor requests additional clarification including documentary evidence thereof.

(3) A reflection on a statement of goods or services not accepted by the obligor or his designee or not delivered to the obligor or his designee in accordance with the agreement made at the time of a transaction.

(4) The creditor's failure to reflect properly on a statement a payment made by the obligor or a credit issued to the obligor

(5) A computation error or similar error of an accounting nature of the creditor on a statement.

(6) Failure to transmit the statement required under section 127(b) of this Act to the last address of the obligor which has been disclosed to the creditor, unless that address was furnished less than twenty days before the end of the billing cycle for which the statement is required.

(7) Any other error described in regulations of the Board.

(c) For the purposes of this section, "action to collect the amount, or any part thereof, indicated by an obligor under paragraph (2)" does not include the sending of statements of account, which may include finance charges on amounts in dispute, to the obligor following written notice from the obligor as specified under subsection (a), if—

(1)   the obligor's account is not restricted or closed because of the failure of the obligor to pay the amount indicated under paragraph (2) of subsection (a), and

(2)   the creditor indicates the payment of such amount is not required pending the creditor's compliance with this section. Nothing in this section shall be construed to prohibit any action by a creditor to collect any amount which has not been indicated by the obligor to contain a billing error.

(d) Pursuant to regulations of the Board, a creditor operating an open-end consumer credit plan may not, prior to the sending of the written explanation or clarification required under paragraph (B)(ii), restrict or close an account with respect to which the obligor has indicated pursuant to subsection (a) that he believes such account to contain a billing error solely because of the obligor's failure to pay the amount indicated to be in error. Nothing in this subsection shall be deemed to prohibit a creditor from applying against the credit limit on the obligor's account the amount indicated to be in error.

(e) Any creditor who fails to comply with the requirements of this section or section 162 forfeits any right to collect from the obligor the amount indicated by the obligor under paragraph (2) of subsection (a) of this section, and any finance charges thereon, except that the amount required to be forfeited under this subsection may not exceed $50.

[15 USC 1666. As added by act of Oct. 28, 1974 (88 Stat. 1512) and amended by acts of March 31, 1980 (94 Stat. 177, 184) and Dec. 26, 1981 (95 Stat. 1515).]

SECTION 162—REGULATION OF CREDIT REPORTS

(a) After receiving a notice from an obligor as provided in section 161(a), a creditor or his agent may not directly or indirectly threaten to report to any person adversely on the obligor's credit rating or credit standing because of the obligor's failure to pay the amount indicated by the obligor under section 161 (a)(2), and such amount may not be reported as delinquent to any third party until the creditor has met the requirements of section 161 and has allowed the obligor the same number of days (not less than ten) thereafter to make payment as is provided under the credit agreement with the obligor for the payment of undisputed amounts.

(b) If a creditor receives a further written notice from an obligor that an amount is still in dispute within the time allowed for payment under subsection (a) of this section, a creditor may not report to any third party that the amount of the obligor is delinquent because the obligor has failed to pay an amount which he has indicated under section 161 (a)(2), unless the creditor also reports that the amount is in dispute and, at the same time, notifies the obligor of the name and address of each party to whom the creditor is reporting information concerning the delinquency.

(c) A creditor shall report any subsequent resolution of any delinquencies reported pursuant to subsection (b) to the parties to whom such delinquencies were initially reported.

[15 USC 1666a. As added by act of Oct. 28, 1974 (88 Stat. 1513).]

SECTION 163—LENGTH OF BILLING PERIOD

(a) If an open-end consumer credit plan provides a time period within which an obligor may repay any portion of the credit extended without incurring an additional finance charge, such additional finance charge may not be imposed with respect to such portion of the credit extended for the billing cycle of which such period is a part unless a statement which includes the amount upon which the finance charge for that period is based was mailed at least fourteen days prior to the date specified in the statement by which payment must be made in order to avoid imposition of that finance charge.

(b) Subsection (a) does not apply in any case where a creditor has been prevented, delayed, or hindered in making timely mailing or delivery of such periodic statement within the time period specified in such subsection because of an act of God, war, natural disaster, strike, or other excusable or justifiable cause, as determined under regulations of the Board.

[15 USC 1666b. As added by act of Oct. 28, 1974 (88 Stat. 1514).]

SECTION 164—PROMPT CREDITING OF PAYMENTS

Payments received from an obligor under an open-end consumer credit plan by the creditor shall be posted promptly to the obligor's account as specified in regulations of the Board. Such regulation shall prevent a finance charge from being imposed on any obligor if the creditor has received the obligor's payment in readily identifiable form in the amount, manner, location, and time indicated by the creditor to avoid the imposition thereof.

[15 USC 1666c. As added by act of Oct. 28, 1974 (88 Stat. 1514).]

SECTION 165—TREATMENT OF CREDIT BALANCES

Whenever a credit balance in excess of $1 is created in connection with a consumer credit transaction through (1) transmittal of funds to a creditor in excess of the total balance due on an account, (2) rebates of unearned finance charges or insurance premiums, or (3) amounts otherwise owed to or held for the benefit of an obligor, the creditor shall—

    (A)   credit the amount of the credit balance to the consumer's account;

    (B)   refund any part of the amount of the remaining credit balance, upon request of the consumer; and

    (C)   make a good faith effort to refund to the consumer by cash, check, or money order any part of the amount of the credit balance remaining in the account for more than six months, except that no further action is required in any case in which the consumer's current location is not known by the creditor and cannot be traced through the consumer's last known address or telephone number.

[15 USC 1666d. As added by act of Oct. 28, 1974 (88 Stat. 1514) and amended by acts of March 31, 1980 (94 Stat. 185) and Dec. 26, 1981 (95 Stat. 1515).]

SECTION 166—PROMPT NOTIFICATION OF RETURNS

With respect to any sales transaction where a credit card has been used to obtain credit, where the seller is a person other than the card issuer, and where the seller accepts or allows a return of the goods or forgiveness of a debit for services which were the subject of such sale, the seller shall promptly transmit to the credit card issuer, a credit statement with respect thereto and the credit card issuer shall credit the account of the obligor for the amount of the transaction.

[15 USC 1666e. As added by act of Oct. 28, 1974 (88 Stat. 1514).]

SECTION 167—USE OF CASH DISCOUNTS

(a) With respect to credit card which may be used for extensions of credit in sales trans-actions in which the seller is a person other than the card issuer, the card issuer may not, by contract or otherwise, prohibit any such seller from offering a discount to a cardholder to induce the cardholder to pay by cash, check, or similar means rather than use a credit card.

(b) With respect to any sales transaction, any discount from the regular price offered by the seller for the purpose of inducing payment by cash, checks, or other means not involving the use of an open-end credit plan or a credit card shall not constitute a finance charge as determined under section 106 if such discount is offered to all prospective buyers and its availability is disclosed clearly and conspicuously.

[15 USC 1666f. As added by act of Oct. 28, 1974 (88 Stat. 1515) and amended by acts of Feb. 17, 1976 (90 Stat. 197) and July 27, 1981 (95 Stat. 144).]

SECTION 168—PROHIBITION OF TIE-IN SERVICES

Notwithstanding any agreement to the contrary, a card issuer may not require a seller, as a condition to participating in a credit card plan, to open an account with or procure any other service from the card issuer or its subsidiary or agent.

[15 USC 1666g. As added by act of Oct. 28, 1974 (88 Stat. 1515).]

SECTION 169—PROHIBITION OF OFFSETS

(a) A card issuer may not take any action to offset a cardholder's indebtedness arising in connection with a consumer credit transaction under the relevant credit card plan against funds of the cardholder held on deposit with the card issuer unless—

(1) such action was previously authorized in writing by the cardholder in accor-dance with a credit plan whereby the cardholder agrees periodically to pay debts incurred in his open-end credit account by permitting the card issuer periodically to deduct all or a portion of such debt from the cardholder's deposit account, and

(2) such action with respect to any outstanding disputed amount not be taken by the card issuer upon request of the cardholder.

In the case of any credit card account in existence on the effective date of this section, the previous written authorization referred to in clause (1) shall not be required until the date (after such effective date) when such account is renewed, but in no case later than one year after such effective date. Such written authorization shall be deemed to exist if the card issuer has previously notified the cardholder that the use of his credit card account will subject any funds which the card issuer holds in deposit accounts of such cardholder to off-set against any amounts due and payable on his credit card account which have not been paid in accordance with the terms of the agreement between the card issuer and the cardholder

(b) This section does not alter or affect the right under State law of a card issuer to attach or otherwise levy upon funds of a cardholder held on deposit with the card issuer if that remedy is constitutionally available to creditors generally.

[15 USC 1666h. As added by acts of Oct. 28, 1974 (88 Stat. 1515).]

SECTION 170—RIGHTS OF CREDIT CARD CUSTOMERS

(a) Subject to the limitation contained in subsection (b), a card issuer who has issued a credit card to a cardholder pursuant to an open-end consumer credit plan shall be subject to all claims (other than tort claims) and defenses arising out of any transaction in which the credit card is used as a method of payment or extension of credit if (1) the obligor has made a good faith attempt to obtain satisfactory resolution of a disagreement or problem relative to the transaction from the person honoring the credit card; (2) the amount of the initial transaction exceeds $50; and (3) the place where the initial transaction occurred was in the same State as the mailing address previously provided by the cardholder or was within 100 miles from such address, except that the limitations set forth in clauses (2) and (3) with respect to an obligor's right to assert claims and defenses against a card issuer shall not be applicable to any transaction in which the person honoring the credit card (A) is the same person as the card issuer, (B) is controlled by the card issuer, (C) is under direct or indirect common control with the card issuer, (D) is a franchised dealer in the card issuer's products or services, or (F) has obtained the order for such transaction through a mail solicitation made by or participated in by the card issuer in which the cardholder is solicited to enter into such transaction by using the credit card issued by the card issuer.

(b) the amount of claims or defenses asserted by the cardholder may not exceed the amount of credit outstanding with respect to such transaction at the time the cardholder first notifies the card issuer or the person honoring the credit card of such claim or defense. For the purpose of determining the amount of credit outstanding in the preceding sentence, payments and credits to the cardholder's account are deemed to have been applied, in the order indicated, to the payment of: (1) late charges in the order of their entry to the account; (2) finance charges in order of their entry to the account; and (3) debits to the account other than those set forth above, in the order in which each debit entry to the account was made.

[15 USC 1666i. As added by act of Oct. 28, 1974 (88 Stat. 1515).]

SECTION 171—RELATION TO STATE LAWS

(a) This chapter does not annul, alter, or affect, or exempt any person subject to the provisions of this chapter from complying with the laws of any State with respect to credit billing practices, except to the extent that those laws are inconsistent with any provision of this chapter, and then only to the extent of the inconsistency. The Board is authorized to determine whether such inconsistencies exist. The Board may not determine that any State law is inconsistent with any provision of this chapter if the Board determines that such law gives greater protection to the consumer.

(b) The Board shall by regulation exempt from the requirements of this chapter any class of credit transactions within any State if it determines that under the law of the State that class of transactions is subject to requirements substantially similar to those imposed under this chapter or that such law gives greater protection to the consumer, and that there is adequate provision for enforcement.

(c) Notwithstanding any other provisions of this title, any discount offered under section 167(b) of this title shall not be considered a finance charge or other charge for credit under the usury laws of any State or under the laws of any State relating to disclosure of information in connection with credit transactions, or relating to the types, amounts or rates of charges, or to any element or elements of charges permissible under such laws in connection with the extension or use of credit.

[15 USC 1666j. As added act of Oct. 28, 1974 (88 Stat. 1516) and amended by act of Feb. 27, 1976 (90 Stat. 198).]

Board of Governors of the Federal Reserve System

AMENDMENTS AND CORRECTIONS TO REGULATION Z TRUTH IN LENDING
FEBRUARY 1992*

1. *Section 226.5a(a)(3) is corrected by adding the words "of the type" before the words "subject to the requirements of section 226.5b."*

2. *Section 226.5a(g)(2) is corrected by deleting "and is figured in the same way as the first balance" from the last sentences of subparagraphs (i) and (ii).*

3. *Section 226.9(e)(1) and (f)(1) are corrected by adding the words "of the type" before the words "subject to section 226.5a."*

4. *Effective October 8, 1991, appendix I is amended by revising the entry for savings institutions to read as follows:*

   Savings institutions insured under the Savings Association Insurance Fund of the FDIC and federally chartered savings banks insured under the Bank Insurance Fund of the FDIC (but not including state-chartered savings banks insured under the Bank Insurance Fund).

*A complete Regulation Z, as amended and corrected effective October 8, 1991, consists of—
  • the pamphlet dated July 1989 (see inside cover) and
  • this slip sheet.
Items 4 and 5 are new. Items 1 through 3 were included in the previous slip sheet.

Office of Thrift Supervision regional director for the region in which the institution is located.

TRUTH IN LENDING ACT

5. *Effective December 19, 1991, section 108(a)(1), (2), and (4) of the Truth in Lending Act is amended to read as follows:*

   (a) Compliance with the requirements imposed under this title shall be enforced under (1) section 8 of the Federal Deposit Insurance Act, in the case of—

      (A) national banks, and Federal branches and Federal agencies of foreign banks, by the Office of the Comptroller of the Currency;

      (B) member banks of the Federal Reserve System (other than national banks), branches and agencies of foreign banks (other than Federal branches, Federal agencies, and insured State branches of foreign banks), commercial lending companies owned or controlled by foreign banks, and organizations operating under section 25 or 25A of the Federal Reserve Act, by the Board; and

      (C) banks insured by the Federal Deposit Insurance Corporation (other than members of the Federal Reserve System) and insured State branches of foreign banks, by the Board of Directors of the Federal Deposit Insurance Corporation.

   (2) section 8 of the Federal Deposit Insurance Act, by the Director of the Office of Thrift Supervision, in the case of a savings association the deposits of which are insured by the Federal Deposit Insurance Corporation.

   *   *   *   *   *

   (4) the Federal Aviation Act of 1958, by the Civil Aeronautics Board with respect to any air carrier or foreign air carrier subject to that Act.

COMPETITIVE EQUALITY BANKING ACT OF 1987 SECTION 1204

12 USC 3806; 101 Stat. 662; Pub. L. 100-86 (August 10, 1987)

SECTION 1204—ADJUSTABLE RATE MORTGAGE CAPS

(a) Any adjustable rate mortgage loan originated by a creditor shall include a limitation on the maximum interest rate that may apply during the term of the mortgage loan.

(b) The Board of Governors of the Federal Reserve System shall prescribe regulations to carry out the purposes of this section.

(c) Any violation of this section shall be treated as a violation of the Truth in Lending Act and shall be subject to administrative enforcement under section 108 or civil damages under section 130 of such Act, or both.

(d) For purpose of this section—

(1)   the term "creditor" means a person who regularly extends credit for personal, family, or household purposes; and

(2)   the term "adjustable rate mortgage loan" means any loan secured by a lien on a one- to four-family dwelling unit, including a condominium unit, cooperative housing unit, or mobile home, where the loan is made pursuant to an agreement under which the creditor may, from time to time, adjust the rate of interest.

(e)   This section shall take effect upon the expiration of 120 days after the date of enactment of this Act.

[12 USC 3806.]

CHAPTER 13

Equal Credit Opportunity Act

Denying credit because the applicant was a woman or a minority was so prevalent in the 60s and 70s that a major segment of the population almost accepted this as a fact of life. In passing the Truth In Lending Act, Congress addressed not only the major areas of discrimination, such as that involving women and minorities, but also prohibited discrimination in areas such as age and marital status. A key part of the Act is Regulation B, entitled the Equal Credit Opportunity Act. Congress stated that if credit is to be extended, the lending institution must consider only the creditworthiness of the applicant and must confine its entire evaluation to whether the applicant has the ability to repay the money. The creditor will not be allowed to evaluate other qualities, characteristics, status, or nature of the particular applicant.

The purpose of the Equal Credit Opportunity Act is to promote the availability of credit to all creditworthy applicants without regard to race, color, religion, national origin, sex, marital status, or age. In addition, an applicant should not be denied credit because income is derived from a public assistance program or due to the fact that the applicant has in good faith exercised any right under the Consumer Credit Protection Act (making a claim or starting a suit against the creditor for a violation of a law). The Regulation prohibits creditor practices which discriminate on the basis of any of these factors.

Regulation B and the commentary to Regulation B are textbook explanations of exactly what the credit grantor is prohibited from considering and evaluating when granting credit. This chapter is designed to provide an overview of the Regulation to apprise the credit grantor of the areas to be considered before

651

extending credit. A thorough reading of both the Regulation and the commentary is recommended.

The Omnibus Consolidated Appropriation Act of 1997 urges lenders to self-correct any violations of the Equal Credit Opportunity Act by granting a privilege to the lender with regard to any programs that involve self-testing to determine whether their compliance programs are effective. If the creditor meets the conditions set forth in these amendments, any reports or results of the self-testing are privileged and may not be obtained or used by any applicant, department, or agency in any proceeding or civil action in which violations of the ECOA are alleged.

RACE, COLOR, RELIGION AND NATIONAL ORIGIN

A creditor shall not inquire about the race, color, religion, or national origin of an applicant or of any other person in connection with a credit transaction.[1] No questions of this nature may be included in any credit application. A creditor may inquire about the permanent residence or the immigration status of the applicant, and appropriate inquiries may appear on the credit application, since residence and status are germane to a credit decision. Regulation B expressly states that a creditor may request any information in connection with an application for credit except the information prohibited by this law.[2]

Once the product has been offered to a particular area, credit cannot be refused because of race, color, religion, age, sex, marital status or national origin. The only basis for refusing to extend credit is that the individual does not satisfy credit standards in compliance with the Equal Credit Opportunity Act.

SEX

No inquiry as to the sex of an applicant is allowed, although the applicant may designate a title on the application (Ms., Mrs., Mr., and Miss) so long as the form discloses that the designation of title is optional. The application shall use terms that are neutral as to sex.

CHILDBEARING

A creditor may not inquire about birth control practices, intentions concerning the bearing of children, or the ability to bear children. An inquiry may be made con-

---

[1]Sec. 202.1.

[2]Sec. 202.5 (b).

cerning the number and ages of applicant's dependents or dependent-related financial obligations, providing the information is requested without regard to sex, marital status, or other prohibited reasons.[3]

AGE AND PUBLIC ASSISTANCE

An applicant's age, unless a minor, or whether applicant is receiving public assistance, shall not be considered except as permitted by the Act. Age may be a variable in an empirically derived (through experience and observation), demonstrably and statistically sound credit scoring system. Age and public assistance may be considered for the purpose of determining a pertinent element of creditworthiness in a judgmental system (see below). The age of an elderly person may be used to favor an elderly applicant in extending credit,[4] but the age of an elderly person may not be assigned a negative value in the scoring system.

CREDIT APPLICATION

The creditor may request any information in connection with an application for credit providing the request is not prohibited under the Equal Credit Opportunity Act or another law. The Act sets forth specific rules as to accepting applications and separate rules for evaluating applications.

The Act lists other criteria for considering items in an application for credit:

A. The likelihood that any group will bear or rear children and thus will receive diminished or interrupted income in the future may not be considered.

B. A lack of a telephone listing may not be considered, but having a telephone listing may be considered.

C. Income from a part-time employment annuity or a pension may be considered as well as the continuation of that income.

D. Alimony and child support may be considered to the extent the income is consistently received.

E. Immigration status and a permanent residency may be considered.

SPOUSE OR FORMER SPOUSE

Information concerning a spouse or a former spouse may be requested if:

---

[3]Sec. 202.6 (b) 3.

[4]Sec. 202.6 (b) 2.

1. the spouse is permitted to use the account
2. the spouse is liable on the account
3. the creditor is relying on the income of the spouse as a basis of repayment, including alimony or child support.

In all other instances, the creditor cannot request information on the application concerning a spouse. At the same time, a creditor cannot inquire whether income is derived from alimony or child support unless the creditor is relying on such income as a basis for repayment of the loan.

SPOUSE AS GUARANTOR

A creditor shall not require the signature of a spouse on any credit instrument if the applicant qualifies under the creditor's standards of creditworthiness for the amount and terms of the credit requested. Requesting the spouse to sign the application merely because "there is a spouse" may be a violation of the Equal Credit Opportunity Act (Regulation B).[5] If the creditor relies entirely upon the creditworthiness of the applicant and still seeks the spouse's signature, the creditor may fear that the applicant will transfer some of the assets to the spouse and file bankruptcy or leave for parts unknown. The Act prohibits the creditor requiring the spouse to guarantee a loan under these circumstances.

The law protects the creditor if transfers are made to defraud creditors for the purpose of not repaying the loan. If the borrower does not meet the credit requirements, the creditor can seek an additional guarantor, but may not specify that the spouse be the guarantor. An exception to the rule is where secured credit is offered and the wife's signature is needed to create a valid lien, such as property held by joint tenancy or in community property states.

RECOUPMENT—SPOUSE

Under the Equal Credit Opportunity Act, a Statute of Limitations of two years is set for a spouse to declare his or her guarantee void and seek damages. The expiration of the Statute of Limitations calculated from the execution of said guarantee may bar the institution of such an independent action. No such prohibition exists, however, to the utilization of such grounds as a defense. The court stated that whereas the Statute of Limitations may apply to the institution of the suit against the lender to seek damages or declare the guarantee void, the Statute of Limitations is of no effect when the spouse uses it as a defense to an action to collect the debt. This is the same concept that applies to situations where we have a

---

[5]Sec. 202.7 (d).

usurious contract. The party may declare that the contract is usurious and be subject to the Statute of Limitations, but where the creditor seeks to collect the money due under the contract, the Statute of Limitations is not a bar to the use of this defense.[6]

Unfortunately, most spouses do not assert this violation until they are sued by the bank on their guarantee and some states take the position that the spouse cannot assert the defense of a violation of the Equal Credit Opportunity Act in a civil commercial suit based on the loan or the guarantee. The Equal Credit Opportunity Act sets forth a specific remedy for violation of the Act. A federal civil action may be maintained against the creditor for damages, punitive damages not to exceed $10,000 and attorney's fees with a two-year Statute of Limitations. Under these provisions, many courts deny the right of the spouse to assert any claim in a civil suit and state that the spouse is confined to the remedies available under the Equal Credit Opportunity Act to a suit in the federal courts.

The Equal Credit Opportunity Act also provides that a court of competent jurisdictions may issue "equitable and declaratory relief as necessary" to enforce the requirement of the act. Under this theory, many courts take the position that a spouse may assert a violation as a counterclaim for recoupment in a civil suit, or as an affirmative defense to a collection case, even after the running of the two-year Statute of Limitations. The courts seem to reason that the Statute of Limitations is not applicable until such time as the lender decides to institute suit based on the spouse's guarantee—at least in those states that recognize this decision (New Jersey, Kansas, Pennsylvania, Virginia, and Iowa).

While these courts may allow the spouse to assert a claim for recoupment or a counterclaim in a civil action by the lender, no authority exists in any of the cases or in any of the statutory language that a violation of the Equal Credit Opportunity Act renders any instrument or contract void because of said violation. The defense is unique and peculiar to the spouse and may be asserted only within the framework of the Equal Credit Opportunity Act. Recoupment tolls the Statute of Limitations providing the recoupment limits itself to the same transaction upon which the lender is instituting suit. If the counterclaim arises from a different transaction or a transaction that did not deal with the actual basis of the suit of the lender, some courts feel the Statute of Limitations is tolled. In such cases, creditors may be faced with counterclaims based on these violations that occurred with regard to lending transactions that took place years before the one upon which the lending institution is instituting suit.[7]

A recent case in the Connecticut Superior Court did not allow the invalidation of the entire obligation (consisting of promissory notes) based upon an ECOA violation against some of the individual defendants. The court allowed the creditor to proceed against the husbands. The wives could assert a counterclaim

---

[6]*Silverman v. Eastrich Multiple Investor Fund, L.P.*, 51 F.3d 28 (3rd Cir. 1995).

[7]*Hammons v. Ehney*, 924 S.W.2d 843 (Mo. 1996).

against the creditors, but the court did not allow the violation to stand as a special defense for the husbands who are not the subject of the discrimination.[8]

JOINT APPLICANTS

A joint applicant is someone who applies contemporaneously with the applicant for shared or joint credit and not someone whose signature is required by the creditor as a condition for granting the credit requested. In a recent case, a wife was the co-owner of the corporation and the financial application detailed the joint ownership of the assets. While the wife did not have a major role in the day-to-day operation of the corporation or any of its subsidiaries, she clearly had an equal stake with her husband in the assets that secured the borrowing. The court held that she was a bona fide joint applicant for the loans and that the Equal Credit Opportunity Act does not protect her from liability upon Plaintiff's claim.

The emphasis of the court was on her ownership of the business. The court distinguished other cases where the spouses who were required to sign the notes were not connected to the underlying transactions for which the loans were sought, and played no ownership interest in the business and no role in the negotiations of the loans. In most of the other cases, the wives were neither officers nor shareholders in the business and had no material participation in its activities. In this particular case, the husband and wife used the proceeds of the loan to jointly purchase another business and the bank relied on the documents setting forth jointly owned properties in granting the loans.[9]

ADVERSE ACTION

Under Regulation B, a creditor must notify an applicant of any negative action taken with regard to an application for credit[10] within:

1. thirty days after receiving a completed application concerning the creditor's approval of the credit application, the creditor must give notice of or counter offer to the request for credit by the applicant, or adverse action on the credit application.
2. thirty days after taking adverse action on an incomplete application.
3. thirty days after taking adverse action on an existing account.
4. ninety days after notifying the applicant of a counter offer if the applicant does not expressly accept or use the credit offered.

---

[8]*Union Trust v. Sirois*, No. CV94-038058S, 1997 WL 600392 (Conn. Super. Ct. Sept. 19, 1997).

[9]*Midlantic National Bank v. Hansen*, 48 F.3d 693 (3rd Cir. 1995), *cert. dismissed*, 116 S. Ct. 32, 132 L. Ed. 2d 914 (1995).

[10]Sec. 202.9

A notification of adverse action shall be in writing and shall contain a statement of the reasons for the adverse action or of applicant's right to request the reason for the action taken.

Statements of the adverse action based on the creditor's internal standards or policies, or the fact that the applicant failed to achieve the qualifying score on the creditor's credit scoring system, are insufficient.

The Federal Trade Commission has issued a manual for creditors on "How to Write Adverse Action Notices" and it is available free from the Federal Trade Commission. Needless to say, obtaining a copy of this manual is recommended for any creditor extending credit under Regulation B.

FURNISHING OF CREDIT INFORMATION

A creditor who furnishes credit information to a credit reporting agency shall designate the participation of both spouses if the applicant's spouse is permitted to use or is contractually liable on the account. With regard to any existing account, the creditor shall designate any such participation ninety days after receiving a written request. If a creditor reports to a credit reporting agency, the participation of both spouses shall be reported where both spouses are participating in the loan. If responding to an inquiry, the creditor must furnish the information to reflect the participation of both spouses.

RETENTION OF RECORDS

The Act specifically allows a creditor to retain in its files information that is received from consumer reporting agencies, an applicant, or others without the specific request of the creditor. The creditor must retain for 25 months applications received and all other information used in evaluating the application that is not returned to the applicant.[11]

ENFORCEMENT AND PENALTIES

The Equal Credit Opportunity Act allows the applicant to sue for civil damages as well as punitive damages, but limits punitive damages to $10,000 in an individual action and the lesser of $500,000 or one percent of the creditor's net worth, in a class action.[12]

---

[11]Sec. 202.12

[12]Sec. 202.14.

LEGISLATION

Regulation B of the Equal Credit Opportunity Act was amended on April 2, 1998, becoming effective on April 30, 1998, with respect to the forms to be used that should reflect the changes in the Fair Credit Reporting Act.

COMMENT

The regulations provide a full set of forms for credit applications including open-end unsecured credit, closed-end unsecured/secured credit, community property, and residential and mortgage loans. The Appendix to Regulation B also provides notification forms and other examples.

CHAPTER 13
APPENDIX I

Regulation B
Equal Credit Opportunity 12 CFR 202;
as revised effective December 8, 1989

REGULATION B
EQUAL CREDIT OPPORTUNITY

12 CFR 202; effective March 23, 1977; as amended effective December 8, 1989*

---

*Board of Governors of the Federal Reserve System. Any inquiry relating to this regulation should be addressed to the Federal Reserve Bank of the District in which the inquiry arises. February 1990

Section 202.1—Authority, Scope, and Purpose

(a) *Authority and scope.* This regulation is issued by the Board of Governors of the Federal Reserve System pursuant to title VII (Equal Credit Opportunity Act) of the Consumer Credit Protection Act, as amended (15 USC 1601 et seq.). Except as otherwise provided herein, the regulation applies to all persons who are creditors, as defined in section 202.2(l). Information-collection requirements contained in this regulation have been approved by the Office of Management and Budget under the provisions of 44 USC 3501 et seq. and have been assigned OMB No. 7100–0201.

(b) *Purpose.* The purpose of this regulation is to promote the availability of credit to all creditworthy applicants without regard to race, color, religion, national origin, sex, marital status, or age (provided the applicant has the capacity to contract); to the fact that all or part of the applicant's income derives from a public assistance program; or to the fact that the applicant has in good faith exercised any right under the Consumer Credit Protection Act. The regulation prohibits creditor practices that discriminate on the basis of any of these factors. The regulation also requires creditors to notify applicants of action taken on their applications; to report credit history in the names of both spouses on an account; to retain records of credit applications; and to collect information about the applicant's race and other personal characteristics in applications for certain dwelling-related loans.

Section 202.2—Definitions

For the purposes of this regulation, unless the context indicates otherwise, the following definitions apply.

(a) *Account* means an extension of credit. When employed in relation to an account, the word use refers only to open-end credit.

(b) *Act* means the Equal Credit Opportunity Act (title VII of the Consumer Credit Protection Act).

(c) *Adverse action.* (1) The term means—

  (i)   a refusal to grant credit in substantially the amount or on substantially the terms requested in an application unless the creditor makes a counteroffer (to grant credit in a different amount or on other terms) and the applicant uses or expressly accepts the credit offered;

  (ii) a termination of an account or an unfavorable change in the terms of an account that does not affect all or a substantial portion of a class of the creditor's accounts; or

  (iii) a refusal to increase the amount of credit available to an applicant who has made an application for an increase.

(2) The term does not include—

  (i)   a change in the terms of an account expressly agreed to by an applicant;

  (ii) any action or forbearance relating to an account taken in connection with inactivity, default, or delinquency as to that account;

---

*Creditors have the option of continuing to comply with the previous version of the regulation until April 1, 1990, when compliance with this amended version becomes mandatory.

        (iii)   a refusal or failure to authorize an account transaction at a point of sale or loan, except when the refusal is a termination or an unfavorable change in the terms of an account that does not affect all or a substantial portion of a class of the creditor's accounts, or when the refusal is a denial of an application for an increase in the amount of credit available under the account;

        (iv)   a refusal to extend credit because applicable law prohibits the creditor from extending the credit requested; or

        (v)   a refusal to extend credit because the creditor does not offer the type of credit or credit plan requested.

   (3)   An action that falls within the definition of both paragraphs (c)(l) and (c)(2) of this section is governed by paragraph (c)(2).

(d) *Age* refers only to the age of natural persons and means the number of fully elapsed years from the date of an applicant's birth.

(e) *Applicant* means any person who requests or who has received an extension of credit from a creditor, and includes any person who is or may become contractually liable regarding an extension of credit. For purposes of section 202.7(d), the term includes guarantors, sureties, endorsers and similar parties.

(f) *Application* means an oral or written request for an extension of credit that is made in accordance with procedures established by a creditor for the type of credit requested. The term does not include the use of an account or line of credit to obtain an amount of credit that is within a previously established credit limit. A *completed application* means an application in connection with which a creditor has received all the information that the creditor regularly obtains and considers in evaluating applications for the amount and type of credit requested (including, but not limited to, credit reports, any additional information requested from the applicant, and any approvals or reports by governmental agencies or other persons that are necessary to guarantee, insure, or provide security for the credit or collateral). The creditor shall exercise reasonable diligence in obtaining such information.

(g) *Business credit* refers to extensions of credit primarily for business or commercial (including agricultural) purposes, but excluding extensions of credit of the types described in section 202.3(a), (b), and (d).

(h) *Consumer credit* means credit extended to a natural person primarily for personal, family, or household purposes.

(i) *Contractually liable* means expressly obligated to repay all debts arising on an account by reason of an agreement to that effect.

(j) *Credit* means the right granted by a creditor to an applicant to defer payment of a debt, incur debt and defer its payment, or purchase property or services and defer payment therefor.

(k) *Credit card* means any card, plate, coupon book, or other single credit device that may be used from time to time to obtain money, property, or services on credit.

(l) *Creditor* means a person who, in the ordinary course of business, regularly participates in the decision of whether or not to extend credit. The term includes a creditor's assignee, transferee, or subrogee who so participates. For purposes of sections 202.4 and 202.5(a), the term also includes a person who, in the ordinary course of business, regularly refers applicants or prospective applicants to creditors, or selects or offers to select creditors to whom requests for credit may be made. A person is not a creditor regarding any violation of the act or this regulation committed by another creditor unless the person knew or had reasonable notice of the act, policy, or practice that constituted the violation before becoming involved in the credit transaction. The term does not include a person whose only participation in a credit transaction involves honoring a credit card.

(m) *Credit transaction* means every aspect of an applicant's dealings with a creditor regarding an application for credit or an existing extension of credit (including, but not limited to, information requirements; investigation procedures; standards of creditworthiness; terms of credit; furnishing of credit information; revocation, alteration, or termination of credit; and collection procedures).

(n) *Discriminate against an applicant* means to treat an applicant less favorably than other applicants.

(o) *Elderly* means age 62 or older.

(p) *Empirically derived and other credit scoring systems.*

    (1)   A *credit scoring system* is a system that evaluates an applicant's creditworthiness mechanically, based on key attributes of the applicant and aspects of the transaction, and that determines, alone or in conjunction with an evaluation of additional information about the applicant, whether an applicant is deemed creditworthy. To qualify as an *empirically derived, demonstrably and statistically sound, credit scoring system,* the system must be—

        (i)   based on data that are derived from an empirical comparison of sample groups or the population of creditworthy and noncreditworthy applicants who applied for credit within a reasonable preceding period of time;

        (ii)   developed for the purpose of evaluating the creditworthiness of applicants with respect to the legitimate business interests of the creditor utilizing the system (including, but not limited to, minimizing bad debt losses and operating expenses in accordance with the creditor's business judgment);

        (iii)   developed and validated using accepted statistical principles and methodology; and

        (iv)   periodically revalidated by the use of appropriate statistical principles and methodology and adjusted as necessary to maintain predictive ability.

    (2)   A creditor may use an empirically derived, demonstrably and statistically sound, credit scoring system obtained from another person or may obtain credit experience from which to develop such a system. Any such system must satisfy the criteria set forth in paragraph (p)(1)(i) through (iv) of this section; if the creditor is unable during the development process to validate the system based on its own credit experience in accordance with paragraph (p) (1) of this section, the system must be validated when sufficient credit experience becomes available.

A system that fails this validity test is no longer an empirically derived, demonstrably and statistically sound, credit scoring system for that creditor.

(q) *Extend credit and extension of credit* mean the granting of credit in any form (including, but not limited to, credit granted in addition to any existing credit or credit limit; credit granted pursuant to an open-end credit plan; the refinancing or other renewal of credit, including the issuance of a new credit card in place of an expiring credit card or in substitution for an existing credit card; the consolidation of two or more obligations; or the continuance of existing credit without any special effort to collect at or after maturity).

(r) *Good faith* means honesty in fact in the conduct or transaction.

(s) *Inadvertent error* means a mechanical, electronic, or clerical error that a creditor demonstrates was not intentional and occurred notwithstanding the maintenance of procedures reasonably adapted to avoid such errors.

(t) *Judgmental system of evaluating applicants* means any system for evaluating the creditworthiness of an applicant other than an empirically derived, demonstrably and statistically sound, credit scoring system.

(u) *Marital status* means the state of being unmarried, married, or separated, as defined by applicable state law. The term "unmarried" includes persons who are single, divorced, or widowed.

(v) *Negative factor or value*, in relation to the age of elderly applicants, means utilizing a factor, value, or weight that is less favorable regarding elderly applicants than the creditor's experience warrants or is less favorable than the factor, value, or weight assigned to the class of applicants that are not classified as elderly and are most favored by a creditor on the basis of age.

(w) *Open-end credit* means credit extended under a plan under which a creditor may permit an applicant to make purchases or obtain loans from time to time directly from the creditor or indirectly by use of a credit card, check, or other device.

(x) *Person* means a natural person, corporation, government or governmental subdivision or agency, trust, estate, partnership, cooperative, or association.

(y) *Pertinent element of creditworthiness*, in relation to a judgmental system of evaluating applicants, means any information about applicants that a creditor obtains and considers and that has a demonstrable relationship to a determination of creditworthiness.

(z) *Prohibited basis* means race, color, religion, national origin, sex, marital status, or age (provided that the applicant has the capacity to enter into a binding contract); the fact that all or part of the applicant's income derives from any public assistance program; or the fact that the applicant has in good faith exercised any right under the Consumer Credit Protection Act or any state law upon which an exemption has been granted by the Board.

(aa) *State* means any state, the District of Columbia, the Commonwealth of Puerto Rico, or any territory or possession of the United States.

Section 202.3—Limited Exceptions for Certain Classes of Transactions

(a) *Public-utilities credit.* (1) *Definition.* Public-utilities credit refers to extensions of credit that involve public-utility services provided through pipe, wire, or other connected facilities, or radio or similar transmission (including extensions of such facilities), if the charges for service, delayed payment, and any discount for prompt payment are filed with or regulated by a government unit.

(2) *Exceptions.* The following provisions of this regulation do not apply to public-utilities credit:

    (i) section 202.5(d)(l) concerning information about marital status;

    (ii) section 202.10 relating to furnishing of credit information; and

    (iii) section 202.12(b) relating to record retention.

(b) *Securities credit.* (1) *Definition.* Securities credit refers to extensions of credit subject to regulation under section 7 of the Securities Exchange Act of 1934 or extensions of credit by a broker or dealer subject to regulation as a broker or dealer under the Securities Exchange Act of 1934.

(2) *Exceptions.* The following provisions of this regulation do not apply to securities credit:

    (i) section 202.5(c) concerning information about a spouse or former spouse;

    (ii) section 202.5(d)(l) concerning information about marital status;

    (iii) section 202.5(d) (3) concerning information about the sex of an applicant;

    (iv) section 202.7(b) relating to designation of name, but only to the extent necessary to prevent violation of rules regarding an account in which a broker or dealer has an interest, or rules necessitating the aggregation of accounts of spouses for the purpose of determining controlling interests, beneficial interests, beneficial ownership, or purchase limitations and restrictions;

    (v) section 202.7(c) relating to action concerning open-end accounts, but only to the extent the action taken is on the basis of a change of name or marital status;

    (vi) section 202.7(d) relating to the signature of a spouse or other person;

    (vii) section 202.10 relating to furnishing of credit information; and

    (viii) section 202.12(b) relating to record retention.

(c) *Incidental credit.* (1) *Definition.* Incidental credit refers to extensions of consumer credit other than credit of the types described in paragraphs (a) and (b) of this section—

    (i) that are not made pursuant to the terms of a credit card account;

    (ii) that are not subject to a finance charge (as defined in Regulation Z, 12 CFR 226.4); and

    (iii) that are not payable by agreement in more than four installments.

(2) *Exceptions.* The following provisions of this regulation do not apply to incidental credit:

    (i) section 202.5(c) concerning information about a spouse or former spouse;

    (ii) section 202.5(d)(l) concerning information about marital status;

(iii)   section 202.5(d) (2) concerning information about income derived from alimony, child support, or separate maintenance payments;

(iv)   section 202.5(d)(3) concerning information about the sex of an applicant, but only to the extent necessary for medical records or similar purposes;

(v)   section 202.7(d) relating to the signature of a spouse or other person;

(vi)   section 202.9 relating to notifications;

(vii)   section 202.10 relating to furnishing of credit information; and

(viii) section 202.12(b) relating to record retention.

(d) *Government credit.* (1) *Definition.* Government credit refers to extensions of credit made to governments or governmental subdivisions, agencies, or instrumentalities.

(2)   *Applicability of regulation.* Except for section 202.4, the general rule prohibiting discrimination on a prohibited basis, the requirements of this regulation do not apply to government credit.

Section 202.4—General Rule Prohibiting Discrimination

A creditor shall not discriminate against an applicant on a prohibited basis regarding any aspect of a credit transaction.

Section 202.5—Rules Concerning Taking of Applications

(a) *Discouraging applications.* A creditor shall not make any oral or written statement, in advertising or otherwise, to applicants or prospective applicants that would discourage on a prohibited basis a reasonable person from making or pursuing an application.

(b) *General rules concerning requests for information.* (1) Except as provided in paragraphs (c) and (d) of this section, a creditor may request any information in connection with an application.[1]

(2)   *Required collection of information.* Notwithstanding paragraphs (c) and (d) of this section, a creditor shall request information for monitoring purposes as required by section 202.13 for credit secured by the applicant's dwelling. In addition, a creditor may obtain information required by a regulation, order, or agreement issued by, or entered into with, a court or an enforcement agency (including the attorney general of the United States or a similar state official) to monitor or enforce compliance with the act, this regulation, or other federal or state statute or regulation.

(3)   *Special-purpose credit.* A creditor may obtain information that is otherwise restricted to determine eligibility for a special-purpose credit program, as provided in section 202.8(c) and (d).

(c) *Information about a spouse or former spouse.* (1) Except as permitted in this paragraph, a creditor may not request any information concerning the spouse or former spouse of an applicant.

---

[1]This paragraph does not limit or abrogate any federal or state law regarding privacy, privileged information, credit reporting limitations, or similar restrictions on obtainable information.

(2) *Permissible inquiries.* A creditor may request any information concerning an applicant's spouse (or former spouse under paragraph (c) (2) (v)) that may be requested about the applicant if—

(i) the spouse will be permitted to use the account;

(ii) the spouse will be contractually liable on the account;

(iii) the applicant is relying on the spouse's income as a basis for repayment of the credit requested;

(iv) the applicant resides in a community property state or property on which the applicant is relying as a basis for repayment of the credit requested is located in such a state; or

(v) the applicant is relying on alimony, child support, or separate maintenance payments from a spouse or former spouse as a basis for repayment of the credit requested.

(3) *Other accounts of the applicant.* A creditor may request an applicant to list any account upon which the applicant is liable and to provide the name and address in which the account is carried. A creditor may also ask the names in which an applicant has previously received credit.

(d) *Other limitations on information requests.*

(1) *Marital status.* If an applicant applies for individual unsecured credit, a creditor shall not inquire about the applicant's marital status unless the applicant resides in a community property state or is relying on property located in such a state as a basis for repayment of the credit requested. If an application is for other than individual unsecured credit, a creditor may inquire about the applicant's marital status, but shall use only the terms "married," "unmarried," and "separated." A creditor may explain that the category "unmarried" includes single, divorced, and widowed persons.

(2) *Disclosure about income from alimony, child support, or separate maintenance.* A creditor shall not inquire whether income stated in an application is derived from alimony, child support, or separate maintenance payments unless the creditor discloses to the applicant that such income need not be revealed if the applicant does not want the creditor to consider it in determining the applicant's creditworthiness.

(3) *Sex.* A creditor shall not inquire about the sex of an applicant. An applicant may be requested to designate a title on an application form (such as Ms., Miss, Mr., or Mrs.) if the form discloses that the designation of a title is optional. An application form shall otherwise use only terms that are neutral as to sex.

(4) *Childbearing, childrearing.* A creditor shall not inquire about birth control practices, intentions concerning the bearing or rearing of children, or capability to bear children. A creditor may inquire about the number and ages of an applicant's dependents or about dependent-related financial obligations or expenditures, provided such information is requested without regard to sex, marital status, or any other prohibited basis.

(5) *Race, color, religion, national origin.* A creditor shall not inquire about the race, color, religion, or national origin of an applicant or any other person in con-

nection with a credit transaction. A creditor may inquire about an applicant's permanent residence and immigration status.

(e) *Written applications.* A creditor shall take written applications for the types of credit covered by section 202.13(a) but need not take written applications for other types of credit.

Section 202.6—Rules Concerning Evaluation of Applications

(a) *General rule concerning use of information.* Except as otherwise provided in the act and this regulation, a creditor may consider any information obtained, so long as the information is not used to discriminate against an applicant on a prohibited basis.[2]

(b) *Specific rules concerning use of information.* (1) Except as provided in the act and this regulation, a creditor shall not take a prohibited basis into account in any system of evaluating the creditworthiness of applicants.

    (2) *Age, receipt of public assistance.* (i) Except as permitted in this paragraph, a creditor shall not take into account an applicant's age (provided that the applicant has the capacity to enter into a binding contract) or whether an applicant's income derives from any public assistance program.

        (ii) In an empirically derived, demonstrably and statistically sound, credit scoring system, a creditor may use an applicant's age as a predictive variable, provided that the age of an elderly applicant is not assigned a negative factor or value.

        (iii) In a judgmental system of evaluating creditworthiness, a creditor may consider an applicant's age or whether an applicant's income derives from any public assistance program only for the purpose of determining a pertinent element of creditworthiness.

        (iv) In any system of evaluating creditworthiness, a creditor may consider the age of an elderly applicant when such age is used to favor the elderly applicant in extending credit.

    (3) *Childbearing, childrearing.* In evaluating creditworthiness, a creditor shall not use assumptions or aggregate statistics relating to the likelihood that any group of persons will bear or rear children or will, for that reason, receive diminished or interrupted income in the future.

    (4) *Telephone listing.* A creditor shall not take into account whether there is a telephone listing in the name of an applicant for consumer credit but may take into account whether there is a telephone in the applicant's residence.

    (5) *Income.* A creditor shall not discount or exclude from consideration the income of an applicant or the spouse of an applicant because of a prohibited basis or because the income is derived from part-time employment or is an annuity, pension, or other retirement benefit; a creditor may consider the amount and probable continuance of any income in evaluating an applicant's creditwor-

---

[2]The legislative history of the act indicates that the Congress intended an "effects test" concept, as outlined in the employment field by the Supreme Court in the cases of *Griggs v. Duke Power Co..* 401 U.S. 424 (1971), and *Albemarle Paper Co. v. Moody.* 422 U.S. 405 (1975), to be applicable to a creditor's determination of creditworthiness.

thiness. When an applicant relies on alimony, child support, or separate maintenance payments in applying for credit, the creditor shall consider such payments as income to the extent that they are likely to be consistently made.

(6) *Credit history.* To the extent that a creditor considers credit history in evaluating the creditworthiness of similarly qualified applicants for a similar type and amount of credit, in evaluating an applicant's creditworthiness a creditor shall consider—

(i) the credit history, when available, of accounts designated as accounts that the applicant and the applicant's spouse are permitted to use or for which both are contractually liable;

(ii) on the applicant's request, any information the applicant may present that tends to indicate that the credit history being considered by the creditor does not accurately reflect the applicant's creditworthiness; and

(iii) on the applicant's request, the credit history, when available, of any account reported in the name of the applicant's spouse or former spouse that the applicant can demonstrate accurately reflects the applicant's creditworthiness.

(7) *Immigration status.* A creditor may consider whether an applicant is a permanent resident of the United States, the applicant's immigration status, and any additional information that may be necessary to ascertain the creditor's rights and remedies regarding repayment.

(c) *State property laws.* A creditor's consideration or application of state property laws directly or indirectly affecting creditworthiness does not constitute unlawful discrimination for the purposes of the act or this regulation.

Section 202.7—Rules Concerning Extensions of Credit

(a) *Individual accounts.* A creditor shall not refuse to grant an individual account to a creditworthy applicant on the basis of sex, marital status, or any other prohibited basis.

(b) *Designation of name.* A creditor shall not refuse to allow an applicant to open or maintain an account in a birth-given first name and a surname that is the applicant's birth-given surname, the spouse's surname, or a combined surname.

(c) *Action concerning existing open-end accounts.* (1) *Limitations.* In the absence of evidence of the applicant's inability or unwillingness to repay, a creditor shall not take any of the following actions regarding an applicant who is contractually liable on an existing open-end account on the basis of the applicant's reaching a certain age or retiring or on the basis of a change in the applicant's name or marital status:

(i) require a reapplication, except as provided in paragraph (c) (2) of this section;

(ii) change the terms of the account; or

(iii) terminate the account.

(2) *Requiring reapplication.* A creditor may require a reapplication for an open-end account on the basis of a change in the marital status of an applicant who is contractually liable if the credit granted was based in whole or in part on income of the applicant's spouse and if information available to the creditor indicates that the applicant's income may not support the amount of credit currently available.

(d) *Signature of spouse or other person.* (1) *Rule for qualified applicant.* Except as provided in this paragraph, a creditor shall not require the signature of an applicant's spouse or other person, other than a joint applicant, on any credit instrument if the applicant qualifies under the creditor's standards of creditworthiness for the amount and terms of the credit requested.

    (2)   *Unsecured credit.* If an applicant requests unsecured credit and relies in part upon property that the applicant owns jointly with another person to satisfy the creditor's standards of creditworthiness, the creditor may require the signature of the other person only on the instrument(s) necessary, or reasonably believed by the creditor to be necessary, under the law of the state in which the property is located, to enable the creditor to reach the property being relied upon in the event of the death or default of the applicant.

    (3)   *Unsecured credit—community property states.* If a married applicant requests unsecured credit and resides in a community property state, or if the property upon which the applicant is relying is located in such a state, a creditor may require the signature of the spouse on any instrument necessary, or reasonably believed by the creditor to be necessary, under applicable state law to make the community property available to satisfy the debt in the event of default if—

        (i)   applicable state law denies the applicant power to manage or control sufficient community property to qualify for the amount of credit requested under the creditor's standards of creditworthiness; and

        (ii)   the applicant does not have sufficient separate property to qualify for the amount of credit requested without regard to community property.

    (4)   *Secured credit.* If an applicant requests secured credit, a creditor may require the signature of the applicant's spouse or other person on any instrument necessary, or reasonably believed by the creditor to be necessary, under applicable state law to make the property being offered as security available to satisfy the debt in the event of default, for example, an instrument to create a valid lien, pass clear title, waive inchoate rights, or assign earnings.

    (5)   *Additional parties.* If, under a creditor's standards of creditworthiness, the personal liability of an additional party is necessary to support the extension of the credit requested, a creditor may request a cosigner, guarantor, or the like. The applicant's spouse may serve as an additional party, but the creditor shall not require that the spouse be the additional party.

    (6)   *Rights of additional parties.* A creditor shall not impose requirements upon an additional party that the creditor is prohibited from imposing upon an applicant under this section.

(e) *Insurance.* A creditor shall not refuse to extend credit and shall not terminate an account because credit life, health, accident, disability, or other credit-related insurance is not available on the basis of the applicant's age.

Section 202.8—Special-Purpose Credit Programs

(a) *Standards for programs.* Subject to the provisions of paragraph (b) of this section, the act and this regulation permit a creditor to extend special-purpose credit to applicants who meet eligibility requirements under the following types of credit programs:

(1)   any credit assistance program expressly authorized by federal or state law for the benefit of an economically disadvantaged class of persons;

(2)   any credit assistance program offered by a not-for-profit organization, as defined under section 501(c) of the Internal Revenue Code of 1954, as amended, for the benefit of its members or for the benefit of an economically disadvantaged class of persons; or

(3)   any special-purpose credit program offered by a for-profit organization or in which such an organization participates to meet special social needs, if-

    (i)   the program is established and administered pursuant to a written plan that identifies the class of persons that the program is designed to benefit and sets forth the procedures and standards for extending credit pursuant to the program; and

    (ii)   the program is established and administered to extend credit to a class of persons who, under the organization's customary standards of creditworthiness, probably would not receive such credit or would receive it on less favorable terms than are ordinarily available to other applicants applying to the organization for a similar type and amount of credit.

(b)   *Rules in other sections. (1) General applicability.* All of the provisions of this regulation apply to each of the special-purpose credit programs described in paragraph (a) of this section unless modified by this section.

(2)   *Common characteristics.* A program described in paragraph (a)(2) or (a)(3) of this section qualifies as a special-purpose credit program only if it was established and is administered so as not to discriminate against an applicant on any prohibited basis; however, all program participants may be required to share one or more common characteristics (for example, race, national origin, or sex) so long as the program was not established and is not administered with the purpose of evading the requirements of the act or this regulation.

(c)   *Special rule concerning requests and use of information.* If participants in a special-purpose credit program described in paragraph (a) of this section are required to possess one or more common characteristics (for example. race, national origin, or sex) and if the program otherwise satisfies the requirements of paragraph (a), a creditor may request and consider information regarding the common characteristic(s) in determining the applicant's eligibility for the program.

(d)   *Special rule in the case of financial need.* If financial need is one of the criteria under a special-purpose program described in paragraph (a) of this section, the creditor may request and consider, in determining an applicant's eligibility for the program, information regarding the applicant's marital status; alimony, child support, and separate maintenance income; and the spouse's financial resources. In addition, a creditor may obtain the signature of an applicant's spouse or other person on an application or credit instrument relating to a special-purpose program if the signature is required by federal or state law.

Section 202.9—Notifications

(a)   *Notification of action taken, ECOA notice, and statement of specific reasons. (1) When notification is required.* A creditor shall notify an applicant of action taken within—

(i)   30 days after receiving a completed application concerning the creditor's approval of, counteroffer to, or adverse action on the application;

(ii)   30 days after taking adverse action on an incomplete application, unless notice is provided in accordance with paragraph (c) of this section;

(iii)   30 days after taking adverse action of an existing account; or

(iv)   90 days after notifying the applicant of a counteroffer if the applicant does not expressly accept or use the credit offered.

(2)   *Content of notification when adverse action is taken.* A notification given to an applicant when adverse action is taken shall be in writing and shall contain: a statement of the action taken; the name and address of the creditor; a statement of the provisions of section 701(a) of the act; the name and address of the federal agency that administers compliance with respect to the creditor; and either—

(i)   a statement of specific reasons for the action taken; or

(ii)   a disclosure of the applicant's right to a statement of specific reasons within 30 days, if the statement is requested within 60 days of the creditor's notification. The disclosure shall include the name, address, and telephone number of the person or office from which the statement of reasons can be obtained. If the creditor chooses to provide the reasons orally, the creditor shall also disclose the applicant's right to have them confirmed in writing within 30 days of receiving a written request for confirmation from the applicant.

(3)   *Notification to business credit applicants.* For business credit, a creditor shall comply with the requirements of this paragraph in the following manner:

(i)   With regard to a business that had gross revenues of $1,000,000 or less in its preceding fiscal year (other than an extension of trade credit, credit incident to a factoring agreement, or other similar types of business credit), a creditor shall comply with paragraphs (a)(l) and (2), except that—

(A)   The statement of the action taken may be given orally or in writing, when adverse action is taken;

(B)   Disclosure of an applicant's right to a statement of reasons may be given at the time of application, instead of when adverse action is taken, provided the disclosure is in a form the applicant may retain and contains the information required by paragraph (a) (2) (ii) and the ECOA notice specified in paragraph (b) (1) of this section;

(C)   For an application made solely by telephone, a creditor satisfies the requirements of this paragraph by an oral statement of the action taken and of the applicant's right to a statement of reasons for adverse action.

(ii)   With regard to a business that had gross revenues in excess of $1,000,000 in its preceding fiscal year or an extension of trade credit, credit incident to a factoring agreement, or other similar types of business credit, a creditor shall—

(A) Notify the applicant, orally or in writing, within a reasonable time of the action taken; and

(B) Provide a written statement of the reasons for adverse action and the ECOA notice specified in paragraph (b) (1) of this section if the applicant makes a written request for the reasons within 60 days of being notified of the adverse action.

(b) *Form of ECOA notice and statement of specific reasons.*

    (1) ECOA notice. To satisfy the disclosure requirements of paragraph (a) (2) of this section regarding section 701(a) of the act, the creditor shall provide a notice that is substantially similar to the following:

    The federal Equal Credit Opportunity Act prohibits creditors from discriminating against credit applicants on the basis of race, color, religion, national origin, sex, marital status, age (provided the applicant has the capacity to enter into a binding contract); because all or part of the applicant's income derives from any public assistance program; or because the applicant has in good faith exercised any right under the Consumer Credit Protection Act. The federal agency that administers compliance with this law concerning this creditor is (name and address as specified by the appropriate agency listed in appendix A of this regulation).

    (2) *Statement of specific reasons.* The statement of reasons for adverse action required by paragraph (a)(2)(i) of this section must be specific and indicate the principal reason(s) for the adverse action. Statements that the adverse action was based on the creditor's internal standards or policies or that the applicant failed to achieve the qualifying score on the creditor's credit scoring system are insufficient.

(c) *Incomplete applications.* (1) *Notice alternatives.* Within 30 days after receiving an application that is incomplete regarding matters that an applicant can complete, the creditor shall notify the applicant either—

    (i) of action taken, in accordance with paragraph (a) of this section or

    (ii) of the incompleteness, in accordance with paragraph (c) (2) of this section.

    (2) *Notice of incompleteness.* If additional information is needed from an applicant, the creditor shall send a written notice to the applicant specifying the information needed, designating a reasonable period of time for the applicant to provide the information, and informing the applicant that failure to provide the information requested will result in no further consideration being given to the application. The creditor shall have no further obligation under this section if the applicant fails to respond within the designated time period. If the applicant supplies the requested information within the designated time period, the creditor shall take action on the application and notify the applicant in accordance with paragraph (a) of this section.

    (3) *Oral request for information.* At its option, a creditor may inform the applicant orally of the need for additional information; but if the application remains incomplete the creditor shall send a notice in accordance with paragraph (c) (1) of this section.

(d) *Oral notifications by small-volume creditors.* The requirements of this section (including statements of specific reasons) are satisfied by oral notifications in the case of any creditor that did not receive more than 150 applications during the preceding calendar year.

(e) *Withdrawal of approved application.* When an applicant submits an application and the parties contemplate that the applicant will inquire about its status, if the creditor approves the application and the applicant has not inquired within 30 days after applying, the creditor may treat the application as withdrawn and need not comply with paragraph (a)(l) of this section.

(f) *Multiple applicants.* When an application involves more than one applicant, notification need only be given to one of them but must be given to the primary applicant where one is readily apparent.

(g) *Applications submitted through a third party.* When an application is made on behalf of an applicant to more than one creditor and the applicant expressly accepts or uses credit offered by one of the creditors, notification of action taken by any of the other creditors is not required. If no credit is offered or if the applicant does not expressly accept or use any credit offered, each creditor taking adverse action must comply with this section, directly or through a third party. A notice given by a third party shall disclose the identity of each creditor on whose behalf the notice is given.

Section 202.10—Furnishing of Credit Information

(a) *Designation of accounts.* A creditor that furnishes credit information shall designate—

    (1)   any new account to reflect the participation of both spouses if the applicant's spouse is permitted to use or is contractually liable on the account (other than as a guarantor, surety, endorser, or similar party); and

    (2)   any existing account to reflect such participation, within 90 days after receiving a written request to do so from one of the spouses.

(b) *Routine reports to consumer reporting agency.* If a creditor furnishes credit information to a consumer reporting agency concerning an account designated to reflect the participation of both spouses, the creditor shall furnish the information in a manner that will enable the agency to provide access to the information in the name of each spouse.

(c) *Reporting in response to inquiry.* If a creditor furnishes credit information in response to an inquiry concerning an account designated to reflect the participation of both spouses, the creditor shall furnish the information in the name of the spouse about whom the information is requested.

Section 202.11—Relation to State Law

(a) *Inconsistent state laws.* Except as otherwise provided in this section, this regulation alters, affects, or preempts only those state laws that are inconsistent with the act and this regulation and then only to the extent of the inconsistency. A state law is not inconsistent if it is more protective of an applicant.

(b) *Preempted provisions of state law.* (1) A state law is deemed to be inconsistent with the requirements of the act and this regulation and less protective of an applicant within the meaning of section 705(f) of the act to the extent that the law—

(i)   requires or permits a practice or act prohibited by the act or this regulation;

(ii)   prohibits the individual extension of consumer credit to both parties to a marriage if each spouse individually and voluntarily applies for such credit;

(iii)   prohibits inquiries or collection of data required to comply with the act or this regulation;

(iv)   prohibits asking or considering age in an empirically derived, demonstrably and statistically sound, credit scoring system to determine a pertinent element of creditworthiness, or to favor an elderly applicant; or

(v)   prohibits inquiries necessary to establish or administer a special-purpose credit program as defined by section 202.8.

(2)   A creditor, state, or other interested party may request the Board to determine whether a state law is inconsistent with the requirements of the act and this regulation.

(c)   *Laws on finance charges, loan ceilings.* If married applicants voluntarily apply for and obtain individual accounts with the same creditor, the accounts shall not be aggregated or otherwise combined for purposes of determining permissible finance charges or loan ceilings under any federal or state law. Permissible loan ceiling laws shall be construed to permit each spouse to become individually liable up to the amount of the loan ceilings, less the amount for which the applicant is jointly liable.

(d)   *State and federal laws not affected.* This section does not alter or annul any provision of state property laws, laws relating to the disposition of decedents' estates, or federal or state banking regulations directed only toward insuring the solvency of financial institutions.

(e)   *Exemption for state-regulated transactions.* (1) *Applications.* A state may apply to the Board for an exemption from the requirements of the act and this regulation for any class of credit transactions within the state. The Board will grant such an exemption if the Board determines that—

(i)   the class of credit transactions is subject to state law requirements substantially similar to the act and this regulation or that applicants are afforded greater protection under state law; and

(ii)   there is adequate provision for state enforcement.

(2)   *Liability and enforcement.* (i) No exemption will extend to the civil-liability provisions of section 706 or the administrative-enforcement provisions of section 704 of the act.

(ii)   After an exemption has been granted, the requirements of the applicable state law (except for additional requirements not imposed by federal law) will constitute the requirements of the act and this regulation.

Section 202.12—Record Retention

(a)   *Retention of prohibited information.* A creditor may retain in its files information that is prohibited by the act or this regulation in evaluating applications, without violating the act or this regulation, if the information was obtained—

(1)   from any source prior to March 23, 1977;

(2)   from consumer reporting agencies, an applicant, or others without the specific request of the creditor; or

(3)   As required to monitor compliance with the act and this regulation or other federal or state statutes or regulations.

(b) *Preservation of records.* (1) *Applications.* For 25 months (12 months for business credit) after the date that a creditor notifies an applicant of action taken on an application or of incompleteness, the creditor shall retain in original form or a copy thereof—

    (i)   any application that it receives, any information required to be obtained concerning characteristics of the applicant to monitor compliance with the act and this regulation or other similar law, and any other written or recorded information used in evaluating the application and not returned to the applicant at the applicant's request;

    (ii)   a copy of the following documents if furnished to the applicant in written form (or, if furnished orally, any notation or memorandum made by the creditor):

        (A)   the notification of action taken: and

        (B)   the statement of specific reasons for adverse action; and

    (iii)   any written statement submitted by the applicant alleging a violation of the act or this regulation.

(2)   *Existing accounts.* For 25 months (12 months for business credit) after the date that a creditor notifies an applicant of adverse action regarding an existing account, the creditor shall retain as to that account. in original form or a copy thereof—

    (i)   any written or recorded information concerning the adverse action; and

    (ii)   any written statement submitted by the applicant alleging a violation of the act or this regulation.

(3)   *Other applications.* For 25 months (12 months for business credit) after the date that a creditor receives an application for which the creditor is not required to comply with the notification requirements of section 202.9, the creditor shall retain all written or recorded information in its possession concerning the applicant, including any notation of action taken.

(4)   *Enforcement proceedings and investigations.* A creditor shall retain the information specified in this section beyond 25 months (12 months for business credit) if it has actual notice that it is under investigation or is subject to an enforcement proceeding for an alleged violation of the act or this regulation by the attorney general of the United States or by an enforcement agency charged with monitoring that creditor's compliance with the act and this regulation, or if it has been served with notice of an action filed pursuant to section 706 of the act and section 202.14 of this regulation. The creditor shall retain the information until final disposition of the matter, unless an earlier time is allowed by order of the agency or court.

(5)   *Special rule for certain business-credit applications.* With regard to a business with gross revenues in excess of $1,000,000 in its preceding fiscal year, or an extension of trade credit, credit incident to a factoring agreement or other similar types of business credit, the creditor shall retain records for at least 60 days

after notifying the applicant of the action taken. If within that time period the applicant requests in writing the reasons for adverse action or that records be retained, the creditor shall retain records for 12 months.

Section 202.13—Information for Monitoring Purposes

(a) *Information to be requested.* A creditor that receives an application for credit primarily for the purchase or refinancing of a dwelling occupied or to be occupied by the applicant as a principal residence, where the extension of credit will be secured by the dwelling, shall request as part of the application the following information regarding the applicant(s):

   (1) race or national origin, using the categories American Indian or Alaskan Native; Asian or Pacific Islander; Black; White; Hispanic; Other (Specify);

   (2) sex;

   (3) marital status, using the categories Married, Unmarried, and Separated; and

   (4) age.

"Dwelling" means a residential structure that contains one to four units, whether or not that structure is attached to real property. The term includes, but is not limited to, an individual condominium or cooperative unit, and a mobile or other manufactured home.

(b) *Obtaining of information.* Questions regarding race or national origin, sex, marital status, and age may be listed, at the creditor's option, on the application form or on a separate form that refers to the application. The applicant(s) shall be asked but not required to supply the requested information. If the applicant(s) chooses not to provide the information or any part of it, that fact shall be noted on the form. The creditor shall then also note on the form, to the extent possible, the race or national origin and sex of the applicant(s) on the basis of visual observation or surname.

(c) *Disclosure to applicant(s).* The creditor shall inform the applicant(s) that the information regarding race or national origin, sex, marital status, and age is being requested by the federal government for the purpose of monitoring compliance with federal statutes that prohibit creditors from discriminating against applicants on those bases. The creditor shall also inform the applicant(s) that if the applicant(s) chooses not to provide the information, the creditor is required to note the race or national origin and sex on the basis of visual observation or surname.

(d) *Substitute monitoring program.* A monitoring program required by an agency charged with administrative enforcement under section 704 of the act may be substituted for the requirements contained in paragraphs (a), (b), and (c).

Section 202.14—Enforcement, Penalties, and Liabilities

(a) *Administrative enforcement.* (1) As set forth more fully in section 704 of the act, administrative enforcement of the act and this regulation regarding certain creditors is assigned to the Comptroller of the Currency, Board of Governors of the Federal Reserve System, board of directors of the Federal Deposit Insurance Corporation, Office of Thrift Supervision, National Credit Union Administration, Interstate Commerce Commission, secretary of agriculture, Farm Credit Administration,

Securities and Exchange Commission, Small Business Administration, and secretary of transportation.

(2) Except to the extent that administrative enforcement is specifically assigned to other authorities, compliance with the requirements imposed under the act and this regulation is enforced by the Federal Trade Commission.

(b) *Penalties and liabilities.* (1) Sections 706(a) and (b) and 702(g) of the act provide that any creditor that fails to comply with a requirement imposed by the act or this regulation is subject to civil liability for actual and punitive damages in individual or class actions. Pursuant to sections 704(b), (c), and (d) and 702(g) of the act, violations of the act or regulation also constitute violations of other federal laws. Liability for punitive damages is restricted to nongovernmental entities and is limited to $10,000 in individual actions and the lesser of $500,000 or 1 percent of the creditor's net worth in class actions. Section 706(c) provides for equitable and declamatory relief and section 706(d) authorizes the awarding of costs and reasonable attorney's fees to an aggrieved applicant in a successful action.

(2) As provided in section 706(f), a civil action under the act or this regulation may be brought in the appropriate United States district court without regard to the amount in controversy or in any other court of competent jurisdiction within two years after the date of the occurrence of the violation, or within one year after the commencement of an administrative enforcement proceeding or of a civil action brought by the attorney general of the United States within two years after the alleged violation.

(3) Sections 706(g) and (h) provide that, if an agency responsible for administrative enforcement is unable to obtain compliance with the act or this regulation, it may refer the matter to the attorney general of the United States. On referral, or whenever the Attorney General has reason to believe that one or more creditors are engaged in a pattern or practice in violation of the act or this regulation, the attorney general may bring a civil action.

(c) *Failure of compliance.* A creditor's failure to comply with sections 202.6(b)(6), 202.9, 202.10, 202.12 or 202.13 is not a violation if it results from an inadvertent error. On discovering an error under sections 202.9 and 202.10, the creditor shall correct it as soon as possible. If a creditor inadvertently obtains the monitoring information regarding the race or national origin and sex of the applicant in a dwelling-related transaction not covered by section 202.13, the creditor may act on and retain the application without violating the regulation.

APPENDIX A—FEDERAL ENFORCEMENT AGENCIES

The following list indicates the federal agencies that enforce Regulation B for particular classes of creditors. Any questions concerning a particular creditor should be directed to its enforcement agency.

National Banks
Comptroller of the Currency
Consumer Examinations Division
Washington, D.C. 20219

State Member Banks
Federal Reserve Bank serving the District in which the state member bank is located.

Nonmember Insured Banks
Federal Deposit Insurance Corporation Regional Director for the region in which the nonmember insured bank is located.

Savings institutions under the Savings Association Insurance Fund of the FDIC and federally chartered savings banks insured under the Bank Insurance Fund of the FDIC (but not including state-chartered savings banks insured under the Bank Insurance Fund)
The district director of the Office of Thrift Supervision in the district in which the institution is located.

Federal Credit Unions
Regional office of the National Credit Union Administration serving the area in which the federal credit union is located.

Air Carriers
Assistant General Counsel for Aviation Enforcement and Proceedings
Department of Transportation
400 Seventh Street, S.W.
Washington, D.C. 20590

Creditors Subject to Interstate Commerce Commission
Office of Proceedings
Interstate Commerce Commission
Washington, D.C. 20523

Creditors Subject to Packers and Stockyards Act
Nearest Packers and Stockyards Administration area supervisor.

Small Business Investment Companies
U.S. Small Business Administration
1441 L Street, NW.
Washington, D.C. 20416

Brokers and Dealers
Securities and Exchange Commission
Washington, D.C. 20549

Federal Land Banks, Federal Land Bank Associations, Federal Intermediate Credit Banks, and Production Credit Associations
Farm Credit Administration
1501 Farm Credit Drive
McLean, Virginia 22102-5090

Retailers. Finance Companies, and All Other Creditors Not Listed Above
FTC regional office for region in which the creditor operates or

Federal Trade Commission
Equal Credit Opportunity
Washington, D.C. 20580

APPENDIX B—MODEL APPLICATION FORMS

This appendix contains five model credit application forms, each designed for use in a particular type of consumer credit transaction as indicated by the bracketed caption on each form. The first sample form is intended for use in open-end, unsecured transactions; the second for closed-end, secured transactions; the third for closed-end transactions, whether unsecured or secured; the fourth in transactions involving community property or occurring in community property states; and the fifth in residential mortgage transactions. The appendix also contains a model disclosure for use in complying with section 202.13 for certain dwelling-related loans. All forms contained in this appendix are models; their use by creditors is optional.

The use or modification of these forms is governed by the following instructions. A creditor may change the forms by asking for additional information not prohibited by section 202.5; by deleting any information request; or by rearranging the format without modifying the substance of the inquiries. In any of these three instances, however, the appropriate notices regarding the optional nature of courtesy titles; the option to disclose alimony, child support, or separate maintenance; and the limitation concerning marital status inquiries must be included in the appropriate places if the items to which they relate appear on the creditor's form.

If a creditor uses an appropriate appendix B model form, or modifies a form in accordance with the above instructions, that creditor shall be deemed to be acting in compliance with the provisions of paragraphs (c) and (d) of section 202.5 of this regulation.

[Open-end, unsecured credit]

CREDIT APPLICATION

IMPORTANT: Read these Directions before completing this Application.

Check
Appropriate
Box

☐ If you are applying for an individual account in your own name and are relying on your own income or assets and not the income or assets of another person as the basis for repayment of the credit requested, complete only Sections A and D.

☐ If you are applying for a joint account or an account that you and another person will use, complete all Sections, providing information in B about the joint applicant or user.

☐ If you are applying for an individual account, but are relying on income from alimony, child support, or separate maintenance or on the income or assets of another person as the basis for repayment of the credit requested, complete all Sections to the extent possible, providing information in B about the person on whose alimony, support, or maintenance payments or income or assets you are relying.

SECTION A—INFORMATION REGARDING APPLICANT

Full Name (Last, First, Middle): .... Birthdate: / /

Present Street Address: .... Years there: ....

City: .... State: .... Zip: .... Telephone: ....

Social Security No.: .... Driver's License No.: ....

Previous Street Address: .... Years there: ....

City: .... State: .... Zip: ....

Present Employer: .... Years there: .... Telephone: ....

Position or title: .... Name of supervisor: ....

Employer's Address: ....

Previous Employer: .... Years there: ....

Previous Employer's Address: ....

Present net salary or commission: $ .... per .... No. Dependents: .... Ages: ....

Alimony, child support, or separate maintenance income need not be revealed if you do not wish to have it considered as a basis for repaying this obligation.

Alimony, child support, separate maintenance received under: court order ☐ written agreement ☐ oral understanding ☐

Other income: $ .... per .... Source(s) of other income: ....

Is any income listed in this Section likely to be reduced in the next two years?
☐ Yes (Explain in detail on a separate sheet.) No ☐

Have you ever received credit from us? .... When? .... Office: ....

Checking Account No.: .... Institution and Branch: ....

Savings Account No.: .... Institution and Branch: ....

Name of nearest relative
not living with you: .... Telephone: ....

Relationship: .... Address: ....

SECTION B—INFORMATION REGARDING JOINT APPLICANT, USER, OR OTHER PARTY (Use separate sheets if necessary.)

Full Name (Last, First, Middle): .... Birthdate: / /

Relationship to Applicant (if any): ....

Present Street Address: .... Years there: ....

City: .... State: .... Zip: .... Telephone: ....

Social Security No.: .... Driver's License No.: ....

Present Employer: .... Years there: .... Telephone: ....

Position or title: .... Name of supervisor: ....

Employer's Address: ....

Previous Employer: .... Years there: ....

Previous Employer's Address: ....

Present net salary or commission: $ .... per .... No. Dependents: .... Ages: ....

Alimony, child support, or separate maintenance income need not be revealed if you do not wish to have it considered as a basis for repaying this obligation.

Alimony, child support, separate maintenance received under: court order ☐ written agreement ☐ oral understanding ☐

Other income: $ .... per .... Source(s) of other income: ....

Is any income listed in this Section likely to be reduced in the next two years?
☐ Yes (Explain in detail on a separate sheet.) ☐ No

Checking Account No.: .... Institution and Branch: ....

Savings Account No.: .... Institution and Branch: ....

Name of nearest relative not living
with Joint Applicant, User, or Other Party: .... Telephone: ....

Relationship: .... Address: ....

SECTION C—MARITAL STATUS
(Do not complete if this is an application for an individual account.)

Applicant: ☐ Married   ☐ Separated   ☐ Unmarried (including single, divorced, and widowed)
Other Party: ☐ Married   ☐ Separated   ☐ Unmarried (including single, divorced, and widowed)

SECTION D—ASSET AND DEBT INFORMATION (If Section B has been completed, this Section should be completed giving information about both the Applicant and Joint Applicant, User, or Other Person. Please mark Applicant-related information with an "A." If Section B was not completed, only give information about the Applicant in this Section.)

ASSETS OWNED (Use separate sheet if necessary.)

Description of Assets	Value	Subject to Debt? Yes/No	Name(s) of Owner(s)
Cash	$		
Automobiles (Make, Model, Year)			
Cash Value of Life Insurance (Issuer, Face Value)			
Real Estate (Location, Date Acquired)			
Marketable Securities (Issuer, Type, No. of Shares)			
Other (List)			
Total Assets	$		

OUTSTANDING DEBTS (Include charge accounts, instalment contracts, credit cards, rent, mortgages, etc. Use separate sheet if necessary.)

Creditor	Type of Debt or Acct. No.	Name in Which Acct. Carried	Original Debt	Present Balance	Monthly Payments	Past Due? Yes, No
1. (Landlord or Mortgage Holder)	☐ Rent Payment ☐ Mortgage		$ (Omit rent)	$ (Omit rent)	$	
2.						
3.						
4.						
5.						
6.						
Total Debts			$	$	$	

(Credit References) Date Paid

| 1 | $ | |
| 2. | | |

Are you a co-maker, endorser, or guarantor on any loan or contract?	Yes ☐ No ☐	If "yes" for whom?	To whom?
Are there any unsatisfied judgments against you?	Yes ☐ No ☐	Amount $	If "yes" to whom owed?
Have you been declared bankrupt in the last 14 years?	Yes ☐ No ☐	If "yes" where?	Year

Other Obligations—(E.g., liability to pay alimony, child support, separate maintenance. Use separate sheet if necessary.)

Everything that I have stated in this application is correct to the best of my knowledge. I understand that you will retain this application whether or not it is approved. You are authorized to check my credit and employment history and to answer questions about your credit experience with me.

Applicant's Signature	Date	Other Signature (Where Applicable)	Date

[Closed-end, secured credit]

CREDIT APPLICATION

IMPORTANT: Read these Directions before completing this Application.

Check Appropriate Box

☐ If you are applying for individual credit in your own name and are relying on your own income or assets and not the income or assets of another person as the basis for repayment of the credit requested, complete Sections A, C, D, and E, omitting B and the second part of C.

☐ If this is an application for joint credit with another person, complete all Sections, providing information in B about the joint applicant.

☐ If you are applying for individual credit, but are relying on income from alimony, child support, or separate maintenance or on the income or assets of another person as the basis for repayment of the credit requested, complete all Sections to the extent possible, providing information in B about the person on whose alimony, support, or maintenance payments or income or assets you are relying.

Amount Requested   Payment Date Desired   Proceeds of Credit

$................................   .... To be Used For................................

SECTION A—INFORMATION REGARDING APPLICANT

Full Name (Last, First, Middle): .... Birthdate: / /

Present Street Address: .... Years there: ....

City: .... State: .... Zip: .... Telephone: ....

Social Security No.: .... Driver's License No.: ....

Previous Street Address: .... Years there: ....

City: .... State: .... Zip: ....

Present Employer .... Years there: .... Telephone: ....

Position or title: .... Name of supervisor: ....

Employer's Address: ....

Previous Employer: .... Years there: ....

Previous Employer's Address: ....

Present net salary or commission: $ .... per .... No. Dependents: .... Ages: ......

Alimony, child support, or separate maintenance income need not be revealed if you do not wish to have it considered as a basis for repaying this obligation.

Alimony, child support, separate maintenance received under: court order ☐ written agreement ☐ oral understanding ☐

Other income: $ .... per .... Source(s) of other income: ....

Is any income listed in this Section likely to be reduced before the credit requested is paid off?
☐ Yes (Explain in detail on a separate sheet.) No ☐

Have you ever received credit from us? .... When? .... Office: ....

Checking Account No. .... Institution and Branch: ....

Savings Account No. .... Institution and Branch:

Name of nearest relative not living with you: .... Telephone: ....

Relationship: .... Address: ....

SECTION B—INFORMATION REGARDING JOINT APPLICANT OR OTHER PARTY (Use separate sheets if necessary.)

Full Name (Last, First, Middle): .... Birthdate: / /

Relationship to Applicant (if any): ....

Present Street Address: .... Years there: ....

City: .... State: .... Zip .... Telephone: ....

Social Security No.: .... Driver's License No.: ....

Present Employer: .... Years there: .... Telephone: ....

Position or title: .... Name of supervisor: ....

Employer's Address: ....

Previous Employer: .... Years there: ....

Previous Employer's Address: ....

Present net salary or commission: $ .... per .... No. Dependents: .... Ages: ....

Alimony, child support, or separate maintenance income need not be revealed if you do not wish to have it considered as a basis for repaying this obligation.

Alimony, child support, separate maintenance received under: court order ☐ written agreement ☐ oral understanding ☐

Other income: $ .... per .... Source(s) of other income: ....

Is any income listed in this Section likely to be reduced before the credit requested is paid off?
☐ Yes (Explain in detail on a separate sheet.) No ☐

Checking Account No.: .... Institution and Branch: ....

Savings Account No.: .... Institution and Branch: ....

Name of nearest relative not living with Joint Applicant or Other Party: ....

Relationship: .... Address: ....

SECTION C—MARITAL STATUS

Applicant: ☐ Married   ☐ Separated   ☐ Unmarried (including single, divorced, and widowed)
Other Party: ☐ Married   ☐ Separated   ☐ Unmarried (including single, divorced, and widowed)

SECTION D—ASSET AND DEBT INFORMATION (If Section B has been completed, this Section should be completed giving information about both the Applicant and Joint Applicant or Other Person. Please mark Applicant-related information with an "A." If Section B was not completed, only give information about the Applicant in this Section.)

ASSETS OWNED (Use separate sheet if necessary.)

Description of Assets	Value	Subject to Debt? Yes/No	Name(s) of Owner(s)
Cash	$		
Automobiles (Make, Model, Year)			
Cash Value of Life Insurance (Issuer, Face Value)			
Real Estate (Location, Date Acquired)			
Marketable Securities (Issuer, Type, No. of Shares)			
Other (List)			
Total Assets	$		

OUTSTANDING DEBTS (Include charge accounts, instalment contracts, credit cards, rent, mortgages, etc. Use separate sheet if necessary.)

Creditor	Type of Debt or Acct. No.	Name in Which Acct. Carried	Original Debt	Present Balance	Monthly Payments	Past Due? Yes No
1. (Landlord or Mortgage Holder)	☐ Rent Payment ☐ Mortgage		$ (Omit rent)	$ (Omit rent)	$	
2.						
3.						
Total Debts			$	$	$	

(Credit References) Date Paid

1. $

2.

Are you a co-maker, endorser, or guarantor on any loan or contract?	Yes ☐ No ☐	If "yes" for whom?		To whom?
Are there any unsatisfied judgments against you?	Yes ☐ No ☐	Amount $	If "yes" to whom owed?	
Have you been declared bankrupt in the last 14 years?	Yes ☐ No ☐	If "yes" where?		Year

Other obligations—(E.g., liability to pay alimony, child support, separate maintenance. Use separate sheet if necessary.)

SECTION E—SECURED CREDIT Briefly describe the property to be given as security:

....

and list names and addresses of all co-owners of the property:

Name   Address

....

If the security is real estate, give the full name of your spouse (if any): ....

Everything that I have stated in this application is correct to the best of my knowledge. I understand that you will retain this application whether or not it is approved. You are authorized to check my credit and employment history and to answer questions about your credit experience with me.

_____   _____   _____   _____
Applicant's Signature   Date   Other Signature   Date
                                               (Where Applicable)

[Closed-end, unsecured/secured credit]

CREDIT APPLICATION

IMPORTANT: Read these Directions before completing this Application.

Check Appropriate Box

☐ If you are applying for individual credit in your own name and are relying on your own income or assets and not the income or assets of another person as the basis for repayment of the credit requested, complete only Sections A and D. If the requested credit is to be secured, also complete the first part of Section C and Section E.

☐ If you are applying for joint credit with another person, complete all Sections except E, providing information in B about the joint applicant. If the requested credit is to be secured, then complete Section E.

☐ If you are applying for individual credit, but are relying on income from alimony, child support, or separate maintenance or on the income or assets of another person as the basis for repayment of the credit requested, complete all Sections except E to the extent possible, providing information in B about the person on whose alimony, support, or maintenance payments or income or assets you are relying. If the requested credit is to be secured, then complete Section E.

Amount Requested	Payment Date Desired	Proceeds of Credit
$...............		To be Used For ....

SECTION A—INFORMATION REGARDING APPLICANT

Full Name (Last, First, Middle): ....   Birthdate: / /

Present Street Address: ....   Years there: ....

City: .... State: .... Zip: .... Telephone: ....

Social Security No.: .... Driver's License No.: ....

Previous Street Address: ....   Years there: ....

City: .... State: .... Zip: ....

Present Employer: .... Years there: .... Telephone: ....

Position or title: .... Name of supervisor: ....

Employer's Address: ....

Previous Employer: ....   Years there: ....

Previous Employer's Address: ....

Present net salary or commission: $ .... per .... No. Dependents: .... Ages: ....

Alimony, child support, or separate maintenance income need not be revealed if you do not wish to have it considered as a basis for repaying this obligation.

Alimony, child support, separate maintenance received under: court order ☐ written agreement ☐ oral understanding ☐

Other income: $ .... per .... Source(s) of other income: ....

Is any income listed in this Section likely to be reduced before the credit requested is paid off?

☐ Yes (Explain in detail on separate sheet.)   ☐ No

Have you ever received credit from us? .... When? .... Office ....

Checking Account No.: .... Institution and Branch: ....

Savings Account No.: .... Institution and Branch: ....

Name of nearest relative not living with you: .... Telephone: ....

Relationship: .... Address: ....

SECTION B—INFORMATION REGARDING JOINT APPLICANT OR OTHER PARTY (Use separate sheets if necessary.)

Full Name (Last, First, Middle): ....   Birthdate: / /

Relationship to Applicant (if any): ....

Present Street Address: ....   Years there: ....

City: .... State: .... Zip: .... Telephone: ....

Social Security No.: .... Driver's License No.: ....

Present Employer: .... Years there: .... Telephone: ....

Position or title: .... Name of supervisor: ....

Employer's Address: ....

Previous Employer: ....   Years there: ....

Previous Employer's Address: ....

Present net salary or commission: $ .... per .... No. Dependents: .... Ages: ....

Alimony, child support, or separate maintenance income need not be revealed if you do not wish to have it considered as a basis for repaying this obligation.

Alimony, child support, separate maintenance received under: court order ☐ written agreement ☐ oral understanding ☐

Other income: $ .... per .... Source(s) of other income: ....

Is any income listed in this Section likely to be reduced before the credit requested is paid off?

☐ Yes (Explain in detail on separate sheet.)   ☐ No

Checking Account No.: .... Institution and Branch: ....

Savings Account No.: .... Institution and Branch: ....

Name of nearest relative not living with Joint Applicant or Other Party: .... Telephone: ....

Relationship: .... Address: ....

SECTION C—MARITAL STATUS
(Do not complete if this is an application for individual unsecured credit.)
Applicant: ☐ Married   ☐ Separated   ☐ Unmarried (including single. divorced, and widowed)
Other Party: ☐ Married   ☐ Separated   ☐ Unmarried (including single, divorced, and widowed)

SECTION D—ASSET AND DEBT INFORMATION (If Section B has been completed, this Section should be completed giving information about both the Applicant and Joint Applicant or Other Person. Please mark Applicant-related information with an "A." If Section B was not completed, only give information about the Applicant in this Section.)

ASSETS OWNED (Use separate sheet if necessary.)

Description of Assets	Value	Subject to Debt? Yes/No	Name(s) of Owner(s)
Cash	$		
Automobiles (Make, Model, Year)			
Cash Value of Life Insurance (Issuer, Face Value)			
Real Estate (Location, Date Acquired)			
Marketable Securities (Issuer, Type, No. of Shares)			
Other (List)			
Total Assets	$		

OUTSTANDING DEBTS (Include charge accounts. instalment contracts, credit cards, rent, mortgages, etc. Use separate sheet if necessary.)

Creditor	Type of Debt or Acct. No.	Name in Which Acct. Carried	Original Debt	Present Balance	Monthly Payments	Past Due? Yes/No
1. Landlord or Mortgage Holder)	☐ Rent Payment ☐ Mortgage		$ (Omit rent)	$ (Omit rent)	$	
2.						
3.						
Total Debts			$	$	$	

Credit References)		Date Paid
1.	$	
2.		

Are you a co-maker, endorser, or guarantor on any loan or contract?   Yes ☐   No ☐   If "Yes," for whom?   To whom?

Are there any unsatisfied judgments against you?   Yes ☐   No ☐   Amount $ If "Yes," to whom owed?

Have you been declared bankrupt in the last 14 years?   Yes ☐   No ☐   If "Yes," where?   Year

Other obligations—(E.g. liability to pay alimony, child support, separate maintenance. Use separate sheet if necessary.)

SECTION E—SECURED CREDIT (Complete only if credit is to be secured. Briefly describe the property to be given as security.

and list names and addresses of all co-owners of the property:

Name   Address

If the security is real estate, give the full name of your spouse (if any).

Everything that I have stated in this application is correct to the best of my knowledge. I understand that you will retain this application whether or not it is approved. You are authorized to check my credit and employment history and to answer questions about your credit experience with me.

Applicant's Signature   Date   Other Signature (Where Applicable)   Date

[Community property]

CREDIT APPLICATION
IMPORTANT: Read these Directions before completing this Application.

Check Appropriate Box

☐ If you are applying for individual credit in your own name, are not married, and are not relying on alimony, child support, or separate maintenance payments or on the income or assets of another person as the basis for repayment of the credit requested, complete only Sections A and D. If the requested credit is to be secured, also complete Section E.

☐ In all other situations, complete all Sections except E, providing information in B about your spouse, a joint applicant or user, or the person on whose alimony, support, or maintenance payments or income or assets you are relying. If the requested credit is to be secured, also complete Section E.

Amount Requested   **Payment Date Desired**   **Proceeds of Credit To be Used For**
$..............................

SECTION A—INFORMATION REGARDING APPLICANT

Full Name (Last, First, Middle): .... Birthdate: / /

Present Street Address .... Years there: ......

City: .... State: .... Zip: .... Telephone: ....

Social Security No.: .... Driver's License No.: ....

Previous Street Address: .... Years there: ......

City: .... State: .... Zip: ....

Present Employer: .... Years there: ...... Telephone: ....

Position or title: .... Name of supervisor: ....

Employer's Address: ....

Previous Employer: .... Years there: ......

Previous Employer's Address: ....

Present net salary or commission: $ .... per .... No. Dependents: ...... Ages: ....

Alimony, child support, or separate maintenance income need not be revealed if you do not wish to have it considered as a basis for repaying this obligation.

Alimony, child support, separate maintenance received under: court order ☐ written agreement ☐ oral understanding ☐

Other income: $ .... per .... Source(s) of other income: ....

Is any income listed in this Section likely to be reduced in the next two years or before the credit requested is paid off?
☐ Yes (Explain in detail on a separate sheet.) No ☐

Have you ever received credit from us? .... When? .... Office: ....

Checking Account No.: .... Institution and Branch: ....

Savings Account No.: .... Institution and Branch: ....

Name of nearest relative not living with you .... Telephone: ....

Relationship: .... Address: ....

SECTION B—INFORMATION REGARDING SPOUSE, JOINT APPLICANT, USER, OR OTHER PARTY (Use separate sheets if necessary.)

Full Name (Last, First, Middle): .... Birthdate: / /

Relationship to Applicant (if any): .... Years there: ......

Present Street Address: ....

City: .... State: .... Zip: .... Telephone: ....

Social Security No.: .... Driver's License No.: ....

Present Employer: .... Years there: ...... Telephone: ....

Position or title: .... Name of supervisor: ....

Employer's Address: ....

Previous Employer: .... Years there: ......

Previous Employer's Address: ....

Present net salary or commission: $ .... per .... No. Dependents: ...... Ages: ....

Alimony, child support, or separate maintenance income need not be revealed if you do not wish to have it considered as a basis for repaying this obligation.

Alimony, child support, separate maintenance received under: court order ☐ written agreement ☐ oral understanding ☐

Other income: $ .... per .... Source(s) of other income: ....

Is any income listed in this Section likely to be reduced in the next two years or before the credit requested is paid off?
☐ Yes (Explain in detail on a separate sheet.) ☐ No

Checking Account No.: .... Institution and Branch: ....

Savings Account No.: .... Institution and Branch: ....

Name of nearest relative not living with Spouse, Joint Applicant, User, or other Party: .... Telephone: ....

Relationship: .... Address: ....

SECTION C—MARITAL STATUS

Applicant: ☐ Married   ☐ Separated   ☐ Unmarried (including single, divorced, and widowed)

Other Party: ☐ Married   ☐ Separated   ☐ Unmarried (including single, divorced, and widowed)

SECTION D—ASSET AND DEBT INFORMATION (If Section B has been completed, this Section should be completed giving information about both the Applicant and Spouse, Joint Applicant, User, or Other Person. Please mark Applicant-related information with an "A." If Section B was not completed, only give information about the Applicant in this Section.)

ASSETS OWNED (Use separate sheet if necessary.)

Description of Assets	Value	Subject to Debt? Yes/No	Name(s) of Owner(s)
Cash	$		
Automobiles (Make, Model, Year)			
Cash Value of Life Insurance (Issuer, Face Value)			
Real Estate (Location, Date Acquired)			
Marketable Securities (Issuer, Type, No. of Shares)			
Other (List)			
Total Assets	$		

OUTSTANDING DEBTS (Include charge accounts, instalment contracts, credit cards, rent, mortgages, etc. Use separate sheet if necessary.)

Name of Creditor	Type of Debt or Acct. No.	Name in Which Acct. Carried	Original Debt	Present Balance	Monthly Payments	Past Due? Yes/No
1. (Landlord or Mortgage Holder)	☐ Rent Payment ☐ Mortgage		$ (Omit rent)	$ (Omit rent)	$	
2.						
3.						
Total Debts			$	$	$	

(Credit References)   Date Paid

1. $

2.

Are you a co-maker, endorser, or guarantor on any loan or contract? Yes ☐ No ☐   If "yes," for whom?   To whom?

Are there any unsatisfied judgments against you? Yes ☐ No ☐ Amount $ If "yes," to whom owed?

Have you been declared bankrupt in the last 14 years Yes ☐ No ☐ If "yes," where?   Year

Other obligations—(E.g., Liability to pay alimony, child support, separate maintenance. Use separate sheet if necessary.)

SECTION E—SECURED CREDIT (Complete only if credit is to be secured.) Briefly describe the property to be given as security:

and list names and addresses of all co-owners of the property:

Name   Address

Everything that I have stated in this application is correct to the best of my knowledge. I understand that you will retain this application whether or not it is approved. You are authorized to check my credit and employment history and to answer questions about your credit experience with me.

Applicant's Signature   Date   Other Signature (Where Applicable)   Date

[Residential real estate mortgage loan]

RESIDENTIAL LOAN APPLICATION

MORTGAGE APPLIED FOR	☐ Conventional ☐ FHA ☐ VA ☐ _____	Amount $	Interest Rate %	No. of Months	Monthly Payment Principal & Interest $	Escrow/Impounds (to be collected monthly) ☐ Taxes ☐ Hazard Ins. ☐ Mtg. Ins. ☐ _____

Prepayment Option

1. SUBJECT PROPERTY

Property Street Address	City	County	State	Zip	No. Units

Legal Description (Attach description if necessary.) — Year Built

Purpose of Loan: ☐ Purchase ☐ Construction-Permanent ☐ Construction ☐ Refinance ☐ Other (Explain)

Complete this line if Construction-Permanent or Construction Loan

	Lot Value Data	Original Cost	Present Value (a)	Cost of Improv. (b)	Total (a + b)	ENTER TOTAL AS PURCHASE PRICE IN DETAILS OF '93 PURCHASE.
Year Acquired ___	$	$	$	$	

Complete this line if a Refinance Loan

Year Acquired	Original Cost	Amt. Existing Liens	Purpose of Refinance	Describe Improvements [ ] made [ ] to be made
	$	$		Cost: $

Title Will Be Held In What Name(s) — Manner in Which Title Will Be Held

Source of Down Payment and Settlement Charges

This application is designed to be completed by the borrower(s) with the lender's assistance. The Co-Borrower Section and all other Co-Borrower questions must be completed and the appropriate boxes(es) checked if ☐ another person will be jointly obligated with the Borrower on the loan, ☐ the Borrower is relying on income from alimony, child support, or separate maintenance or on the income or assets of another person as a basis for repayment of the loan, or ☐ the Borrower is married and resides, or the property is located, in a community property state.

2. BORROWER		**3. CO-BORROWER**	
Name	Age / School Yrs.	Name	Age / School Yrs.
Present Address No. Years ___ ☐ Own ☐ Rent		Present Address No. Years ___ ☐ Own ☐ Rent	
Street		Street	
City/State/Zip		City/State/Zip	
Former address if less than 2 years at present address		Former address if less than 2 years at present address	
Street		Street	
City/State/Zip		City/State/Zip	
Years at former address ☐ Own ☐ Rent		Years at former address ☐ Own ☐ Rent	
Marital: ☐ Married ☐ Separated	Dependents other than listed by Co-borrower No. / Ages	Marital: ☐ Married ☐ Separated	Dependents other than listed by Borrower No. / Ages
Status: ☐ Unmarried (incl. single, divorced, widowed)		Status: ☐ Unmarried (incl. single, divorced, widowed)	
Name and Address of Employer	Years employed in this line of work or profession? ___ years Years on this job ___ ☐ Self Employed	Name and Address of Employer	Years employed in this line of work or profession? ___ years Years on this job ___ ☐ Self Employed
Position/Title	Type of Business	Position/Title	Type of Business
Social Security Number	Home Phone / Business Phone	Social Security Number	Home Phone / Business Phone

4. GROSS MONTHLY INCOME				**5. MONTHLY HOUSING EXPENSE**			**6. DETAILS OF PURCHASE**	
Item	Borrower	Co-Borrower	Total		Present*	Proposed		
Base Empl. Income	$	$	$	Rent	$		a. Purchase Price	$
Overtime				First Mortgage (P&I)		$	b. Total Closing Costs (Est.)	
Bonuses				Other Financing (P&I)			c. Pre Paid Escrows (Est.)	
Commissions				Hazard Insurance			d. Total (a+b+c)	$
Dividends/Interest				Real Estate Taxes			e. Amount of Mortgage	( )
Net Rental Income				Mortgage Insurance			f. Other Financing	( )
Other† (Before completing, see notice under Describe Other Income below.)				Homeowner Assn. Dues			g. Present Equity in Lot	( )
				Other:			h. Amount of Cash Deposit	( )
				Total Monthly Pmt.	$	$	i. Closing Costs Paid by Seller	( )
				Utilities			j. Cash Reqd. For Closing (Est.)	$
Total	$	$	$	Total	$	$		

7. DESCRIBE OTHER INCOME

	B-Borrower C-Co-Borrower	NOTICE: † Alimony, child support, or separate maintenance income need not be revealed if the Borrower or Co-Borrower does not choose to have it considered as a basis for repaying this loan.	Monthly Amount $

8. IF EMPLOYED IN CURRENT POSITION FOR LESS THAN TWO YEARS COMPLETE THE FOLLOWING

B/C	Previous Employer/School	City/State	Type of Business	Position/Title	Dates From/To	Monthly Income
						$

9. THESE QUESTIONS APPLY TO BOTH BORROWERS

If a "yes" answer is given to a question in this column, explain on an attached sheet.   Borrower Yes/No   Co-Borrower Yes/No

	Borrower Yes/No Co-Borrower Yes/No		Borrower Yes/No Co-Borrower Yes/No
Have you any outstanding judgments?		Do you have health and accident insurance?	
In the last 14 years, have you been bankrupt? Have you had property foreclosed upon or given title or a deed in lieu thereof?		Do you have major medical coverage?	
Are you a co-maker or endorser on a note?		Do you intend to occupy the property?	
Are you a party in a law suit?		Will this property be your primary residence?	
Are you obligated to pay alimony, child support, or separate maintenance?		Have you previously owned a home?	
Is any part of the down payment borrowed?		Sale price of previously owned home $ ___ $ ___	

* All Present Monthly Housing Expenses of the Borrower and Co-Borrower should be listed on a combined basis.

This statement and any applicable supporting schedules may be completed jointly by both married and unmarried co-borrowers if their assets and liabilities are sufficiently joined so that the statement can be meaningfully and fairly presented on a combined basis; otherwise separate statements and schedules are required. If the Co-Borrower section was completed about a spouse, this statement and supporting schedules must be completed about that spouse also.

☐ Completed Jointly   ☐ Not Completed Jointly

10. ASSETS			11. LIABILITIES			
Indicate by (*) those liabilities that will be satisfied upon sale of real estate owned or upon refinancing of property.						
Description	Cash or Market Value	Creditor's Name, Address, Account Number	Acct. Name if Not Borrower(s)	Mo. Pmt. and Mos. left to pay	Unpaid Balance
Cash Deposit Toward Purchase Held By	$	Instalment Debts (include "revolving" charge accounts)		$ Pmt./Mos. /	$
Checking and Savings Accounts (Names of Institutions/ Acct. Nos.)				/	
				/	
				/	
Stocks and Bonds (No./description)		Automobile Loans		/	
Life Insurance Net Cash Value				/	
Face Amount ($)		Real Estate Loans			
SUBTOTAL LIQUID ASSETS $					
Real Estate Owned (Enter Market Value from Schedule of Real Estate Owned)					
Vested Interest in Retirement Fund		Other Debt, Including Stock Pledges			
Net Worth of Business Owned (Attach Financial Stat.)					
Automobiles (Make and Year)				/	
Furniture and Personal Property		Alimony, Child Support, and Maintenance Payments (Owed To)			
Other Assets (Itemize)					
		TOTAL MONTHLY PAYMENTS		$	
TOTAL ASSETS A $		NET WORTH (A minus B) $		TOTAL LIABILITIES B	$

SCHEDULE OF REAL ESTATE OWNED (If Additional Properties Owned Attach Separate Schedule)

Address of Property (Indicate S if Sold, PS if Pending Sale or R if Rental being held for income)		Type of Property	Present Market Value	Amount of Mortgages & Liens	Gross Rental Income	Mortgage Payments	Taxes, Ins. Maintenance and Misc.	Net Rental Income
	⇩		$	$	$	$	$	$
TOTALS			$	$	$	$	$	$

12. LIST PREVIOUS CREDIT REFERENCES

⇩ B-Borrower C-Co-Borrower	Creditor's Name and Address	Account Number	Purpose	Highest Balance	Date Paid

List any additional names under which credit has previously been received _____

AGREEMENT: The Undersigned applies for the loan indicated in this application, to be secured by a first mortgage or deed of trust on the property described herein, and represents that the property will not be used for any illegal or restricted purpose and that all statements made in this application are true and are made for the purpose of obtaining the loan. Verification may be obtained from any source named in this application. The original or a copy of this application will be retained by the lender, even if the loan is not granted.

Borrower's Signature_____Date / /   Co-Borrower's Signature_____Date / /

INFORMATION FOR GOVERNMENT MONITORING PURPOSES

The following information is requested by the federal government for certain types of loans related to a dwelling in order to monitor the lender's compliance with equal credit opportunity and fair housing laws. You are not required to furnish this information, but are encouraged to do so. The law provides that a lender may neither discriminate on the basis of this information, nor on whether you choose to furnish it. However, if you choose not to furnish the information, under federal regulations the lender is required to note race or national origin and sex on the basis of visual observation or surname. If you do not wish to furnish the information, please check below.

BORROWER:	I do not wish to furnish this information ☐	CO-BORROWER:	I do not wish to furnish this information ☐
RACE OR NATIONAL ORIGIN	☐ American Indian, Alaskan Native ☐ Asian, Pacific Islander ☐ Black ☐ Hispanic ☐ White ☐ Other (specify) _____	RACE OR NATIONAL ORIGIN	☐ American Indian, Alaskan Native ☐ Asian, Pacific Islander ☐ Black ☐ Hispanic ☐ White ☐ Other (specify) _____
SEX	☐ Female ☐ Male	SEX	☐ Female ☐ Male

FOR LENDER'S USE ONLY

APPENDIX C—SAMPLE NOTIFICATION FORMS

This appendix contains eight sample notification forms. Forms C-1 through C-4 are intended for use in notifying an applicant that adverse action has been taken on an application or account under section 202.9(a) (1) and (2) (i) of this regulation. Form C-5 is a notice of disclosure of the right to request specific reasons for adverse action under section 202.9(a)(l) and (2)(ii). Form C-6 is designed for use in notifying an applicant, under section 202.9(c)(2), that an application is incomplete. Forms C-7 and C-8 are intended for use in connection with applications for business credit under section 202.9(a) (3).

Form C-1 contains the Fair Credit Reporting Act disclosure as required by sections 615(a) and (b) of that act. Forms C-2 through C-5 contain only the section 615(a) disclosure (that a creditor obtained information from a consumer reporting agency that played a part in the credit decision). A creditor must provide the section 615(b) disclosure (that a creditor obtained information from an outside source other than a consumer reporting agency that played a part in the credit decision) where appropriate.

The sample forms are illustrative and may not be appropriate for all creditors. They were designed to include some of the factors that creditors most commonly consider. If a creditor chooses to use the checklist of reasons provided in one of the sample forms in this appendix and if reasons commonly used by the creditor are not provided on the form, the creditor should modify the checklist by substituting or adding other reasons. For example, if "inadequate downpayment" or "no deposit relationship with us" are common reasons for taking adverse action on an application, the creditor ought to add or substitute such reasons for those presently contained on the sample forms.

If the reasons listed on the forms are not the factors actually used, a creditor will not satisfy the notice requirement by simply checking the closest identifiable factor listed. For example, some creditors consider only references from banks or other depository institutions and disregard finance company references altogether; their statement of reasons should disclose "insufficient bank references," not "insufficient credit references." Similarly, a creditor that considers bank references and other credit references as distinct factors should treat the two factors separately and disclose them as appropriate. The creditor should either add such other factors to the form or check "other" and include the appropriate explanation. The creditor need not, however, describe how or why a factor adversely affected the application. For example, the notice may say "length of residence" rather than "too short a period of residence."

A creditor may design its own notification forms or use all or a portion of the forms contained in this appendix. Proper use of Forms C- 1 through C-4 will satisfy the requirement of section 202.9(a)(2)(i). Proper use of Forms C-5 and C-6 constitutes full compliance with sections 202.9(a)(2)(ii) and 202.9(c) (2), respectively. Proper use of Forms C-7 and C-8 will satisfy the requirements of section 202.9(a) (2) (i) and (ii), respectively, for applications for business credit.

FORM C-l—SAMPLE NOTICE OF ACTION TAKEN AND STATEMENT OF REASONS

Statement of Credit Denial, Termination, or Change

Date_____

Applicant's Name: _____

Applicant's Address: _____

Description of Account, Transaction, or Requested Credit:

_____

Description of Action Taken:

_____
_____

Part I—**PRINCIPAL REASON(S) FOR CREDIT DENIAL, TERMINATION, OR OTHER ACTION TAKEN CONCERNING CREDIT.** This section must be completed in all instances.

— Credit application incomplete
— Insufficient number of credit references provided
— Unacceptable type of credit references provided
— Unable to verify credit references
— Temporary or irregular employment
— Unable to verify employment
— Length of employment
— Income insufficient for amount of credit requested
— Excessive obligations in relation to income
— Unable to verify income
— Length of residence
— Temporary residence
— Unable to verify residence
— No credit file
— Limited credit experience
— Poor credit performance with us
— Delinquent past or present credit obligations with others
— Garnishment, attachment, foreclosure, repossession, collection action, or judgment
— Bankruptcy
— Value or type of collateral not sufficient
— Other, specify: _____

Part II—**DISCLOSURE OF USE OF INFORMATION OBTAINED FROM AN OUT-SIDE SOURCE.** This section should be completed if the credit decision was based in whole or in part on information that has been obtained from an outside source.

__ Our credit decision was based in whole or in part on information obtained in a report from the consumer reporting agency listed below. You have a right under the Fair Credit Reporting Act to know the information contained in your credit file at the consumer reporting agency. The reporting agency played no part in our decision and is unable to supply specific reasons why we have denied credit to you.

Name: _____

Address: _____

Telephone number: _____

__ Our credit decision was based in whole or in part on information obtained from an outside source other than a consumer reporting agency. Under the Fair Credit Reporting Act, you have the right to make a written request, no later than 60 days after you receive this notice, for disclosure of the nature of this information.

If you have any questions regarding this notice, you should contact:

Creditor's name: _____

Creditor's address: _____

Creditor's telephone number: _____

NOTICE: The federal Equal Credit Opportunity Act prohibits creditors from discriminating against credit applicants on the basis of race, color, religion, national origin, sex, marital status, age (provided the applicant has the capacity to enter into a binding contract); because all or part of the applicant's income derives from any public assistance program; or because the applicant has in good faith exercised any right under the Consumer Credit Protection Act. The federal agency that administers compliance with this law concerning this creditor is (name and address as specified by the appropriate agency listed in appendix A).

FORM C-2—SAMPLE NOTICE OF ACTION TAKEN AND STATEMENT OF REASONS

Date

Dear Applicant:

Thank you for your recent application. Your request for [a loan/a credit card/an increase in your credit limit] was carefully considered, and we regret that we are unable to approve your application at this time, for the following reason(s):

Your Income:

__ is below our minimum requirement.

__ is insufficient to sustain payments on the amount of credit requested.

__ could not be verified.

Your Employment:

__ is not of sufficient length to qualify.

__ could not be verified.

Your Credit History:

__ of making payments on time was not satisfactory.

__ could not be verified.

Your Application:

__ lacks a sufficient number of credit references.

__ lacks acceptable types of credit references.

__ reveals that current obligations are excessive in relation to income.

Other:_____

The consumer reporting agency contacted that provided information that influenced our decision in whole or in part was [name, address and telephone number of the reporting agency]. The reporting agency is unable to supply specific reasons why we have denied credit to you. You do, however, have a right under the Fair Credit Reporting Act to know the information contained in your credit file. Any questions regarding such information should be directed to [consumer reporting agency].

If you have any questions regarding this letter you should contact us at [creditor's name, address and telephone number].

NOTICE: The federal Equal Credit Opportunity Act prohibits creditors from discriminating against credit applicants on the basis of race, color, religion, national origin, sex, marital status, age (provided the applicant has the capacity to enter into a binding contract); because all or part of the applicant's income derives from any public assistance program; or because the applicant has in good faith exercised any right under the Consumer Credit Protection Act. The federal agency that administers compliance with this law concerning this creditor is (name and address as specified by the appropriate agency listed in appendix A).

Form C-3—Sample Notice of Action Taken and Statement of Reasons (Credit Scoring)

Date

Dear Applicant:

Thank you for your recent application for _____. We regret that we are unable to approve your request.

Your application was processed by a credit scoring system that assigns a numerical value to the various items of information we consider in evaluating an application. These numerical values are based upon the results of analyses of repayment histories of large numbers of customers.

The information you provided in your application did not score a sufficient number of points for approval of the application. The reasons you did not score well compared with other applicants were:

- Insufficient bank references
- Type of occupation
- Insufficient credit experience

In evaluating your application the consumer reporting agency listed below provided us with information that in whole or in part influenced our decision. The reporting agency played no part in our decision other than providing us with credit information about you. Under the Fair Credit Reporting Act, you have a right to know the information provided to us. It can be obtained by contacting: [name, address, and telephone number of the consumer reporting agency].

If you have any questions regarding this letter, you should contact us at

Creditor's Name: _____

Address: _____

_____

Telephone: _____

Sincerely,

NOTICE: The federal Equal Credit Opportunity Act prohibits creditors from discriminating against credit applicants on the basis of race, color, religion, national origin, sex, marital status, age (with certain limited exceptions); because all or part of the applicant's income derives from any public assistance program; or because the applicant has in good faith exercised any right under the Consumer Credit Protection Act. The federal agency that administers compliance with this law concerning this creditor is (name and address as specified by the appropriate agency listed in appendix A).

FORM C-4—SAMPLE NOTICE OF ACTION TAKEN, STATEMENT OF REASONS, AND COUNTEROFFER

Date

Dear Applicant:

Thank you for your application for _____. We are unable to offer you credit on the terms that you requested for the following reason(s):

We can, however, offer you credit on the following terms: _____

_____.

If this offer is acceptable to you, please notify us within [amount of time] at the following address: _____.

Our credit decision on your application was based in whole or in part on information obtained in a report from [name, address and telephone number of the consumer reporting agency]. You have a right under the Fair Credit Reporting Act to know the information contained in your credit file at the consumer reporting agency.

You should know that the federal Equal Credit Opportunity Act prohibits creditors, such as ourselves, from discriminating against credit applicants on the basis of their race, color, religion, national origin, sex, marital status, age because they receive income from a public assistance program, or because they may have exercised their rights under the Consumer Credit Protection Act. If you believe there has been discrimination in handling your application you should contact the [name and address of the appropriate federal enforcement agency listed in appendix A].

Sincerely,

FORM C-5—SAMPLE DISCLOSURE OF RIGHT TO REQUEST SPECIFIC REASONS FOR CREDIT DENIAL

Date

Dear Applicant:

Thank you for applying to us for _____.

After carefully reviewing your application, we are sorry to advise you that we cannot [open an account for you/grant a loan to you/increase your credit limit] at this time.

If you would like a statement of specific reasons why your application was denied, please contact [our credit service manager] shown below within 60 days of the date of this letter. We will provide you with the statement of reasons within 30 days after receiving your request.

Creditor's Name
Address
Telephone number

If we obtained information from a consumer reporting agency as part of our consideration of your application, its name, address, and telephone number is shown below. You can find out about the information contained in your file (if one was used) by contacting:

Consumer reporting agency's name
Address
Telephone number

Sincerely,

NOTICE: The federal Equal Credit Opportunity Act prohibits creditors from discriminating against credit applicants on the basis of race, color, religion, national origin, sex, marital status, age (provided the applicant has the capacity to enter into a binding contract); because all or part of the applicant's income derives from any public assistance program; or because the applicant has in good faith exercised any right under the Consumer Credit Protection Act. The federal agency that administers compliance with this law concerning this creditor is (name and address as specified by the appropriate agency listed in appendix A).

FORM C-6—SAMPLE NOTICE OF INCOMPLETE APPLICATION AND REQUEST FOR ADDITIONAL INFORMATION

Creditor's name
Address
Telephone number

Date

Dear Applicant:

Thank you for your application for credit. The following information is needed to make a decision on your application: _____.

We need to receive this information by ____(date) . If we do not receive it by that date, we will regrettably be unable to give further consideration to your credit request.

Sincerely,

FORM C-7—SAMPLE NOTICE OF ACTION TAKEN AND STATEMENT OF REASONS (BUSINESS CREDIT)

Creditor's Name
Creditor's address

Date

Dear Applicant:
Thank you for applying to us for credit. We have given your request careful consideration, and regret that we are unable to extend credit to you at this time for the following reasons:
[Insert appropriate reason, such as
Value or type of collateral not sufficient
Lack of established earnings record
Slow or past due in trade or loan payments]

Sincerely,

NOTICE: The federal Equal Credit Opportunity Act prohibits creditors from discriminating against credit applicants on the basis of race, color, religion, national origin, sex, marital status, age (provided the applicant has the capacity to enter into a binding contract); because all or part of the applicant's income derives from any public assistance program; or because the applicant has in good faith exercised any right under the Consumer Credit Protection Act. The federal agency that administers compliance with this law concerning this creditor is [name and address as specified by the appropriate agency listed in appendix A].

FORM C-8—SAMPLE DISCLOSURE OF RIGHT TO REQUEST SPECIFIC REASONS FOR CREDIT DENIAL GIVEN AT TIME OF APPLICATION (BUSINESS CREDIT)

Creditor's name
Creditor's address

If your application for business credit is denied, you have the right to a written statement of the specific reasons for the denial. To obtain the statement, please contact [name, address and telephone number of the person or office from which the statement of reasons can be obtained] within 60 days from the date you are notified of our decision. We will send you a written statement of reasons for the denial within 30 days of receiving your request for the statement.

NOTICE: The federal Equal Credit Opportunity Act prohibits creditors from discriminating against credit applicants on the basis of race, color, religion, national origin, sex, marital status, age (provided the applicant has the capacity to enter into a binding contract); because all or part of the applicant's income derives from any public assistance program; or because the applicant has in good faith exercised any right under the Consumer Credit Protection Act. The federal agency that administers compliance with this law concerning this creditor is [name and address as specified by the appropriate agency listed in appendix A].

APPENDIX D—ISSUANCE OF STAFF INTERPRETATIONS

Official Staff Interpretations

Officials in the Board's Division of Consumer and Community Affairs are authorized to issue official staff interpretations of this regulation. These interpretations provide the protection afforded under section 706(e) of the act. Except in unusual circumstances, such interpretations will not be issued separately but will be incorporated in an official commentary to the regulation, which will be amended periodically.

Requests for Issuance of Official Staff Interpretations

A request for an official staff interpretation should be in writing and addressed to the Director, Division of Consumer and Community Affairs, Board of Governors of the Federal Reserve System, Washington, D.C. 20551. The request should contain a complete statement of all relevant facts concerning the issue, including copies of all pertinent documents.

Scope of Interpretations

No staff interpretations will be issued approving creditors' forms or statements. This restriction does not apply to forms or statements whose use is required or sanctioned by a government agency.

EQUAL CREDIT OPPORTUNITY ACT

15 USC 1691; as added by Pub. L. 93-495, Title V, 88 Stat. 1521 (October 28, 1974)

PUBLIC LAW 93–495, TITLE V

Section
502   Findings and purpose
503   Amendment to the Consumer Credit Protection Act

Section 502—Findings and Purpose

The Congress finds that there is a need to insure that the various financial institutions and other firms engaged in the extensions of credit exercise their responsibility to make credit available with fairness, impartiality, and without discrimination on the basis of sex or marital status. Economic stabilization would be enhanced and competition among the various financial institutions and other firms engaged in the extension of credit would be strengthened by an absence of discrimination on the basis of sex or marital status, as well as by the informed use of credit which Congress has heretofore sought to promote. It is the purpose of this Act to require that financial institutions and other firms engaged in the extension of credit make that credit equally available to all creditworthy customers without regard to sex or marital status.

[15 USC 1691 note.]

Section 503—Amendment to the Consumer Credit Protection Act

The Consumer Credit Protection Act (Public Law 90-321) is amended by adding at the end thereof a new title VII:

TITLE VII—EQUAL CREDIT OPPORTUNITY

Section

Section 701—Prohibited Discrimination; Reasons for Adverse Action*

(a)   It shall be unlawful for any creditor to discriminate against any applicant, with respect to any aspect of a credit transaction—

    (1)   on the basis of race, color, religion, national origin, sex or marital status, or age (provided the applicant has the capacity to contract);

    (2)   because all or part of the applicant's income derives from any public assistance program; or

    (3)   because the applicant has in good faith exercised any right under the Consumer Credit Protection Act.

(b)   It shall not constitute discrimination for purposes of this title for a creditor—

    (1)   to make an inquiry of marital status if such inquiry is for the purpose of ascertaining the creditor's rights and remedies applicable to the particular extension of credit and not to discriminate in a determination of creditworthiness;

    (2)   to make an inquiry of the applicant's age or of whether the applicant's income derives from any public assistance program if such inquiry is for the purpose of determining the amount and probable continuance of income levels, credit history, or other pertinent element of creditworthiness as provided in regulations of the Board;

(3)   to use any empirically derived credit system which considers age if such system is demonstrably and statistically sound in accordance with regulations of the Board, except that in the operation of such system the age of an elderly applicant may not be assigned a negative factor or value; or

(4)   to make an inquiry or to consider the age of an elderly applicant when the age of such applicant is to be used by the creditor in the extension of credit in favor of such applicant.

(c)   It is not a violation of this section for a creditor to refuse to extend credit offered pursuant to—

(1)   any credit assistance program expressly authorized by law for an economically disadvantaged class of persons;

(2)   any credit assistance program administered by a nonprofit organization for its members or an economically disadvantaged class of persons; or

(3)   any special purpose credit program offered by a profitmaking organization to meet special social needs which meets standards prescribed in regulations by the Board; if such refusal is required by or made pursuant to such program.

(d) (1)   Within thirty days (or such longer reasonable time as specified in regulations of the Board for any class of credit transaction) after receipt of a completed application for credit, a creditor shall notify the applicant of its action on the application.

(2)   Each applicant against whom adverse action is taken shall be entitled to a statement of reasons for such action from the creditor. A creditor satisfies this obligation by—

(A)   providing statements of reasons in writing as a matter of course to applicants against whom adverse action is taken; or

(B)   giving written notification of adverse action which discloses (i) the applicant's right to a statement of reasons within thirty days after receipt by the creditor of a request made within sixty days after such notification, and (ii) the identity of the person or office from which such statement may be obtained. Such statement may be given orally if the written notification advises the applicant of his right to have the statement of reasons confirmed in writing on written request.

(3)   A statement of reasons meets the requirements of this section only if it contains the specific reasons for the adverse action taken.

(4)   Where a creditor has been requested by a third party to make a specific extension of credit directly or indirectly to an applicant, the notification and statement of reasons required by this subsection may be made directly by such creditor, or indirectly through the third party, provided in either case that the identity of the creditor is disclosed.

(5)   The requirements of paragraph (2), (3), or (4) may be satisfied by verbal statements or notifications in the case of any creditor who did not act on more than 150 applications during the calendar year preceding the calendar year in which the adverse action is taken, as determined under regulations of the Board.

(6)   For purposes of this subsection, the term "adverse action" means a denial or revocation of credit, a change in the terms of an existing credit arrangement, or a refusal to grant credit in substantially the amount or on substantially the terms requested. Such term does not include a refusal to extend additional credit under an existing credit arrangement where the applicant is delinquent or otherwise in default, or where such additional credit would exceed a previously established credit limit.

[15 USC 1691. As amended by act of March 23, 1976 (90 Stat. 251).]

Section 702—Definitions

(a) The definitions and rules of construction set forth in this section are applicable for the purposes of this title.

(b) The term "applicant" means any person who applies to a creditor directly for an extension, renewal, or continuation of credit, or applies to a creditor indirectly by use of an existing credit plan for an amount exceeding a previously established credit limit.

(c) The term "Board" refers to the Board of Governors of the Federal Reserve System.

(d) The term "credit" means the right granted by a creditor to a debtor to defer payment of debt or to incur debt and defer its payment or to purchase property or services and defer payment therefor.

(e) The term "creditor" means any person who regularly extends, renews, or continues credit; any person who regularly arranges for the extension, renewal, or continuation of credit; or any assignee of an original creditor who participates in the decision to extend, renew, or continue credit.

(f) The term "person" means a natural person, a corporation, government or governmental subdivision or agency, trust, estate, partnership, cooperative, or association.

(g) Any reference to any requirement imposed under this title or any provision thereof includes reference to the regulations of the Board under this title or the provision thereof in question.

[15 USC 1691a.]

Section 703—Regulations

(a) (1) The Board shall prescribe regulations to carry out the purposes of this title. These regulations may contain but are not limited to such classifications, differentiation, or other provision, and may provide for such adjustments and exceptions for any class of transactions, as in the judgment of the Board are necessary or proper to effectuate the purposes of this title, to prevent circumvention or evasion thereof, or to facilitate or substantiate compliance therewith.

(2)   Such regulations may exempt from the provisions of this title any class of transactions that are not primarily for personal, family, or household purposes, or business or commercial loans made available by a financial institution, except that a particular type within a class of such transactions may be

*Effective date for amendments to section 701 is March 23, 1977. All other amendments are effective upon enactment.

exempted if the Board determines, after making an express finding that the application of this title or of any provision of this title of such transaction would not contribute substantially to effecting the purposes of this title.

(3) An exemption granted pursuant to paragraph (2) shall be for no longer than five years and shall be extended only if the Board makes a subsequent determination, in the manner described by such paragraph, that such exemption remains appropriate.

(4) Pursuant to Board regulations, entities making business or commercial loans shall maintain such records or other data relating to such loans as may be necessary to evidence compliance with this subsection or enforce any action pursuant to the authority of this Act. In no event shall such records or data be maintained for a period of less than one year. The Board shall promulgate regulations to implement this paragraph in the manner prescribed by chapter 5 of title 5, United States Code.

(5) The Board shall provide in regulations that an applicant for a business or commercial loan shall be provided a written notice of such applicant's right to receive a written statement of the reasons for the denial of such loan.

(b) The Board shall establish a Consumer Advisory Council to advise and consult with it in the exercise of its functions under the Consumer Credit Protection Act and to advise and consult with it concerning other consumer related matters it may place before the Council. In appointing the members of the Council, the Board shall seek to achieve a fair representation of the interests of creditors and consumers. The Council shall meet from time to time at the call of the Board. Members of the Council who are not regular full-time employees of the United States shall, while attending meetings of such Council, be entitled to receive compensation at a rate fixed by the Board, but not exceeding $100 per day, including travel time. Such members may be allowed travel expenses, including transportation and subsistence, while away from their homes or regular place of business.

[15 USC 1691b. As amended by acts of March 23, 1976 (90 Stat. 252) and Oct. 25, 1988 (102 Stat. 2692).]

Section 704—Administrative Enforcement

(a) Compliance with the requirements imposed under this title shall be enforced under:

(1) Section 8 of the Federal Deposit Insurance Act, in the case of—

(A) national banks, by the Comptroller of the Currency;

(B) member banks of the Federal Reserve System (other than national banks), by the Board;

(C) banks insured by the Federal Deposit Insurance Corporation (other than members of the Federal Reserve System), by the Board of Directors of the Federal Deposit Insurance Corporation.

(2) Section 8 of the Federal Deposit Insurance Act, by the Director of the Office of Thrift Supervision, in the case of a savings association the deposits of which are insured by the Federal Deposit Insurance Corporation.

(3) The Federal Credit Union Act, by the Administrator of the National Credit Union Administration with respect to any Federal Credit Union.

(4)   The Acts to regulate commerce, by the Interstate Commerce Commission with respect to any common carrier subject to those Acts.

(5)   The Federal Aviation Act of 1958, by the Secretary of Transportation with respect to any air carrier or foreign air carrier subject to that Act.

(6)   The Packers and Stockyards Act, 1921 (except as provided in section 406 of that Act), by the Secretary of Agriculture with respect to any activities subject to that Act.

(7)   The Farm Credit Act of 1971, by the Farm Credit Administration with respect to any Federal land bank, Federal land bank association, Federal intermediate credit bank, and production credit association.

(8)   The Securities Exchange Act of 1934, by the Securities and Exchange Commission with respect to brokers and dealers; and

(9)   The Small Business Investment Act of 1958, by the Small Business Administration, with respect to small business investment companies.

(b) For the purpose of the exercise by any agency referred to in subsection (a) of its powers under any Act referred to in that subsection, a violation of any requirement imposed under this title shall be deemed to be a violation of a requirement imposed under that Act. In addition m its powers under any provision of law specifically referred to in subsection (a), each of the agencies referred to in that subsection may exercise for the purpose of enforcing compliance with any requirement imposed under this title, any other authority conferred on it by law. The exercise of the authorities of any of the agencies referred to in subsection (a) for the purpose of enforcing compliance with any requirement imposed under this title shall in no way preclude the exercise of such authorities for the purpose of enforcing compliance with any other provision of law not relating to the prohibition of discrimination on the basis of sex or marital status with respect to any aspect of a credit transaction.

(c) Except to the extent that enforcement of the requirements imposed under this title is specifically committed to some other Government agency under subsection (a), the Federal Trade Commission shall enforce such requirements. For the purpose of the exercise by the Federal Trade Commission of its functions and powers under the Federal Trade Commission Act, a violation of any requirement imposed under this title shall be deemed a violation of a requirement imposed under that Act. All of the functions and powers of the Federal Trade Commission under the Federal Trade Commission Act are available to the Commission to enforce compliance by any person with the requirements imposed under this title, irrespective of whether that person is engaged in commerce or meets any other jurisdictional tests in the Federal Trade Commission Act, including the power to enforce any Federal Reserve Board regulation promulgated under this title in the same manner as if the violation had been a violation of a Federal Trade Commission trade regulation rule.

(d) The authority of the Board to issue regulations under this title does not impair the authority of any other agency designated in this section to make rules respecting its own procedures in enforcing compliance with requirements imposed under this title.

[15 USC 1691c. As amended by acts of March 23, 1976 (90 Stat. 253): Oct. 3, 1984 (98 Stat. 1708); and Aug. 9, 1989 (103 Stat. 439).]

Section 705—Relation to State Laws

(a) A request for the signature of both parties to a marriage for the purpose of creating a valid lien, passing clear title, waiving inchoate rights to property, or assigning earnings, shall not constitute discrimination under this title. *Provided, however,* that this provision shall not be construed to permit a creditor to take sex or marital status into account in connection with the evaluation of creditworthiness of any applicant.

(b) Consideration or application of State property laws directly or indirectly affecting creditworthiness shall not constitute discrimination for purposes of this title.

(c) Any provision of State law which prohibits the separate extension of consumer credit to each party to a marriage shall not apply in any case where each party to a marriage voluntarily applies for separate credit from the same creditor: *Provided,* that in any case where such a State law is so preempted, each party to the marriage shall be solely responsible for the debt so contracted.

(d) When each party to a marriage separately and voluntarily applies for and obtains separate credit accounts with the same creditor, those accounts shall not be aggregated or otherwise combined for purposes of determining permissible finance charges or permissible loan ceilings under the laws of any State or of the United States.

(e) Where the same act or omission constitutes a violation of this title and of applicable State law, a person aggrieved by such conduct may bring a legal action to recover monetary damages either under this title or under such State law, but not both. This election of remedies shall not apply to court actions in which the relief sought does not include monetary damages or to administrative actions.

(f) This title does not annul, alter, or affect, or exempt any person subject to the provisions of this title from complying with, the laws of any State with respect to credit discrimination, except to the extent that those laws are inconsistent with any provision of this title, and then only to the extent of the inconsistency. The Board is authorized to determine whether such inconsistencies exist. The Board may not determine that any State law is inconsistent with any provision of this title if the Board determines that such law gives greater protection to the applicant.

(g) The Board shall by regulation exempt from the requirements of sections 701 and 702 of this title any class of credit transactions within any State if it determines that under the law of that State that class of transactions is subject to requirements substantially similar to those imposed under this title or that such law gives greater protection to the applicant, and that there is adequate provision for enforcement. Failure to comply with any requirement of such State law in any transaction so exempted shall constitute a violation of this title for the purposes of section 706.

[15 USC 1691d. As amended by act of March 23, 1976 (90 Stat. 253).]

Section 706—Civil Liability

(a) Any creditor who fails to comply with any requirement imposed under this title shall be liable to the aggrieved applicant for any actual damages sustained by such applicant acting either in an individual capacity or as a member of a class.

(b) Any creditor, other than a government or governmental subdivision or agency, who fails to comply with any requirement imposed under this title shall be liable to the aggrieved applicant for punitive damages in an amount not greater than $10,000, in addition to any actual damages provided in subsection (a), except that in the case of a class action the total recovery under this subsection shall not exceed the lesser of $500,000 or 1 per centum of the net worth of the creditor. In determining the amount of such damages in any action, the court shall consider, among other relevant factors, the amount of any actual damages awarded, the frequency and persistence of failures of compliance by the creditor, the resources of the creditor, the number of persons adversely affected, and the extent to which the creditor's failure of compliance was intentional.

(c) Upon application by an aggrieved applicant, the appropriate United States district court or any other court of competent jurisdiction may grant such equitable and declaratory relief as is necessary to enforce the requirements imposed under this title.

(d) In the case of any successful action under subsection (a), (b), or (c), the costs of the action, together with a reasonable attorney's fee as determined by the court, shall be added to any damages awarded by the court under such subsection.

(e) No provision of this title imposing any liability shall apply to any act done or omitted in good faith in conformity with any official rule, regulation, or interpretation thereof by the Board or in conformity with any interpretation or approval by an official or employee of the Federal Reserve System duly authorized by the Board to issue such interpretations or approvals under such procedures as the Board may prescribe therefor, notwithstanding that after such act or omission has occurred, such rule, regulation, interpretation, or approval is amended, rescinded, or determined by judicial or other authority to be invalid for any reason.

(f) Any action under this section may be brought in the appropriate United States district court without regard to the amount in controversy, or in any other court of competent jurisdiction. No such action shall be brought later than two years from the date of the occurrence of the violation, except that—

(1) whenever any agency having responsibility for administrative enforcement under section 704 commences an enforcement proceeding within two years from the date of the occurrence of the violation,

(2) whenever the Attorney General commences a civil action under this section within two years from the date of occurrence of the violation, then any applicant who has been a victim of the discrimination which is the subject of such proceeding or civil action may bring an action under this section not later than one year after the commencement of that proceeding or action.

(g) The agencies having responsibility for administrative enforcement under section 704, if unable to obtain compliance with section 701, are authorized to refer the matter to the Attorney General with a recommendation that an appropriate civil action be instituted.

(h) When a matter is referred to the Attorney General pursuant to subsection (g), or whenever he has reason to believe that one or more creditors are engaged in a pattern or practice in violation of this title, the Attorney General may bring a civil action in any appropriate United States district court for such relief as may be appropriate, including injunctive relief.

(i) No person aggrieved by a violation of this title and by a violation of section 805 of the Civil Rights Act of 1968 shall recover under this title and section 812 of the Civil Rights Act of 1968, if such violation is based on the same transaction.

(j) Nothing in this title shall be construed to prohibit the discovery of a creditor's credit granting standards under appropriate discovery procedures in the court or agency in which an action or proceeding is brought.

[15 USC 1691e. As amended by act of March 23, 1976 (90 Stat. 253).]

Section 707—Annual Reports to Congress

Each year, the Board and the Attorney General shall, respectively, make reports to the Congress concerning the administration of their functions under this title, including such recommendations as the Board and the Attorney General, respectively, deem necessary or appropriate. In addition, each report of the Board shall include its assessment of the extent to which compliance with the requirements of this title is being achieved, and a summary of the enforcement actions taken by each of the agencies assigned administrative enforcement responsibilities under section 704.

[15 USC 1691f. As added by act of March 23, 1976 (90 Stat. 255) and amended by act of March 31, 1980 (94 Stat. 174).]

Section 708—Effective Date

This title takes effect upon the expiration of one year after the date of its enactment. The amendments made by the Equal Credit Opportunity Act Amendments of 1976 shall take effect on the date of enactment thereof and shall apply to any violation occurring on or after such date, except that the amendments made to section 701 of the Equal Credit Opportunity Act shall take effect 12 months after the date of enactment.

[15 USC 1691 note.]

Section 709—Short Title

This title may be cited as the "Equal Credit Opportunity Act."

[15 USC 1691 note.]

CHAPTER 13
Appendix II

Amendments to Regulation B and the Equal Credit Opportunity Act
February 1998*

1. Effective December 14, 1993, the last sentence of section 202.1(b) is amended to read as follows:
The regulation also requires creditors to notify applicants of action taken on their applications; to report credit history in the names of both spouses on an account; to retain records of credit applications; to collect information about the applicant's race and other personal characteristics in applications for certain dwelling-related loans; and to provide applicants with copies of appraisal reports used in connection with credit transactions.

2. Effective December 14, 1993, a new section 202.5a is added:

SECTION 202.5a—Rules on Providing Appraisal Reports
(a) *Providing appraisals.* A creditor shall provide a copy of the appraisal report used in connection with an application for credit that is to be secured by a lien on a dwelling. A creditor shall comply with either paragraph (a)(I) or (a)(2) of this section.

    (1) *Routine delivery.* A creditor may routinely provide a copy of the appraisal report to an applicant (whether credit is granted or denied or the application is withdrawn).

    (2) *Upon request.* A creditor that does not routinely provide appraisal reports shall provide a copy upon an applicant's written request.

---

*   A complete Regulation B, as amended January 30, 1998, consists of—
- the regulation pamphlet dated February 1990 (see inside front cover) and
- this slip sheet.

Items 3, 5, and II are new. The other items were included in the May 1994 slip sheet.

(i) *Notice.* A creditor that provides appraisal reports only upon request shall notify an applicant in writing of the right to receive a copy of an appraisal report. The notice may be given at any time during the application process but no later than when the creditor provides notice of action taken under section 202.9 of this part. The notice shall specify that the applicant's request must be in writing, give the creditor's mailing address, and state the time for making the request as provided in paragraph (a)(2)(ii) of this section.

(ii) *Delivery.* A creditor shall mail or deliver a copy of the appraisal report promptly (generally within 30 days) after the creditor receives an applicant's request, receives the report, or receives reimbursement from the applicant for the report, whichever is last to occur. A creditor need not provide a copy when the applicant's request is received more than 90 days after the creditor has provided notice of action taken on the application under section 202.9 of this part or 90 days after the application is withdrawn.

(b) *Credit unions.* A creditor that is subject to the regulations of the National Credit Union Administration on making copies of appraisals available is not subject to this section.

(c) *Definitions.* For purposes of paragraph (a) of this section, the term dwelling means a residential structure that contains one to four units whether or not that structure is attached to real property. The term includes, but is not limited to, an individual condominium or cooperative unit, and a mobile or other manufactured home. The term appraisal report means the document(s) relied upon by a creditor in evaluating the value of the dwelling.

3. *Effective January 30, 1998, section 202.12(b)(6) is added to read as follows:*

(6) *Self-tests.* For 25 months after a self-test (as defined in section 202.15) has been completed, the creditor shall retain all written or recorded information about the self-test. A creditor shall retain information beyond 25 months if it has actual notice that it is under investigation or is subject to an enforcement proceeding for an alleged violation, or if it has been served with notice of a civil action. In such cases, the creditor shall retain the information until final disposition of the matter, unless an earlier time is allowed by the appropriate agency or court order.

4. *Effective December 14, 1993, section 202.14(b) is amended by revising paragraph (3) and by adding new paragraphs (4) and (5), to read as follows:*

(3) If an agency responsible for administrative enforcement is unable to obtain compliance with the act or this regulation, it may refer the matter to the attorney general of the United States. In addition, if the Board, the Comptroller of the Currency, the Federal Deposit Insurance Corporation, the Office of Thrift Supervision, or the National Credit Union Administration has reason to believe that one or more creditors engaged in a pattern or practice of discouraging or denying applications in violation of the act or this regulation, the agency shall refer the matter to the attorney general. Furthermore, the agency may refer a matter to the attorney general if the agency has reason to believe that one or more creditors violated section 701(a) of the act.

(4) On referral, or whenever the attorney general has reason to believe that one or more creditors engaged in a pattern of practice in violation of the act or this regulation, the attorney general may bring a civil action for such relief as may be appropriate, including actual and punitive damages and injunctive relief.

(5) If the Board, the Comptroller of the Currency, the Federal Deposit Insurance Corporation, the Office of Thrift Supervision, or the National Credit Union Administration has reason to believe (as a result of a consumer complaint, conducting a consumer compliance examination, or otherwise) that a violation of the act or this regulation has occurred which is also a violation of the Fair Housing Act, and the matter is not referred to the attorney general, the agency shall notify—

(i)   the secretary of Housing and Urban Development; and

(ii) the applicant that the secretary of Housing and Urban Development has been notified and that remedies for the violation may be available under the Fair Housing Act.

5. *Effective January 30, 1998, section 202.15 is added to read as follows:*

SECTION 202.15—Incentives for Self-Testing and Self-Correction

(a) General rules.

    (1) *Voluntary self-testing and correction.* The report or results of the self-test that a creditor voluntarily conducts (or authorizes) are privileged as provided in this section. Data collection required by law or by any governmental authority is not a voluntary self-test.

    (2) *Corrective action required.* The privilege in this section applies only if the creditor has taken or is taking appropriate corrective action.

    (3) *Other privileges.* The privilege created by this section does not preclude the assertion of any other privilege that may also apply.

(b) *Self-test defined.*

    (1) *Definition.* A self-test is any program, practice, or study that—

        (i)   is designed and used specifically to determine the extent or effectiveness of a creditor's compliance with the act or Regulation B; and

        (ii) creates data or factual information that is not available and cannot be derived from loan or application files or other records related to credit transactions.

    (2) *Types of information privileged.* The privilege under this section applies to the report or results of the self-test, data or factual information created by the self-test, and any analysis, opinions, and conclusions pertaining to the self-test report or results. The privilege covers workpapers or draft documents as well as final documents.

    (3) *Types of information not privileged.* The privilege under this section does not apply to—

        (i)   information about whether a creditor conducted a self-test, the methodology used or the scope of the self-test, the time period covered by the self-test, or the dates it was conducted; or

(ii) loan and application files or other business records related to credit transactions, and information derived from such files and records, even if it has been aggregated, summarized, or reorganized to facilitate analysis.

(c) *Appropriate corrective action.*

(1) *General requirement.* For the privilege in this section to apply, appropriate corrective action is required when the self-test shows that it is more likely than not that a violation occurred, even though no violation has been formally adjudicated.

(2) *Determining the scope of appropriate corrective action.* A creditor must take corrective action that is reasonably likely to remedy the cause and effect of a likely violation by—

(i) identifying the policies or practices that are the likely cause of the violation; and

(ii) assessing the extent and scope of any violation.

(3) *Types of relief.* Appropriate corrective action may include both prospective and remedial relief, except that to establish a privilege under this section—

(i) a creditor is not required to provide remedial relief to a tester used in a self-test;

(ii) a creditor is only required to provide remedial relief to an applicant identified by the self-test as one whose rights were more likely than not violated; and

(iii) a creditor is not required to provide remedial relief to a particular applicant if the statute of limitations applicable to the violation expired before the creditor obtained the results of the self-test or the applicant is otherwise ineligible for such relief.

(4) *No admission of violation.* Taking corrective action is not an admission that a violation occurred.

(d) (1) *Scope of privilege.* The report or results of a privileged self-test may not be obtained or used—

(i) by a government agency in any examination or investigation relating to compliance with the act or this regulation; or

(ii) by a government agency or an applicant (including a prospective applicant who alleges a violation of section 202.5(a)) in any proceeding or civil action in which a violation of the act or Regulation B is alleged.

(2) *Loss of privilege.* The report or results of a self-test are not privileged under paragraph (d)(1) of this section if the creditor or a person with lawful access to the report or results)—

(i) voluntarily discloses any part of the report or results, or any other information privileged under this section, to an applicant or government agency or to the public;

(ii) discloses any part of the report or results, or any other information privileged under this section, as a defense to charges that the creditor has violated the act or regulation; or

(iii)   fails or is unable to produce written or recorded information about the self-test that is required to be retained under section 202.12(b)(6) when the information is needed to determine whether the privilege applies. This paragraph does not limit any other penalty or remedy that may be available for a violation of section 202.12.

(3)   *Limited use of privileged information.* Notwithstanding paragraph (d)(l) of this section, the self-test report or results and any other information privileged under this section may be obtained and used by an applicant or government agency solely to determine a penalty or remedy after a violation of the act or this regulation has been adjudicated or admitted. Disclosures for this limited purpose may be used only for the particular proceeding in which the adjudication or admission was made. Information disclosed under (d)(3) remains privileged under paragraph (d)(1) of this section.

6. Effective May 1, 1992, the introductory text and the first three items of appendix A are amended to read as follows:

APPENDIX A—FEDERAL ENFORCEMENT AGENCIES

The following list indicates the federal agencies that enforce Regulation B for particular classes of creditors. Any questions concerning a particular creditor should be directed to its enforcement agency. Terms that are not defined in the Federal Deposit Insurance Act (12 USC 1813(s)) shall have the meaning given to them in the International Banking Act of 1978 (12 USC 3101).

National banks and federal branches and federal agencies of foreign banks
        District office of the Office of the Comptroller of the Currency for the district in which the institution is located

State member banks, branches and agencies of foreign banks (other than federal branches, federal agencies, and insured state branches of foreign banks), commercial lending companies owned or controlled by foreign banks, and organizations operating under section 25 or 25A of the Federal Reserve Act
        Federal Reserve Bank serving the District in which the institution is located

Nonmember insured banks and insured state branches of foreign banks
        Federal Deposit Insurance Corporation regional director for the region in which the institution is located

                    *   *   *   *   *

7. Effective December 14, 1993, the first and last paragraphs of the introductory text to appendix C are amended to read as follows:

APPENDIX C—SAMPLE NOTIFICATION FORMS

This appendix contains nine sample notification forms. Forms C-1 through C-4 are intended for use in notifying an applicant that adverse action has been taken on an application or account under section 202.9(a)(l) and (2)(i) of this regulation. Form C-5 is a notice of disclosure of the right to request specific reasons for adverse action under section 202.9(a)(l) and

(2)(ii). Form C-6 is designed for use in notifying an applicant, under section 202.9(c)(2), that an application is incomplete. Forms C-7 and C-8 are intended for use in connection with applications for business credit under section 202.9(a)(3). Form C-9 is designed for use in notifying an applicant of the right to receive a copy of an appraisal under section 202.5a.

*   *   *   *   *

A creditor may design its own notification forms or use all or a portion of the forms contained in this appendix. Proper use of Forms C-1 through C-4 will satisfy the requirement of section 202.9(a)(2)(i). Proper use of Forms C-5 and C-6 constitutes full compliance with sections 202.9(a)(2)(ii) and 202.9(c)(2), respectively. Proper use of Forms C-7 and C-8 will satisfy the requirements of section 202.9(a)(2)(i) and (ii), respectively, for applications for business credit. Proper use of Form C-9 will satisfy the requirements of section 202.5a of this part.

8. Effective December 14, 1993, appendix C is amended by adding a new Form C-9:

FORM C-9—SAMPLE DISCLOSURE OF RIGHT TO RECEIVE A COPY OF AN APPRAISAL

You have the right to a copy of the appraisal report used in connection with your application for credit. If you wish a copy, please write to us at the mailing address we have provided. We must hear from you no later than 90 days after we notify you about the action taken on your credit application or you withdraw your application.
[In your letter, give us the following information:]

EQUAL CREDIT OPPORTUNITY ACT

9. Effective December 19, 1991, section 701 is amended by adding a new paragraph (e):
(e) Each creditor shall promptly furnish an applicant, upon written request by the applicant made within a reasonable period of time of the application, a copy of the appraisal report used in connection with the applicant's application for a loan that is or would have been secured by a lien on residential real property. The creditor may require the applicant to reimburse the creditor for the cost of the appraisal.

10. Effective December 19, 1991, section 704(a) is amended by revising paragraph (1) and by adding a sentence following paragraph (9):

SECTION 704—ADMINISTRATIVE ENFORCEMENT

(a) Compliance with the requirements imposed under this title shall be enforced under:
  (1) Section 8 of the Federal Deposit Insurance Act, in the case of—
    (A) national banks, and Federal branches and Federal agencies of foreign banks, by the Office of the Comptroller of the Currency;
    (B) member banks of the Federal Reserve System (other than national banks), branches and agencies of foreign banks (other than Federal branches, Federal agencies, and insured State branches of foreign

banks), commercial lending companies owned or controlled by foreign banks, and organizations operating under section 25 or 25A of the Federal Reserve Act, by the Board of Governors of the Federal Reserve System; and

(C)   banks insured by the Federal Deposit Insurance Corporation (other than members of the Federal Reserve System) and insured State branches of foreign banks, by the Board of Directors of the Federal Deposit Insurance Corporation;

*   *   *   *   *

The terms used in paragraph (1) that are not defined in this title or otherwise defined in section 3(s) of the Federal Deposit Insurance Act (12 U.S.C. 1813(s)) shall have the meaning given to them in section 1(b) of the International Banking Act of 1978 (12 U.S.C. 3101).

11. Effective September 30, 1996, section 704A was added to read as follows:

SECTION 704A—Incentives for Self-Testing and Self-Correction

(a)   *Privileged information.*

  (1)   A report or result of a self-test (as that term is defined by regulations of the Board) shall be considered to be privileged under paragraph (2) if a creditor—

  (A)   conducts, or authorizes an independent third party to conduct, a self-test of any aspect of a credit transaction by a creditor, in order to determine the level or effectiveness of compliance with this title by the creditor; and

  (B)   has identified any possible violation of this title by the creditor and has taken, or is taking, appropriate corrective action to address any such possible violation.

  (2)   If a creditor meets the conditions specified in subparagraphs (A) and (B) of paragraph (1) with respect to a self-test described in that paragraph, any report or results of that self-test—

  (A)   shall be privileged; and

  (B)   may not be obtained or used by any applicant, department, or agency in any—

   (i)   proceeding or civil action in which one or more violations of this title are alleged; or

   (ii)   examination or investigation relating to compliance with this title.

(b)   *Results of self-testing.*

  (1)   No provision of this section may be construed to prevent an applicant, department, or agency from obtaining or using a report or results of any self-test in any proceeding or civil action in which a violation of this title is alleged, or in any examination or investigation of compliance with this title if—

  (A)   the creditor or any person with lawful access to the report or results—

      (i)   voluntarily releases or discloses all, or any part of, the report or results to the applicant, department, or agency, or to the general public; or

      (ii)   refers to or describes the report or results as a defense to charges of violations of this title against the creditor to whom the self-test relates; or

   (B)   the report or results are sought in conjunction with an adjudication or admission of a violation of this title for the sole purpose of determining an appropriate penalty or remedy.

(2)   Any report or results of a self-test that are disclosed for the purpose specified in paragraph (l)(B)—

   (A)   shall be used only for the particular proceeding in which the adjudication or admission referred to in paragraph (1)(B) is made; and

   (B)   may not be used in any other action or proceeding.

(c) *Adjudication.* An applicant, department, or agency that challenges a privilege asserted under this section may seek a determination of the existence and application of that privilege in—

(1)   a court of competent jurisdiction; or

(2)   an administrative law proceeding with appropriate jurisdiction.

---

12. *Effective December 19, 1991, section 706 is amended by revising subsections (g) and (h) and by adding a new subsection (k), to read as follows:*

    (g) The agencies having responsibility for administrative enforcement under section 704, if unable to obtain compliance with section 701, are authorized to refer the matter to the Attorney General with a recommendation that an appropriate civil action be instituted. Each agency referred to in paragraphs (1), (2), and (3) of section 704(a) shall refer the matter to the Attorney General whenever the agency has reason to believe that 1 or more creditors has engaged in a pattern or practice of discouraging or denying applications for credit in violation of section 701(a). Each such agency may refer the matter to the Attorney General whenever the agency has reason to believe that 1 or more creditors has violated section 701(a).

    (h) When a matter is referred to the Attorney General pursuant to subsection (g), or whenever he has reason to believe that one or more creditors are engaged in a pattern or practice in violation of this title, the Attorney General may bring a civil action in any appropriate United States district court for such relief as may be appropriate, including actual and punitive damages and injunctive relief.

           *   *   *   *   *

    (k) *Notice to HUD of violations.* Whenever an agency referred to in paragraph (1), (2), or (3) of section 704(a)—

   (1)   has reason to believe, as a result of receiving a consumer complaint, conducting a consumer compliance examination, or otherwise, that a violation of this title has occurred;

    (2)   has reason to believe that the alleged violation would be a violation of the Fair Housing Act; and

    (3)   does not refer the matter to the Attorney General pursuant to subsection (g),

the agency shall notify the Secretary of Housing and Urban Development of the violation, and shall notify the applicant that the Secretary of Housing and Urban Development has been notified of the alleged violation and that remedies for the violation may be available under the Fair Housing Act.

CHAPTER 14

Fair Credit Reporting Act

The use of credit reporting agencies blossomed in the 60s when a large number of local and national credit reporting agencies entered the arena to feast on the credit boom. They furnished information to just about anyone who asked and was willing to pay a fee. The information being provided to these agencies was accepted and recorded by many with little regard for accuracy and completeness. The reporting agencies were growing at such a phenomenal rate that they found it difficult to respond to consumers' requests concerning mistakes and inaccurate information, and in many instances some of the smaller agencies totally ignored the consumer. Blatant mistakes occurred where a consumer's credit was ruined because the name was similar to that of another consumer. Most states were not too concerned with the consumer, and little state regulation was enacted in this area, especially in those states where the major reporting agencies employed a large staff. Congress sought to correct the problem in the 70s and created stringent requirements for the credit reporting agencies.

The Fair Credit Reporting Act, effective in 1971, achieved two goals. First, the Act enabled consumers to obtain information from credit reporting agencies. Second, the Act compelled the reporting agencies, and those supplying the agencies with information, to comply with certain procedures and regulations regarding the availability of information about the consumer. The Act applies only to consumer credit transactions; it does not apply to commercial credit transactions or commercial agencies which distribute information to businesses.

In 1997 a significant amendment to the act was passed, effective October 1998, and it is reviewed later in the chapter.

CONSUMER REPORT

A consumer report is any written, oral, or other communication of any information by a consumer reporting agency consisting of the following seven characteristics about a consumer.[1]

1. Creditworthiness.
2. Credit standing.
3. Credit capacity.
4. Character.
5. General reputation.
6. Personal characteristics.
7. Mode of living.

A consumer report must be used primarily for personal, family, household, or employment purposes and utilized in whole or in part to establish a consumer's eligibility for credit or insurance.

A report of owners of motor vehicles, which lists the names of creditworthy individuals, is a consumer report, while a report limited solely to the consumers' names and addresses is not a consumer report, since no other information is disclosed. A telephone directory is not considered a consumer report nor is a list of names of persons with a checking account, since the mere fact that the party has a checking account is not evidence of creditworthiness. Trade directories of attorneys, insurance agencies, or accountants are not consumer reports.

Reports to determine whether the financial worth of a prospective defendant in a law suit is substantial enough to justify instituting a suit are not permitted, and a consumer report may not be obtained for use in discrediting a witness at a trial. Neither of the aforementioned reports are used to determine the creditworthiness of a consumer.

Collection agencies and creditors become consumer reporting agencies if they regularly furnish information beyond the transaction or experience with the consumer to third parties to use in connection with another consumer transaction.

Under Section 2, the amendment has spelled out what a consumer report does not include in Subdivisions A–D.

CONSUMER REPORTING AGENCY

A consumer reporting agency is a firm that receives compensation on a cooperative non-profit basis and regularly engages in whole or in part in the practice of

---

[1]16 CFR 603; *Hoke v. Retail Credit Corp*, 521 F. 2d 1079 (1975), cert. denied 4-23 U.S. 1087; 15 U.S.C. 1681a(d).

assembling or evaluating information on consumers for the purpose of furnishing said report to their customers. Therefore, a creditor providing information to the credit bureau for a fee does not become a consumer reporting agency.

PERMISSIBLE PURPOSES OF A CONSUMER REPORT

A consumer report may be issued only for permissible purposes. The concept of "legitimate business need" has been broadly interpreted, but the amendments to the Act have addressed specifically the definition of a "legitimate business." In Section 4, (F) the permissible purpose requires a legitimate business need for the information in connection with a business transaction that is initiated by the consumer or to review an account to determine whether the consumer continues to meet the terms of the account.

Under the old Fair Credit Reporting Act, we had three recent decisions dealing with obtaining a credit report. In the 8th Circuit, the court held that you could not obtain a credit report for purposes of extracting a settlement from an insurance carrier in a malpractice case. The court zeroed in on the fact that the credit report was obtained for commercial or professional use and not in connection with the consumer transaction.[2]

In another case in the 11th Circuit, the court held there was no permissible purpose for obtaining a credit report by a party who made a claim under his policy even where the insurance company felt that the claim asserted might have been fraudulent. The insurance company argued that the credit report was not in a sense a "consumer report." The court felt that the report was a "consumer report" because the agency expected the report to be used for a permissible purpose and collected the information to satisfy what it thought was a permissible request.[3]

Bear in mind that both of these decisions were based on the Fair Credit Reporting Act as it was set forth prior to October of 1998. The new Act became effective in October of 1998 and there have been few decisions interpreting the new Act.

The Internal Revenue Service inquired whether they could obtain a report on the spouse of a taxpayer in a community property state where the taxpayer owed money to the Internal Revenue Service and the Federal Commission responded that there was no permissible purpose if the spouse herself is not personally liable for the tax.[4]

---

[2]*Bakker v. McKinnon*, 152 F.3d 1007 (8th Cir. 1998).

[3]*Yang v. Government Employee's Insurance*, 146 F.3d 1320 (11th Cir. 1998).

[4]Bauchner, FTC Informal Staff Letter, August 5, 1998.

RECORD KEEPING

A consumer reporting agency is not obligated to convey a consumer's dispute statement in the same identical form so long as it is a clear and accurate codification or summary of the statement. In this instance, the consumer reporting agency altered the capitalization, punctuation, and paragraph arrangement of a consumer statement.[5]

With regard to keeping records, the Fair Credit Reporting Act is silent on this issue, but consumer reporting agencies must take note of the fact that the Fair Credit Reporting Act imposes a two-year statute of limitations on suits. This is more than the one-year statute that applies to the Fair Debt Collection Practices Act.

CREDIT REPORTS ON BUSINESS

A report that is not a consumer report does not become a consumer report just because it is used for the permissible purposes itemized. Credit reports on businesses, such as a D&B Report, are not consumer reports.[6] A report to determine the credit eligibility of a business is not a consumer report even if it contains information on individuals.[7]

A reporting agency is allowed to furnish identifying information and other limited information concerning consumers to a governmental agency providing a permissible purpose exists.

A 6th Circuit court held that drawing a credit report in preparation for a trial is not a permissible purpose within the Fair Credit Reporting Act.[8]

INVESTIGATIVE REPORTS

An investigative report is one in which the consumer's character, general reputation, personal characteristics, or mode of living is determined through personal interviews with neighbors and friends or associates of the consumer.[9] Insurance companies and employers use this type of report. The information is gathered by use of the telephone or by sending a representative to the neighborhood of the

---

[5]Edwards, FTC Informal Staff Letter, July 15, 1998.

[6]*Levy v. Boron Oil Co.*, 419 F. Supp., 1240 (1976).

[7]*Wrigley v. Dun & Bradstreet, Inc.*, 375 F. Supp. 969 (1974).

[8]*Duncan v. Handmaker, Middletown and Reutlinger*, 149 F.3d 424 (6th Cir. 1998).

[9]16 CFR 606.

consumer. The agency must disclose in writing that the report is being prepared and that the consumer is entitled to certain information.

The disclosure that an investigative report may be made must be mailed to the consumer not later than three days after the report is first requested by the client. Such disclosure is not necessary if the report is being used for employment purposes. Thus, a person or business requesting an investigative report must recognize that the consumer will be notified by the reporting agency, unless the report is for employment purposes.

Upon written request by the consumer after receiving the above disclosure, any person or business that procures an investigative report must furnish a complete and accurate disclosure of the nature and the scope of the investigation requested. This written disclosure must be mailed no later than five days after the date of the request from the consumer.

OBSOLETE INFORMATION

A consumer reporting agency may not issue or include in its report[10]

1. Bankruptcies older than ten years.
2. Suits and judgments older than seven years or past the statute of limitations, whichever is longer.
3. Unpaid taxes and tax liens older than seven years.
4. Accounts placed for collection or charged to profit which antedates the report by more than seven years.
5. Records of arrest, indictment, or conviction of a crime older than seven years.
6. Any adverse information which antedates the report by more than seven years.

The amendment attempted to clarify when the seven-year period commences and states as follows:

> "the seven-year period referred to in paragraphs 4 (6) of Subsection A shall begin, with respect to any delinquent account that is placed for collection (internally or by referral to a third party, whichever is early) charged to profit or loss, or subjected to any single action, upon the expiration of the 180-day period beginning on the day of the commencement of the delinquency which immediately precede the collection activity, charged to profit or loss or similar action"

---

[10]16 CFR 605.

This seems to say that the seven-year period begins when the delinquent account is placed with a collection agency or a law firm or is sent to a collection department in the creditor's organization, whichever is earlier. It also can commence if it is charged to a profit or loss or subject to any similar action. With regard to the last part of the Section, there have been many presentations made and interpretations of what the exact meaning of these last three lines are. Rather than join the other opinions, some of which are very cautious and others of which are broad, I prefer to wait until we have some type of interpretation by the legal system.

PRE-SCREENING

A pre-screened consumer list is a list of consumers meeting certain requirements with respect to income, jobs, sex, age, house ownership, or auto ownership. The data bases of the reporting agency provide specific information concerning prospective customers for a particular product or service. Pre-screening is also known as "target marketing." Some companies request additional information from survivors of a pre-screen by sending a credit application and then rejecting the credit. In some instances, additional promotional material is sent and credit is reviewed a second time if the consumer seeks to make a purchase. The Federal Trade Commission interprets the Act to prohibit these additional activities to qualify for the credit offer, and asserts that any survivor of a pre-screen must receive a credit offer without qualification. Sending credit applications or promotional material after a pre-screen is a violation of the Act. Bankruptcy or a similar change in financial circumstances does permit a creditor to reexamine the offer of credit.

COMPLIANCE PROCEDURES

The credit reporting agency must use due diligence to require prospective users of the information to certify the specific purpose for which the information is being sought. In addition, the information may not be used for any other purpose.[11]

The party requesting information does not have to provide certification for each name if the purpose is the same for all requests. A single certification that the information will be used for the proper purpose is sufficient to support many requests.[12]

---

[11]*Bryant v. TRW Inc.*, 487 F. Supp. 1234 (1980).

[12]16 CFR 607.

An agency must use reasonable procedures to assure the greatest possible accuracy of the information. No specific guidelines or definitions are provided for "reasonable procedures." Cases have gone both ways on the extent of the due diligence that the agency must expend to obtain the information.

To show that the credit reporting agency did not use due diligence, the consumer must prove both the inaccuracy of the information and that the credit reporting agency was not acting reasonably in obtaining the information. Due to continuous litigation in this area, specific criteria are difficult to provide since different courts considering similar facts arrive at different conclusions.

An agency is obligated to correct inaccurate information supplied by third parties. The extent of this obligation is uncertain and probably rests on the facts and circumstances of each case. Some courts hold that there is no obligation to investigate information supplied by creditors. But knowledge by an agency that the information is incorrect may provide a different result. Of course, if the final report is accurate, then the procedure used to produce the report is reasonable.[13]

If a married consumer's file does not designate whether the information belongs to either the joint or the individual credit of the two spouses, the reporting agency must honor a request by the consumer to segregate the information and report only the information that applies to one of the respective spouses.

A creditor must notify a credit reporting agency when a past due account has been paid or discharged in bankruptcy. The reporting agency is not in violation if the account is not marked "paid," if it was not informed by the creditor of the payment or discharge in bankruptcy.

DISCLOSURE TO CONSUMER

Every reporting agency, upon request of the consumer and with proper identification, shall disclose accurately the nature and substance of the information on file at the time of the request. The source of the information need not be disclosed.[14]

The agency must disclose the name of any employer that has received a report within two years or any report that has been issued within one year. The reporting agency must furnish to the consumer the identity of any firm that has received a pre-screen list which contains the consumer's name.

The consumer may appear in person or make a written request with proper identification. The agency may disclose by mail, by telephone, or in person, if requested by the consumer. The consumer may have a third party present when making such a request.

---

[13]*McPhee v. Chilton Corp.*, 468 F. Supp. 494 (1978).

[14]16 CFR 609.

AMENDMENT TO FAIR CREDIT REPORTING ACT

The amendments to the Fair Credit Reporting Act which were part of the Omnibus Budget Bill became effective on October 1, 1997. A copy of the Fair Credit Reporting Act appears in the Appendix. As reported by the Associated Credit Bureau, one of the major disappointments was that the bill does not allow credit bureaus to sell information to direct marketers. There was an effort on behalf of the industry to include direct marketing as a permissible purpose, but these efforts failed because the Federal Trade Commission felt that consumer identification information would be included. The Commission wanted this consumer identification information to qualify as a consumer report and thus be limited to dissemination. This position seemed to defy logic in that this requirement only applied to consumer reporting agencies and did nothing to deal with all other databases that sell or provide the same type of identification information. As a compromise, the bill does order the Federal Reserve System to conduct a study on the subject of sensitive consumer identification information and to report back to Congress. The major revisions are as follows:

1. *Banks—Sharing Information.* Under the new amendments, banks are permitted to share consumer data among affiliates without having to comply with the Fair Credit Reporting Act. Under the original law, the banks felt that they became consumer reporting agencies if one division shared information about a consumer with another division, such as an automobile finance division furnishing information to the mortgage lending division.

2. *Private Right of Action.* One of the significant provisions in the Act is that there is a civil cause of action for consumers and consumer reporting agencies against individuals who knowingly or under false pretenses obtain a consumer report without a permissible purpose. The perpetrator is now subject to actual damages of $1,000.

3. *Free Disclosure.* A free disclosure upon request is required to be given to an individual at least once a year. If the consumer is unemployed or is on welfare or has been the victim of fraud, there is no cost.

4. *Adverse Action.*The Act has equivocated the definition of adverse action within the meaning set forth in Section 701(d)(6) of the Equal Credit Opportunity Act. All appropriate file findings, decisions, commentary, and orders issued under the Equal Credit Opportunity Act by the Board of Governors of the Federal Reserve System shall apply. The amendment provides almost a page of definition of what the term "adverse action" really means.

   In the event of an adverse action, the person taking the adverse action must provide oral, written, or electronic notice to the consumer of the name and address of the agency that furnished the report and a statement that the agency did not make the decision to take the action. The consumer must also be provided with an oral or written notice of the right to obtain the consumer report and to dispute the consumer report.

5. *Employment—Notices.* A new subsection has been added dealing with employment purposes and requires certain notification to the consumer of the consumer's rights under this title. The person who procures the report must notify the consumer. If the consumer is declined employment, a copy of the report must also be furnished to the consumer with a description, in writing, of the rights of the consumer. The requirements continue for another page and a careful reading is required.

6. *Exemptions.* The monetary exemptions as to obsolete information have been increased from $50,000 to $150,000. The employment of any individual at an annual salary which equals or may be expected to equal $20,000 has been increased to $75,000, and the life insurance exemption has increased from $50,000 to $150,000.

7. *Bankruptcy.* If a consumer reporting agency reports a bankruptcy, it must identify whether it is a Chapter 7 or a Chapter 13 bankruptcy and if the bankruptcy is withdrawn before a final judgment, the agency shall include in the report that such case was withdrawn upon receipt of documentation of such withdrawal.

8. *Closing an Account.* A consumer reporting agency must report the voluntary closing of a credit account by the consumer as well as a disputed account. If the account is disputed by the consumer, the agency must indicate that fact in each consumer report.

9. *Verification of Accuracy.* A reporting agency that furnishes an investigative report that includes information of a public record that relates to an arrest, indictment, conviction, civil judicial action, tax lien, or outstanding judgment may not issue said report unless the agency has verified the accuracy of the information during the thirty-day period.

10. *Interviews.* With regard to obtaining information through a personal interview with a neighbor, friend, or associate of the consumer, the agency may not issue a report unless it has followed reasonable procedures to obtain confirmation of the information from an additional source that has independent and direct knowledge of the person interviewed and is the best possible source of the information.

11. *Adverse Action—Disclosure.* A consumer reporting agency may not prohibit a user of a consumer report furnished by the agency from disclosing the contents of the report to the consumer if adverse action against the consumer has been taken by the user based in whole or in part on the report.

The agency must provide to any person who furnishes the information or to whom a consumer report is provided a notice of the person's responsibilities under this particular amendment.

12. *Resale of Report.* There is a strict prohibition against reselling a consumer report unless the person discloses to the consumer reporting agency that originally furnished the report the identity of the end user and the permissible purposes under the act for which the report is furnished to the end user. Any person who is reselling the report shall comply with the reasonable procedures to insure that the report is resold by the person only for a purpose for which the report may be furnished.

13. *Disclosure of Credit Scores.* The consumer reporting agency is under no obligation to disclose information concerning credit scores or other risk scores or predictors related to the consumer.

14. *Disclosures of Name of Inquirer.* The agency must disclose to each consumer anyone who procured the report for employment purposes during the two-year period preceding the date on which the request was made or for any other purposes during the one-year period preceding the date on which the request was made, as well as all inquiries during that one-year period in connection with a credit or insurance transaction.

15. *Disclosure Notice.* The amendment also sets forth the summary of the rights to be disclosed with each written disclosure to the consumer. The contents of this disclosure notice are specific and list several items, including a listing of all the federal agencies responsible for enforcing the provisions of the Fair Credit Reporting Act.

16. *Writing Requirement of Disclosure.* All disclosures to the consumer must be in writing, although the consumer may request disclosure by telephone, in person, by electronic means, or by any other responsible means.

17. *Disputed Report.* If the consumer disputes the accuracy of the information, the agency must reinvestigate free of charge before the end of the 30-day period beginning on the date on which the agency receives notice. The 30-day period may only be extended by an additional 15 days.

    Before the end of a 5-day period after the 30-day period, the agency must provide notification of the dispute to any person who has been provided with the information. The agency may terminate a reinvestigation if it has reasonable grounds to believe that the dispute is frivolous or irrelevant, including the failure of the consumer to provide sufficient information to investigate. The consumer must be notified of this determination no later than 5 business days after said determination of frivolousness is made. The amendment does provide the form and notice to be provided to the consumer.

    If after the reinvestigation the information is determined to be inaccurate, it shall be promptly removed. It cannot be reinserted into the credit report of the consumer unless the person who furnishes the information certifies that the information is complete and accurate. In that event the agency shall notify the consumer of the reinsertion not more than 5 business days later. The Act does provide a form of notice to the consumer. In general, a consumer reporting agency shall provide written notice to the consumer of the results of the reinvestigation not later than 5 business days after the completion of the reinvestigation. The notice to the consumer shall provide a statement that the reinvestigation is completed and that the file has been revised by reason of the reinvestigation, a description of the procedure used to determine the completeness of the information, and a notice to the consumer that the consumer has a right to add a statement to the file disputing the accuracy or completeness of the information.

18. *Cost and Charges for Service.* The costs and charges that the agencies may impose for the services they render are set forth, and a reasonable charge may not exceed $8.00. Disclosure of a consumer report is free to the consumer for up to 60 days after adverse action.

19. *Reliance on Reports.* Separate sections deal with users of the reports who make written, credit, or insurance solicitations on the basis of consumer reports or who take certain actions based on information provided by affiliates who are using consumer reports.

20. *Attorney Fee.* The court may award attorney's fees to the successful party in an action instituted by the consumer in bad faith or for purposes of harassment. Whether this particular clause will be successful in deterring technical violations or minor violations is questionable. Under other consumer laws such as the Truth in Lending or the Fair Debt Collection Practice Act, the courts rarely award attorney's fees to defendants even though the suits may be frivolous and instituted purely for the purpose of harassment.

21. *Penalties.* The amendment has increased the time for imprisonment for willfully obtaining information on a consumer (or an officer or an employee of an agency who willfully provides information) in violation of the Act to a period of 2 years in prison as opposed to the prior Act which limited the time in prison to 1 year. The amendment also adds minimum actual damages of $100 and a maximum of $1,000 for noncompliance.

22. *Accurate and Inaccurate Information.* Furnishers of information must provide accurate information. The Act expressly states that a person shall not furnish any information relating to a consumer to any consumer reporting agency if the person knows or consciously avoids knowing the information is inaccurate. A person shall not furnish information relating to a consumer to any consumer reporting agency if the person has been notified by the consumer at the address specified by the person for such notice that specific information is inaccurate and the information is in fact inaccurate.

23. *Updating Information.* The agency must correct and update any information that has been furnished to the agency as well as provide notice of any dispute, notice of any closed account, and notice of any delinquency of account.

24. *Enforcement.* The state's chief law enforcement agencies may bring an action to enjoin violations in any federal court or other court of competent juris-

diction. If there is a knowing violation that constitutes a pattern or practice of violation, penalties are capped at $2,500 per violation.

25. *Requirements on Users of Consumer Reports.* This particular topic has been totally rewritten, runs approximately two and a half pages, and sets forth the obligations upon users of consumer reports. It covers the subject of the duties of the users with regard to taking adverse action on the basis of information contained in the reports and requires the user to provide oral, written or electronic notice of the adverse action to the consumer. It specifically sets forth not only the requirements that must be furnished to the consumer, but the method of transmission to the consumer to the extent of requiring a toll-free telephone number by the credit reporting agency if the agency compiles and maintains files on consumers on a nationwide basis. Whenever credit is denied, upon the consumer's request, certain procedures must be utilized when the consumer submits a written request for the reasons of such adverse action, with specific time limits and duties and the information that must be provided. The amendment protects the user from any lawsuits (the Act now allows a private right of action) in that if reasonable procedures are used, the agency shall not be liable for a violation. The Act does not set forth what the reasonable procedures are, but states that no person shall be held liable for any violation if by a preponderance of the evidence at the time of the alleged violations, reasonable procedures were in place to assure compliance with the provisions of the section. Somehow I feel that this will probably lead to more litigation against the agencies, for it follows the "bona fide error" defense in the Fair Debt Collection Practice Act, which has been of little assistance to agencies and law firms because of the high level of reasonable procedures required by the courts.

CONSUMER REPORTS

A mailing list consists of collections of names and addresses. Trans Union used special criteria to cull names from its database so that a buyer of the list knows that every person named has at least two separate credit accounts (known as a tradeline). The lists of persons also satisfied a particular sub-criteria. Trans Union sold the list for marketing purposes.

The Federal Trade Commission claimed that this information transformed Trans Union's list from legally innocuous mailing lists to consumer reports covered by the Fair Credit Reporting Act. Trans Union denied that the lists are consumer reports because it did not collect or furnish the information therein to serve as a factor in determining credit eligibility. The Federal Trade Commission found to the contrary. Trans Union objected on the grounds that it was entitled to a hearing and that, even if the lists are consumer reports, selling to mass mailers is a permissible purpose under the Act.

The Court noted that in a settlement with Trans Union's competitor, TRW, the Commission permitted TRW to market lists from its credit reporting database based on such identifying information as name, zip code, age, social security number, plus substantially similar identifiers. The Federal Trade Commission distinguished its position on TRW based on the principle that the data there related only to identification. The Court found a problem with the Commission's position because they rely entirely on their "labeling theory" despite an affidavit by the director of marketing of Trans Union stating that the base list does not contain information upon which a credit grantor may make a judgment as to a consumer's eligibility for credit.

The Court also was not content with the idea that selling a mailing list to catalogers and other users of mass mailings necessarily created a consumer report. The Court remanded the matter to the Federal Trade Commission for further hearing and stated that the Federal Trade Commission made sweeping and arbitrary inferences about the purposes for which the lists had been collected. The Court said such further proceedings that would be taken by the Federal Trade Commission must be consistent with the opinion rendered.[15]

Another case in Missouri also emphasized that a report limited solely to the consumer's name and address, with no connotation as to creditworthiness or other characteristics, does not constitute a consumer report if it does not bear on any of the seven factors specified in the Act. In this case, TRW supplied an address update containing plaintiff's name and current and former addresses as well as social security information. The information did not bear on plaintiff's credit or general character, nor was it used to establish eligibility for credit, employment, or any of the other purposes listed in the statute.[16]

FEDERAL TRADE COMMISSION BOOKLETS

The Federal Trade Commission has published three booklets on the Fair Credit Reporting Act which may interest employers "Fair Credit Reporting," "Credit Reports: What Employers Need to Know," and "Using Credit Reports: What Information Providers Need to Know." These reports are available through the Consumer Response Center, Federal Trade Commission, Washington, DC 20580 or call 202-326-2222.

---

[15]*Trans Union Corp. v. Federal Trade Commission*, 81 F.3d 228 (D.C. Cir. 1996).

[16]*Dotzler v. Perot*, 914 F.Supp. 328 (E.D. Mo. 1996).

CHAPTER 14
APPENDIX I

FAIR CREDIT REPORTING ACT

As a public service, the staff of the Federal Trade Commission (FTC) has prepared the following complete text of the Fair Credit Reporting Act (FCRA), 15 U.S.C. § 1681 et seq. Although staff generally followed the format of the U.S. Code as published by the Government Printing Office, the format of this text does differ in minor ways from the Code (and from West's U.S. Code Annotated). For example, this version uses FCRA section numbers (§§ 601-625) in the headings. (The relevant U.S. Code citation is included with each section heading and each reference to the FCRA in the text.)

This version of the FCRA is complete as of November 27, 1998. It includes the amendments to the FCRA set forth in the Consumer Credit Reporting Reform Act of 1996 (Public Law 104-208, the Omnibus Consolidated Appropriations Act for Fiscal Year 1997, Title II, Subtitle D, Chapter 1), Section 311 of the Intelligence Authorization for Fiscal Year 1998 (Public Law 105-107), and the Consumer Reporting Employment Clarification Act of 1998 (Public Law 105-347).

TABLE OF CONTENTS

§ 601. Short title
This title may be cited as the Fair Credit Reporting Act

§ 602. Congressional findings and statement of purpose

(a) *Accuracy and fairness of credit reporting.* The Congress makes the following findings:

    (1)   The banking system is dependent upon fair and accurate credit reporting. Inaccurate credit reports directly impair the efficiency of the banking system, and unfair credit reporting methods undermine tile public confidence which is essential to the continued functioning of the banking system.

    (2)   An elaborate mechanism has been developed for investigating and evaluating the creditworthiness, credit standing, credit capacity, character, and general reputation of consumers.

    (3)   Consumer reporting agencies have assumed a vital role in assembling and evaluating consumer credit and other information on consumers.

    (4)   There is a need to insure that consumer reporting agencies exercise their grave responsibilities with fairness, impartiality, and a respect for the consumer's right to privacy.

(b) *Reasonable procedures.* It is the purpose of this title to require that consumer reporting agencies adopt reasonable procedures for meeting the needs of commerce for consumer credit, personnel, insurance, and other information in a manner which is fair and equitable to the consumer, with regard to the confidentiality, accuracy, relevancy, and proper utilization of such information in accordance with the requirements of this title.

15 U.S.C. 1681

§ 603. Definitions; rules of construction

(a) Definitions and rules of construction set forth in this section are applicable for the purpose of this title.

(b) The term "person" means any individual, partnership, corporation, trust, estate, cooperative, association, government or governmental subdivision or agency, or any other entity.

(c) The term "consumer" means an individual.

(d) Consumer report.

    (1)   *In general.* The term "consumer report" means any written, oral, or other communication of any information by a consumer reporting agency bearing on a consumer's creditworthiness, credit standing, credit capacity, character, general reputation, personal characteristics, or mode of living which is used or

expected to be used or collected in whole or in part for the purpose of serving as a factor in establishing the consumer's eligibility for

(A)   credit or insurance to be used primarily for personal, family, or household purposes:

(B)   employment purposes; or

(C)   any other purpose authorized under section 604 [§ 168 1b].

(2)   *Exclusions.* The term "consumer report" does not include

    (A)   any

        (i)   report containing information solely as to transactions or experiences between the consumer and the person making the report:

        (ii)   communication of that information among persons related by common ownership or affiliated by corporate control; or

        (iii)   communication of other information among persons related by common ownership or affiliated by corporate control, if it is clearly and conspicuously disclosed to the consumer that the information may be communicated among such persons and the consumer is given the opportunity, before the time that the information is initially communicated, to direct that such information not be communicated among such persons;

    (B)   any authorization or approval of a specific extension of credit directly or indirectly by the issuer of a credit card or similar device;

    (C)   any report in which a person who has been requested by a third party to make a specific extension of credit directly or indirectly to a consumer conveys his or her decision with respect to such request, if the third party advises the consumer of the name and address of the person to whom the request was made, and such person makes the disclosures to the consumer required under section 615 [§ 1681m]; or

    (D)   a communication described in subsection (o).

(e)   The term "investigative consumer report" means a consumer report or portion thereof in which information on a consumer's character, general reputation, personal characteristics, or mode of living is obtained through personal interviews with neighbors, friends, or associates of the consumer reported on or with others with whom he is acquainted or who may have knowledge concerning any such items of information. However, such information shall not include specific factual information on a consumer's credit record obtained directly from a creditor of the consumer or from a consumer reporting agency when such information was obtained directly from a creditor of the consumer or from the consumer.

(f)   The term "consumer reporting agency" means any person which, for monetary fees, dues, or on a cooperative nonprofit basis, regularly engages in whole or in part in the practice of assembling or evaluating consumer credit information or other information on consumers for the purpose of furnishing consumer reports to third parties, and which uses any means or facility of interstate commerce for the purpose of preparing or furnishing consumer reports.

(g) The term "file," when used in connection with information on any consumer, means all of the information on that consumer recorded and retained by a consumer reporting agency regardless of how the information is stored.

(h) The term "employment purposes" when used in connection with a consumer report means a report used for the purpose of evaluating a consumer for employment, promotion, reassignment or retention as an employee.

(i) The term "medical information" means information or records obtained, with the consent of the individual to whom it relates, from licensed physicians or medical practitioners, hospitals, clinics, or other medical or medically related facilities.

(j) Definitions relating to child support obligations.

    (1) *Overdue support.* The term "overdue support has the meaning given to such term in section 666(e) of title 42 [Social Security Act, 42 U.S.C. § 666(e)].

    (2) *State or local child support enforcement agency.* The term "State or local child support enforcement agency" means a State or local agency which administers a State or local program for establishing and enforcing child support obligations.

(k) Adverse action.

    (1) *Actions included.* The term "adverse action"

        (A) has the same meaning as in section 701(d)(6) of the Equal Credit Opportunity Act; and

        (B) means

            (i) a denial or cancellation of, an increase in any charge for, or a reduction or other adverse or unfavorable change in the terms of coverage or amount of, any insurance, existing or applied for, in connection with the underwriting of insurance;

            (ii) a denial of employment or any other decision for employment purposes that adversely affects any current or prospective employee;

            (iii) a denial or cancellation of, an increase in any charge for, or any other adverse or unfavorable change in the terms of, any license or benefit described in section 604(a)(3)(D) [§ 168 1b]; and

            (iv) an action taken or determination that is

                (I) made in connection with an application that was made by, or a transaction that was initiated by, any consumer, or in connection with a review of an account under section 604(a)(3)(F)(ii) [§ 1681b]; and

                (II) adverse to the interests of the consumer.

    (2) *Applicable findings, decisions, commentary, and orders.* For purposes of any determination of whether an action is an adverse action under paragraph (1)(A), all appropriate final findings, decisions, commentary, and orders issued under section 701(d)(6) of the Equal Credit Opportunity Act by the Board of Governors of the Federal Reserve System or any court shall apply.

(l) *Firm offer of credit or insurance.* The term "firm offer of credit or insurance" means any offer of credit or insurance to a consumer that will be honored if the consumer is determined, based on information in a consumer report on the consumer, to meet the specific criteria used to select the consumer for the offer, except that the offer may be further conditioned on one or more of the following:

(1)   The consumer being determined, based on information in the consumer's application for the credit or insurance, to meet specific criteria bearing on creditworthiness or insurability, as applicable, that are established

    (A)   before selection of the consumer for the offer; and

    (B)   for the purpose of determining whether to extend credit or insurance pursuant to the offer.

(2)   Verification

    (A)   that the consumer continues to meet the specific criteria used to select the consumer for the offer, by using information in a consumer report on the consumer, information in the consumer's application for the credit or insurance, or other information bearing on the creditworthiness or insurability of the consumer; or

    (B)   of the information in the consumer's application for the credit or insurance, to determine that the consumer meets the specific criteria bearing on creditworthiness or insurability.

(3)   The consumer furnishing any collateral that is a requirement for the extension of the credit or insurance that was

    (A)   established before selection of the consumer for the offer of credit or insurance; and

    (B)   disclosed to the consumer in the offer of credit or insurance.

(m) *Credit or insurance transaction that is not initiated by the consumer.* The term "credit or insurance transaction that is not initiated by the consumer" does not include the use of a consumer report by a person with which the consumer has an account or insurance policy, for purposes of

(1)   reviewing the account or insurance policy: or

(2)   collecting the account.

(n) *State.* The term "State" means any State, the Commonwealth of Puerto Rico, the District of Columbia, and any territory or possession of the United States.

(o) *Excluded communications.* A communication is described in this subsection if it is a communication

(1)   that, but for subsection (d)(2)(D), would be an investigative consumer report;

(2)   that is made to a prospective employer for the purpose of

    (A)   procuring an employee for the employer; or

    (B)   procuring an opportunity for a natural person to work for the employer;

(3)   that is made by a person who regularly performs such procurement;

(4)   that is not used by any person for any purpose other than purpose described in subparagraph (A) or (B) of paragraph (2) and

(5)   with respect to which

    (A)   the consumer who is the subject of the communication

(i) consents orally or in writing to the nature and scope of the communication, before the collection of any information for the purpose of making the communication.

(ii) consents orally or in writing to the making of the communication to a prospective employer, before the making of the communication; and

(iii) in the case of consent under clause (i) or (ii) given orally, is provided written confirmation of that consent by the person making the communication, not later than 3 business days after the receipt of the consent by that person;

(B) the person who makes the communication does not, for the purpose of making the communication, make any inquiry that if made by a prospective employer of the consumer who is the subject of the communication would violate any applicable Federal or State equal employment opportunity law or regulation; and

(C) the person who makes the communication

(i) discloses in writing to the consumer who is the subject of the communication, not later than 5 business days after receiving any request from the consumer for such disclosure, the nature and substance of all information in the consumer's file at the time of the request, except that the sources of any information that is acquired solely for use in making the communication and is actually used for no other purpose, need not be disclosed other than under appropriate discovery procedures in any court of competent jurisdiction in which an action is brought; and

(ii) notifies the consumer who is the subject of the communication, in writing, of the consumer's right to request the information described in clause (i).

(p) *Consumer reporting agency that compiles and maintains files on consumers on a nationwide basis.* The term "consumer reporting agency that compiles and maintains files on consumers on a nationwide basis" means a consumer reporting agency that regularly engages in the practice of assembling or evaluating, and maintaining, for the purpose of furnishing consumer reports to third parties bearing on a consumer's creditworthiness, credit standing, or credit capacity, each of the following regarding consumers residing nationwide:

(1) Public record information.

(2) Credit account information from persons who furnish that information regularly and in the ordinary course of business.

15 U.S.C. 1681a

§ 604. Permissible purposes of consumer reports

(a) *In general.* Subject to subsection (c), any consumer reporting agency may furnish a consumer report under the following circumstances and no other:

(1) In response to the order of a court having jurisdiction to issue such an order, or a subpoena issued in connection with proceedings before a Federal grand jury.

(2) In accordance with the written instructions of the consumer to whom it relates.

(3)   To a person which it has reason to believe

    (A)   intends to use the information in connection with a credit transaction involving the consumer on whom the information is to be furnished and involving the extension of credit to, or review or collection of an account of, the consumer; or

    (B)   intends to use the information for employment purposes; or

    (C)   intends to use the information in connection with the underwriting of insurance involving the consumer; or

    (D)   intends to use the information in connection with a determination of the consumer's eligibility for a license or other benefit granted by a governmental instrumentality required by law to consider an applicant's financial responsibility or status; or

    (E)   intends to use the information, as a potential investor or servicer, or current insurer, in connection with a valuation of, or an assessment of the credit or prepayment risks associated with, an existing credit obligatior; or

    (F)   otherwise has a legitimate business need for the information

        (i)   in connection with a business transaction that is initiated by the consumer; or

        (ii)   to review an account to determine whether the consumer continues to meet the terms of the account.

(4)   In response to a request by the head of a State or local child support enforcement agency (or a State or local government official authorized by the head of such an agency), if the person making the request certifies to the consumer reporting agency that

    (A)   the consumer report is needed for the purpose of establishing an individual's capacity to make child support payments or determining the appropriate level of such payments;

    (B)   the paternity of the consumer for the child to which the obligation relates has been established or acknowledged by the consumer in accordance with State laws under which the obligation arises (if required by those laws);

    (C)   the person has provided at least 10 days' prior notice to the consumer whose report is requested, by certified or registered mail to the last known address of the consumer, that the report will be requested; and

    (D)   the consumer report will be kept confidential, will be used solely for a purpose described in subparagraph (A), and will not be used in connection with any other civil, administrative, or criminal proceeding, or for any other purpose.

(5)   To an agency administering a State plan under Section 454 of the Social Security Act (42 U.S.C. § 654) for use to set an initial or modified child support award.

(b) Conditions for furnishing and using consumer reports for employment purposes.

    (1)   *Certification from user.* A consumer reporting agency may furnish a consumer report for employment purposes only if

       (A)   the person who obtains such report from the agency certifies to the agency that

             (i)   the person has complied with paragraph (2) with respect to the consumer report, and the person will comply with paragraph (3) with respect to the consumer report if paragraph (3) becomes applicable; and

             (ii) information from the consumer report will not be used in violation of any applicable Federal or State equal employment opportunity law or regulation; and

       (B)   the consumer reporting agency provides with the report, or has previously provided, a summary of the consumer's rights under this title, as prescribed by the Federal Trade Commission under section 609(c)(3) [§ 1681g].

  (2)   *Disclosure to consumer.*

       (A)   In general. Except as provided in subparagraph (B), a person may not procure a consumer report, or cause a consumer report to be procurred, for employment purposes with respect to any consumer, unless—

             (i)   a clear and conspicuous disclosure has been made in writing to the consumer at any time before the report is procured or caused to be procured, in a document that consists solely of the disclosure, that a consumer report may be obtained for employment purposes; and

             (ii) the consumer has authorized in writing (which authorization may be made on the document referred to in clause (i)) the procurement of the report by that person.

       (B)   Application by mail, telephone, computer, or other similar means. If a consumer described in subparagraph (C) applies for employment by mail, telephone, computer, or other similar means, at any time before a consumer report is procured or caused to be procured in connection with that application—

             (i)   the person who procures the consumer report on the consumer for employment purposes shall provide to the consumer, by oral, written, or electronic means, notice that a consumer report may be obtained for employment purposes, and a summary of the consumer's rights under section 615(a)(3); and

             (ii) the consumer shall have consented, orally, in writing, or electronically to the procurement of the report by that person.

       (C)   Scope. Subparagraph (B) shall apply to a person procuring a consumer report on a consumer in connection with the consumer's application for employment only if—

             (i)   the consumer is applying for a position over which the Secretary of Transportation has the power to establish qualifications and maximum hours of service pursuant to the provisions of section 31502 or title 49, or a position subject to safety regulation by a State transportation agency; and

             (ii) as of the time at which the person procures the report or causes the report to be procured the only interaction between the consumer and the person in connection with that employment application has been by mail, telephone, computer, or other similar means.

(3) *Conditions on use for adverse actions.*

(A) *In general.* Except as provided in subparagraph (B), in using a consumer report for employment purposes, before taking any adverse action based in whole or in part on the report, the person intending to take such adverse action shall provide to the consumer to whom the report relates—

(i) a copy of the report; and

(ii) a description in writing of the rights of the consumer under this title, as prescribed by the Federal Trade under section 609(c)(3).

(B) *Application by mail, telephone, computer, or other similar means.*

(i) If a consumer described in subparagraph (C) applies for employment by mail, telephone, computer, or other similar means, and if a person who has procured a consumer report on the consumer for employment purposes takes adverse action on the employment application based in whole or in part on the report, then the person must provide to the consumer to whom the report relates, in lieu of the notices required under subparagraph (A) of this section and under section 615(a), within 3 business days of taking such action, an oral, written or electronic notification—

(I) that adverse action has been taken based in whole or in part on a consumer report received from a consumer reporting agency;

(II) of the name, address and telephone number of the consumer reporting agency that furnished the consumer report (including a toll-free telephone number established by the agency if the agency compiles and maintains files on consumers on a nationwide basis);

(III) that the consumer reporting agency did not make the decision to take the adverse action and is unable to provide to the consumer the specific reasons why the adverse action was taken; and

(IV) that the consumer may, upon providing proper identification, request a free copy of a report and may dispute with the consumer reporting agency the accuracy or completeness of any information in report.

(ii) If, under clause (B)(i)(IV), the consumer requests a copy of a consumer report from the person who procured the report, then, within 3 business days of receiving the consumer's request, together with proper identification, the person must send or provide to the consumer a copy of a report and a copy of the consumer's rights as prescribed by the Federal Trade Commission under section 609(c)(3).

(C) *Scope.* Subparagraph (B) shall apply to a person procuring a consumer report on a consumer in connection with the consumer's application for employment only if—

(i)   the consumer is applying for a position over which the Secretary of Transportation has the power to establish qualifications and maximum hours of service pursuant to the provisions of section 31502 of title 49, or a position subject to safety regulation by a State transportation agency; and

(ii)   as of the time at which the person procures the report or causes the report to be procured the only interaction between the consumer and the person in connection with that employment application has been by mail, telephone, computer, or other similar means.

(4)   Exception for national security investigations.

    (A)   *In general.* In the case of an agency or department of the United States Government which seeks to obtain and use a consumer report for employment purposes, paragraph (3) shall not apply to any adverse action by such agency or department which is based in part on such consumer report, if the head of such agency or department makes a written finding that—

       (i)   the consumer report is relevant to a national security investigation of such agency or department;

       (ii)   the investigation is within the jurisdiction of such agency or department;

       (iii)   there is reason to believe that compliance with paragraph (3) will—

          (I)   endanger the life or physical safety of any person;

          (II)   result in flight from prosecution;

          (III) result in the destruction of, or tampering with, evidence relevant to the investigation;

          (IV) result in the intimidation of a potential witness relevant to the investigation;

          (V)   result in the compromise of classified information; or

          (VI) otherwise seriously jeopardize or unduly delay the investigation or another official proceeding.

    (B)   *Notification of consumer upon conclusion of investigation.* Upon the conclusion of a national security investigation described in subparagraph (A), or upon the determination that the exception under subparagraph (A) is no longer required for the reasons set forth in such subparagraph, the official exercising the authority in such subparagraph shall provide to the consumer who is the subject of the consumer report with regard to which such finding was made—

       (i)   a copy of such consumer report with any classified information redacted as necessary;

       (ii)   notice of any adverse action which is based, in part, on the consumer report; and

       (iii)   the identification with reasonable specificity of the nature of the investigation for which the consumer report was sought.

(C)   *Delegation by head of agency or department.* For purposes of subparagraphs (A) and (B), the head of any agency or department of the United States Government may delegate his or her authorities under this paragraph to an official of such agency or department who has personnel security responsibilities and is a member of the Senior Executive Service or equivalent civilian or military rank.

(D)   *Report to the congress.* Not later than January 31 of each year, the head of each agency and department of the United States Government that exercised authority under this paragraph during the preceding year shall submit a report to the Congress on the number of times the department or agency exercised such authority during the year.

(E)   *Definitions.* For purposes of this paragraph, the following definitions shall apply:

   (i)   Classified information. The term 'classified information' means information that is protected from unauthorized disclosure under Executive Order No. 1 2958 or successor orders.

(c)   Furnishing reports in connection with credit or insurance transactions that are not initiated by the consumer.

   (1)   *In general.* A consumer reporting agency may furnish a consumer report relating to any consumer pursuant to subparagraph (A) or (C) of subsection (a)(3) in connection with any credit or insurance transaction that is not initiated by the consumer only if

      (A)   the consumer authorizes the agency to provide such report to such person; or

      (B)   (i)   the transaction consists of a firm offer of credit or insurance;

         (ii)   the consumer reporting agency has complied with subsection (e); and

         (iii)   there is not in effect an election by the consumer, made in accordance with subsection (e), to have the consumer's name and address excluded from lists of names provided by the agency pursuant to this paragraph.

   (2)   *Limits on information received under paragraph (1)(B).* A person may receive pursuant to paragraph (1)(B) only

      (A)   the name and address of a consumer;

      (B)   an identifier that is not unique to the consumer and that is used by the person solely for the purpose of verifying the identity of the consumer; and

      (C)   other information pertaining to a consumer that does not identify the relationship or experience of the consumer with respect to a particular creditor or other entity.

   (3)   *Information regarding inquiries.* Except as provided in section 609(a)(5) [§ 1681g], a consumer reporting agency shall not furnish to any person a record of inquiries in connection with a credit or insurance transaction that is not initiated by a consumer.

(d)   [Reserved.]

(e) Election of consumer to be excluded from lists.

    (1)   *In general.* A consumer may elect to have the consumer's name and address excluded from any list provided by a consumer reporting agency under subsection (c)(1)(B) in connection with a credit or insurance transaction that is not initiated by the consumer, by notifying the agency in accordance with paragraph (2) that the consumer does not consent to any use of a consumer report relating to the consumer in connection with any credit or insurance transaction that is not initiated by the consumer.

    (2)   *Manner of notification.* A consumer shall notify a consumer reporting agency under paragraph (1)

        (A)   through the notification system maintained by the agency under paragraph (5); or

        (B)   by submitting to the agency a signed notice of election form issued by the agency for purposes of this subparagraph.

    (3)   *Response of agency after notification through system.* Upon receipt of notification of the election of a consumer under paragraph (1) through the notification system maintained by the agency under paragraph (5), a consumer reporting agency shall

        (A)   inform the consumer that the election is effective only for the 2-year period following the election if the consumer does not submit to the agency a signed notice of election form issued by the agency for purposes of paragraph (2)(B); and

        (B)   provide to the consumer a notice of election form, if requested by the consumer, not later than 5 business days after receipt of the notification of the election through the system established under paragraph (5), in the case of a request made at the time the consumer provides notification through the system.

    (4)   *Effectiveness of election.* An election of a consumer under paragraph (1)

        (A)   shall be effective with respect to a consumer reporting agency beginning 5 business days after the date on which the consumer notifies the agency in accordance with paragraph (2);

        (B)   shall be effective with respect to a consumer reporting agency

            (i)   subject to subparagraph (C), during the 2-year period beginning 5 business days after the date on which the consumer notifies the agency of the election, in the case of an election for which a consumer notifies the agency only in accordance with paragraph (2)(A); or

            (ii)   until the consumer notifies the agency under subparagraph (C), in the case of an election (or which a consumer notifies the agency in accordance with paragraph (2)(B);

        (C)   shall not be effective after the date on which the consumer notifies the agency, through the notification system established by the agency under paragraph (5), that the election is no longer effective; and

        (D)   Shall be effective with respect to each affiliate of the agency.

    (5)   *Notification system.*

(A) *In general.* Each consumer reporting agency that, under subsection (c)(1)(B) furnishes a consumer report in connection with a credit or insurance transaction that is not initiated by a consumer, shall

(i) establish and maintain a notification system, including a toll-free telephone number, which permits any consumer whose consumer report is maintained by the agency to notify the agency, with appropriate identification, of the consumer's election to have the consumer's name and address excluded from any such list of names and addresses provided by the agency for such a transaction; and

(ii) publish by not later than 365 days after the date of enactment of the Consumer Credit Reporting Reform Act of 1996, and not less than annually thereafter, in a publication of general circulation in the area served by the agency

(I) a notification that information in consumer files maintained by the agency may be used in connection with such transactions; and

(II) the address and toll-free telephone number for consumers to use to notify the agency of the consumer's election under clause (I).

(B) *Establishment and maintenance as compliance.* Establishment and maintenance of a notification system (including a toll-free telephone number) and publication by a consumer reporting agency on the agency's own behalf and on behalf of any of its affiliates in accordance with this paragraph is deemed to be compliance with this paragraph by each of those affiliates.

(6) *Notification system by agencies that operate nationwide.* Each consumer reporting agency that compiles and maintains files on consumers on a nationwide basis shall establish and maintain a notification system for purposes of paragraph (5) jointly with other such consumer reporting agencies.

(f) *Certain use or obtaining of information prohibited.* A person shall not use or obtain a consumer report for any purpose unless

(1) the consumer report is obtained for a purpose for which the consumer report is authorized to be furnished under this section; and

(2) the purpose is certified in accordance with section 607 [§ 1681e] by a prospective user of the report through a general or specific certification.

(g) *Furnishing reports containing medical information.* A consumer reporting agency shall not furnish for employment purposes, or in connection with a credit or insurance transaction, a consumer report that contains medical information about a consumer, unless the consumer consents to the furnishing of the report.

15 U.S.C. 1681b

§ 605. Requirements relating to information contained in consumer reports

(a) *Information excluded from consumer reports.* Except as authorized under subsection (b) of this section, no consumer reporting agency may make any consumer report containing any of the following items of information:

(1) Cases under title 11 [United States Code] or under the Bankruptcy Act that, from the date of entry of the order for relief or the date of adjudication, as the case may be, antedate the report by more than 10 years.

(2) Civil suits, civil judgments, and records of arrest that from date of entry, antedate the report by more than seven years or until the governing statute of limitations has expired, whichever is the longer period.

(3) Paid tax liens which, from date of payment, antedate the report by more than seven years.

(4) Accounts placed for collection or charged to profit and loss which antedate the report by more than seven years.*

(5) Any other adverse item of information, other than records of convictions of crimes which antedates the report by more than seven years.*

(b) *Exempted cases.* The provisions of subsection (a) of this section are not applicable in the case of any consumer credit report to be used in connection with

(1) a credit transaction involving, or which may reasonably be expected to involve, a principal amount of $150,000 or more;

(2) the underwriting of life insurance involving, or which may reasonably be expected to involve, a face amount of $150,000 or more; or

(3) the employment of any individual at an annual salary which equals, or which may reasonably be expected to equal $75,000, or more.

(c) *Running of reporting period.*

(1) *In general.* The 7-year period referred to in paragraphs (4) and (6) of subsection (a) shall begin, with respect to any delinquent account that is placed for collection (internally or by referral to a third party, whichever is earlier), charged to profit and loss, or subjected to any similar action, upon the expiration of the 180-day period beginning on the date of the commencement of the delinquency which immediately preceded the collection activity, charge to profit and loss, or similar action.

(2) *Effective date.* Paragraph (1) shall apply only to items of information added to the file of a consumer on or after the date that is 455 days after the date of enactment of the Consumer Credit Reporting Reform Act of 1996.

(d) *Information required to be disclosed.* Any consumer reporting agency that furnishes a consumer report that contains information regarding any case involving the consumer that arises under title 11, United States Code, shall include in the report an identification of the chapter of such title 11 under which such case arises if provided by the source of the information. If any case arising or filed under title 11, United States Code, is withdrawn by the consumer before a final judgment, the consumer reporting agency shall include in the report that such case or filing was withdrawn upon receipt of documentation certifying such withdrawal.

---

*The reporting periods have been lengthened for certain adverse information pertaining to U.S. Government insured or guaranteed student loans, or pertaining to national direct student loans. See sections 430A(f) and 463(c)(3) of the Higher Education Act of 1965. 20 U.S.C. 1080a(f) and 20 U.S.C. 1087cc(c)(3), respectively.

(e)   *Indication of closure of account by consumer.* If a consumer reporting agency is notified pursuant to section 623(a)(4) [§ 1681s-2] that a credit account of a consumer was voluntarily closed by the consumer, the agency shall indicate that fact in any consumer report that includes information related to the account.

(f)   *Indication of dispute by consumer.* If a consumer reporting agency is notified pursuant to section 623(a)(3) [§ 1681s-2] that information regarding a consumer who was furnished to the agency is disputed by the consumer, the agency shall indicate that fact in each consumer report that includes the disputed information.

---

15 U.S.C. 1681c

§ 606. Disclosure of investigative consumer reports

(a)   *Disclosure of fact of preparation.* A person may not procure or cause to be prepared an investigative consumer report on any consumer unless

   (1)   it is clearly and accurately disclosed to the consumer that an investigative consumer report including information as to his character, general reputation, personal characteristics and mode of living, whichever are applicable, may be made, and such disclosure

      (A)   is made in a writing mailed, or otherwise delivered, to the consumer, not later than three days after the date on which the report was first requested, and

      (B)   includes a statement informing the consumer of his right to request the additional disclosures provided for under subsection (b) of this section and the written summary of the rights of the consumer prepared pursuant to section 609(c) [§ 1681g]; and

   (2)   the person certifies or has certified to the consumer reporting agency that

      (A)   the person has made the disclosures to the consumer required by paragraph (1); and

      (B)   the person will comply with subsection (b).

(b)   *Disclosure on request of nature and scope of investigation.* Any person who procures or causes to be prepared an investigative consumer report on any consumer shall, upon written request made by the consumer within a reasonable period of time after the receipt by him of the disclosure required by subsection (a)(1) of this section. make a complete and accurate disclosure of the nature and scope of the investigation requested. This disclosure shall be made in a writing mailed, or otherwise delivered, to the consumer not later than five days after the date on which the request for such disclosure was received from the consumer or such report was first requested, whichever is the later.

(c)   *Limitation on liability upon showing of reasonable procedures for compliance with provisions.* No person may be held liable for any violation of subsection (a) or (b) of this section if he shows by a preponderance of the evidence that at the time of the violation he maintained reasonable procedures to assure compliance with subsection (a) or (b) of this section.

(d)   Prohibitions.

   (1)   *Certification.* A consumer reporting agency shall not prepare or furnish investigative consumer report unless the agency has received a certification under subsection (a)(2) from the person who requested the report.

(2) *Inquiries.* A consumer reporting agency shall not make an inquiry for the purpose of preparing an investigative consumer report on a consumer for employment purposes if the making of the inquiry by an employer or prospective employer of the consumer would violate any applicable Federal or State equal employment opportunity law or regulation.

(3) *Certain public record information.* Except as otherwise provided in section 613 [§ 1681k], a consumer reporting agency shall not furnish an investigative consumer report that includes information that is a matter of public record and that relates to an arrest, indictment, conviction, civil judicial action, tax lien, or outstanding judgment, unless the agency has verified the accuracy of the information during the 30-day period ending on the date on which the report is furnished.

(4) *Certain adverse information.* A consumer reporting agency shall not prepare or furnish an investigative consumer report on a consumer that contains information that is adverse to the interest of the consumer and that is obtained through a personal interview with a neighbor, friend, or associate of the consumer or with another person with whom the consumer is acquainted or who has knowledge of such item of information, unless

(A) the agency has followed reasonable procedures to obtain confirmation of the information, from an additional source that has independent and direct knowledge of the information; or

(B) the person interviewed is the best possible source of the information.

15 U.S.C. 1681d

§ 607. Compliance procedures

(a) *Identity and purposes of credit users.* Every consumer reporting agency shall maintain reasonable procedures designed to avoid violations of section 605 [§ 1681e] and to limit the furnishing of consumer reports to the purposes listed under section 604 [§ 1681b] of this title. These procedures shall require that prospective users of the information identify themselves, certify the purposes for which the information is sought, and certify that the information will be used for no other purpose. Every consumer reporting agency shall make a reasonable effort to verify the identity of a new prospective user and the uses certified by such prospective user prior to furnishing such user a consumer report. No consumer reporting agency may furnish a consumer report to any person if it has reasonable grounds for believing that the consumer report will not be used for a purpose listed in section 604 [§ 1681b] of this title.

(b) *Accuracy of report.* Whenever a consumer reporting agency prepares a consumer report it shall follow reasonable procedures to assure maximum possible accuracy of the information concerning the individual about whom the report relates.

(c) *Disclosure of consumer reports by users allowed.* A consumer reporting agency may not prohibit a user of a consumer report furnished by the agency on a consumer from disclosing the contents of the report to the consumer, if adverse action against the consumer has been taken by the user based in whole or in part on the report.

(d) Notice to users and furnishers of information.

(1) *Notice requirement.* A consumer reporting agency shall provide to any person

(A) who regularly and in the ordinary course of business furnishes information to the agency with respect to any consumer; or

        (B)   to whom a consumer report is provided by the agency; a notice of such person's responsibilities under this title.

    (2)   *Content of notice.* The Federal Trade Commission shall prescribe the content of notices under paragraph (1), and a consumer reporting agency shall be in compliance with this subsection if it provides a notice under paragraph (1) that is substantially similar to the Federal Trade Commission prescription under this paragraph.

(e) Procurement of consumer report for resale.

    (1)   *Disclosure.* A person may not procure a consumer report for purposes of reselling the report (or any information in the report) unless the person discloses to the consumer reporting agency that originally furnishes the report

        (A)   the identity of the end-user of the report (or information); and

        (B)   each permissible purpose under section 604 [§ 1681b] for which the report is furnished to the end-user of the report (or information).

    (2)   *Responsibilities of procurers for resale.* A person who procures a consumer report for purposes of reselling the report (or any information in the report) shall

        (A)   establish and comply with reasonable procedures designed to ensure that the report (or information) is resold by the person only for a purpose for which the report may be furnished under section 604 [§ 1681b], including by requiring that each person to which the report (or information) is resold and that resells or provides the report (or information) to any other person

           (i)   identifies each end user of the resold report (or information);

           (ii) certifies each purpose or which the report (or information) will be used; and

           (iii) certifies that the report (or information) will be used for no other purpose; and

        (B)   before reselling the report, make reasonable efforts to verify the identifications and certifications made under subparagraph (A).

15 U.S.C. 1681e

§ 608. Disclosures to governmental agencies

Notwithstanding the provisions of section 604 (§ 1681b] of this title, a consumer reporting agency may furnish identifying information respecting any consumer, limited to his name, address, former addresses, places of employment, or former places of employment, to a governmental agency.

15 U.S.C. 1681f

§ 609. Disclosures to consumers

(a) *Information on file; sources; report recipients.* Every consumer reporting agency shall, upon request, and subject to 610(a)(1) [§ 1681h], clearly and accurately disclose to the consumer:

    (1)   All information in the consumer's file at the time of the request except that nothing in this paragraph shall be construed to require a consumer reporting

agency to disclose to a consumer any information concerning credit scores or any other risk scores or predictors relating to the consumer.

(2)   The sources of the information; except that the sources of information acquired solely for use in preparing an investigative consumer report and actually used for no other purpose need not be disclosed: Provided, that in the event an action is brought under this title, such sources shall be available to the plaintiff under appropriate discovery procedures in the court in which the action is brought.

(3)   (A)   Identification of each person (including each end-user identified under section 607(e)(1) [§ 1681e]) that procured a consumer report

      (i)   for employment purposes, during the 2-year period preceding the date on which the request is made; or

      (ii)   for any other purpose, during the 1-year period preceding the date on which the request is made.

  (B)   An identification of a person under subparagraph (A) shall include

      (i)   the name of the person or, if applicable, the trade name (written in full) under which such person conducts business; and

      (ii)   upon request of the consumer, the address and telephone number of the person.

  (C)   Subparagraph (A) does not apply if—

      (i)   the end user is an agency of department of the United States Government that procures the report from the person for purposes of determining the eligibility of the consumer to whom the report relates to receive access or continued access to classified information (as defined in section 604(b)(4)(E)(i)); and

      (ii)   the head of the agency or department makes a written finding as prescribed under section 604(b)(4)(A).

(4)   The dates, original payees, and amounts of any checks upon which is based any adverse characterization of the consumer, included in the file at the time of the disclosure.

(5)   A record of all inquiries received by the agency during the 1-year period preceding the request that identified the consumer in connection with a credit or insurance transaction that was not initiated by the consumer.

(b)   *Exempt information.* The requirements of subsection (a) of this section respecting the disclosure of sources of information and the recipients of consumer reports do not apply to information received or consumer reports furnished prior to the effective date of this title except to the extent that the matter involved is contained in the files of the consumer reporting agency on that date.

(c)   Summary of rights required to be included with disclosure.

(1)   *Summary of rights.* A consumer reporting agency shall provide to a consumer, with each written disclosure by the agency to the consumer under this section

  (A)   a written summary of all of the rights that the consumer has under this title; and

  (B)   in the case of a consumer reporting agency that compiles and maintains files on consumers on a nationwide basis, a toll-free telephone number established by the agency, at which personnel are accessible to consumer during normal business hours.

(2)   *Specific items required to be included.* The summary of rights required under paragraph (1) shall include:

(A)   a brief description of this title and all rights of consumers under this title;

(B)   an explanation of how the consumer may exercise the rights of the consumer under this title;

(C)   a list of all Federal agencies responsible for enforcing any provision of this title and the address and any appropriate phone number of each such agency, in a form that will assist the consumer in selecting the appropriate agency;

(D)   a statement that the consumer may have additional rights under State law and that the consumer may wish to contact a State or local consumer protection agency or a State attorney general to learn of those rights; and

(E)   a statement that a consumer reporting agency is not required to remove accurate derogatory information from a consumer's file, unless the information is outdated under section 605 [§ 1681c] or cannot be verified.

(3)   *Form of summary of rights.* For purposes of this subsection and any disclosure by a consumer reporting agency required under this title with respect to consumers' rights, the Federal Trade Commission (after consultation with each Federal agency referred to in section 621(b) [§ 1681s]) shall prescribe the form and content of any such disclosure of the rights of consumers required under this title. A consumer reporting agency shall be in compliance with this subsection if it provides disclosures under paragraph (1) that are substantially similar to the Federal Trade Commission prescription under this paragraph.

(4)   *Effectiveness.* No disclosures shall be required under this subsection until the date on which the Federal Trade Commission prescribes the form and content of such disclosures under paragraph (3).

15 U.S.C. 1681g

§ 610. Conditions and form of disclosure to consumers

(a)   In general.

(1)   *Proper identification.* A consumer reporting agency shall maintain, as a condition of making the disclosures required under section 609 [§ 1681g], that the consumer furnish proper identification.

(2)   *Disclosure in writing.* Except as provided in subsection (b), the disclosures required to be made under section 609 [§ 1681g] shall be provided under that section in writing.

(b)   Other forms of disclosure.

(1)   *In general.* If authorized by a consumer, a consumer reporting agency may make the disclosures required under 609 [§ 1681g]

(A)   other than in writing; and

(B)   in such form as may be

(i)   specified by the consumer in accordance with paragraph (2); and

(ii) available from the agency.

(2) *Form.* A consumer may specify pursuant to paragraph (1) that disclosures under section 609 [§ 1681g] shall be made

    (A) in person, upon the appearance of the consumer at the place of business of the consumer reporting agency where disclosures are regularly provided, during normal business hours, and on reasonable notice;

    (B) by telephone, if the consumer has made a written request for disclosure by telephone;

    (C) by electronic means, if available from the agency; or

    (D) by any other reasonable means that is available from the agency.

(c) *Trained personnel.* Any consumer reporting agency shall provide trained personnel to explain to the consumer any information furnished to him pursuant to section 609 [§ 1681g] of this title.

(d) *Persons accompanying consumer.* The consumer shall be permitted to be accompanied by one other person of his choosing, who shall furnish reasonable identification. A consumer reporting agency may require the consumer to furnish a written statement granting permission to the consumer reporting agency to discuss the consumer's file in such person's presence.

(e) *Limitation of liability.* Except as provided in sections 616 and 617 [§§ 1681n and 1681o] of this title, no consumer may bring any action or proceeding in the nature of defamation, invasion of privacy, or negligence with respect to the reporting of information against any consumer reporting agency, any user of information, or any person who furnishes information to a consumer reporting agency, based on information disclosed pursuant to section 609, 610, or 615 [§§ 1681g, 1681h, or 1681m] of this title or based on information disclosed by a user of a consumer report to or for a consumer against whom the user has taken adverse action, based in whole or in part on the report, except as to false information furnished with malice or willful intent to injure such consumer.

____
15 U.S.C. 1681h

§ 611. Procedure in case of disputed accuracy

(a) Reinvestigations of disputed information.

    (1) Reinvestigation required.

        (A) *In general.* If the completeness or accuracy of any item of information contained in a consumer's file at a consumer reporting agency is disputed by the consumer and the consumer notifies the agency directly of such dispute, the agency shall reinvestigate free of charge and record the current status of the disputed information, or delete the item from the file in accordance with paragraph (5), before the end of the 30-day period beginning on the date on which the agency receives the notice of the dispute from the consumer.

        (B) *Extension of period to reinvestigate.* Except as provided in subparagraph (C), the 30-day period described in subparagraph (A) may be extended for not more than 15 additional days if the consumer reporting agency receives information from the consumer during that 30-day period that is relevant to the reinvestigation.

(C)   *Limitations on extension of period to reinvestigate.* Subparagraph (B) shall not apply to any reinvestigation in which, during the 30-day period described in subparagraph (A), the information that is the subject of the reinvestigation is found to be inaccurate or incomplete or the consumer reporting agency determines that the information cannot be verified.

(2)   Prompt notice of dispute to furnisher of information.

(A)   *In general.* Before the expiration of the 5-business-day period beginning on the date on which a consumer reporting agency receives notice of a dispute from any consumer in accordance with paragraph (1), the agency shall provide notification of the dispute to any person who provided any item of information in dispute, at the address and in the manner established with the person. The notice shall include all relevant information regarding the dispute that the agency has received from the consumer.

(B)   *Provision of other information from consumer.* The consumer reporting agency shall promptly provide to the person who provided the information in dispute all relevant information regarding the dispute that is received by the agency from the consumer after the period referred to in subparagraph (A) and before the end of the period referred to in paragraph (1)(A).

(3)   Determination that dispute is frivolous or irrelevant.

(A)   *In general.* Notwithstanding paragraph (1), a consumer reporting agency may terminate a reinvestigation of information disputed by a consumer under that paragraph if the agency reasonably determines that the dispute by the consumer is frivolous or irrelevant, including by reason of a failure by a consumer to provide sufficient information to investigate the disputed information.

(B)   *Notice of determination.* Upon making any determination in accordance with subparagraph (A) that a dispute is frivolous or irrelevant, a consumer reporting agency shall notify the consumer of such determination not later than 5 business days after making such determination, by mail or, if authorized by the consumer for that purpose, by any other means available to the agency.

(C)   *Contents of notice.* A notice under subparagraph B shall include

(i)   the reasons for the determination under subparagraph (A); and

(ii)   identification of any information required to investigate the disputed information, which may consist of a standardized form describing the general nature of such information.

(4)   *Consideration of consumer information.* In conducting any reinvestigation under paragraph (1) with respect to disputed information in the file of any consumer, the consumer reporting agency shall review and consider all relevant information submitted by the consumer in the period described in paragraph (1)(A) with respect to such disputed information.

(5)   Treatment of inaccurate or unverifiable information.

(A)   *In general.* If, after any reinvestigation under paragraph (1) of any information disputed by a consumer, an item of the information is found to be inaccurate or incomplete or cannot be verified, the consumer reporting agency shall promptly delete that item of information from the consumer's file or modify that item of information, as appropriate, based on the results of the reinvestigation.

(B) Requirements relating to reinsertion of previously deleted material.

  (i) *Certification of accuracy of information.* If any information is deleted from a consumers file pursuant to subparagraph (A), the information may not be reinserted in the file by the consumer reporting agency unless the person who furnishes the information certifies that the information is complete and accurate.

  (ii) *Notice to consumer.* If any information that has been deleted from a consumer's file pursuant to subparagraph (A) is reinserted in the file, the consumer reporting agency shall notify the consumer of the reinsertion in writing not later than 5 business days after the reinsertion or, if authorized by the consumer for that purpose, by any other means available to the agency.

  (iii) *Additional information.* As part of, or in addition to, the notice under clause (ii), a consumer reporting agency shall provide to a consumer in writing not later than 5 business days after the date of the reinsertion

    (I) a statement that the disputed information has been reinserted;

    (II) the business name and address of any furnisher of information contacted and the telephone number of such furnisher, if reasonably available, or of any furnisher of information that contacted the consumer reporting agency, in connection with the reinsertion of such information; and

    (III) a notice that the consumer has the right to add a statement to the consumer's file disputing the accuracy or completeness of the disputed information.

(C) *Procedures to prevent reappearance.* A consumer reporting agency shall maintain reasonable procedures designed to prevent the reappearance in a consumer's file, and in consumer reports on the consumer, of information that is deleted pursuant to this paragraph (other than information that is reinserted in accordance with subparagraph (B) (i)).

(D) *Automated reinvestigation system.* Any consumer reporting agency that compiles and maintains files on consumers on a nationwide basis shall implement an automated system through which furnishers of information to that consumer reporting agency may report the results of a reinvestigation that finds incomplete or inaccurate information in a consumer's file to other such consumer reporting agencies.

(6) Notice of results of reinvestigation.

(A) *In general.* A consumer reporting agency shall provide written notice to a consumer of the results of a reinvestigation under this subsection not later than 5 business days after the completion of the reinvestigation, by mail or, if authorized by the consumer for that purpose, by other means available to the agency.

     (B)   *Contents.* As part of, or in addition to, the notice under subparagraph (A), a consumer reporting agency shall provide to a consumer in writing before the expiration of the 5-day period referred to in subparagraph (A)

          (i)   a statement that the reinvestigation is completed;

          (ii)   a consumer report that is based upon the consumer's file as that file is revised as a result of the reinvestigation;

          (iii) a notice that, if requested by the consumer, a description of the procedure used to determine the accuracy and completeness of the information shall be provided to the consumer by the agency, including the business name and address of any furnisher of information contacted in connection with such information and the telephone number of such furnisher, if reasonably available;

          (iv) a notice that the consumer has the right to add a statement to the consumer's file disputing the accuracy or completeness of the information; and

          (v)   a notice that the consumer has the right to request under subsection (d) that the consumer reporting agency furnish notifications under that subsection.

  (7)   *Description of reinvestigation procedure.* A consumer reporting agency shall provide to a consumer a description referred to in paragraph (6)(B)(iii) by not later than 15 days after receiving a request from the consumer for that description.

  (8)   *Expedited dispute resolution.* If a dispute regarding an item of information in a consumer's file at a consumer reporting agency is resolved in accordance with paragraph (5)(A) by the deletion of the disputed information by not later than 3 business days after the date on which the agency receives notice of the dispute from the consumer in accordance with paragraph (1)(A), then the agency shall not be required to comply with paragraphs (2), (6), and (7) with respect to that dispute if the agency

     (A)   provides prompt notice of the deletion to the consumer by telephone;

     (B)   includes in that notice, or in a written notice that accompanies a confirmation and consumer report provided in accordance with subparagraph (C), a statement of the consumer's right to request under subsection (d) that the agency furnish notifications under that subsection; and

     (C)   provides written confirmation of the deletion and a copy of a consumer report on the consumer that is based on the consumer's file after the deletion, not later than 5 business days after making the deletion.

(b) *Statement of dispute.* If the reinvestigation does not resolve the dispute, the consumer may file a brief statement setting forth the nature of the dispute. The consumer reporting agency may limit such statements to not more than one hundred words if it provides the consumer with assistance in writing a clear summary of the dispute.

(c) *Notification of consumer dispute in subsequent consumer reports.* Whenever a statement of a dispute is filed, unless there is reasonable grounds to believe that it is frivolous or irrelevant, the consumer reporting agency shall, in any subsequent consumer report containing the information in question, clearly note that it is disputed by the consumer and provide either the consumer's statement or a clear and accurate codification or summary thereof.

(d) *Notification of deletion of disputed information.* Following any deletion of information which is found to be inaccurate or whose accuracy can no longer be verified or any notation as to disputed information, the consumer reporting agency shall, at the request of the consumer, furnish notification that the item has been deleted or the statement, codification or summary pursuant to subsection (b) or (c) of this section to any person specifically designated by the consumer who has within two years prior thereto received a consumer report for employment purposes, or within six months prior thereto received a consumer report for any other purpose. which contained the deleted or disputed information.

15 U.S.C. 1681i

§ 612. Charges for certain disclosures

(a) Reasonable charges allowed for certain disclosures.

    (1)   *In general.* Except as provided in subsections (b), (c), and (d), a consumer reporting agency may impose a reasonable charge on a consumer

        (A)   for making a disclosure to the consumer pursuant to section 609 [§ 1681g], which charge

            (i)   shall not exceed $8; and

            (ii)   shall be indicated to the consumer before making the disclosure; and

        (B)   for furnishing, pursuant to 611(d) [§ 1681i], following a reinvestigation under section 611(a) [§ 1681i], a statement, codification, or summary to a person designated by the consumer under that section after the 30-day period beginning on the date of notification of the consumer under paragraph (6) or (8) of section 611(a) [§ 1681i] with respect to the reinvestigation, which charge

            (i)   shall not exceed the charge that the agency would impose on each designated recipient for a consumer report; and

            (ii)   shall be indicated to the consumer before furnishing such information.

    (2)   *Modification of amount.* The Federal Trade Commission shall increase the amount referred to in paragraph (1)(A)(I) on January 1 of each year, based proportionally on changes in the Consumer Price Index, with fractional changes rounded to the nearest fifty cents.

(b) *Free disclosure after adverse notice to consumer.* Each consumer reporting agency that maintains a file on a consumer shall make all disclosures pursuant to section 609 [§ 1681g] without charge to the consumer if, nor later than 60 days after receipt by such consumer of a notification pursuant to section 615 [§ 1681m], or of a notification from a debt collection agency affiliated with that consumer reporting agency stating that the consumer's credit rating may be or has been adversely affected, the consumer makes a request under section 609 [§ 1681g].

(c) *Free disclosure under certain other circumstances.* Upon the request of the consumer, a consumer reporting agency shall make all disclosures pursuant to section 609 [§ 1681g] once during any 12-month period without charge to that consumer if the consumer certifies in writing that the consumer

    (1)   is unemployed and intends to apply for employment in the 60-day period beginning on the date on which the certification is made;

    (2)   is a recipient of public welfare assistance; or

    (3)   has reason to believe that the file on the consumer at the agency contains inaccurate information due to fraud.

(d)   *Other charges prohibited.* A consumer reporting agency shall not impose any charge on a consumer for providing any notification required by this title or making any disclosure required by this title, except as authorized by subsection (a).

15 U.S.C. 1681j

§ 613. Public record information for employment purposes

(a) *In general.* A consumer reporting agency which furnishes a consumer report for employment purposes and which for that purpose compiles and reports items of information on consumers which are matters of public record and are likely to have an adverse effect upon a consumer's ability to obtain employment shall

    (1)   at the time such public record information is reported to the user of such consumer report, notify the consumer of the fact that public record information is being reported by the consumer reporting agency, together with the name and address of the person to whom such information is being reported; or

    (2)   maintain strict procedures designed to insure that whenever public record information which is likely to have an adverse effect on a consumer's ability to obtain employment is reported it is complete and up to date. For purposes of this paragraph, items of public record relating to arrests, indictments, convictions, suits, tax liens, and outstanding judgments shall be considered up to date if the current public record status of the item at the time of the report is reported.

(b) *Exemption for national security investigations.* Subsection (a) does not apply in the case of an agency or department of the United States Government that seeks to obtain and use a consumer report for employment purposes, if the head of the agency or department makes a written finding as prescribed under section 604(b)(4)(A).

15 U.S.C. 1681k

§ 614. Restrictions on investigative consumer reports

Whenever a consumer reporting agency prepares an investigative consumer report, no adverse information in the consumer report (other than information which is a matter of public record) may be included in a subsequent consumer report unless such adverse information has been verified in the process of making such subsequent consumer report, or the adverse information was received within the three-month period preceding the date the subsequent report is furnished.

15 U.S.C. 1681l

§ 615. Requirements on users of consumer reports

(a) *Duties of users taking adverse actions on the basis of information contained in consumer reports.* If any person takes any adverse action with respect to any consumer that is based in whole or in part on any information contained in a consumer report, the person shall

    (1)   provide oral, written, or electronic notice of the adverse action to the consumer;

(2) provide to the consumer orally, in writing, or electronically

   (A) the name, address, and telephone number of the consumer reporting agency (including a toll-free telephone number established by the agency if the agency compiles and maintains files on consumers on a nationwide basis) that furnished the report to the person; and

   (B) a statement that the consumer reporting agency did not make the decision to take the adverse action and is unable to provide the consumer the specific reasons why the adverse action was taken; and

(3) provide to the consumer an oral, written, or electronic notice of the consumer's right

   (A) to obtain, under section 612 [§ 1681j], a free copy of a consumer report on the consumer from the consumer reporting agency referred to in paragraph (2), which notice shall include an indication of the 60-day period under that section for obtaining such a copy; and

   (B) to dispute, under section 611 [§ 1681i], with a consumer reporting agency the accuracy or completeness of any information in a consumer report furnished by the agency.

(b) Adverse action based on information obtained from third parties other than consumer reporting agencies.

(1) *In general.* Whenever credit for personal, family, or household purposes involving a consumer is denied or the charge for such credit is increased either wholly or partly because of information obtained from a person other than a consumer reporting agency bearing upon the consumer's creditworthiness, credit standing, credit capacity, character, general reputation, personal characteristics, or mode of living, the user of such information shall, within a reasonable period of time, upon the consumer's written request for the reasons for such adverse action received within sixty days after learning of such adverse action, disclose the nature of the information to the consumer. The user of such information shall clearly and accurately disclose to the consumer his right to make such written request at the time such adverse action is communicated to the consumer.

(2) Duties of person taking certain actions based on information provided by affiliate.

   (A) *Duties, generally.* If a person takes an action described in subparagraph (B) with respect to a consumer, based in whole or in part on information described in subparagraph (C), the person shall

      (i) notify the consumer of the action, including a statement that the consumer may obtain the information in accordance with clause (ii); and

      (ii) upon a written request from the consumer received within 60 days after transmittal of the notice required by clause (I), disclose to the consumer the nature of the information upon which the action is based by not later than 30 days after receipt of the request.

   (B) *Action described.* An action referred to in subparagraph (A) is an adverse action described in section 603(k)(1)(A) [§ 1681a], taken in connection with a transaction initiated by the consumer, or any adverse action described in clause (i) or (ii) of section 603(k)(1)(B) [§ 1681a].

(C) *Information described.* Information referred to in subparagraph (A)

  (i) except as provided in clause (ii), is information that

   (I) is furnished to the person taking the action by a person related by common ownership or affiliated by common corporate control to the person taking the action; and

   (II) bears on the creditworthiness, credit standing, credit capacity, character, general reputation, personal characteristics, or mode of living of the consumer; and

  (ii) does not include

   (I) information solely as to transactions or experiences between the consumer and the person furnishing the information; or

   (II) information in a consumer report.

(c) *Reasonable procedures to assure compliance.* No person shall be held liable for any violation of this section if he shows by a preponderance of the evidence that at the time of the alleged violation he maintained reasonable procedures to assure compliance with the provisions of this section.

(d) Duties of users making written credit or insurance solicitation on the basis of information contained in consumer files.

  (1) *In general.* Any person who uses a consumer report on any consumer in connection with any credit or insurance transaction that is not initiated by the consumer, that is provided to that person under section 604(c)(1)(B) [§ 1681b], shall provide with each written solicitation made to the consumer regarding the transaction a clear and conspicuous statement that

   (A) information contained in the consumer's consumer report was used in connection with the transaction;

   (B) the consumer received the offer of credit or insurance because the consumer satisfied the criteria for creditworthiness or insurability under which the consumer was selected for the offer;

   (C) if applicable, the credit or insurance may not be extended if. after the consumer responds to the offer, the consumer does not meet the criteria used to select the consumer for the offer or any applicable criteria bearing on credit worthiness or insurability or does not furnish any required collateral;

   (D) the consumer has a right to prohibit information contained in the consumer's file with any consumer reporting agency from being used in connection with any credit or insurance transaction that is not initiated by the consumer; and

   (E) the consumer may exercise the right referred to in subparagraph (D) by notifying a notification system established under section 604(e) [§ 1681b].

  (2) *Disclosure of address and telephone number.* A statement under paragraph (1) shall include the address and toll-free telephone number of the appropriate notification system established under section 604(e) [§ 1681b].

  (3) *Maintaining criteria on file.* A person who makes an offer of credit or insurance to a consumer under a credit or insurance transaction described in paragraph

(1) shall maintain on file the criteria used to select the consumer to receive the offer, all criteria bearing on creditworthiness or insurability, as applicable, that are the basis for determining whether or not to extend credit or insurance pursuant to the offer, and any requirement for the furnishing of collateral as a condition of the extension of credit or insurance, until the expiration of the 3-year period beginning on the date on which the offer is made to the consumer.

(4) *Authority of federal agencies regarding unfair or deceptive acts or practices not affected*. This section is not intended to affect the authority of any Federal or State agency to enforce a prohibition against unfair or deceptive acts or practices, including the making of false or misleading statements in connection with a credit or insurance transaction that is not initiated by the consumer.

15 U.S.C. 1681m

§ 616. Civil liability for willful noncompliance

(a) *In general*. Any person who willfully fails to comply with any requirement imposed under this title with respect to any consumer is liable to that consumer in an amount equal to the sum of

(1)   (A)   any actual damages sustained by the consumer as a result of the failure or damages of not less than $100 and not more than $1,000; or

      (B)   in the case of liability of a natural person for obtaining a consumer report under false pretenses or knowingly without a permissible purpose, actual damages sustained by the consumer as a result of the failure or $1,000, whichever is greater;

(2) such amount of punitive damages as the court may allow; and

(3) in the case of any successful action to enforce any liability under this section, the costs of the action together with reasonable attorney's fees as determined by the court.

(b) *Civil liability for knowing noncompliance*. Any person who obtains a consumer report from a consumer reporting agency under false pretenses or knowingly without a permissible purpose shall be liable to the consumer reporting agency for actual damages sustained by the consumer reporting agency or $1,000, whichever is greater.

(c) *Attorney's fees*. Upon a finding by the court that an unsuccessful pleading, motion, or other paper filed in connection with an action under this section was filed in bad faith or for purposes of harassment, the court shall award to the prevailing party attorney's fees reasonable in relation to the work expended in responding to the pleading, motion, or other paper.

15 U.S.C. 1681n

§ 617. Civil liability for negligent noncompliance

(a) *In general*. Any person who is negligent in failing to comply with any requirement imposed under this title with respect to any consumer is liable to that consumer in an amount equal to the sum of

(1) any actual damages sustained by the consumer as a result of the failure;

(2) in the case of any successful action to enforce any liability under this section, the costs of the action together with reasonable attorney's fees as determined by the court.

(b) *Attorney's fees*. On a finding by the court that an unsuccessful pleading, motion, or other paper filed in connection with an action under this section was filed in bad faith or for purposes of harassment, the court shall award to the prevailing party attorney's fees reasonable in relation to the work expended in responding to the pleading, motion, or other paper.

15 U.S.C. 1681o

§ 618. Jurisdiction of courts; limitation of actions

An action to enforce any liability created under this title may be brought in any appropriate United States district court without regard to the amount in controversy, or in any other court of competent jurisdiction, within two years from the date on which the liability arises, except that where a defendant has materially and willfully misrepresented any information required under this title to be disclosed to an individual and the information so misrepresented is material to the establishment of the defendant's liability to that individual under this title, the action may be brought at any time within two years after discovery by the individual of the misrepresentation.

15 U.S.C. 1681p

§ 619. Obtaining information under false pretenses

Any person who knowingly and willfully obtains information on a consumer from a consumer reporting agency under false premises shall be fined under title 18, United States Code, imprisoned for not more than 2 years, or both.

15 U.S.C. 1681q

§ 620. Unauthorized disclosures by officers or employees

Any officer or employee of a consumer reporting agency who knowingly and willfully provides information concerning an individual from the agency's files to a person not authorized to receive that information shall be fined under title 18, United States Code, imprisoned for not more than 2 years, or both.

15 U.S.C. 1681r

§ 621. Administrative enforcement

(a) (1) *Enforcement by Federal Trade Commission*. Compliance with the requirements imposed under this title shall be enforced under the Federal Trade Commission Act [15 U.S.C. §§ 41 et seq.] by the Federal Trade Commission with respect to consumer reporting agencies and all other persons subject thereto, except to the extent that enforcement of the requirements imposed under this title is specifically committed to some other government agency under subsection (b) hereof. For the purpose of the exercise by the Federal Trade Commission of its functions and powers under the Federal Trade Commission Act, a violation of any requirement or prohibition imposed under this title shall constitute an unfair or deceptive act or practice in commerce in violation of section 5(a) of the Federal Trade Commission Act [15 U.S.C. § 45(a)] and shall be subject to enforcement by the Federal Trade Commission under section 5(b) thereof [15 U.S.C. § 45(b)] with respect to any consumer reporting agency or person subject to enforcement by the Federal Trade Commission pursuant to this subsection, irrespective of whether that person is engaged in commerce or meets any other jurisdictional tests in the Federal Trade Commission Act. The Federal Trade Commission shall have such procedural, investigative, and enforcement powers, including the power to issue procedural rules in enforcing compliance with the requirements imposed under this title and to require the filing of reports, the production of documents, and the appearance of witnesses as though the applicable terms and conditions of the Federal Trade Commission Act were part of this title. Any person violating any of the provisions of this title shall be subject to the penalties and entitled to the privileges and immunities provided in the Federal Trade Commission Act as though the applicable terms and provisions thereof were part of this title.

(2)   (A)   In the event of a knowing violation, which constitutes a pattern or practice of violations of this title, the Commission may commence a civil action to recover a civil penalty in a district court of the United States against any person that violates this title. In such action, such person shall be liable for a civil penalty of not more than $2,500 per violation.

     (B)   In determining the amount of a civil penalty under subparagraph (A), the court shall take into account the degree at culpability, any history of prior such conduct, ability to pay, effect on ability to continue to do business, and such other matters as justice may require.

(3)   Notwithstanding paragraph (2), a court may not impose any civil penalty on a person for a violation of section 623 (a)(1) [§ 1681s-2] unless the person has been enjoined from committing the violation, or ordered not to commit the violation, in an action or proceeding brought by or on behalf of the Federal Trade Commission, and has violated the injunction or order, and the court may not impose any civil penalty for any violation occurring before the date of the violation of the injunction or order.

(4)   Neither the Commission nor any other agency referred to in subsection (b) may prescribe trade regulation rules or other regulations with respect to this title.

(b)   *Enforcement by other agencies.* Compliance with the requirements imposed under this title with respect no consumer reporting agencies, persons who use consumer reports from such agencies, persons who furnish information to such agencies, and users of information that are subject to subsection (d) of section 615 [§ 1681m] shall be enforced under

(1)   section 8 of the Federal Deposit Insurance Act [12 U.S.C. § 1818], in the case of

     (A)   national banks, and Federal branches and Federal agencies of foreign banks, by the Office of the Comptroller of the Currency;

     (B)   member banks of the Federal Reserve System (other than national banks), branches and agencies of foreign banks (other than Federal branches, Federal agencies, and insured State branches of foreign banks), commercial lending companies owned or controlled by foreign banks, and organizations operating under section 25 or 25(a) [25A] of the Federal Reserve Act [12 U.S.C. §§ 601 et seq., §§ 611 et seq.], by the Board of Governors of the Federal Reserve System; and

     (C)   banks insured by the Federal Deposit Insurance Corporation (other than members of the Federal Reserve System) and insured State branches of foreign banks, by the Board of Directors of the Federal Deposit Insurance Corporation:

(2)   section 8 of the Federal Deposit Insurance Act [12 U.S.C. §1818], by the Director of the Office of Thrift Supervision, in the case of a savings association the deposits of which are insured by the Federal Deposit Insurance Corporation;

(3)   the Federal Credit Union Act [12 U.S.C. §§ 1751 et seq.], by the Administrator of the National Credit Union Administration [National Credit Union Administration Board] with respect to any Federal credit union;

(4)   subtitle IV of title 49 [49 U.S.C. §§ 10101 et seq.], by the Secretary of Transportation, with respect to all carriers subject to the jurisdiction of the Surface Transportation Board;

(5)   the Federal Aviation Act of 1958 [49 U.S.C. Appx §§ 1301 et seq.], by the Secretary of Transportation with respect to any air carrier or foreign air carrier subject to that Act [49 U.S.C. Appx §§ 1301 et seq.]; and

(6)   the Packers and Stockyards Act, 1921 [7 U.S.C. §§ 181 et seq.] (except as provided in section 406 of that Act [7 U.S.C. §§ 226 and 227]), by the Secretary of Agriculture with respect to any activities subject to that Act.

The terms used in paragraph (1) that are not defined in this title or otherwise defined in section 3(s) of the Federal Deposit Insurance Act (12 U.S.C. § 1813(s)) shall have the meaning given to them in section 1(b) of the International Banking Act of 1978 (12 U.S.C. § 3101).

(c) State action for violations.

(1)   *Authority of states.* In addition to such other remedies as are provided under State law, if the chief law enforcement officer of a State, or an official or agency designated by a State, has reason to believe that any person has violated or is violating this title, the State

(A)   may bring an action to enjoin such violation in any appropriate United States district court or in any other court of competent jurisdiction;

(B)   subject to paragraph (5), may bring an action on behalf of the residents of the State to recover

(i)   damages for which the person is liable to such residents under sections 616 and 617 [§§ 1681n and 1681o] as a result of the violation;

(ii)   in the case of a violation of section 623(a) [§ 1681s-2], damages for which the person would, but for section 623(c) [§ 1681s-2], be liable to such residents as a result of the violation; or

(iii) damages of not more than $1,000 far each willful or negligent violation; and

(C)   in the case of any successful action under subparagraph (A) or (B), shall be awarded the casts of the action and reasonable attorney fees as determined by the court.

(2)   *Rights of federal regulators.* The State shall serve prior written notice of any action under paragraph (1) upon the Federal Trade Commission or the appro-

priate Federal regulator determined under subsection (b) and provide the Commission or appropriate Federal regulator with a copy of its complaint, except in any case in which such prior notice is not feasible, in which case the State shall serve such notice immediately upon instituting such action. The Federal Trade Commission or appropriate Federal regulator shall have the right

(A)   to intervene in the action;

(B)   upon so intervening, to be heard on all matters arising therein;

(C)   to remove the action to the appropriate United States district court; and

(D)   to file petitions for appeal.

(3)   *Investigatory powers.* For purposes of bringing any action under this subsection, nothing in this subsection shall prevent the chief law enforcement officer, or an official or agency designated by a State, from exercising the powers conferred on the chief law enforcement officer or such official by the laws of such State to conduct investigations or to administer oaths or affirmations or to compel the attendance of witnesses or the production of documentary and other evidence.

(4)   *Limitation on state action while federal action pending.* If the Federal Trade Commission or the appropriate Federal regulator has instituted a civil action or an administrative action under section 8 of the Federal Deposit Insurance Act for a violation of this title, no State may, during the pendency of such action, bring an action under this section against any defendant named in the complaint of the Commission or the appropriate Federal regulator for any violation of this title that is alleged in that complaint.

(5)   Limitations on state actions for violation of section 623(a)(1) [§ 1681s-2].

(A)   *Violation of injunction required.* A State may not bring an action against a person under paragraph (1)(B) for a violation of section 623(a)(1) [§ 1681 s-2], unless

(i)   the person has been enjoined from committing the violation, in an action brought by the State under paragraph (1)(A); and

(ii)   the person has violated the injunction.

(B)   *Limitation on damages recoverable.* In an action against a person under paragraph (1)(B) for a violation of section 623(a)(1) [§ 1681 s-2], a State may not recover any damages incurred before the date of the violation of an injunction on which the action is based.

(d) *Enforcement under other authority.* For the purpose of the exercise by any agency referred to in subsection (b) of this section of its powers under any Act referred to in that subsection, a violation of any requirement imposed under this title shall be deemed to be a violation of a requirement imposed under that Act. In addition to its powers under any provision of law specifically referred to in subsection (b) of this section, each of the agencies referred to in that subsection may exercise, for the purpose of enforcing compliance with any requirement imposed under this title any other authority conferred on it by law. Notwithstanding the preceding, no agency referred to in subsection (b) may conduct an examination of a bank. savings association, or credit union regarding compliance with the provisions of this title, except in response to a complaint (or if the agency otherwise has knowledge) that the bank, savings association, or credit union has violated a provision of this title, in which case, the agency may conduct an examination as necessary to investigate the complaint. If an agency determines during an investigation in response to a complaint that a violation of this title has occurred, the agency may, during its next 2 regularly scheduled examinations at the bank, savings association, or credit union, examine for compliance with this title.

(e) *Interpretive authority.* The Board of Governors of the Federal Reserve System may issue interpretations of any provision of this title as such provision may apply to any persons identified under paragraph (1), (2), and (3) of subsection (b), or to the holding companies and affiliates of such persons, in consultation with Federal agencies identified in paragraphs (1), (2), and (3) of subsection (b).

----
15 U.S.C. 1681s

§ 622. Information on overdue child support obligations

Notwithstanding any other provision of this title, a consumer reporting agency shall include in any consumer report furnished by the agency in accordance with section 604 [§ 1681b] of this title, any information on the failure of the consumer to pay overdue support which

(1)   is provided

(A)   to the consumer reporting agency by a State or local child support enforcement agency; or

(B)   to the consumer reporting agency and verified by any local, State, or Federal government agency; and

(2)   antedates the report by 7 years or less.

----
15 U.S.C. 1681s-1

§ 623. Responsibilities of furnishers of information to consumer reporting agencies

(a)   Duty of furnishers of information to provide accurate information.

(1)   Prohibition.

(A)   *Reporting information with actual knowledge of errors.* A person shall not furnish any information relating to a consumer to any consumer reporting agency if the person knows or consciously avoids knowing that the information is inaccurate.

(B)   *Reporting information after notice and information of errors.* A person shall not furnish information relating to a consumer to any consumer reporting agency if

(i)   the person has been notified by the consumer, at the address specified by the person far such notices, that specific information is inaccurate; and

(ii)   the information is, in fact, inaccurate.

(C)   *No address requirement.* A person who clearly and conspicuously specifies to the consumer an address for notices referred to in subparagraph (B) shall not be subject to subparagraph (A); however, nothing in subparagraph (B) shall require a person to specify such an address.

(2) *Duty to correct and update information.* A person who

    (A) regularly and in the ordinary course of business furnishes information to one or more consumer reporting agencies about the person's transactions or experiences with any consumer; and

    (B) has furnished to a consumer reporting agency information that the person determines is not complete or accurate, shall promptly notify the consumer reporting agency of that determination and provide to the agency any corrections to that information, or any additional information, that is necessary to make the information provided by the person to the agency complete and accurate, and shall not thereafter furnish to the agency any of the information that remains not complete or accurate.

(3) *Duty to provide notice of dispute.* If the completeness or accuracy of any information furnished by any person to any consumer reporting agency is disputed to such person by a consumer, the person may not furnish the information to any consumer reporting agency without notice that such information is disputed by the consumer.

(4) *Duty to provide notice of closed accounts.* A person who regularly and in the ordinary course of business furnishes information to a consumer reporting agency regarding a consumer who has a credit account with that person shall notify the agency of the voluntary closure of the account by the consumer, in information regularly furnished for the period in which the account is closed.

(5) *Duty to provide notice of delinquency of accounts.* A person who furnishes information to a consumer reporting agency regarding a delinquent account being placed for collection, charged to profit or loss, or subjected to any similar action shall, not later than 90 days after furnishing the information, notify the agency of the month and year of the commencement of the delinquency that immediately preceded the action.

(b) Duties of furnishers of information upon notice of dispute.

    (1) *In general.* After receiving notice pursuant to section 611(a)(2) [§ 1681i] of a dispute with regard to the completeness or accuracy of any information provided by a person to a consumer reporting agency, the person shall

        (A) conduct an investigation with respect to the disputed information;

        (B) review all relevant information provided by the consumer reporting agency pursuant to section 611(a)(2) [§ 1681i];

        (C) report the results of the investigation to the consumer reporting agency; and

        (D) if the investigation finds that the information is incomplete or inaccurate, report those results to all other consumer reporting agencies to which the person furnished the information and that compile and maintain files on consumers on a nationwide basis.

    (2) *Deadline.* A person shall complete all investigations, reviews, and reports required under paragraph (1) regarding information provided by the person to a consumer reporting agency, before the expiration of the period under section 611(a)(1) [§ 1681i] within which the consumer reporting agency is required to complete actions required by that section regarding that information.

(c) *Limitation on liability.* Sections 616 and 617 [§§ 1681n and 1681o] do not apply to any failure to comply with subsection (a), except as provided in section 621(c)(1)(B) [§ 1681s].

(d) *Limitation on enforcement.* Subsection (a) shall be enforced exclusively under section 621 [§ 1681s] by the Federal agencies and officials and the State officials identified in that section.

---

15 U.S.C. 1681s-2

§ 624. Relation to State laws

(a) *In general.* Except as provided in subsections (b) and (c), this title does not annul, alter, affect, or exempt any person subject to the provisions of this title from complying with the laws of any State with respect to the collection, distribution, or use of any information on consumers, except to the extent that those laws are inconsistent with any provision of this title, and then only to the extent of the inconsistency.

(b) *General exceptions.* No requirement or prohibition may be imposed under the laws of any State

  (1)   with respect to any subject matter regulated under

    (A)   subsection (c) or (e) of section 604 [§ 1681b], relating to the prescreening of consumer reports;

    (B)   section 611 [§ 1681i], relating to the time by which a consumer reporting agency must take any action, including the provision of notification to a consumer or other person, in any procedure related to the disputed accuracy of information in a consumer's file, except that this subparagraph shall not apply to any State law in effect on the date of enactment of the Consumer Credit Reporting Reform Act of 1996:

    (C)   subsections (a) and (b) of section 615 [§ 1681m], relating to the duties of a person who takes any adverse action with respect to a consumer;

    (D)   section 615(d) [§ 1681m] relating to the duties of persons who use a consumer report of a consumer in connection with any credit or insurance transaction that is not initiated by the consumer and that consists of a firm offer of credit or insurance;

    (E)   section 605 [§ 1681c], relating to information contained in consumer reports, except that this subparagraph shall not apply to any State law in effect on the date of enactment of the Consumer Credit Reporting Reform Act of 1996; or

    (F)   section 623 [§ 1681s-2], relating to the responsibilities of persons who furnish information to consumer reporting agencies, except that this paragraph shall nor apply

      (i)   with respect to section 54A(a) of chapter 93 of the Massachusetts Annotated Laws (as in effect on the date of enactment of the Consumer Credit Reporting Reform Act of 1996); or

      (ii)   with respect to section 1785.25(a) of the California Civil Code (as in effect on the date of enactment of the Consumer Credit Reporting Reform Act of 1996);

(2) with respect to the exchange of information among persons affiliated by common ownership or common corporate control, except that this paragraph shall not apply with respect to subsection (a) or (c)(1) of section 2480e of title 9, Vermont Statutes Annotated (as in effect on the date of enactment of the Consumer Credit Reporting Reform Act of 1996); or

(3) with respect to the form and content of any disclosure required to be made under section 609(c) [§ 1681g].

(c) *Definition affirm offer of credit or insurance.* Notwithstanding any definition of the term "firm offer of credit or insurance" (or any equivalent term) under the laws of any State, the definition of that term contained in section 603(l) [§ 1681a] shall be construed to apply in the enforcement and interpretation of the laws of any State governing consumer reports.

(d) Limitations. Subsections (b) and (c)

(1) do not affect any settlement, agreement, or consent judgment between any State Attorney General and any consumer reporting agency in effect on the date of enactment of the Consumer Credit Reporting Reform Act of 1996; and

(2) do not apply to any provision of State law (including any provision of a State constitution) that

(A) is enacted after January 1, 2004;

(B) states explicitly that the provision is intended to supplement this title; and

(C) gives greater protection to consumers than is provided under this title.

---

15 U.S.C. 1681t

§ 625. Disclosures to FBI for counterintelligence purposes

(a) *Identity of financial institutions.* Notwithstanding section 604 [§ 1681b] or any other provision of this title, a consumer reporting agency shall furnish to the Federal Bureau of Investigation the names and addresses of all financial institutions (as that term is defined in section 1101 of the Right to Financial Privacy Act of 1978 [12 U.S.C. §3401]) at which a consumer maintains or has maintained an account, to the extent that information is in the files of the agency, when presented with a written request for that information, signed by the Director of the Federal Bureau of Investigation, or the Director's designee, which certifies compliance with this section. The Director or the Director's designee may make such a certification only if the Director or the Director's designee has determined in writing that

(1) such information is necessary for the conduct of an authorized foreign counterintelligence investigation; and

(2) there are specific and articulable facts giving reason to believe that the consumer

(A) is a foreign power (as defined in section 101 of the Foreign Intelligence Surveillance Act of 1978 [50 U.S.C. § 1801]) or a person who is not a United States person (as defined in such section 101) and is an official of a foreign power; or

(B) is an agent of a foreign power and is engaging or has engaged in an act of international terrorism (as that term is defined in section 101(c) of the

Foreign Intelligence Surveillance Act of 1978 [50 U.S.C. § 1801(c)]) or clandestine intelligence activities that involve or may involve a violation of criminal statutes of the United States.

(b) *Identifying information.* Notwithstanding the provisions of section 604 [§ 1681b] or any other provision of this title, a consumer reporting agency shall furnish identifying information respecting a consumer, limited to name, address, former addresses, places of employment, or former places of employment, to the Federal Bureau of Investigation when presented with a written request, signed by the Director or the Director's designee, which certifies compliance with this subsection. The Director or the Director's designee may make such a certification only if the Director or the Director's designee has determined in writing that

(1)   such information is necessary to the conduct of an authorized counterintelligence investigation; and

(2)   there is information giving reason to believe that the consumer has been, or is about to be, in contact with a foreign power or an agent of a foreign power (as defined in section 101 of the Foreign Intelligence Surveillance Act of 1978 [50 U.S.C. § 1801]).

(c) *Court order for disclosure of consumer reports.* Notwithstanding section 604 [§ 1681b] or any other provision of this title, if requested in writing by the Director of the Federal Bureau of Investigation, or a designee of the Director, a court may issue an order ex parte directing a consumer reporting agency to furnish a consumer report to the Federal Bureau of Investigation, upon a showing in camera that

(1)   the consumer report is necessary for the conduct of an authorized foreign counterintelligence investigation; and

(2)   there are specific and articulable facts giving reason to believe that the consumer whose consumer report is sought

(A)   is an agent of a foreign power, and

(B)   is engaging or has engaged in an act of international terrorism (as that term is defined in section 101(c) of the Foreign Intelligence Surveillance Act of 1978 [50 U.S.C. § 1801(c)]) or clandestine intelligence activities that involve or may involve a violation of criminal statutes of the United States.

The terms of an order issued under this subsection shall not disclose that the order is issued for purposes of a counterintelligence investigation.

(d) *Confidentiality.* No consumer reporting agency or officer, employee, or agent of a consumer reporting agency shall disclose to any person, other than those officers, employees, or agents of a consumer reporting agency necessary to fulfill the requirement to disclose information to the Federal Bureau of Investigation under this section, that the Federal Bureau of Investigation has sought or obtained the identity of financial institutions or a consumer report respecting any consumer under subsection (a), (b), or (c), and no consumer reporting agency or officer, employee, or agent of a consumer reporting agency shall include in any consumer report any information that would indicate that the federal Bureau of Investigation has sought or obtained such information or a consumer report.

(e) *Payment of fees.* The Federal Bureau of Investigation shall, subject to the availability of appropriations, pay to the consumer reporting agency assembling or providing report of information in accordance with procedures established under this section a fee for reimbursement for such costs as are reasonably necessary and which have been directly incurred in searching, reproducing, or transporting books, papers, records, or other data required or requested to be produced under this section.

(f) *Limit on dissemination.* The Federal Bureau of Investigation may not disseminate information obtained pursuant to this section outside of the Federal Bureau of Investigation, except to other Federal agencies as may be necessary for the approval or conduct of a foreign counterintelligence investigation, or, where the information concerns a person subject to the Uniform Code of Military Justice, to appropriate investigative authorities within the military department concerned as may be necessary for the conduct of a joint foreign counterintelligence investigation.

(g) *Rules of construction.* Nothing in this section shall be construed to prohibit information from being furnished by the Federal Bureau of Investigation pursuant to a subpoena or court order, in connection with a judicial or administrative proceeding to enforce the provisions of this Act. Nothing in this section shall be construed to authorize or permit the withholding of information from the Congress.

(h) *Reports to Congress.* On a semiannual basis, the Attorney General shall fully inform the Permanent Select Committee on Intelligence and the committee on Banking, Finance and Urban Affairs of the House of Representatives, and the Select Committee on Intelligence and the Committee on Banking, Housing, and Urban Affairs of the Senate concerning all requests made pursuant to subsections (a), (b), and (c).

(i) *Damages.* Any agency or department of the United States obtaining or disclosing any consumer reports, records, or information contained therein in violation of this section is liable to the consumer to whom such consumer reports, records, or information relate in an amount equal to the sum of

    (1) $100, without regard to the volume of consumer reports, records, or information involved;

    (2) any actual damages sustained by the consumer as a result of the disclosure;

    (3) if the violation if found to have been willful or intentional, such punitive damages as a court may allow; and

    (4) in the case of any successful action to enforce liability under this subsection, the costs of the action, together with reasonable attorney fees, as determined by the court.

(j) *Disciplinary actions for violations.* if a court determines that any agency or department of the United States has violated any provision of this section and the court finds that the circumstances surrounding the violation raise questions of whether or not an officer or employee of the agency or department acted willfully or intentionally with respect to the violation, the agency or department shall promptly initiate a proceeding to determine whether or not disciplinary action is warranted against the officer or employee who was responsible for the violation.

(k) *Good-faith exception.* Notwithstanding any other provision of this title, any consumer reporting agency or agent or employee thereof making disclosure of consumer reports or identifying information pursuant to this subsection in good-faith reliance upon a certification of the Federal Bureau of Investigation pursuant to provisions of this section shall not be liable to any person for such disclosure under this title, the constitution of any State, or any law or regulation of any State or any political subdivision of any State.

(l) *Limitation of remedies.* Notwithstanding any other provision of this title, the remedies and sections set forth in this section shall be the only judicial remedies and sanctions for violation of this section.

(m) *Injunctive relief.* In addition to any other remedy contained in this section, injunctive relief shall be available to require compliance with the procedures of this section. In the event of any successful action under this subsection, costs together with reasonable attorney fees, as determined by the court, may be recovered.

―――――――――
15 U.S.C. 1681u

LEGISLATIVE HISTORY

House Reports: No. 91-975 (Comm. on Banking and Currency) and
                  No. 91-1587 (Comm. of Conference)

Senate Reports: No. 91-1139 accompanying S. 3678 (Comm. on Banking and Currency)

Congressional Record, Vol. 116(1970)
                  May 25, considered and passed House.
                  Sept. 18, considered and passed Senate, amended.
                  Oct. 9, Senate agreed to conference report.
                  Oct. 13, House agreed to conference report.
Enactment: Public Law No. 91-508 (October 26, 1970):

Amendments: Public Law Nos. 95-473 (October 17, 1978)
                                   95-598 (November 6,1978)
                                   98-443 (October 4, 1984)
                                   101-73 (August 9, 1989)
                                   102-242 (December 19, 1991)
                                   102-537 (October 27, 1992)
                                   102-550 (October 28, 1992)
                                   103-325 (September 23, 1994)
                                   104-88 (December 29, 1995)
                                   104-93 (January 6, 1996)
                                   104-193 (August 22, 1996)
                                   104-208 (September 30, 1996)
                                   105-107 (November 20, 1997)
                                   105-347 (November 2, 1998)

CHAPTER 15

Fair Credit Billing

Prior to the "consumer decade" of the 70s, many major credit grantors ignored debtors' requests regarding billing errors. Frequently, a complaint by the consumer to the credit grantor, department store, credit card issuer, bank, or financial institution would be disregarded, or a form response would be used, stating that the consumer's questions would be reviewed in due course. As a result consumers never received adequate answers and, in many instances, credit standings were severely impaired by this lack of attention. Furthermore, the creditor continued efforts to collect the debt from the consumer by mailing statements demanding payment. If the consumer failed to pay the erroneous balance due, the collection agency or law firm entered the picture and dunned the consumer with letters and telephone calls. In many cases, the debt was paid despite the fact that the creditor was not entitled to payment. Congress did not overlook this problem when it passed the Truth in Lending Act (see Chapter 12), a portion of which has become known as the Fair Credit Billing Act.

The Fair Credit Billing Act prohibits a creditor from engaging in any efforts to collect the balance due without first responding to consumer disputes or requests for information by providing a full response and explanation. The Act also addresses other minor abuses. The creditor must treat the consumer in a fair and equitable manner when computing billing and balances.

The Act deals with credit card accounts (open-end credits) as to billing errors, the ability of the consumer to correct billing errors, and the prohibition of credit card issuers from ignoring the complaints of the consumer.[1] Agreements payable in more than four installments or for which the payment of a finance charge is or may be required are covered under the Fair Credit Billing Act.

---

[1]15 USC 1666; 33 *Business Lawyer* 981 (1978); *W.T. Grant Company v. C.I.R.*, 483 2d 1115 (1973).

CONSUMER ACTION

To trigger the obligation of the creditor under the Fair Credit Billing Act, the consumer must send a notice "in writing." An oral notification is insufficient. The creditor must not mislead or deceive the consumer into believing that a telephone call is sufficient notice. Printing on the monthly statement that all complaints and billing errors will be resolved if the consumer contacts the creditor by using a certain telephone number would constitute a violation of the Act.

NOTIFICATION

When a creditor, within sixty days after having sent a bill to the purchaser, receives a written notice from the purchaser which sets forth any one or more of the following:

1. information permitting the mailer to identify the name, address and account number,
2. a claim that there is a billing error,
3. the reasons for the billing error,
4. a statement that the charge made to the consumer was not incurred by the consumer,
5. a statement that the consumer requests clarification and documentary evidence to support the clarification,
6. an allegation that goods have not been delivered to the consumer in accordance with the purchase order,
7. a statement that the creditor failed to reflect a payment or credit made by this consumer,
8. a computation error,
9. any other computation, delivery, or billing error.

The creditor shall, unless the debtor has, after giving such written notice, and before the expiration of the time limits set forth herein, agreed that the billing statement was correct:

A. Not later than 30 days after receipt of notice, send a written acknowledgement unless the action in subdivision B is taken within such 30 day period
B. Not later than two complete billing cycles, and in no event later than ninety days after the receipt of the notice
   1. make the appropriate corrections and notify the debtor of the corrections and explanations thereof, and if the debtor requests, provide copies of documentary evidence of the debtor's indebtedness.

2. after an investigation, send a written explanation or clarification setting forth the reasons why the creditor believes the account is correct, and upon request of the debtor, provide copies of the documentary evidence of the debtor's obligation.

The creditor has only two choices: either correct the error and notify the debtor or send a written explanation of why the debtor is wrong. If the creditor resolves the dispute during this procedure, no further notification to the debtor is necessary. During this period of time, the creditor may not impose additional charges, but the creditor may reduce the credit limit by the amount in dispute. If the creditor reports to a credit reporting agency, the matter must be communicated to the agency as a disputed account.

MORATORIUM ON COLLECTION ACTIVITY

The law requires the creditor to respond to the consumer complaint before commencing any collection activity During the period that the creditor does not respond to the consumer, collection activity must be suspended by the creditor and cannot be re-commenced until after compliance with the provisions of the Act.[2]

FAILURE TO COMPLY

A creditor who fails to comply with the above provisions forfeits any right to collect the amount of the error, including any finance charges. The creditor may not directly or indirectly threaten to report any person adversely to a credit reporting agency because of the consumer's failure to pay the amount of the billing error until the creditor has complied with all the conditions of the act. If, after receiving the explanation from the creditor, the consumer continues to claim that the amount is still in dispute, the creditor may not report the amount as delinquent to any third party, unless the creditor also reports that the amount is in dispute and notifies the consumer of the name and address of the third party or the credit reporting agency. Naturally, a resolution of the dispute must be reported.

CONSUMER DEFENSE

The card issuer is subject to all defenses asserted by the consumer against the seller of the goods or provider of the service. For example, the consumer purchases

---

[2]15 USC 1666.

a toaster for $55. The purchaser uses her credit card. The toaster does not operate properly in that the toast is ejected before it is toasted. The credit card issuer cannot ignore this defense even if the toaster is not returned, and cannot charge the credit card account for the $55 after notification by the consumer of the existence of this defense. In order for the consumer to take advantage of these provisions in the Act, the following conditions must be met:

1. The consumer has made a good faith attempt to resolve the dispute with the merchant.
2. The amount of the transaction exceeds $50.
3. The place where the initial transaction occurred was in the same state as the mailing address provided by the card holder or was within 100 miles from the address.

If the card issuer and merchant are one and the same or the merchant is under the direct control of the card issuer, then there is but one creditor and the above requirement of a good faith attempt to resolve the dispute does not apply.

FINANCE CHARGES

The consumer is entitled to a window of fourteen days to pay before a finance charge is imposed. A statement including the amount upon which the finance charge is based must be mailed at least fourteen days prior to the date specified in the statement by which payment must be made.[3] If an open-end consumer credit plan provides a time period within which a debtor may repay any portion of the credit extended without an additional finance charge, such a charge may not be imposed unless a statement is mailed within 14 days prior to the time period specified.

CREDIT BALANCE

Credit balances in excess of one dollar should be refunded to the consumer upon written request. Every effort should be made to refund credit balances every six months or upon request. Each state has separate laws concerning credit balances and the creditor should consult with counsel as to specific requirements for its state.[4]

---

[3] 15 USC 1666b.

[4] 15 USC 1666d.

CASH DISCOUNTS

The credit card issuer may not enter into any agreement with a merchant to prohibit the merchant from offering a discount to a consumer to pay by cash rather than by credit card. If the discount offered by the merchant is less than five percent, it shall not be considered a finance charge as determined under the Truth in Lending Act.

UNAUTHORIZED USE OF A CREDIT CARD

A consumer is only liable up to $50 for the "unauthorized use" of a credit card, defined as someone using the credit card who has no authority to do so and where the card holder has not received the merchandise or the service offered. To utilize this limited liability, the consumer must notify the credit card issuer.

The credit card issuer initially approving the credit card account must advise the consumer of:

1. the limitation of liability up to $50.
2. the method the consumer should use to notify the creditor as to the loss of the card.

Most credit card accounts provide for oral notification to any employee of the credit card issuer[5] by use of an identified telephone number. The consumer can use someone else authorized by the consumer to notify the credit card issuer.

CONSUMER'S STATEMENTS

Some companies routinely print the entire Fair Credit Billing Act word for word on the back of customers' statements, or the Act may be rephrased.

PROMPT POSTING

All payments must be posted promptly if identifiable.[6]

---

[5]A debit card or check guarantee card is not covered by this section of the Fair Credit Billing Act.

[6]15 USC 1666c.

SELLER OBLIGATION

A seller who accepts a return of merchandise or issues credit for services must notify the credit card issuer promptly so that the consumer's account is credited.[7]

OFFSETS

A card issuer, such as a bank, may not deduct monies from a deposit account (bank account) to make payments on the consumer's credit card account unless previously authorized to do so in writing by the cardholder.[8]

UNMATCHED FUNDS

Unmatched accounts sometimes include credit balances, unclaimed refunds, unclaimed vouchers, or unclaimed bonus certificates. The customer has moved, has left for parts unknown, or, for whatever reason, cannot be located. As a result, the credit balance cannot be refunded. This occurs when companies go out of business and no bankruptcy is filed. Gift certificates and credit vouchers which are never cashed fall into this category.

Most states require the above items to be treated as abandoned property and refunded to the state after a specified period of time. The laws vary from state to state and consultation with counsel is recommended.[9]

> COLLECTION TIP: *Have a carefully prepared manual for use by your staff which sets forth the procedures necessary to comply with the Fair Credit Billing Act. An investigation commenced by an administrative agency always begins with a request for records and documents. Furnishing the commission with a procedural manual prepared for use by the staff is a positive step in the right direction. If human error occurred on the part of an employee, you will have shown a good faith intent to comply with the Act.*

BIBLIOGRAPHY

(1) Amendments to the Truth and Lending Act, 53 *North Carolina Law Review* 1270 (1974).

(2) Clasky, Levally and Taylor—Truth and Lending, Fair Credit Billing and Fair Credit Reporting, 33 *Business Law* 981 (1978).

---

[7] "See supra note 6."

[8] 15 USC 1666h.

[9] *Gary v. American Express Co.*, 743 F. 2d 10 (1984); *American Express Co. v. Koerner,* 452 U.S. 233 (1981); *Mourning v. Family Publications Service, Inc.,* 411 U.S. 356 (1973); *Lincoln First Bank, N.A. v. Carlson,* 426 NYS 2d 433 (1980).

CHAPTER 15
APPENDIX I

S8 STAT, 1511

PUBLIC LAW 93–495
93RD CONGRESS,
H. R. 11221
OCTOBER 28, 1974

TITLE III—FAIR CREDIT BILLING

§ 301. Short title

Fair Credit Billing
Act. 15 USC 1601
note.

This title may be cited as the "Fair Credit Billing Act."

§ 302. Declaration of purpose

The last sentence of section 102 of the Truth in Lending Act (15 U.S.C. 1601) is amended by striking out the period and inserting in lieu thereof a comma and the following: "and to protect the consumer against inaccurate and unfair credit billing and credit card practices."

§ 303. Definitions of creditor and open-end credit plan

The first sentence of section 103(f) of the Truth in Lending Act (15 U.S.C. 1602(f)) is amended to read as follows: "The term 'creditor' refers only to creditors who regularly extend, or arrange for the extension of, credit which is payable by agreement in more than four installments or for which the payment of a finance charge is or may be required, whether in connection with loans, sales of property or services, or otherwise. For the purposes of the requirements imposed under Chapter 4 and sections 127(a)(6), 127(a)(7), 127(a)(8), 127(b)(1), 127(b)(2), 127(b)(3), 127(b)(9), and 127(b)(11) of Chapter 2 of this Title, the term 'creditor' shall also include card issuers whether or not the amount due is payable by agreement in more than four installments or the payment of a finance charge is or may be required, and the Board shall, by regulation, apply these requirements to such card issuers, to the extent appropriate, even though the requirements are by their terms applicable only to creditors offering open end credit plans.

Post, p. 1512.

Infra, 15 USC 1637.

§ 304. Disclosure of fair credit billing rights

(a) Section 127(a) of the Truth in Lending Act (15 U.S.C. 1637(a)) is amended by adding at the end thereof a new paragraph as follows:

Post, pp. 1512, 1515.

"(8) A statement, in a form prescribed by regulations of the Board of the protection provided by sections 161 and 170 to an obligor and the creditor's responsibilities under sections 162 and 170. With respect to each of two billing cycles per year, at semiannual intervals, the creditor shall transmit such statement to each obligor to whom the creditor is required to transmit a statement pursuant to section 127(b) for such billing cycle."

(b) Section 127(c) of such Act (15 U.S.C. 1637(c)) is amended to read:

"(c) In the case of any existing account under an open end consumer credit plan having an outstanding balance of more than $1 at or after the close of the creditor's first full billing cycle under the plan after the effective date of subsection (a) or any amendments thereto, the items described in subsection (a), to the extent applicable and not previously disclosed, shall be disclosed in a notice mailed or delivered to & obligor not later than the time of mailing the next statement required by subsection (b)."

§ 305. Disclosure of billing contact

Section 127(b) of the Truth in Lenclim, Act (15 U.S.C. 1637(b)) is amended by adding at the end thereof a new paragraph as follows:

88 STAT. 1512

"(11) The address to be used by the creditor for the purpose of receiving billing inquiries from the obligor."

§ 306. Billing practices

The Truth in Lending Act (15 U.S.C. 1601-1665) is amended by adding at the end thereof a new chapter as follows:

CHAPTER 4—CREDIT BILLING

"Sec.

"161.   Correction of billing errors.
"162.   Regulation of credit reports.
"163.   Length of billing period.
"164.   Prompt crediting of payments.
"165.   Crediting excess payments.
"166.   Prompt notification of returns.
"167.   Use of cash discounts.
"168.   Prohibition of tie-in services.
"169.   Prohibition of offsets.
"170.   Rights of credit card customers.
"171.   Relation to State laws.

"§ 161. Correction of billing errors

15 USC 1666.

"(a) If a creditor, within sixty days after having transmitted to an obligor a statement of the obligor's account in connection with an extension of consumer credit, receives at the address

Ante, p. 1511.

disclosed under section 127(b) (11) a written notice (other than notice on a payment stub or other payment medium supplied by the creditor if the creditor so stipulates with the disclosure required under section 127(a) (8)) from the obligor

Ante, p. 1511.

in which the obligor—

"(1) sets forth or otherwise enables the creditor to identify the name and account number (if any) of the obligor,

"(2) indicates the obligor's belief that the statement contains a billing error and the amount of such billing error, and

"(3) sets forth the reasons for the obligor's belief (to the extent applicable) that the statement contains a billing error, the creditor shall, unless the obligor has, after giving such written notice and before the expiration of the time limits herein specified, agreed that the statement was correct—

"(A) not later than thirty days after the receipt of the notice, send a written acknowledgment thereof to the obligor, unless the action required in subparagraph (B) is taken within such thirty-day period, and

"(B) not later than two complete billing cycles of the creditor (in no event later than ninety days) after the receipt of the notice and prior to taking any action to collect the amount, or any part thereof, indicated by the obligor under paragraph (2) either

"(i) make appropriate corrections in the account of the obligor, including the crediting of any finance charges on amounts erroneously billed, and transmit to the obligor a notification of such corrections and the creditor's explanation of any change in the amount indicated by the obligor under paragraph (2) and, if any such change is made and the obligor so requests, copies of documentary evidence of the obligor's in debtedness; or

"(ii) send a written explanation or clarification to the obligor, after having conducted an investigation, setting forth to the extent applicable the reasons why the creditor believes the account of the obligor was correctly shown in the statement and, upon request of the obligor, provide copies of documentary evidence of the obligor's indebtedness. In the case of a billing error where the obligor alleges that the creditor's

88 STAT. 1513

billing statement reflects goods not delivered-to the obligor or his designee in accordance with the agreement made at the time of the transaction, a creditor may not construe such amount to be correctly shown unless he determines that such goods were actually delivered, mailed, or other wise sent to the obligor and provides the obligor with a statement of such determination.

After complying with the provisions of this subsection with respect to an alleged billing error, a creditor has no further responsibility under this section if the obligor continues to make substantially the same allegation with respect to such error.

Definitions.

"(b) For the purpose of this section, a 'billing error' consists of any of the following:

"(1) A reflection on a statement of an extension of credit which was not made to the obligor or, if made, was not in the amount reflected on such statement.

"(2) A reflection on a statement of an extension of credit for which the obligor requests additional clarification including documentary evidence thereof.

"(3) A reflection on a statement of goods or services not accepted by the obligor or his designee or not delivered to the obligor or his designee in accordance with the agreement made at the time of a transaction.

"(4) The creditor's failure to reflect properly on a statement a payment made by the obligor or a credit issued to the obligor.

"(5) A computation error or similar error of an accounting nature of the creditor on a statement.

"(6) Any other error described in regulations of the Board.

"(c) For the purposes of this section, 'action to collect the amount, or any part thereof, indicated by an obligor under paragraph (2)' does not include the sending of statements of account to the obligor following written notice from the obligor as specified under subsection (a), if—

"(1) the obligor's account is not restricted or closed because of the failure of the obligor to pay the amount indicated under paragraph (2) of subsection (a), and

"(2) the creditor indicates the payment of such amount is not required pending the creditor's compliance with this section. Nothing in this section shall be construed to prohibit any action by a creditor to collect any amount which has not been indicated by the obligor to contain a billing error.

"(d) Pursuant to regulations of the Board, a creditor operating an open end consumer credit plan may not, prior to the sending of the written explanation or clarification required under paragraph (B) (ii), restrict or close an account with respect to which the obligor has indicated Pursuant to subsection (a) that he believes such ac count to contain a billing error solely because of the obligor's failure to pay the amount indicated to be in error. Nothing in this sub section shall be deemed to prohibit a creditor from applying against the credit limit on the obligor's account the amount indicated to be in error.

Noncompliance.

"(e) Any creditor who fails to comply with the requirements of this section or section 162 forfeits any right to collect from the obligor the amount indicated by the obligor under paragraph (2) of subsection (a) of this section, and any finance charges thereon, except that the amount required to be forfeited under this subsection may not exceed $50.

"§ 162. Regulation of credit reports

15 USC 1666a.

88 STAT. 1514

"(a) After receiving a notice from an obligor as provided in section 161(a), a creditor or his agent may not directly or indirectly threaten to report to any person adversely on the obligor's credit rating or credit standing because of the obligor's failure to pay the amount indicated by the obligor under section 161(a)(2), and such amount may not be reported as delinquent to any third party until the creditor has met the requirements of section 161 and has al lowed the obligor the same number of days (not less than ten) thereafter to make payment as is provided under the credit agreement with the obligor for the payment of undisputed amounts.

"(b) If a creditor receives a further written notice from an obligor that an amount is still in dispute within the time allowed for payment under subsection (a) of this section, a creditor may not report to any third party that the amount of the obligor is delinquent because the obligor has failed to pay an amount which he has indicated under section 161(a)(2), unless the creditor also reports that the amount is in dispute and, at the same time, notifies the obligor of the name and address of each party to whom the creditor is reporting information concerning the delinquency.

"(c) A creditor shall report any subsequent resolution of any delinquencies reported pursuant to subsection (b) to the parties to whom such delinquencies were initially reported.

"§ 163. Length of billing period

15 USC 1666b.

"(a) If an open end consumer credit plan provides a time period within which an obligor may repay any portion of the credit extended without incurring an additional finance charge, such additional finance charge may not be imposed with respect to such portion of the credit extended for the billing cycle of which such period is a part unless a statement which includes the amount upon which the finance charge for that period is based was mailed at least fourteen days prior to the date specified in the statement by which payment must be made in order to avoid imposition of that finance charge.

"(b) Subsection (a) does not apply in any case where a creditor has been prevented, delayed, or hindered in making timely mailing or delivery of such periodic statement within the time period specified in such subsection because of an act of God, war, natural disaster, strike, or other excusable or justifiable cause, as determined under regulations of the Board.

"§ 164. Prompt crediting of payments

15 USC 1666c.

"Payments received from an obligor under an open end consumer credit plan by the creditor shall be posted promptly to the obligor's account as specified in regulations of the Board. Such regulations shall prevent a finance charge from being imposed on any obligor if the creditor has received the obligor's payment in readily identifiable form in the amount, manner, location, and time indicated by the creditor to avoid the imposition thereof.

"§ 165. Crediting excess payments

15 USC 1666d.

"Whenever an obligor transmits funds to a creditor in excess of the total balance due on an open end consumer credit account, the creditor shall promptly (1) upon request of the obligor refund the amount of the overpayment, or (2) credit such amount to the obligor's account.

"§ 166. Prompt notification of returns

15 USC 1666e.

"With respect to any sales transaction where a credit card has been used to obtain credit, where the seller is a person other than the card issuer, and where the seller accepts or allows a return of the goods or forgiveness of a debit for services which were the subject of such sale, the seller shall promptly transmit to the credit card issuer, a credit statement with respect thereto and the credit card issuer shall credit the account of the obligor for the amount of the transaction.

88 STAT 1515

15 USC 1666f.

"§ 167. Use of cash discounts

"(a) With respect to credit card which may be used for extensions of credit in sales transactions in which the seller is a person other than the card issuer, the card issuer may not, by contract or other wise, prohibit any such seller from offering a discount to a cardholder to induce the cardholder to pay by cash, check, or similar means rather than use a credit card.

"(b) With respect to any sales transaction, any discount not in excess of 5 per centum offered by the seller for the purpose of inducing payment by cash, check, or other means not involving the use of a credit card shall not constitute a finance charge as determined under section 106, if such discount is offered to all prospective buyers and its availability is disclosed to all prospective buyers clearly and conspicuously in accordance with regulations of the Board.

"§ 168. Prohibition of tie-in services

15 USC 1666g.

"Notwithstanding any agreement to the contrary a card issuer may not require a seller, as a condition to participating in a credit card plan, to open an account with or procure any other service from the card issuer or its subsidiary or agent.

"§ 169. Prohibition of offsets

15 USC 1666h.

"(a) A card issuer may not take any action to offset a cardholder's indebtedness arising in connection with a consumer credit transaction under the relevant credit card plan against funds of the cardholder held on deposit with the card issuer unless—

"(1) such action was previously authorized in writing by the cardholder in accordance with a credit plan whereby the cardholder agrees periodically to pay debts incurred in his open end credit account by permitting the card issuer periodically to deduct all or a portion of such debt from the card holder's deposit account, and

"(2) such action with respect to any outstanding disputed amount not be taken by the card issuer upon request of the cardholder.

In the case of any credit card account in existence on the effective date of this section, the previous written authorization referred to in clause (1) shall not be required until the date (after such effective date) when such account is renewed, but in no case later than one year after such effective date. Such written authorization shall be deemed to exist if the card issuer has previously notified the cardholder that the use of his credit card account will subject any funds which the card issuer holds in deposit accounts of such cardholder to offset against any amounts due and payable on his credit card account which have not been paid in accordance with the terms of the agreement between the card issuer and the cardholder.

"(b) This section does not alter or affect the right under State law of a card issuer to attach or otherwise levy upon funds of a cardholder held on deposit with the card issuer if that remedy is constitutionally available to creditors generally.

"§ 170. Rights of credit card customers

15 USC 1666i.

"(a) Subject to the limitation contained in subsection (b), a card issuer who has issued a credit card to a cardholder pursuant to an open end consumer credit plan shall be subject to all claims (other than tort claims) and defenses arising out of any transaction in which the credit card is used as a method of payment or extension of credit if (1) the obligor has made a good faith attempt to obtain satisfactory resolution of a disagreement or problem relative to the transaction from the person honoring the credit card; (2) the amount of the initial

SS STAT. 1516

transaction exceeds $50; and (3) the place where the initial transaction occurred was in the same State as the mailing address previously provided by the cardholder or was within 100 miles from such address, except that the limitations set forth in clauses (2) and (3) with respect to an obligor's right to assert claims and defenses against a card issuer shall not be applicable to any transaction in which the person honoring the credit card (A) is the same person as the card issuer, (B) is controlled by the card issuer, (C) is under direct or indirect common control with the card issuer, (D) is a franchised dealer in the card issuer's products or services, or (E) has obtained the order for such transaction through a mail solicitation made by or participated in by the card issuer in which the cardholder is solicited to enter into such transaction by using the credit card issued by the card issuer.

"(b) The amount of claims or defenses asserted by the cardholder may not exceed the amount of credit outstanding with respect to such transaction at the time the cardholder first notifies the card issuer or the person honoring the credit card of such claim or defense. For the purpose of determining the amount of credit out standing in the preceding sentence, payments and credits to the cardholder's account are deemed to have been applied, in the order indicated, to the payment of: (1) late charges in the order of their entry to the account; (2) finance charges in order of their entry to the account; and (3) debits to the account other than those set forth above, in the order in which each debit entry to the account was made.

"§ 171. Relation to State laws

15 USC 1666j.

"(a) This chapter does not annul, alter, or affect, or exempt any person subject to the provisions of this chapter from complying with, the laws of any State with respect to credit billing practices, except to the extent that those laws are inconsistent with any provision of this chapter, and then only to the extent of the inconsistency. The Board is authorized to determine whether such inconsistencies exist. The Board may not determine that any State law is inconsistent with any provision of this chapter if the Board determines that such law gives greater protection to the consumer.

"(b) The Board shall by regulation exempt from the requirements of this chapter any class of credit transactions within any State if it determines that under the law of that State that class of transactions is subject to requirements substantially similar to those imposed under this chapter or that such law gives greater protection to the consumer, and that there is adequate provision for enforcement."

§ 307. Conforming amendments

(a) The table of chapters of the Truth in Lending Act is amended by adding immediately under item 3 the following:

"4. CREDIT BILLING _ 161"

(b) Section 111(d) of such Act (15 U.S.C. 1610(d)) is amended by striking out "and 130" and inserting in lieu thereof a comma and the following: "130, and 166."

(c) Section 121(a) of such Act (15 U.S.C. 1631(a)) is amended—

   (1) by striking out "and upon whom a finance charge is or may be imposed"; and

   (2) by inserting "or chapter 4" immediately after "this chapter."

(d) Section 121(b) of such Act (15 U.S.C. 1631(b)) is amended by inserting "or chapter 4" immediately after "this chapter."

(e) Section 122(a) of such Act (15 U.S.C. 1632(a)) is amended by inserting "or chapter 4" immediately after "this chapter."

88 STAT. 1517

(f) Section 122(b) of such Act (15 U.S.C. 1632(b)) is amended by inserting "or chapter 4" immediately after "this chapter."

§ 308. Effective date

15 USC 1666 note.

This title takes effect upon the expiration of one year after the date of its enactment.

CHAPTER 16

Skiptracing

A credit and collection manager is often faced with the task of locating a debtor who has left for parts unknown. Some skiptrace firms mislead creditors and promote their services by implying to the creditor that certain information is available to them which is unavailable to others. The creditor incorrectly speculates that the firm is either connected with someone in the social security department or the local utility company, or connected to some state agency which will provide information which is not available to the general public. Since neither may be the case, set forth here are the legal means known to most people in the collection industry which enables the creditor to locate a debtor.

APPLICATION

A complete review of the application should be made before any skiptracing is done, including a review of credit references, prior addresses and prior places of employment.

TELEPHONE DIRECTORY

Searching the telephone directory in the county in which the debtor was located is probably the quickest, cheapest, and most efficient method. Some of the regional Bell telephone companies provide CD-Roms of an entire state or region, enabling searches statewide or over a specified geographic area. The problem with the CD-Rom is that the telephone companies update the information quarterly or semiannually, whereas a request on the telephone to 555-1212 (information) provides up-to-date changes in any telephone number. At the same time some of the Bell companies allow access to their databases (the same database that the information operator uses) and this type of access would provide current telephone numbers and addresses. The latter access is expensive. AT&T now provides information service which covers the country. Several Web sites also provide telephone numbers.

CRISS-CROSS TELEPHONE DIRECTORY

Directories are available which list telephone numbers by street address. With this type of directory, a call to neighbors in the building in which an individual formerly resided may provide information. Another type of criss-cross directory is a listing of all the telephone numbers in numerical order with an identifying address for each telephone number. If the debtor's telephone number is known, but the address is unknown, the address is available. These types of directories are mostly in the major metropolitan areas in the country.

> COLLECTION TIP: *Debt collectors and creditors should comply with the Fair Debt Collection Practices Act when contacting neighbors and follow the procedures for locating debtors prescribed by the Act.*

DATA BASES

Many data bases have been created for the direct marketing industry to target market the consumer. These data bases contain the age, vehicle ownership, house ownership, credit information, buying habits, social security numbers, and other information on wide cross sections of from 75 million to 100 million residents of the United States. The data bases of the major credit reporting agencies provide significant information about a prospective borrower or a delinquent debtor and hence are useful in locating people and collecting debts. Some provide programs to assist credit and collection managers.

The credit reporting agencies are principal purveyors of this information (see chapter on Fair Credit Reporting Act). Most data bases are designed to service the creditor attempting to locate the debtor. In addition to the data bases listed in the Appendix, the three major credit reporting agencies—Experian, Equifax, and Trans Union—all have extensive data bases on millions of individuals, and can provide detailed information for the creditor attempting to locate a debtor.

U.S. POSTAL SERVICE

A letter may be sent by certified mail or registered mail requesting that the Postal Service disclose the delivery address, if it is not the address on the envelope. This information is available for six months after the debtor moves and requests the Post Office to forward the mail to the new address. The letter must be marked "return receipt requested." To be sure that the debtor receives the letter, indicate "restrictive delivery." If the mail is to be forwarded, indicate "forward."

The Postal Service will provide the forwarding address of an individual to an attorney who wants the information for purposes of instituting suit.

RETURNED MAIL

Mail that is returned to the sender as undeliverable may be marked with various wording which provides useful information.

(1) "Refused" may indicate that the debtor is still at the address and the notation on the envelope is usually the handwriting of the mail carrier.

(2) "Not there" usually indicates that the debtor is no longer at the address and is also probably written by the mail carrier, although the debtor may have written the notation to mislead the creditor. The debtor may be accepting other mail.

(3) "Moved, Left No Forwarding Address" probably means that the debtor has left for parts unknown. This also is usually written by the mail carrier but the mail is probably accumulating at the Post Office and not being picked up.

(4) "Moved, Forwarding Expired," written by the mail carrier or an employee at the post office, means that when the debtor left, a forwarding address was provided but the retention of said forwarding address has expired. This is usually about six months, and the Postal Service does not forward mail after that time nor does it provide the new address if you request it.

Any other wording on the envelope, such as "not here" or "unknown" or "left," indicates that someone else wrote this on the envelope and returned it to the mail carrier. The party kind enough to write the message could know where the debtor is and some effort might be made to contact that party at the address to which the envelope was delivered. Sometimes cross directories can provide this information, especially if the address is a private or two-family house.

COURT RECORDS

Court records reveal judgments against the debtor, tax liens, and pending litigation. Sometimes these court proceedings may reveal new addresses or other information which may be helpful in locating the debtor. This information may be provided by service bureaus, which are local in nature. To identify these service bureaus, contact a clerk of the court, county clerk or an attorney located in the state or county familiar with collection.

LANDLORD

To know the name of the landlord where the debtor lives or used to live is helpful. This information is available from the county clerk or the register where deeds are recorded, or may be obtained from a title company or other local abstract company. An inquiry to an attorney should produce the organization providing this information. Once the name is obtained, an inquiry may be addressed to the landlord to provide where the debtor has relocated. If he or she refuses to cooperate, after a judgment is entered an information subpoena may be served on the landlord to provide information such as the name and address of the moving company which moved the debtor's property. A further inquiry to the moving company may produce positive results.

PROPERTY OWNERS

Some states have alphabetical listings of property owners showing the ownership of property statewide. Contact the title company. For those states that do not provide this information, the next best source is the local tax assessor. Verify ownership of property by using local tax assessors to furnish the block and lot of the property, and conduct a search to determine whether the debtor has mortgages, liens, etc. on the property. Service organizations also provide this service.

VOTER REGISTRATION

Usually the county clerk can tell you where voter registration lists are maintained. The name, address, and telephone number of the registered voter is available.

MOTOR VEHICLE SEARCHES

In most states, the Department of Motor Vehicles will furnish information at a cost of a few dollars if provided with a name. Contact the state motor vehicle bureau and obtain the proper form to determine what information must be furnished for a search. Service bureaus provide this type of retrieval service for law firms and financial institutions. Due to the concerns for the privacy of the individual, some states have passed laws which restrict access to this type of information.

LICENSE BUSINESS

If the debtor is a licensed business or the debtor has obtained a license to operate a profession, information can be obtained from the state. Service companies such as plumbers, electricians, barbers, contractors, and home improvement firms all require licensing and information can be obtained from the proper agency. Professions such as attorneys, doctors, architects, accountants, and dentists also are on file with appropriate state agencies and trade associations. In addition, insurance brokers, real estate brokers, and stock brokers are licensed by the state or an administrative agency of the state or federal government. Searches can be made with the state agencies furnishing a name and the agency will respond to Freedom of Information requests furnishing the name and address of the particular debtor or business.

A wide range of businesses require licensing: restaurants and bars, liquor stores, taxi cab drivers, and beauticians, as well as most service businesses involved in health care, care of animals, and the control of insects.

UNION MEMBERSHIPS

If the debtor is practicing a trade, a call to the trade union should provide information, at least as to whether the debtor is a dues-paying member. Any additional information is up to union policy and procedures, but sometimes the extra effort produces results.

SECRETARY OF STATE

All corporations must file with the secretary of state a certificate of incorporation which provides an address where service of process may be served on the corporation. An inquiry to the state will provide the proper name of the corporation and the address. The names and addresses of the principals of the corporation appear in the franchise tax returns filed, and usually can be obtained from the proper state office. Sometimes the incorporator of the corporation is a principal but more often the incorporator resigns immediately upon incorporation. Obtaining a copy of the certificate of incorporation will provide the name and address of the incorporators.

GOVERNMENTAL AGENCIES

Agencies such as the Securities and Exchange Commission, the Federal Communication Commission, the Civil Airlines Bureaus, and other types of agencies maintain records on businesses that are involved in their industry, and information may be obtained upon request.

MILITARY SERVICE

Contact can be made with the debtor in military service through one of the following:

- CNC Military Records Bureau, U.S. Marine Corp., Washington, D.C. 20380
- The Navy Locator Service #21, Naval Dept., Washington, D.C. 20350
- Commander U.S. Army Enlisted Records and Evaluation Center 46249
- Airforce World Wide Locator, Randolph Airforce Base, TX 78150

The best place to start is with the army, since it has more personnel than the rest of the branches.

RECORDINGS

The county clerk's office will indicate whether a debtor is doing business under his/her own name or a partnership name and will show the name and address of the debtor and the partners.

BANKRUPTCY PETITIONS

If the debtor has filed bankruptcy, searching the records of the Bankruptcy Court where the debtor resides will provide information which may assist in locating the debtor. Sometimes relatives listed as creditors may be helpful; even other creditors may help, and may share information. Sometimes a review of the bankruptcy papers will indicate the home state of the debtor to which a debtor may return if financial difficulties are encountered.

CENTRAL OFFICE VITAL STATISTICS

This agency provides information as to births, deaths, marriages, divorces, and other special events.

BETTER BUSINESS BUREAU

If complaints have been made against the debtor, the Better Business Bureau will furnish information concerning the firm and the nature of the complaints against the business.

ESTATES

If a relative of the debtor has recently passed away and the estate has been probated, court records may provide information as to residence and also whether the particular debtor will be a beneficiary of any funds of the deceased relative. The probate records may also furnish the names of other relatives of the debtor. If the deceased owed the debtor any monies or the debtor is a beneficiary under the will, and judgment has been obtained against the debtor, consult with counsel since proceedings may be available to execute on any monies that may be paid to the debtor.

MORTGAGES

If a debtor has sold a house and has executed a purchase money mortgage in favor of the buyer, a call to the buyer might produce the address where the payment is being sent. Consult with counsel since proceedings may be available to attach the payments being made to the debtor if a judgment has been obtained.

CITY RECORDS

Sometimes information can be obtained from Water Department records, utility records, dog and fishing license records, Board of Education records, high school and college records, etc.

CREDIT REPORTING AGENCIES

Inquiry to Equifax, Experian, Trans Union, or Dun & Bradstreet will provide information as to credit inquiries, litigation, and background on businesses and individuals. Be sure you comply with the Fair Credit Reporting Act as to permissible purposes.

SOCIAL SECURITY NUMBER

The first three digits of the social security number indicate the state where it was obtained, which is usually the debtor's home state. Often a debtor returns to his/her family (home state), and efforts to locate the debtor should be targeted there.

FORMER EMPLOYERS

If the application lists an employer, contacting the employer may provide the address where the last W-2 form was sent to the debtor. Sometimes a former employer even knows the debtor's new employer.

REMEDIES AFTER JUDGMENT

If the debtor leaves for parts unknown after a judgment is obtained, the number of tracing devices available increases substantially. One of the major devices is the use of the information subpoena, which can be served on a wide variety of third parties to obtain information about the debtor. It can be served on the telephone company, utilities, insurance companies, landlords, banks, security brokers, real estate brokers, and other third parties such as friends, relatives, accountants, and attorneys. The use of this device is limited only by the creativity of the attorney handling the collection case. In addition to this device, the attorney also has available the use of a subpoena to produce books and records which may be addressed not only to the debtor, if service can be effected upon the debtor, but also other third parties listed above. The use of the subpoena by the attorney is often successful. Unfortunately, these legal tools are only available after a judgment is obtained and should be in the hands of an experienced collection attorney.

CHAPTER 16

Appendix I

Examples of Major Databases

Metromail Corp.
360 East 22nd Street
Lomabard, IL 60148

Acollaid Services
Metro Phoenix Commerce Park
2101 West Alice
Phoenix, AZ 85021

Donnelly Marketing
1901 South Meyers Road
Suite 700
Oakbrook Terrace, IL 60181

Reverse Directory
Cole Publication
901 West Bond Street
Lincoln, NC 68521

Pro CD
Dauvers, Mass.

Database America
Montvale, NJ

Verifacts
2321 E. Lincolnway
Sterling, IL 61081

Equifax
Atlanta, GA

Experian (TRW)
Orange, CA

Transunion
Chicago, IL

Internet
Switchboard
www.switchboard.com

PC411
www.411.com

CHAPTER 16
APPENDIX II

SOCIAL SECURITY NUMBERS BY STATE

The location of where the debtor obtained a social security number (usually before the first job) is indicated in most instances by the first three numbers.

New Hampshire	001-003	Mississippi (also 587)	425-428
Maine	004-007	Arkansas	429-432
Vermont	008-009	Louisiana	433-439
Massachusetts	010-034	Oklahoma	440-448
Rhode Island	035-039	Texas	449-467
Connecticut	040-049	Minnesota	468-477
New York	050-134	Iowa	478-485
New Jersey	135-258	Missouri	486-500
Pennsylvania	259-211	North Dakota	501-502
Maryland	212-220	South Dakota	503-504
Delaware	221-222	Nebraska	505-508
Virginia	223-231	Kansas	509-515
West Virginia	232-236	Montana	516-517
North Carolina	237-246	Idaho	518-519
South Carolina	247-251	Wyoming	520
Georgia	252-260	Colorado	521-524
Florida	261-267	New Mexico (also 585)	525
Ohio	268-302	Arizona	526-527
Indiana	303-317	Utah	528-529
Illinois	318-361	Nevada	530
Michigan	362-389	Washington	531-539
Wisconsin	390-399	California	545-57

Index